Lecture Notes of the Institute for Computer Sciences, Social Informatics and Telecommunications Engineering 274

More information about this series at http://www.springer.com/series/8197

Fasikaw Atanaw Zimale ·
Temesgen Enku Nigussie ·
Solomon Workneh Fanta (Eds.)

Advances of Science and Technology

6th EAI International Conference, ICAST 2018
Bahir Dar, Ethiopia, October 5–7, 2018
Proceedings

 Springer

Editors
Fasikaw Atanaw Zimale
Faculty of Civil and Water Resources
Engineering
Bahir Dar Institute of Technology
Bahir Dar University
Bahir Dar, Ethiopia

Temesgen Enku Nigussie
Faculty of Civil and Water Resources
Engineering
Bahir Dar Institute of Technology
Bahir Dar University
Bahir Dar, Ethiopia

Solomon Workneh Fanta
Faculty of Chemical and Food Engineering
Bahir Dar Institute of Technology
Bahir Dar University
Bahir Dar, Ethiopia

ISSN 1867-8211   ISSN 1867-822X (electronic)
Lecture Notes of the Institute for Computer Sciences, Social Informatics
and Telecommunications Engineering
ISBN 978-3-030-15356-4   ISBN 978-3-030-15357-1 (eBook)
https://doi.org/10.1007/978-3-030-15357-1

Library of Congress Control Number: 2019934094

This Springer imprint is published by the registered company Springer Nature Switzerland AG
The registered company address is: Gewerbestrasse 11, 6330 Cham, Switzerland

Preface

We are delighted to introduce the proceedings of the 6th EAI International Conference on Advancement of Science and Technology (ICAST 2018). This conference brought together scholars, scientists, researchers in academia and institutes, as well as experts from industry to exchange knowledge, experiences, the latest technological advancements, research findings, innovations, and applications in all aspects of science and technology.

The technical program of ICAST 2018 consisted of 47 full papers, in oral presentation sessions during the main conference tracks, and eight poster presentations. The conference tracks were: Track 1 – Agro-Processing Industries for Sustainable Development; Track 2 – Water Resources Development for the Shared Vision in the Blue Nile Basin; Track 3 – IT and Computer Technology Innovation; Track 4 – Recent Advances in Electrical and Computer Engineering; Track 5 – Progresses in Product Design and System Optimization. Aside from the high-quality technical paper presentations, the technical program also featured four keynote speeches and three session keynote speakers. The four keynote speeches were Professor Mammo Muchie from DST-NRF SARChI Chair in Innovation Studies, Tshwane University of Technology, South Africa, Prof. Chiuhsiang Joe Lin from the Department of Industrial Management, National Taiwan University of Science and Technology, Taiwan, Prof. Zhiyan Pan from the Department of Environmental Engineering Zhejiang University of Technology, China, Prof. Yunghsiang S. Han (Distinguished Professor) from the School of Electrical Engineering and Intelligentization, Dongguan University of Technology, China. The three session keynote speakers were Prof. Muluneh Yitayew, University of Arizona, USA, Dr. Yilma Seleshi, School of Civil and Environmental Engineering, AAiT, Addis Ababa University, and Dr. Shimelis Emire, School of Chemical and Bio Engineering AAiT, Addis Ababa University. The five tracks were conducted as parallel sessions in four halls and poster presentations were held during the coffee breaks.

Coordination with the Steering Committee chair, Prof. Imrich Chlamtac, the Organizing Committee chair, Dr. Seifu A. Tilahun, the co-chairs, Dr. Atikilt Abebe and Mr. Endalkachew Chanie, and the Technical Program Committee chair was essential for the success of the conference. We sincerely appreciate their constant support and guidance. It was also a great pleasure to work with such an excellent Organizing Committee who worked hard in organizing and supporting the conference. In particular, the Technical Program Committee, led by Prof. Kibret Mequanint, and the co-chairs, Dr. Bereket Haile, Dr. Gebeyehu Belay, and Prof. A. Pushparaghavan, were instrumental in organizing the peer-review process of the technical papers, which led to a high-quality technical program. We are also grateful to the conference manager, Radka Pincakova, for her support, and all the authors who submitted their papers to the ICAST 2018 conference and workshops.

This volume contains the papers presented at the 6th EAI International Conference on Advancement of Science and Technology (ICAST 2018), which was held during October 5–7, 2018, at Grand Resort and Spa, Bahir Dar, Ethiopia. All submissions were strictly peer reviewed by the Technical Program Committee and only the papers accepted were presented.

We strongly believe that ICAST 2018 provided a good forum for all researchers, developers, and practitioners to discuss all science and technology aspects that are relevant to advancements in this subject. We also expect that future ICAST conferences will be as successful and stimulating, as indicated by the contributions presented in this volume.

February 2019

Seifu A. Tilahun
Kibret Mequanint
Fasikaw Atanaw Zimale

Organization

Steering Committee Chair

Imrich Chlamtac — Bruno Kessler Professor, University of Trento, Italy

Organizing Committee

General Chair

Seifu A. Tilahun — Bahir Dar University, Ethiopia

General Co-chairs

Endalkachew Chanie — Bahir Dar University, Ethiopia
Atikilt Ketema — Bahir Dar University, Ethiopia

TPC Co-chairs

Kibret Mequanint — University of Western Ontario, Canada
Bereket Haile National — Taiwan University of Science and Technology, Taiwan
Gebeyehu Belay — Bahir Dar University, Ethiopia
A. Pushparaghavan — Bahir Dar University, Ethiopia
Tammos S. Steenhuis — Cornell University, USA

Sponsorship and Exhibit Chair

Tesfa Tegegne — Bahir Dar University, Ethiopia

Local Chair

Sisay Geremew — Bahir Dar University, Ethiopia

Workshops Chair

Zenamarkos Bantie — Bahir Dar University, Ethiopia

Publicity and Social Media Chairs

Abaynesh Yehedgo — Katholieke Universiteit Leuven, Belgium
Fikreselam Gared — Bahir Dar University, Ethiopia
Sewunet Alemu — Bahir Dar University, Ethiopia

Publications Chair

Fasikaw Atanaw — Bahir Dar University, Ethiopia

Web Chair

Tewodros Worku   Bahir Dar University, Ethiopia

Posters and PhD Track Chair

Sam Goundar   Victoria University, New Zealand

Panels Chair

Moges Ashagre   Katholieke Universiteit Leuven, Belgium

Demos Chair

Temesgen Enku Nigussie   Bahir Dar University, Ethiopia

Tutorials Chair

Yenenh Tamirat   Asia University, Taiwan

Technical Program Committee

Kibret Mequanint   University of Western Ontario, Canada
Bereket Haile National   Taiwan University of Science and Technology, Taiwan
Gebeyehu Belay   Bahir Dar University, Ethiopia
A. Pushparaghavan   Bahir Dar University, Ethiopia
Tammos S. Steenhuis   Cornell University, USA

Contents

Application of Lean Tools for Reduction of Manufacturing Lead Time

Star Abrham[✉] and Sisay Geremew

Faculty of Mechanical and Industrial Engineering,
Bahir Dar Institute of Technology, Bahir Dar University, Bahir Dar, Ethiopia
`star.abrham@gmail.com`, `sisayg78@gmail.com`

Abstract. In the recent years, manufacturing industries are trying to improve customer service by reducing wastes, reducing lead time, improving quality and improving productivity using lean tools. Value Stream Mapping is one of the lean tools for analyzing the current state and designing a future state for the series of events that take a product from its beginning through delivery to the customer. The goal of this study is to apply Value Stream Mapping in production line of Fuel tank semi trailers at XYZ PLC Metal Industry for reducing the manufacturing lead time. In this case study, the existing state of the production line is mapped with the help of Value Stream Mapping process symbols and the biggest improvement areas like excessive work in process and long lead time are identified. Some improvements in current state Value Stream Mapping are suggested and with these improvements future state Value Stream Mapping is developed. Current state and future state of the production line are compared; the results show that 47.45% reduction in lead time, 50.2% reduction in work in process time, 59.2% reduction in total waiting time, 72.72% reduction in number of work in process products, 7% reduction in number of workers and over 89.65% increase in the yearly throughput of products.

Keywords: Manufacturing lead time · Value stream mapping · Lean tools

1 Introduction

In this competitive world, the competitive edge of manufacturing industries depends largely on their ability of delivering their goods at low cost and high quality to customers [1]. To achieve this edge, manufacturing industries use lean tools because of their systematic approach in manufacturing waste and lead time reduction. Value Stream Mapping is a powerful lean tool that combines material processing steps with information flow as well as other important related data. The ultimate goal of Value Stream Mapping is identifying and eliminating the different types of wastes in the production line in order to increase its efficiency and productivity. This paper presents a case study on the application of Value Stream Mapping in one of the metal industries in Ethiopia facing different problems related to overall work efficiency, throughput and production lead time. It addresses the implementation of lean manufacturing in the production line of Fuel tank semi trailers with a focus on analyzing the processes; identifying and minimizing wastes and reducing the manufacturing lead time.

© ICST Institute for Computer Sciences, Social Informatics and Telecommunications Engineering 2019
Published by Springer Nature Switzerland AG 2019. All Rights Reserved
F. A. Zimale et al. (Eds.): ICAST 2018, LNICST 274, pp. 1–10, 2019.
https://doi.org/10.1007/978-3-030-15357-1_1

2 Literature Review

Lean manufacturing is a systematic method for waste minimization within a manufacturing system without sacrificing productivity. Lean also takes into account waste created through overburden and waste created through unevenness in workloads. Working from the perspective of the client who consumes a product or service, value is any action or process that a customer would be willing to pay for. Lean manufacturing has different tools like Value Stream Mapping, Single-minute exchange of die (SMED), Five S, Kanban, poka-yoke (error-proofing), total productive maintenance, kaizen, cellular manufacturing, standardized work and one piece flow that assist in the identification and steady elimination of waste. As waste is eliminated; quality improves while production time and cost are reduced. Today the use of lean tools in the manufacturing world has been increased because of their capability in manufacturing waste and lead time reduction. Value Stream Mapping is a lean tool that helps users see and understand the flow of material and information as products make their way through the value stream [2]. The value stream includes the value adding and non value-adding activities that are required to bring a product from raw material through delivery to the customer. According to Hines and Rich [3] value stream includes the complete value added as well as non-value added activities, from conception of requirement back through to raw material source and back again to the consumer's receipt of product. Jones and Womack [4] explain Value Stream Mapping as the process of visually mapping the existing stage of manufacturing as it now occurs and preparing a future state map with better methods and performance. Singh et al. [6] have carried out a case study to identify areas of wastes in manufacturing of components to meet the maintenance need of diesel traction fleet, Indian railways. They have tried to discuss the lean implementation process with the help of Value Stream Mapping. As a result many benefits are reported such as reduction in lead time by 83.14%, reduction in processing time by 12.62%, reduction in Work in process inventory by 89.47%, reduction in manpower requirement by 30% and rise in productivity per operator by 42.86%. Vinodh et al. [7] apply Value Stream Mapping for enabling leanness in the manufacturing process of stiffer camshaft in an Indian camshaft manufacturing organization. As a result, idle time has been decreased from 19,660 to 19,449 min; total cycle time has been reduced from 539 to 525 min, number of work-in-progress inventory has been reduced from 4,660 to 4,610 units. On time delivery of products has been improved from 70% to 85%. Defects have been reduced by 4% and uptime has been increased by 1.72%. Seth and Gupta [8] have made an attempt to use Value Stream Mapping as a technique to achieve productivity improvement at supplier end for an auto industry. They reported a reduction in number of work in process inventory and finished goods inventory as well as an improvement in production output per person. Like these promising studies the authors were provoked to conduct this study with the lean tools in one of the metal industries in Ethiopia to reduce the manufacturing lead time.

3 Research Methodology

To conduct this case study research we start with the review of different research works on lean manufacturing and Value Stream Mapping applications in manufacturing industries. This is followed by identification of critical shop floor and selection of a product for the case study. And then, all important data related to the product such as material & information flow, cycle time, value added time and non-value added time for each process has been collected and current state Value Stream Mapping has been developed to show the existing status of the selected production line. Then the current state Value Stream Mapping has been analyzed; some improvements are suggested and with these process improvements a future state Value Stream Mapping is prepared to design a lean process flow.

4 Case Study

The case study has been carried out at XYZ PLC Metal Industry located in Mekelle, Ethiopia. The company deals with manufacturing of truck mounted fuel tankers, 2 axle; 3 axle dry cargo trailers and semitrailers for transporting heavy duty equipment. Truck mounted fuel tanker has been chosen as the candidate product for the case study. The reason behind the selection of this product family is that they have high volume of production; high number of manufacturing processes over the others and are highly demanded by the customers when compared to other family of products. Figure 1

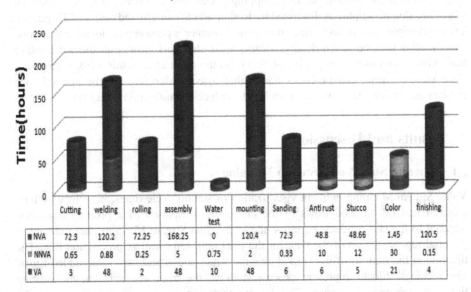

Ratio of VA, NVA & NNVA in each work station

	Cutting	welding	rolling	assembly	Water test	mounting	Sanding	Anti rust	Stucco	Color	finishing
■ NVA	72.3	120.2	72.25	168.25	0	120.4	72.3	48.8	48.66	1.45	120.5
■ NNVA	0.65	0.88	0.25	5	0.75	2	0.33	10	12	30	0.15
■ VA	3	48	2	48	10	48	6	6	5	21	4

Fig. 1. Ratio of value added time, non value added time and necessary non value added time in each work station

shows us the amount of value added time, necessary non value added time and non value added times in each work station of Fuel tank semi trailers production line.

As it is shown in Fig. 1, there is a high amount of waiting time or non value added time in each work station. So by reducing this waiting time or non value added time, the manufacturing lead time can be reduced. The pie chart below displays the contribution of value added time, non value added time and necessary non value added time to a total time of the current Fuel tank semi trailers production line (Fig. 2).

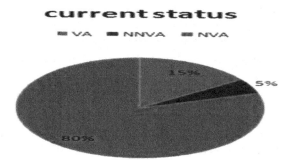

Fig. 2. Percentage of value added time, non value added time and necessary non value added time in the production line

This study continues with mapping of current state of Fuel tank semi trailers production line. The mapping is done in software using various process symbols of Value Stream Mapping to visualize the flow of material and information as the product takes its way in the production line. Mapping is carried out keeping in view of the lean manufacturing principles as discussed by Rother and Shook [5] and Seth and Gupta [6]. These principles are: define value from your customer's perspective; identify the value stream; eliminate the seven deadly wastes; make the work flow; pull the work rather than push it; and pursue to perfection level. So the main idea of this work is to give a clear view of how lean practices and Value Stream Mapping can be applied to a production line of Fuel tank semi trailers to reduce manufacturing lead time.

5   Results and Discussion

5.1   Current State Value Stream Mapping

Value Stream Mapping helps in visualization of station cycle times, inventory buffers, material and information flows in the entire transformation of a product from raw material to the end product. Figure 4 shows a Value Stream Mapping that indicates a pictorial representation of the data for the Fuel tank semi trailers production line. The timeline at the bottom of the map shows the value added and non value added times. The rectangle blocks represent process stations, the triangles represent the waiting times at each process station. The figure inside the rectangular box represents the average value added time and the figures under the triangles in-between process stations represent the non-value added time. The cycle time is calculated in hours/batch. The available time is calculated based on regular production time of 8 h per shift. As it is shown in the timeline of the current state value stream mapping, the total task time or cycle time of the fuel tanker is 263.01 h consisting of 201 h of value added time and 62.01 h of necessary non-value added time. This indicates that the fuel tanker spends a total of 263.01 h being processed at different work stations. The fuel tanker also stays for about 1252.3 h as work in process product starting from the cutting station to the last finishing work station. There is a total of 1059.9 h of waiting time through all stations that indicates the average waiting time of the fuel tanker per work station is about 96.51 h. The sum of the value added and non-value added time also known as the lead time is also calculated to be 1324.6 h. This means a single fuel tanker that could be made in 263.01 h is taking 1324.6 h to be produced due to non value added activities in the current state Value Stream Mapping. The total distance travelled by the worker and materials in the current production process is also calculated to be 1787 m. The Takt time; the rate at which one product has to come out of the manufacturer to meet the customer demand is calculated to be 53.5 h by dividing the available working hours per year which is 5940 h to customer requirement of products per year which is 111 fuel tankers. The comparison analysis of Takt time and cycle time of the processes is shown in figure below (Fig. 3).

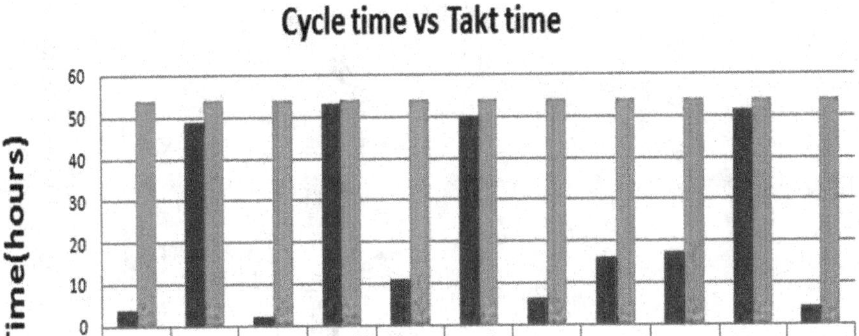

Cycle time vs Takt time

	Cutting	welding	rolling	assembly	Water test	mounting	Sanding	Anti rust	Stucco	Color	finishing
CYCLE TIME	3.65	48.88	2.25	53	10.75	50	6.33	16	17	51	4.15
TAKT TIME	53.5	53.5	53.5	53.5	53.5	53.5	53.5	53.5	53.5	53.5	53.5

Fig. 3. Takt time versus cycle time before improvement

As the graph shows, the production line is not balanced because the tasks are not uniformly distributed among the work stations. In some of the work stations, there is a lot of free time for workers. This shows that the line is capable of making more products but there is a need to have the line balanced. The line balancing efficiency for the workloads at the eleven work stations of the production line is calculated as the ratio of total processing time and the value of multiplication of actual workstation number with the largest assigned cycle time. The total processing time is equivalent to

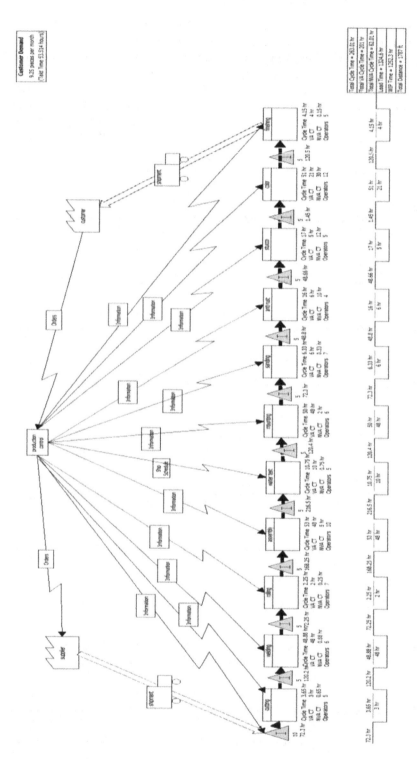

Fig. 4. Current state value stream mapping

the sum of the operation cycle times which gives 263 h whereas the actual number of workstations is 11 and the largest assigned cycle time is 53 h (assembly work station). Thus, the line balancing efficiency is found to be 45.1% as calculated below.

$$\begin{aligned} &\text{Line balancing efficiency} \\ &= \sum \text{Total processing time}/(\text{No of stations} * \text{Longest processing time}) \\ &\text{Line balancing efficiency} = 263\,\text{h}/(11 * 53\,\text{h}) \\ &\text{Line balancing efficiency} = 45.1\% \end{aligned} \quad (1)$$

Once the current state Value Stream Mapping is completed, the next step is to look for possible improvements and start outlining a future state Value Stream Mapping. The main goal of developing future state Value Stream Mapping is to eliminate identified wastes and make a continuous and smooth flow that generates shortest lead-time, highest quality and lowest cost. Different types of wastes have been identified from the current state Value Stream Mapping. The identified wastes have been reduced by applying different lean tools such as line balancing and First in First Out rule to prepare a future state Value Stream Mapping. The Future State Value Stream Mapping shows how the shop floor will operate after lean improvements are implemented.

5.2 Combining Similar Operations and Line Balancing

In sanding, anti rust, stucco and painting work stations; the cycle time and the number of operators were high. So to reduce that, the operations have been combined to be performed in one big work station by balancing the line; and the sanding operation has been started to be performed by the workers of anti rust and stucco painting work stations since it takes a small amount of time. As a result, the number of workers has been reduced from 72 to 67. The comparison analysis of Takt time and cycle time of processes after balancing the line is shown in figure below.

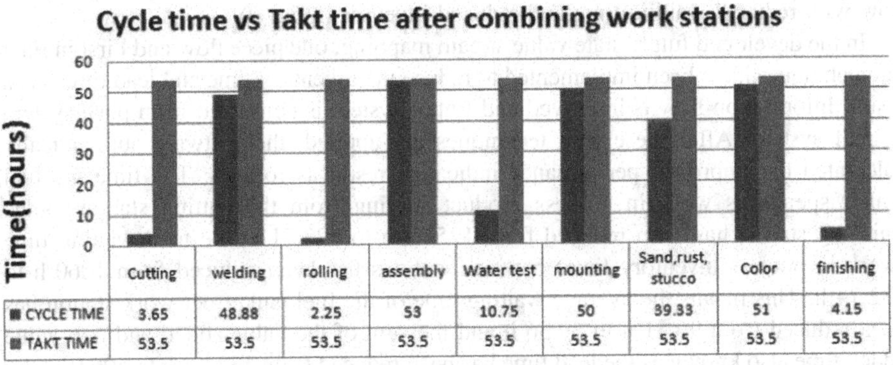

Cycle time vs Takt time after combining work stations

	Cutting	welding	rolling	assembly	Water test	mounting	Sand,rust, stucco	Color	finishing
CYCLE TIME	3.65	48.88	2.25	53	10.75	50	39.33	51	4.15
TAKT TIME	53.5	53.5	53.5	53.5	53.5	53.5	53.5	53.5	53.5

Fig. 5. Takt time versus cycle time after combining work stations

As it is shown in Fig. 5, the tasks are uniformly distributed among work stations and the line is balanced with all processes. This means that the line is capable of making more products than before and on the basis of the collected processing time data, line balancing efficiency is calculated to see the improvements in the proposed state of a value Stream. The total processing time is equivalent to the sum of the operation cycle times which gives 263 h whereas the actual number of workstation is nine as a result of combining the sanding, antirust and stucco operations to be performed in one work station and the largest assigned cycle time is 53 h (assembly work station). Thus, the line balancing efficiency is found to be 55.13% as calculated below.

$$\text{Line balancing efficiency}$$
$$= \sum \text{Total processing time}/(\text{no of stations} * \text{longest processing time})$$
$$\text{Line balancing efficiency} = 263\,\text{h}/(9 * 53\,\text{h})$$
$$\text{Line balancing efficiency} = 55.13\%$$

(2)

From the above result, the improved line balancing efficiency of the production line is 55.13%. This result is better in comparison with the previous line balancing efficiency but there is a room for improvement of the production line using other lean tools and techniques.

5.3   One Piece Flow and First in First Out (FIFO) Techniques

One piece flow means components are produced one by one, and each component progresses instantly from one operation to the next without having to wait in a buffer. In the current production process, the product passes through the work stations in a batch mode. This results in high travelling distance, high lead time and high work in process time. In order to keep the flow continuous that leads to reduction in buffer time, one piece flow and FIFO technique have been applied. One piece flow technique has been applied in the production line to transfer the products from one station to another station one by one rather than in a batch in order to eliminate all the waste. The FIFO technique has been also applied to process and deliver the products to the next station in the same order they entered the first work station. This results in clear and smooth flow with reduced waiting time and reduced inventory (Fig. 6).

In the developed future state value stream mapping, one piece flow and First in First out techniques have been implemented to reduce the inventory time and lead time. As a result, Information flow is improved and Entire system is converted from push system to pull system. After these lean techniques are applied, the software automatically calculated the improved performance indicators result as follows. The time the fuel tanker spends as work in process product starting from the cutting station to the finishing station has been reduced from 1252.3 h to 623.71 h; the total waiting time (work in process inventory time) between stations has been reduced from 1060 h to 432.74 h. This means the average waiting time of the fuel tanker per work station has been reduced from 96.51 h to 39.36 h and the sum of the value added and non-value added time also known as the lead time has been reduced from 1324.6 h to 696.01 h by combining similar operations, balancing the line and applying FIFO rule. This indicates that a single fuel tanker that could be made in 263.01 h is taking 696.01 h to be produced in the improved Value Stream Mapping. The total travelled distance between stations has been also reduced from 1787 m to 1017 m. As it is observed from the result of the Value Stream Mapping, every unit of fuel tanker come out with in 53.5 h's

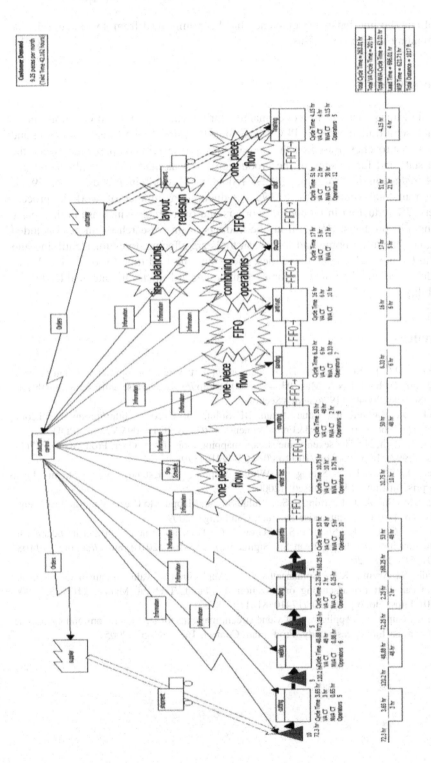

Fig. 6. Future state value stream mapping after lean tools implementation

interval and the line balancing efficiency has been improved from 45.13% to 55.13% by combining similar operations.

6 Conclusion

The goal of this paper was to reduce manufacturing lead time in the production line of Fuel tank semi trailers at XYZ PLC Metal Industry using Value Stream Mapping and other lean approaches. Based on the findings of the research; comparison between the current state and future state of the production line was made. The results show that 47.45% reduction in lead time, 50.2% reduction in work in process time, 59.2% reduction in total waiting time, 72.72% reduction in number of work in process products, 7% reduction in number of workers and over 89.65% increase in the yearly throughput of products. Hence, from the findings of this research it can be concluded that Value Stream Mapping and other lean tools are effective tools for identifying and reducing the non-value added activities, shortening the lead time for on-time delivery of products and enabling the companies to move towards their ultimate goal leading to profitability.

References

1. Onesime, O.C.T., Xu, X., Zhan, D.: A decision support system for supplier selection process. Int. J. Inf. Technol. Decis. Mak. **03**, 453 (2004). http://www.worldscientific.com/doi/abs/10.1142/S0219622004001197#citedBySection
2. Lovelle, J.: Mapping the value stream. IIE Solut. **33**(2) (2001). http://proquest.umi.com/pqdweb?did=68597087&sid=3&Fmt=4&clientId=10342&RQT=309&VName=PQD
3. Hines, P., Rich, N.: The seven value stream mapping tools. Int. J. Oper. Prod. Manag. **17**(1), 46–64 (1997). https://doi.org/10.1108/01443579710157989
4. Jones, D., Womack, J.: Seeing the Whole: Mapping the Extended Value Stream. Lean Enterprise Institute, Massachusetts (2000)
5. Rother, M., Shook, J.: Learning to See–Value-Stream Mapping to Create Value and Eliminate Muda, pp. 1–4. Lean Enterprise Institute, Cambridge (2009)
6. Singh, B., Garg, S.K., Sharma, S.K., Grewal, C.: Lean implementation and its benefits to production industry. Int. J. Lean Six Sigma **1**(2), 157–168 (2010). https://doi.org/10.1108/20401461011049520
7. Vinodh, S., Arvind, K.R., Somanaathan, M.: Application of value stream mapping in an Indian camshaft manufacturing organization. J. Manuf. Technol. Manag. **21**(7), 888–900 (2010). https://doi.org/10.1108/17410381011077973
8. Seth, D., Gupta, V.: Application of value stream mapping for lean operations and cycle time reduction: an Indian case study. Prod. Plan. Control. **16**(1), 44–59 (2005)

Predicting Runoff, Sediment and Management Scenarios for Reducing Soil Erosion in Data Scarce Regions, Blue Nile Basin

Berhanu M. Mekuria[1] and Mamaru A. Moges[2,3(✉)]

[1] Amhara Design Supervision Works Enterprise, Bahir Dar, Ethiopia
[2] Faculty of Civil and Water Resources Engineering, Bahir Dar Institute of Technology, Bahir Dar University, P.O. Box 26, Bahir Dar, Ethiopia
[3] Blue Nile Water Institute, Watershed Hydrology Directorate, Bahir Dar University, Bahir Dar, Ethiopia
mamarumoges@gmail.com

Abstract. This study presents modeling runoff and sediment with management scenarios for watershed management and resource erosion in Koga watershed using AnnAGNPS model. Calibration of the model was carried from 1988–2001 and validation from 2002–2007. The result of sensitivity analysis indicated that the CN was the most sensitive parameter to runoff and peak runoff rate whereas LS and K-factor were for sediment yield following RF, and these parameters were subjected to calibration. For model calibration, R^2 of 0.69, 0.35, 0.55; NSE of 0.69, −0.38, 0.55; RSR of 0.54, 1.14, 0.67; and PBIAS of 0.07%, −80.56% and 4.09% were obtained for surface runoff, peak runoff rate, and sediment load, respectively. Similarly validation results indicated an R^2 of 0.76, 0.54, 0.62; NSE of 0.76, 0.38, 0.62; RSR of 0.43, 0.71, 0.56, and PBIAS of 2.31%, −36.58% and 5.68% for surface runoff, peak runoff rate, and sediment load, respectively. Where the model efficiency was rated at the range of fair to excellent for three of the outputs of the model for both calibration and validation period. Only 21.5% of the area was able to generate the 78.8% of total soil erosion, with higher than tolerable limit. Hence converting of 21.5% of highest eroding cropland cells either to forest or grassland would reduce soil erosion, sediment yield and load significantly. Ultimately it would help to reduce the sedimentation in Koga dam which could result in reduction of storage capacity.

Keywords: Blue Nile basin · Koga watershed · Runoff · Sediment yield · AnnAGNPS

1 Introduction

1.1 Background

Soil erosion, which accelerated by anthropogenic effects which is resulting soil degradation and becoming a severe ecological challenge worldwide [1]. Mainly it is aggravated by rapid population growth, deforestation, unsuitable land cultivation, uncontrolled and overgrazing [2]. It results the non-point source (NPS) pollutants is inflow in to surface water system from agricultural watersheds. Intensive agriculture has been long

F. A. Zimale et al. (Eds.): ICAST 2018, LNICST 274, pp. 11–31, 2019.
https://doi.org/10.1007/978-3-030-15357-1_2

recognized as a major source of NPS pollutants such as sediment, nutrients and pesticides which are the major cause of water-quality degradation [3]. This results eutrophication on reservoirs and loss of valuable essential nutrients and fertile topsoil [4] and reduces productivity. Across the globe soil erosion causes the largest contaminant of surface water which the leading pollution problem in rivers and streams [5].

In Ethiopia soil erosion is considered as the main challenge for agriculture due to its capability to reduce productivity [6]. Particularly in the highland areas and which with 43% of the total area of the country [7] soil erosion is at high rate and threatening productivity. In the Blue Nile basin, specifically in In Koga Watershed there was continuous soil erosion challenges in Koga watershed [8] and it decreases farm income [9]. In order to rescue the soil erosion best management practices has to be identified and targeted for watershed management. To accomplish this watershed models could play key role for evaluating the runoff, sediment and source areas in the watersheds to reduce soil erosion.

Watershed models were developed to describe help to understand the watersheds management dynamics [10]. For example it helps to understand the land degradation related to soil erosion [11], and help to identify recommendable solutions through best management practices [12]. In addition models also could help for planning effective landscape interventions to reduce land degradation and requires knowledge on spatial distribution of runoff [13]. Hence models for predicting sediment yield based on different management scenario are very important for reducing threats of the soil erosion.

There have been different watershed models for predicting runoff, sediment load and other hydrological variables including Areal Non-point Source Watershed Environment Response Simulation-2000, ANSWERS-2000 [14], Soil and Water Assessment Tool, SWAT [15], Annualized Agricultural Non-Point Source, AnnAGNPS [16]. The AnnAGNPS model has been applied worldwide and proved as very effective tool for identifying erosion source areas. It helps in decision-making processes for adopting BMPs and/or conservation programs. Where NPS pollution control can be achieved in the most efficient way [17, 18]. Some of the models have been developed and tested in different part of the world such as in the United States [17], Norway [19], China [18], Island [20], Canada [21], Spain [22], Belgium [23], and Portugal [24]. In Ethiopia, AnnAGNPS model has been used in some parts of the country by [25–28]. Among these models AnnAGNPS was widely applicable in the range of watershed to predict flow, sediment, and nutrients [29].

Predicting the sediment load from rivers is important for estimating the siltation of artificial and natural reservoirs [30]. Modeling of runoff and sediment would help evaluation of soil erosion and loss of nutrient [31] from watersheds. Hence looking for the model which will mainly predict the runoff and sediment in identifying the source areas for simulating the management scenario for reducing erosion is paramount. In this regard this study chooses the AnnAGNPS model for predicting runoff, peak runoff rate and sediment yield in the study area. Simulation and investigation of sources soil erosion in the agricultural watersheds such as in the Koga watershed was vital. Because in less than 2 km upstream of the watershed was existing dam with an irrigation potential of 7000 ha which has been started since 2007. Hence effective watershed management and planning is critically needed reduce the soil erosion. This will help to minimize the inflow of sediment in to the reservoir. Therefore the objectives of this study were trifold (1) to evaluate capability of the AnnAGNPS model to predict the runoff and sediment yield, (2) to assess the sediment yield and runoff generation with respect to different land use practice and (3) to identify the source areas (hot spots) of erosion and evaluate the effectiveness of alternative BMPs scenarios with its impact on soil erosion, sediment yield and sediment load of Koga watershed.

2 Research Methodology

2.1 Description of the Study Area

Koga watershed with 293 km^2 in lies in the head water of the Blue Nile basin. Geographically it is located at 37°2′0″ to 37°19′0″E longitude and 11°10′0″ to 11°25′0″N latitude with altitude range 1883 to 3084 a.m.s.l. (Fig. 1). The upland of the watershed is narrow and mountainous while the downstream flat and gentle slope [32]. The climate in the watershed is categorized under subtropical climate zone (Yeshaneh et al. 2013). Where the weather condition is characterized by distinct dry and wet seasons and cold locally known as "woina dega". The rainfall is mono-modal which lasts from end of May to end of September. The mean annual rainfall in the watershed was 1403 mm from 1988 to 2007. The annual average minimum and maximum temperature in the watershed was 11.5 °C and 27 °C, respectively. The major crops grown in the watershed were teff, millet, maize, barley, wheat, rice, pulses, oilseed and potatoes. The soil type constitutes 32.2% Nitosols, 24.7% Vertisols, 16.4% Alisols, 15.4% Luvisols, 9.7% Leptosols and 1.6% Regosols. The land use in the watershed was characterized as 71.32% cropland, 12.76% forest, 10.29% pasture and 5.62% built up.

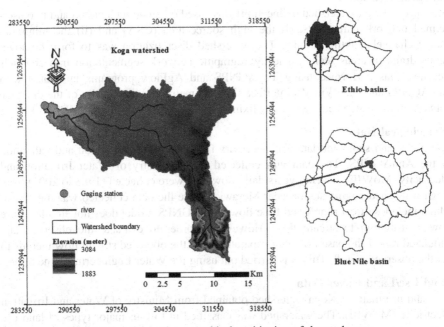

Fig. 1. Relative and geographical positioning of the study area

2.2   Data

Primary data such as observation of operation and management in the watershed, hydro-geological features, visiting detail investigation for specific sites for a confidential conceptual model and confirmation of the secondary data collected at the deskwork were performed. Main data type used for this study was presented in Table 1 with the source availability and duration. Details on description of data input types used were presented in the following sub sections.

Climate Data

Daily climate variables such as precipitation, maximum and minimum temperature, dew-point temperature, solar radiation and wind speed were required by AnnAGNPS model. This helps for the model simulation to consider the temporal and spatial climate variability. The nearest weather stations for Koga watershed were Meshanti, Adet, Dangila and Bahir Dar. Precipitation was obtained from Meshanti, Adet and Dangila. Temperature data was used from stations of Adet, Dangila and Bahir Dar stations. Similarly from Adet and Bahir Dar stations relative humidity for calculating of dew point temperature Sunshine for computation of solar radiation and wind speed. Thiessen polygon method was used for estimating the areal climate data from the selected stations. Climatic data quality has also been be carried out. The consistency of the data was tested by a double mass curve whereas homogeneity and trend analysis of the data were tested using RAINBO software version 2.2 [33]. The data quality tests indicated that the time series of climatic data was found consistent and homogenous. Station-average method (for missing data less 10%) and normal ratio method (for stations with missing data greater than 10%) was used to fill the missed data [34].

Topography Data

DEM processing (Watershed delineation) was based on an outlet location and two user-defined network parameters, (i) the high source area (CSA) and (ii) the minimum source channel length (MSCL). The watershed discretization was to form homogeneous drainage areas (cells). The hydrographic network segmentation into channels (reaches) was performed using TopAGNPS and AgFlow programs integrated with AnnAGNPS and MapWinGIS interface. The geometry and the density of the drainage network in the watershed were set by fixing the CSA to 20 ha and the MSCL to 140 m.

Hydrological Data

The runoff and sediment data was necessary for performing calibration and validation of the AnnAGNPS. The data was collected from Ministry of Water Irrigation and Electricity (MoWIE). Twenty years daily flow data were collected (1988 to 2007) from Koga watershed gaging station near Merawi. Where the data collected was the stream which includes direct runoff and base flow. AnnAGNPS model does not simulate base flow contribution to stream flow. However in order to evaluate the observed and simulated runoff the base flow was separated from the observed stream flow records to get the observed runoff. This was carried out using the Water Engineering Time Series.

Land Use/Land Cover Data

The land use map for Koga watershed obtained from Ministry of Water and Irrigation Electricity (MoWIE). The watershed was classified in to four major types of land use

(Table 2). The major crops grown in the watershed were teff, millet, maize, barley, wheat, rice, pulses, oilseed, and potatoes. The dominant land use was assigned to each AnnAGNPS cell. There were five types of land use identifier (cropland, pasture, forest, rangeland, and urban) in the AnnAGNPS model. Crop management operation in the watershed was vital to estimate the sediment yield [18]. It was prepared based on field observation in the watershed and RUSLE as recommended by [35].

Soil Data

Soil physical properties such as particle size fraction, depth, texture, field capacity and wilting point were required by the AnnAGNPS model. Organic matter content, PH, bulk density, saturated hydraulic conductivity, soil hydrologic group and soil erodibility factor were also required as the model input. Soil layer particle size fraction, depth, texture, PH and organic matter content were extracted from the soil data obtained from the Amhara Design and Supervision Works Enterprise [36]. Soil Plant Air Water, SPAW [37] was used to estimate the soil hydraulic parameters such as saturated hydraulic conductivity, field capacity, bulk density and wilting point of the soil. The soil erodibility (K) was computed based on [38].

Sediment Data

The sediment data collected at the gaging station of the Koga watershed was used for was used for calibration and validation of the runoff from 1988 to 2007. Nevertheless, for sediment data is not enough to carry out the calibration and validation as measured values obtained from the Ministry of Water and Electricity were scarce where the 63 event sediment data in the years of 1990–2011 were used to generate the observed data for calibration using the rating curve.

2.3   AnnAGNPS Model Description

The AnnAGNPS [16] model is a distributed physically based, continuous simulation, daily time step model. It was developed through a project between the USDA Agricultural Research Service (ARS) and the Natural Resources Conservation Service (NRCS). AnnAGNPS model was planned to be used as a decision support tool to evaluate the NPS pollution from the agricultural watersheds ranging in size up to 300,000 ha [39]. The AnnAGNPS hydrologic sub-model the SCS curve number technique [40] was used to determine the surface runoff on the basis of a continuous soil moisture balance. The model only needs an initial values of curve number (CN) for antecedent moisture condition (AMC) II. Despite the model updates the hydrologic soil conditions based on the soil moisture balance and crop cycle [41].

The model requires physical parameters of the watershed, soil data, climate data, and land use and management data. Topographic Parameterization, TOPAGNPS [42] used to extract the physical parameters including the cell and stream network information from DEM. The output from TOPAGNPS was used by Agricultural Watershed Flownet generation (AGFLOW) convert the output in to the format required by AnnAGNPS [41]. Climate data can be either simulated by using t Generation of Weather Elements for Multiple Applications (GEM) program or manually using historical data [43]. Spatial data such as DEM, soils, and land use for AnnAGNPS model was prepared by using MAPWinGIS. It also makes an intersection of each generated cell with land use and soil spatial to assign each cell with specific land use and soil type. The AnnAGNPS Input editor has a spreadsheet with all the data collected from the cell and the reaches. After importing the parameters in the cell it will automatically sort and check all the information within each cell. At the end the model simulation was taken place.

2.4 Sensitivity Analysis

Sensitivity analysis is a measure of the response of selected output variables to variations in input parameters and/or driving variables [44]. It helps to look for the most sensitive parameters which can significantly play role in the simulation of runoff, peak runoff, and sediment. According to [25, 26, 44] parameters such as CN, RF, RUSLE LS-factor, SRR, 10 Year Energy Intensity factor (EI10), soil erodibility factor (K), sheet flow manning's (SFM), concentrated flow manning's (CFM) were selected for sensitivity analysis. Likewise this study has also used this parameter for sensitivity analysis. The relative parameter importance was evaluated by using [45]. Accordingly, each selected parameter was changed with an increment of $\pm 10\%$, ± 20, ± 30 and ± 50 and by fixing the values of the remaining parameters.

2.5 Model Performance

The model performance during calibration and validation periods was evaluated on the monthly time scale by using both qualitative and quantitative approaches. The qualitative procedure consisted of visually comparing in data-display graphics of the observed and predicted values. Quantitative evaluation was based on the range of statistical summary. Mainly the model performance efficiency of the AnnAGNPS model was evaluated by using statistical criteria's. Which include the Coefficient of determination (R^2), Nash-Sutcliff efficiency, NSE [46], percentage bias (PBIAS), Root Mean Square Error (RMSE) and RMSE-observation standard deviation ratio (RSR) as presented Table 4. Where each statistical output of the model efficiencies were evaluated by using the class category based on [29].

3 Result and Discussion

3.1 Sensitivity Analysis of AnnAGNPS Model

CN was found the most sensitive parameter to surface runoff and peak runoff rate with high output variations. For instance, the percent deviation of runoff and peak runoff rate were -35.04 to $+129.52\%$, and 17.05 to $+17.34\%$ respectively due to changes in CN from -10% to $+10\%$ (Fig. 2). Similarly changes in precipitation had a great impact on the output variations of runoff and peak runoff rate. LS-factor, soil erodibility factor (K), concentrated flow manning's (CFM) and surface random roughness (SRR) did not significantly resulted variation in the hydrological outputs. Sediment yield was highly sensitive to RF. Following RF, change in LS, K, CN, CFM, and SRR had an impact on sediment yield in decreasing order. Unlike these parameters EI10 was less sensitive and did not have significant effect variation of the model output.

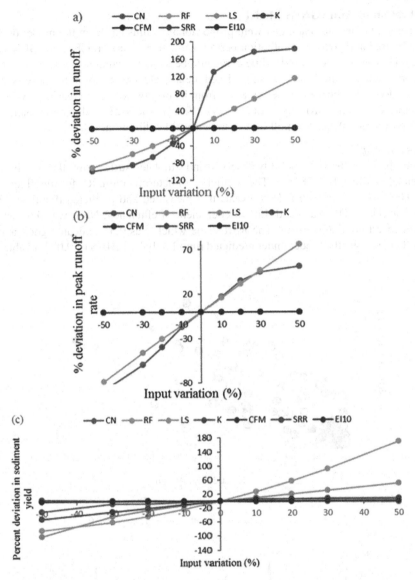

Fig. 2. Sensitivity of (a) runoff, (b) peak runoff rate, (c) sediment yield by ±10, ±20, ±30 and ±50 input variation

The same trend with outputs was observed to ±20%, ±30% and ±50% change in input parameters as the response to ±10% input changes but with a higher magnitude. In Ethiopia sensitivity of CN by using the AnnAGNPS model has been observed from studies by [25, 28]. In addition, CN higher sensitivity was reported in studies carried out worldwide on as indicated by [20, 29, 44, 47, 48].

Calibration of AnnAGNPS Model

The curve numbers for each cell were proportionally adjusted, from the model default value by trial and error for calibration period. LS-factor, K-factor, CFM and SRR were varied, increased or decreased, while curve numbers were decreased or increased in the contrary until the predicted runoff and sediment yield came closer to the observed outputs. Reducing curve number by 8.8% from its original value, increasing LS-factor, K-factor, CFM and SRR by 40%, 31.7%, 1250% and 625%, the best result was obtained for runoff, peak runoff and sediment yield calibration.

Surface Runoff

The comparisons between monthly observed and simulated surface runoff amounts were presented in Table 1 and Fig. 3. The coefficient of determination, R^2, for runoff amount was 0.69 (good correlation). This reveals that measured and predicted runoff was linearly correlated. The Nash and Sutcliff coefficient of efficiency, NSE, was 0.69 which demonstrated good agreement. The RSR value which was 0.54 indicated good agreement. On average, the model under predicted runoff only by PBIAS of 0.07% (Table 1).

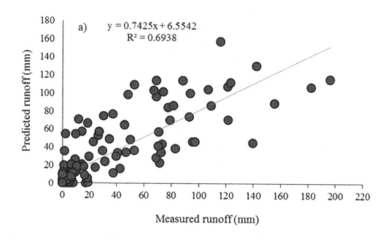

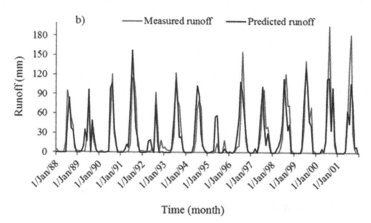

Fig. 3. Observed and predicted runoff (a) scatter plot (b) hydrograph for calibration period on monthly scale

Based on o model performance measuring criteria classification by [29] the results indicated a good to an excellent agreement of simulated runoff by the AnnAGNPS model. Closely related model prediction performance values were obtained during calibration period time for AnnAGNPS model by [28] an R^2 of 0.83 and NSE of 0.76, [27] an R^2 of 0.78 and NSE of 0.73, [24] an R^2 0.87 and NSE of 0.73. The model prediction for the runoff was relatively better than by [25] in Augucho catchment, Ethiopia with an R^2 of 0.57 and NSE of −0.69. The poor model prediction performance was attributed to the shortfalls of Soil Conservation Research Program database and inconsistencies in data collection.

Peak Runoff Rate
The model performance in predicting peak runoff rate was fair with an R^2 value of 0.35 although according to the NSE, RSR and PBIAS value unsatisfactory correlation between observed and simulated data exist (Table 1 and Fig. 4). The model over predicted peak runoff rate by PBIAS of 80.56%. The over prediction of the model for peak runoff rate was also found by [25–28] The model prediction for peak runoff rate (NSE of −0.38) was better than in the study conducted by [28] reported the NSE values of −33.

Table 1. Estimated statistical parameters of model performance for calibration and validation period

	Calibration on monthly scale (1988–2001)					Validation on monthly scale (2002–2007)				
	R^2	NSE	RMSE	RSR	PBIAS	R^2	NSE	RMSE	RSR	PBIAS
Surface runoff	0.69	0.69	22.08	0.54	0.07	0.75	0.75	20.17	0.433	2.31
Peak runoff	0.35	−0.38	18.23	1.14	−80.56	0.54	0.38	13.25	0.71	−36.58
Sediment	0.54	0.54	0.20	0.67	4.09	0.62	0.62	0.19	0.56	5.68

Sediment Load
The evaluation of model performance observed and simulated sediment load provided an R^2, NSE, RSR and PBIAS were 0.55, 0.55, 0.67 and 4.09% respectively (Table 2 and Fig. 5). This indicated fair to an excellent agreement with the simulated value. Similarly the study by [26] with NSE of 0.9; [28] with NSE of 0.71; [27] with NSE of 0.47; [25] found less result of NSE value of 0.158 during calibration. Comparing the average monthly values of measured and predicted sediment load, the model under predicted sediment load by 4.09%. The result in this study indicated better statistical performance than the study conducted by [26] which reported that the model under predicted sediment yield by 15%. Similarly in terms of performance the result provided better result by [23] reported NSE values of 0.16, and [22] found NSE values of 0.2.

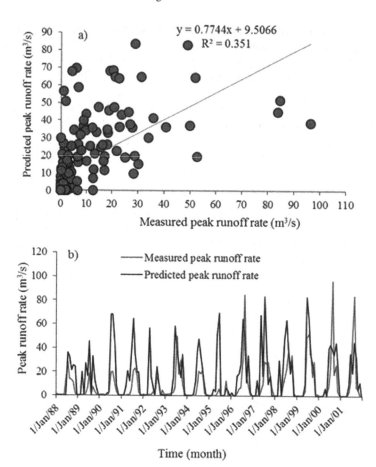

Fig. 4. Observed & predicted peak runoff rate (a) scatter plot (b) hydrograph for calibration period on monthly scale

Validation of AGNPS Model

Validation of AnnAGNPS was performed on a monthly time scale from 2002–2007. The observed and validated output results were presented in Table 3 and the statistical parameters of the model performance were summarized in Table 1. Surface runoff validation provided a very good agreement of 0.75 for both R^2 and NSE, also the value of RSR and PBIAS were 0.43 and 2.31%. This illustrated a very good to excellent agreement respectively (Table 1). The comparisons between monthly observed and simulated surface runoff amounts were improved during validation period (Fig. 6).

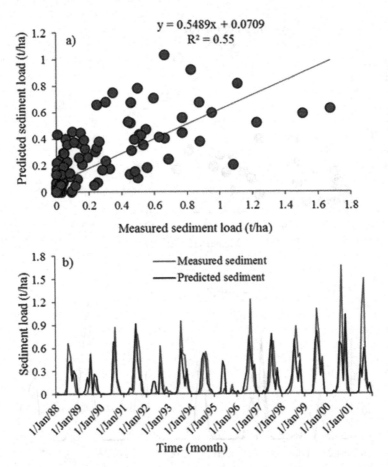

Fig. 5. Observed & predicted sediment load (a) scatter plot (b) hydrograph for calibration period on monthly scale

Peak runoff rate during validation was in a satisfactory agreement with 0.54 and 0.38 value for R^2 and NSE respectively and the model overestimated peak runoff rate by 36.58% (Table 1). This indicated improved agreement than during calibration. The comparisons between monthly observed and predicted peak runoff rate was indicated in Fig. 7.

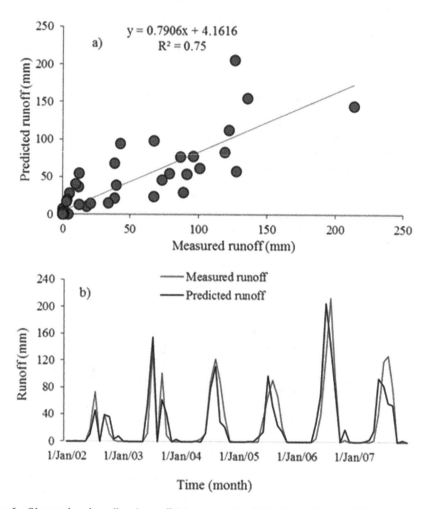

Fig. 6. Observed and predicted runoff (a) scatter plot (b) hydrograph for validation period on monthly scale

The overall efficiency for predicted peak runoff rate was a little bit improved during the validation period. The comparisons between observed and predicted sediment load were shown in Fig. 8. The attained statistical parameters value of R^2, NSE, RSR and PBIAS were 0.62, 0.62, 0.56 and 5.68% respectively (Table 1 and Fig. 8). These indicated a good to an excellent agreement. All statistical model performance measuring parameters except PBIAS were improved during validation period.

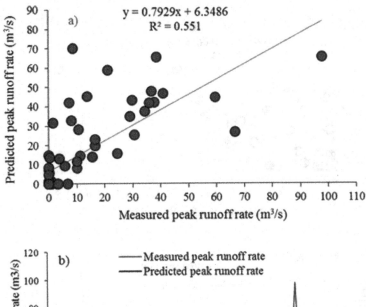

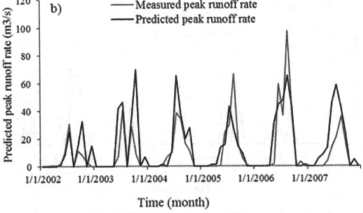

Fig. 7. Observed and predicted peak runoff rate (a) scatter plot (b) hydrograph for validation period on monthly scale

3.2 Sediment Yield and Soil Erosion

The soil erosion amount varied greatly with different land use types (Table 2). The results indicated that the highest amounts of average annual runoff and soil erosion, 405.17 mm/ha and 10.99 ton/ha respectively. It were generated from cropland (culti-vated agricultural land), followed by pasture (grass land) and urban (residential area) which had contributed average annual soil erosion of 0.05 and 0.03 t/ha respectively. Forestland had contributed the least soil erosion (0.001 t/ha). The study indicated that erosion increases as the land use changed from grassland/forest land to crop land for agricultural crop production. The spatial distribution in soil loss ranges from insignificant amount (nearly zero) up to moderate in around middle of the watersheds. It also ranges from low up to severe in lower parts and very severe to extremely severe

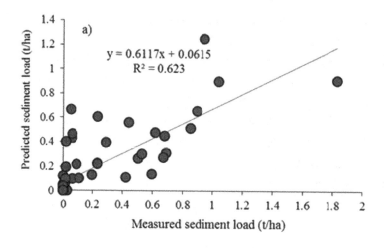

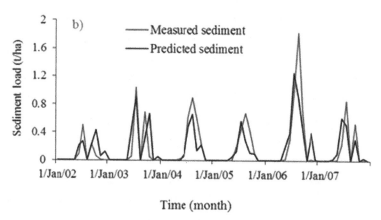

Fig. 8. Observed and predicted sediment load (a) scatter plot (b) hydrograph for validation period on monthly scale

in the upper part of the watershed. Soil erosion highly affected areas were spatially located in the narrow steep slope which is the mid upper part of the watershed. In addition to the steep slope (>30%) mainly the cultivated agricultural land was more highly susceptible to erosion.

Table 2. Average soil erosion of different land use types predicted by AnnAGNPS

Land use types	Area (ha)	Percent of area (%)	Average soil erosion (t/year)	Percent of soil erosion (%)	Average soil erosion rate t/ha/year
Cropland	21,027.4	71.70	249.91	99.37	10.99
Forest	3,738.4	12.75	0.02	0.01	0.001
Pasture	3,061.8	10.44	1.00	0.40	0.05
Urban	1,501.1	5.12	0.56	0.22	0.03
Total	29,328.7	100	251.49	100	11.07

Soil erosion rates/soil loss predicted was spatially variable and reached up 82 t/ha/year (Fig. 9). The total soil erosion from the study watershed was estimated to be 276.37×10^3 t/year (Table 3). The overall average soil erosion estimation was 9.4 t/ha/year. This result was in line with the range of the average annual soil erosion estimated for Ethiopian highlands with an average soil erosion of 9.7 t/ha/year by [49].

Soil loss tolerance was the maximum amount of soil erosion that can occur without any reduction in crop productivity [50]. Worldwide accepted maximum limit of soil loss tolerance was 11.2 t/ha/year [51]. Whereas for Ethiopia maximum tolerable soil

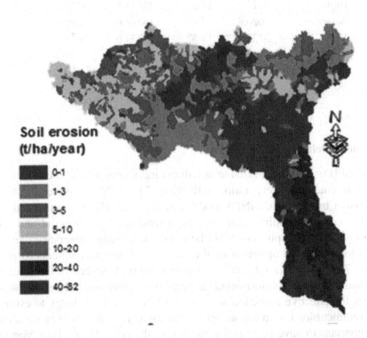

Fig. 9. Spatial distribution of soil erosion rates in Koga watershed

loss of 18 t/ha/year was recommended by [52]. Similarly [53] recommended 10 t/ha/year as the tolerable limit of soil loss. Therefore, by considering the recommended value of 10 t/ha/year, a soil loss less than 10 t/ha was on 78.53% of the watershed area of land and accounts only 21.2% of the total soil erosion. The remaining area of land with 21.47% accounts 78.8% of total soil erosion indicating above the recommended tolerable limit of soil loss. Out of the area that was above the tolerable limit of soil loss 4.99% belongs to severe, 39.71% to very severe and 34.10% to the extremely severe erosion classes (Table 3). Thus priority watershed management should be carried out on those areas considered and found as highly affected area. Where the best management practices recommended would reduce the soil erosion in the watershed.

Table 3. Soil erosion rates numeric classification according to [11]

Soil erosion rate (t/ha/year)	Soil erosion risk class	Area (ha)	Percent of total area (%)	Soil erosion (t/year)	Percent of total soil loss (%)	Average annual soil erosion rate (t/ha/year)
0–1	Very low	8750.0	29.83	449.4	0.16	9.4
1–3	Low	4778.8	16.29	10352.7	3.75	
3–5	Moderate	5332.4	18.18	20740.7	7.50	
5–10	High	4173.2	14.23	27053.1	9.79	
10–20	Severe	1020.8	3.48	13788.6	4.99	
20–40	Very severe	3422.9	11.67	109734.0	39.71	
40–82	Extremely severe	1850.7	6.31	94251.2	34.10	
Total		29328.7	100.00	276369.9	100.00	

3.3   Sediment Delivery Ratio (SDR)

Sediment yield is usually not available as a direct measurement, but it can be estimated by using a sediment delivery ratio, SDR [54]. The SDR estimated in the Koga watershed outlet by the AnnAGNPS model was about 25.5%. This indicated that soil materials that carry non-point source pollutant loadings (soil material and nutrients such as nitrogen and phosphorus) could be delivered to Koga watershed dam. Where this dam is located 1 km upstream of the gaging station and commenced started in 2007. While 74.5% of the eroded soil materials were re-deposited in the catchment of the watershed. The SDR information is helpful in planning future the watershed management for effective reduction soil erosion [18] because it helps to estimate the amount of sediment load from the soil loss estimation. To reduce soil erosion/sediment loss it is important to have more soil deposited in the cells. Hence Best Management Strategies has to focus on cells or sub basins which have more soil loss rate to reduce further siltation of Koga reservoir.

3.4   Best Management Practices

Best Management Practices (BMPs) are treatment alternatives. Such as conversion from cropland cells having erosion risk class of severe and above to forest or grassland. It was demonstrated and simulated run in the AnnAGNPS model as a means to reduce soil erosion within the watershed. Similarly to minimize and sediment load from the watershed i.e. the cells that produce erosion above tolerance limit should be converted to forest or grassland. Average annual values of soil erosion, sediment yield and sediment load over twenty years of simulations (1988–2007) were presented in Table 4. It was summarized based on reference to the different management practices that were implemented. By implementing scenario III or V, the maximum soil erosion in the watershed was reduced to less than 10 t/ha/year. This indicates that the landscape soil loss became within the tolerable limit of soil loss. Converting croplands cells having severe and above soil erosion risk classes to grassland have the same trend as converting to a forest (Table 4). Therefore converting the traditional agriculture in to conservation agriculture with and afforestation in degraded areas could bring tolerable soil loss in the watershed. The systems (scenarios) considered in this study have a reasonable chance of being implemented with appropriate rural policy of development including with some incentive for encouragement programs.

Table 4. Summary (1988–2007) of management scenario analysis and results of reduction for sediment load & yield

Scenario		Average				Reduction (%)			Maximum
No	Description	Runoff amount (mm)	Landscape erosion (t/ha/yr)	Sed. yield (t/ha/yr)	Sed. loading (t/ha/yr)	Soil erosion	Sed. yield	Sed. load	landscape erosion (t/ha/year
I	Baseline condition (no change of original land use)	354.25	9.42	3.08	2.41	0	0	0	81.34
II	Cropland cell having soil erosion risk classes of extremely severe (40–82 t/ha/year) changed to forest	338.73	6.21	1.89	1.53	34.10	38.53	36.51	39.90
III	Cropland cell having soil erosion risk classes of sever and above (10–82 t/ha/year) changed to forest	301.26	2.00	0.45	0.39	78.79	85.41	83.63	9.91
IV	Cropland cell having soil erosion risk classes of extremely severe (40–82 t/ha/year) changed to grassland	345.02	6.25	1.91	1.55	33.65	38.01	35.75	39.90
V	Cropland cell having soil erosion risk classes of very sever and above (10–81.34 t/ha/year) changed to grassland	322.82	2.10	0.48	0.42	77.75	84.28	82.42	9.91

4 Conclusion

The total annual erosion of the Koga watershed was 0.3 million metric tons, and of which about 74.5% of the eroded soil materials was re-deposited in the catchment of the watershed, with the rest (25.5%) delivered to the watershed outlet. The simulations result of alternative management practices showed that converting 21.47% of highest eroding cropland cells, to either forest or grassland would reduce soil erosion, sediment yield and sediment load by 78.79%, 85.41% and 83.63% respectively, indicating that the maximum soil erosion in the watershed was reduced to less than 10 t/ha/year which means that the landscape soil loss was became within the tolerable limit of soil loss. Above all the results obtained from applying AnnAGNPS on Koga watershed demonstrate that the model has significant potential as a management tool for evaluation of the effectiveness of alternative BMPs scenarios and their impact on soil erosion, sediment yield and sediment load, long term monthly estimation of runoff, peak runoff rate and sediment load, identification of hot spot area of erosion, and investigation of sediment delivery characteristics. Hence, the method could be replicated in other parts of Lake Tana sub-basin in general in the country for similar watersheds to predict of runoff and sediment, assessment of conservation prioritization, to evaluate the effectiveness management practices to reduce soil erosion.

Acknowledgment. We would like to than Bahir Dar University, Blue Nile Water Institute for funding this research project. In addition our thanks also extended to the National Meteorological agency (NMA) and Ministry of Water Irrigation and Electricity of Ethiopia for providing climatic and hydrological data respectively.

References

1. Bai, Z.G., Dent, D.L., Olsson, L., Schaepman, M.E.: Proxy global assessment of land degradation. Soil Use Manag. **24**(3), 223–234 (2008)
2. Hurni, H., et al.: Land degradation and sustainable land management in the highlands of Ethiopia (2010)
3. Tim, U.S., Jolly, R., Liao, H.H.: Impact of landscape feature and feature placement on agricultural non-point-source-pollution control. J. Water Resour. Plan. Manag. **121**, 463–470 (1995)
4. Suir, G.M.: Validation of AnnAGNPS at the field and farm-scale using an integrated AGNPS/GIS system (2002)
5. Koltun, G., Landers, M., Nolan, K., Parker, R.: Sediment transport and geomorphology issues in the water resources division. In: Proceedings of the US Geological Survey (USGS) Sediment Workshop: Expanding Sediment Research Capabilities in today's USGS, 4–7 February 1997. Reston, VA. and Harpers Ferry, WV (1997)
6. Easton, Z., et al.: A multi basin SWAT model analysis of runoff and sedimentation in the Blue Nile, Ethiopia. Hydrol. Earth Syst. Sci. **14**, 1827–1841 (2010)
7. Constable, M.: Ethiopian Highlands Reclamation Study (EHRS): Summary EHRS. FAO/MoA Joint Project, Addis Ababa (1985)
8. Gelagay, H.S., Minale, A.S.: Soil loss estimation using GIS and Remote sensing techniques: a case of Koga watershed, Northwestern Ethiopia. Int. Soil Water Conserv. Res. **4**, 126–136 (2016)
9. Erkossa, T., Wudneh, A., Desalegn, B., Taye, G.: Linking soil erosion to on-site financial cost: lessons from watersheds in the Blue Nile basin. Solid Earth **6**, 765 (2015)
10. Oeurng, C., Sauvage, S., Sánchez-Pérez, J.-M.: Assessment of hydrology, sediment and particulate organic carbon yield in a large agricultural catchment using the SWAT model. J. Hydrol. **401**, 145–153 (2011)

11. Borrelli, P., Märker, M., Schütt, B.: Modelling post-tree-harvesting soil erosion and sediment deposition potential in the Turano River basin (Italian Central Apennine). Land Degrad. Dev. **26**, 356–366 (2015)
12. Borah, D., Bera, M.: Watershed-scale hydrologic and nonpoint-source pollution models: review of mathematical bases. Trans. ASAE **46**, 1553 (2003)
13. Moges, M.A., et al.: Suitability of watershed models to predict distributed hydrologic response in the Awramba watershed in Lake Tana Basin. Land Degrad. Dev. **28**, 1386–1397 (2017)
14. Beasley, D.B., Huggins, L.F.: ANSWERS, areal nonpoint source watershed environment response simulation: User's manual (1981)
15. Arnold, J.G., Srinivasan, R., Muttiah, R.S., Williams, J.R.: Large area hydrologic modeling and assessment part I: model development. J. Am. Water Resour. Assoc. **34**, 73–89 (1998)
16. Bingner, R., Theurer, F.: AnnAGNPS: estimating sediment yield by particle size for sheet and rill erosion. In: Proceedings of the Seventh Interagency Sedimentation Conference, Reno, NV, pp. 1–7 (2001)
17. Yuan, Y., Locke, M., Bingner, R.: Annualized agricultural non-point source model application for Mississippi Delta Beasley Lake watershed conservation practices assessment. J. Soil Water Conserv. **63**, 542–551 (2008)
18. Hua, L., He, X., Yuan, Y., Nan, H.: Assessment of runoff and sediment yields using the AnnAGNPS model in a three-gorge watershed of China. Int. J. Environ. Res. Public Health **9**, 1887–1907 (2012)
19. Eriksson, N.:. Adaption of the Agricultural Non-point Source Pollution Model to the Morsa Watershed (2003)
20. Polyakov, V., Fares, A., Kubo, D., Jacobi, J., Smith, C.: Evaluation of a non-point source pollution model, AnnAGNPS, in a tropical watershed. Environ. Model Softw. **22**, 1617–1627 (2007)
21. Das, S., Rudra, R., Gharabaghi, B., Gebremeskel, S., Goel, P., Dickinson, W.: Applicability of AnnAGNPS for Ontario conditions. Can. Biosyst. Eng. **50**, 1.1–1.11 (2008)
22. Chahor, Y., Casalí, J., Giménez, R., Bingner, R., Campo, M., Goñi, M.: Evaluation of the AnnAGNPS model for predicting runoff and sediment yield in a small Mediterranean agricultural watershed in Navarre (Spain). Agric. Water Manag. **134**, 24–37 (2014)
23. Zema, D., Bingner, R., Denisi, P., Govers, G., Licciardello, F., Zimbone, S.: Evaluation of runoff, peak flow and sediment yield for events simulated by the AnnAGNPS model in a Belgian agricultural watershed. Land Degrad. Dev. **23**, 205–215 (2012)
24. Duarte, A.F.C., Mateos, L.I., Fereres, E.C.: Modeling runoff with AnnAGNPS model in a small agricultural catchment, in Mediterranean environment. In: 21st Century Watershed Technology: Improving Water Quality and Environment Conference Proceedings, Bari, Italy, May 27–June 1 2012. American Society of Agricultural and Biological Engineers (2012)
25. Haregeweyn, N., Yohannes, F.: Testing and evaluation of the agricultural non-point source pollution model (AGNPS) on Augucho catchment, western Hararghe, Ethiopia. Agr. Ecosyst. Environ. **99**, 201–212 (2003)
26. Mohammed, H., Yohannes, F., Zeleke, G.: Validation of agricultural non-point source pollution model in Kori watershed, South Wollo, Ethiopia. Int. J. Appl. Earth Obs. Geoinf. **6**, 97–109 (2004)
27. Amare, A.: Study of sediment yield from the Watershed of Angereb reservoir. MSc thesis, Department of Agricultural Engineering, Alemaya University, Ethiopia (2005)
28. Lindi, S.: Prediction of runoff and sediment yield using Annualized Agricultural nonpoint source (AnnAGNPS) pollution model: case of Ereguda catchment, East Hararghe, Ethiopia. ARPN J. Sci. Technol. **4**(10) (2014)

29. Parajuli, P.B., Nelson, N.O., Frees, L.D., Mankin, K.R.: Comparison of AnnAGNPS and SWAT model simulation results in USDA-CEAP agricultural watersheds in south-central Kansas. Hydrol. Process. **23**, 748–763 (2009)
30. Ali, Y.S.A., Crosato, A., Mohamed, Y.A., Abdalla, S.H., Wright, N.G.: Sediment balances in the Blue Nile River Basin. Int. J. Sedim. Res. **29**, 13 (2014)
31. Walling, D.E.: Assessing the accuracy of suspended sediment rating curves for a small basin. Water Resour. Res. **13**, 531–538 (1977)
32. Assefa, T.T., Jha, M.K., Tilahun, S.A., Yetbarek, E., Adem, A.A., Wale, A.: Identification of erosion hotspot area using GIS and MCE technique for Koga watershed in the Upper Blue Nile Basin, Ethiopia. Am. J. Environ. Sci. **11**, 245 (2015)
33. Raes, D., Willems, P., Gbaguidi, F.: RAINBOW – a software package for analyzing data and testing the homogeneity of historical data sets. In: Proceedings of the 4th International Workshop on 'Sustainable Management of Marginal Drylands', Islamabad, Pakistan (2006)
34. McCuen, R.H.: Hydrologic Design and Analysis, p. 814. Prince Hall, New Jersey (1998)
35. Renard, K.G.: Predicting soil erosion by water: a guide to conservation planning with the revised universal soil loss equation (RUSLE) (1997)
36. Amhara Design Supervision Water Enterprise (2015)
37. Saxton, K., Rawls, W.: Soil and water characteristics, version 6.02. 74. USDA Agricultural Research Service in cooperation with Department of Biological Systems Engineering Washington State University (2006)
38. Williams, J.: The EPIC model in: Computer Models of Watershed Hydrology. Water Resources Publications, Highlands Ranch (1995). Singh, VP
39. Bosch, D., Theurer, F., Bingner, R., Felton, G., Chaubey, I.: Evaluation of the AnnAGNPS water quality model. In: Agricultural Non-Point Source Water Quality Models: Their Use and Application, pp. 45–54 (1998)
40. SCS: Urban hydrology for small watersheds. USDA-NRCS Technical Release, 55 (1986)
41. Bingner, R.L., Theurer, F.D., Yuan, Y.: AnnAGNPS Technical Processes Documentation, Version 5.4 (2015)
42. Garbrecht, J., Martz, L.W.: TOPAZ user manual (2004)
43. Johnson, G.L., Daly, C., Taylor, G.H., Hanson, C.L.: Spatial variability and interpolation of stochastic weather simulation model parameters. J. Appl. Meteorol. **39**, 778–796 (2000)
44. Liu, J., Zhang, L., Zhang, Y., Hong, H., Deng, H.: Validation of an agricultural non-point source (AGNPS) pollution model for a catchment in the Jiulong River watershed, China. J. Environ. Sci. **20**, 599–606 (2008)
45. Crow, F., Ghermazien, T., Pathak, C.: The effect of land use parameters on runoff simulation by the USDAHL hydrology model [Oklahoma]. Transactions of the ASAE [American Society of Agricultural Engineers] (USA) (1983)
46. Nash, J.E., Sutcliffe, J.V.: River flow forecasting through conceptual models. Hydrol **10**, 280–292 (1970)
47. Licciardello, F., Zema, D., Zimbone, S., Bingner, R.: Runoff and soil erosion evaluation by the AnnAGNPS model in a small Mediterranean watershed. Trans. ASABE **50**, 1585–1593 (2007)
48. Shamshad, A., Leow, C., Ramlah, A., Hussin, W.W., Sanusi, S.M.: Applications of AnnAGNPS model for soil loss estimation and nutrient loading for Malaysian conditions. Int. J. Appl. Earth Obs. Geoinf. **10**, 239–252 (2008)
49. Nyssen, J., Poesen, J., Haile, M., Moeyersons, J., Deckers, J., Hurni, H.: Effects of land use and land cover on sheet and rill erosion rates in the Tigray highlands, Ethiopia. Zeitschrift für Geomorphologie **53**, 171–197 (2009)
50. Hurni, H.: Soil erosion and soil formation in agricultural ecosystems: Ethiopia and Northern Thailand. Mt. Res. Dev. **3**, 131–142 (1983)

51. Wischmeier, W.H., Smith, D.D.: Predicting rainfall erosion losses-a guide to conservation planning. Predicting rainfall erosion losses-a guide to conservation planning (1978)
52. Hurni, H.: A Simplified Version of the USLE Adapted for Prediction of Soil Loss in the Ethiopian Highlands, p. 11. University of Berne/Ministry of Agriculture, Addis Ababa (1985)
53. Rose, C.W.: Research methods in soil erosion processes. In: Lal, R. (ed.) Soil Erosion Research Methods. Soil and Water Conservation Society, pp. 159–178. St. Luice Press, Boca Raton (1994)
54. Ouyang, D., Bartholic, J.: Predicting sediment delivery ratio in Saginaw Bay watershed. In: Proceedings of the 22nd National Association of Environmental Professionals Conference, Orlando, FL, USA, 19–23 May 1997 (1997)

Morphological Changes in the Lower Reach of Megech River, Lake Tana Basin, Ethiopia

Getachew Asmare[1]([✉]) and Mengiste Abate[2]

[1] Amhara Design and Supervision Works Enterprise,
P.O. Box-1921, Bahir Dar, Ethiopia
chadgallery@gmail.com
[2] Faculty of Civil and Water Resources Engineering,
Bahir Dar Institute of Technology, Bahir Dar University,
P.O. Box-26, Bahir Dar, Ethiopia
mengisteaba@gmail.com

Abstract. This study examined and identify, map the plan-form changes and to evaluate, investigate and explore the effect and impact or influence of drivers/catchment process induces for the plan-form changes along a 44.43-km stretch of Lower Reach of Megech River, Lake Tana Ethiopia, for the last 30 years by using secondary climate data, catchment characteristics, field observation, key informant interview and Satellite images of the year 1984, 1995, 2000, 2006, 2009 and 2014. For data preparation and analysis, Image analysis software (ERDAS 2014), Arc GIS and Terrain analysis tools were used. Lower reach of Megech River has undergone major plan-form changes for the past 30 years. At a distance about 19.3 km from the Lake, the river abounded the old channel course and shifted from west to east and developed new channel which directly drains to Lake Tana. The sinuosity of Megech River shows an overall increase of 8.2% for the 30-year study period. Generally, the plan form alteration of Megech River at different reach is due to natural and artificial influences. Hence, appropriate river engineering works should be practiced so as to minimize the negative aspects of channel bank retreats.

Keywords: Anthropogenic impacts · Megech River · Plan form · Sinuosity · Meandering

1 Introduction

Morphology of river is a field of science which deals with the change of river plan form and the shapes of river channels and how they change over time (Uddin et al. 2011). Rivers can degrade or aggrade, widen or narrow, become coarser or finer, meander or straighten, and braid. The response and the change can also change over the time and space of adjustment.

The continuous change of river channels over time has been a major focus study in geomorphology various techniques, such as sediment logical, historical sources, plan metric resurvey, repeated cross-profiling, erosion pins and terrestrial photogrammetric, have been used to measure riverbank erosion, bank collapse, deposition, channel direction change and channel change.

Published by Springer Nature Switzerland AG 2019. All Rights Reserved
F. A. Zimale et al. (Eds.): ICAST 2018, LNICST 274, pp. 32–49, 2019.
https://doi.org/10.1007/978-3-030-15357-1_3

Plan-form/pattern or adjustment of an alluvial river is organized through a feedback between channels, floodplain, bars and vegetation which in turn is controlled by the spatial sorting of aggradation and degraded bed load and wash load sediments. The migration of meandering rivers results from interactions among flow, sediment transport, channel, land use land cover, human interaction and environmental activities form that create complicated sedimentary structures and lead to the evolution of channel plan form over time (Singh 2014). The interference of anthropogenic activities on the natural river or environment influences the nature of the landscape processes and their activities also the increasing extent of the human disturbances or anthropogenic activities such as land feature changes, irrigation practice, urbanization, quarry mining or production for construction material, channelization, gravel and sand mining and hydraulic structures construction along or across the river have brought changes to a power of changing the river channel characteristics'.

The variables that affect channel or river system, such as climate, geology, vegetation, valley dimensions, hydrology, channel morphology and sediment load, have different causal relationships one with another, depending upon the time scale of analysis which means spatial and temporal analysis. However, channel form in particular is mainly a result of the interaction between river flows, sediment yields (driving variables), valley characteristics (boundary characteristics) and human activity (Taylor 2002). River form at all scales is controlled by a complex interaction of many environmental variables and the relative importance of any particular variable in shaping channel form depends on the time and geographic scale being considered (Taylor 2002) which those factors can be either natural or human-induced and can act at different spatial and temporal scales and river morphology investigates the evolution of fluvial environments through the analysis of qualitative and quantitative aspects to interpret valuable relationships.

The existence of infrastructural projects, urbanization, road construction, dam constructions, sand and gravel mining activities, quarry production for construction materials also lead to increase or decrease the stream transport capacity and thereby aggradation or degradation processes could occur which impacts the plan form and shape of the river (Abate et al. 2015).

Morphometric parameters, such as channel width, water surface area and sinuosity, were calculated in several studies to evaluate the migration of channel plan form morphology. Bank erosion and deposition, channel pattern identification, bank line and centerline shift and channel change caused by human intervention have been investigated on the basis of remotely sensed data (Yang et al. 2015).

The river Megech is one of the four main rivers of Lake Tana sub basin, which contributes flow for Lake Tana. The river is a major contributor to the building up of the delta which was evidenced of severe bank erosion and rapid rates of bank line retreat along the Dembia plain as we observed during site observation. The lateral migration (right and left bank shifting) of the river results in displacement of population and loss of fertile agricultural land as it is one of the most potential irrigation scheme of lake Tana (Getachew et al. 2013).

This study examined and identify, map the plan-form changes and to evaluate, investigate and explore the effect and impact or influence of drivers'/catchment process induces for the plan-form changes along a 44.43-km stretch of Lower Reach of Megech

River, Lake Tana Ethiopia, for the last 30 years by using secondary climate data, catchment characteristics, field observation, key informant interview and Satellite images.

The characteristics and dynamics of meandering rivers have been the subject of extensive research, Megech River channel plan form geometry has been changed over past years. Lateral migration of Megech River path specifically at the lower reach of Dembiya Woredas is enormous. Though, the mechanism involved, causes of shifting, migration, bank erosion, Valuable irrigated lands are lost because of riverbank erosion are not yet well investigated. In addition, Investigation of interaction of human activities and rivers has become an important problem because they have essential role on rivers morphology. This study is equally important as it will offer the option of using the capabilities of GIS and highly resolution Remote Sensing data or images (like Spot Images, rectified Google earth images, topo map and latest DEM) rather than using low resolution images like land sat image and 90 by 90 m DEM to solve problem associated with river course changing, channel pattern, channel shifting, bank erosion, bank line shifting, active and previous channel width and meandering at the study area, but land sat data will show only center line of the river, does not show bank line, width, delta, island and river spatial extents. This high resolution data's can help in under-standing how river features are clearly identified and showed, how fast or slow is the river morphology is change. Previously studied shows researchers and other organizations use different catchment area and catchment stream length for their work still now a day they use the previous outlet for their watershed delineation. But now this research will provide and answer as to why and how changes of channel occur by using time series high resolution remote sensing data over decadal time scales are essential to study plan form change.

2   Materials and Methods

2.1   Descriptions of the Study Area

The Megech River is one of the four tributary of Lake Tana, Ethiopia (Fig. 1). It rises just from the nearest highlands of Gondar City, and has a catchment area of about 741.8 km^2 and the catchment elevation is ranging between 1784–2960.65 m above sea level. Approximately, the area where Megech River lays found between 12°45′25″N to 12°16′8″N latitudes and 37°33′19″E to 37°24′5″E longitudes. Megech River flows southward crossing the Denbia floodplain into Lake Tana for a total river stream length of about 92.6 km from the source to lake Tana but the studied reach of Megech River has length of about 44.43 km; it starts from Bahir Dar- Gondar bridge and ends at Lake Tana among the total stream length of 92.6 km of Megech River.

Major tributaries of Megech River are the Lesser Angereb, Keha Mezoriya and there are small intermittent and perennial rivers in the catchment, which flow into the main stem, Megech.

The farmers used the river for traditional irrigation agriculture for long years. Recently, the Federal Government of Ethiopia and regional government of Amhara plans a medium dam at the upper course of the river to irrigate the downstream of the

Dembia plain. Denbia is one of the most important potential areas for irrigation like that of Fogera floodplain in the above part of Lake Tana. Sand mining activity has also practiced in Megech River.

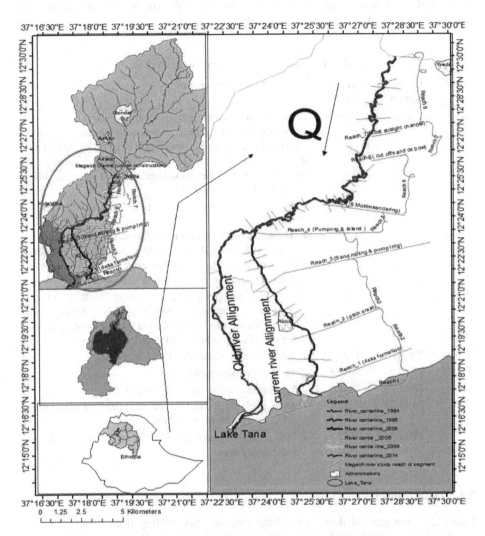

Fig. 1. Location map of study area (Megech catchment and Megech River)

2.2   Delineation and Characterization of the Study Reaches

The study of lower reach of Megech river is divided into 8 sub reaches of channel reaches and 34 cross sections (trans versed sections cross sections) based on channel characteristics the above criteria (Table 1) that reflect changes in channel pattern, dominant types of channel movement, channel bed morphology, and channel shifting, widening, erosion, observation of cut off and confinement.

The division of Megech study was made based on observations in channel pattern change, channel bed morphology, channel shifting, widening, erosion, observation of cut off and confinement. The methods described by Abate et al. (2015) were followed for reach demarcation. In addition to that for this study the subdivision of reaches was based up on the following criteria (Table 1).

Table 1. Characterization of the study reaches

Reach	Cross section	Length (m)	Demarcation characteristics
1	1 to 2	1850.6	Formation of delta and islands when the lake level fluctuates (spatially or plain extent) which means when the lake level decreases or drops there is delta and island when the lake level increases or rises the island or delta was submerged in the other hand back water effect affects the outlet point to other direction
2	2 to 4	3210.9	✓ Is located immediately u/s of Lake Tana, it is flat and plain area ✓ There is more irrigation during winter when the lake rerates (lake level drops and the water leaves the plain) ✓ There is over grazing land for cattle and facilitate for sediment input in to lake during site observation
3	4 to 9	4761.3	✓ Most sand mining activity area, pump irrigation in the right bank of the river, construction of dyke during flood mitigation area and artificial sand bag for ponding water for pump suction hose during pump irrigation
4	9 to 13	4128.7	✓ Pump irrigation and island formation
5	13 to 20	8946.5	✓ Most river meandering area
6	20 to 28	7932.7	✓ Formation of different river features area
7	28 to 29	1478.4	✓ Most stable river channel formation (straight plan form which is a more defined channel area
8	29 to 34	9612.8	✓ U/s of the study area up to bridge and most regular meandering area

2.3 Data Collection

Figure 2 shows general flow chart of the methodology starting from data collection. Satellite images (1984, 1995, 2000, 2006 (Spot 5), 2009 and 2014 (Spot 5)), 12.5 m by 12.5 m DEM, field observation and information obtained from local people were the main data for the analysis of Megech channel planform change. The Spot 5 imagery has a ground resolution of 2.5 m by 2.5 m and gives clear channel information.

"On 11 Jan 2016, field observation and measurements were made on channel width, available infrastructures around the river, sand mining activities, the extent of bank erosion, over bank deposition, breaching points and existing irrigation practice."

GPS points were also taken for accuracy assessment and for the interpretation of satellite images.

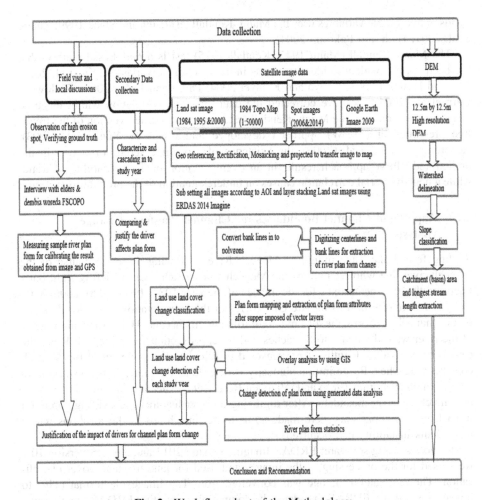

Fig. 2. Work flow chart of the Methodology

"River cross-sections was measured by role meter and staff roads for analyzing the existing river condition on existing gauge discharge site, reaches affected by bank erosion, and local bridge along the river site."

Information has also gathered from the local people and from the Dembia Woreda office on the recent and past channel conditions/alignments through unstructured interview. DEMs used as an input for Arc GIS for catchment delineation and for extraction of physical catchment characteristics.

Secondary data of rainfall, flow and sediment data were obtained from Ministry of Water, Irrigation and Electricity (MoWIE).

Trend analysis of rainfall and stream flow was done by using Spearman's rank correlation.

Both statistical analysis and a semi-distributed rainfall– runoff model was used to assess trends in the discharge in the Megech Catchment. The statistical analysis of trends in hydrologic variables uses the Mann–Kendall test (Lins and Slack 1999; Zhang et al. 2001; Huth and Pokorna 2004).

The Mann–Kendall (Mann 1945; Kendall 1975) test is a rank-based method that has been applied widely to identify trends in hydro climatic variables (Xu et al. 2003; Yue and Hashino 2003; Kahya and Kalayci 2004; Partal and Kalya 2006). Following Burn et al. (2004), we have corrected the data for serial correlation within the time series prior to applying the Mann–Kendall test using the modified version of the trend-free prewhitening (TFPW) approach developed and tested by Yue et al. (2003). According to Yue et al. (2003), the existence of a positive serial correlation in the unmodified TFPW approach results in an overestimation of the probability of trend, while a negative serial correlation causes an underestimation of the probability of trend.

2.4   Mapping of Channel Boundaries for Channel Planform Change Analysis

Starting from Lake Tana mouth of Megech River following the main course of the Megech river, the whole length of the Megech study reach, channel left & right bank lines and the river centerlines for the images of the year 1984, 1995, 2000, 2006, 2009 and 2014 were digitized using Arc GIS 10.1. For the interpretation of the local effects on the channel planform, the 44 km length (old alignment) and 41 km (new alignment) of the river were divided into 8 reaches and 34 cross sections. For Megech River the centerline and valley lengths were measured to calculate the sinuosity of the Megech considered reaches. By definition sinuosity is defined as the ratio of channel length to valley length (Schumm 1985) and (Van den Berg 1995). The sinuosity gives an idea of how much the river meanders. After digitizing all river features and existing condition in each year, comparisons were made so as to get insight about the locations where major bank instability had occurred.

Remote sensing software: ERDAS Imagine version 2014 and ArcGIS version 10.1 were used for the processing of the images and used for land use land cover classification. The raw satellite image was converted from Tag Image file format (Tiff) to image format using EDRAS in order to be compatible with other ERDAS Imagine file.

The advantage of ERDAS Imagine version 2014 direct linked with Google earth during classification. So it avoids accuracy assessment checking from other methods.

All acquired Landsat images and spot images are rectified, 2009 google earth is downloaded as rectified image but it should be mosaicked and sub setting by ERDAS imagine 2014. After rectified identifying the areas of the catchment which by using Megech catchment to fix area of interest by clipping (sub setting) it. The clipping process is done using ERDAS Imagine 2014 subset tool.

For Land use cover classification supervised classification scheme with maximum likelihood classifier decision rule was used. Supervised classification is the most common type of classification technique in which all pixels with similar spectral value are categorized in to land cover classes or themes. Supervised classification relies on the prior knowledge of pattern recognition of the study area. It requires the manual identification of point of interest areas as reference within the images, to determine the spectral signature of identified features.

3   Results and Discussion

3.1   Change in Watershed

The channel course of Megech River has been shifted from west to east since 1996. As a result of this shift, two watershed areas were found; before and after 1996. About 741.8 km² and 693.1 Km² watershed areas were calculated by delineating the

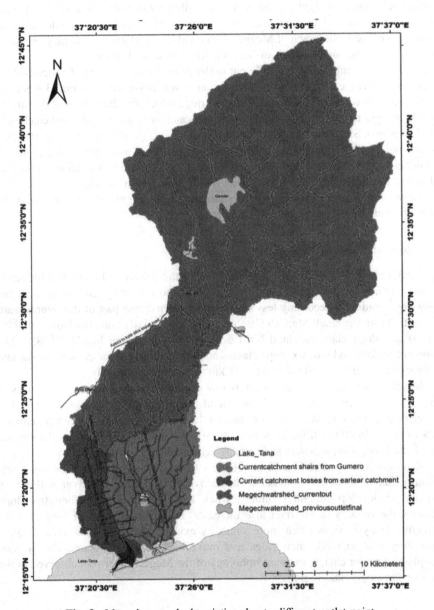

Fig. 3. Megech watershed variation due to different outlet point

catchment areas using the current outlet and the old outlet of Megech River to the Lake respectively (Fig. 3). The overlying analysis of the current and the old watershed boundaries clearly demonstrated that the Megech watershed boundary is shifted to eastward and lost about 48.1 km^2 area from the old watershed and gained 96.1 km^2 area from Gumero watershed, east of Megech Watershed. The overall result showed that the Megech River and its catchment boundary shifted to the east ward and now the left side of the old catchment boundary line has become the divide line for the current drainage flow. The increased watershed area contributes much flow and sediment to the Dembia floodplain and to the Lake Tana. This result or increasing could facilitate aggradation of the lower reach of Megech River and its outlet point. This may be one of the reason why the lower course of Megech River is shifted to east.

By using the same DEM but different outlet point for delineation of watershed we get different catchment size. From site observation and as shown from Fig. 3 when we use the previous outlet the river was followed ridge which the drainage and the stream flows from right to the left. In case of the current catchment gains additional catchment from Gummero. Since the amount of flood for Megech is greater than Gummero while flood comes from upstream and the Megech flood overflows over the plain and moves the Gumero flood back and dumps its sediment as a check structures and trap boulders and debris to the Gumero plain and formation of boundary of divide line.

The result indicates plan form or river morphological alignment change affects the watershed and watershed parameters and vice versa.

3.2 Slope of Megech Watershed

According to Shields 1982, channel slope is one of the important factors that influence the flow velocity in the channel and the profile of most river systems is steep in the headwaters, gradually becoming less steep on the downstream part of the river toward the mouth. From the result Megech Catchment has slope classes ranging from 0 to 25% (Fig. 4) and slope class and land form description is based on Shields (1982). The catchment is classified into six slope classes and the dominant slope classes are flat and gently slope 303.6 km^2 (40.9%) and 1.97 km^2 (26.5%) respectively.

Megech at downstream of the study is low gradient streams with the slope class of 0–3% (flat slope) and channel bank lines tend to shift sideways by meandering. The flow velocity is greatest on the concave side of the meander bend. This is where erosion tends to occur. In contrast, the flow velocity of lower reach of Megech on the convex side of the bend. This is where sediment is deposited.

According to (Ward 1957), Slope of the stream channel is one of the most significant parameters studied to understand the river behavior and the river will have a tendency to develop straight channels, when the slope is more. When the slope increases, the velocity of the river also increases. In the lower reach of Megech river overlaying analysis shown that more sinuosity exists at the flat slope areas (0–3%), where they tend to erode their sides and move back and forth across the megech floodplain. A major change in the morphology of the Megech river was observed in the lower or flat slope class regions.

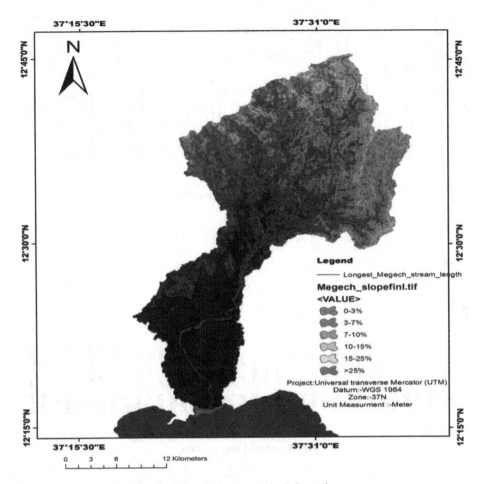

Fig. 4. Megech river watershed slope classes.

3.3 Trend Analysis of Rainfall, Stream Flow and Sediment Concentration

From the graph shown the trend analysis of annual rainfall in the Megech catchment does not show significant changes for the years 1952 to 2014 (Fig. 5), The Megech river precipitation at Gondar station has no clear trend for precipitation, both increasing and decreasing trend observed in the catchment but there is a minor change in precipitation for the precedent record slightly decreasing reduction in precipitation in major rainy season (Kiremit) and an increment of precipitation in Bega season. This indicates that although the river exhibit plan form alteration the rainfall pattern in the area is almost homogeneous. But, the trend analysis of Megech catchment reported annual stream flows starting from 2006 to 2012 has shown an increased trend on flow magnitude (Fig. 6). It is uncertain however whether higher levels of water on the staff gauge have been correctly interpreted and/or the upstream catchment is highly

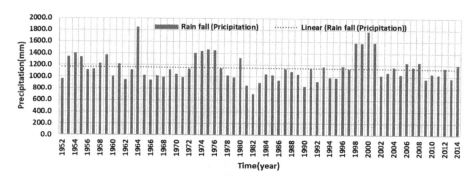

Fig. 5. Annual average precipitation

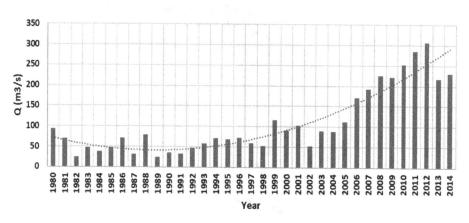

Fig. 6. Annual average flow

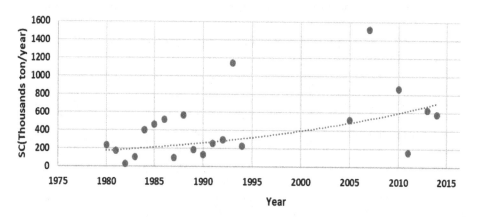

Fig. 7. Annual average Sediment concentration trends

impervious which leads to high runoff generation. The sediment concentration trend has also showed an increasing trend (Fig. 7). These all factors lead to Megech River channel modification in its planform and bed level raise at its outlet.

Therefore, any factor affecting the hydrological response and sediment delivery of a catchment and discharge and sediment yields will influence the channel geomorphological conditions. Finally, these factors are also modified by human activity either directly. Human activities, including land use changes, irrigation practice, quarry production, urbanization, construction of road and infra structures, affect discharge and sediment supply indirectly, typically by increasing peak flows and increasing the quantities of sediment and direct impact on river systems, particularly channelization and in stream mining.

3.4   Land Use Land Cover Changes

The land use, land cove change dynamics of the Megech catchment has been analyzed for the years 1984, 2000, 2006, 2009 and 2014. Field observations that we made in the catchment, information obtained from satellite images and Google maps showed that the major portions of the forest land and bush and shrubs including grass land have decreased continuously in these years. The results show that there was a significant agricultural development from 1984 (57.4%) to 2009 (90.6%) (Fig. 8 and Table 2). Based on the land use map, about 63.2% of the vegetation (forest) covers and 34.0% of bush and shrubs were lost or converted to other land use.

Table 2. Megech catchment land use land cover classification

Land use type code (ha)	Change assessment year and area coverage in ha from the total watershed area									
	1984	%	2000	%	2006	%	2009	%	2014	%
Bush and shrub land	27712.6	35.1	26398.9	33.5	19156.7	24.3	4142.4	5.3	4058.100	5.15
Wetland	541.5	0.7	620.7	0.8	20.5	0.0	104.5	0.1	282.100	0.36
Built-up area	541.5	0.7	334.9	0.4	552.3	0.7	646.6	0.8	722.340	0.92
Water body	358.4	0.5	446.2	0.6	488.7	0.6	470.9	0.6	534.980	0.68
Cultivated land	45277.0	57.4	48108.0	61.0	55783.8	70.8	71400.1	90.6	71621.180	90.84
Forest land	4413.1	5.6	2935.7	3.7	2842.4	3.6	2079.9	2.6	1625.660	2.06
Total	78844.4	100.0	78844.4	100.0	78844.4	100.0	78844.4	100.0	78844.4	100.0

An error matrix that is established using 56 ground control points and Google earth image in the Megech Catchment. From the error matrix four measures of accuracy are estimated that are the overall accuracy, user's accuracy, producer's accuracy, and the kappa statistic. The kappa coefficient (k) of 0.79 and 0.86 of the maximum likelihood classification in the periods 2006 and 2009 represents it is better accuracy. According to Monserud (1990) suggested a kappa value, the classification in this study has very good agreement with the validation data set.

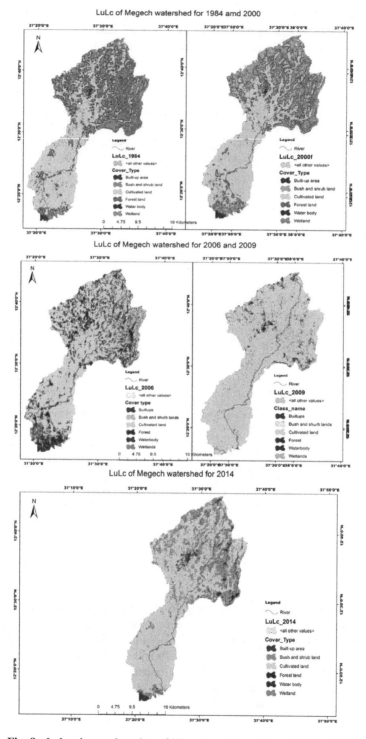

Fig. 8. LuLc change detection of Megech catchment from 1984 to 2014

From land use land cove change (Fig. 8 a to c) most of the vegetation covers showed a decrease in the last 30 years. Forest land and bush and shrubs including grass land have decreased continuously in these years. As expected, water body and wetlands showed small variation as compared to the other cover types. Another well expectation was the increase of cultivated lands. It progressed from 57.4 to 90.6 in the year 2009 and decrease to 77.7 in present instead build up area increases because there is high expansion of urbanization.

Based on the land use map, about (table) 63.2% of the vegetation (forest) covers and 34.0% of bush and shrubs were lost or converted to other land use. In case of the Megech River, it is observed that the highly affected areas by erosion throughout the years are agricultural land followed by river channel and forest land followed by agricultural land and building area. Erosion and deposition by both the rivers affected settlement areas in the floodplains. Naturally bush and shrubs are very use full for soil stability and infiltration purpose but from the local people interviews bushes and shrubs are used for fire wood.

Replacement of forest land by agriculture and use for bush and shrubs for their domestic fire wood usage are a common trend within the study area and is seen to be one of the major causes of erratic river bank erosion and channel breaching or shifting of channel. It has been observed that bank erosion has increased by instability of the river behavior due to deforestation and inadequate land use in the upper reach of land use land cover from u/s makes the catchments of Lay Armachiho, Wogera and including urbanization and drainage network from Gondar and Azezo towns which ultimately led to excessive sediment load into the rivers.

Land use\Land cover is one of the most important factors that affect surface erosion, runoff, and evapo-transpiration in a watershed. As shown in the result soil bank erosion is high in the lower reach of Mgeche River; this is because of soil degradation, deforestation, over grazing, plowing steeply slope areas for the purpose of expanding agricultural land and sedimentation is high around the Lake; this creates competition of settlement near the Lake.

From observation, qualitative analysis or interview of elder people, Dembia Woreda Food Security Coordination and Disaster Prevention Office, the river breaches the previous alignment in 1996 and the stable channel bank collapse, tree and other types of sediment traps was pushed and closed the river alignment as a check dam due to an expected flood because of u/s deforestation and replace to agriculture and set-tlement (urbanization). This indicates there is highly fluctuation of land use land cover fluctuation and followed by high run off.

All land uses and practices in the drainage catchment (e.g., deforestation, agri-culture, mining, urbanization and fires) affect runoff and sediment yield. Human activities, including land use changes, affect discharge and sediment supply indirectly, typically by increasing peak flows and increasing the quantities of sediment and direct impact on river systems, particularly channelization and in stream mining.

The high runoff response and sediment load of Megech River are reported to occur due to strong degradation of the catchment.

The agricultural intensification by land clearing and deforestation has resulted in increasing the area of degraded soil. This suggests high runoff response and sediment load of Megech River to the delta and the floodplain. The increasing population pressure and the continuous cultivation caused a loss of organic matter of the soil that has a binding effect (Tebebu et al. 2015). This leds to more bare and plowed soil and decrease the aggregate stability of soil. This, in turn, resulted in higher sediment concentrations in Megech river. All that has led to greater sediment transport by Megech River towards the lake and this changes the Megech River characteristics.

3.5   Plan Form Changes

Sinuosity

The general trend shows that; the sinuosity of Megech River is increasing from 1984 to 2014 (Fig. 9). The sinuosity of Megech River shows an overall increase of 8.187% for the 30-year study period. The valley length and channel length of Megech river decreases from 1984 to present 2014. Overall net channel area ranged from a minimum of 1.635 km^2 during 1984–2006 to 3.103 km^2 in period 2009 to 2014. The Megech River registered an overall net percentage change increase or gain of 74.14% in channel area over 30 years.

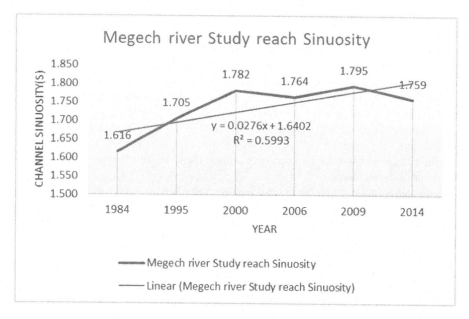

Fig. 9. Megech river sinuosity for different years

Channel Width and Cross Section

The channel width of the study reach increased by 25.42 m on average. The change in width was highest in the middle part of the river along Reach 6. In the present study, the width of the Megech River has increased and eroded a large part of land along the both banks of the river. Considering the cross-section of 2000 as a base for comparison, there was high erosion in the right side even there was island in 2000 and it was removed by flood and deposition in the left side by the year 2007, there was high erosion in the left side (1.5 m) and deposition in the right (0.5 m) side by deposition in 2014. There was 12.4 m extent bank erosion and widening in 2014 in the left bank of the river. There is bank narrowing in the left side of the river by 2010. It is clear that the bed level fluctuation in 2000 was relatively the maximum. The variation in 2007 was the minimum which can be attributed to some factors.

River Bank Erosion and Lateral Migration

The total area of bank erosion from 1984 to 2014 were about 437 ha, of which 293 ha were on the left bank and 144 ha on the right bank. The total area of bank accretion (deposition) from 1984 to 2014 equaled 221 ha, of which 120 ha were on the left bank and 101 ha on the right bank. It has been found that the total area lost as a result of erosion were 437 ha and the total area gained as a result of sediment deposition along its bank were about 221 ha. These totals translate into annual bank erosion rates of 2.9 ha/year from 1984 to 2006, 31 ha/year from 2006 to 2009, 56 ha/year from 2009 to 2014 and total of 89.87 ha/year from 1984 to 2014 and became part of channel and the trend shows increase.

The gain could be attributed to widening of the channel due to starting of neck cut-off, bank erosion & deposition, bend migration, extreme irrigation practice. The lateral erosion on the river banks led to a decrease in agricultural lands bordering the river banks and decrease in the areas of the river islands, which in turn led to a decrease in agricultural production. Both the erosion and deposition rates are increased during the period 1984 to 2014. High rates of erosion are observed, the increase in erosion and deposition rates resulted in formation of new islands, change in island areas, erosion, and deposition of river banks which resulted in disturbance of cultivated lands. An effect of the plan form change is the loss of agricultural land is estimated about 172.903 ha in the left bank and 43.206 ha in the right side total area loosed from 1984 to 2014 was 216.109 ha. Annually total net area lose is 7.203 ha per year from the bank.

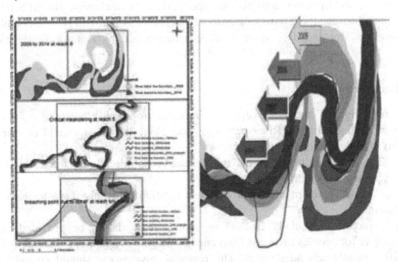

Fig. 10. Typical bend migration, formation of neck cut off and ox-bow lakes at reach 6 in different years

In general erosion is more dominant in the Megech river because of which the width of the river has increased significantly.

Bends migrated followed by expansion, extension, rotation, and translation and all are combination process and exist through the process. The bend migration was determined by comparing the images of different years given from the study year. Active meandering occurs when the channel banks were eroded, which also drives channel widening. The meander oscillation has been observed in all study reaches. In reach 6 cut-off has been created and an oxbow Lake was formed (Fig. 10).

4   Conclusion and Recommendations

4.1   Conclusion

The River had undergone a significant plan form changes over the past and last 30 years (1984 to 2014). Significant channel widening, channel course change, loss of land due to bank erosion, formation of different river features like cut off and oxbow lakes were found. Stream bank failures were very common along the study reaches. The collapsed banks contributed huge sediment to the channel bed, facilitates bar and the collapsed materials contributes delta development. The sinuosity of Megech River shows an overall increase of 8.2% for the 30-year study period. The Megech River is a meandering with sinuosity index values varying in between 1.6 to 1.8 in terms of general sinuosity and 1.01 to 2.39 for reach based sinuosity. The channel width of Megech River is increasing year after year, eroding a large part of land along both banks of the river and the overall shifting of the river towards east. It was found that erosion is more pronounced in both banks than the deposition while calculating river bank migration. The principal causes of the observed dynamics in Megech River were deforestation and intensive agriculture in the upper and lower catchments, gravel and quarry mining and irrigation activities in upper part of the catchment, the left and right banks of the river and these have worsened stream bank erosion. The present conditions of channel erosion and deposition have been aggravated by Anthropogenic effects which changes the morphology of Megech River.

4.2   Recommendations

While managing and studying rivers, it is important to identify potential causes and impacts of channel change. River training works along the River should be in place where river bank erosion occurs.

Effective catchment treatment should be done so as to minimize the flashy nature and the sediment concentration of the river.

There should be sediment and flow gauging station near Lake Tana to model the river system.

Infra structures especially Bridges or foot bridges should be provided across Megech River for peoples to access from one kebele/gote to another, to market or other to satisfice people around dembia. The regional government should consider this assignment.

References

Abate, M., et al.: Morphological changes of Gumara River channel over 50 years, Upper Blue Nile basin, Ethiopia. J. Hydrol. **525**, 152–164 (2015). https://doi.org/10.1016/j.jhydrol.2015.03.044

Burn, D.H., et al.: Hydrological trends and variability in the Liard River basin. Hydrol. Sci. J. **49**(1), 53–68 (2004)

Getachew, T., et al.: Evaluation of Operation of Lake Tana Reservoir Future Water Use under Emerging Scenario with and without climate Change Impacts, Upper Blue Nile. Int. J. Comput. Technol. **4**(2c2), 654–663 (2013)

Huth, R., Pokorna. L.: Parametric versus non-parametric estimates of climatic trends. Theo. Appl. Climatol. **77**(1–2), 107–112 (2004)

Kahya, E., Kalayci, S.: Trend analysis of streamflow in Turkey. J. Hydrol. **289** (1–4), 128–144 (2004)

Kendall, M.G.: Rank Correlation Methods. Griffin, London (1975)

Lins, H.F., Slack, J.R.: Streamflow trends in the United States. Geophys. Res. Lett. **26**(2), 227–230 (1999)

Mann, H.B.: Nonparametric tests against trend. Econometrica: J. Econometric Soc. **13**(3), 245–259 (1945)

Monserud, R.A.: Methods for comparing global vegetation maps. International Institute for Applied Systems Analysis a 14-2361 Laxenburg a Austria (1990)

Partal, T., Kalya, E.: Trend analysis in Turkish precipitation data. Hydrol. Process. **20**, 2011–2026 (2006)

Schumm, S.: Patterns of alluvial rivers. Annu. Rev. Earth Planet. Sci. **13**, 5 (1985)

Shields, W.M.: Philopatry, inbreeding, and the evolution of sex. SUNY press (1982)

Singh, S.M.: Morphology changes of Ganga River over time at Varanasi. J. River Eng. **2**, 4–6 (2014)

Taylor, D.C.: Recognising channel and floodplain forms (2002)

Tebebu, T.Y., et al.: Improving efficacy of landscape interventions in the (sub) humid Ethiopian highlands by improved understanding of runoff processes. Front. Earth Sci. **3**, 49 (2015) https://doi.org/10.3389/feart.2015.00049

Trading-Economics. 2016. Ethiopa Population. http://www.tradingeconomics.com/ethiopia/population. Accessed 15 Apr 2016

Uddin, K., Shrestha, B.A., Alam, M.S.: Assessment of morphological changes and vulnerability of river bank erosion alongside the River Jamuna using remote sensing. J;. Earth Sci. Eng. **1**(1), 29–34 (2011)

Van den Berg, J.H.: Prediction of alluvial channel pattern of perennial rivers. Geomorphology **12**, 259–279 (1995)

Ward, W.: Playmaking with children from kindergarten through junior high school. Appleton-Century-Crofts (1957)

Xu, et. al.: Monotonic trend and step changes in Japanese precipitation. J. Hydrol. **279**, 144–150 (2003)

Yang, C., et al.: Remotely sensed trajectory analysis of channel migration in lower Jingjiang Reach during the period of 1983–2013. Remote Sens. **7**(12), 16241–16256 (2015)

Yue, S., Hashino M.: Long term trends of annual and monthly precipitation in Japan. J. Am. Water Resour. Assoc. **39**, 587–596 (2003)

Yue, S., et al.: Power of the Mann–Kendall and Spearman's rho tests for detecting monotonic trends in hydrological series. J. Hydrol. **259**(1–4), 254–271 (2003)

Zhang, X., et al.: Trends in Canadian streamflow. Water Res. Res. **37**(4), 987–998 (2001)

Development of Rainfall Disaggregation Model in the Awash River Basin, Ethiopia

Tsegamlak D. Beyene[1], Mamaru A. Moges[2(✉)],
and Seifu A. Tilahun[2]

[1] School of Hydraulic and Water Resource Engineering,
College of Engineering and Technology, Dilla University, Dila, Ethiopia
[2] Faculty of Civil and Water Resource Engineering, Bahir Dar Technology
Institute, Bahir Dar University, P.O. Box 26, Bahir Dar, Ethiopia
mamarumoges@gmail.com

Abstract. This study aims at developing a model that can generate synthetic hourly rainfall data from the existing daily rainfall data of Awash river basin. Fifteen minutes rainfall data collected from national meteorological agency for 13 active stations and daily data collected from 54 stations were considered. Stochastic rainfall disaggregation and Hyetos temporal precipitation model was tested using the available fifteen minutes data. Three regions with close climate condition and rainfall pattern were identified and tested to be homogeneous in the stochastic method. Both methods are tested by using statistical comparison of variance, skew-ness, probability of dry period, and Lag-1 ACF. The result of the stochastic method showed very good performance in preserving the probability of zero rainfall and the daily rainfall total. But it has limitation in disaggregating rainfall magnitudes with high return period. Statistical comparison of Hyetos model indicated very good agreement with the original data. Especially the daily total statistical properties were well preserved. The comparison of the two methods showed that Hyetos is better in preserving the statistical property. Generally the methods are capable in preserving statistical properties and the daily total rainfall depth. Therefore, Hyetos model is pertinent for only temporal disaggregation, whereas the stochastic method is applicable for both spatial and temporal disaggregation in the basin.

Keywords: Rainfall · Disaggregation · Stochastic · Hyetos

1 Introduction

1.1 Background

The need for higher resolution of temporal and spatial distribution of rainfall data has become higher in most of water resources assessment studies all over the world. Recently, the use of satellites for producing the quality of high resolution rainfall data both temporally and spatially was popular and possible [1]. But the access to such data in most cases was hardly possible to obtain at low cost anywhere and anytime [2]. Still rainfall data collection of finer time scale is possible by the use of different types of recording rain gauges. The number and distribution of such instruments in our country

F. A. Zimale et al. (Eds.): ICAST 2018, LNICST 274, pp. 50–64, 2019.
https://doi.org/10.1007/978-3-030-15357-1_4

is not developed [3]. Therefore this calls for a scientific approach to fulfill the need of such data by extracting from the ones we have.

Stochastic models have a wide range of application in fields such as flood risk estimation, river flow forecasting and water resources engineering [4]. For areas where only daily rainfall records are available synthetic short-time period rainfall may be used as input for time varying infiltration models [5]. In a multitude of hydrological computation including rainfall-runoff and water balance modeling, flood forecasting and computer models of pollutant transport and many others, the access to high resolution temporal rainfall data is the crucial step [2].

Generating the higher temporal resolution rainfall from coarser time scale in our country context has not addressed very well. But there are few related studies such as by [6] which generated a maximum hourly rainfall data from existing daily rainfall records by regionalizing the rainfall stations of the basin. [7] showed the effect of temporal distribution of rainfall intensity in altering timing and magnitude of peak flood from a given catchment. To fulfill the gap of data shortage for such uses disaggregation models are vital approaches. But, model development for disaggregating daily rainfall data to hourly timescale is difficult with small record length of finer time scale record data.

Hardly available high temporal resolution data would have an impact in design water resource structure especially in developing countries such as Ethiopia. Most of these structures fail due to under estimation or are expressive due to over estimation peak flood, which is related to hourly rainfall distribution [6]. Irrigation and drainage design (IDD) manual [8] for the design of irrigation structures states the maximum hourly rainfall to be 50% of daily rainfall for areas less than 5 km^2 according to ministry of agriculture, with high uncertainty. The technique used in estimating design flood for such structures throughout is old and unreliable. In addition most drainage structure design is based on Ethiopian Road Authority (ERA) design manual [9] which divides the country in to five regional IDF curve. This would have uncertainty in higher rainfall variability across the country. [6] has indicated that these curves are satisfactorily reasonable for rainfall durations of one-half hour or more. The methods could over estimate or under estimate the maximum hourly rainfall magnitude [10]. Not only such methods need update but the effect of temporal rainfall variability needs to be addressed. Currently small numbers of recording stations are available in Awash River basin with small record length.

Even though the recording gauging stations with hourly time scale are unevenly scattered still the existing records are useful for disaggregating the daily rainfall data [1]. Extraction of hourly maximum from daily rainfall data is an important approach to capture the catchment response to rainfall and minimize error induced in lump [10]. Where, disaggregating daily rainfall to hourly and sub hourly time scale of rainfall data should be available. Hence these could be solved by developing a method for extracting hourly rainfall depth from available daily data. One way of doing would be by using available models of disaggregation by testing the performance of the models for our climate condition.

Therefore the aim of this paper was developing rainfall disaggregation model to generate synthetic data of hourly time scale from available daily rainfall data for Awash River basin. Particularly the original methodology developed by [11] with some modification. In addition a disaggregation model for temporal stochastic simulation of rainfall at fine time scales known as Hyetos, which was developed by the Department of Water Resources, Hydraulic and Maritime Engineering, National Technical University of Athens, was tested for generating hourly rainfall data from available daily rainfall data.

2 Research Methodology

2.1 Description of the Study Area

The Awash River basin (Fig. 1) is one of the main basins among the twelve basins of Ethiopia. It covers total area of 110,000 Km². Awash River basin extends from latitude 8° 30' N to 12° 00' N and 38° 05' E to 43° 25' E longitude. The mean annual rainfall in the basin varies from maximum of 1600 mm to minimum of 160 mm with annual average of 557 mm. The mean annual temperature varies from a minimum of 20.8 °C to the maximum of 29 °C in the basin [12]. The basin incorporates climate zones Arid and semi-arid in its most part. The basin is located mainly in the central highlands of Ethiopia, with water resource potential of 4.9 Bm³ of surface flow [13]. The elevation in the basin ranges from 250 m to 4100 m a.m.s.l. showing with high variable range of topography.

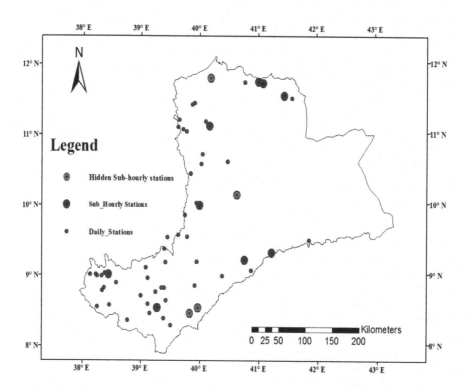

Fig. 1. Rainfall stations distribution in the Awash river basin

2.2   Rainfall Disaggregation Method

In this paper two main rainfall disaggregation methods were used to convert available daily rainfall record of Awash River basin in to hourly time scale. These methods includes: (i) Stochastic precipitation disaggregation method by [11] and (ii) Hyetos rainfall disaggregation model. Details of two methods are explained in the following sub sections.

Stochastic Method of Disaggregation

This method was developed by [11], whose overall process consists of creating event database (i.e. event rainfall depth with corresponding hourly depth) and constructing Cumulative Density Function (CDF) of event depth. Stochastic precipitation disaggregation method was selected because of limited data record. It was also known to perform well in preserving the intermittency and the characteristics of the rainfall process.

The procedure of disaggregation (Fig. 2) starts by setting ordinate 'a' from event CDF for month to be disaggregated of known daily rainfall depth (D_T), where $D(a) \leq D_T$. Then a random number (u_i) between 0 and 'a' was generated from uniform distribution and for the generated random number event depth Di was taken from the monthly CDF (Fig. 3b). This is the initial event depth, hence the process continues by subtracting Di from D_T until convergence condition ($\varepsilon < Dt$) was met. Where ε is assigned minimum threshold value of single, 1-h event for each month. Once the individual events Di are selected, the hourly depth, for these events are taken from the event database (Fig. 3a). For detail assumptions and procedure of the method readers are advised to view study by [11].

Two modifications have been applied on the method by [11]. The first modification was to adjust the method to properly fit our data limitation. The data were from the events which are from multiple stations within the basin. The second modification was the climate similarity between stations, which was approximated by regionalization in addition to comparison of station elevation and monthly rainfall record. Data from thirteen stations was utilized for this method, of which four stations are used as hidden stations for validation purpose.

Regionalization

This method considers climate proximity to cluster the stations in the basin. The aim was to form groups of sites that approximately satisfy the homogeneity condition. This suggests the sites with similar frequency distributions are statistically identical apart from a site specific scale factor [14].

Selection of Regionalization Parameters. For the purpose of disaggregation model three parameters which affect and related to rainfall variability have been chosen. The proposed parameters were elevation of the stations, geographical locations, and mean monthly maximum rainfall depth derived from sub hourly stations. But the last parameter for daily stations was the mean annual rainfall.

MINITAB statistical software was used to obtain the initial clustering of the daily and hourly stations. This statistical software has different types of clustering methods.

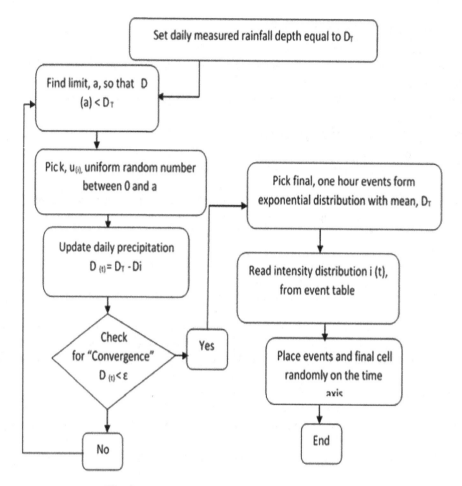

Fig. 2. Flow chart of disaggregation procedure (11)

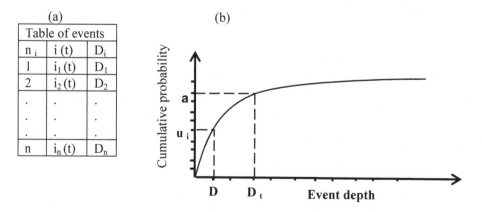

Fig. 3. Stochastic disaggregation procedure [11] [(a) Event table; (b) Event depth CDF;]

Among these clustering approaches K-means clustering mechanism was chosen and used for this study. The result of daily stations regionalization (Fig. 4) is in good agreement with elevation range.

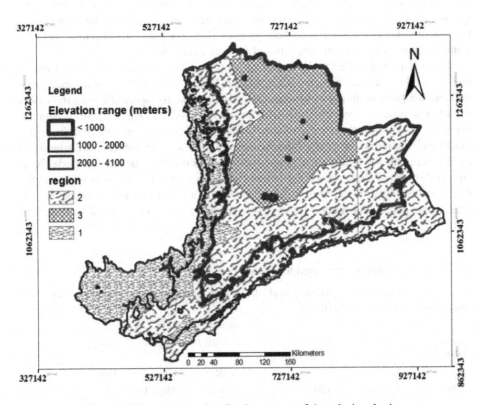

Fig. 4. Daily station regionalization output of Awash river basin

When comparing data at hand for this study with that of data utilized in the original work, it emphasizes the resulting disaggregation process was poor in dry months. This was because events recorded in dry months were smaller in number when compared to rainy months. Due to this reason three months i.e. July, August, and September were considered for this method.

The stochastic disaggregation procedure starts with finding events from the aggregated hourly rainfall data record. From stations in similar region hourly data were collected from months with no missing data. Once separate rainfall events collected in each event depth were calculated by summing observed hourly rainfall depths in each event. Then CDF's was calculated on monthly base using event depth.

Hyetos Rainfall Disaggregation Model

Based upon the Bartlett-Lewis process Hyetos rainfall disaggregation model combines a rainfall simulation model with proven techniques implemented for the purpose of adjusting the finer scale (hourly) to obtain the required coarser scale (daily) values [15]. The Bartlett-Lewis rainfall model is a continuous time model whereas the disaggregation operates on discrete time with two characteristic time scales, the higher level (e.g., daily) and lower-level (e.g., hourly) ones [15]. For detail assumptions and procedure of the method readers are advised to view study by [16].

Three stations (Table 1) with sufficient short duration data were chosen for use in this study. The stations namely Addis Ababa, Meiso, and Dubti were selected from different weather conditions in the basin so as to illustrate the applicability of the model in different weather conditions. In addition as the model requires monthly data for application, two months (with sufficient data record length) are selected from dry month and wet month for each of the stations. Test modes one and three are conducted on each continuous data, with separate validation period for application mode three. Due to shortage of data selected dry month for Meiso station is not necessarily from the driest, rather from "belg" season. Detail explanations and references of the Hyetos rainfall disaggregation model are available from the link http://www.itia.ntua.gr/en/softinfo/3/.

Table 1. Data used for Hyetos rainfall disaggregation model

Station name	Elevation (m)	Mean annual (mm)	Month for test mode I		Month for test mode III
			Dry month	Wet month	
Addis Ababa	2,277	1165	February	August	August
Meiso	1,338	792	April	June	June
Dubty	376	134	October	August	-

3 Result and Discussion

3.1 Disaggregation Result

Stochastic Method of Disaggregation Result

The results from the event data base event with duration of one hour were averaged to find the monthly threshold value. The event depths indicated in the monthly CDF of each region (Fig. 5). It was clearly observed that a rainfall characteristic that monthly threshold value the peak in august and decreases as we go to the dry months (Fig. 6). The observed data from each station, which was used in establishing the CDF and monthly convergence parameter (ε), ranges from three to seven years. This clarifies the representativeness of events, but it lacks to accommodate extreme event depths with higher return period.

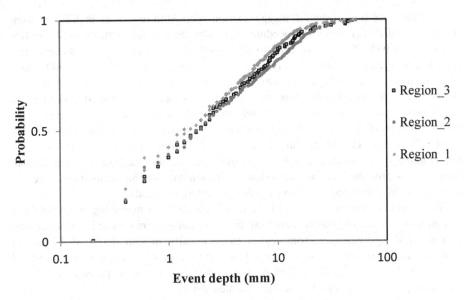

Fig. 5. August's CDF of event depth

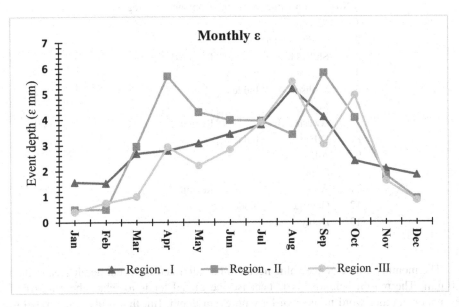

Fig. 6. Monthly convergence parameter

Stochastic method of rainfall disaggregation adapted in this study is different from other forms of disaggregation procedure especially from those methods which utilize frequency analysis. When compared to such methods it is advantageous since it provides full disaggregation of the daily rainfall depth and gives temporal variability also, rather than resulting in single intensity of rainfall depth for a given return period and duration. The process of using this method requires monthly event CDF and monthly convergence value. Therefore in this study the resulting methodology is presented in the form of monthly CDF with respective monthly convergence value. The monthly event CDF are developed for July, August and September month, plus the monthly convergence value presented in Fig. 6 is the result of this method for each region. Generally as presented in the methodology section this stochastic method of disaggregation is implemented by following the procedure outlined.

Three regions having three stations each (Table 2) for constructing event database was proven to be homogeneous based on the above parameters for use in the stochastic method of disaggregation. From region three a daily rainfall depth of 12 mm at Gewane station on 7/8/2015 was recorded, where the region's August month threshold value is 5.46; so as an illustration (Table 3) the disaggregation process resulted 4 events of 3 h, 4 h, 7 h and 1 h of the indicated depth.

Table 2. Sub hourly stations region with hidden stations

S/No	Station name	Remark	Homogeneous region
1	Erer		
2	Addis Ababa		
3	Sh/Robit		Region-1
4	Abomsa	hidden	
5	Woliso	hidden	
6	Meiso		
7	Awash Arba		Region-2
8	D/Fage	hidden	
9	Adama		
10	Semera		
11	Assaita		Region-3
12	Gewane	hidden	
13	Dubty		

The monthly convergence value needs to be calibrated for event depth greater than 20 mm. The reason behind this is because the model tends to relate the number of events or in other word number of Di with event depth. But this study was limited to conduct calibration of convergence value for larger values due to data limitation from different year.

Table 3. Disaggregation illustration for region-3

D_T (mm)	"a"	u_i	D_i	D_t	Selected hourly depth patern for each D_i from database of August of the region (mm/hr)						
12	0.846	0.521	2.2	9.8	1	0.2	1				
	0.811	0.578	2.8	7	0.2	1.8	0.6	0.2			
	0.746	0.725	6.8	0.2	3.8	0.2	0.6	0.2	0.4	0.4	1.2
			0.2		0.2						

After getting hourly rainfall depth for each Di event the starting time is taken randomly from a normal distribution constrained that no event should overlap. The illustration of disaggregation from region-1 and 2 (Table 4) showed the randomness of the method in spite of daily depth, in allocating different pattern of depth and duration.

Table 4. Disaggregation illustration for region-1 and 2

St. name	Day	D_T	"a"	u_i	D_i	D_t	Selected hourly depth patern for each D_i from database of August of the region		
Dalli fage (region-2)	5/8/2016	25.4	0.96	0.78	8.4	17	2.8	5	0.6
			0.91	0.83	11.2	5.8	0.4	8.8	2
			0.71	0.67	5	0.8	2.6	2.4	
					0.8		0.8		
Woliso (region-1)	27/8/2016	11.2	0.57	0.36	6.8	4.4	3.4	3.4	
					4.4		4.4		

Stochastic Method of Disaggregation Validation

In this study the stochastic model performs well with longer record year of shorter time scale. Besides, available data was less representative to rainfall depth with higher return period both in statistical representativeness and in predicting maximum hourly rainfall depth. Hence the model was poor in predicting intense rainfall occurring in short duration with large magnitude.

The validation process for this study was conducted by using separate stations in each region. For example the validation of region one using Woliso station for the month of August (Table 5) showed the method well conserved daily statistics more than the hourly statistics. Similarly result was observed on the other regions; that is the daily magnitude was well preserved, but the hourly predicted values were not in agreement with the observed value with some level of error. Especially the variance and skewness values are under estimated. The value of lag-1 Acf of observed and predicted hourly rainfall depth is over estimated. The reason for such variation between observed and predicted value is due to the problem of the model in disaggregating larger rainfall magnitudes.

Table 5. Statistical comparison of validation process

Probability of zero				Variance			
Observed		Predicted		Observed		Predicted	
Hourly	Daily	Hourly	Daily	Hourly	Daily	Hourly	Daily
0.90995	0.16129	0.9207	0.16129	0.41087	8.36928	0.21163	8.36928
Lag-1 ACF coeff.				Skewness			
Observed		Predicted		Observed		Predicted	
Hourly	Daily	Hourly	Daily	Hourly	Daily	Hourly	Daily
0.033767	0.030806	0.115606	0.030806	12.3464	1.8974	6.58969	1.8974

The hourly rainfall temporal distribution in the month of August at Woliso station clearly showed that the peak rainfall were under estimated whereas the lower magnitudes of rainfall were overestimated (Fig. 7). The other observation was the displacement of time of occurrence of disaggregated rainfall depth.

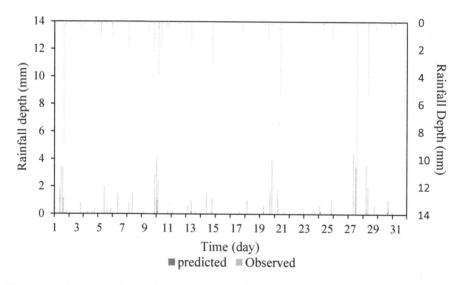

Fig. 7. Hourly rainfall distribution of observed and predicted rainfall depth for August month of at Woliso station

One of the purposes of disaggregation is enabling determination of peak events. Collecting the peak hourly events on daily base from both observed and predicted data of August month for Woliso station (Fig. 8) indicated a better prediction of hourly peak than taking 50% of the daily total which is the case presented by Irrigation Drainage Design Manual. But still the stochastic method of disaggregation needs adjustment by including ample fine time scale recorded data for a better prediction of higher depth of rainfall.

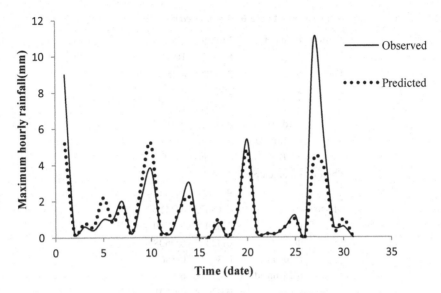

Fig. 8. Hourly maximum of August month at Woliso station

Hyetos Model Result

Hyetos model accesses available finer time scale rainfall data to calculate site specific model parameters in order to disaggregate daily rainfall depth. The BLM parameters were estimated for each station listed in the methodology section (Table 6). A principally similar model of Modified Bartlett-Lewis Rectangular Pulse Model (MBLRPM) was implemented in Upper Blue Nile River Basin and it was due to MBLRPM alone has poor result which suggested stochastic redistribution of the outputs of the model using Beta probability distribution function [3]. An adjusting procedure indicated in methodology section has proven the result of Hyetos model in this study.

Table 6. BLM parameter values

Station	Parameters	Month	
		8	2
Addis Ababa	α	97.99	3.07977
	κ	65.87	11.2771
	ϕ	25	0.2272
	λ (d–1)	2.25	0.1133
	μ_X (mm d^{-1})	95.94	93.025
	ν (d)	0.92839	0.000324

(continued)

Table 6. (*continued*)

Station	Parameters	Month	
		8	10
Dubty	α	3.24884	4.46
	κ	100	4.916
	ϕ	0.9864	1.477
	λ (d–1)	0.46623	0.0417
	μ_X (mm d^{-1})	10	110
	ν (d)	0.01066	0.0392

Station	Parameters	Month	
		4	6
Meiso	α	5.13323	17.414
	κ	1.65925	7.4219
	ϕ	0.02407	0.0608
	λ (d–1)	0.40659	0.3863
	μX (mm d^{-1})	16.5776	60
	ν (d)	0.02884	0.010118

Hyetos Model Validation

The model has shown to perform the disaggregation process by preserving the statistical property of original observed both at hourly and daily time scale. The comparison of disaggregated rainfall data for Meiso station on month six (Table 7) with obseved statistical property resulted poor comparison of variance and Lag-1 Acf than skewness and probability of zero. The comparison is conducted for all wet and dry periods. The daily statistical property is well preserved whereas on hourly time scale the Lag-1 autocorrelation coefficient shows over estimation when compared to the others. Compared to the case study performed on Heathrow airport rain gauge (London, UK) by Koutsoyiannis, Onof [15] generally the result of this study has slightly lower performance. Comparably better result was obtained on skew-ness and probability of dry period. Other case studies by [17] in Malaysia also indicated similar results. The result of Meiso station on month six had better predicted skew-ness than the previously mentioned studies.

Table 7. Validation result of Hyetos disaggregation model

Probability of zero				Variance			
Observed		Predicted		Observed		Predicted	
Hourly	Daily	Hourly	Daily	Hourly	Daily	Hourly	Daily
0.9681	0.667	0.9792	0.7	0.6785	20.766	0.732	20.887
Lag-1 autocorrelation coefficient				Skew-ness			
Observed		Predicted		Observed		Predicted	
Hourly	Daily	Hourly	Daily	Hourly	Daily	Hourly	Daily
0.1328	0.2852	0.1720	0.2820	16.092	2.6287	16.0869	2.631

3.2   Model Comparison

The result showed that both methods were capable preserving the daily total magnitude. On the other hand the stochastic method under estimate the rest values. The anticipated cause of this problem is related to under estimation of large rainfall magnitudes. Statistical comparison of both methods with observed magnitude of Meiso station for June 2010 (Fig. 9) was better conserved by Hyetos model.

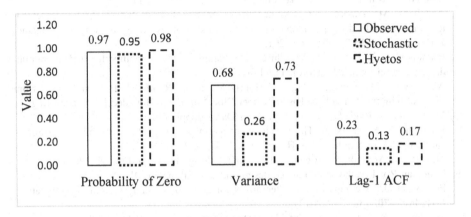

Fig. 9. Statistical comparison of models with observed

Skewness indicated similar pattern similar to the other comparisons. The probability of zero rainfall is the statistical property that is well preserved compared to the other. The comparison is performed by also altering the observed values i.e. by removing large rainfall depths. And it has been observed the performance of the stochastic method improves (particularly the skewness and variance). In general, comparison of the two methods showed that Hyetos is better, since the statistical property is from one station.

4   Conclusion

The stochastic method, which enables spatial disaggregation, has been found to be uncomplicated and stingy. Even though this method seems to have randomness in process it's showed to have good performance for small rainfall values. Acceptable performance was shown by the method for higher rainfall; this is due to data shortage to accommodate larger rainfall events from the recorded value. Hyetos model was tested on three climate conditions for rainy and dry seasons. Since the model was for specific site, stations having sufficient data from different climate conditions were selected. Hytoes model performance was consistent in preserving the statistical property on different data sets. In general it was understood that the specific disaggregation, where small records are available, can be extended by using Hyetos model. Whereas the problem of less and or shorter time scale in a given area can be alleviated by using the stochastic method.

References

1. Pluntke, T., et al.: Use of past precipitation data for regionalisation of hourly rainfall in the low mountain ranges of Saxony, Germany. Nat. Hazards Earth Syst. Sci. **10**(2), 353 (2010)
2. Güntner, A., et al.: Cascade-based disaggregation of continuous rainfall time series: the influence of climate. Hydrol. Earth Syst. Sci. Discuss. **5**(2), 145–164 (2001)
3. Engida, A.N., Esteves, M.: Characterization and disaggregation of daily rainfall in the Upper Blue Nile Basin in Ethiopia. J. Hydrol. **399**(3–4), 226–234 (2011)
4. Abdellatif, M., Atherton, W., Alkhaddar, R.: Application of the stochastic model for temporal rainfall disaggregation for hydrological studies in north western England. J. Hydroinform. **15**(2), 555–567 (2013)
5. Econopouly, T., Davis, D., Woolhiser, D.: Parameter transferability for a daily rainfall disaggregation model. J. Hydrol. **118**(1–4), 209–228 (1990)
6. Alem, A.M.: Developing a Regional Hourly Maximum Rainfall Extraction Method from Daily Maximum Rainfall for Part of Upper Blue Nile Basin Bounded by Amhara Region, Masters thesis. Bahir Dar University, Bahir Dar, Ethiopia (2015)
7. Knoesen, D., Smithers, J.: The development and assessment of a daily rainfall disaggregation model for South Africa. Hydrol. Sci. J. **54**(2), 217–233 (2009)
8. Ministry Of Agriculture: Irrigation and drainage design mannual, Ethiopia (2001)
9. Ethiopian Road Authority: Drainage design manual, Ethiopia (2013)
10. Pui, A., et al.: A comparison of alternatives for daily to sub-daily rainfall disaggregation. J. Hydrol. **470**, 138–157 (2012)
11. Socolofsky, S., Adams, E.E., Entekhabi, D.: Disaggregation of daily rainfall for continuous watershed modeling. J. Hydrol. Eng. **6**(4), 300–309 (2001)
12. Behailu, S.: Stream Flow Simulation For The Upper Awash Basin. Faculty of Technology Department of Civil Engineering, Addis Ababa University (2004)
13. Berhanu, B., Seleshi, Y., Melesse, A.M.: Surface water and groundwater resources of Ethiopia: potentials and challenges of water resources development. In: Melesse, A.M., Abtew, W., Setegn, S.G. (eds.) Nile River Basin, pp. 97–117. Springer, Cham (2014). https://doi.org/10.1007/978-3-319-02720-3_6
14. Hosking, J.R.M., Wallis, J.R.: Regional Frequency Analysis: An Approach Based on L-Moments. Cambridge University Press, Cambridge (2005)
15. Koutsoyiannis, D., Onof, C., Wheater, H.S.: Multivariate rainfall disaggregation at a fine timescale. Water Resour. Res. **39**(7) (2003)
16. Koutsoyiannis, D.: Rainfall disaggregation methods: theory and applications. In: Workshop on Statistical and Mathematical Methods for Hydrological Analysis, Rome (2003)
17. Hanaish, I.S., Ibrahim, K., Jemain, A.A.: Daily rainfall disaggregation using HYETOS model for Peninsular Malaysia. Matrix **2**, 1 (2011)

Evaluation of Processing Conditions for Lentil and Corn Blend Extrudate

Tadesse Fenta[1](✉) and Yogesh Kumar[2]

[1] Faculty of Chemical and Food Engineering,
Bahir Dar University, P.O. Box 26, Bahir Dar, Ethiopia
tadeyfenta@gmail.com
[2] Faculty of Chemical and Bio Engineering, Addis Ababa University,
P.O. Box 1176, Addis Ababa, Ethiopia
jhaykl697@rediffmail.com

Abstract. An expanded food product was obtained from lentil-corn flour mixture by extrusion cooking. The lentil flour addition was maintained at 10%, 30% and 50% mixed with cereal or (corn) flour which was maintained at 50%, 70% and 90%. Operating conditions were cooking temperature; blend ratio and moisture contents of the feed mixture. Physicochemical properties of the extruded product were investigated.

The proportions of lentil and corn were selected using a unique 17-run, three-factor, and three-level using response surface methodology. Response variables were physical properties (specific length, degree of expansion and bulk density) and functional properties (water absorption index, water solubility index and water hydration capacity) and then sensory quality of the product.

It was demonstrated that lentil has good potential for making extruded products rich in protein and fiber. The best model which gives a protein rich extruded product with desirable physical and functional attributes were 47.8% lentil flour, 52.2% corn flour (db) processed at 15.82% moisture content and 181.97 °C temperature. The product was fully expanded and well cooked with almost uniform in sizes and shapes at these optimum conditions. Hence, the processing factors must be at its optimal values to achieve high extrudate quality and consistence.

Keywords: Extrusion · Corn · Lentil · Physicochemical properties · Response surface methodology

1 Introduction

Cereal grains are staple foods worldwide. They are used for production of different classes of foods; these include breakfast cereals such as corn flakes, breads, and pastries, brewing of both alcoholic and non-alcoholic drinks. In different cultures and societies staple foods, are also produced for use as accompaniments for soups, gravies and stews and they supply the basic energy requirement of the consumers. They are also used for the production of different snack foods which are eaten to prevent hunger before main meals or just (as enjoyment) for the fun of eating them, but they are deficient in some essential amino acids like lysine. To produce nutritious products,

F. A. Zimale et al. (Eds.): ICAST 2018, LNICST 274, pp. 65–82, 2019.
https://doi.org/10.1007/978-3-030-15357-1_5

cereals are usually fortified with pulse proteins (lysine). Maize is the most important cereal crop both in area coverage and production in Ethiopia [1]. In nutritional terms, maize grain is mainly useful as a source of carbohydrate and energy. In recent years; the use of maize in Ethiopia has increased at a more rapid rate than other cereals. It is being used for human consumption, animal feed and as a source of raw materials in various industries. Lentil (*Lens culinaris Medic.*) on the other hand is an important crop belonging to the *Leguminosae* family used predominantly as a human food source. It is one of the prominent sources of plant proteins, having a protein content of 21–31% (w/w) [2]. Storage proteins of lentils consist of about 80% (w/w) of total seed proteins [3]. Legumes are important sources of nutrition in developing countries and in vegetarian diets. Lentils are leguminous crops that are excellent sources of protein, carbohydrate, fiber, minerals and nutrients. Lentils are produced in the high altitude areas of Ethiopia. National average lentil yields of Ethiopia since 2002 have been 509 and 876 (2008) kilograms per hectare. Ethiopia is the 6th lentil producing country in the world. Chickpeas, a variety of beans and their mixtures, peas, cowpeas, sorghum and legume blends has been extruded, but there are very few studies on lentils (*lens culinaris*).

Extrusion cooking technologies are used to manufacture many forms of food stuff from cereals and other ingredients. The range of products includes breakfast cereals, snack foods, pregels (modified starches used in food products), breading crumbs and animal feeds. Ingredients, such as maize flour and grits, wheat flour and other food components, are passed through an extrusion cooker under pressure, mechanical shearing stresses and elevated temperature, and expand rapidly as they are forced through the outlet die [4]. Extrusion cooking of cereal flours into a wide variety of products is well documented, but extrusion of starchy legumes has been studied to a lesser extent. Extrusion cooking is used to texturize starch and protein based materials. Extruders minimize the operating costs and higher productivity than other cooking process, combining energy efficiency and versatility [5]. The evolution of snack foods has been classified as the first, second, and third generation snacks. Third-generation snacks are indirectly, expanded snacks made by extrusion processing followed by additional puffing steps by deep-fat frying or hot air stream to achieve the final texture [6].

Several researchers have reported that inclusion of lentil in the daily diet has many beneficial effects in controlling and preventing various metabolic diseases, such as diabetes mellitus and coronary heart disease [6]. In addition, pulses have been considered to be appropriate for weight management; they have low fat content and are rich in protein, fiber and resistant starch, which lead to delayed gastric emptying, resulting in an earlier sense of fullness during a meal, reduced hunger, and increased satiety after a meal [7].

In developing countries like Ethiopia, where many people can hardly afford high protein foods due to their expensive costs. There is urgent need for cheaper foods rich in protein for individuals, taking into consideration their age, sex, physical activity and physiological needs. The diet of an average Ethiopian consists of foods that are mostly carbohydrate based. Therefore, there is the need for strategic use of inexpensive high protein resources that complement the balanced amino acid profile of the staple diet in order to enhance their nutritive value and overcome malnutrition problem. This research intends to show the possibility of enriching the starchy foods with legumes.

The ultimate goal of this work is to develop Ready-to-Eat snack food product from a blend of lentil-cornmeal bled by using a Twin screw extruder and optimize extrusion conditions or parameters for the extrudate. Additionally, the study describes changes in the physicochemical properties of the product with parameters of moisture content of feed, barrel temperature and screw speed of the extruder and functional properties of the products such as water absorption index (*WAI*), water holding/hydration capacity (*WHC*), water solubility index (*WSI*) and sensory as well as textural analysis.

2 Materials and Methods

Red lentil (*Lens culinaris*), Alemaya variety were obtained from Debre Zeit Agricultural Research Center (DZARC) and BH-660 maize variety was taken from Bako area. Red lentil type was selected due to its relatively higher yield in the farm and white maize due to its high yield and area coverage of farming.

Based on the preliminary proximate composition and physicochemical studies, three blends of flours A, B and C were developed. The three different flour mixture were prepared in a ribbon blender (Model AB, Alvan blanch Type, England) for 20 min.

After blending, the mixture was packed in plastic bags and stored at 4 ± 1 °C for further use. The moisture content of each blend was adjusted to 13, 16, and 19% (on wet basis) directly in the extruder before extrusion processing using a calibrated, proportioning pump (water injection pump). This approach was used because the lentil and corn flour blend became sticky and difficult to feed if adjusted to 13, 16, and 19% moisture prior to extrusion. The ratio used for the combination of the flours for products was arrived at using the material balance calculations.

The flour mixture was then subjected to extrusion test at all combinations of the operating parameters (feed moisture and processing temperature) (Table 1).

Table 1. The formulated blends of flours A, B and C; barrel temperature and feed moisture content.

Factor/variable	Coded levels		
	−1	0	+1
BT (°C)	160	180	200
FMC (%)	13	16	19
BR % (g/100 g)	10:90	30:70	50:50

Where BT - barrel temperature; FMC - feed moisture content; BR - lentil: corn blending ratio

The raw and extruded samples were milled with laboratory miller and proximate analysis (in Duplicates) was performed on each sample according to [8] procedures for proximate analysis. Proximate composition of both flours was reported on dry mass basis. The software, Design-Expert 7, Response surface method, Box-Behnken Design with one-way ANOVA (analysis of variance) were used for comparison of means [15]. Significance was accepted at 0.05 level of probability ($p < 0.05$). The extrusion variables studied was feed moisture content, barrel temperature and legume/cereal blend ratio. Treatments were done in replicate (Table 2).

Table 2. Experimental set up with feed flow rate of 51 g/min at the working atmospheric Po of 45 bars.

Pattern	Runs	Barrel Temp (°C)	Blend ratio (% lentil)	Moisture content (%)	Liquid-flow rate or stroke (%)
+−0	1	200	10	16	9.22
++0	2	200	50	16	9.20
0−−	3	180	10	13	9.00
0−+	4	180	10	19	9.68
0+−	5	180	50	13	9.05
−0−	6	160	30	13	9.30
−+0	7	160	50	16	8.58
−−0	8	160	10	16	8.47
000	9	180	30	16	9.65
−0+	10	160	30	19	10.3
000	11	180	30	16	11.2
+0+	12	200	30	19	10.7
000	13	180	30	16	8.90
0++	14	180	50	19	9.17
+0−	15	200	30	13	9.30
000	16	180	30	16	9.68
000	17	180	30	16	9.80

The samples were extruded based on the above experimental setup and steady state is reached when there is no visible drift in torque and dies pressure [9]. The extrudate were manually cut to a uniform length of 4 cm to calculate some physical properties. The extruded products were placed on a table and allowed to cool for 30 min at room temperature for the measurement of weight and diameter [10].

Physical properties (specific length, degree of expansion and bulk density) and Functional Properties (water absorption index (WAI), water solubility index (WAI) and water hydration capacity (WHC)) and sensory evaluation of the product has been carried out.

3   Results and Discussion

3.1   Chemical Composition of Raw Materials and the Extrudate

The chemical composition of corn and dehulled lentil flour used in this study is presented in (Table 3) below. The crude protein content of the corn was 7.88%, which is the lowest when compared with other cereals, whereas crude protein content of lentil was 17%.

Table 3. Proximate composition of raw corn and dehulled lentil flours.

Component (%)	Corn*	Lentil*
Moisture (%db)	1.78 ± 0.06	1.40 ± 0.06
Protein (N * 6.25)	7.88 ± 0.13	17.00 ± 0.57
Crude fat	4.56 ± 0.44	1.15 ± 0.08
Crude fiber	2.14 ± 0.40	2.65 ± 0.40
Total ash	1.40 ± 0.28	2.38 ± 0.56
Total carbohydrate**	82.24 ± 0.55	75.42 ± 0.36
Energy (Kcal/100 gm)	416.52 ± 0.08	380.03 ± 0.02

In extrusion of cereal flour and starch-based products, the qualities of the raw material such as the composition of starch, protein, lipid and fiber dictates that product quality attributes, among others are the expansion and functional properties [5].

As presented in (Table 4), raw blends of lentil and corn flour were significantly ($p < 0.05$) higher in protein than corn, fat and carbohydrate content than lentil alone. The same could be said with regard to ash and crude fiber contents. The increase in nutrients content of blend with legume over the blend with corn could be because of the balancing of the nutrients among the cereals and legumes. The carbohydrate content decreased along the increase in the legume content, in the blend ratio. The decrease in carbohydrate content although appears to be mostly significant, it could be because of increased solubility of carbohydrates due to the addition of legumes were expected to enrich protein and mineral content in the final snack product.

In (Table 5), below the mixture of lentil and corn after extrusion contained a better content of crude protein (as an example protein content of 12.36% at processing condition of 50:50 blend ratio at 160 °C barrel temperature and 16% feed moisture content) than the mixture of corn and lentil before extrusion (11.94% for 50:50 blend ratio). Corn has the highest total carbohydrate 82.24% (g/100 g) than lentil which contained 75.42% (g/100 g). Generally, the mixture has the higher total carbohydrate than lentil alone. Crude fiber (2.14%) and total ash (1.40%) of corn were lower than crude fiber (2.65%) and total ash (2.38%) of lentil. Crude fiber (2.14%) of corn before extrusion were greater than crude fiber (1.86%) after extrusion of the mixture and crude fat (1.15%) of lentil before extrusion is lower than crude fat (1.31%) after extrusion as seen at 50:50 blend ratio, 160 °C barrel temperature and 16% moisture content processing condition as an example. The value of extrudate total ash increases as blend

Table 4. Proximate composition and mineral contents of lentil and corn raw flour blends.

Component (%db)	Raw blends (n = 3)		
	10:90(LF:MF)*	30:70(LF:MF)*	50:50(LF:MF)*
Moisture	1.74 ± 0.081	1.66 ± 0.062	1.60 ± 0.13
Protein (N × 6.25)	8.80 ± 0.23	10.62 ± 0.38	11.94 ± 0.03
Crude fat	4.22 ± 0.50	3.54 ± 0.22	2.86 ± 0.42
Crude fiber	2.60 ± 0.41	2.50 ± 0.38	2.40 ± 0.23
Total ash	2.28 ± 0.33	2.08 ± 0.18	1.89 ± 0.37
Total carbohydrate**	76.10 ± 0.31	77.46 ± 0.14	79.31 ± 0.05
Energy (Kcal/100 gm)	377.58 ± 0.72	384.18 ± 0.21	390.82 ± 0.01
*Total minerals (***mg/100 g)*			
Calcium	11.90	21.7	31.5
Magnesium	126.51	125.5	124.5
Phosphorus	234.11	282.3	330.5
Iron	3.21	4.15	91.60
Potassium	353.82	487.40	621.01

ratio of lentil increases. The addition of lentil to corn for snack production shows increment in mineral content in the final product as mentioned by previous research findings for lentil in Pakistan [11]. This result revealed that lentil may also provide sufficient amount of minerals to meet the human daily mineral requirement besides protein content.

3.2   Effects of Extrusion Conditions on Physical Properties

The amount of complexed amylose decreased, the expansion ratio increases and percentage of water soluble carbohydrate decrease leading to decreased in bulkiness [12]. In this study the bulk density at 50:50(LF: MF) blend ratio is 0.44 g/cm^3 while it is 0.36 g/cm^3 at 10:90(LF:MF) blend ratio shows that when the corn ratio increases the water insoluble carbohydrate also increases that gives lower bulk density than lower corn flour extrudate. Higher temperatures had been reported to enhance extrudate expansion [13]. For example at 200 °C barrel temperature expansion ratio is 1.326 while at 160 °C the expansion ratio is 1.164 as shown in (Table 6) below.

Bulk density is a very important parameter in the production of expanded and formed food products, as the bulk density considers expansion in all directions [14]. A quadratic model was selected in the design program for this response to test for its adequacy and to describe its variation with independent variables.

$$\text{Bulk density} = \frac{\text{Mass of sample}}{\text{Volume of sample}} \tag{1}$$

Table 5. Proximate chemical composition of extruded snack products produced at different operating conditions.

*g/100 g

Extruded Blends (n = 3)

	BR	BT	MC	BR	BT	MC	BR	BT	MC	BR	BT	MC	BR	BT	MC	BR	BT	MC
	10:90 LF:MF	200 °C	16%	50:50 LF:MF	200 °C	16%	50:50 LF:MF	160 °C	16%	30:70 LF:MF	160 °C	13%	30:70 LF:MF	180 °C	16%	50:50 LF:MF	180 °C	19%
Moisture	8.55 ± 0.03			8.63 ± 0.50			8.32 ± 0.23			8.16 ± 0.02			9.34 ± 0.07			8.48 ± 0.01		
Protein (N × 6.25)	9.05 ± 0.05			12.17 ± 0.19			12.36 ± 0.13			9.96 ± 0.04			10.00 ± 0.01			13.13 ± 0.04		
Crude fat	1.51 ± 0.03			1.45 ± 0.08			1.31 ± 0.04			1.42 ± 0.06			1.47 ± 0.03			1.294 ± 0.01		
Crude fiber	1.49 ± 0.05			1.85 ± 0.02			1.86 ± 0.03			1.64 ± 0.06			1.72 ± 0.02			1.83 ± 0.021		
Total ash	1.20 ± 0.03			2.10 ± 0.68			2.40 ± 0.68			1.99 ± 0.06			1.69 ± 0.06			2.80 ± 0.04		
Carbohydrate **	78.22 ± 0.25			73.80 ± 0.73			73.75 ± 0.04			76.83 ± 0.35			75.87 ± 0.11			72.46 ± 0.16		
Energy (Kcal/100gm)	362.65 ± 0.33			356.93 ± 0.04			356.23 ± 0.05			359.94 ± 0.30			356.71 ± 0.07			354.02 ± 0.33		
*Total minerals (***mg/100 g)*																		
Calcium	11.76			31.40			31.50			21.72			21.72			31.52		
Magnesium	126.30			124.30			124.52			125.46			125.45			124.52		
Phosphorus	234.05			330.05			330.53			282.33			282.23			330.45		
Iron	3.11			91.53			91.50			4.25			4.15			91.54		
Potassium	353.78			487.34			621.06			487.04			621.10			487.41		

Table 6. Data for physical properties of the extruded products.

Run	F-1 BT (°C)	F-2 BR (%)	F-3 FMC (%)	R-1 Bd	R-2 Lsp	R-3 ER
1	200	10:90	16	0.51 ± 0.52	3.44 ± 0.33	1.326 ± 0.34
2	200	50:50	16	0.44 ± 0.43	2.35 ± 0.47	1.432 ± 0.34
3	180	10:90	13	0.54 ± 0.32	1.09 ± 0.37	1.162 ± 0.35
4	180	10:90	19	0.36 ± 0.11	2.09 ± 0.44	1.123 ± 0.45
5	180	50:50	13	0.45 ± 0.47	1.59 ± 0.25	1.396 ± 0.21
6	160	30:70	13	0.47 ± 0.37	1.66 ± 0.12	1.398 ± 0.35
7	160	50:50	16	0.52 ± 0.62	1.77 ± 0.11	1.421 ± 0.42
8	160	10:90	16	0.41 ± 0.31	1.62 ± 0.41`	1.164 ± 0.44
9	180	30:70	16	0.37 ± 0.26	3.89 ± 0.72	1.321 ± 0.72
10	160	30:70	19	0.48 ± 0.32	2.50 ± 0.74	1.083 ± 0.47
11	180	30:70	16	0.43 ± 0.33	3.48 ± 0.65	1.271 ± 0.66
12	200	30:70	19	0.37 ± 0.22	2.83 ± 0.18	1.184 ± 0.34
13	180	30:70	16	0.37 ± 0.29	3.88 ± 0.43	1.326 ± 0.23
14	180	50:50	19	0.47 ± 0.35	1.74 ± 0.66	1.102 ± 0.25
15	200	30:70	13	0.49 ± 0.27	1.28 ± 0.25	1.321 ± 0.33
16	180	30:70	16	0.41 ± 0.31	3.72 ± 0.33	1.25 ± 0.27
17	180	30:70	16	0.38 ± 0.32	3.90 ± 0.13	1.31 ± 0.11

Where: BR = lentil proportion with corn flour (g lentil flour/100 g blend flour), FMC = feed moisture content (%), BT = barrel temperature (°C), Lsp = specific length, Bd = bulk density, ER = expansion ratio. F = factor and R = response; mean values ± SD

Final equation in terms of coded factors for Bulk Density is:

$$\text{Bulk Density} = + 0.38 - 8.750E - 003 * A + 7.500E - 003 * B - 0.034 * C - 0.045 * A * B - 0.033 * A * C + 0.050 * B * C + 0.043 * A^2 + 0.045 * B^2 + 0.028 * C^2$$

$$(2)$$

Where; *A: Barrel temperature, B: Blend ratio, C: Feed moisture content and E - Exponetial function.*

As it can be observed in Eq. (2), the linear terms of C, interaction term of A * B, B * C and square terms of A^2, B^2 and C^2 were highly influencing variable coefficients affected the model of bulk density of extrudate. There was strong correlation between the feed moisture content and bulk density of extrudate than other factors as seen from the design. As the value of feed moisture content decreased the value of bulk density decreased [22].

The Model F-value of 6.85 implies the model is significant. There is only a 1.47% chance that a "Model F-Value" this large could occur due to noise. Values of "Prob > F" less than 0.050 indicate model terms are significant.

"Adeq Precision" measures the signal to noise ratio. A ratio greater than 4 is desirable. The ratio of 7.376 indicates an adequate signal. This model can be used to navigate the design space [15].

Inorder to come across the variation of responses with respect to independent variables, series of a three dimensional response surfaces were drawn using Design-Expert 7. Since the study involved three variables with constant variable of screw speed (200 rpm), it was necessary to fix the value of two variables to see the effect of the other variable to interpret their interaction effect up on the responses. The relation ship developed between dependent and independent variables were used to plot response surfaces and representative plots. As shown from the graph below (Fig. 1) the increase in barrel temperature will leads to a decrease in bulk density with increasing blend ratio. Results on bulk density showed that the linear terms of moisture content and blend ratio were significant, indicating their strong linear effects. The interaction effects were positive with moisture content and blend ratio. Whereas the interaction effect of barrel temperature and blend ratio were positive until barrel temperature reaches 180 °C and then negatively interacted. The interaction effect of barrel temperature and moisture content is negative. When the results were compared with those at 13 and 19% moisture content, decrease in bulk density with increase in moisture content was observed. An increase in bulk density was noticed at 10% and 50% lentil blend ratio. The graph is concaved down showing that the bulk density was significantly decreasing ($p < 0.05$) as the increase in these variables.

Sample extruded at barrel temperature of 180 °C had the highest product moisture (9.34%). In this study, a decreasing trend of product moisture content from 9.34% to 8.55% and 8.16% for barrel temperature of 180 °C, 200 °C and 160 °C were observed, respectively.

Products extruded at 160 °C showed lower product moisture (8.16%). This was due to moderate bulk density and lower feed moisture content retains the lowest moisture puffing. On the other hand, high moisture contents were associated with less expanded

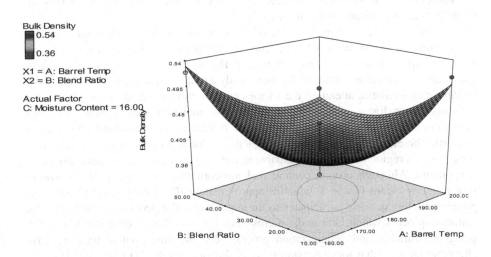

Fig. 1. Effect of barrel temperature and blend ratio on bulk density.

extrudate and required additional energy input to remove the water [16]. Moisture content of products showed increment from 8.16% to 9.34% for extruder feed moisture content of 13% and 19% respectively. Extrusion at 160 °C gave the lowest product moisture for extrudate. Samples extruded at 19% feed moisture content was relatively soft and moist as compared to extrudate at 13%. Insufficient vaporization occurring at high feed moisture content might be one of the causes for softness of the extrudate [17].

Expansion ratio (E_R) is an important quality parameter in products like breakfast cereals and ready-to-eat snack foods. In products intended for further cooking, this may not be important; in fact, large E_R which promotes increased porosity, may result in softer texture in cooked products. The maximum values of E_R for the expanded extrudate were lied between 180 and 200 °C barrel temperature; 13 and 17% moisture content and 30 to 50% blend ratio beyond that the value of E_R decreases from 3D. Blending with legume flours increased leads to decrease in expansion ratio of extrudate.

$$D_r = \left(\frac{D_e}{D_d}\right) \qquad (3)$$

Where: D_r is diametric expansion ratio, D_e is diameter of extrudate in cm, D_d is diameter of die whole in cm.

$$\text{Expansion Ratio} = +\ 1.32 + 0.025 * A + 0.072 * B - 0.098 * C - 0.038 * A * B + 0.044 * A * C$$
$$-\ 0.064 * B * C + 0.031 * A^2 - 0.019 * B^2 - 0.11 * C^2$$

$$(4)$$

Where: *A: Barrel temperature, B: Blend ratio, C: Moisture content of Feed, A * B: Barrel temperature * Blend ratio, A * C: Barrel temperature ** Moisture *content of Feed, B * C: Blend ratio * Moisture content of feed.*

Values of "Prob > F" was less than 0.0500 (i.e. 0.0057) indicate model terms (B, C, BC,C^2) are significant model terms.

The graphic (Fig. 2) representation of the expansion ratio is somewhat concaves down showed maxima for both temperature and blend ratio. More uniform texture and the most expanded products were obtained at 180 °C and 16% moisture of the feed. The predictive equations obtained for these analyses, allowed a range of products with variable characteristics attending the various consumption standards to be obtained.

Thus direct linear relationship between low moisture feed content and high expansion ratios of the extruded products are typical for cereals (due to high starch content). Therefore, this paper shows that lentil, behaves as proteinaceous food component with a region of maximum expansion ratio for feed moisture content and barrel temperature. Although protein content in lentil-corn flour is seem relatively low as shown in raw blends (Table 5) which is approximately 10.5% on dry solid basis. This protein probably actively participates to the super molecular network formed upon the extrusion process which later make a cross linkage with that of corn starch's undergoing denaturation and gelatinization process. But moisture content have negative effects up on the value for expansion ratio as shown from the 3D plot (Fig. 3).

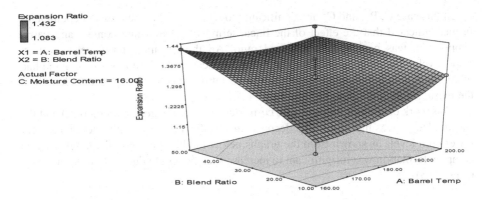

Fig. 2. Effect of barrel temperature and blend ratio on expansion ratio.

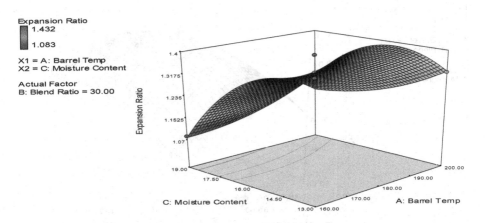

Fig. 3. Effect of barrel temperature and moisture content on expansion ratio.

Both bulk density (B_{den}) and *expansion ration(E_R)* represent the extent of puffing of the extrudate. Therefore, it might be expected that these two properties would be negatively correlated, with higher E_R contributing to lower B_{den}, but this may not always be the case. The reason could be as E_R only considers the expansion in the radial direction, perpendicular to extrudate flow, whereas B_{den} considers the expansion in all directions.

Specific length is also another deteriminental factor of the extrudates. The second degree polynomial model for L_{SP} versus feed moisture content, blend ratio and barrel temperature resulted into an equation:

$$\text{Specific Length} = +\,3.79 + 0.29 * A - 0.099 * B + 0.44 * C - 0.31 * A * B + 0.18 * A * C$$
$$- 0.21 * B * C - 0.53 * A^2 - 0.97 * B^2 - 1.19 * C^2$$

(5)

Where: *A: barrel temperature, B: blend ratio, C: moisture content of feed.*

In this case C, B^2, and C^2 are significant model terms. The linear model coefficients further indicated that the effect of the linear term of feed moisture content and barrel temperature was positive except blend ratio. All the quadratic term were positive, respectively. The magnitude of the coefficients indicated that feed moisture content had more effect than barrel temperature and blend ratio respectively on specific length of the extrudate as seen from Eq. 4 above.

This work confirmed for moderate corn (rich in oil in the germ portion of it) and the specific length was increased. The decrease in specific length for higher lentil and very lower corn levels as shown from the graphs below might be because the amylose-lipid complex formation was insignificant to increase specific length due to dilution of the oil (Figs. 4, 5).

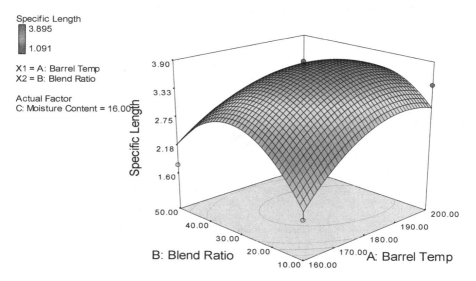

Fig. 4. Effect of barrel temperature and blend ratio of the feed on specific length.

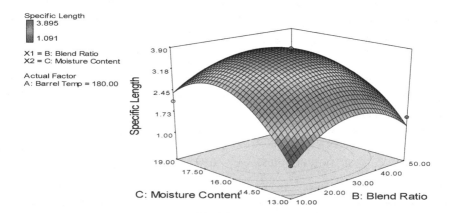

Fig. 5. Effect of feed moisture and blend ratio on specific length.

3.3   Effects on Functional Properties

Gelatinization which leads to transformation of raw starch to a cooked digestible material is one of the important effects that extrusion has on starch component of foods. As extruded product characteristics, water absorption index (*WAI*), water solubility index (*WSI*) and water holding capacity (*WHC*) are very important parameters in describing the degree of gelatinization (cooking) in the Twin extruder to process the blends [18]. Pure Corn has WAI and WSI value of 5.793 ± 0.06 and 11.79 ± 1.42, respectively [19] at operating conditions of 16% moisture content, 200 °C and 6.84 kg/h flow rate which has similarity with the result in (Table 7) below.

Table 7. Data for functional properties of the extruded product.

Run	F-1 BT (°C)	F-2 BR (%)	F-3 FMC (%)	R-1 WAI	R-2 WSI	R-3 WHC
1	200	10:90	16	5.73 ± 0.27	6.54 ± 0.32	3.43 ± 0.25
2	200	50:50	16	8.17 ± 0.04	9.22 ± 0.74	6.32 ± 0.09
3	180	10:90	13	4.77 ± 0.52	6.41 ± 0.29	3.94 ± 0.14
4	180	10:90	19	6.02 ± 0.41	7.02 ± 0.62	5.18 ± 0.53
5	180	50:50	13	7.06 ± 0.14	9.54 ± 0.49	6.32 ± 0.45
6	160	30:70	13	4.78 ± 0.45	6.72 ± 0.36	6.63 ± 0.06
7	160	50:50	16	7.08 ± 0.23	11.74 ± 0.24	7.83 ± 0.74
8	160	10:90	16	4.76 ± 0.42	10.36 ± 0.22	2.64 ± 0.33
9	180	30:70	16	6.20 ± 0.28	9.51 ± 0.52	5.23 ± 0.12
10	160	30:70	19	5.69 ± 0.27	8.89 ± 0.36	4.57 ± 0.27
11	180	30:70	16	6.20 ± 0.21	9.50 ± 0.52	5.23 ± 0.12
12	200	30:70	19	4.96 ± 0.31	7.98 ± 0.25	3.864 ± 0.21
13	180	30:70	16	6.20 ± 0.21	9.50 ± 0.52	5.23 ± 0.12
14	180	50:50	19	8.23 ± 0.47	11.36 ± 0.26	8.83 ± 0.37
15	200	30:70	13	4.11 ± 0.54	9.38 ± 0.78	5.01 ± 0.55
16	180	30:70	16	6.30 ± 0.26	8.10 ± 0.33	5.43 ± 0.11
17	180	30:70	16	6.41 ± 0.35	9.31 ± 0.21	5.12 ± 0.52

Where: *WAI - water absorbing index, WSI - water solubility index and WHC - water holding capacity; F - Factor; R - Response. Values are triplicate means ± SD*

Studied water absorption index, water absorption capacity, oil absorption capacity, and emulsifying capacity in the extrusion process of normal bean cultivars flour. The influence of process variables on functional properties have been shown to be generally significant in all these studies [20]. In this work similar finding were obtained.

The texture analysis by compression test of extruded foods are mainly composed mainly cereals, starch, and vegetable proteins. The major role of these ingredients is to give structure, texture, mouth feel, bulk and many other characteristics desired for specific finished products [21].The compression tests (or Texture analyzing) were performed at room temperature (25 °C) using cylindrical probe TA-XT (stable micro systems, surrey, England). The samples were compressed between two parallel plates of 10 cm diameter each, at a crosshead speed of 5 mm/min, with a 100 N load cell. Force and deformation were recorded and gives the values range from 0.4 to 0.80 N/mm^2 for 17 samples.

Crispness of extrudate was affected by extrusion temperature and material characteristics. Feed moisture content decreased crispness of extrudate. Hardness of the samples was found to be affected by feed moisture content, extrusion temperature and blend ratio $(p < 0.001)$. When lentil level increased, the force of deformation increased as show from the (Table 8) below. The temperature rise also resulted to softer products.

Table 8. Texture analysis results for sample extrudate

Run	BT (°C)	BR (%)	FMC (%)	Breaking strength/texture value (N/mm^2)
1	180	50:50	13	0.75 ± 0.11
2	180	10:90	13	0.80 ± 0.14
3	160	10:90	16	0.78 ± 1.55
4	180	50:50	19	0.47 ± 1.40
5	180	10:90	19	0.54 ± 2.07
6	160	50:50	16	0.73 ± 0.16
7	160	30:70	19	0.62 ± 1.40
8	180	30:70	16	0.40 ± 1.32
9	200	50:50	16	0.53 ± 0.54
10	160	30:70	13	0.75 ± 2.22
11	180	30:70	16	0.35 ± 1.11
12	200	10:90	16	0.38 ± 0.11
13	180	30:70	16	0.37 ± 1.50
14	200	30:70	19	0.51 ± 2.01
15	180	30:70	16	0.42 ± 1.62
16	200	30:70	13	0.44 ± 1.52
17	180	30:70	16	0.46 ± 0.78

The optimization was to get maximum expansion ratio, *WAI, WSI, WHC*, specific length and minimum bulk density as much as possible. Under these conditions the optimum response values were found out within the boundaries of the experimental region following the method of ridge analysis [22]. The values showed that for verification of models optimum temperature, feed moisture, and blend ratios could be taken as 181.97 °C, 15.82% and 47.8:52.2% lentil-corn blends, respectively, for all the six responses (Table 9). Since moisture content had less effect on expansion ratio and bulk density as compared to that on hardness, 16% moisture content was assumed to be the optimum for these responses. At these optimum values the model was tested

Table 9. Optimum conditions for all responses in the experiment.

Barrel temp.	Blend ratio	Feed moisture content	Bulk density	Expansion ratio	Specific length	WAI	WSI	WHI	Desirability	Remark
181.97	47.76%	15.82	0.42	1.38	2.91	7.94	10.15	6.87	0.74	Selected

3.4   Effects on Sensory Evaluation

Regarding to sensory analysis; as shown (Table 10) below, It was found that lentil content had significant effect on all the characteristics of product in visual color, appearance, flavor and crispiness, whereas feed moisture had only significant effect on appearance and texture but it can be maximized with increase in food additives. However, the operating conditions at 50:50% lentil-corn blend ratio content 180 °C barrel temperature and 19% feed moisture had higher preference in overall acceptability than other conditions according to the recipes formulation.

There was significant difference between the overall acceptability of the extrudate ($p < 0.05$). Generally more accepted extrudate for overall acceptability were those extrudate that had relatively higher scores for color or appearance, taste or flavor, mouth feel and crispiness. Lentil flour addition significantly affected over all acceptability ($p < 0.05$). The 50:50% lentil-corn blend extrudate were most accepted. As discussed above, the corn used for this study had lower protein content than several

Table 10. Sensory analysis of extruded snack products.

Blend ratio and operating conditions				*Panelist score			
Run	BT (°C)	BR (%)	FMC (%)	Color	Flavor	Crispiness	Overall acc.
1	180	50:50	13	7.00 ± 0.71	7.25 ± 0.40	7.5 ± 1.12	7.00 ± 0.00
2	180	10:90	13	3.4 ± 0.4	6.00 ± 1.41	7.20 ± 1.16	5.20 ± 1.16
3	160	10:90	16	6.5 ± 1.87	7.00 ± 1.41	7.25 ± 1.64	6.50 ± 1.73
4	180	50:50	19	4.67 ± 2.40	5.67 ± 1.40	7.22 ± 0.92	8.24 ± 2.10
5	180	10:90	19	5.80 ± 1.47	7.20 ± 1.56	7.20 ± 1.47	6.40 ± 1.36
6	160	50:50	16	8.33 ± 0.46	7.67 ± 0.74	8.83 ± 0.37	7.83 ± 0.90
7	160	30:70	19	5.20 ± 2.40	4.80 ± 2.10	6.00 ± 1.41	4.80 ± 1.72
8	180	30:70	16	5.80 ± 1.10	7.3 ± 0.50	7.0 ± 0.60	6.20 ± 0.40
9	200	50:50	16	7.33 ± 0.47	7.67 ± 0.47	8.17 ± 1.07	7.17 ± 0.69
10	160	30:70	13	6.5 ± 1.12	5.25 ± 2.17	5.25 ± 0.43	4.75 ± 1.48
11	200	30:70	19	5.50 ± 1.12	7.25 ± 0.43	7.75 ± 0.80	6.75 ± 0.83
12	180	30:70	16	5.80 ± 1.10	7.3 ± 0.50	7.00 ± 0.60	6.20 ± 0.40
13	200	30:70	13	6.80 ± 1.10	5.50 ± 2.13	6.40 ± 0.41	4.7 ± 1.46
14	180	30:70	16	5.80 ± 1.10	7.3 ± 0.50	7.01 ± 0.60	6.20 ± 0.40
15	200	10:90	16	4.33 ± 1.87	5.67 ± 1.88	6.16 ± 0.90	5.66 ± 1.11
16	180	30:70	16	5.67 ± 1.20	7.01 ± 0.33	6.82 ± 0.55	6.81 ± 0.35
17	180	30:70	16	5.70 ± 0.89	6.91 ± 0.22	7.36 ± 0.41	7.10 ± 0.26

*BT - barrel temperature (°C), FMC - feed moisture content (%), SS - screw speed (rpm) and n - number of panelist*Samples were evaluated in rod form.

cereals and moderate amount of lentil flour addition was needed to improve sensory properties associated with protein content. The barrel temperature, feed moisture and blend ratio had significantly affected overall acceptability of extrudate ($p < 0.05$).

4 Conclusions

This study was conducted to investigate the effect of blend ratio and operating conditions (feed moisture and barrel temperature) on the physicochemical, functional and sensory properties of extruded product from corn and lentil flour. Extrusion tests were conducted using co-rotating twin screw extruder at three levels of blend ratio [10:90 (LF:MF), 30:70(LF:MF), and 50:50(LF:MF)], feed moisture [13,16 and 19%] and barrel temperature [160,180 and 200 °C] using Design-Expert 7.

Blend ratio, temperature and feed moisture content were found to have significant effects on the product properties. Lentil blending increased protein, total ash and fiber content of the product but reduced fat and carbohydrate content of the extrudate. Blend ratio was the most dominant factor affecting physical, functional and sensory properties of extruded products. Increased lentil proportion affected diametric expansion ratio, WSI, WAI, WHC, bulk density and hardness positively. On the other hand, the effects of addition of lower lentil levels were positive while higher levels were negative on specific length. The effect of feed moisture content was observed on WSI, WAI, specific length and bulk density of products was positive and negatively affects expansion ratio. Barrel temperature significantly affected bulk density negatively.

It is interesting to mention here that extrusion at feed moisture (16%) and high temperature (180 °C) was good to produce puffed product from 50:50% corn and lentil blend using 9 mm die size and reduced residence time. Sample extruded at barrel temperature of 180 °C had the highest product moisture (9.34%). In this study, a decreasing trend of product moisture content from 9.34% to 8.55% and 8.16% for barrel temperature of 180 °C, 200 °C and 160 °C were observed respectively. Products extruded at 160 °C showed lower product moisture (8.16%). This was due to moderate bulk density and lower feed moister content retains the lowest moisture puffing.

This product had a mean value (at least for three measurements) of specific length of 2.44 cm/g, expansion ratio of 1.28, bulk density of 0.44 g/cm^3, WAI of 6.01%, WSI of 8.95%and WHC of 5.34%. The sensory scores (a mean value of 22 panelists) for color, flavor, crispness and overall acceptability were also 5.92, 6.58, 7.06 and 6.24 respectively on nine-point hedonic scale.

Acknowledgments. All experimentation and study were conducted with the help of Addis Ababa university for research funding, Ethiopian health and nutrition research institute (EHNRI) and Bahir Dar university, Ethiopia. The first author thankfully acknowledges all mentioned institutions for providing all kinds of possible laboratory facilities and funding during the study in Ethiopia.

References

1. CSA, Central Statistical Agency: Agricultural sample survey: report on area and production for major crops. Statistical Bulletin 427, Addis Ababa, Ethiopia (2006). http://www.ecx.com. et/commodities.aspx. Accessed 6 March 2013
2. Urbano, G., Porres, J.M., Frías, J., Vidal-Valverde, C.: Nutritional value. In: Yadav, S.S., McNeil, D.L., Stevenson, P.C. (eds.) Lentil, pp. 47–93. Springer, Dordrecht (2007). https:// doi.org/10.1007/978-1-4020-6313-8_5
3. Adsule, R.N., Kadam, S.S., Leung, H.K.: Lentil. In: Salunkhe, D.K., Kadam, S.S. (eds.) Handbook of World Food Legumes: Nutritional Chemistry, Processing Technology, and Utilization, vol. 11, p. 131. CRC (Cyclic Redundancy Check) Press, Boca Raton (1989)
4. Riaz, M.N.: Extruders in Food Applications. Head, Extrusion Technology Program, Food Protein Research and Development Center. CRC (Cyclic Redundancy Check) Press, Taylor and Francis Group, Texas A&M University (2000)
5. Mercier, C., Feillet, P.: Modification of carbohydrate component by extrusion cooking of cereal product. Cereal Chem. **52**, 283–297 (1975)
6. Moore, G.: Snack food extrusion. In: Frame, N.D. (ed.) The Technology of Extrusion Cooking, pp. 110–143. Blackie Academic & Professional, London (1994)
7. Dilis, V., Trichopoulou, A.: Nutritional and health properties of pulses. Mediterr. J. Nutr. **1**, 149–157 (2009)
8. AACC, American Association of Cereal Chemists: Approved Methods of the American Association of Cereal Chemists, 10th edn. AACC, St. Paul, Minnesota, US (2000)
9. Garber, B.W., Hsieh, F., Huff, H.E.: Influence of particle size on the twin screw extrusion of corn meal. Cereal Chem. **74**(5), 656–661 (1997)
10. Ibanoglu, Ş., Ainworth, P., Ozer, E.A., Plunkett, A.: Physical and sensory evaluation of nutritionally balanced gluten free extruded snack. J. Food Eng. **75**, 469–472 (2005)
11. Amjad, L., Khalil, A.L., Ateeq, N., Khan, M.S.: Nutritional quality of important food legumes. Food Chem. **97**, 331–335 (2006)
12. Bhatnagar, S., Hanna, M.A.: Amylose–lipid complex formationduring single-screw extrusion of various corn starches. Cereal Chem. **71**, 582–587 (1994)
13. Alverez-Martinez, L., Kondury, K.P., Harper, J.M.: A general model for expansion of extrudated products. J. Food Sci. **53**, 609–615 (1988)
14. Wang, W.M., Klopfenstein, C.F.: Effects of twin-screw extrusion on the nutritional quality of wheat, barley, oats. Cereal Chem. **6**, 94–98 (1993)
15. Montgomery, C.: Design and Analysis of Experiments, 5th edn. Wiley, New York (2001)
16. Cammire, M., Clykink, C., Bittner, R.: Characteristics of extruded mixture of corn meal and glandless cottonseed flour. Cereal Chem. **68**(64), 419–424 (1991)
17. Harris, P.L., Cuppett, S.L., Lee, K.W.: A scanning electron microscope study of maize gluten meal and soy co-extrudates. Cereal Chem. **65**, 228–232 (1988)
18. Jyothi, A.N., Sheriff, J.T., Sanjeev, M.S.: Physical and functional properties of arrowroot starch extrudates. J. Food Sci. **74**(2), 97–104 (2009)
19. Lazou, A., Krokida, M.: Structural and textural characterization of corn-lentil extruded snacks. J. Food Eng. **100**, 392–408 (2011)

20. Rocha-Gozman, N.E., Gallegos-Infante, J.A., Gonzalez-Laredo, R.F., Castillo-Antonio, P.A., Delgado-Licon, E., Ibarra-Perez, F.: Functional properties of three common bean (Phaseolus Vulgaris) cultivars stored under accelerated condition followed by extrusion. Lebensm-wiss u-Technol **39**, 6–10 (2006)
21. Launay, B., Lisch, L.M.: Twin-screw extrusion cooking of starches: Flow behavior of starch pastes, expansion and mechanical properties of extrudates. J. Food Eng. **52**, 1746–1747 (1983)
22. Khuri, A.I., Cornell, J.A.: Response Surface Design and Analysis. Marcel Dekker, Inc., New York (1987)

Machine Repair Problem with Preventive Maintenance and Multi Criteria Prioritization of Machines

Ahmed Abide[(✉)], Jeyaraju Jayaprakash, Bereket Haile,
and Sisay Geremew

Faculty of Mechanical and Industrial Engineering,
Bahir Dar Institute of Technology, Bahir Dar University, Bahir Dar, Ethiopia
wubied@gmail.com, ahmedat@bdu.edu.et

Abstract. Queues of failed machines in machine repairing problem occur due to the failure of machines at random in the manufacturing industries, while different jobs are performed on the machines. Due to failures of machines, the manufacturing system may face significant loss of production, revenue, and customer goodwill. Most existing studies of the machine repair problem founded their study on the assumption of machines are repaired only after failure and with first come first served service discipline. That means preventive maintenance and machine priority based service are ignored. Our study extends this model by incorporating preventive maintenance and multi-criteria based prioritization of machines. Analytical network process tool is used to obtain the priority of machineries. And age based repair differential equations governing the model are constructed. We have established some indices for the system performance in terms of optimal preventive maintenance age t and system's long run expected cost. An illustrative case is considered to justify solution quality by comparing the result with the previous model study results.

Keywords: Maintenance · Machine repair problem ·
Machine interference problem · Queues

1 Introduction

The technological advancement forced every area of work to be associated with machine. As a result humans are becoming more dependent on machine than before. Consequently any interruption due to failure of machines will affect both the quality of the service delivered by the machines, and also increases the cost of operating the machine. The machine interference and the machine repair/failure problems occur in almost all the areas including the computer networks, communication systems, production systems, transportation systems, flexible manufacturing systems, etc. Due to wide applications, various researchers working in the area of queuing theory devoted their attention on this topic considering various concepts (Jain et al. 2014). When a machine breaks down, it is repaired by one of a crew of R repair persons, thus this repair person cannot repair other broken machines for a period of time. Thus, during

F. A. Zimale et al. (Eds.): ICAST 2018, LNICST 274, pp. 83–92, 2019.
https://doi.org/10.1007/978-3-030-15357-1_6

this busy period of time, it is possible that there are broken machines have to wait and are interfered with by the machine being repaired (Chen 2006).

Different researchers try to model machine repair/interference problem based on diverse important factors. The factors may include: arrival pattern/distribution, queuing model, number of server, service discipline, queuing discipline, characteristics of server, etc. In a classical machine repair model, it is assumed that the servers remain idle until the failed machines present (Wu and Ke 2014). While others like Yang et al. 2005 proposed a queuing network model for a single operator, machine interference problem with external operations, i.e., those tasks that can be completed while the machine is running.

By considering a policy in relation to either the server wait the entire working time or leave the working facility for other tasks one may have a range of models. The primary goal of leaving the repair facility (Vacation) is to improve the utility of the work force (support for other departments), or increase the abilities of personnel by joining a training course (Ke and Wu 2012). Ke et al. 2009 modeled an M/M/R machine repair problem with spares and server with single, multiple and hybrid vacations. On the other hand Ke and Wu 2012 proposed "(R, V, K) synchronous multiple vacation policy" and could be used to expresses a queuing system with R servers and K teams/groups (with size V) are allowed to take synchronous vacation. Baba 2005 extended on the concept of working vacation policy. The researchers in their GI/M/1 queue model considered the server works with different rates rather than completely stop working during a vacation period. Here, most of the researches done consider single phase processing while Ke and Lin 2008 extended the concept of multiple phase maintenance operation studied by Wang and Kuo 1997 by adding random failure of servers in their model.

Wang et al. 2007 studied an M/M/R machine repair problem with balking and reneging involving spare switching failures. Wang et al. 2011 further studied by considering only variable servers and balking concept. Maheshwari and Ali 2013, in their investigation, a machine repair model with balking reneging, spares and additional repairmen were developed. While, Sharma 2015 extended similar problem with N-policy and server vacation instead of switching failure. Except slight alteration the working vacation may look similar with the concept of service pressure coefficient; which models the fact that the mean service rate increases with the queue length. When the queue grows then the system load becomes heavier, and the repairpersons may quicken their repair rate by working overtime or neglecting other tasks (Taha 1992) because of pressure. Wang et al. 2013 investigated warm-standby M/M/R machine repair problem with multiple imperfect coverage which involving the service pressure condition. While Hsu et al. 2014 examined an M/M/R machine repair problem with warm standbys, switching failures, reboot delays and a repair pressure coefficient. On the other hand Sharma 2015 explored a Machine repair problem with balking, reneging and vacation with N-policy.

The concept of N-policy has the same logic with batch processing of items in a manufacturing setup. Wang et al. 2007 and Parthasarathy and Sudhesh 2008 investigated an M/M/c queuing system with N-policy queue, though, they have considered different number of server and service model. Kumar and Jain 2013 in their work they introduced the concept of F-policy for the controlling of arrivals whereas N-policy is applied for controlling the repair to the failed machines in similar fashions with the previous studies. On the contrary, Ke et al. 2013 in their paper modeled an infinite capacity M/M/R queue system with a second optional service channel.

A lot of research has been done by varying the nature of standby units and their switching characteristics. Jain et al. 2015 considered the assumption of if all the spares are exhausted and there are less than M but more than m (m < M) operating machines in operation (m, M) policy. Many studies on machine repairing systems with standbys assumed that it is perfect to switch over the standby to operating one. However, in real-life situations, the possibility of failure to switch a standby to an operating one exists (Ke et al. 2016). Thus, they explored the performance measures and optimization analysis of machine repairing systems with standby switching failure. In another study they further investigated the switching failure concept by introducing in their model different service discipline (Ke et al. 2018).

In order to accommodate realistic situations, the concept of fuzzy system deliberated with machine repair problem. Pardo and Fuente 2008 developed finite input source fuzzy queuing model. Shekhar et al. 2014 investigated Fuzzy Machine Repair Problem with Switching Failure and Reboot.

From the exhaustive analysis of literature the following research gaps is identified:

- Most of the studies conducted by earlier researchers concentrate modeling the queue system either deterministic arrival pattern of a machine or stochastic arrival of a machine. But in real life problems both a combination of deterministic and stochastic arrival patterns could be experienced like in the case of the maintenance facility may be expected to serve both preventive (scheduled) and corrective maintenance services. Thus to accommodate this problem the model should consider the scheduled and random arrival of machines (M/M/R+D/M/R).

- In addition, most studies considered first come first served (FCFS) service discipline instead of considering machine priority. But in reality different machineries may have different priorities. And thus, the impact on long term cost of service will be different. In order to avoid any loss due to priority a research should consider priority based service discipline. Furthermore, multi-criteria decision making approach should be used to assign realistic priority.

- Almost all the studies in machine repair problem do not incorporate the concept of learning effect in the repair personnel. For both preventive and breakdown maintenance activities the repair person may experience doing a task in faster rate and simpler method every time.

- Finally, integration of two different sections each having their own maintenance crew with optimal vacation policy is another gap identified. Where maintenance personnel will take vacation from one section to the other by looking the queue in their system.

In the coming sections by considering the first two research gaps we will present the model and its characteristics, formulation of critical age policy, priority determination, illustrative case study and conclusion.

2 Model Description

2.1 Assumptions

We considered the assumptions of Armstrong 2002 with some extension of the service discipline. From first come first served to priority based. The assumptions made by the previous author are the following.

- A machine repair problem consisting of M *identical* operating machines,
- N repairmen in the repair facilities,
- The random operating life of each machine has distribution $F(x)$,
- Survival function, $\bar{F}(x) = 1 - F(x)$
- Density $f(x)$,
- Hazard function $z(x)$, where x is the age of that particular machine since its last repair. Here it is assumed that $z(x)$ is strictly increasing in x, so that the machines have an increasing failure rate (IFR).
- A machine can be repaired either before it has failed (preventive) or after (corrective) repair; for both forms of repairs,
- The repair duration has exponential distribution with mean R.
- It is also assumed that the machines will be as good as new after repair.

2.2 Cost Characteristics

The objective is to determine a preventive maintenance policy which will minimize the long run expected cost and improve the relation with customers as well as try to minimize different damages. The long run expected cost rate $C_{m, n}$ (policy) of operating the system, given the following four non-negative costs.

1. A shortage cost is incurred at rate k per unit time per machine unavailable.
2. A repair cost c is incurred when every time a repair (corrective or preventive), and in addition pay
3. A breakage cost b for every machine which fails in use.
4. While running, a machine incurs an operating cost at rate $aq\ (t)$, where, a is cost coefficient and $q\ (t)$ is a non-negative non-decreasing function of the machine age; this cost can represent increasing power consumption, decreasing productivity, and quality as well.

2.3 Critical Age Policy

A specified age t for a machine to go for preventive maintenance is a critical age. A machine that fails before the critical age t will immediately be sent for corrective repair, while any machine that reaches age t without having failure will be sent for preventive maintenance.

$$U(t) = \int_0^t \bar{F}(x)\,dx \tag{1}$$

= Mean machine life time, given t;

$$\text{yi} = [u(t)^{m-i}R^i[(m-i)!i!]^{-1} \text{ for } 0 \leq i \leq n \tag{2a}$$

$$\text{yi} = [u(t)]^{m-i}R^i[(m-i)!n!n^{i-n}]^{-1} \text{ for } n \leq i \leq m \tag{2b}$$

Based on the above relation; one can use a given critical age t to determine the probability of having i machines inoperative as;

$$\text{prob}_i(t) = \text{yi}\left[\sum_{j=0}^{m} \text{yj}\right]^{-1} \tag{3}$$

By using steady state formulas derived by Armstrong, the steady state measures of operating performance for expected number of machine operating (up) and expected number of machines inoperative (down).

$$E[\text{down}(t)m, n] = \sum_{i=0}^{m} i\text{prob}_i(t) \tag{4}$$

$$E[\text{Up}(t)m, n] = m - \sum_{i=0}^{m} i\text{probi}(t) \tag{5}$$

The cost rate for the failed machine is k, and for each operational

$$\text{rate}(t) = \left[c + bF(t) + a\int_0^t q(x)F(x)dx\right][u(t)]^{-1} \tag{6}$$

Taking the summation of the products of costs and their probability yields the following equation for the system's long run expected cost rate:

$$C_{m,n}(t) = \sum_{i=0}^{m}[ik + (m-i)\text{rate}(t)]\text{probi}(t) \tag{7}$$

Alternatively, it can be rewritten in terms of the number of machines up and down;

$$C_{m,n}(t) = \text{rate}(t)\left[m - \sum_{i=0}^{m} i\text{probi}(t)\right] + k\left[\sum_{i=0}^{m} i\text{probi}(t)\right] \tag{8}$$

$$= \text{rate}(t)E\left[up(t)_{m,n}\right] + kE\left[down(t)_{m,n}\right] \tag{9}$$

These equations (Eqs. 8 and 9) are useful to calculate the expected cost rate resulting from the use of an age t policy in a given system.

All developments until now are without the consideration of priority of a certain machine over the other. Instead the considered service discipline is FCFS. However in real maintenance practices we may need some sophistication to include the priority of a machine in its total cost. Here we can introduce the priority factor p of a machine available for maintenance by affecting Shortage cost incurred by priority factor. The priority factor can be determined by separate techniques like AHP, as the case in this study. Thus, Eqs. 7 and 9 would be come as follows:

$$C_{m,n}(t) = \sum_{i=0}^{m} [(1/Pj)ik + (m-i)rate(t)]probi(t) \qquad (10)$$

$$C_{m,n}(t) = rate(t)E\left[up(t)_{m,n}\right] + \left(\frac{1}{Pj}\right)kE\left[down(t)_{m,n}\right] \qquad (11)$$

$$pj = p_1, p_2, \ldots, p_m \qquad (12)$$

Where, j = 1, 2…m
Pj should be different from zero (P$\neq$0), 0 < Pj $\leq$ 1,
For $C_{m,n}(t)$ and its optimal age $t_{m,n}$ we have

1. The optimal repair age $t_{m,n}$ is increasing in the number of machines m and decreasing in the number of repair men n;
2. The optimal repair age $t_{m,n}$ is increasing in the shortage cost rate k and the repair cost c, and is decreasing in the breakage penalty b and the operating cost rate a;
3. Both the expected total number of machines down and the expected number of machines idle are decreasing in t.

By using different constraints the problem can be treated as a constrained optimization problem.

3   Priority Determination

In order to determine the priority of each machine we have used super decision software v-3.0.0. The software helps to apply the concept of hierarchical approach. Thus, to compute the priorities there are four phases in the process.

Phase 1: First one need to set the goal. In our case the goal is maintenance priority setting. Then, identify and set major criteria to achieve the goal. Here three major criterions are assigned such as cost, damage and customer relation. Within each major criteria, sub criteria's need to be determined. As shown in Table 1 the sub criteria are feed in to the network module.

Phase 2: The pair-wise comparison was undertaken among major criterion.

Phase 3: Pair wise comparison among sub criterion will be undertaken in this phase.

Phase 4: Computation of priority was done in this phase. The final priority can be either idealized or normalized priority (Fig. 1).

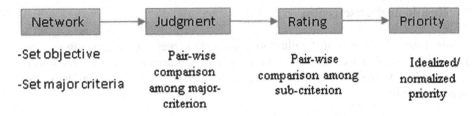

Fig. 1. Priority setting steps in super decision

4 Illustrative Case Study

For this study the data considered by Armstrong (2002), for his investigation were used. The given data sets are, m would take from elements {2, 4, 6}, n = 1, R would take values from the element {0.05, 0.10}, c = 0, a = 0, k would be either of the elements {2, 16}, and b = 1 for the machine lifetime distribution F (t) we choose a Weibull distribution with scale λ = 1 and shape η = 4 to give a mean life of $\approx$ 1.

The priority of failed machines is computed by using super decision tool; the steps followed are as stated in the previous section. The input data essential for the determination of priority were collected by using work study techniques.

In the table above the major factors (i.e. cost, damage and customer relation) and their respective sub factors (such as: MTBF, production loss, etc.) are presented. In order to determine the priority for each machine, a collected data for a given four failed machines for each criteria is considered. The individual values multiplied by the priority and summing all values will give the total sum priority value. The simple formula

$$\text{Total sum} = \sum_{i=1}^{11}(priority_i * data_i)$$

By considering the larger value among the total sum as a factorizing element normalized priority (pj) will be generated for each machine as in the last row of Table 1.

Table 1. Priority determination

No	Major criteria	Criteria	Priority	M_1	M_2	M_3	M_4
1	Cost	11MTBF of each machine	0.8365	10	13	11	8
2		12MTTR of each machine	0.8141	30	20	60	4
3		13Spare part availability	1	9	4	3	5
4	Damage	21production loss	0.5299	9	6	4	3
5		22plant damage by the failure	0.1848	9	6	8	2
6		23product damage	0.2768	3	5	4	9
7		24Environmental damage	0.1970	5	3	8	4
8		25people damage (safety)	0.1887	8	4	9	6
9	Customer relation	31Due date of the product	0.7239	9	7	5	4
10		32Penalty of the agreement	0.5947	6	1	5	7
11		33loss of loyalty	0.5241	4	6	9	8
			Total	63.73	46.98	80.34	32.57
			pj	0.793	0.58	1	0.4

5 Result and Discussion

In this section the results of the illustrative example is presented in two sub sections. The first sub section will dealt with the long term maintenance cost without priority consideration. While in the second section the analysis would be by considering priority of machines.

5.1 Without Priority

As it can be realized from Table 2, the long term cost is decreasing with an increasing number of machine m, keeping n constant.

Table 2. Long term cost with FCFS service discipline

$C_{m,n}$	R = 0.05, K = 2			R = 0.1, K = 2			R = 0.05, K = 16			R = 0.1, K = 16		
	$C_{2,1}$	$C_{4,1}$	$C_{6,1}$	$C_{2,1}$	$C_{4,1}$	$C_{6,1}$	$C_{2,1}$	$C_{4,1}$	$C_{6,1}$	$C_{2,1}$	$C_{4,1}$	$C_{6,1}$
value	0.05	0.01	0.01	0.11	0.02	0.02	0.36	0.07	0.04	0.79	0.16	0.09

5.2 Considering Priority

As it can be depicted from Table 3, in all cases considering priority will have cost saving of the allotted value in percentage over FCFS service discipline. Here, in the analysis a system of six machines is considered and the situation is when four machines are failed. Each machine do have its own priority as it is computed in Sect. 4. If we fail to maintain highly prioritized machine first, we will incur additional costs. For Example in R = 0.05, K = 2, the highly prioritized machine is M_3. If the maintenance crew served M_3 first; the long term cost will be 0.007 unit. Otherwise, additional cost of 28.57%, 57.14% and 114.3%, will be incurred if M_1, M_2 and M_4 are considered respectively.

Table 3. Long term cost with Priority based service discipline

	R = 0.05, K = 2				R = 0.1, K = 2			
Machine (m)	M_1	M_2	M_3	M_4	M_1	M_2	M_3	M_4
Priority (pj)	0.793	0.585	1	0.405	0.793	0.585	1	0.405
$C_{6,1}$ with pj	0.009	0.011	0.007	0.015	0.018	0.022	0.015	0.03
Δ in %	28.57	57.14	0	114.3	20	46.67	0	100
	R = 0.05, K = 16				R = 0.1, K = 16			
Machine (m)	M_1	M_2	M_3	M_4	M_1	M_2	M_3	M_4
Priority (pj)	0.793	0.585	1	0.405	0.793	0.585	1	0.405
$C_{6,1}$ with pj	0.053	0.07	0.042	0.101	0.108	0.145	0.087	0.207
Δ in %	26.19	66.66	0	140.5	24.14	66.66	0	137.9

6 Conclusion

This paper presented an extension of both preventive and corrective maintenance model for the machine repair problem with a multi-criteria based priority. Here the arrival pattern do have both deterministic (scheduled) and stochastic or random features. In the previous studies the service discipline were first come first served. While in this model based on the requirement for the super decision software multi-criteria based priorities of machineries is developed. The paper considers long term cost of the maintenance service for both FCFS and priority based service discipline. Though, this research focuses on the single-operator machine interference problem, it can be further expanded to multiple operator problem. In addition, the multiple-operator with different skill levels problem is important in practice and becomes another subject for future research.

References

Shekhar, C., Jain, M., Bhatia, S.: Fuzzy analysis of machine repair problem with switching failure and reboot. J. Reliab. Stat. Stud. **7**(S), 41–55 (2014)

Wu, C.-H., Ke, J.-C.: Multi-server machine repair problems under a (V, R) synchronous single vacation policy. Appl. Math. Model. **38**(7–8), 2180–2189 (2014)

Ke, J.C., Lin, C.H.: Sensitivity analysis of machine repair problems in manufacturing systems with service interruptions. Appl. Math. Model. **32**(10), 2087–2105 (2008)

Ke, J.-C., Hsu, Y.-L., Liu, T.-H., Zhang, Z.G.: Computational analysis of machine repair problem with unreliable multi-repairmen. Comput. Oper. Res. **40**(3), 848–855 (2013)

Ke, J.-C., Wu, C.-H.: Multi-server machine repair model with standbys and synchronous multiple vacation. Comput. Ind. Eng. **62**(1), 296–305 (2012)

Ke, J.-C., Lee, S.-L., Liou, C.-H.: Machine repair problem in production systems with spares and server vacations. Rairo Oper. Res. **43**(1), 35–54 (2009)

Ke, J.-C., Liu, T.-H., Yang, D.-Y.: Machine repairing systems with standby switching failure. Comput. Ind. Eng. **99**, 223–228 (2016)

Ke, J.-C., Liu, T.-H., Yang, D.-Y.: Modeling of machine interference problem with unreliable repairman and standbys imperfect switchover. Reliab. Eng. Syst. Saf. **174**, 12–18 (2018)

Kumar, K., Jain, M.: Controlling F-policy and threshold N-policy for the machine repair system with provision of warm standbys (2013)

Wang, K.H., Ke, J.B., Ke, J.C.: Profit analysis of the M/M/R machine repair problem with balking, reneging, and standby switching failures. Comput. Oper. Res. **34**(3), 835–847 (2007a)

Wang, K.-H., Kuo, M.-Y.: Profit analysis of the M/Et/1 machine repair problem with a non-reliable service station. Comput. Ind. Eng. **32**(3), 587–594 (1997)

Wang, K.-H., Liou, C.-D., Lin, Y.-H.: Comparative analysis of the machine repair problem with imperfect coverage and service pressure condition. Appl. Math. Model. **37**(5), 2870–2880 (2013)

Wang, K.-H., Wang, T.-Y., Pearn, W.L.: Optimal control of the N policy M/G/1 queuing system with server breakdowns and general startup times. Appl. Math. Model. **31**(10), 2199–2212 (2007b)

Wang, K.-H., Liouand, Y.-C., Yang, D.-Y.: Cost optimization and sensitivity analysis of the machine repair problem with variable servers and balking. Procedia-Soc. Behav. Sci. **25**, 178–188 (2011)

Jain, M., Shekhar, C., Shukla, S.: Vacation queuing model for a machining system with two unreliable repairmen. Int. J. Oper. Res. **20**(4), 469–491 (2014a)

Jain, M., Mittal, R., Kumari, R.: (m, M) Machining system with two unreliable servers, mixed spares and common-cause failure. J. Ind. Eng. Int. **11**(2), 171–178 (2015)

Jain, M., Rakhee, Maheshwari, S.: N-policy for a machine repair system with spares and reneging. Appl. Math. Model. **28**(6), 513–531 (2014b)

Pardo, M.J., De La Fuente, D.: Optimal selection of the service rate for a finite input source fuzzy queuing system. Fuzzy Sets Syst. **159**(3), 325–342 (2008)

Armstrong, M.J.: Age repair policies for the machine repair problem. Eur. J. Oper. Res. **138**(1), 127–141 (2002)

Sharma, P.: Machine repair problem with spares, balking, reneging and n-policy for vacation. J. Rajasthan Acad. Phys. Sci. **14**(3–4), 337–343 (2015)

Sudhesh, R., Parthasarathy, P.R.: Transient solution of a multi-server Poisson queue with N-policy. Int. J. Comput. Math. Appl. **55**(3), 550–562 (2008)

Maheshwari, S., Ali, S.: Machine repair problem with mixed spares, balking and reneging. Int. J. Theor. Appl. Sci. **5**(1), 75–83 (2013)

Chen, S.-P.: A mathematical programming approach to the machine interference problem with fuzzy parameters. Appl. Math. Comput. **174**(1), 374–387 (2006)

Taha, H.A.: Operations research: An introduction, 5th edn. Macmillan, New York (1992)

Yang, T., Lee, R.-S., Chen, M.-C., Chen, P.: Queuing network model for a single-operator machine interference problem with external operations. Eur. J. Oper. Res. **167**(1), 163–178 (2005)

Baba, Y.: Analysis of a GI/M/1 queue with multiple working vacations. Oper. Res. Lett. **32**(2), 201–209 (2005)

Hsu, Y.-L., Ke, J.-C., Liu, T.-H., Wu, C.H.: Modeling of multi-server repair problem with switching failure and reboot delay and related profit analysis. Comput. Ind. Eng. **69**, 21–28 (2014)

Cascaded Hybrid Device Multilevel Converters for Wind Mill Applications

P. Palanivel[1](✉), R. Selvarasu[1], B. Barani Sundaram[2],
and Hinsermu Alemayehu[1]

[1] Adama Science and Technology University, Adama, Ethiopia
drpalanivelres@gmail.com, selvarasunaveen@gmail.com,
hialex98@gmail.com
[2] Defense Engineering College, Bishoftu, Ethiopia
bsundar2@gmail.com

Abstract. In recent years Multilevel Converter (MLC) plays a vital role in wind power genration. In this paper, Shifted Carrier - Pulse Width Modulation (SC-PWM) based hybrid device multilevel converter configuration for 5 MW wind mill are proposed. A five level cascaded hybrid device MLC is developed and the simulations are performed using MATLAB/Simulink. The simulation results are offered and their performances are analyzed by implementing FPGA SPARTAN-3 processor. The proposed MLC reduces the THD and increases the output voltage.

Keywords: Wind mill · Shifted carrier-pulse width modulation · Hybrid device multilevel inverter

1 Introduction

The power generation through wind mill has been introduced in Ethiopia in the year 2010. The generated power from wind mill need to be integrated with the existing power system and it becomes a challenging one for system engineers. The integration of wind power with the existing system needs the power electronic converters, which affect the quality of power supplied to the consumer. Since the introduction of power electronic converters for integration of wind power to the existing system may generate Total Harmonic Distortion (THD), which affects the power quality. Hence system operator to be ensured for supplying the quality power to the consumer [1]. A review has been made for the application of power electronic devices for wind power generation and their integration to the existing power system for supplying quality power to the consumer [2].

The cost of power semiconductor devices used for medium voltage MLC for industrial application has been compared [3]. In order to overcome the loss occurs in semiconductor devices of inverter, a NPC inverter has been applied in multi level inverter and their operation also discussed [4, 5]. A three phase MLI with novel switching strategy has been proposed for grid integration, which reduces the switching count and improves the higher levels in output voltage [6]. SHE-PWM technique has been proposed for cascaded H-bridge inverter containing single DC source [7]. A hybrid MLC has been developed for interfacing wind energy system with the grid. The

F. A. Zimale et al. (Eds.): ICAST 2018, LNICST 274, pp. 93–101, 2019.
https://doi.org/10.1007/978-3-030-15357-1_7

developed system reduces the capacitor ripple voltage which helps to choose the reduced capacitor value [8]. A different PWM technique has been applied for MLI in order to reduce THD and enhance the output voltage [9, 10]. A Fuzzy and PI technique has been applied for cascaded H-bridge MLI for reducing THD [11].

In this paper, SC-PWM based hybrid device MLC configuration for wind mill applications are proposed and designed. SC-PWM technique is applied to hybrid device MLC for analyzing performance of proposed MLC. The SC-PWM technique is able to reduce THD and improve the output voltage. The simulations results are compared with the experimental results.

2   Hybrid Multilevel Converters (MLC) for Wind Turbine

Wind power converter system plays a vital role for interfacing the wind mill generator and an electric grid as shown in Fig. 1. Hybrid MLC is the main component of wind power converter system. The MLC has to fulfill the requirement of generator and electric grid to provide the quality power to the consumer.

The MLC has to get greatest possible real power from the wind mill generator. Also it should be able to control the generator frequency and voltage magnitude. Similarly the MLC should have the ability to absorb/inject the reactive power in electric grid side. Also MLC helps to maintain voltage magnitude and frequency in the electric grid constant. In order to fulfill the need of generator and grid side wind power converter system containing a five level MLC is proposed for 5 MW wind mill.

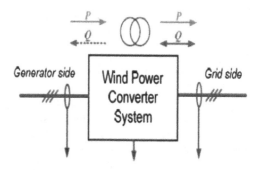

Fig. 1. Wind power converter system.

The proposed 5 MW wind mill system is shown in Fig. 2. In the proposed system 5 MW at 8.2 m/s is generated with the output voltage of 24 V and speed of 300 RPM. The battery is used to store the generated electric power and constant 400 V DC is supplied to the inverter from the step up chopper (24/400).

A three phase 180° conduction mode of five-level inverter is designed and implemented to deliver 400 V AC power to the grid. A feedback is introduced with a pulse generator between grid and inverter for controlling action.

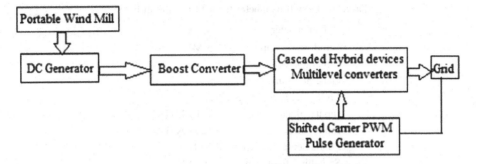

Fig. 2. Block diagram of cascaded hybrid device multilevel converters.

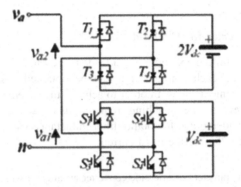

Fig. 3. Cascaded hybrid device MLC circuit diagram

The proposed cascade MLC circuit diagram is presented in Fig. 3. The proposed inverter contains one IGBT and one IGCT H-bridge inverter. The IGCT are used to operate at high voltage and current ratings. The IGBT inverter is used to operate at higher switching frequency. Since the proposed system contains one IGCT and one IGBT H-bridge inverter it is termed as hybrid inverter and can be operated at high volt-Amp rating than a conventional inverter.

3 Design Criteria

In order to conduct evaluation of each converter candidate, the parameters of generator and basic design for converters are needed.

The parameters considered for the proposed system is given in Table 1. The voltage rating for IGBT is chosen as 3.3 kV. Three 20 kV and 50 Hz AC voltage sources are considered for analysis. The resistance of the conductor is not considered and transformer is considered as ideal.

Table 1. Design parameter for 5 MW wind turbine.

WT parameter	Value
Wind power capacity	5 MW
Generator voltage	2200 V
Generator current	852 A
Multilevel inverter rating	2 MVA
Input voltage	3110 V (DC)
Input current	1204 A (DC)
Fundamental frequency	50 Hz
Switching frequency	5000 Hz
IGBT voltage rating	3.3 kV
IGBT current rating	1.5 KA

3.1 Design of Converter for Grid Side

The parameters chosen for the converter of grid side is presented in Table 2. The output voltage of DC bus and each configuration can be obtained based on commutated voltage of power electronic devices. In order to achieve the acceptable switching losses of power electronic devices, the switching frequency is chosen as 5000 Hz. The filter capacitance is not considered and the output filter inductance value is chosen to bound the ripple of current to 25% of the rated current.

Table 2. Parameters of grid side converter at different wind speeds.

Wind speed VW (m/s)	5	8	11	14
Generator power PG (MW)	2	3	4	5
Primary side voltage (Vrms)	2200 V			
Fundamental frequency (Fg)	50 Hz			
Switching frequency (Fs)	5000 Hz			

3.2 Design of Converter for Generator Side

The parameters chosen for the generator side converter is presented in Table 3. Switching frequency is chosen as 10 times of generator fundamental frequency. i.e. 800 Hz. The filters are not considered in order to avoid complexity. The wind speed is greater than 14 m/s the stator voltage control are used, if the wind speed is less than 14 m/s, the maximum torque control is used.

Table 3. Parameters of generator side converter at different wind speeds.

Wind speed VW (m/s)	5	8	11	14
Generator power PG (MW)	1.5	2.3	3.4	4.5
Primary side voltage (V_{rms})	1800 V			
Fundamental frequency (F_g)	50 Hz			
Switching frequency (F_s)	800 Hz			

4 Modulation Technique

In this work, SC-PWM technique is considered. The wave form of SC-PWM is presented in Fig. 4. The sinusoidal and bipolar pulse width modulation is considered for modulating each cell separately. The each cell of shifted carrier signal is continuously compared with the reference voltage signal. A phase shift of 180° for each full bridge inverter in a multilevel phase leg is introduced.

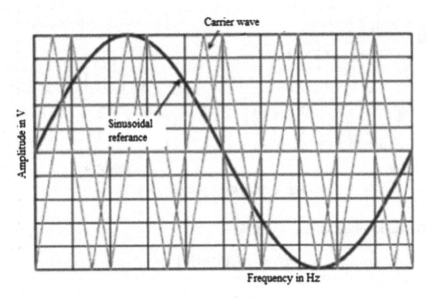

Fig. 4. SC-PWM.

The waveform of SC-PWM signal is presented in Fig. 5. The n − 1 phase shifted carrier signal is generated for a n- level inverter.

A five level inverter is designed and simulations are performed. PS-PWM technique is considered and their operating procedure is as follows.

- n = level of the inverter.
- n − 1. i.e. four carrier waveforms are arranged. The phase shift of 90° is chosen for carriers among the full bridge inverter.
- If the reference is more than all the carrier wave form than the converter switches to + V_{dc}.
- If the reference is lower than the upper most carrier waveform and more than all other carriers than the converter switches to $V_{dc}/2$.
- If the reference is lower than the two upper most carrier waveform and more than two lower most carriers than the converter switches to 0.
- If the reference is more than lower most carrier and lesser than all other carriers, than the converter switches to - $V_{dc}/2$.
- If the reference is lower than all carriers, than the converter switches to - V_{dc}.

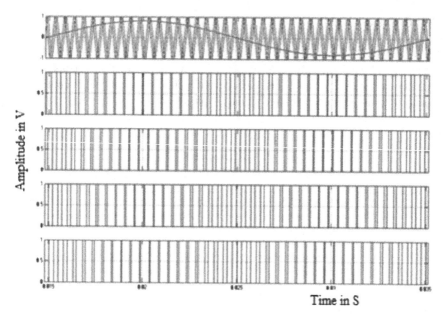

Fig. 5. SC-PWM signal generation

The carrier phase shifting is as follows,

$$Pcr = \frac{(S-1)\prod}{n} \tag{1}$$

Where, S = Sth bridge.
n = Number inverter.

$$n = (P-1)/2 \tag{2}$$

Where, P = Number of switched DC levels, which can be attained in each phase Leg.

The output voltage of power cell 'i' is given by

$$V_{oi} = 1/T_{cr} \cdot \int V_{oi}(t)\, dt \tag{3}$$

$$V_{oi} = T_{on}/T_{cr} \cdot V_{dc} \tag{4}$$

$$V_{oi} = V \tag{5}$$

Where, V_{oi} = Output voltage of cell i,

The three phase sinusoidal modulating signals are generated by using phase shift oscillator. The generated signal is compared with (n−1) phase shifted carrier waves and PWM pulses are generated. These PWM pulses are applied to 3 phase 5 level inverter.

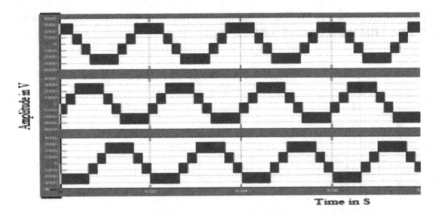

Fig. 6. Simulation results of five level output voltage

The simulation and experimental results of five level output voltage is presented in Figs. 6 and 7 respectively. The output voltage is 3212 V. But input voltage is only 3110 V. Here output voltage is enhanced for nearly 5%. So, PS-PWM is used to enhance output voltage. This technique used to wind power converter systems. The hardware output voltage shown in Fig. 7. The hardware and simulation output voltage more or less same output level. The SC-PWM frequency spectrum is presented in Fig. 8.

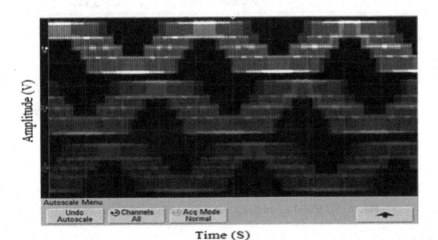

Fig. 7. Experimental output voltage of five level inverter.

Switching frequency of 5 kHz and fundamental frequency 50 Hz is considered in switching spectrum. The output voltage obtained by SC-PWM is about 3212 V for input voltage of 1550 V from each source. As switching frequency is 5 kHz and fundamental frequency is 50 Hz, so harmonic order is about 100 which is shown in Fig. 9. The THD value is about 3.84%.

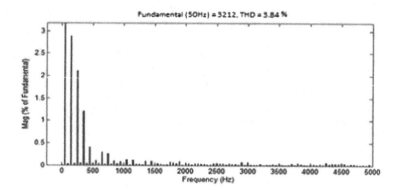

Fig. 8. SC-PWM based five level converter frequency spectrum.

It is observed that the SC-PWM gives better result compared to the other methods. Here, the SC-PWM technique lowers the THD and improves the output voltage. The output voltage V_{ac} is maintained at 3212 V. The THD value is 3.84%.

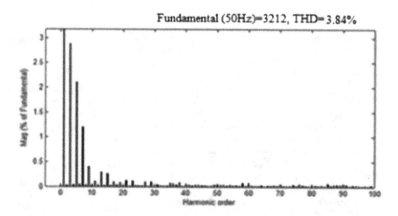

Fig. 9. SC-PWM based five level converter harmonic spectrum.

5   Conclusion

A five level inverter is designed for 5 MW wind mill. The shifted carrier PWM technique is considered and it gives superior performance in terms of enhanced output voltage and reduced THD when compared to other techniques. The results are analyzed by simulation using MATLAB/Simulink and validated by implementing FPGA,

SPARTAN-3 processor. The results are obtained from experimental work which is almost similar to the simulation work.

References

1. Blaabjerg, F., Chen, Z., Kjaer, S.B.: Power electronics as efficient interface in dispersed power generation systems. IEEE Trans. Power Electron. **19**(4), 1184–1194 (2004)
2. Chen, Z., Guerrero, J.M., Blaabjerg, F.: A review of the state of the art of power electronics for wind turbines. IEEE Trans. Power Electron. **24**(8), 1859–1875 (2009)
3. Krug, D., Bernet, S., Fazel, S.S., Jalili, K., Malinowski, M.: Comparison of 2.3-kV medium-voltage multilevel converters for industrial medium-voltage drives. IEEE Trans. Industr. Electron. **54**(6), 2979–2992 (2007)
4. Rodriguez, J., Bernet, S., Steimer, P.K., Lizama, I.E.: A survey on neutral-point-clamped inverters. IEEE Trans. Ind. Electron. **57**(7), 2219–2230 (2010)
5. Bruckner, T., Bernet, S., Guldner, H.: The active NPC converter and its loss-balancing control. IEEE Trans. Ind. Electron. **52**(3), 855–868 (2005)
6. Amamra, S.-A., Meghriche, K., Cherifi, A., Francois, B.: Multilevel inverter topology for renewable energy grid integration. IEEE Trans. Ind. Electron. **64**(11), 8855–8866 (2017)
7. Sharifzadeh, M., Vahedi, H., Al-Haddad, K.: SHE-PWM applied on single DC source CHB with self regulation of capacitors voltages. In: IEEE International Conference on Industrial Technology (ICIT) 2018, pp. 1893–1897 (2018)
8. Debnath, S., Saeedifard, M.: A new hybrid modular multilevel converter for grid connection of large wind turbines. IEEE Trans. Sustain. Energy **4**(4), 1051–1064 (2013)
9. Palanivel, P., Dash, S.S.: analysis of THD and output voltage performance for cascaded multilevel inverter using carrier pulse width modulation techniques. IET Power Electron. **4** (8), 951–958 (2011)
10. Palanivel, P., Dash, S.S., Premalatha, S.: Performance analysis of multilevel inverters using variable switching frequency carrier based PWM techniques. Renew. Energy Power Qual. J. **10**, 32–37 (2012)
11. Kannan, C., Mohanty, N.K., Selvarasu, R.: A new topology for cascaded H-bridge multilevel inverter with PI and Fuzzy control. Energy Procedia **117**, 916–927 (2017)

Evaluation of Workplace Environmental Ergonomics and Method Development for Manufacturing Industries

Tomas C. Kassaneh[✉] and Ahmed A. Tadesse

Faculty of Mechanical and Industrial Engineering, Bahir Dar Institute
of Technology, Bahir Dar University, P.O. Box 26, Bahir Dar, Ethiopia
tomaspoly@gmail.com, wubied@gmail.com

Abstract. Though workplace safety is relatively satisfactory in developed countries, it does not receive proper attention in developing countries yet. It is known that productivity improvement mainly in labor intensive factories like metal and textile, is not easy without considering the workforce safety. Studies on Ethiopian manufacturing industries show that there are different workplace safety problems, and as a result of less attention, there are also very few practices on prevention and control. Even the few studies done on the area do not yet see the workplace physical factors in terms of complying standards and being causes for injuries and low performance. Thus, this study focused to assess and ergonomically evaluate the workplace environment and develop a control method. It is conducted on purposely selected 10 metal and 4 textile factories. Workplace observation, focus group discussion and measurement are methods applied and digital light, sound level and heat stress meters are measurement equipment used. The factories' environmental measurements compared to the Occupational Safety and Health Administration (OSHA) and National Institute for Occupational Safety and Health (NOISH) standards shows incompliance and even some textile and garment factory work sections has lighting reading level less than 250 lx where 2000 lx is the standard, and metal factory work sections have also up to 128 dB from 85 dB noise exposure standard. Hazardous sections are identified as an intervention and the major causes and impact of the factors is assessed. Finally, a factory level strategic approach model is developed for workplace hazard prevention and control.

Keywords: Workplace safety · Environmental factors · Hazard control method

1 Introduction

Physical Environmental Ergonomic hazards are workplace conditions that pose the risk of injury to an employee. It includes vibration, temperature extremes, illumination, and noise exposures. Fasunloro (2004) defined occupational hazard as the "potential risk to the health of a person emerging from an unhealthy environment" which is a significant public health issue. Generally, the hazards at workplace can be classified as health hazards and physical hazards (Fatonade and Allotey 2016). As it is stated also by

© ICST Institute for Computer Sciences, Social Informatics and Telecommunications Engineering 2019
Published by Springer Nature Switzerland AG 2019. All Rights Reserved
F. A. Zimale et al. (Eds.): ICAST 2018, LNICST 274, pp. 102–112, 2019.
https://doi.org/10.1007/978-3-030-15357-1_8

Stephen (1998), the physical hazards include noise, temperature, illumination, vibration, radiation. The quality of working environment in any organization is a critical factor and may simply determine the level of employee's motivation, subsequent performance and productivity (Jonny and Nwonu 2014). Among the above types of physical hazards, most of them are prevalent in the metal, iron and steel, textile and garment industries. The World Health Organization (WHO) (2010) considers the workplace a priority setting for health promotion in the 21st century. Safe work and workplace are necessary for increased production and higher productivity and hence promotion and protection of safe work and workplace is the complementary aspect of industrial development (Upadhyaya 2002; Devanand 2015). The interdependence between working conditions and productivity is increasingly recognized.

In manufacturing industries of Ethiopia, development and labor market demand is increasing from year to year. The manufacturing industries increment alone without workplace safety improvement approaches is considered to be unproductive especially in metal and textile manufacturing industries-labor intensive sectors. Workplace accidents and work errors occur in the process of production as a result of unsafe working condition, unsafe acts, personal failure and lack of awareness on the side of both the employers and workers. As per the Ethiopian Ministry of Labor and Social Affairs (MOLSA) (2016), though accident reports don't clearly show the nature and causes of work accidents, the highest percentage (56.05%) occurred in the manufacturing industries. To enhance the metal and textile sector development which has been given priority by Ethiopian government, workplace safety is found to be mandatory and so; a company-wide ergonomic assessment should be developed.

2 Problem Description

Though occupational health and safety of workers has recently improved and is relatively satisfactory in developed countries, it receives yet little attention and comes at low level in the list of national priorities (ILO 2010). This is also true for Ethiopia, where slight consideration is given for workplace safety and associated problems are savior (Yessuf et al. 2014; Zeleke 2015; BOLSA 2017; Seife 2017; Kassu 2017). Moreover, some researches in Ethiopia shows that occupational health data collection and harmonization is in beginning stages and even the available data often done by different organizations, different criteria, infrequently and no information management system. As per the literature, few researches were conducted on metal, textile and garment industries in relation to occupational safety and health control in Ethiopia; with special focus on accident identification and severity for the reactive purpose. However, the factory working conditions in terms of complying standards in lighting, temperature and noise, and the associated impacts are not yet studied in the way that shows the specific sections of a factory. The above mentioned physical environmental factors are also a kind of root causes for the occurrence of different injuries identified by previous studies. For example, due to high temperature environment, a worker may be forced to unsafe act of working which leads to body injuries and as a result error on the product quality. Therefore, the ergonomics hazards related to the physical environmental factors are becoming one of the major workplace problems which affect the safety and performance of Ethiopian metal and textile factories and needs a scientific evaluation and corrective measure.

3 Objective of the Study

The major aim of the study is to measure and evaluate the workplace physical environmental ergonomics factors in Ethiopian metal and textile manufacturing factories and develop strategic approach model with its implementation strategy. Specifically, it is to assess working practices of the case companies with respect to ergonomics and safety, to measure the level and intensity of factors, to identify the gap compared to the OSHA & NOISH standards, to identify hazardous work sections, to investigate the causes and show the impact of the incompliance.

4 Methodology of the Research

This research used workplace observation, interview and workplace environment measurement as primary data collection methods. Each workplace of the selected factories is scientifically observed in the view of ergonomics and safety. Then identification of abnormal sections or work sections having discomfort is made so as to be used for measurement. The measurement equipment used includes Sound level meter (Model HD600), Lux level meter (Model 407026) and Heat stress meter (Model HT30). Interview in the form of discussion is used to get information from workers and experts regarding to safeness and suitability of the working environment, the workplace hazards faced and prevention practices. Books, articles, government and company reports and previous studies are also used. The study is conducted in 10 metal and 4 textile and garment factories as samples which are selected using purposive sampling technique. The researchers selected Metal Industries and Textile and Garment Factories as a case because these factories are labor intensive, have exposed work nature for physical environmental factors and have also more manual works than other types of industries. Moreover, prior attention is given by government on these sectors. Comparison of the case factories' environmental measurements is done with the OSHA and NOISH standards. After the data analysis, discussion and identification of major hazardous work sections, the major causes and impact on the safety and productivity of the factories is assessed so as to use for the development of hazard prevention and control method.

5 Result and Discussion

5.1 Workplace Measurements, Analysis and Findings

The light, noise and temperature measured data from the sample factories are organized, analyzed and the summary of results are presented in Table 1. The analysis of each individual factory is undertaken in similar fashion as of the lighting analysis of Ak garment shown for instance with Fig. 1.

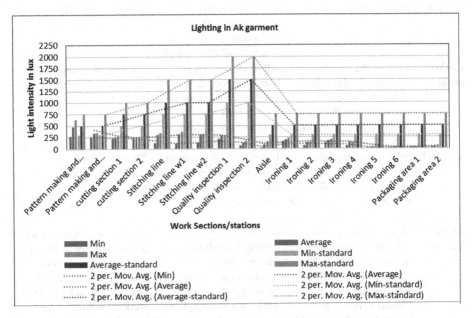

Fig. 1. Lighting data compared with standard for AK garment factory

Table 1. Summarized result of the measured and analyzed data of the case factories

Factory	Noise	Lighting	Temperature
KTSC textile	Out of 12 sections assessed almost all does not comply the standard level except one section	With the exception of grey inspection, all other sections have below standard lighting levels expected for the task	All sections are in good temperature except the Ring frame section which have much higher temperature of 34 °C
MA garment & textiles	Knitting and open-end machines have higher noise but ring frame is normal	Except Sewing line, cutting machine, cutting manual and Ring frame all other sections are to standard	Boiler section has 31.6 °C where the standard is 30 °C. Other sections are normal

(*continued*)

Table 1. (*continued*)

Factory	Noise	Lighting	Temperature
BTSC textile	Sections like open end, Picanol and Somet machines in weaving area, and other workshop sections do not comply with the standard	With the exception of packaging, sewing, cutting and inspection sections, all other sections have lighting level of below standard	Except fractional difference of 0.1–0.4 °C in spinning, wood workshop, Printing, bleaching and dying sections, others are normal
AK garment	Here noise has no impact in the factory	All measurements lag behind the minimum standard with the exception of pattern making and cutting 1 & 2	The temperature in the factory is normal
HMMBI metal	Most of the sections have noise levels above the standard. Hammering activities have the reading of above 108 dB which is very risky	All work sections are normal except the Leath machine area & grounding room which have low light level as compared from the standard	All sections comply with the standard except heat treatment area
KO steel	Except shearing m/c, corrugation m/c, Nail making m/c 1, Collusion m/c, all other sections are up to the standard	Lighting level is almost around the standard range and has no effect on the worker and the work	The factory has comparably good temperature
Ak metal industry	Most sections are very risky for workers to accomplish their task without any PPE even some sections have over 100 dB which is much higher from the standard, 85 dB	In milling section, the lighting is slightly lower, whereas, the minimum lighting in platting room is far behind the standard, while maximum lighting is comparable with the standard	The melting shop is risky and also causes the rise of air temperature in room. There is also the sparkling of molten particles and the working practice is very hazardous in the shop
MI metal	In dome welding and hammering the noise reading reach 128 dB which is very hazardous	The lighting condition in the factory is normal	Temp. is normal except dome manufacturing area which is hazardous due to smoke and poor ventilation

Both metal industries and Textile and garment factories have workplaces with under the standard requirement of lighting and above the standard limit of noise and heat exposure. Lighting factor problem is affecting the textile and garment factories whereas noise exposure problem is visible in metal factories. Temperature or heat stress problem is not significantly shown in both of the industry types except few sections like furnace areas in metal and ring frame section in some textile factories. However, the metal melting work and practice shown is very hazardous as there is sparkling of molten metal that can injure workers. In some of the textile factories, specifically garment section, there is a light bulb which can provide standard lighting level;

however, due to afraid of the warming resulted from such bulb, they are not using it and as a result they are working with poor lighting. Due to the different technologies used in textile factories, the level and intensity of the factors is different and it is found that in the factories having recent technology machines, there is less intensity of generating heat and noise.

5.2   Identification of Causal Factors and Impact Assessment for the Incompliance of Workplace Environment

After the study founds the presence of incompliance in the workplaces, it is tried to identify the major causes/factors and assess the impacts of it. This will help the researchers in developing the mitigation ways.

Identification of Causal Factors. From the observation of work places and discussion made with factory workers and experts, the major causes identified are briefly presented below.

Lighting. The major possible causes identified for the lighting factor includes poor lighting design, lack of proper maintenance on failed bulbs, deliberately making some bulbs off to avoid the heat generated, and farness of the light source from a work station. Moreover, lack of awareness about the advantage and disadvantages of proper lighting on health and productivity contributed for the problems listed above. For instance, rather than making off intentionally some bulbs to reduce the heat generated, they can fully on the bulbs and prevent the heat through proper ventilation. The incorrect lighting design and poor installation of lighting source can cause disability glare from a light fitting, color effects and distracting reflection.

Noise exposure. Regarding to the noise factor, poor work practices, lack of regular maintenance of machines, lack of sound protecting guards, poor workplace design (nearness or collecting of high sound generating tasks in one station/section), use of old technology, are the major factors identified.

Temperature/heat stress. The high temperature recorded in some sections of the case factories is due to high heat generating machines, lack of protecting guards, poor ventilation system, confined working area, maintenance and use of old technology.

Generally, the failure on the part of the management in realizing and applying prevention methods and not giving attention for safety could be considered as one of the major causes to the incompliance which in turn affects workers' safety.

Impact of the Incompliance. It is difficult to quantify the impact of the environmental workplace problems because of lack of recorded data. The assessments made from different reports and expert discussions are summarized shortly below so as to show the criticality of the issue and thus get attention by the factory management or owners. Medical, lost wages, sick leave with pay, absenteeism expenses for replacement are included impacts from the cost perspective. For instance, a study revealed that the medical expenses due to accidents or diseases impoverished by metal, steel and iron industries incurred costs in sum of ETB 2,320,707.27 only from 19 industries in 2007 E.C. and sum of ETB 776,699.93 from 24 industries in 2008 E.C. (BOLSA 2017). While from health side, different body injuries, MSDs, hearing loss, sight problems are impacts shown. On the other hand, individual or team productivity will decrease, error increases, delivery time will increase and generally affects the performance (productivity and quality). Researches in the quality field suggests that around 30–50% of quality defects are related to poor ergonomics (Axelsson 2000; Drury 2000; Lin et al. 2001, as cited in Neumann et al. (2002).

6 Strategic Approach for Hazard Prevention and Control

6.1 The Need for a Strategic Approach

In many of the studies made in Ethiopian industries, numerous accidents found to emanate from the less concern of safety and health at workplace by the organization's management, absence of guidelines and easily implementable methods, and enforcement possibilities. Moreover, as discussed earlier, the incompliance of the physical workplace environments are also causes for the accidents. Such safety problems are not one time and so difficult to solve by proposing specific methods to be implemented, rather it needs sustainable and strategic ways to follow. As it is supported by our assessment and other studies (Habtu et al. (2014); Zeleke (2015); BOLSA (2017)), though majority of factories provide some PPEs for their workers, it is not utilized properly by workers all the time while they are on duty. Accordingly, recommending PPE alone or some other specific method is not significant and effective measure. Regarding on improving company productivity, safety and work environment through strategic way, recommendations were given by Seife (2017) for Ethiopian textile industries and Kasu (2017) for manufacturing industries. In addition, Kasu (2017) develops an integrated model for OSH practice of Ethiopian manufacturing industries. Though we found that the model is good at national level as a framework, it will be a little bit complex and difficult for a company level at this OSH stage of our industries. These all calls up to develop a strategic approach than trying to implement single, specific and short-term mitigation methods.

6.2 The Proposed Strategic Approach Model

An integrated model (Fig. 2) is developed from a hierarchical hazard prevention and control method and hazard prevention and control program implementation model. The model is developed considering different practices, literature, case companies existing condition, and demand and results of the study so as to customize the general ergonomics and safety principles.

Model-1: Hierarchical Hazard Prevention and Control Framework. The model will serve as a framework for OSH experts on determination of the most effective and feasible corrective actions to be undertaken. The approach groups actions by their likely effectiveness in reducing or removing a hazard. Accordingly, safety department experts of factories can use this method to select and implement feasible and effective controls. Following this hierarchy normally leads to the implementation of essentially safer systems, where the risk of illness or injury has been considerably reduced. The Hierarchy breaks down as follows, with the most effective measures at the top of the inverted pyramid and the least effective at the bottom.

1. *Elimination (Physically Remove the hazard)*. This is the preferred method and most effective solution at reducing hazards; however, it is also tend to be the most difficult to implement in an existing process.
2. *Substitution (Replace the hazard)*. It is substituting or replacing the known hazard with a material, process, or equipment that is less hazardous.
3. *Engineering controls (a physical change to the workplace)*. It focuses on changing the structure of the work area by installing physical barriers/ using safety devices.
4. *Administrative and work practice controls* (change the way people work).
5. *Personal protective equipment (PPE) (protect the worker with PPE)*. When all options mentioned above are exhausted, introduction of PPE is recommended.

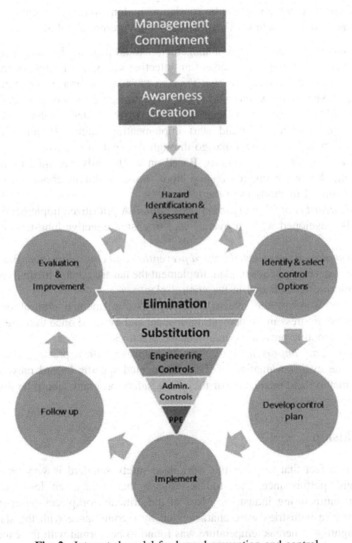

Fig. 2. Integrated model for hazard prevention and control

Here it should be noted that instead of relying on the lowest methods, safety department of a factory should look up the pyramid to the higher order solutions and risk elimination strategies. Moreover, the full control of some hazards may require the combined use of two or more control methods.

Model-2: Hazard Prevention and Control Program Implementation Model. Based on OSHA's recommended practices for safety and health program an eight step modified strategic hazard prevention and control program implementation model is developed. The model is modified to integrate with the NOISH hazard prevention and control framework (inverted pyramid) and to make it easily applicable for manufacturing industries and government agencies. Management commitment and awareness creation are introductory steps of the safety program to a factory. Whereas, the next six steps are major tasks which should be continuously done in order to implement safety prevention and control method. The detail steps are presented below.

1. *Management commitment.* The management should provide the leadership, vision, and resources required to implement an effective safety and health program.
2. *Company-wide awareness creation through training.* Awareness creation training has to be given to the whole workers of the company on safety program.
3. *Hazard identification and assessment.* At this step, safety department experts/supportive team should start implementing safety programs by hazard identification and assessment and go through the next five steps.
4. *Identify and select control options.* Based on the hazards identified in step 3, the team with the involvement of shop floor workers should choose feasible and effective control methods from the hierarchy.
5. *Develop hazard control plan for implementation.* A prioritized implementation plan should be developed with an overall goal to ensure effective long-term control of hazards.
6. *Implementation of the selected hazard prevention and control method.* Based on the previously developed control plan, implement the hazard control methods according to the priorities established in the control plan.
7. *Follow up.* Confirm the effectiveness of the implemented control options by tracking the progress in implementing, inspect and evaluate once they are installed, and follow routine preventive maintenance practices.
8. *Evaluation and Improvement.* Lastly, to improve safety practice continuously through the cycle, evaluation of the implemented specific hazard prevention and control method and evaluation of the whole safety program should be done.

7 Conclusion

Though it is a fact that meeting the workplace safety standard is very essential for organizations' performance, the studies indicate that it is given less attention in Ethiopian manufacturing industries. Most of the critical workplaces observed in the metal and textile industries were characterized by incompliance with the standard in noise and lighting, whereas temperature was found to be normal with the exception of few sections. Some sections in textile industries, such as weaving sections has noise up to 102 dB and in metal industries, it rises up to 128 dB in hammering activity from 85 dB of standard. While, lighting level in textile and garment quality inspection areas measured less than 250 lx from 2000 lx of standard which is very far from the standard. Lack of attention and commitment from factory owners or management in realizing and applying properly guarded machine for reducing heat and noise, proper illumination and ventilation, workplace design are the major causes for the incompliance. From the interview and discussion made, it is concluded that the incompliance is affecting workers on their health and efficiency. The study also concludes that the use of specific, single and short term temporary measures will not be effective and brings continuous improvement on the safety and health issues of manufacturing industries. Hence, a strategic approach model is developed that helps industries to introduce easily, implement hazard prevention and control at a company level and bring continuous safety and health improvement sustainable. Workplace assessment other than light, temperature, noise; for instance, dust in textile and cement factories, vibration in metal industries and chemicals in processing industries are highly recommended as a future study.

References

BOLSA: A report on workplace Safety and Health Assessment of Metal, Iron and Steel Manufacturing Industries in Addis Ababa City. AA city adm. bureau of labor and social affairs (2017)

Devanand, U.: Lighting in textile industry. Int. J. Adv. Res. 4(2), 17–26 (2015)

Ethiopian Ministry of Labor and Social affair (MOLSA): A report on work accident (2016)

Fasunloro, A., Owotade F.J.: Occupational hazards among clinical dental staff. J. Contemp. Dent. Pract. 5(2), 134–152 (2004)

Habtu, Y., Kumie, A., Tefera, W.: Magnitude and factors of occupational injury among workers in large scale metal manufacturing industries in Ethiopia. Open Access Libr. J. 1, e1087 (2014). https://doi.org/10.4236/oalib.1101087

ILO: Work related accidents and diseases take a heavy toll worldwide (2010)

Johnny, C.E., Nwonu, C.O.: A Critical review of the effect of working conditions on employee performance: evidence from Nigeria. EBS J. Manage. Sci. 9, 1–11 (2014)

Kasu, J.: An Integrated Approach of Occupational Safety and Health Practice for Ethiopian Manufacturing Industries (Ph.D dissertation). Addis Ababa University, Ethiopia (2017)

National Institute for Occupational Safety and Health (NIOSH): Hierarchy of Controls. Division of Applied Research and Technology (DART), USA (2016)

Neumann, W., Kihlberg, S., Medbo, P., Mathiassen, S., Winkel, J.: A case study evaluating the ergonomic and productivity impacts of partial automation strategies in the electronics industry. Int. J. Prod. Res. 40(16), 4059–4075 (2002)

Occupational Safety and Health Administration (OSHA): Recommended Practices for Safety and Health Programs (2016). www.osha.gov/shpguidelines

Fatonade, O.O., Allotey, S.E.: An assessment of health hazards in the Ghanaian building industry: sources and preventive measures. Int. J. Eng. Res. Technol. (IJERT) 5(7), 239–247 (2016)

Seife, E.: Improvement of productivity through ergonomics-a case of edget yarn and sewing thread S. C. (Master's thesis). Addis Ababa University, Ethiopia (2017)

Stephen, P.: Organizational Behavior, 8th edn. Prentice Hall, Upper Saddle River (1998)

Upadhyaya, U.: Occupational health, safety and environment in the construction sector. A report organized and presented by OSHE Institute (2002)

World Health Organization (WHO): The Health Promoting Work Place (2010). https://en.wikipedia.org/wiki/Workplace_health_promotion

Yessuf, S., Moges, H., Ahmed, A.: Determinants of occupational injury in Kombolcha textile factory, Ethiopia. Int. J. Occup. Environ. Med. **4**(5), 84–93 (2014)

Zeleke, T.: Prevalence and factors associated with work related injuries among iron and steel industries workers in Addis Ababa. (Master's thesis). School of Public Health, College of Health Science, Addis Ababa University, Ethiopia (2015). Accessed 21 Nov 2016

CSN 12050 Carbon Steel Mechanical Property Enhancement Using Thermal Treatment to Optimize Product Sustainability

Melesse Workneh Wakjira[1,2]([⊠]), Holm Altenbach[1] [iD],
and Perumalla Janaki Ramulu[3] [iD]

[1] Otto-Von-Guericke-Universität Magdeburg, Magdeburg, Germany
melewine@yahoo.com, holm.altenbach@ovgu.de
[2] Adama Science and Technology University, Adama, Ethiopia
[3] Program of Mechanical Design and Manufacturing Engineering,
School of Mechanical, Chemical and Materials Engineering,
Adama Science and Technology University, Adama, Ethiopia
perumalla.janaki@astu.edu.et

Abstract. Many of the mechanical properties of steel can be improved under controlled sequence of heating and cooling to modify their properties and to meet the desired engineering applications. In this study, the effect of heat treatment cycles (hardening, normalizing, annealing, tempering and recrystallization) on the mechanical properties of CSN 12050 carbon steel have been studied. The aim of the study of this paper is to enhance the ease of machinability for CSN 12050 carbon steel products and to achieve the ultimate goal of product sustainability optimization. The treated and untreated samples change in properties is examined using standard methods. Spectro test TXC25 machine model number 2010, Vickers Hardness tester (HV), and WP310 universal material tester is used to analyze chemical composition and mechanical properties of the specimens respectively. The standard mathematical equations are used to calculate the experimental results of mean values for the test samples of HV and the stress-strain values obtained from the tensile test; later converted to true stress-strain values. Results showed that the mechanical properties of CSN 12050 carbon steel can be changed and improved through annealing and recrystallization process for the ease of machinability. Moreover, the enhanced mechanical properties of CSN 12050 carbon steel can be enlighten the goal of product sustainability through the achieved ease of machinability in dry turning condition.

Keywords: Mechanical-properties · Heat-treatment · Machinability · Product-sustainability

M. W. Wakjira—Research scholar under sandwich program.

F. A. Zimale et al. (Eds.): ICAST 2018, LNICST 274, pp. 113–121, 2019.
https://doi.org/10.1007/978-3-030-15357-1_9

1 Introduction

Manufacturing engineers are often challenged to find ways to improve machinability without harming material performance, which are much focused on the machining efficiency and productivity. However, unlike most material properties machinability cannot be simplified into exclusive work material property. It is a subsequent property of the machining system which is mainly affected by cutting tool materials, and work materials properties etc.

Engineering materials could be developed with improved machinability or more uniform machinability through chemical component adjustment, modification of microstructure, and mechanical properties enhancement. Hence, to achieve the improved work material for better machinability the most important and appropriate properties enhancing operations are heat treatment. To investigate the effect of heat treatment in-relation to the mechanical properties (tensile and hardness), CSN 12050 carbon steel is the best candidate. This steel is widely used for industrial applications like Shafts, Gears, Bolts, Pins, connecting rods, Rams, Axles, Crankshafts, Studs, Rams, Guide rods, Spindles and Hydraulic clamps etc. Among these products the Pin product which is used for cane carrier chains of Sugar Mills is selected to optimize the machinability. It is predominantly manufactured at Hibret Manufacturing and Machine Building Industry (HMMBI) of Ethiopia. The motive to investigate the CSN 12050 carbon steel is initiated from the outcome of preliminary case study at HMMBI Ethiopia and the problem identified thorough onsite observation of the manufactured product quality and defects.

The CSN 12050 carbon steel is usually recommended by the suppliers to carry out heat treatment after initial stock removal to achieve better mechanical properties. "Many of the important mechanical properties of steel, including yield strength and hardness, the ductile-brittle transition temperature and susceptibility to environmental embrittlement can be improved considerably by refining the grain size", [1, 2]. The mechanical properties of steel are strongly connected to their microstructure obtained after heat treatments which are performed to achieve good hardened and tensile strength with sufficient ductility [3, 4].

Different types of steels are heat treated in manufacturing industries and represent a major demand for property enhancement [5, 6]. There is an abundant amount of research work done on the heat treatment process and different steel materials properties [7], but sustainability issues of heat treatment processes have rarely been given much attention. So far, there is hardly any reported work focus on heat treatment process of CSN 12050 carbon steel to optimize its mechanical properties for machinability in the aspect of product sustainability. Therefore, in this research effect of heat treatment process on CSN 12050 carbon steel product sustainability issues that relate to machinability is presented. Due to time, budget and others constraints among many properties of CSN 12050 carbon steel, in this research chemical component adjustment, and mechanical properties (hardness and tensile) test is conducted.

1.1 Materials and Methods

The selected candidate material used for the test in this investigation is CSN 12050 carbon steel rolling bar. To examine the effect of thermal treatment on the CSN 12050 carbon steel, the experimentation is carried out in relation to; examine the chemical composition, sample preparation and investigation of mechanical properties of CSN 12050 carbon steel material.

1.2 Aim and Objective of the Study

The aim of the study is to enhance the performance of machinability for CSN 12050 carbon steel products and to achieve the ultimate goal of product sustainability optimization.

1.3 The Objectives of Research

To understand and analyze the alloying elements, improve tensile strength, ductility and hardness. Accordingly, to eliminate the need of cutting fluids or reduce the cost needed for the cutting fluids and reduce the power consumption during machining the CSN 12050 carbon steel.

2 Material Chemical Composition

The experimental investigation of the study taking place by identifying CSN 12050 carbon steel chemical composition analysis of Spectro test TXC25 machine as shown in Fig. 1 (Table 1).

Fig. 1. Spectro test TXC25 machine set up for sample calibrations for CSN 12050 carbon steel experimentation.

Table 1. CSN 12050 carbon steel chemical composition analysis of Spectro test TXC25 machine.

CSN 12050 carbon steel mechanical composition weight by percent										
C	Si	Mn	P	S	Cr	Mo	Ni	Al	Cu	Fe
0.47	0.24	0.59	0.045	0.085	0.074	0.003	0.017	0.016	0.079	98.4

3 Thermal Treatment of CSN 12050 Carbon Steel and Sample Preparation

Heat treated CSN 12050 carbon steel can possesses good homogenous metallurgical structures, giving consistent machining properties to achieve the goal of product sustainability optimization. The mechanism of heat treatment mainly categorized into thermochemical, thermal treatment and thermo mechanical processes. Thermochemical process which consist of boronising, carburizing, and nitriding. Thermal treatment consists softening (annealing and normalizing) and hardening (hardening and tempering) processes. Thermo mechanical processes which consist of mechanical working operation through the heat-treatment operation like hot forging, rolling etc. The experimentation of this study is conducted on the thermal treatment (hardening, normalizing, annealing, tempering and recrystallization) processes. Samples used for standard cylindrical specimens (12 mm outside diameter/gripping head, 5 mm inside diameter/gauge length, 32.5 mm minimum gripping length and 55 mm gauge length) is prepared by turning using CNC lathe machine.

4 Mechanical Property Experimental Examination of CSN 12050 Carbon Steel

Determination of mechanical properties of materials is more complicated due to the role of different mechanisms. The treated and untreated samples shown in Fig. 5 are used to determine the mechanical properties. The mean value of hardness number experimental results is determined by taking five hardness readings at different orientations on the samples using Vickers Hardness tester (HV). The Vickers hardness tester uses a square-based pyramid diamond indenter with an angle of 136^0 between the opposite faces at the vertex, which is pressed into the surface of the test piece using a prescribed force (F). Measuring ranges from 5–2900 HV and test force 9.807, 49.03, 98.07, 196.1, 294.2, and 490.3 N (1, 5, 10, 20, 30, and 50 kgf). The mean values for the test samples of HV experimental result reports are expressed as:

$$\overline{X} = \frac{\sum\limits_{i=1}^{n} X_i}{n} \tag{1}$$

Where, $\overline{X}$, the mean of X_i, n, the number of data point, and X_i, each of the value of data point.

For tensile properties a cylindrically turned tensile specimens are loaded into a WP310 universal material tester 50 kN (Table 2).

Table 2. Thermal treatment conditions to investigate the mechanical properties test.

Conditions	Temperature (°C)	Handling time (min)	Cooling medium
Hardened	850	40	Water
Normalized	850	40	Air
Annealed	850	40	Furnace
Tempered	540	40	Air
Recrystallized	550	60	Air

The testing machines Vickers Hardness tester, WP310 universal material tester 50 KN and finished/tested sample of specimens are shown in Figs. 2, 3, 4, and 5 respectively.

Fig. 2. Vickers Hardness tester

Fig. 3. WP310 universal material tester 50 kN

Fig. 4. Starting point for tensile testing

Fig. 5. Tested specimens at fracture point

The general mathematical equations used to compute the experimental result expressed as:

$$HV = \frac{0.102 \times 2F\left(\sin \frac{136^0}{2}\right)}{d^2} \tag{2}$$

Where, HV, Hardness measured value and F, test force and d, is diagonal of square-based pyramid diamond indenter.

The WP310 universal material tester 50 kN recorded the force elongation, stress elongation, and tensile strength for all the specimens which is used for further analysis.

The stress–strain values obtained from the tensile test gives the engineering stress–train values which is based on the original cross-sectional area of the test specimens. These values are later converted to true stress–strain values which is more important in manufacturing. The basic equations used to evaluate the engineering/true stress and engineering/true strain derived from [8]. The engineering stress (σ_E) at any point on the curve is defined as the force divided by the original area (A_0), and the equations for engineering strain, % elongation, % area reduction, true stress and true strain are respectively expressed as:

$$\sigma_E = \frac{F}{A_o} \tag{3}$$

$$\varepsilon_E = \frac{L - L_o}{L_o} \tag{4}$$

$$\%EL = \frac{L_f - L_o}{L_o} \tag{5}$$

$$\%RA = \frac{A_o - A_f}{A_o} \tag{6}$$

$$\sigma_T = \frac{F}{A_o}(1 + \varepsilon_E) = \sigma(1 + \varepsilon_E) \tag{7}$$

$$\varepsilon_T = \ln(1 + \varepsilon_E) \tag{8}$$

5 Results and Discussion

The WP310 universal material tester which is calibrated in unit of 50 kN were subjected to test the heat-treated specimens. The thermal treatment effects of hardened, normalized, annealed, tempered and recrystallized specimens are examined in-relation to their mechanical properties (hardness, tensile strength, percentage elongation, and percentage reduction) [5, 6].

The variability in tensile strength, percentage elongation, percentage reduction, hardness, true stress and true strain of heat treated and untreated CSN 12050 carbon steel are shown in Figs. 6, 7 and 8, respectively.

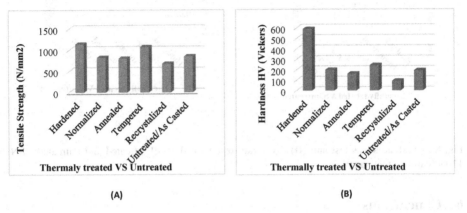

(A)   (B)

Fig. 6. (A) Tensile strength and (B) hardness test result for treated and untreated CSN 12050 carbon steel samples

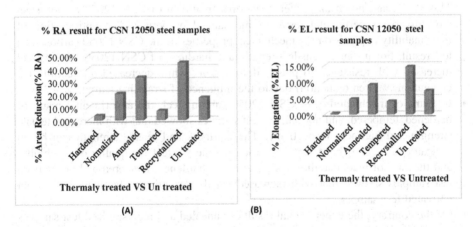

(A)   (B)

Fig. 7. (A) % of Area Reduction (% RA) and (B) % of Elongation test result for thermally treated and untreated CSN 12050 carbon steel samples

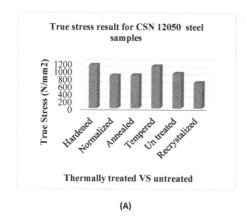
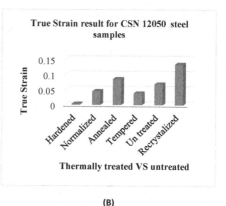

(A)   (B)

Fig. 8. (A) True stress test and (B) true strain result for thermally treated and untreated CSN 12050 carbon steel samples

6 Conclusions

This study set out to investigate thermal treatment of CSN 12050 carbon steel to optimize machinability some of the key findings are as follows:

- This study has shown that different thermal treatment of CSN 12050 carbon steel gave diverse experimental result of mechanical properties. The optimization of machinability depends on the mechanical properties of the CSN 12050 carbon steel test result. For instance, tensile strength, and hardness of CSN 12050 carbon steel increased with resistance to plastic deformation, while decreased its ductility (% elongation, % area reduction) due to the influence of strain hardening.
- In terms of machinability of CSN 12050 carbon steel, the experimental result of hardened, tempered, and normalized test samples showed that with increased tensile strength and hardness respectively. The hardness and tensile strength can be an indicator of machinability but, too much hardness affect the quality of machining and the ease of machinability. As a result, the hardened, tempered and normalized test samples showed that with increased tensile strength and hardness value than untreated test sample.
- On the contrary, the experimental result of annealed and recrystallized test samples showed that with decreased tensile strength and hardness, and increased ductility (% elongation, % reduction) respectively. These results showed that the improvement of the tensile strength and hardness of the CSN 12050 carbon steel for better quality of machining and high productivity. Moreover, it is possible to machine in dry condition and reduce the cost of cutting fluids.

Finally; from the above thermally treated mechanical properties investigation result of CSN 12050 carbon steel samples recrystallization is selected for product sustainability optimization:

By heating the CSN 12050 carbon steel to the recrystallization temperature before deformation, the amount of straining can endure substantially, as a result it can be predicted the forces and power required to carry out the process significantly reduced. Which means through the reduction of cutting forces and power requirement during machining the product can be manufactured with minimized cost, reduced carbon emissions along with safe personal health. Also, by heating to the recrystallized temperature the machining process can be carried out in dry condition to reduce the cost needed for cutting fluids, the associated environmental and personal health risks.

- If the CSN 12050 carbon steel is heated to sufficiently elevated temperature and then deformed, strain hardening does not occur. Instead, new grains are formed that are free of strain, and the CSN 12050 carbon steel behaves as a perfectly plastic material; that is, with a strain-hardening exponent n = 0.
- Recrystallization is a temperature dependent characteristic of metals that can be exploited in manufacturing industries. Hence, in this study among the test sample of thermally treated CSN 12050 carbon steel recrystallized sample test result highly enhanced for successful machinability to achieve the triple bottom line goal of sustainability (environmentally, economically, and societally) sound full. This is a good opportunity for HMMB METEC Ethiopia to optimize machinability and manufacture sustainable pin product for their customer's satisfaction with other surplus benefits.

References

1. Qamar, S.Z.: Effect of heat treatment on mechanical properties of H11 tool steel. J. Achiev. Mater. Manuf. Eng. **35**(2), 115–120 (2009)
2. Liu, K., Shan, Y., Yang, Z., Liang, J., Lu, L., Yang, K.: Effect of heat treatment on prior grain size and mechanical property of a maraging stainless steel. J. Mater. Sci. Technol. **22**(6), 769–774 (2006)
3. Adnan, C.: Effect of cooling rate on hardness and Microstructure of AISI 1020, AISI 1040 and AISI 1060 steels. Int. J. Phys. Sci. **4**(9), 514–518 (2009)
4. Dossett, J.L., Boyer, H.E.: Practical Heat Treating, 2nd edn. ASM International, Novelty (2006)
5. ASTM E8, Standard Test Method for Tension Testing of Metallic Materials, American Society of Testing and Materials (2008)
6. Babu, S.S., Totten, G.E.: Steel Heat Treatment Handbook, 2nd edn. CRC Taylor and Francis, Boca Raton (2006)
7. Valeria, L., Lorusso, H.N., Svoboda, H.G.: Effect of carbon content on microstructure and mechanical properties of dual phase steels. Procedia Mater. Sci. **8**, 1047–1056 (2015)
8. Callister, W.D., Rethwisch, D.G.: Materials Science and Engineering: An Introduction, 8th edn., pp. 131–195. Wiley, Hoboken (2010)

Physico-Chemical Characterizations of Ethiopian Kaolin for Industrial Applications: Case Study WDP Propoxur Formulations

Tadele Assefa Aragaw$^{(\boxtimes)}$ and Feleke Kuraz

Faculty of Chemical and Food Engineering, Bahir Dar Institute of Technology,
Bahir Dar University, Bahir Dar, Ethiopia
taaaad82@gmail.com, felek2004@gmail.com

Abstract. This research aims to investigate chemical, physical, mineralogical and optical properties of Ethiopian kaolin with mechanical, wet beneficiation, chemical modification and thermal treatment (calculations) for their appropriateness of industrial application. The effect of beneficiation and calculation methods of treatment on the structure of kaolin was studied using complete chemical analysis (AAS), X-ray diffraction, Fourier transforms infrared spectrometer analysis (FTIR) and Thermal analysis comparatively with the reference kaolin were studied. Complete silicate analysis showed that the Fe_2O_3 and TiO_2 were reduced via beneficiation and beneficiation with surfactant from 1.908% to 0.201% and 0.87% to 0.056%, respectively. Physico-chemical characterizations, thermal analysis effect of calculations results show that improvement to a very high grade with a chemical composition close to that of ideal kaolin. Beneficiation with a surfactant, followed by calcination at 850 °C, showed a further decrease in Fe_2O_3 and TiO_2 impurities. XRD results revealed that all characteristics reflection of kaolin and quartz were showed as major peaks upon calculations and as well as the reference kaolin. The basic properties for industrial grade specification significantly increased after a certain treatment in comparison with reference (imported) kaolin.

Keywords: Kaolin · Calcinations · Beneficiation · Surfactant · WDP propoxur

1 Introduction

Kaolinite is hydrous aluminum silicate member belonging to the dioctahedral1:1 kaolin mineral group. Indeed, kaolinite is the most widespread phase amongst the other kaolin polymorphs, namely halloysite, dickite and nacrite [1].

The theoretical structural formula of kaolin minerals is $Al_2Si_2O_5$ (OH) 4 that means 46.54% SiO_2, 39.50% Al_2O_3 and 13.96% loss on ignition as structurally bonded hydroxyls. Raw kaolin, however, shows some contents of other elements, due to the presence of the cited associated mineral impurities [2, 3]. Kaolinite normally appears as stacked pseudo hexagonal platelets, <2 μm in size, with a common booklet like shape. Each kaolinite layer is considered as a strong dipole, where the siloxane surface is

F. A. Zimale et al. (Eds.): ICAST 2018, LNICST 274, pp. 122–134, 2019.
https://doi.org/10.1007/978-3-030-15357-1_10

hydrophobic and dominated by negative charges, while the aluminum surface exhibits positive charges and is hydrophilic. Thus, the individual layers of kaolinite are strongly bonded by hydrogen and dipolar interactions [4].

Industrial usage of kaolin minerals exhibits physicochemical and mineralogical characteristics which make them very useful in many different applications [5–7]. These characteristics is important for the utilization of kaolinite in a varied field of industrial applications [2, 7]. The applications depend on the physical, chemical, mechanical, and rheological properties of kaolin minerals that act as an active component or as excipient by controlling the efficiency of the dosage forms, and/or improving the drug bioavailability [3, 8–14]. Amorphous calcined kaolin is the water-soluble, more unstable and dissolves more quickly than its crystalline form. Consequently, an amorphizing agent (dispersant) is necessary to help this process and to stabilize amorphous active ingredient in the solid dosage form [15].

The most important physical tests and parameters recommended to qualify kaolin grades as diluents in solid dosage forms include bulk and tapped density of powder, powder fineness, moisture or loss on drying, hardness, friability, disintegration time, dissolution or active ingredient release profile [16, 17].

Currently; Ethiopia imports the China kaolin for Water Dispersible Powder (WDP) propoxur formulation even though there is kaolin deposit here in Ethiopia. This is because Ethiopian kaolin expected to be high in impurity prior to iron compounds as the information gathered from the Ethiopian geological survey. This is the problem not to use for different industrial application including for propoxur WDP formulation as a carrier. To confirm this problem, the raw Ethiopian kaolin has undergone a certain treatment phase and characterization to form the amorphous alumina-silicate kaolin. Thus, investigating physic-chemical characterizations of the domestic kaolin together with different treatment methods (beneficiation, is aimed at removing impurities like feldspar, iron oxide, etc. and thermal (calcination) make it suitable for different industrial application grade is an important issue specifically propoxur WDP formulation.

2 Methodology

2.1 Materials and Chemicals

Kaolin (bombowuha kaolin) used in this study was supplied from Ethiopian petroleum, minerals and biofuel corporation, Addis Ababa. The reference (China) kaolin was supplied from Adamitulu pesticide factory sharing company. All chemicals, reagents, and material that were used are of analytical grade and were purchased from Addis Ababa, Ethiopia.

2.2 Beneficiation

For the separation of impurities from kaolin, produce kaolin products to meet the needs of various industrial applications; wet treatment (beneficiation) process is an important step according to the procedures reported by [18]. Ground kaolin were dispersed in water and surfactants (1% of dried kaolin) were added. The powdered sample was soaked in deionized water for 24 h (one day). The layers were separated by decantation. The fine clay slurry has been dried at 60 °C and sieved about less than 75 μm so as to the fine grits for further analysis and characterization.

2.3 Thermal Treatment (Calcinations)

The beneficiated kaolin was activated through calcination in a muffled furnace from 550–850 °C for 3 h to form reactive state metakaolin. The heating processes derive off water from the mineral kaolin and collapse the material structure, resulting in an amorphous alumina-silicate ($Al_2O_3.2SiO_2$).

2.4 Thermal Analysis

Thermogravimeter (model ATAT2012) was used for the thermal studies. The TG/DSC measurements were carried out from room temperature up to 1000 °C with air atmosphere in a flow rate approximately 15 mL/min.

Instrument temperature was calibrated by heating indium (melting point = 156.6 °C) as a standard at 10, 15 and 20 °C/min [19].

2.5 Mineralogy Study with XRD

Qualitative and quantitative characterizations of the phases and the number of phases that is present in were determined by Rigaku MiniFlex 300/600) with Ni-filtered Cu Ka radiation at different calcinations temperature and as well the reference (China) kaolin having D/teX Ultra 1D silicon strip detector and Standard Sample Holder. Scan axis = 2theta/theta, continuous scanning measurement mode, wave length 1 of 1.54059, with a speed of 0.12 s/step.

2.6 Chemical Analysis

There are different methods accessible for the determinations of elemental analysis techniques for clay minerals (kaolin). In this study notably lithium metaborate fusion, HF attack, gravimetric and AAS analytical methods, from the geological survey of Ethiopia to determine oxide compositions. Digestion of samples with hydrofluoric and nitric acids (total decomposition) and fusion with lithium metaborate at 950 °C was employed [20]. Analytical Procedures were used as the method reported by [21] and elemental concentrations in milligram per liter in the solution have been converted into weight percentage oxide composition as shown in Eq. 1.

$$\text{Elements(wt\%)} = \frac{\text{mg/l*(dilution factor)} * (0.01)}{\text{grams of sample}} \qquad (1)$$

2.7   Fourier Transformation Infrared (FTIR) Analysis

The FTIR spectra were used for qualitative characterization of surface functional groups of the kaolin. The samples were mixed with KBr and then ground, desorbed and pressed to obtain IR transparent pellets. The percent transmittance was recorded using a PerkinElmer frontier spectrophotometer. The spectra were collected within a scanning range of 400–4000 cm^{-1}.

2.8   Performance Analysis of Formulated WDP Propoxur

Dissolution Rate: The dissolution rate of the propoxur formulations in water medium was done according to USP XXIII paddle method [22]. The stirring speed was 80 rpm and the temperature was maintained ambient. Aliquots (10 ml) were withdrawn at the 0–180 min with 20-min interval and analyzed for the amount of active ingredient dissolved with spectrophotometry at 410 nm using a UV–visible spectrophotometer (PerkinElmer lambda 35) as the Eq. 2.

$$\%\text{propoxur released} = \frac{\text{Amount of propoxur released (mg)} * 100}{\text{dose (mg)}} \quad (2)$$

Where, df = dilution factor; Vd = volume of dilution medium

Dispersion Stability: Dispersion stability was carried out by accurately weighing 0.5 g of the sample, which was added to 200 ml of distilled water and was stirred on an orbital shaker for about 20 min at ambient temperature and allowed to stand in cylinder. 30–180 min with 30 min' interval and residue settled at the bottom was separated by decanting the solution, which was dried on an aluminum foil and weighed, from which percentage yield of complex dispersed in water was calculated, which indicates its dispersion stability [23]. The Dispersion stability is determined by calculating the % yield of dispersion as shown in Eq. 3.

$$\%\text{Yield of dispersion} = \frac{P}{P0} * 100 \quad (3)$$

Where P = weight of sample dispersed in water and
P0 = weight of original sample

Wettability: About 2 g of the sample was weighed and pour uniformly and quickly in the beaker containing 100 ml of hard water (342 ppm) and start the stopwatch simultaneously [24]. The time (seconds) was noted when the whole material is completely submerged in the water.

3 Results and Discussions

3.1 Differential Scanning Calorimeter (DSC) Analysis

Ethiopian kaolin, where the samples are taken, is poorly ordered kaolin as the dehydroxylation peak shows 514 °C. The thermal analysis gives information on weight loss; recrystallization, decomposition and phase transformation reveal the thermal behavior of the kaolinite structure [25]. A large release of moisture and volatile matters has seen concurrent with the weight loss and endothermic in the TG/DSC data. In kaolin composition as can be seen in Fig. 1, DSC/TG signatures a strong case for the presence of lattice energy. Information about interactions between mineral components is obtained from DSC value where the thermal effects at temperatures up to 514 °C have clearly observed. Beneficiated kaolin showed two endothermic and exothermic peaks at 309 and 940 °C, and 85 and 514 °C respectively Fig. 1. The DSC curve of kaolin showed a broad characteristic melting endotherm with a maximum at 940 °C. Finally, the recrystallization and transformation of dehydrated substance to mullite, cristobalite, and quartz were observed at the endothermic peaks at 940 °C is characteristic for metakaolin dissociation and formation of spinel. That means a higher degree of structural order produces a higher endothermic peak while a smaller particle size leads to a lower endothermic peak [26].

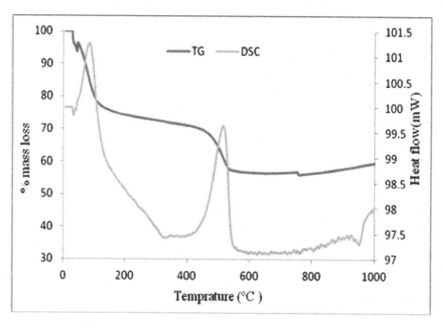

Fig. 1. TG–DSC signals of beneficiated Ethiopian kaolin.

3.2   Mineralogy with XRD

X-ray diffraction (XRD) result reveals structural defects in kaolin because of variability in the peak positions and modulation of their intensities in kaolin XRD patterns. XRD identification of order/disorder is challenging because of overlapping peaks and interferences in kaolin [27, 28]. The degree of kaolinite XRD patterns exhibits broadband between 2theta = 21.03 and 28.12 showed diffuse halo peak which is a characteristic amorphous phase present metakaolins [29]. At those peaks of kaolin was observed in all calcination temperatures with an intensity which increases the rate of calcination. This corresponds with the variation of loss on ignition in metakaolin. The diffraction pattern shown in Fig. 2 give kaolin and quartz as the major minerals in kaolin as well as reference (China) kaolin. The Pattern illustrates the beneficiated kaolin at different calcination temperature and reference kaolin. It was clear that the kaolin is mainly composed of kaolinite mineral as indicated from peaks existing at 2θ values are 21.03, 24.11, 25.133, 27.95, 27.91 and 53.29 has been reported in previous studies [30]. This indicates that the kaolin used in this research is ideal kaolin with anorthic (triclinic) lattice structure. High proportion of quartz mineral was detected from peaks existing at 2θ values 26.88 both in the reference and domestic kaolin and small proportions 39.92 and 50.75 [31] from the reference kaolin but not the domestic kaolin and also it is clearly shown by the patter, as the temperature increases the intensity increases together with amorphousness increase by decreasing the quartz peak at 2θ values 26.88. Therefore, thermally activate kaolin produces structural changes promoting its reactivity. Figure 2 shows a small proportion of titanium oxide (anatase) 2θ values 24.4–25.28 both in reference and Ethiopian kaolin.

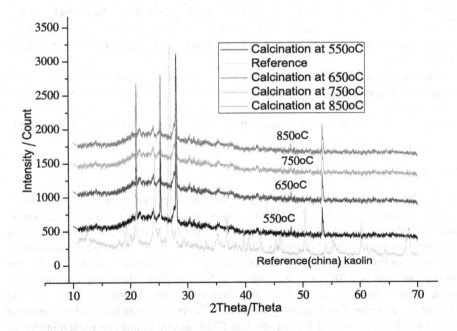

Fig. 2. X-ray diffraction patterns of kaolin at different calcination temprature (550 °C, 650 °C, 750 °C and 850 °C) and reference (china) kaolin

3.3 Chemical Composition

The chemical composition of kaolin was determined by AAS as summarized in Table 1. The common chemical composition analysis detected is the basic components of the kaolin mineral aluminum oxide, silicon oxide and (LoI). It can be seen that the treated kaolin shows better improves the quality of the raw kaolin to almost pure kaolin. It is unluckily that the composition of Fe_2O_3 decreases from 1.908 to 0.201 in Calcined kaolin with a surfactant which is even lower than the china kaolin. This made known a slight decrease in TiO_2 and Fe_2O_3 contents in the kaolin with a simple calcination temperature but further reduction in both TiO_2 and Fe_2O_3 was obtained after beneficiation with a surfactant. It can be seen that anatase (titanium oxide) is concentrated in the fine end of the kaolin particle size distribution [32]. Characteristically, kaolin with less than one percent of iron oxide is considered to be the best quality for a variety of applications. Thus, most important is the increase of the Al_2O_3 content from 32.71 to 39.80% and the SiO_2 increase from 44.8 to 51.37% with drops of LOI from 15.9 to 1.9 due to simple moisture removal and hydroxyl removal of kaolin to produce metakaolin, which is the most active form of kaolin. The major oxide composition analysis tells us a substantial reduction from the kaolin to beneficiation with a surfactant. This confirms that the chemical composition of the treated kaolin with different treatment mechanisms having 51.37% SiO_2 and 39.80% Al_2O_3 which is high-quality grade kaolin for industrial application [33].

Table 1. Chemical composition of raw, reference (china), beneficiated, Beneficiated with surfactant and calcined (850 °C) kaolin

SAMPLES	SiO_2	Al_2O_3	CaO	Fe_2O_3	MgO	K_2O	Na_2O	TiO_2	LOI
Raw	44.8	32.71	0.434	1.908	1.51	0.79	0.019	0.87	**15.9**
Metakaolin without beneficiation	46.4	37.1	0.289	0.983	1.12	0.427	0.038	0.67	**2.03**
Calcined with beneficiation	47.48	38.80	0.325	0.462	0.27	0.544	0.050	0.52	**2.01**
Calcined and beneficiation with surfactant	51.37	39.80	0.325	0.201	0.17	0.104	0.050	0.056	**1.90**
Reference (China) kaolin	46.6	38.8	0.06	0.51	0.08	0.03	0.12	0.48	**1.93**

3.4 FTIR Analysis

As can be seen from the spectra Fig. 3, the bands placed between 3702.17 cm^{-1} regions corresponds to Si-OH stretching vibration from the raw and reference kaolin and the 3628.54 cm^{-1} bands correspond to the inner layer OH (Al-O-H) stretching the raw and reference kaolin obtained by [28, 34]. But no any peak at those of the calcined kaolin. From this, it can be deduced that there is no OH from the calcined kaolin. The absorption band at 1107 cm^{-1} is assigned to Si-O in-plane stretching vibration. The bands placed at 1080.21 cm^{-1} regions correspond to skeleton Si-O-Si in-plane stretching vibration. The frequency vibration 910 cm^{-1} indicated as OH deformation linked to cationic iron and aluminum. The FTIR spectra depict the predominance of kaolin mineral in the studied sample and did not show any peak for impurity such as smectite. The spectral region between 803.89 cm^{-1} is very sensitive against the crystalline and purity of the kaolin mineral. AL-OH ("gibbsite-like") layer shows at 785.68 cm^{-1} [35]. Si-O-Al bending vibration and Si-O bending vibration shows at 564.78 and 463.8 cm^{-1} respectively. The bending vibrations of water molecules adsorbed to kaolin surface (hygroscopic moisture) are responsible for the bands at 1660 cm^{-1}. As can be seen from Fig. 3, the raw kaolin clearly shows a sharp peak at those bands but the calcined and reference kaolin is an insignificant exhibit. Calcined kaolin has enhanced percent transmittance than the raw kaolin also higher than the reference kaolin. Behind to this is, the structure of kaolin breaks down and the iron-containing minerals are converted to oxides compositions that pass on color with low brightness to the product.

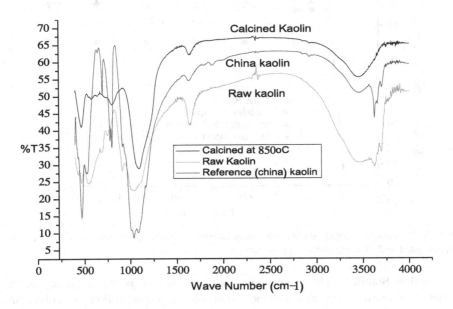

Fig. 3. FTIR- spectra of kaolin (Raw, Calcined and reference (China) kaolin)

3.5 Performance Analysis of Formulated WDP Propoxur

Dissolution Rate: The dissolution profiles of the formulated WDP propoxur can be observed that with raw kaolin, calcined kaolin, beneficiated kaolin and beneficiated kaolin with surfactant have shown Fig. 4 us in increasing the solubility of the propoxur technical ingredient. It is seen that the formulation with surfactant gives higher Dissolution of formulated product with kaolin have been observed that the formulations with raw, calcined, beneficiated and beneficiated with surfactant increase its solubility of propoxur technical. As can be seen the formulated WDP propoxur with beneficiated kaolin surfactant gives a higher percentage of the dissolved active ingredient as compared to that of raw, calcined and simple beneficiated kaolin. This is due to the fact that interaction between the chemical modifiers (surfactant) mixed together on the kaolin surface. Dissolutions were compared to modified and without modified kaolin. The dissolution percentage was lower with formulated WDP propoxur in raw kaolin as compared to that of beneficiated kaolin, calcined kaolin and beneficiated kaolin with a surfactant. This excellent percent dissolution is due to the role of surfactant which can form suspensions of the propoxur technical. It is observed that active ingredient showed no significant change in UV absorbance after that room temperature. The values ranged from 65.8% to 95.96% for solutions at room temperature in raw and treated kaolin. This insured solution stability of active propoxur during the period of dissolution testing.

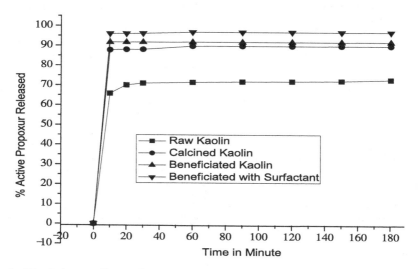

Fig. 4. Dissolution profile studies on formulations of WDP propoxur for raw, calcined, beneficiated and of beneficiated with surfactant.

Dispersion Stability: The dispersion stability expressed as the constancy of the number of particles per unit volume, point out the confrontation to settling and coagulation. In uneven dispersions, the concentrations of particles in the upper dispersion layers decrease because of settling and/or flocculation. As can be seen, Ethiopian raw kaolin has low dispersion stability but the beneficiated with surfactant have high dispersion ability [36].

Dispersion stability depends on the surface area, the particle size distribution, and the solubility of the kaolin mineral in the dispersion medium that is water. If dispersion is stabilized to hinder flocculation and the particle size remains in the colloidal state, below about 0.3 mm, the Brownian motion will prevent settling of particles [36]. The colliding particles become attached to each other unless their surface is modified or some measure has been taken to overcome the attraction between particles. One of the most important functions of a dispersant/surfactant chemical modifier is to hinder the approach of the particles to the close distance where attractive forces dominate and stabilize the dispersion against formulations of WDP propoxur flocculation.

As it can be seen from Fig. 5, the dispersion stability of formulated product with calcined kaolin, beneficiated kaolin and of beneficiated kaolin with surfactant increased sequentially when compared to that of raw Ethiopian kaolin, which indicated that the treatment of kaolin with thermal wet and chemical not only affects the solubility but also the dispersion stability. It can be interpreted from Fig. 5 that the formulated product with beneficiated kaolin and with surfactant show much better dispersion stability that can be attributed to the presence of surfactant molecules in the kaolin structure have the power to form a suspension. Also, the dispersion stability of formulation simple beneficiated with water is slightly comparable to that of the formulation of beneficiated with a surfactant, while that of formulation calcined indicates that the dispersion stability of the formulation which is lower. But have moderate dispersion stability than the raw kaolin.

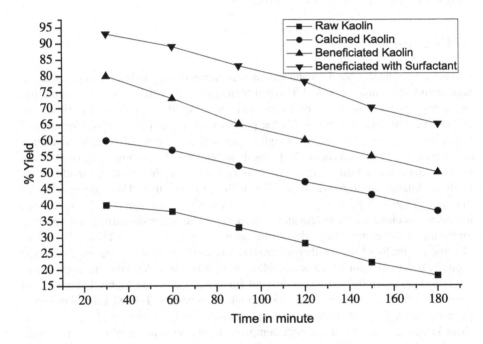

Fig. 5. Dispersion studies on formulations of WDP propoxur for raw, calcined, beneficiated and of beneficiated with surfactant

Wettability: The wetting property studied is immersion wetting. From the results (Table 2) of the wettability test, it is quite evident that the wetting time for formulation of beneficiated with surfactant is lower as compared to that of calcined and beneficiated, which is much lower when compared to raw kaolin, and had resulted due to the decrease in interfacial tension at the solid-liquid interface by the adsorption of the chemical modifier (surfactant) mix together on the kaolin surface causing an enhancement of the wetting property.

Table 2. Wetting time of formulation on raw, calcined, beneficiated and of beneficiated with surfactant kaolin

Formulation	Wetting time (second)
Raw	34.2
Calcined without beneficiation	13.5
Beneficiated with water	10.1
Of beneficiated with surfactant	6.87

Further, it can be made clear that surfactant molecule adsorbed on the surface by Van der Waals attraction get used to the hydrophilic group towards the aqueous solution, thus increasing the hydrophilicity of the absorbent particles and depiction them more wettable with an aqueous solution [37].

4 Conclusion

Ethiopian specifically bombowuha kaolin was successfully modified using beneficiation, chemical modification, and Thermal treatments. The calcination temperature has an ability to increase the brightness and decrease the color values giving an improvement in optical properties. In the present research, a successful beneficiation of Ethiopian kaolin was achieved through a mechanical process of particle separation based on a wet beneficiation method. The beneficiation of the kaolin improves it to a suitable grade for industrial materials. It is demonstrated that chemical modification (with surfactant) can improve the quality of the kaolin further. The characteristics of Ethiopian kaolin clays from western region deposit of the bombowuha led to the following conclusions: the calcination treatment can be adequate starting from 500 °C for the thermal treatments to produce metakaolin as can be seen from TG/DSC analysis. The low weight loss from the thermal analysis conforms as no more organic matter and is poorly ordered kaolin which is suitable to use for the different industrial application.

The china clays (reference kaolin) and Ethiopian kaolin are highly kaolinitic and have same in physic-chemical and mineralogical properties. Treated Ethiopian kaolin (with mechanical and thermal treatment) is found to have properties closer to that of chain kaolin even by far it is better compared to the reference kaolin based on their particle property and pH value. Impurities in raw Ethiopian kaolin are much higher than the chain kaolin clay and it is the 'iron-containing titania' which impacts the optical, chemical and mineralogical properties. However, the treatment processes (beneficiation and calcination) reduces the iron percentage to a lower level than that the reference kaolin. These titania particles with iron in their structure influence the white shade of clay and make it inferior to the domestic kaolin. Calcination first decreases (up to 700 °C) the brightness and whiteness and increases (up to 1200 °C) giving an overall improvement in optical properties. In the end, it can be concluded that treated Ethiopian kaolin (calcined, beneficiated and with surfactant) significantly increased the kaolin high-grade quality for industrial application.

Acknowledgement. We sincere gratefulness goes to Bahir Dar Institute of Technology for their financial support to do this research. Also, my deep gratitude goes to different company and university, Ethiopian geological survey, Ethiopian petroleum and Biofuel Corporation, Adamitulu pesticide factory and Addis Ababa University. We would like to thank the Faculty of Chemical and Food Engineering, Bahir Dar Institute of Technology staffs for their help and accessing all materials for successful completion.

References

1. Weaver, C.E., Pollard, L.D.: The Chemistry of Clay Minerals, vol. 15, 1st edn, pp. 52–59. Elsevier, Amsterdam (1973)
2. Kogel, J.E., Trivedi, N.C., Barker, J.M.: Industrial Minerals and Rocks: Commodities, Markets and Uses Society for Mining. Metallurgy, and Exploration, Inc, Littleton (2006)
3. Williams, L.B.: Geomimicry: harnessing the antibacterial action of clays. Clay Miner. **52**, 1–24 (2017)
4. Chun-Hui, Z., John, K.: Clays, and clay minerals: geology, properties and uses. Appl. Clay Sci. **74**, 58–65 (2013)
5. Peter, A.C.: Industrial Minerals and Their Uses: A Handbook and Formulary, pp. 125–136. William Andrew, Norwich (1996)
6. Murray, H.H.: Applied Clay Mineralogy, 1st edn. Elsevier, Amsterdam (2007)
7. Chatterjee, K.K.: Uses of Industrial Minerals, Rocks and Freshwater. Nova Science Publishers Inc, New York (2009)
8. Carretero, M.I., Gomes, C.S.F., Tateo, F.: Clays, drugs, and human health. In: (Eds.) 5, Handbook of Clay Science. Elsevier, Amsterdam, pp. 711–764 (2013)
9. Zhu, H., Njuguna, J.: Nanolayered silicates/clay minerals: uses and effects on health: In: Health and Environmental Safety of Nanomaterials. Woodhead Publishing Ltd., Elsevier, Amsterdam, pp. 133–146 (2014)
10. Ghadiri, M., Chrzanowskiab, W., Rohanizadeh, R.: Biomedical applications of cationic clay miner. RSC Adv. **7**, 29467–29481 (2015)
11. Khurana, I.S., Kaur, S., Kaur, H., Khurana, R.K.: Multifaceted role of clay minerals in pharmaceuticals. Future Sci. OA **1**, 3 (2015). https://doi.org/10.4155/fso.15.6
12. Kim, M.H., Choi, G., Elzatahry, A., Vinu, A., Choy, Y.B., Choy, J.: Review of clay drug hybrid material for biomedical applications: administration routes. Clays Clay Miner. **64**(2), 115–130 (2016)
13. Yuan, P., Thill, A., Bergaya, F.: Nanosized Tubular Clay Minerals Halloysite and Imogolite, Developments in Clay Science, vol. 7, 1st edn, pp. 203–215. Elsevier Ltd., Amsterdam (2016)
14. Rautureau, M., Figueiredo Gomes, C.S., Liewig, N., Katouzian-Safadi, M.: Clays and Health. Springer, Cham (2017). https://doi.org/10.1007/978-3-319-42884-0
15. Conley, R.F.: Practical Dispersion: A Guide to Understanding and Formulating Slurries, 1st edn, pp. 78–82. VCH Publishers, New York (1996)
16. Mathur, N., Kumar, R., Tiwari, K., Singh, S., Fatima, N.: Evaluation of quality control parameters on various brands of paracetamol tablet formulation. World J. Pharm. Pharm. Sci. **4**(7), 976–984 (2015)
17. Shahabuddin, M.D., Al Mamun, A., Tasnu, T., Asaduzzaman, M.: In-process, and finished products quality control tests for pharmaceutical tablets according to Pharmacopoeias. J. Chem. Pharm. Res. **7**(9), 180–185 (2015)

18. Aroke, U.O., El-Nafaty, U.A., Osha, O.A.: Properties and characterization of kaolin clay from Alkaleri, NorthEastern Nigeria. Inte. J. Emerg. Technol. Adv. Eng. **3**, 387–392 (2013)
19. Archer, J.D., Douglas, W.M., Brad, S.: The effects of instrument parameters and sample properties on thermal decomposition: interpreting thermal analysis data from Mars. Planet. Sci. **2**(2), 1–21 (2013). https://doi.org/10.1186/2191-2521-2-2
20. Twyman, R. M. Wet Digestion. Elsevier Ltd. Online (2005)
21. Potts, P.S.: A Handbook of Silicate Rock Analysis, pp. 47–58. Blackie and Sons Ltd., Glasgow (1992)
22. King, R.E.: Tablets, capsules and pills. In: Oslo, A. (ed.) Remington's Pharmaceutical Sciences, pp. 1559–1560. Mack, Philadelphia (1980)
23. Robert, J.P., Toshiaki, M., Frederick, M.F.: The dispersibility and stability of carbon black in media of low dielectric constant, Electrostatic and steric contributions to colloidal stability. Colloids Surf. **7**(3), 183–207 (1983)
24. IS 6940: Indian Standard Methods of Test for Pesticides and their Formulations (FAD 1): Pesticides and Pesticides first revision (1982)
25. Hongfei, C., Qinfu, L., Jing, Y., Songjiang, M., Ray, L.F.: The thermal behavior of kaolinite intercalation complexes-A review. Thermochim. Acta **545**, 1–13 (2012)
26. Bontle, M., Nadiye-Tabbiruka, M.S.: Chemical and thermal characterization of a clayey material found near gaborone dam. J. Appl. Sci. Environ. Manage. **11**, 77–80 (2007)
27. Hu, P., Yang, H.: Insight into the physicochemical aspects of kaolins with different morphologies. Appl. Clay Sci. **47**, 58–65 (2013)
28. Peter, A.A., Yahaya, M.S., Wan, M.A.W.D.: Kaolinite properties and advances for solid acid and basic catalyst synthesis. RSC Adv **5**, 101127–101147 (2015). https://doi.org/10.1039/c5ra18884a
29. Kenne, D.B.B., Elimbi, A., Cyr, M., Dika, M.J., Tchakoute, H.K.: Effect of the rate of calcination of kaolin on the properties of metakaolin-based geopolymers. J. Asian Ceram. Soc. **3**, 130–138 (2015)
30. Goulash, M., Buhl, J.-C.H.: Geochemical and mineralogical characterization of the Jabal Al-Harad Jordan for its possible utilization. Clay Miner. Mineral. Soc. **45**(4), 281–294 (2010)
31. Liew, Y.M., Kamarudin, H., Mustafa Al Bakri, A.M., Luqman, M., KhairulNizar, I., Ruzaidi, C.M., Heah, C.Y.: Processing and characterization of calcined kaolin cement powder. Constr. Build. Mater. **30**, 794–802 (2012)
32. Bundy, W.M., Murray, H.H.: The effect of aluminum on the surface properties of kaolinite. Clays Clay Miner. **21**(5), 295–302 (1973)
33. https://www.indiamart.com/proddetail/olinpowder7107133755.html. Accessed June 2018
34. Burhan, D., Emin, C.: Investigation of central anatolian clays by FTIR Spectroscopy. Int. J. Nat. Eng. Sci. **3**, 154–161 (2009)
35. Giese, R.F.: Kaolin minerals: structure and stabilities. In: Bailey, S.W. (ed.) Hydrous Phyllosilicates, pp. 29–66. Mineralogical Society of America, Washington DC (1988)
36. Kissa, E.: Stabilization with dispersants and dispersibility. In: Dispersions Characterization, Testing, and Measurement; (surfactant science no, 84), p. 173. Marcel Dekker, New York (1999)
37. Attwood, D., Florence, A.T.: Surfactant System Their Chemistry, Pharmacy, and Biology, EC4P 4EE, pp. 31–37. Chapman and Hall, London (1983)

Effect of Biochar Application Rate, Production (Pyrolysis) Temperature and Feedstock Type (Rice Husk/Maize Straw) on Amendment of Clay-Acidic Soil

Brook Tesfamichael[1]([⊠]) [iD] and Nebiyeleul Gessese[2]

[1] Environmental Engineering Division, School of Chemical
and Bio Engineering, Addis Ababa University, Addis Ababa, Ethiopia
brookutd@gmail.com
[2] Global Development Solutions LLC (GDS), Reston, VA 20190, USA

Abstract. Biochar is a porous solid material produced by pyrolysis (oxygen-free burning) of biomass for the sake of improving soil quality. The aim of this study was to examine the effect of biochar application rate, pyrolysis temperature and feedstock type on the fertility of leached, acidic, clay soil. The biochars used in the study were produced from rice husk (RH) and maize straw (MS) at pyrolysis temperatures of 350, 450 and 550 °C, so in total six biochars were used. To examine the effects of biochar on soil amendment, the six biochars were mixed with the acidic, clay soil at four different levels of applications (0.5, 2.0, 5.0 and 10.0% w/w) then they were chemically characterized. pH, electrical conductivity, CEC, exchangeable basic cations, WHC, organic carbon and total nitrogen content were determined. The increment in the application rate of biochar resulted in a significant increment in soil pH, CEC, exchangeable basic cations, WHC, Organic carbon content. Increasing the biochar production temperature from 350 to 550 °C brought slight increment in pH, Electrical conductivity and Organic carbon content of the soil. Incorporating RH biochar in the soil resulted in higher soil pH but higher organic carbon content of the soil was acquired by incorporating MS biochar.

Keywords: Biochar · Pyrolysis temperature · Soil amendment · Rice husk · Maize straw

1 Introduction

Ethiopia is among the developing countries with majority (about 85%) of the people earn their living mainly by agriculture. Agriculture in Ethiopia has a significant role in securing economic development since the sector generates over 46% of GDP and 80% of export earnings [1]. Nonetheless, many challenges are facing the sector which makes it difficult to attain the pre-planned targets. Among these challenges, the soil fertility issue is the main one. Some of the reasons that bring a poor soil quality in the country include poor agronomic practices, limited awareness of communities, absence of proper

© ICST Institute for Computer Sciences, Social Informatics and Telecommunications Engineering 2019
Published by Springer Nature Switzerland AG 2019. All Rights Reserved
F. A. Zimale et al. (Eds.): ICAST 2018, LNICST 274, pp. 135–144, 2019.
https://doi.org/10.1007/978-3-030-15357-1_11

land policies and inappropriate agricultural techniques. The low nutrient concentration and high acidity are becoming the major challenges of the country's soil.

Agricultural residue management is recommended in several researches as one method for enhancement of soil fertility [2, 3]. However, a problem of agricultural residue management is widely available in Ethiopia although residues are found in surplus. Few amounts of the country's agricultural residues are utilized as a fodder but huge amount is un-utilized as transformation of the residues to an asset is lacking. As a result of this, the surplus residues are typically burnt on-farm [4]. The burning of these residues leads to a release of GHGs to the atmosphere and contributed to bring the agricultural sector as a leader in GHGs emission compared to other sectors [5]. Ethiopia's GHGs emission has shown an increment from time to time despite it has insignificant contribution at global scale. If current practices prevail, GHG emissions in Ethiopia will more than double from 150 Mt CO_2e to 400 Mt CO_2e in 2030 [5].

Therefore, it is very important for developing inexpensive and efficient solution that enhances soil fertility and reduces the emission of GHGs before they bring a devastating problem on human life and the ecosystem of Ethiopia. Many studies have proposed biochar technology as a viable option to offer an integrated approach to contribute to the challenges [6]. In the last decade an interest in biochar and its impact on soil properties has boomed worldwide. The use of biochar amendments to replenish soil organic carbon (SOC) pools, restore soil fertility and sequester carbon has been recommended by the United Nations Convention to Combat Desertification (UNCCD) during Climate Change Conference held in Copenhagen in 2009 [7].

Biochar is solid material produced by pyrolysis (oxygen-free burning) of biomass. Although biochar and charcoal are used interchangeably in many literatures, there is a major distinction between the two. Unlike charcoal, biochar is produced at specific temperature with the intent to be added to a soil as a means of enhancing soil quality and sequestering carbon. Biochar has different properties depending on the type of biomass feedstock and the pyrolytic conditions used in its production [8].

The outputs of several researches have shown the potential of biochar to improve soil quality by retaining nutrients and water, reducing the acidity, enhancing the cation exchange capacity (CEC) of the soil and attracting more beneficial fungi and microbes to the soil [9–12]. On the other hand, biochar's environmental benefit is a straight forward mechanism. The organic matter used for biochar production forms a stable structure while it is pyrolyzed. The stable form of the biochar is highly resistant to chemical and biological degradation and makes it stable in the soil for a long term; even for centuries and millennia. Consequently, it sequesters carbon derived from the organic matter for a long period which leads to withdrawal of CO_2 from the atmosphere [8].

Upon the author review, no scientific study has been carried out regarding the simultaneous impact of biochar production temperature, application rate and feedstock type despite many researches are conducted around the area. Hence, the motivation behind this research is assessing the simultaneous impact of the above three parameters on the amendment of clay, acidic soil which is the common problematic type among wide variety of soils available in Ethiopia.

2   Materials and Methods

2.1   Raw Material Collection

The major raw materials used in this study are soil and agricultural residues (rice husk and maize straw). The soil for the study was collected from farmer's field in Entoto area, North of Addis Ababa. The area was selected based on the recommendation of soil experts of the Agricultural research center. The study outcome of the center has shown the agriculture around the area is currently facing a severe problem of intensive run-off and erosion due to reduction in organic matter, water filtration, and water and nutrient retention capacity of the soil. The rice husk was acquired from Fogera district of South Gondor zone in the Amhara regional state, one of high rice producing place in Ethiopia. The maize straw was collected from government farm in Ziway town.

2.2   Soil Sampling and Preparation

Soil was sampled with a soil auger at a depth of 20 cm after clearing the top 10 cm of the soil surface. Thereafter soil samples were subjected to air-drying, and further crushed to reduce heterogeneity and provide maximum surface area for physical and chemical reactions. After crushing, soil samples sieved through a mechanically vibrating 2-mm mesh for 10 min so as to sort out coarse fragments and also bigger organic materials, whose nutrients might influence the results of the upcoming analyses. Because the soil samples were not allowed to stay moist for extended periods of time, the sieved soil was spread on plastic covers and left to dry in the sun for one day. Finally, soil used for laboratory analyses was put into polythene bags.

2.3   Biochar Production

Biochar was produced using a lab-scale slow pyrolysis process after preparing a new pyrolysis set up in the School of Chemical and Bio-Engineering laboratory of Addis Ababa University. All runs in the experimentation of this research were conducted in a batch process of pyrolysis. First pretreated feedstocks of approximately 100 grams were added into the reactor tube. The reactor was then flushed with N_2 gas at a pressure of 5 bar to maintain anoxic environment. Whenever there was N_2 flushing the other hole that was closed with a lid becomes uncovered to allow the release of the unwanted oxygen. The flushed reactor was then placed in the furnace at room temperature for the start of the charring process and the temperature was raised at an average rate of 10 °C min^{-1} until the specific desired temperature was reached and held constant. The series of experiments were conducted to pyrolyze the rice husk and maize straw at 350 °C, 450 °C and 550 °C to obtain six samples (RH350, RH450, RH550, MS350, MS450 and MS550). After one hour of heating and charring the power supply was turned off and the system was cooled over night to reach room temperature. Then, the biochar were grounded and sieved through a mechanically vibrating 2-mm mesh for 10 min so as to have the same particle size as that of the soil.

2.4   Preparation of Soil-Biochar Mixtures

The six biochars produced from RH and MS at 350, 450 and 550 °C pyrolysis temperatures were applied to the soil at 0.5%, 2%, 5% and 10% application rates and mixed thoroughly. Therefore, a total of 24 soil-biochar mixtures were prepared.

2.5   Laboratory Analysis

The raw soil's and soil-biochar mixtures' pH and Electrical conductivity (EC) were measured in water at a soil-water ratio of 1:2.5 using pH and conductivity meter respectively. The water holding capacity (WHC) was determined by putting the soil or soil-biochar mixtures into a glass funnel fitted with filter paper then saturating it with water and determines the quantity of water it retained after one day. The organic carbon and total nitrogen (N) content of the soil and soil-biochar mixtures were determined by Walkley-Black and Kjeldahl methods respectively [13, 14]. Total exchangeable K and Na amounts were analyzed using flame photometer whereas total exchangeable Ca and Mg were analyzed by atomic absorption spectrophotometer from the soil leached by 1 N ammonium acetate at pH 7 [15]. In similar fashion, CEC was determined after leaching the soil using 1 N ammonium acetate at pH 7 then titrimetrical estimation by distillation of ammonium that was displaced by sodium [16].

2.6   Statistical Analysis

One-way analysis of variance (ANOVA) was performed to assess the significance differences in soil parameters and plant growth between different soil-biochar treatments, using the general factorial procedure of Design-expert@7.1.

3   Result and Discussion

3.1   Effect of Biochar Application Rate, Biochar Production (Pyrolysis) Temperature and Biochar Production Feedstock on Soil PH and EC Content

The effect of biochar application rate, biochar production (pyrolysis) temperature and biochar production feedstock on clay acidic soil pH and EC are given in Figs. 1 and 2 respectively. The statistical analysis revealed that the soil pH and EC values were significantly ($p < 0.05$) affected by biochar application rate and biochar production (pyrolysis) temperature. However, the biochar feedstock (being RH or MS) does not have significant ($p > 0.05$) effect on soil pH and EC.

The highest values of pH and EC were observed in soil treated with 10% biochar application rate, while the lowest values were recorded at the untreated soil. In consistence with these results, Agusalim et al. also reported increment of soil pH from 3.75 to 4.90 after applying 10 tones/ha of rice husk biochar [17]. The existence of alkaline carbonates, oxides, and hydroxide in the ash fraction of the biochar is the main potential reason for the observed increment of soil pH in the biochar treated soil compared to the control is likely due to [6].

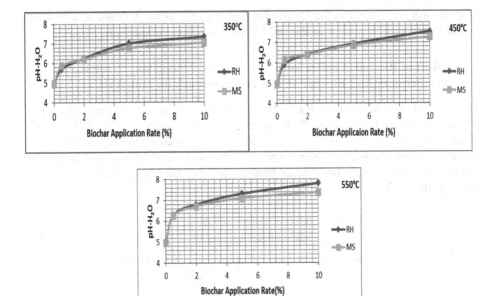

Fig. 1. Effect of application rate and feedstock type of biochars produced at pyrloysis temperature of 350 °C (top left), 450 °C (top right) and 550 °C (bottom) on soil pH

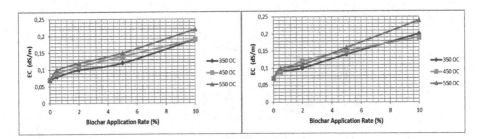

Fig. 2. Effect of application rate and production (pyrolysis) temperature of biochars derived from rice husk (left) and maize straw (right) on soil EC

According to the results of this study, the soil pH and EC increases with the biochar production (pyrolysis) temperature. The highest pH and EC values were observed in soil treated with biochar produced at 550 °C pyrolysis temperature. The potential reason for increment of the soil pH with pyrolysis temperature of the biochar might be the destruction of acidic functional groups on the biochar surface and the reduction of oxygen that resulted in the removal of various acidic functional oxides at high temperature. In agreement to this result, the pH increment also observed with increasing the pyrolysis temperature between 300 and 500 °C during rice husk and sugar cane bagasse pyrolysis from the research output of Shinogi and Kanri [18]. On the other hand, the ash content of biochar obtained at higher pyrolysis temperatures is a possible reason to bring an increment in the soil EC with pyrolysis temperature.

3.2   Effect of Biochar Application Rate, Biochar Production (Pyrolysis) Temperature and Biochar Production Feedstock on Soil WHC

The effect of biochar application rate, biochar production (pyrolysis) temperature and biochar production feedstock on WHC of clay acidic soil is given in Fig. 3. The WHC of the soil was significantly ($p < 0.05$) affected by biochar application rate only. However, the pyrolysis temperature to produce the biochars and the type of feedstocks (being either RH or MS) for biochar production don't have a significant ($p > 0.05$) effect on the WHC of the soil.

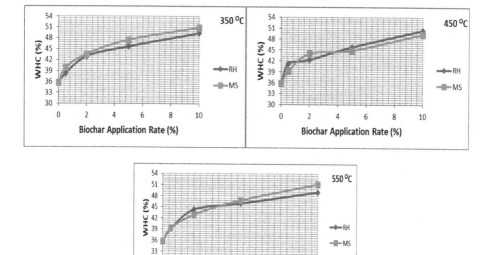

Fig. 3. Effect of application rate and feedstock type of biochars produced at pyrloysis temperature of 350 °C (top left), 450 °C (top right) and 550 °C (bottom) on soil WHC

The highest values of WHC were observed in soil treated with 10% biochar application rate, while the lowest values were recorded at the control (0%) or untreated soil.

The potential increment of WHC with the application rate of biochar is due to the ability of the porous structure of the biochar to retain water. The other hypothesized reason is the improved aggregation or structure of the soil after biochar incorporation. Therefore, it is quite logical that soil applied with biochar had the highest WHC. The results of this study is similar to those reported by Agusalim et al., Sokchea et al. and Sisomphone et al. where WHC was increased from 11.3 to 15.5%, 43 to 53% and 40 to 50% respectively due to the application of biochar [17, 19, 20].

3.3 Effect of Biochar Application Rate, Biochar Production (Pyrolysis) Temperature and Biochar Production Feedstock on Soil Organic C and Total N

The mean values of Soil Organic Carbon (SOC) and Total Nitrogen (TN) across different biochar application rates, pyrolysis feedstocks and temperatures are given in Figs. 4 and 5 respectively. The SOC was significantly ($P < 0.05$) affected by the biochar application rate and pyrolysis temperature. Nevertheless, it was not significantly ($P > 0.05$) affected by the biochar production feedstock either being RH or MS. On the other hand, the TN content of the soil was not significantly ($P > 0.05$) affected by all the three parameters.

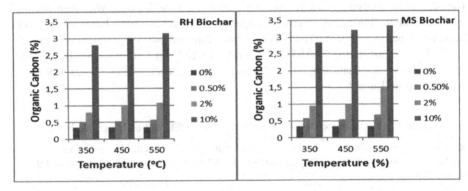

Fig. 4. Effect of application rate and production (pyrolysis) temperature of biochars derived from rice husk (left) and maize straw (right) and on SOC

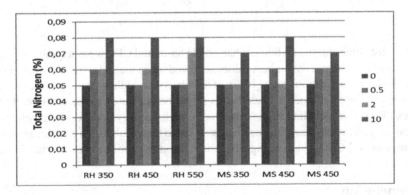

Fig. 5. Effect of application rate, production (pyrolysis) temperature and feedstock type of on soil TN

The soil treated with 10% biochar application rate gives the highest value of SOC. There was a general trend of increasing SOC with increasing biochar application rates. The increase in organic carbon could be resulted from the presence of high amount of carbon in the biochars. In consistent to this study Liang et al. also reported that high organic carbon is available in soils treated with higher biochar rate than lower application rate [21]. Similarly, the SOC increased as the temperature of biochar production increased. Clearly, the reason is due to the fixed carbon content of the biochar increases as the pyrolysis temperature increases. However, the TN increases only by 0.03% compared to the control soil even at the highest biochar application rate (10%). A possible reason could be the insignificant amount of nitrogen in the biochars.

3.4 Effect of Biochar Application Rate, Biochar Production (Pyrolysis) Temperature and Biochar Production Feedstock on Soil CEC and Exchangeable Bases

The statistical analysis showed that application rate of biochar was significantly ($p < 0.05$) affect the cation exchange capacity and exchangeable bases of the soil. However, biochar production (pyrolysis) temperature and biochar production feedstock do not have significant ($p > 0.05$) effect on Soil CEC and Exchangeable Bases: The effect of biochar application rate on CEC and content of exchangeable bases of the soil is presented in Table 1.

Table 1. Effect of biochar application rate on soil CEC and exchangeable bases

Biochar application Rate (%)	Exch. Na (meq/100 g)	Exch. K (meq/100 g)	Exch. Ca (meq/100 g)	Exch. Mg (meq/100 g)	CEC (meq/100 g)
0	0.33	0.42	10.27	6.85	28.84
0.5	0.4	0.73	12.18	8.01	33.94
2	0.43	1.27	13.82	8.64	38.03
10	0.83	1.44	15.55	10.37	40.38

The least values for the all four exchangeable bases and CEC were acquired when the soil is untreated whereas the highest values achieved when the soil is treated with biochar at the highest application rate (10%). The observed highest values of CEC and exchangeable bases at biochar treated soils might be attributed to the inherent characteristics of biochar including high surface area, high porosity and existence negatively charged sites on the biochar surfaces. In agreement to this result, Chan et al. also reported increment of soil CEC and exchangeable bases through application of biochar [22].

4 Conclusion

This study is conducted to investigate the effect of biochar application rate, production temperature and feedstock type on leached acidic soil properties. Rice husk and maize straw biochars were produced at a pyrolytic temperature of 350, 450 and 550 °C and mixed thoroughly at application rates of 0.5, 2, 5 and 10.0% w/w with the leached acidic soil. The chemical laboratory analysis has indicated that the increment biochar application rate led to a significant increment in the soil pH, electrical conductivity, water holding capacity, cation exchange capacity, exchangeable bases and organic carbon content and the highest value of all these soil properties was acquired at 10% biochar application rate. Nonetheless, no significant change has been shown in the total nitrogen content of the soil after biochar application. The presence of ash in the biochar, high surface area and porous nature of the biochar were identified as the main reasons for the increase in the above soil properties. The pH, electrical conductivity and organic carbon content of the soil showed slight increment as the biochar producing temperature increased and this is due to the increment of the ash and carbon content of the biochar with pyrolysis temperature. Incorporating rice husk biochar in the soil results in higher soil pH and electrical conductivity compared to maize straw biochar but higher organic carbon content of the soil was obtained by incorporating maize straw biochar in the soil. In general, the results of this study showed application of biochar derived from rice husk and maize straw on acidic, clay soil increases soil fertility by improving some soil physico-chemical properties. As evident from the present study, it is recommended that the effect of various pyrolysis conditions must be investigated on a variety of feedstocks aimed at producing biochar for different type of soil application.

Acknowledgments. The research is partly financed by Addis Ababa University. Special thanks AAiT and Science Faculty of Addis Ababa University and Water Works Design and Supervision Enterprise for all the valuable inputs and the technical lab support provided.

References

1. FAO Homepage. http://www.fao.org/ag/ca. Accessed 13 Dec 2017
2. Taa, A., Tanner, D., Bennie, A.T.P.: Effects of stubble management, tillage and cropping sequence on wheat production in the South-eastern highlands of Ethiopia. Soil Tillage Res. **76**(1), 69–82 (2004)
3. Mesfin, T., Girma, A., Al-Tawaha, A.M.: Effect of reduced tillage and crop residue ground cover on yield and water use efficiency of sorghum (Sorghum bicolor (L.) Moench) under semi-arid conditions of Ethiopia. World Journal of Agricultural Sciences **1**(2), 152–160 (2005)
4. Zenebe, G.: Household Fuel and Resource use in Rural-Urban Ethiopia. Wageningen University, Wageningen (2007)
5. MO EF: Planning and implementing the Ethiopian Climate Resilient Green Economy, CRGE Strategy. Ethiopian Ministry of Environment and Forest, Ethiopia (2015)
6. Lehmann, J., Joseph, S.: Biochar for environmental management: an introduction, pp. 1–12. ES_BEM_16-2, London, UK, (2009)
7. UNCCD: Use of biochar (charcoal) to replenish soil carbon pools, and restore soil fertility and sequester CO2. In: 5th Session of the Ad Hoc Working Group on Long-term Cooperative Action under the Convention (AWG-LCA 5), Bonn, Germany, 29 March–8 April 2009 (2009)
8. Lehmann, J., Gaunt, J., Rondon, M.: Biochar sequestration in terrestrial ecosystems: a review. Mitig. Adapt. Strat. Glob. Change **11**, 403–427 (2006)
9. Lehmann, J.: A handful of carbon. Nature **447**, 143–144 (2007)

10. Sohi, S., Krull, E., Lopez-Capel, E., Bol, R.: Biochar's roles in soil and climate change: a review of research needs. Adv. Agron. **105**, 47–82 (2009)
11. Atkinson, C.J., Fitzgerald, J.D., Hipps, N.A.: Potential mechanisms for achieving agricultural benefits from biochar application to temperate soils: a review. Plant Soil **337**(1–2), 1–18 (2010)
12. Novak, J.M., Busscher, W.J., Laird, D.L., Ahmedna, M., Watts, D.W., Niandou, M.A.S.: Impact of biochar amendment on fertility of a southeastern coastal plain soil. Soil Sci. **174**(2), 105–112 (2009)
13. Walkley, A., Black, I.A.: An examination of the Degtjareff method for determining soil organic matter and a proposed modification of the chromic acid titration method. Soil Sci. **37**, 29–38 (1934)
14. Kjeldahl, J.: "Neue Methode zur Bestimmung des Stickstoffs in organischen Körpern" (New method for the determination of nitrogen in organic substances). Z. Anal. Chem. **22**(1), 366–383 (1883)
15. Rowell, D.L.: Soil Science: Methods and Applications, p. 350. Addison Wesley Longman Singapore Publishers (Pte) Ltd., England, UK (1994)
16. Chapman, H.: Cation exchange capacity. In: Black, C.A. (ed.) Methods of Soil Analysis, pp. 891–901. Agronomy, Am. Soc. Agro. Inc., Madison, Wisconsin (1965)
17. Agusalim, M., Wani, U., Syechfani, M.: Rice husk biochar for rice based cropping system in acid soil: the characteristics of rice husk biochar and its influence on the properties of acid sulfate soils and rice growth in West Kalimantan. Indonesia. J. Agric. Sci. **2**(1), 39–47 (2010)
18. Shinogi, Y., Kanri, Y.: Pyrolysis of plant, animal and human waste: physical and chemical characterization of the pyrolytic products. Bioresour. Technol. **90**, 241–247 (2003)
19. Sokchea, H., Preston, T.R.: Growth of maize in acid soil amended with biochar, derived from gasifier reactor and gasifier stove, with or without organic fertilizer (biodigester effluent). Livestock Res. Rural Dev. **23**(4), 69 (2011)
20. Simsomphone, S., Preston, T.R.: Growth of rice in acid soils amended with biochar from gasifier or TLUD stove, derived from rice husks, with or without biodigester effluent. Livestock Res. Rural Dev. **23**(2), 32 (2011)
21. Liang, B., et al.: Black carbon increases cation exchange capacity in soil. Soil Sci. Soc. Am. J. **70**, 1719–1730 (2006)
22. Chan, K.Y., Van Zwieten, L., Meszaros, I., Joseph, S.D.: Using poultry litter biochars as soil amendments. Australian J. Soil Res. **46**, 437–444 (2008)

Performance Comparisons of Solar Mixed and Indirect Dryers for Maize Grain Drying

Aynadis Molla[1(✉)], Sajid Alavi[2], Bhadriraju Subramanyam[2],
Solomon Workneh[1], and Nigus Gabbiye[1]

[1] Bahir Dar Institute of Technology, Bahir Dar University,
P.O. Box 79, Bahir Dar, Ethiopia
Aynadism2006@gmail.com
[2] Department of Grain Science and Industry, Kansas State University,
Manhattan, USA

Abstract. This paper presents the design, construction and performance evaluation of mixed (SCMD) and indirect (SCID) -mode solar cabinet dryers for drying of maize grain with varieties of BH-540 and BH-660. The performances of the solar dryers were tested with three levels of sample loading, 21.74 kg/m^2 (thick layer), 16.3 kg/m^2 (medium layer), and 10.87 kg/m^2 (thin layer). In both dryers, the air was heated in the solar collector and passed naturally through a grain bed. For SCMD, the drying cabinet absorbs solar energy directly through the transparent roof. The solar irradiance, temperature and relative humidity distribution for ambient and in different parts of the dryer, and moisture loss of the grain at each try have been recorded. The result revealed that, a temperature raise of 15 °C was found in both dryers with respect to the ambient air. The required drying time was varied depending on the amount of sample loaded. About 32 h was required in thin layer compared to 53 h in thick layers drying process to reduce the moisture content of the grain to its safe storage value of 13% (w,b). The drying rate, collector efficiency and overall system efficiency were varied from 0.41–0.56, kg/h, 44.4–57.2%, and 24.0–32%, for SCID and from 0.47–0.58, kg/h, 44.4–57.2%, and 24.6–33%, for SCMD respectively. Statistically, no significant difference has observed on drying rate and overall dryer efficiency between SCMD and SCID.

Keywords: Drying rate · Dryer efficiency · Solar dryers

1 Introduction

In developing countries, the majority of the population is engaged in farming activeties. Almost 80% of the total food products is cultivated by small farmers [1]. In many rural locations of these countries, grid-connected electricity and supplies of other non-renewable sources of energy are unavailable, unreliable or, too expensive. Hence, open sun drying is the only means to dry crops before harvesting. However, for large-scale production the limitations of open-air drying are well known. Among these are high labor costs, large area requirement, and lack of ability to control the drying process, possible degradation due to biochemical or microbiological reactions, insect infestation, and so on. The drying time required for a given commodity can be quite long and

F. A. Zimale et al. (Eds.): ICAST 2018, LNICST 274, pp. 145–159, 2019.
https://doi.org/10.1007/978-3-030-15357-1_12

resulted in post-harvest losses of up to 30% [2]. The advancement of open sun drying is solar drying, which is drying of food products using solar energy. Solar energy is the primary source of all renewable energy resources. It has enormous potential to meet growing energy requirements of the increasing population of the developing world. Its virtually inexhaustible supply with global distribution and environmentally safe nature make solar energy a very attractive prospect worldwide [3].

In the solar drying process, food products are dried in an enclosed unit to keep them safe from damage from birds, insects, microorganism, pilferage, and unexpected rainfall. Moreover, solar drying of agricultural products in enclosed structures by forced convection is an attractive way of reducing post-harvest losses and low quality of dried products associated with traditional open sun-drying methods [4]. Hence, the introduction of solar dryers in developing countries can reduce crop losses and improve the quality of the dried product significantly when compared to the traditional methods of drying, such as sun or shade drying [5]. Crop grain post-harvest loss in Ethiopia is estimated as high as 10% to 30% [6–8].

Different types of solar dryers have been developed and tested for the efficient utilization of solar energy around the world [9–12]. The literature survey indicates that out of several dryer designs developed and studied, the indirect and mixed mode solar dryers have received the maximum attention of researchers in mathematical modeling and thermal performance evaluation [2]. But, limited work is available in open literature on performance comparisons of those dryers. Simate et al. [13] had developed a lab scale mixed and indirect natural convection dryers using wood for the construction of the dryer chamber part. The authors have reported higher drying rate for mixed mode than indirect type. Singh [3] had also compared the performance of solar mixed and indirect dryer under forced condition by varying the flow rate of the inlet air. The author reported that, higher drying rate and dryer effectiveness for solar mixed type than indirect. From literature, performance of solar dryers may vary depend on the type of construction materials, their working conditions, weather conditions, and so on. So, the main aim of this study was to test the performance of solar mixed and indirect cabinet dryers for drying of freshly harvested maize grain in Amhara Region, Ethiopia, to reduce the large percentage of post-harvest loss of maize grain in the country.

2 Materials and Methods

Freshly harvested maize grains (Zea Mays) with varieties of BH-540 and BH-660 obtained from farmers in the villages of Merawi district, Birakat were used in this study. It was harvested at a moisture content of 22–25% (w.b.).

2.1 Experimental Set up and Description

Solar cabinet mixed dryer (SCMD) and solar cabinet indirect dryer (SCID) were used for drying of freshly harvested maize grain. The dryers were constructed from locally available materials by following rules of thumb [14]. The design specification is presented in Table 1. Both dryers' constructions are almost identical with a difference in drying chamber top cover arrangement. Both dryers consist of a solar air heating

Table 1. Design specifications of solar cabinet indirect and mixed- mode dryers

Parameter	Mixed-mode	Indirect-mode
Mode of heating	Mixed	Indirect
Loading provision	Sliding tray	Sliding tray
Number of trays	6	6
Air outlet provision	Chimney at the top	Chimney at the top
Air circulation	Natural (0.085 m/s)	Natural (0.0085 m/s)
Collector area	3.8.0 m^2	3.8.0 m^2
Drying capacity	150 kg	150 kg
Collector slope	15°	15°
Thinness of plastic sheet	4 mm	4 mm
Drying chamber size	2.0 * 0.6 * 1.5 m, its top part is transparent/glass	2.0 * 0.6 * 1.5 m, its top part is opaque/metal sheet
Size of trays	1.9 * 0.36 * 0.02 m	1.9 * 0.36 * 0.02 m
Chimney with constant cross section	Bottom and top each 0.3 * 0.3 * 0.3 m, Height 1.5 m	Bottom and top each 0.3 * 0.3 * 0.3 m, Height 1.5 m

collector system, drying chamber with a chimney and supporting stand (Fig. 1). The Solar collector was constructed using a galvanized iron sheet at the bottom acting as an absorber and transparent covering (glazing) at its top. The galvanized iron sheet was painted matt black and used as an absorber for maximum absorption of solar heat energy. The drying chamber consists of six trays arranged in parallel fashion and

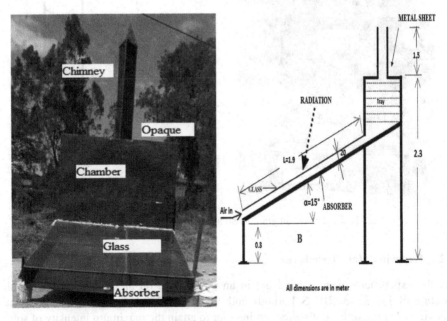

Fig. 1. Schematic diagram of solar cabinet indirect dryer, SCID

chimney located at the center of the chamber. The drying cabinet alongside the structural support of the dryer was built from a galvanized iron sheet which could withstand the unfavorable weather condition. Chimney is used to generate buoyant force on the air, thereby increasing the rate of air flow through the dryer. The chamber and the chimney were fabricated from galvanized iron sheet material. But for SCMD type the top part of the chamber replaced by transparent glass. Galvanized iron wire mesh was used to construct the trays. Both dryers consisted of an inclined flat-plate solar air collector with air flowing between plate and glass cover (Fig. 1) with an average air flow rate of 0.085 m/s. There was pre-heating of inlet air by the solar collector. In a mixed type of solar dryer, grain is dried on a perforated surface and is subjected to direct radiation on its top surface through the transparent drying chamber cover, and hot air current passing through the grain bed from a solar collector. The grain is, therefore, dried by a combination of both direct radiation with conduction of heat from the top layer grains to the bottom ones and the convection of hot air from the solar air heater entering the bottom layers and moving to the top ones. In indirect-mode dryer on the other hand, grain is dried by hot air alone from a solar collector (Fig. 2).

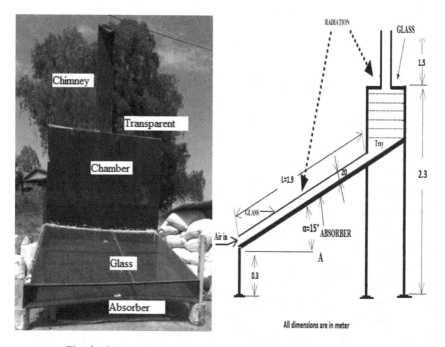

Fig. 2. Schematic diagram of solar cabinet mixed dryer, SCMD

2.2 Experimental Procedures

All the experiments were carried out in an open space on an elevated surface with location of 11° 35' 37.10" N Latitude and 37° 23' 26.77" E Longitude. Both dryers were installed in north, south direction in order to attain the maximum intensity of solar radiation. Freshly harvested maize grain was uniformly placed over each mesh tray inside the drying chamber. Samples were loaded at three different amounts, 21.74 kg/m^2 (thick layer), 16.3 kg/m^2 (medium), and 10.87 kg/m^2 (thin layer) which mean total sample load of 150 kg, 100 kg and 75 kg, respectively in each cabinet dryer. Drying experiments were started at 9:00 AM and continued till 5:00 PM according to the weather condition of the study area, Bahir Dar city. Grain maize sample was loaded in the dryers during night time and the drying was continued until the desired moisture content of 13% (wet basis) was reached. The moisture content of the grain was periodically measured with an interval of 3 h using moisture meter (JOHN DEERE, MOISTURE CHEK PLUS^{TM}, SW08120, and USA). Temperature and relative humidity of ambient air and drying air inside the solar dryers were periodically measured by the Hobo ware data logger (UX 100-011 Temp/RH, Onset HOBO Data Loggers). Each record was taken inside the solar cabinet dryers along the number of trays in loaded or unloaded conditions. Anemometer (CFM/CMM Thermo-Anemometer, model -PMA90, PYLE, and accuracy ± 3%) and Lux meter (Dr Meter Digital Illuminance Meter, model- LX1330B, and accuracy ± 3%) were used to hourly measure the inlet wind speed to solar cabinet dryers and global solar radiation on the ground, respectively. Temperature and relative humidity from the solar collector inlet & outlet, as well as temperature and relative humidity of ambient air temperature were measured from 9:00AM to 05:00PM. A similar standard was followed by Nabnean et al. [15].

2.3   Performance Evaluation of Solar Dryers

According to Augustus Leon *et al.* [9], physical features of the dryer, thermal performance, quality of dried product, and cost of dryer & payback period are parameters generally used for the evaluation of performance of solar dryers. For this study the comparisons of mixed and indirect type solar cabinet dryers were done by their moisture removal and thermal analysis, which are the basic standard procedure for evaluating solar dryer performance [16]. The performances of these systems were evaluated using moisture loss, drying rate, and the system drying efficiency. The drying system was evaluated using the solar collector efficiency, drying rate, percentage moisture loss, and drying efficiency of the dryer. The system performance and the drying characteristics of maize such as moisture content, drying rate, and efficiency were calculated using the following equations.

Moisture Content: The moisture content of maize grain was measured within two hours interval of drying using moisture meter.

   Drying Rate (DR) is expressed as the quantity of moisture removed from the food item over the drying time [16]

$$DR = \frac{M_w}{t_d} \qquad (1)$$

Where M_w is mass of water evaporated (kg) and t_d is drying time per day, (h).

Solar Collector Efficiency

The efficiency of a solar collector is the ratio of heat gained by the air leaving the collector to the incident solar energy over a particular time period [17]. The steady state thermal efficiency of a solar collector is given by Hottel-Whillier-Bliss equation [11].

$$\eta_c = \frac{m_a C_p (T_o - T_a)}{A_c I_T} \tag{2}$$

Where η_c is collector efficiency, %, m_a is the air mass flow rate (kg/s), C_p is specific heat capacity of air, (kJ/kgK), T_o is the temperature of the outgoing air from the collector, (^{0}C), T_a is ambient air temperature (^{0}C), A_c is a collector surface area (m²), and I_T is incident solar radiation on the tilt surface (W/m²).

Dryer Efficiency

Thermal performance or drying rates of the products are the key factors used for the evaluation of the solar drying system efficiency [16]. For natural convection solar dryer, the system efficiency can be expressed as given by [13].

$$\eta_{dryer} = \frac{M_W L_V}{I_T A_c t_d} \tag{3}$$

Where η_{dryer} is the dryer efficiency, and L_V is latent heat of vaporization of water, (kJ/kg).

2.4   Experimental Design

The effects of sample load variation, 150, 100, and 75 kg and solar cabinet dryer type (SCMD and SCID) on the performance of the dryers, were analyzed using R (version 3.3.2, 2016) software T-test at 95% confidence interval. Each experiment was done in triplicate.

3   Results and Discussion

Startup procedures: The dryers were operated at the unloaded condition to equilibrate the atmospheric condition inside the drying chamber. The results for the temperature and relative humidity distribution for ambient and within the dryers are presented in Figs. 3 and 4.

The ambient temperature was quite low, varying from a minimum of 24 °C to a maximum of 31 °C. This is followed by the average temperature of the dyers which ranges from a minimum of 25 °C to a maximum of 41 °C in SCID and a minimum of 25 °C to a maximum of 42 °C in SCMD. Similarly, the average relative humidity of ambient air was varying from 29–45%, whereas in dryers varying from 23–44% and 21–44% in SCID and SCMD, respectively. The average radiation was also ranged from 571–1133 W/m² during the test period. As it can be seen, the air temperature and solar

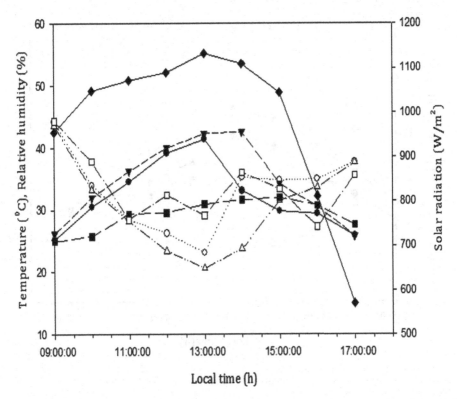

Fig. 3. Average radiation, temperature and relative humidity distribution for the month December, 2016. Temperature distribution; (●) inside SCID, (▼) inside SCMD, & (■) for ambient & relative humidity distribution; (o) inside SCID, (Δ) inside SCMD & (□) for ambient and (♦) solar radiation

radiation increase with hourly sunshine and reaches their pick value of 310C and 1133 W/m², respectively from 11:00 AM to 1:00 PM; whereas, relative humidity was reached the lower curves during this pick time. Thus, drying air temperature inside the dryers was higher than ambient air temperature and relative humidity was lower than the ambient relative humidity in most daily hours of the experiment. This shows that the dryer can perform better than the open sun drying. Warm air can hold more moisture than cold air, so the amount required depends on the temperature to which it is heated in the collector as well as the amount held (absolute humidity) when it entered the collector. The way in which the moisture absorption capability of air is affected by its initial humidity and by the temperature to which it is subsequently heated. Increasing the temperature of the drying air will increase the drying rate in two ways. First, this increases the ability of drying air to hold moisture. Secondly, the heated air will heat the product, increasing its vapor pressure. This will drive the moisture to the surface faster [9].

The hourly variation of the drying air temperature and relative humidity along the number of the trays inside SCID and SCMD chamber are shown in Fig. 4. There is a

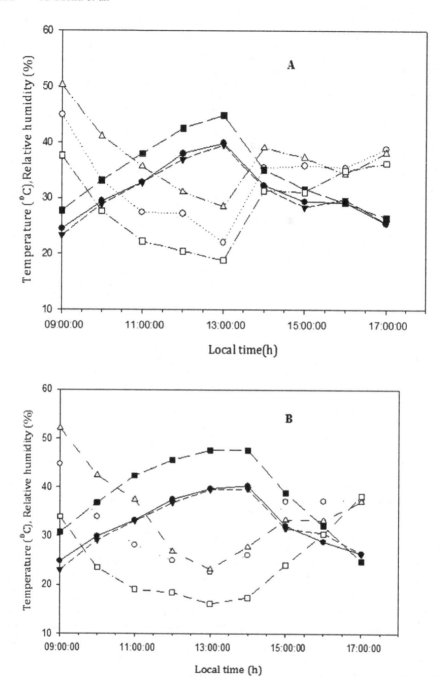

Fig. 4. Average distribution along the number of trays: Temperature (●) tray 1, (▼) tray 3, & (■) tray 6, and relative humidity (o) tray 1, (Δ) tray 3 & (□) tray 6 (A) SICD; (B) SMCD

difference in temperature and relative humidity distribution along the number of trays which is from bottom to top. Higher temperature 48 °C and 45 °C in SCMD and SCID, respectively, and lower relative humidity 16% and 19%, in SCMD and SCID, respectively were recorded at the top tray. Simate *et al.* [13] has reported also the same for mixed type, but lowest temperature for the indirect type at top tray. The authors were using wood for the construction of the indirect dryer chamber and top parts; consequently, the temperature at the top was reduced due to evaporative cooling effect. But, in this study the top part of SCID was metal sheet which has higher thermal conductivity than wood. In SCMD this higher temperature is expected since its top part is transparent. In addition, in SCID top tray temperature was higher, due to the longer time overhead of sun rays at most day time and high thermal conductivity of metal sheet. Daily, higher temperature in the dryer was maintained little bit for a longer time (beyond 15:00) in SCMD than SCID (up to 14:00); this happens due to additional heat supply for SCMD at its top part. However, the average temperature in both dryers was the same.

Lower values of relative humidity were observed at the top tray in both dryers. Relative humidity of drying air is also crucial to the drying process. The ability of air to hold more moisture can be increased by either dehumidifying or heating the air (decreasing its relative humidity or increasing its moisture holding capacity) before it enters the drying chamber or by heating it and thus increasing its evaporative capacity.

Moisture Content and Drying Rate: Figure 5A and B shows the drying curves for freshly harvested maize grain in SCMD and SCID for the drying of both varieties under different sample loading conditions. Generally, an initial moisture content of maize, which varying from 25–33% (db) was dried to the final moisture content of 13.4–15.23% (db) in all conditions. Thus, both dryers have a performance to reduce the moisture content of the grain to the safe storage value which is 15% (db) [6]. As indicated in Fig. 5, the time required to reduce the grain initial moisture content to the safe storage moisture was varying depending on the initial moisture content of the grain, daily solar intensity, and the amount of sample loaded in the dryer. Longer drying time is required for thicker sample load (150 kg) than thin and medium layer (Fig. 5). For example, the desired moisture content of 15% (db) can be reached within 32 h of drying in a thin layer (75 kg) drying, while it takes 53 h of drying in thicker sample load (150 kg) (Fig. 5). Thus, short drying time is required for the thin layer drying process.

Both SCMD and SCID have nearly the same drying rate (Fig. 5) and statistically insignificant difference has been observed. Simate *et al.* [13] has been reported higher drying rate for mixed type than indirect. However, there is a difference in the construction material which is the author was using wood to construct the chamber of the dryers. Under thin layer drying, the drying curves of SCMD have lower value than SCID; because, solar rays lie on the top part of SCMD can pass to the next bottom trays and heat up the grains. However, in thick layer drying conditions, both SCMD and SCID have almost equal drying rate for the whole range of hourly sunshine. This could be due to the increment of the thickness of the sample bed from 3 cm (thin) to 6 cm (thick). Thus, the overhead sun radiation at the top of SCMD can dry only the grain which located at the top and couldn't pass to the lower part of SCMD under this natural

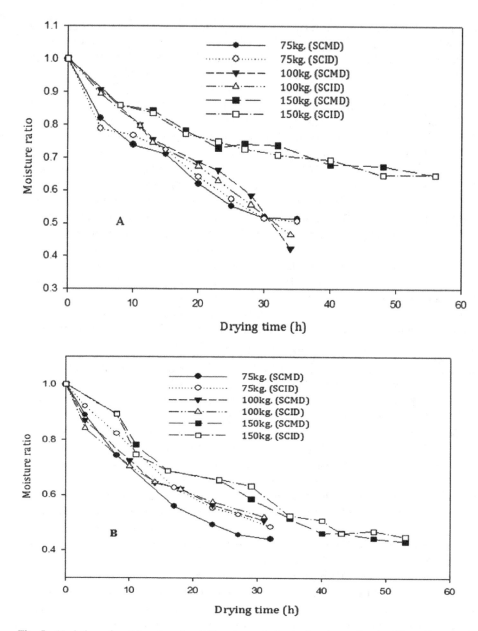

Fig. 5. Variation of moisture loss for different sample load of maize grain; A - BH- 540 variety and B - BH-660 variety

convection system. The other reason could be the flow direction of the air that is from bottom to top; hence lower moisture content was recorded only at the top tray.

All drying rate curves have first and second falling rate periods which are common in all grain drying process [18]. The result also shows that, drying rate of maize was higher at the first falling rate period when compared than the second falling rate. The drying rate was found to decrease with increase in drying time. Drying rate was higher during the initial stages of drying and becomes very low in the later stages; because at the first stage, free water of the grain is evaporated without any restrictions.

Figure 6 shows the drying curve for freshly harvested maize grain in SCID and SCMD for varieties of BH-660 under thin and thick layer conditions at different location of the dryers. Since there is a temperature and relative humidity difference along the number of trays, moisture removal was also varied. As it can be seen in Fig. 6, both in SCMD high moisture removal or lower moisture content of the grain were observed at the top tray both in thin and thick layer sample loading. This is because of presence of higher temperature and lower relative humidity at top tray (Fig. 4). Where as in SCID, lower moisture of the grain was observed at top tray for thin layer and at the bottom for the thick layer drying process. On the other hand, the low moisture removal rate was observed at the center (tray 3) in both thin and thick layers drying. When hot drying air flows from bottom to top, it picks up grain moisture in vapor form. Consequently, the relative humidity of the air increases (Fig. 4) from bottom onwards. At the center (tray 3), the air becomes saturated and its vapor carrying capacity becomes reduced. Hence, lower moisture removal rate or high moisture content of grain was observed weather in thick or thin layer drying process at the center (tray 3).

The drying rate, overall system efficiency, and moisture removal (db) were varied depending on dryer type and amount of sample loaded. The drying rate, collector efficiency and overall system efficiency for drying of freshly harvested maize grain were varied from 0.41–0.56, kgh^{-1}, 44.4–57.2%, and 24.0–32%, and from 0.47–0.58, kgh^{-1}, 44.4–57.2%, and 24.6–33%, for SCID and for SCMD, respectively (Table 2). In this study, almost similar drying rate has been observed in both dryers. But, higher overall dryer efficiency was recorded in SCMD than SCID. However, statistically both dryers have no significant difference in drying rate (with P- value of 0.3676) as well as in overall dryer system efficiency (with P- value of 0.4061) under this natural convection system. The 95% confidence interval for a drying rate was from −0.09265 to 0.03642 and for overall system efficiency was from −5.71122 to 2.43322. However, Singh [3] has reported higher drying rate and larger overall efficiency for forced type mixed than indirect and Simate et al. [13] also reported higher drying rate for mixed type than indirect under natural condition which constructed from wood. In this study, it is observed that, drying rate for thick layer in both SCMD and SCID was much higher than that of thin layer drying process.

Table 2. Comparative study of different drying methods for freshly harvested maize grain

Solar dryer type	Sample weight (kg)	Initial moisture (d.b)	Final moisture (d.b)	Total drying time (h)	Drying rate (kg H_2O/h)	Average radiation (W/m²)	Collector thermal efficiency (%)	Overall dryer system efficiency (%)
SCID	75	29.0	14.1 ± 0.00	32	0.406 ± 0.014	982	57.23	24.69 ± 0.85
	100	28.2	14.7 ± 0.002	31	0.511 ± 0.015	1267	44.36	23.97 ± 0.72
	150	31.1	14.0 ± 0.001	53	0.563 ± 0.015	1039	54.09	32.22 ± 0.87
SCMD	75	30.7	13.6 ± 0.003	32	0.464 ± 0.022	982	57.23	28.09 ± 1.36
	100	28.2	14.3 ± 0.003	31	0.523 ± 0.014	1267	44.36	24.56 ± 0.68
	150	31.1	13.4 ± 0.002	53	0.579 ± 0.008	1039	54.09	33.11 ± 0.47

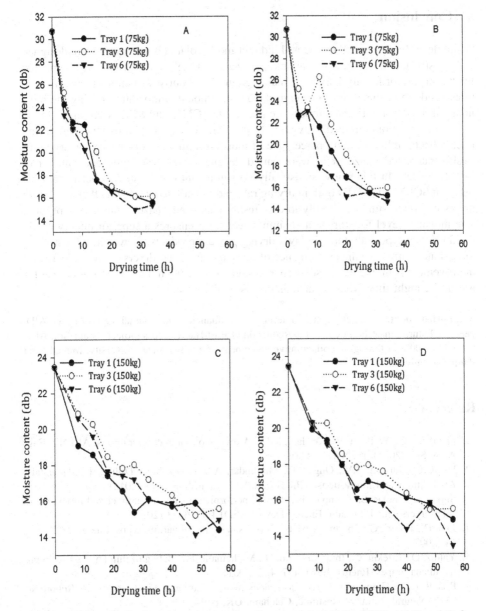

Fig. 6. Moisture distribution along the number of trays; A and C for SCID and B and D for SCMD for drying of BH-660 maize grain

4 Conclusion

A simple and inexpensive mixed and indirect-mode solar cabinet dryers were designed and constructed using locally available materials and their performance was compared for the drying of freshly harvested maize grain. The hourly variation of the temperatures inside the cabinet dryers is higher than the ambient temperature during the most hours of the day-light. The temperature rise inside SCMD and SCID were up to 15 °C for about three hours immediately after 11:00 AM. For a particular experiment, drying rate, collector efficiency and percentage of moisture removed (dry basis) for drying of freshly harvested maize grain were varied depending on dryer type and amount of sample loaded. In this study, statistically no significant difference has been observed between SCID and SCMD both in drying rate and overall dryer system efficiency. Both dryers exhibited sufficient ability to dry freshly harvested maize grain reasonably to a safe moisture level for storage and simultaneously it ensures a superior quality of the dried product especially the thin layer drying process products. However, a lot still has to be done to improve the performance of these passive solar dryers. A possible area of improvement is on the use of solar energy storage systems in the dryer to store heat for use in the night time when solar radiation is totally absent.

Acknowledgment. The authors are grateful for the financial and material support by USAID, Feed the Future Innovation Lab for the Reduction of Post Harvest Loss project (Grant No.: AID-OAA-L-14-00002) through a collaborative agreement of Kansas State University, Mekelle and Bahir Dar university.

References

1. Phadke, P.C., Walke, P.V., Kriplani, V.M.: A review on indirect solar dryers. ARPN J. Eng. Appl. Sci. (2015). ISSN 1819-6608
2. Hii, C.L., Jangam, S.V., Ong, S.P., Mujumdar, A.S. (eds.): Solar Drying: Fundamentals, Applications and Innovations. TPR Group Publication, Singapore (2012)
3. Singh, S., Kumar, S.: Comparative thermal performance study of indirect and mixed-mode solar dryers. Int. J. Sustain. Energy Dev. (IJSED) 1(1), 6–13 (2012)
4. Jain, D., Tiwari, G.: Thermal aspects of open sun drying of various crops. Energy 28(1), 37–54 (2003)
5. Yaldiz, O., Ertekin, C., Ibrahim Uzun, H.: Mathematical modeling of thin layer solar drying of sultana grapes. Energy 26(5), 457–465 (2001)
6. Boxall, R.A.: Grains post-harvest loss assessment in Ethiopia. Final report NRI Report No 2377. Natural Resources Institute, Chatham, UK, p. 44 (1998)
7. Postharvest Loss Challenges. Discussion Paper. Office of Agriculture, Biotechnology, and Textile Trade Affairs Bureau of Economic and Business Affairs. U.S. Department of State (2013)
8. United Nations, Food and Agricultural Organization. Global Food Losses and Food Waste-Extent, Causes and Prevention. Rome (2011)
9. Augustus Leon, M., Kumar, S., Bhattacharya, S.C.: A comprehensive procedure for performance evaluation of solar food dryers. Renew. Sustain. Energy Rev. 6, 367–393 (2002)

10. Ekechukwe, O.V., Norton, B.: Review of solar energy drying systems II: an overview of solar drying technology. Energy Convers. Manag. **40**, 616–655 (1999)
11. Sodha, M.S., Chandra, R.: Solar drying systems and their testing procedures: a review. Energy Convers. Manag. **35**(3), 219–267 (1994)
12. Diamante, L.M., Munro, P.A.: Mathematical modelling of the thin layer solar drying of sweet potato slices. Sol. Energy **51**, 271–276 (1993)
13. Simate, I.: Optimization of mixed-mode and indirect-mode natural convection solar dryers. Renewable Energy **28**(3), 435–453 (2003)
14. Tokar, G.M.: Food drying in Bangladesh. Agro-based industries and technology project (ATDP), IFDC, Dhaka 1213, December 1997
15. Nabnean, S., Janjai, S., Thepa, S., Sudaprasert, K., Songprakorp, R., Bala, B.K.: Experimental performance of a new design of solar dryer for drying osmotically dehydrated cherry tomatoes. Renewable Energy **94**, 147–156 (2016)
16. Tonui, K.S., Mutai, E.B.K., Mutuli, D.A., Mbuge, O.O., Too, K.V.: Design and evaluation of solar grain dryer with a back-up heater. Res. J. Appl. Sci. Eng. Technol. **7**(15), 3036–3043 (2014)
17. Forson, F.K., Nazha, M.A.A., Akuffo, F.O., Rajakaruna, H.: Design of mixed-mode natural convection solar crop dryers: application of principles and rule of thumb. Renewable Energy **32**, 1–14 (2007)
18. Henderson, S.M.: Progress in developing the thin layer drying equation. Trans. ASAE **17**, 1167–1172 (1974)

Test and Characterization of Tensile Strength of Oxytenanthera Abyssinica and Yushania Alpina Bamboos

Fentahun Ayu Muche and Yonas Mitiku Degu$^{(\boxtimes)}$

Faculty of Mechanical and Industrial Engineering,
Bahir Dar Institute of Technology, Bahir Dar University, Bahir Dar, Ethiopia
fentahunayu30@gmail.com, yonasm@bdu.edu.et

Abstract. Bamboo has a long and well-established tradition as a building material throughout the world. Bamboo has various applications such as, for furniture, bicycle structure, unmanned air vehicle structure. Despite the fact that Ethiopia has abundance bamboo, till now the tensile strength of both Oxytenanthera abyssinica (solid) and Yushania Alpina (hollow) bamboo was not studied sufficiently. This research focuses on tensile strength testing and characterization of solid and hollow bamboo found in Amhara region at Jawi and Awi district through standard test procedures. The specimens were prepared and tested according to ISO standard. The tensile strength of specimens were tested and characterized with respect to its species, age and culm position. The test result showed that tensile strength of solid and hollow bamboo without node, increases from bottom to top. Hollow and solid bamboo specimens without node had greater tensile strength than specimens with node. Besides solid bamboo without node had superior average tensile strength (ranges between 211.5 MPa to 260.2 MPa) than hollow bamboo without node (179.7 MPa to 246.1 MPa). Irrespective of the age, specious, with node and without node the lowest strength showed on the bottom portion of the specimens. The test specimen results demonstrated as the age increases from year two to four, the bottom strength increased consistently. To use bamboo for structural and related purpose it is recommended to take the bottom portion strength than the average or the highest strength for safe design.

Keywords: Hollow bamboo · Solid bamboo ·
Oxytenanthera abyssinica and Yushania Alpina bamboo culm · Tensile strength

1 Introduction

The mechanical properties of materials are the most important parameters for structural design. It relates the relationship between a material's responses to the applied load [1]. Tensile test is frequently used parameter to evaluate the mechanical properties of materials. Tensile strength property is one of the most prominent measuring criteria in the design of engineering structures and in the developing new product suit to the specified application [2].

© ICST Institute for Computer Sciences, Social Informatics and Telecommunications Engineering 2019
Published by Springer Nature Switzerland AG 2019. All Rights Reserved
F. A. Zimale et al. (Eds.): ICAST 2018, LNICST 274, pp. 160–169, 2019.
https://doi.org/10.1007/978-3-030-15357-1_13

Bamboo has a long and well established tradition as a building material throughout the world's tropical and sub-tropical regions [3]. It is a naturally occurring composite material consisting of cellulose fibers. It has a maximum tensile strength and flexural strength because of its fibers placed along its length [4]. Bamboo grows mostly in tropical and subtropical areas ranging from sea level to mountain peaks, with a few species reaching into temperate areas [5]. Bamboo is a light weight, flexible, sustainable, eco-friendly, green material and its use, shall be advocated in building construction for sustainable development [6].

Currently, the use of bamboo is well known by craftsman. Unlike other countries, bamboo utilization in Ethiopia has been customary and mainly limited to construction, fencing, handicraft, furniture, water container, baskets, firewood, house utensils, various art-facts, and walking sticks. The study of the mechanical property of bamboo is very important for the industrialization of the material [7]. Although tensile strength of Ethiopian bamboo with node and without node along the grain direction was tested by students for their partial fulfillments of the Bachelor of Science degree, the test procedure was not following the standard test method [8].

The tensile strength of Indian bamboo various species with node and without node was tested. The sample was prepared from four year old green bamboo (*Dendrocalamus strictus*) and the test was done on different region of bamboo. The test result proves that tensile strength increases with height and also increases from inner to outer section [9]. The curved portions of the bamboo split at the end were filled with sand and high strength epoxy resin to prevent the failures of the sample at the grip part. Another research on various species of Indian bamboo and the result shows that bamboo with node has less strength than without node [3].

For the proper utilization of bamboo in structural application the tensile strength characteristic must be known well. Till now the actual tensile strength of Ethiopian bamboo was not studied sufficiently. Hence the objective of this research is to test and characterize the tensile strength of Oxytenanthera abyssinica and Yushania Alpina specious bamboo found in Amhara region at Jawi and Awi district.

2 Materials and Methods

2.1 Materials

Bamboo: Bamboos of age two, three and four were used; the ages of bamboo was selected based on the availability and farmers recommendation from their rich experience in using and planting. Bamboo is mostly used for different applications from the age of two to four. It is mainly characterized by two parts: the main stem above ground called the culm and the underground part called rhizome.

Bamboo Culm: The main stem of a bamboo is a culm, which is the supportive structure of the branches and leaves and contains the main vascular system for the transport of water, nutrients, and food; the culm diameter decrease from bottom to top. The hollow bamboo is larger in diameter compared to the solid bamboo. Figure 1 shows the culm of hollow and solid bamboo.

a) Yushania alpina bamboo culm   b) Oxytenanthera abyssinica bamboo culm

Fig. 1. Culms of bamboo [www.allchile.net]

Study Area: The specimens were prepared from the two species of bamboo found in Ethiopian, Amhara region, outskirt of Jawi (solid bamboo) and Awi zone (hollow bamboo). The two areas were selected for the study due to the abundance availability of bamboo. Solid bamboo is also known as lowland bamboo (Oxytenanthera abyssinica) and it is distributed to Amhara region which is found at Awi zone around Jawi. Hollow bamboo is also known as highland bamboo (Yushania Alpina) which is found at Awi zone around Injibara town.

Node: The jointed segments of the bamboo plant and the area between nodes are called an internode. The nodes of a bamboo are always solid, and the internodes of most bamboos are hollow [11].

Tools and Machines:

- Hand and measuring tools like saw, knife, digital vernier caliper and tape meter were used for sample preparation.
- Universal testing machine: microcomputer controlled UTM YF (Zhejiang Tugong PN0206000031 WAW- 1000B) was used to test the tensile strength of bamboo specimens. The capacity of the machine is 1000 kN at load rating of 0.05 kN/s.

2.2   Methods

The research was carried out based on:

1. *Reviewing prior works:* Searching for different works about mechanical properties and testing techniques of bamboo was the primary task of the research. Here, testing method, specimen preparation from bamboo and other related works were reviewed.
2. *Sample preparation:* Among different standards for wood-based materials, the tensile test was carried out according to ISO/TR 22157-2: 2004 (E) [10]. This standard recommended the suitable size of the specimens for tensile test of bamboo. As bamboo is an anisotropic material, the properties will be varied from the bottom to the top positions. Specimens from the three positions (bottom, middle and top) were taken to check the variation of the properties of bamboo along its length. The three positions were given according to their order from the root to the tip leaves. Figure 2 shows the standard dimension of bamboo specimen for tensile test.

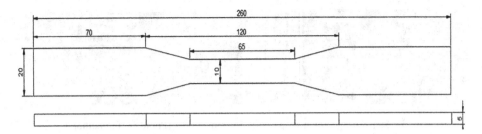

Fig. 2. Standard specimen dimensions for tensile test [dimensions are given in mm]

2.3   Experiment Design

The number of specimens can be determined by the principles of factorial design and fractional factorial design [12]. The mechanical properties of bamboo are dependent on its age, species and culm position. The experiment was done based on these three factors for both solid and hollow bamboo. Here the number of repetitions was determined by the principle of fractional factorial design for the three factors. The equation is given by:

$$\text{Number of specimens a single test} = \frac{2^n}{2} \tag{1}$$

Where: n is the number of factors

$$\text{Number of specimens for a single test} = \frac{2^3}{2} = 4$$

Four specimens were prepared for each position of specimens without node and with node. The total specimens prepared from solid and hollow bamboo were 144.

2.4   Sample Preparation and Testing Procedure

Two types of bamboo were collected from the two areas. The average total lengths of hollow bamboo culm and solid bamboo were found 10 m and 5 m respectively. The culms of hollow and solid bamboo were left in open air until it dries and ready for the sample preparation.

The general procedures used for sample preparation were (depicted Fig. 3):-

1. Cut the bamboo culm from farming site and leave in open space until it gets dries.
2. Remove 1 m from the bottom and then measure again 2.4 m and cut, which is the required portion for the test.
3. Divide the 2.4 m into three equal length (0.8 m each)
4. Split the hollow bamboo prepared in step 3 into four and the solid into two.
5. Plain the bamboo pices until the curved shape become flat.
6. Measure 0.26 m and cut from 0.8 m length from all positions for both with node and without a node.

Fig. 3. Steps of specimen preparation for tensile test [Photo by the authors]

7. Mark to get the bone shape on the prepared specimens according to the standard dimension (refer Fig. 2).
8. Remove the unwanted portion of the sample to get the bon shaped sample.
9. Glued wood at both ends and faces of the specimens for proper gripping during testing.
10. Shaping the sample by sandpaper to obtain the required smooth finished specimen.

After specimens were prepared, the test was performed using universal testing machine which has a sensor connected to the computer. The test results were stored on the computer for each run; after the test was completed the stored data were retrieved for further analysis. The test was done based on the following steps:

1. Specimens gripped by both jaws of the machine at the marked gage length.
2. Run the machine.
3. Save the test files to the appropriate location.
4. Repeat these steps until finishing all the specimens.

The specimens prepared before and after the test are shown in Figs. 4 and 5 respectively.

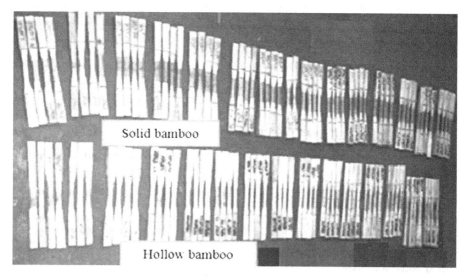

Fig. 4. Specimens prepared for tensile test [Photo by the authors]

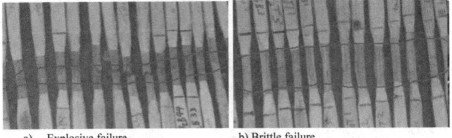

a)   Explosive failure   b) Brittle failure

Fig. 5. Mode of failure of specimens during tensile test [Photo by the authors]

3   Results and Discussion

3.1   Results

The tensile strength of bamboo specimens with node and without node was tested with respect to the type of species, culm position and age. The results obtained during the test are presented from Figs. 6, 7, 8 and 9.

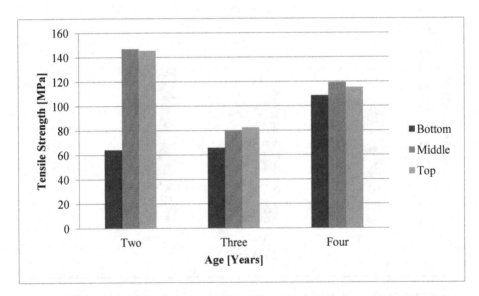

Fig. 6. Tensile strength of hollow bamboo specimens with node vs age and culm position

3.2   Discussion

The tensile strength test result with respect to position and age of both solid and hollow bamboo are plotted from Figs. 6, 7, 8 and 9. Specimens of both types of species without node have higher tensile strength than specimens of with node. Due to the fact

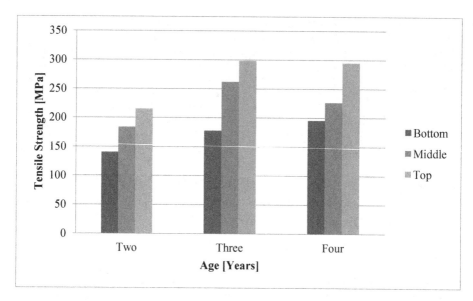

Fig. 7. Tensile strength of hollow bamboo specimens without node vs age and culm position

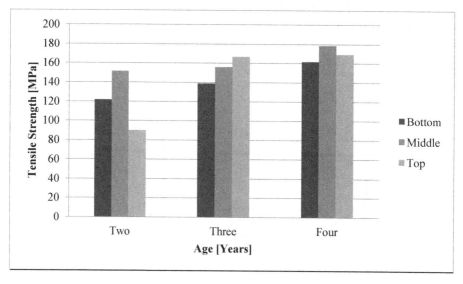

Fig. 8. Tensile strength of solid bamboo specimens with node vs age and culm position

that fiber around the node is discontinuous so it will cause to have lower tensile strength for specimens with node.

The test result demonstrates that the tensile strength of solid and hollow bamboo increases as their ages increased except hollow bamboo with node demonstrate unpredictable behavior in the middle and top portion. The tensile strength of solid

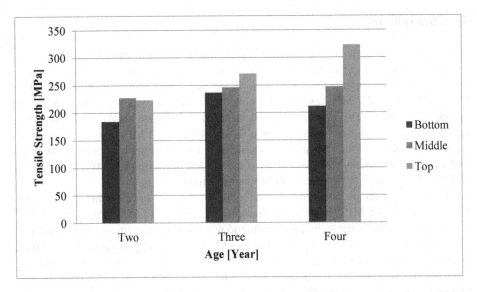

Fig. 9. Tensile strength of solid bamboo specimens without node vs age and culm position

bamboo is directly related to its age for both with and without nodes. As the age of sold bamboo increases from year two, three and four its average tensile strength is also increased from 211.5 MPa, 251 MPa and 260.2 MPa respectively for specimens without node; and from 121.1 MPa, 153.9 MPa and 169.7 MPa respectively for the specimens with nodes.

In the case of hollow bamboo without node registered higher average tensile strength at year three which is 246.1 MPa and followed by year four and two 239 MPa and 179.9 MPa respectively. Hollow bamboo with node got higher average tensile strength at year two followed by four and three 118.8 MPa, 114.3 MPa and 76.0 MPa respectively.

Among all specimens the top position 86.1% specimens' scores higher strength value followed by 13.9% middle portions. Solid bamboo without node 66.67% behave as top portion having higher tensile strength and followed by the middle portion 33.33% Hollow bamboo without node 100% behave as top portion having higher tensile strength and followed by the middle and bottom. Hollow bamboo with node demonstrates random pattern with respect to the culm position. The failures of bamboo with node are different from that of bamboo without a node. As it is shown in Fig. 5 bamboo with node failed in a brittle manner and the failure of culm without node is in an explosive manner.

For conservative design the lowest strength could be taken as the ultimate tensile strength of the whole portion of the bamboo. Irrespective of the age the lowest strength for the hollow and solid bamboo recorded at the bottom portion. It had also a trend of as the age increases the lowest strength of both bamboo increases consistently.

4 Conclusions

Solid bamboo specimens were having higher tensile strength than hollow bamboo specimens with respect to tensile load. The maximum tensile strength of solid bamboo without node specimens for year two, three and four were found 227.5 MPa, 270.9 MPa and 322.7 MPa respectively, at the top portion except year two which is in the middle portion. The maximum tensile strength of hollow bamboo without node specimens were found at the top portion 215.0 MPa, 298.4 MPa and 295.0 MPa at year two, three and four respectively. The lowest tensile strength of hollow bamboo without node specimens were registered at the bottom portion 140.5 MPa, 177.7 MPa and 195.4 MPa at year two, three and four respectively.

The average tensile strength without node of hollow bamboo ranges between 179.7 MPa to 246.1 MPa and solid bamboo ranges between 211.5.0 MPa to 260.2 MPa.

The lowest tensile strength of solid bamboo without node specimens were registered at the bottom portion 183.8 MPa, 236.3 MPa and 211.2 MPa at year two, three and four respectively. The lowest tensile strength of hollow bamboo without node specimens were registered at the bottom portion 140.5 MPa, 177.7 MPa and 195.4 MPa at year two, three and four respectively.

Solid and hollow bamboo specimens without node showing higher tensile strength than bamboo with node. It can also be concluded that bamboo with node having unpredictable behavior of tensile strength, than bamboo without node. To know the unpredictable behavior the microstructure study has to be conducted before testing of the specimens. In addition tensile strength of bamboo with respect to cultivation soil type and environmental conditions need to be studied.

References

1. Scott, M.J.: Material testing lab, engineering innovation section A last modified 4 July 2011, Johns Hopkins University (2011)
2. Favilla, S.: Tensile testing laboratory date of lab exercise, 28 January 2010
3. Bhonde, D., Nagarnaik, P.B., Parbat, D.K., Waghe, U.P.: Physical and mechanical properties of bamboo. Int. J. Sci. Eng. Res. **5**(1) (2014)
4. Soyoye, F.R.: The influence of age and location on selected physical and mechanical properties of bamboo. Int. J. Res. Agric. For. **1**(1), 44–54 (2014)
5. Kassahun, E.: Ecological aspects and resource management of bamboo forest in Ethiopia. Swedish University of Agricultural Sciences, Uppsala (2003)
6. Bhondea, D., Nagarnaik, P.B., Parbatc, D.K., Waghed, U.P.: Experimental analysis of bending stresses in bamboo reinforced concrete beam. In: Proceedings of 3rd International Conference on Recent Trends in Engineering and Technology (ICRTET 2014). Elsevier (2014)
7. Kindu, Y.M.: Status of bamboo resource development, utilization and research in Ethiopia. Ethiop. J. Nat. Resour. **1**, 79–98 (2010)
8. Dereje, D.A.: Testing, determination and characterization of bamboo. Bahir Dar Institute of Technology, Mechanical Engineering Program, BSc. thesis (2016)
9. Verma, V.C.: Tensile strength analysis of bamboo and layered laminate bamboo composites. Int. J. Eng. Res. Appl. (IJERA) **2**(2), 1253–1264 (2012)

10. ISO/TR, 2.-2, Determination of physical and mechanical properties of bamboo part 2 laboratory manual (2004)
11. David, F.: The Book of Bamboo. Library of Congress Cataloging in Publication of Data, San Francisco (1984)
12. Montgomery, D.C.: Design and Analysis of Experiments, 5th edn. Toronto (2001)

Effects of Soil and Water Conservation Practices on Runoff, Soil and Nutrient Losses in Alekt Wenz Watershed, Ethiopian Highland

Simir Birihan Atanaw[1,2](✉), Dessalew Worku Aynalem[2],
Anwar Assefa Adem[2,3] (iD), Wolde Mekuria[4],
and Seifu Admassu Tilahun[2]

[1] Department of Hydraulic and Water Resources Engineering,
Institute of Technology, University of Gondar, Gondar, Ethiopia
simirbirihan80@gmail.com
[2] School of Civil and Water Resources Engineering,
Bahir Dar University, Bahir Dar, Ethiopia
workudessu@gmail.com, satadm86@gmail.com
[3] Department of Natural Resource Management,
Bahir Dar University, Bahir Dar, Ethiopia
anwarasefa@gmail.com,
[4] International Water Management Institute (IWMI), Addis Ababa, Ethiopia
W.Bori@cgiar.org

Abstract. Land degradation caused by soil erosion is a serious problem in northwestern Ethiopian highlands. To reduce the adverse impact of land degradation, soil and water conservation (SWC) measures were implemented. The presented study investigated the hydrological responses of SWC measures implemented in two nested watersheds situated in the northwestern Ethiopian highland. Rainfall, streamflow, sediment concentration, and sediment-associated and dissolved nutrient of N and P for 2015 and 2016 rainy periods were collected and analyzed. The watersheds received 665 mm in 2015 and 795 mm rainfall in 2016 from May to September. The median infiltration rates for treated and untreated watershed were 22 mm hr^{-1}, and 19 mm hr^{-1} respectively. The direct runoff from treated watershed was 8.5 mm yr^{-1} for 2015 and 9.6 mm yr^{-1} for 2016. This is lower than the untreated watershed, which responded 17.3 mm yr^{-1} for 2015 and 15.3 mm yr^{-1} for 2016. The base flow from treated watershed was 180.7 mm yr^{-1} for 2015 and 212 mm yr^{-1} for 2016. It was higher than the untreated watershed, which responded 69.8 mm yr^{-1} for 2015 and 195.4 mm yr^{-1} for 2016. This figure shows that implemented SWC measures reduced the runoff responses by two-fold. Similarly, the SWC measures reduced sediment yield. The sediment yield from treated watershed was 2.4 ton $ha^{-1}yr^{-1}$ and 2.1 ton $ha^{-1}yr^{-1}$ in the year 2015 and 2016, respectively. This is lower than the untreated watershed that lost 6 ton $ha^{-1}yr^{-1}$ and 8.5 ton $ha^{-1}yr^{-1}$ in the year 2015 and 2016, respectively. The effectiveness of the SWC measures between the two watersheds was statistically significant with a significance level of 5%. However, it is important to investigate the long-term effects of SWC in reducing soil and nutrient losses.

© ICST Institute for Computer Sciences, Social Informatics and Telecommunications Engineering 2019
Published by Springer Nature Switzerland AG 2019. All Rights Reserved
F. A. Zimale et al. (Eds.): ICAST 2018, LNICST 274, pp. 170–182, 2019.
https://doi.org/10.1007/978-3-030-15357-1_14

Keywords: Erosion · Nutrient depletion · Runoff · Sediment yield ·
Soil and Water Conservation · Treated · Untreated

1 Introduction

The degradation of land, which declines the quality of land, will remain a global challenge for the 21st century. It results in a negative impact on agricultural productivity [1] and the quality of environmental aspects. It has adverse effects on food security and the quality of life [2]. According to [3] 3.6 billion hectares of land was lost annually due to adverse degradation on a global scale. Overall, the depletion of nutrients in the soil has been estimated at an average rate (kg/ha/year) 18.7 N, 5.1 P, and 38.8 K. This covers 59% N, 85% P and 90% K of harvested areas particularly parts of Africa, Asia, and Latin America [1]. According to [1] the total annual deficit of nutrients was 5.5 Mt (million tons) N, 2.3 Mt P, and 12.2 Mt K, associated with global crop production losses of 1136 Mt yr^{-1}. Land degradation happens all over the world but it is a particular problem in the highlands of sub-Saharan Africa [4].

Ethiopia is one of the hotspot area experiencing continuous natural resources degradation in a century [2]. The rate of land degradation exacerbated in the northwestern Ethiopian highland where 85–90% of the population depends on agriculture and land resources [5]. Its consequences are affecting the food security of the population due to low productivity [6]. The decline of land productivity, which was induced by soil erosion is the major factor responsible for the recurrent malnutrition and famine in Ethiopia [7]. Half of the agricultural land is affected and accounts 1.5–2 billion tons in an annual soil losses rate [6, 8, 9]. This resulting 1.5 million tons of grain reduction for each production period [9]. Ethiopia losses 137 tons ha^{-1} yr^{-1} topsoil through soil erosion by water [10].

Since soil erosion is a natural hazard [11], it is difficult to stop and avoid. It is possible to control and reduce its adverse impact through the implementation of appropriate soil and water conservation (SWC) measures. In Ethiopia, after the declaration of wildlife conservation and development policy, the government initiated various studies and capacity building programs for massive SWC intervention [12]. Various SWC measures have been adopted and implemented by the food for work (FFW) program through government-led national campaign to control soil erosion by water [13].

Similarly, a series SWC practices have been implemented in Northwestern part of Ethiopia by farmers through government led to a national campaign since 2012 [14, 15]. The practices include physical structures (terraces, stone-bund, check dam, and arc weir) and biological (native tree plantations, the establishment of pasturelands with a fence, sesbania (sesbania grandiflora), vetiver grass (chrysopogon zizanioides), and elephant grass (pennistum purpureum).

Soil and water conservation practices could have a role in reducing runoff generation in a rainy season [13]. This is increase base flow of a catchment by improving infiltration rate of the soil. Also, it increases dry season stream flow [16] and prevents rivers from drying up earlier. Generally, it is believed that the impact of conservation practices on hydrological responses mainly related to controlling surface runoff [13], decreasing soil erosion and reservoir sedimentation [17, 18], improving soil fertility of farmland, and enhancing agricultural production [19, 20]. In the northwestern part of the Ethiopian highland, there have been hard enough scientific study to assess the extent of the effectiveness of implemented SWC activities on hydrological responses. In particular, the effectiveness of the implemented SWC practices for reducing soil loss, nutrient depletion and runoff generation have not been studied sufficiently. However, understanding the effects of conservation practices on the hydrological responses is crucial either to design measure that improves the benefits of SWC measures or sustaining existing conservation practices. This study was conducted in Alekt Wenz watershed to investigate the effectiveness of SWC practices on hydrological responses using two experimental nested watersheds under different degree of treatments.

2   Materials and Methods

2.1   Study Area Description

For this particular study, Alekt Wenz watershed was selected and it is found in Lake Tana sub-basin, the Blue Nile, Ethiopia and is located between 38°7'0"E to 38°8'0"E Longitude and 11°46'0"N to 11°48'0"N Latitude. The Alekt Wenz watershed has a total area of 321.6 ha with two adjacent nested watersheds. The adjacent watersheds were treated differently. The one with intensive SWC works and exclosure is called treated. The other watershed with sparse SWC activities and without exclosure is called untreated (Fig. 1). In terms of climatic condition, the study area has an average annual minimum, maximum and mean temperatures of 9.7, 22, 15.5 °C, respectively. The rainfall pattern is unimodal and occurs from May to September. The annual rainfall ranges between 856.8 and 1569.9 mm with a long-term average[1] of 1301 mm. The study area topography is characterized by extremely high relief and over 70% of the land extends from gentle to hill slope landscape. The elevation ranges from 2,779 m to 3000 m (a.s.l). Cultivated land, enclosed-pastureland, grazing land, and forest area are the dominant land use land cover types in the study watershed (Table 1). Cultivated and grazing land facilitated erosion, but forest and enclosed-pastureland reduce runoff generation and soil erosion.

Table 1. Land use/land cover of the two sub-watersheds.

Land use land cover	Treated area		Untreated	
	ha	%	ha	%
Cultivated	29.4	34	126.7	54
Grassland/Exclosure/	19.8	23	1.7	1
Forest	26.3	30	70.9	30
Grazing	11.4	13	35.4	15

---

[1] *Debre-Tabor and Gassay meteorological station from 1951–2014.*

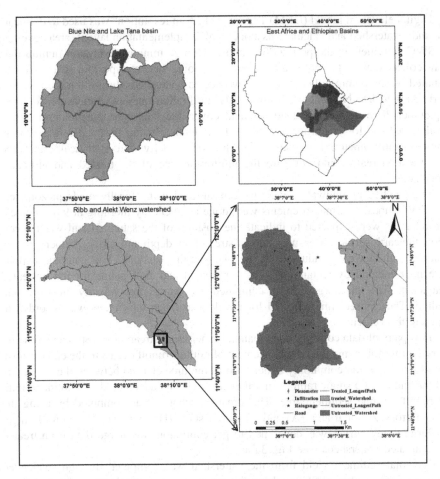

Fig. 1. Location map of the Alekt Wenz watersheds

2.2 Data Collection and Analysis

The land use/land cover map was prepared by supervised image classification. The satellite image was downloaded from earth explorer. To address the objectives of the study, rainfall, infiltration capacity, streamflow, suspended sediment concentration (SSC), dissolved and sediment-associated nutrient were directly measured during the rainy months of the monsoon (May to September) of 2015 and 2016. The remaining months of rainfall and sediment sampling were not measured as it was dry and sediment transport is so negligible. But the base flow was included as stream flow. The spatial information like locations of the outlets, rain gauge, piezometers, SWC structures, and infiltration measurement sites was conducted using GPS.

Digital elevation model (DEM) 12.5 m × 12.5 m resolution[2] was used to delineate the study watershed and calculate its slope, SWC implementation layout, area coverage by SWC activities. In the period 2015 and 2016, five minutes resolution rainfall data were collected with the automatic recording tipping bucket type rain gauge. It was installed on the common border of the two nested watersheds during the rainy season (early June to late November). In this study, infiltration rates were measured in early September 2015 at different land use/land cover and landscape positions on upper, middle, and the lower portion of the study watershed using the single ring (25 cm diameter) infiltrometer. The results of infiltration capacity were statistically analyzed with t-test to realize and compare the infiltration rate of the treated and untreated watersheds.

The perched groundwater levels were monitored using locally made piezometers from PVC tubes. The measurements were done an everyday morning at 9:00 o'clock. The readings were expected to indicate the position of the saturated soil water levels below the earth surface. Measurements of streamflow depth and surface velocity with a floating method were conducted on the two gauging stations. The gauging stations were instrumented by rectangular weir for treated and staff gauge for the untreated watershed. The discharges were computed by using area-velocity measurement method. The elapsed time required for the float to reach the outlets was recorded to compute the velocity.

Two pairs of data collectors had manually measured streamflow depth and velocity every 20 min following the commencement of rainfall-runoff events to the end of storm period. Storm period commonly understood as the time elapsed between the beginning and the ending of a single rainfall-runoff event [21]. The data recording continued until the runoff became sediment free. The stream discharge was computed by using the defined cross-sectional area (A) and measured stage (H). A power function of stage-discharge rating curves was developed to get continuous discharge data from treated and untreated watersheds (see Fig. 3a and b).

The total sediment yield from the watershed was computed through suspended sediment concentration (SSC) analysis. That means storm samples were fetched every 20 min until the flow rate dropped and the flowing water turned clear of sediment. Between three and seven samples of one-liter bottles collected during most of the storm event. The samples were filtered using standard Whatman filter papers with a pore opening of 2.5 μm. The filtered sediments were dried in an oven for 24 h at 105 °C. Suspended sediment was estimated by using the Gravimetric method and sediment yield was computed by using Eq. 1.

$$SY = SSC * V \tag{1}$$

Where SY is sediment yield, SSC has suspended sediment concentration (mg/l) and V is the volume of runoff (liter).

---

[2] Source of DEM (https://www.asf.alaska.edu/).

Time-integrated sampling technique was conducted for nutrient analysis. This was made by mixing equal volumes of sediment mixed water were collected with a regular time interval. The soluble nutrients within the streamflow at the outlets during the rainy season were measured in the water quality laboratory. The nutrient data particularly dissolved phosphorus (DP) and dissolved nitrogen (DN) were organized by making a composite of one storm's samples and took 100 ml after preserved with 2 ml hydrochloric acid (HCl) to conserve from transport losses. The DP and DN were analyzed by palintest photometer model 7100. The lab analysis for sediment-associated nutrients was done in Amhara Design and Supervision Works Enterprise (ADSWE) soil laboratory. Composite sediment data for each month during the rainy period were taken and the associated nutrients (P by ppm for P and percent for N) were extracted. The particulate fraction of phosphorus was determined using the Olsen method while particulate nitrogen was determined using the Kjeldahl method (Fig. 2).

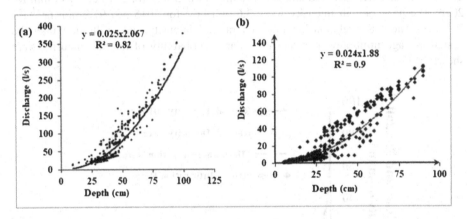

Fig. 2. Stage-discharge rating curve (a) for the untreated and (b) for the treated watershed.

$$N_{Sd} = N_c * S_l + Nd * V \qquad (2)$$

Where N_{sd} is dissolved and sediment-associated nutrient loss (mg), N_c is nutrient concentration (mg/ton) and S_l is the sediment load (ton), Nd is the dissolved nutrient concentration (mg/l) and V is the volume of direct runoff (litter).

The economic value that the farmers incurred to replace the nutrient losses due to runoff is computed based on the price of commercial fertilizers from the local distribution agency (see Tables 4 and 5). Mostly the farmers used UREA and DAP with the proportion of N and P for UREA, (46:0:0) and Diammonium Phosphate (DAP), (18:46:0) in fertilizer analysis system of (N: P: K) ratio, the ratio indicates that 46% of N in UREA and DAP contain 18% N, 46% P2O5 and 20% available P. The economic cost value per 1 kg of N and P were computed as follow:

$$\text{Cost of nitrogen} = \text{Price of 1 kg Urea} / \text{N content in Urea} \qquad (3)$$

$$\text{Cost of phosphorus} = [\text{price of 1 kg DAP} \\ - (\text{price of 1 kg N}_*\text{N content})] / (\text{Available P in DAP}) \quad (4)$$

The average direct purchase price of 100 kg of UREA $70 and DAP $100 in the study period (2015). Also, the price of UREA and DAP including the credited cost were $74.4 UREA and $132.5 DAP per 100 kg. Depending on the value the estimated replacement cost for 1 kg N was $1.6 and available P $5.2.

3   Results and Discussion

3.1   Rainfall Intensity and Infiltration

The study watershed received an annual rainfall of 665 mm for 2015 and 795 mm for 2016. The peak rainfall intensity was 93.6 mm hr^{-1} for 2015 and 91.2 mm hr^{-1} for 2016. To show the relationship between rainfall intensity and infiltration rate, the spatial average infiltration rate and exceedance probability of rainfall intensity were shown in Fig. 3.

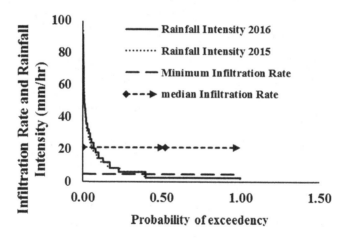

Fig. 3. The exceedance probability of average intensity and median infiltration rate for the Alekt Wenz watersheds in the year 2015 and 2016.

The steady-state infiltration rate for treated watershed ranged from 7 mm hr^{-1} to 122 mm hr^{-1} and for untreated watershed ranged from 5 mm hr^{-1} to 90 mm hr^{-1}. The median infiltration rates from all 24 measurements were 22 mm hr^{-1} for treated and 19 mm hr^{-1} for untreated (Fig. 3). This value showed that the SWC activities enhance the infiltration rate in the treated watershed than the untreated one. To compare rainfall intensity with infiltration rate, median infiltration rate, and exceedance probability is meaningful parameters [21]. As shown in Fig. 3 the median infiltration is exceeded 6% in 2015 and 7% in 2016. Only 6% and 7% of the time infiltration rates were exceeded by rainfall intensity.

3.2 Perched Groundwater Level

Perched groundwater level rose up during August, and declined during September. The average water table level below the surface depth was 0.43 m, 0.83 m and 1.14 m for lower, middle and upper slope of treated watershed respectively (Fig. 4). For untreated watershed, the average water table level below the surface depth was 0.54 m, 0.70 m, and 0.77 m for lower, middle, and upper slope, respectively (Fig. 4). Perched groundwater levels fluctuate more on the untreated watershed because of the rainfall amount. The rainfall in the treated watershed has a chance to infiltrate and stabilize the fluctuation.

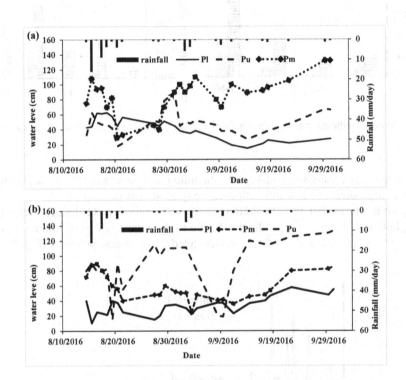

Fig. 4. Perched groundwater level (cm) from the soil surface: (a) from U1 (transect one) the untreated and (b) from treated watersheds (T1) (where Pl = piezometer at the lower slope, Pm = at the middle slope and Pu = at the upper slope.

3.3 Streamflow Responses

The average runoff coefficients from treated watershed were 0.02 for 2015 and 0.04 for 2016 and from untreated watershed 0.1 in both of 2015 and 2016. Therefore, the untreated watershed was generating more direct runoff than the treated watershed in both data recording periods. Table 2 shows that the direct runoff reduced by 50.8% in 2015 and 42.2% in the treated during 2016. This results in 17% base flow increment were detected in the treated watershed.

Table 2. The annual direct runoff and base flow responses from *Alekt Wenz* watersheds.

	Treated		Untreated	
	2015	2016	2015	2016
Direct Runoff (mm)	8.5	9.8	17.3	15.3
Base flow (mm)	180.7	212	69.8	195.4

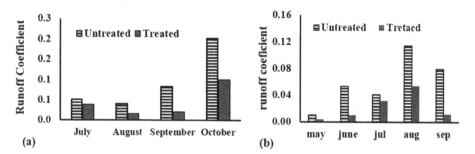

(a)   (b)

Fig. 5. Runoff coefficient monthly distribution of Alekt Wenz watershed (a) for 2015 and (b) for 2016.

During the late rainy season (August), the runoff was generated by low rainfall with saturated watershed and low infiltration capacity as shown in (Fig. 5).

Figure 6 shows that the streamflow depth was higher in the treated watershed during both data recording periods; this is due to the improvement of infiltration rate and base flow increment through the implemented conservation practices (Fig. 7).

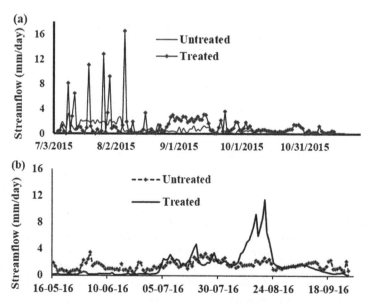

Fig. 6. Time series diagram showing discharge fluctuations obtained from the rating curves for a treated and untreated watershed (a) in 2015 and (b) in 2016.

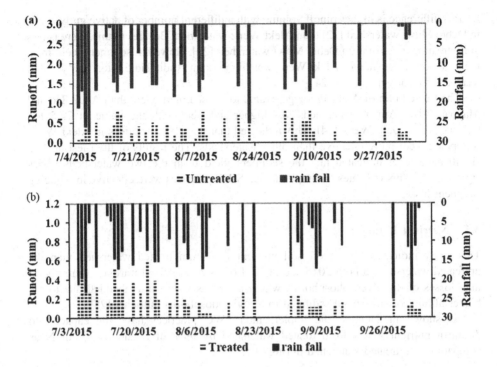

Fig. 7. The rainfall-runoff relationship in 2015 (a), for the untreated and (b), for the treated watershed of the rainy season.

3.4   Suspended Sediment Yield

The reduction of sediment concentration in the treated watershed was due to a decrease in runoff volume and trapped by stone/soil bunds and gabions. Sediment yield was higher during the beginning of the rainfall period because of formation of rills from plowing of the agricultural area. Table 3 shows that a loss from the untreated watershed is higher than the treated watershed. From a total of sediment yield delivery in Alekt Wenz watershed, the treated watershed shares 40.6% in 2015 and 19% in 2016. This is a lower contribution as compared to the untreated watershed sediment yield.

Table 3. Annual sediment yield losses from Alekt Wenz watershed in the year 2015–2016.

Sediment yield (t ha^{-1}yr^{-1})	Treated	Untreated
2015	2.4	6
2016	2.1	8.5

The sediment losses from treated part of Alekt Wenz watershed was very much lower than Debre Mawi watershed which had losses of 13 ton ha^{-1}yr^{-1} [22]. This value was higher as we compared to the untreated part of Alekt Wenz watershed. The reason for this difference is higher runoff volume with a different number of active gully heads in Debre Mawi watershed [22] than Alekt Wenz watershed. Besides to this, there is less gully treatment measure in Debre Mawi watershed [23]. However, sediment yield from the untreated watershed of Alekt Wenz was higher than Andit Tid 5.4 ton $ha^{-1}yr^{-1}$and Maybar (8.8 ton ha^{-1} yr^{-1}) [24].

The treated part of Alekt Wenz generated lower sediment yield than Andit Tid and Maybar. Also, Anjeni watersheds lost higher sediment with the value of 22.5 ton ha^{-1} yr^{-1}than Alekt Wenz [24]. This indicated that the SWC practices in Alekt Wenz watershed were more effective than other watersheds. The results of the t-test at 0.05 significance level indicated that the sediment yield from the two watersheds varies significantly. This indicates the implemented SWC practices were effective in reducing sediment losses.

3.5 Nutrient Losses

This study indicated that lower soil nutrient loss from treated watershed than the untreated watershed in both 2015 and 2016. Losses of dissolved nitrogen were higher than losses of dissolved phosphorus, which is lost as sediment-embedded due to the higher affinity of suspended sediment to absorb phosphorus nutrients [25].

As shown in Table 4, the implemented SWC practices have the capacity to diminish nutrient losses from treated watershed by 99% of P and 67.7% of N as compared to untreated watershed during 2015.

Table 4. Nutrient losses and corresponding replacement cost for *Alekt Wenz* watershed in the year 2015.

Watershed Status	Nutrient type	Nutrient losses (kg ha^{-1})	Replacement Cost ($) $ha^{-1}yr^{-1}$
Treated	Psd*	0.02	0.1
	Nsd**	8.2	13.2
Untreated	Psd	0.2	1.2
	Nsd	25.4	41.1

*P_{sd} (Dissolved and sediment-associated Phosphorus),
**N_{sd} (Dissolved and sediment-associated Nitrogen)

Table 5. Nutrient losses and corresponding replacement cost for Alekt Wenz watershed in 2016.

Watershed Status	Nutrient type	Nutrient losses (kg ha^{-1})	Replacement Cost ($) $ha^{-1}yr^{-1}$
Treated	Psd*	0.16	0.8
	Nsd**	11.92	19.3
Untreated	Psd	0.8	4.1
	Nsd	61.01	98.6

*P_{sd} (Dissolved and sediment-associated Phosphorus), **N_{sd} (Dissolved and sediment-associated Nitrogen).

During 2016, 75% of P and 64.8% of N, dissolved nutrient losses were conserved by SWC activities from treated watershed when we compared with the untreated watershed (Table 6). The farmers who live in the untreated watershed incurred a higher cost ($42.3) than the treated one ($13.3) to replace the lost N-P nutrient in 2015. Also, the untreated watershed incurred $102.8, which is higher than the treated one ($20.1) to replace the nutrient of N and P.

4   Conclusions

This study showed that SWC practices were effective in reducing runoff, losses of sediment and soil nutrients as well as in increasing infiltration rate. The farmers incurred nearly 80.4% cost for fertilizer application in the untreated watershed than the treated watershed. Generally, the conservation practices enhance infiltration rate and contribute water to the groundwater, and base flow in the treated watershed had been improved.

Therefore, implementation of SWC practices according to hydrological characteristics of the watershed is crucially mandatory to reduce sediment losses. To realize the effectiveness of various SWC measure continuous hydrological data recording and evaluation of the data are very important. It is important to investigate the long-term effect of SWC measures in reducing soil and nutrient losses. In addition, it is important in evaluating the linking between watershed characteristics and hydrological responses.

In this study, different SWC measures are proposed for the untreated watershed, such as the treatment of gullies, gabions, land development, biological measures, and exclosures to control soil and nutrient losses.

Acknowledgment. This research was made possible through support provided by CGIAR Research Program on Water, Land and Ecosystem's, East Africa focal regional program. Additional funding was also obtained from the Ethiopian Road Authority (ERA).

References

1. Tan, Z., Lal, R., Wiebe, K.: Global soil nutrient depletion and yield reduction. J. Sustain. Agric. **26**(1), 123–146 (2005)
2. Gashaw, T., Bantider, A., Silassie, H.: Land degradation in Ethiopia: causes, impacts and rehabilitation techniques. J. Environ. Earth Sci. **4**(9), 98–104 (2014)
3. Eswaran, H., Lal, R., Reich, P.: Land degradation: an overview. Responses to Land degradation, pp. 20–35 (2001)
4. Lal, R.: Soil erosion impact on agronomic productivity and environment quality. Crit. Rev. Plant Sci. **17**(4), 319–464 (1998)
5. Amsalu, A., de Graaff, J.: Farmers' views of soil erosion problems and their conservation knowledge at Beressa watershed, central highlands of Ethiopia. Agric. Hum. Values **23**(1), 99–108 (2006)
6. Taddese, G.: Land degradation: a challenge to Ethiopia. Environ. Manag. **27**(6), 815–824 (2001)
7. Bekele, W.: Economics of Soil and Water Conservation, vol. 411 (2003)

8. Brhane, G., Mekonen, K.: Estimating soil loss using universal soil loss equation (USLE) for soil conservation planning at medego watershed, Northern Ethiopia. J. Am. Sci. 5(1), 58–69 (2009)

9. Tamene, L., Vlek, P.L.G.: Soil erosion studies in Northern Ethiopia. In: Braimoh, A.K., Vlek, P.L.G. (eds.) Land Use and Soil Resources, pp. 73–100. Springer, Dordrecht (2008). https://doi.org/10.1007/978-1-4020-6778-5_5

10. Nyssen, J., et al.: How soil conservation affects the catchment sediment budget – a comprehensive study in the north Ethiopian highlands (2009)

11. Hyndman, D., Hyndman, D.: Natural Hazards and Disasters. Cengage Learning (2010)

12. Herweg, K., Ludi, E.: The performance of selected soil and water conservation measures— case studies from Ethiopia and Eritrea. CATENA 36(1–2), 99–114 (1999)

13. Adimassu, Z., Mekonnen, K., Yirga, C., Kessler, A.: Effect of soil bunds on runoff, soil and nutrient losses, and crop yield in the central highlands of Ethiopia. Land Degrad. Dev. 25(6), 554–564 (2014)

14. Birhanu, A., Meseret, D.: Structural soil and water conservation practices in Farta District, North Western Ethiopia: an investigation on factors influencing continued Use. Sci. Technol. Arts Res. J. 2(4), 114–121 (2014)

15. Demelash, M., Stahr, K.: Assessment of integrated soil and water conservation measures on key soil properties in South Gonder, North-Western Highlands of Ethiopia. J. Soil Sci. Environ. Manag. 1(7), 164–176 (2010)

16. Huang, M., Zhang, L.: Hydrological responses to conservation practices in a catchment of the Loess Plateau, China. Hydrol. Process. 18(10), 1885–1898 (2004)

17. Ngetich, K., et al.: Effects of selected soil and water conservation techniques on runoff, sediment yield and maize productivity under sub-humid and semi-arid conditions in Kenya. CATENA 121, 288–296 (2014)

18. Chakela, Q.K., Soil Erosion and Reservoir Sedimentation in Lesotho. Nordic Africa Institute (1981)

19. Bewket, W.: Soil and water conservation intervention with conventional technologies in northwestern highlands of Ethiopia: acceptance and adoption by farmers. Land Use Policy 24(2), 404–416 (2007)

20. Wolka, K.: Effect of soil and water conservation measures and challenges for its adoption: Ethiopia in focus. J. Environ. Sci. Technol. 7(4), 185 (2014)

21. Tilahun, S.A.: Observations and modeling of erosion from spatially and temporally distributed sources in the (semi) humid Ethiopian highlands, pp. 8–67. Cornell University (2012)

22. Dagnew, D.C., et al.: Impact of conservation practices on runoff and soil loss in the sub-humid Ethiopian Highlands: the Debre Mawi watershed. J. Hydrol. Hydromech. 63(3), 214–223 (2015)

23. Mekuria, W.M., et al.: Sustaining the benefits of soil and water conservation in the highlands of Ethiopia (2015)

24. Guzman, C.D.: Suspended sediment concentration and discharge relationships in the Ethiopian highlands. Cornell University (2011)

25. Bertol, I., et al.: Nutrient losses by water erosion (2003)

Optimization of Green Logistic Distribution Routing Problem with Multi Depot Using Improved Simulated Annealing

Teshome Bekele Dagne[✉], Jeyaraju Jayaprakash, Bereket Haile,
and Sisay Geremew

Faculty of Mechanical and Industrial Engineering,
Bahir Dar Institute of Technology, Bahir Dar University, Bahir Dar, Ethiopia
teshome.dagne3@gmail.com

Abstract. The traditional vehicle routing problems (TVRP) are suited for cost minimization. In this study, Green VRP with Multi Depot (G-VRPMD) is addressed. The G-VRPMD, an extension of TVRP, is NP-hard which creates eco-friendly distribution system starting and destination to multiple depots. In the present study, modified probability of accepting criteria (MPAC) has been developed. Clustering of consumer was done based on nearness' to depot using distance saving method. Depot's number, customer number and optimal distance used as performance measures. Comparison of output result with state-of-the-art shows that the performance of Improved Simulated Annealing (ISA) is effective in solving G-VRPMD. The emission rate is proportional to age; therefore in designing distribution network path has to incorporate vehicle age prior to optimization.

Keywords: G-VRPMD · MMAC · Vehicle age · ISA

1 Introduction

Effective logistic distribution requires an efficient delivery system of items from source origin to end consumer. A single origin delivery is called single problem. A multiple problem if the delivery has more than one source origin (Yoshiike and Takefuji 2002). Green routing means designing an eco-friendly distribution system. The green (G-VRPMD) examine the delivery network impacts on transportation environment and cost.

The traditional VRP does not consider delivery impact on environment (Paulo et al. 2018). However, environmental issue becomes a competitive factor for companies and in their corporate social responsibility policy (Lyon and Maxwell 2008). Thus in developing distribution system, impacts on environment has to incorporated. In the present study, G-VRPMD model helps organizations to achieve environmental and cost concern in their distribution system. Under this perspective consumers clustered based distance saving method before distribution assignment and optimization. The aim of study is to design an eco-friendly goods distribution system. A minimum cost attended

F. A. Zimale et al. (Eds.): ICAST 2018, LNICST 274, pp. 183–197, 2019.
https://doi.org/10.1007/978-3-030-15357-1_15

using distance saving whereas the emission model descried in terms of EU 2020 regulation emission factor and vehicle age.

The remainder of this paper is organized as follows: In Sect. 2, literature review on G-VRPMD. Section 3 presents the model development and solution methodology. Section 4 reports the computational study, followed by results and discussion. Section 5 describes illustrative example considered in the work. Finally, the conclusion is given in Sect. 6.

2 Literature Review

Research on routing problem has gain more attention (Lahyani et al. 2015). An extension of TVRP having a constraint including (1) environmental; (2) backhauls; (3) Periodic; (4) maximum route; (5) time window; (6) split delivery (Figliozzi 2010) (see Fig. 1).

Based on addressed problem can be categorized into two such as: - (i) Energy saving models (Erdoğan and Miller-Hooks 2012; Xiao et al. 2012; Ćirović et al. 2014; Kara et al. 2007; Figliozzi 2010; Jabali et al. 2012). (ii) Emission reduction models (Huang et al. 2012; Lin. et al. 2014; Demir et al. 2014; Bektaş and Laporte 2011; Soysal et al. 2015), CMEM (Comprehensive Modal Emission Model) considered by (Bektaş and Laporte 2011; Soysal et al. 2015; Demir et al. 2012), MEET (Emissions and Energy consumption) model used by (Jabali et al. 2012), relate fuel consumption and emissions speed (Figliozzi 2010; Palmer 2007; Jabali et al. 2012), to load and distance (Huang et al. 2012), develop special function (Zhang et al. 2015), speed (Suzuki 2011; Fagerholt et al. 2010), alternative fuel vehicle (Qian and Eglese 2016; Li et al. 2015; Erdoğan and Miller-Hooks 2012; Taha et al. 2014).

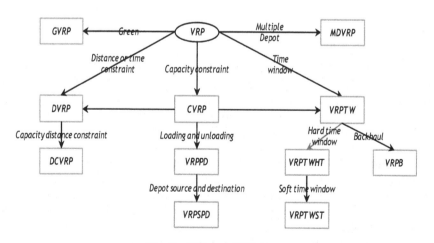

Fig. 1. Different VRP types

Routing problems based on solution approaches categorized into three such as: (i) Exact (ii) Heuristics (iii) Meta-heuristics. Exact methods such as branch and bound

(Laporte and Nobert 1987; Baldacci and Mingozzi 2009; Fischetti et al. 1994), branch and cut (Cordeau 2006), branch and price (Martinelli et al. 2010).

Heuristics such as two-phase heuristics (Beasley 1983), construction heuristics (Clarke and Wright 1964), Iterative heuristics (Gendreau et al. 2001). Meta-heuristics such as simulated annealing, tabu search (Renaud et al. 1996; Li et al. 2012; Prins et al. 2007; Wu et al. 2002; Cordeau et al. 1997), GA (Lacomme et al. 2001; Oliveira et al. 2017; Jorgensen et al. 2007; Haghani and Jung 2005), Ant colony (Donati et al. 2008; Yu et al. 2011), Variable neighborhood search (Hemmelmayr et al. 2009; Affi et al. 2018; Polacek et al. 2004).

Exact methods are only convent for a limited problems in lesser CPU (Kellehauge 2008). The limitation of exact method geared researcher towards heuristic and meta-heuristics for large problems (Kellehauge 2008).

Meta-heuristics suitable for large problems with short CPU time (Zachariadis et al. 2007). This paper deals improved SA performance on green goods distribution system. The contribution is to address logistic supply problems and improve SA convergence mechanism.

3 Methodology

3.1 Mathematical Formulation and Problem Description

A single product supply from m multi-depots to n consumer has been studied. Demand sharing and consumer demand are less than depot storage capacity. In a supply chain a consumer has a successor and predecessor route. The supply route assignment was done using distance saving method. The total cost comprises supply cost and emission cost. Model assumptions are:

(a) A determined demand, vehicle and depot storage
(b) A shortest path b/n depot and consumer is known
(c) Depots location and consumer is known
(d) Origin and destination at depot
(e) A single vehicle visit a depot and a customer exactly once
(f) Homogeneous vehicles are used (capacity, speed and emission parameters are same)

3.2 Model Parameters

Sets	Parameters
F – All depot set	N – Number of vehicles
E – All consumer set	V_i – Product available at f
K – All vehicle set	D_j – Demand at e
Indices	Q_K – Capacity at k
f – depot index	e_{ij} – CO_2 emissions cost between point i to j
e – consumer index	$X_{ij} = 1$, if the arc (i, j) is traveled by vehicle k; 0 otherwise
k – vehicle index	$Z_{ij} = 1$, if customer j is allotted to depot i; 0 otherwise

(continued)

Sets	Parameters
d_{ij} – Distance between point i to j	U_{lk} – auxiliary variable for sub-tour elimination constraints in route k
	C_{ij} – Distribution cost between point i to j

3.3 Model Development

G-VRPMD descried in terms of graph, $G = (A, E)$. Node $j \in A$ indicates consumer or depot and an edge $e \in E$ represent a path in routes. Where $E = \{1, \ldots, n\}$ be consumer set and $F = \{1, \ldots, m\}$ set of depots. Consumer need, $D_j (j \in \{1, 2, 3, \ldots n\})$ to be delivered using a vehicle k. G-VRPMD reduces both cost and CO_2 emissions. G-VRPMD model is shown below:

$$\text{Min} = \sum_{i \in F \cup E} \sum_{j \in F \cup E} \sum_{k \in K} C_{ij}.X_{ij} + \sum_{i \in K} \sum_{J \in F \cup E} e_{ij} \tag{1}$$

Subject to;

$$\sum_{k \in K} \sum_{i \in F \cup E} X_{ijk} = 1, j \in E \tag{2}$$

$$\sum_{j \in E} D_j \sum_{j \in F \cup E} X_{ijk} \le Q_k, k \in K \tag{3}$$

$$\sum_{i \in F \cup E} X_{ijk} = \sum_{j \in F \cup E} X_{jik}, \ k \in K, i, j \in F \cup E \tag{4}$$

$$\sum_{i \in F} \sum_{j \in E} X_{ijk} \le 1, k \in K \tag{5}$$

$$\sum_{j \in E} D_j Z_{ij} \le V_i, i \in F \tag{6}$$

$$-Z_{ij} + \sum_{u \in F \cup E} \left(X_{iuk} - X_{ujk} \right) \le 1, i \in F, j \in E, k \in K \tag{7}$$

$$U_{Ik} - U_{Jk} + Nx_{ijk} \le N - 1, l, j \in J, k \in K \tag{8}$$

$$e_{ij} = \delta.d_{ij}.V_f[(V_A F_V + MF_M).(W_L P_{co2})] \tag{9}$$

Constraint (2) allocated vehicle to customer. Constraint (3) shows the vehicle capacity constraint for all set. Constraint (4) describes vehicles starting and returns point.

(5) Indicates route can serve at once. Constraint (6) states depot capacity. Constraint (7) specifies that a consumer served by depot if there a route exist. Constraint (8) describes sub tour elimination. Constraint (9) CO_2 emission from node i to node j.

3.4   Steps in Simulated Annealing Algorithm (SA)

STEP 1 Select random feasible solution, X_o, randomly, staring temperature (t_o), current solution $(X_i = X_o)$, iteration step (k = 0) and temperature at k^{th} step $(t_k = t_o)$.

STEP 2 Select temperature if satisfies the loop stop condition, go to (3); if not, choose a neighborhood, X_j, randomly and calculate; $\Delta E_{ji} = E(X_j) - E(X_i)$. If $\Delta E_{ji} \leq 0$, thus $(X_i) = (X_j)$; otherwise if $\exp(-\frac{\Delta E_{ji}}{t} > rand(0, 1))$ go to step 2.

STEP 3 Temperature control function; $k = k + 1, t_{k+1} = \alpha t_k, \alpha \in (0.8 - 0.99)$. If it meets the termination conditions, go to step 4; if not, go to (2).

STEP 4 Terminate SA algorithm after all consumers assigned to route

3.5   Modified Simulated Annealing (ISA)

A modified SA is developed to address logistic supply problem. The plugged improvements are shown below:

(1) Distribution representation

A distribution network solution may contain a multiple distribution paths. Loops start and terminate at depot centre (0). For instance a route solution: 0-1-2-0-3-4-0, tells that a route contains two paths, 0-1-2-0 and 0-3-4-0. A route initial solution process is generated using three basic steps: clustering, routing and path optimization (see Fig. 2).

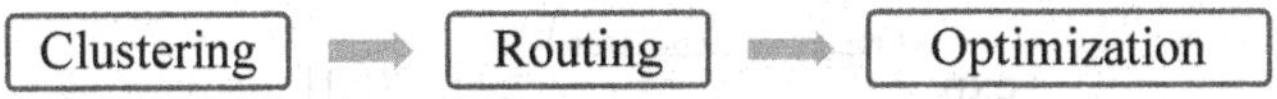

| Clustering | ⟹ | Routing | ⟹ | Optimization |

Fig. 2. SA grouping

(a) Clustering – consumers are grouped based on the distance computation according to the following rule:

$$D_{(c,0)} = \sqrt{(X_c - X_0)^2 + (Y_c - Y_0)^2} \qquad (13)$$

Where, $D_{(c,0)}$ represent the distance between consumer (c) and depot (0).

(b) Routing – each consumers allotted to depot using distance saving matrix $(S_{ci,cj})$ between two consumer c_i and c_j in the same link. The distance saving matrix is shown below;

$$S_{ci,cj} = D_{(0,ci)} + D_{(0,cj)} - D_{(ci,cj)} \qquad (14)$$

(c) Optimization – starting from closest consumer to depot, the logistic supply is sequenced. Logistic supply route optimization is repeated until all unselected customers are sequenced.

(2) Neighborhood. The traditional SA algorithm is $2 - \text{opt}$ exchange to nodes at a time. However, at each temperature, it takes a longer CPU time to get an optimal solution space. In this paper neighborhood switching in-circuit is implemented with randomly using $2 - \text{opt}$ and $3 - \text{opt}$ method to produce a new feasible solution.

(3) Modified probability of accepting criteria (MPAC)

Metropolis accepting criteria determine probability of the accepting a worse solution (see Fig. 3). Suppose there are n times that worse solution is accepted as current solution, we use $(\Delta E_{ji})_k$, the difference of potential energy state values and AC_p as probability of accepting where $k = 1 \ldots n$, and the relation between $(\Delta E_{ji})_k$ and AC_p as shown in Eq. (15).

$$AC_p = \begin{cases} 1, & \text{if } \Delta [E_{ji}]_k \leq 0 \\ \exp^{-\left(\frac{\Delta [E_{ji}]_k}{t_k}\right)}, & \text{if not} \end{cases} \qquad (15)$$

The standard SA accepting criteria is given in Eq. (16).

$$\exp^{-\left(\frac{\text{new soultion} - \text{current solution}}{t_k}\right)} > r_k \epsilon [0, 1] \qquad (16)$$

In present study, modified accepting criteria constructed are given in Eq. (17).

$$MPAC = \exp^{-\left(\frac{\text{new soultion} - \text{current solution}}{\log[t]_k}\right)} > r_k \epsilon [0, 1], t_k = \frac{-\Delta [E_{ji}]_k}{\ln[r]_k} \qquad (17)$$

The MPAC accepting criteria value becomes larger negative us $\log[t]_k$ goes up Therefore; modified accepting criteria of bad solution becomes drastically reduced at high temperature.

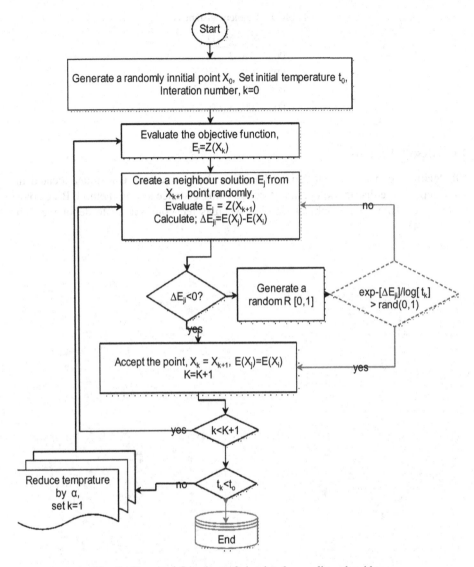

Fig. 3. Proposed flowchart of simulated annealing algorithm

4 Result and Discussion

An Improved Simulated Annealing (ISA) algorithm code was implemented in MATLAB R2016a on Intel core 5 Duo (1.73 GHz), 3 GB RAM PC. A set of test has been carried out to examine ISA performance on problem instance (P03, P05, P06 and P07) known as Cordeaux's instances. These instances are listed in Table 1 where:

I- Problem instance   M- Depot number

N- customer no.   D- Maximum distance traveled

Table 1. Problem instances

I	N	M	D
P03	75	3	∞
P05	100	2	∞
P06	100	3	∞
P07	100	4	∞

4.1 Result Analysis

Clustering – consumers categorized based on depot nearness. Consumer located in same depot route distribution path developed using distance saving method. Blue color indicates consumer geographical location whereas red colors indicate depot location (see Fig. 4).

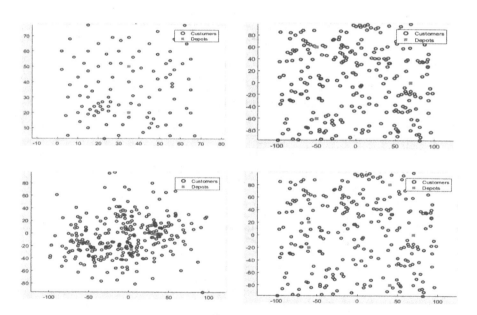

Fig. 4. Illustration of initial consumer location with respect to depot (Color figure online)

Distribution route optimization – consumers with higher distance saving method plugged into same depot (Tables 2, 3, 4 and 5).

Table 2. Distribution network path assignment for P03

Depot	Optimal dist. path	Best opt. distance	Served consumer	No. vehicles
B(30,40)		330.48	25	5
D(10,20)		232.2926	40	6
C(20,10)		101.9574	10	3

Table 3. Distribution network path assignment for P05

Depot	Optimal dist. path	Best opt. distance	Served consumer	No. vehicles
A(20,20)		381.2767	60	7
B(30,40)		370.2926	40	6

Performance – a modified SA performance testing was done with existing literature such as Genetic Clustering (GC) (Thangiah and Salhi 2001) and Genetic Algorithm (GA) (Ombuki-Berman and Hanshar 2009). Performance metrics and output is shown in Table 6. Percentage gap (%GAP) is calculated by,

$$\%GAP = \frac{C_{bod} - C_{bkd}}{C_{bkd}} \times 100$$

Where; C_{bod}, best optimal path using modified SA and C_{bkd}, best known path (Cordeaux instances). The total path distance is closer to optimal distance reported in the literature.

Table 4. Distribution network path assignment for P06

Depot	Optimal dist. path	Best opt. distance	Served consumer	No. vehicles
A(20,30)		324.601	25	5
B(30,20)		275.4021	14	4
C(30,40)		381.2767	60	7

Table 5. Distribution network path assignment for P07

Depot	Optimal dist. path	Best opt. distance	Served consumer	No. vehicles
A(10,10)		257.5058	50	7
B(10,30)		245.4021	14	4
C(20,10)		124.1634	8	3
D(15,25)		294.1318	30	5

Table 6. Comparative analysis for problem instances

I	N	M	Best known distance (km)	Distance reported in literature (km)		Best optimal distance (km) ISA	Best optimal distance (km) SA	% Deviation
				GC (Thangiah and Salhi. 2001)	GA (Ombuki-Berman and Hanshar 2009)			
P03	75	3	641.19	694.49	706.88	664.73	732	3.67
P05	100	2	750.03	-	-	751.5693	794	0.205
P06	100	3	876.5	976.02	908.88	957.1493	1137	9.2
P07	100	4	885.8	-	-	921.2031	1248	3.99

5 Illustrative Example

A depot (O) from its central hub supplies fresh product to n consumer. In order to keep the quality freshness till consumed and minimize cost. The firm requires designing the logistic supply network. Fresh agricultural products are, generally, transported from central to local hub and finally delivered to consumers (see Fig. 5). Costs of vehicle are fixed and variable cost. Fixed cost is 30$ which includes personnel salary and refrigeration equipment. Variable cost includes gasoline price spent 8$ per kilometer. The firm in consideration deliver fresh product from its local warehouse (W_1, W_2, W_3 and W_4) located at Cordeaux coordinate (P03, P05, P06 and P07) respectively to geographically distributed n consumer through assigned m depots.

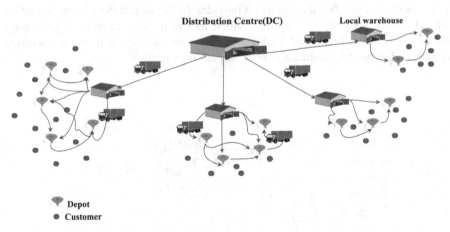

Fig. 5. Illustration of two-echelon logistic distribution

Table 7. Performance metric results

Local warehouse	No. Customer	No. depot	Route	Best optimal distance (km)	Transportation cost	Emission cost/route	Emission cost	Total cost
W_1	75	3	14	664.73	5347.84	155.513	2177.18	7525.02
W_2	100	2	13	751.5693	6042.55	175.829	2285.77	8328.32
W_3	100	3	16	957.1493	7687.19	223.924	3582.78	11269.97
W_4	100	4	19	921.2031	7399.63	215.514	4094.77	11494.40

The total CO_2 emission cost (e_{ij}) from point i to j with distance (d_{ij}) is given by Eq. 18.

$$e_{ij} = \delta.d_{ij}.V_f[(V_A F_V + MF_M).(W_L P_{co2})] \tag{18}$$

Where δ, is vehicle carbon emission factor, V_A is vehicle age, F_V is vehicle constant, M is vehicle mass, W_L is co_2 emission per liter ($W_L = 0.216$ kgco$_2$/Lt), P_{co2} is average fuel price per unit CO_2 ($P_{co2} = 12\$/\text{kgco}_2$), V_f is fuel consumption per unit distance per vehicle ($V_f = 0.614$ Lt/km) and F_M is a road constant. In this study, CO_2 emission as function of age and distance travelled was analyzed by taking other (F_V, M and F_M) parameters constant as shown in Table 7. Emission factor taken for light vehicle as per EU2020 targets as 0.147 kg CO_2/km and Eq. 18 becomes: $e_{ij} = 0.147.d_{ij}V_f[(V_A F_V + MF_M).W_L P_{co2})]$.

The age in [A] region ranges 1 up to 5 years shows an average 8% emission, whereas in [B] region ranges 5 up to 15 years emission increases continually by 27.85%. In [C] region more than 15 ages and afterwards emission increased drastically by 42.31% (see Fig. 6). Therefore using very aged (>15 year) vehicle have more environmental impact than the services it provides. In Developed there is age limitation with a range of 15 year and imposed carbon foot print taxation. But in developing countries like India, Brazil and Ethiopia vehicle used as long as it serve. Therefore decision maker has to consider age prior to path optimization.

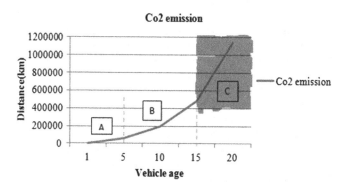

Fig. 6. CO_2 emission per distance travelled

6 Conclusion

A logistic supply network in green vehicle route problem with multi depot (G-VRPMD) is considered. A bi-objective model developed that minimizes emission of vehicles and total cost. Modified accepting criteria have been developed and performance analysis verified using instance. A comparison of modified SA with existing optimal reported results in the literature, ISA performs a better quality solution than other meta-heuristics. A 4.27% gap was found in modified SA, which is smaller than that of GC (9.834%) and GA (6.97%). Utilizing modified SA for G-VRPMD can help organization managers to design eco-friendly distribution network. Emission rate is proportional to vehicle age. Therefore in designing distribution network path vehicle aged has been given priority before route.

References

Affi, M., Derbel, H., Jarboui, B.: Variable neighborhood search algorithm for the green vehicle routing problem. Int. J. Ind. Eng. Comput. **9**, 195–204 (2018)

Anily, S., Federgruen, A.: Simulated annealing methods with general acceptance probabilities. J. Appl. Probab. **24**, 657–667 (1987)

Baldacci, R., Mingozzi, A.: A unified exact method for solving different classes of vehicle routing problems. Math. Program. **120**, 347 (2009)

Beasley, J.E.: Route first—cluster second methods for vehicle routing. Omega **11**, 403–408 (1983)

Bektaş, T., Laporte, G.: The pollution-routing problem. Transp. Res. Part B Methodol. **45**, 1232–1250 (2011)

Ćirović, G., Pamuc, D., Boz'anic, D.: Green logistic vehicle routing problem: routing light delivery vehicles in urban areas using a neuro-fuzzy model. Expert Syst. Appl. **41**, 4245–4258 (2014)

Clarke, G., Wright, J.W.: Scheduling of vehicles from a central depot to a number of delivery points. Oper. Res. **12**, 568–581 (1964)

Cordeau, J.-F.: A branch-and-cut algorithm for the dial-a-ride problem. Oper. Res. **54**, 573–586 (2006)

Cordeau, J.F., Gendreau, M., Laporte, G.: A tabu search heuristic for periodic and multi-depot vehicle routing problems. Networks **30**, 105–119 (1997)

Dell'Amico, M., Righini, G., Salani, M.: A branch-and-price approach to the vehicle routing problem with simultaneous distribution and collection. Transp. Sci. **40**, 235–247 (2006)

Demir, E., Bektas, T., Laporte, G.: The bi-objective pollution-routing problem. Eur. J. Oper. Res. **232**, 464–478 (2014)

Demir, E., Bektaş, T., Laporte, G.: An adaptive large neighborhood search heuristic for the pollution-routing problem. Eur. J. Oper. Res. **223**, 346–359 (2012)

Donati, A.V., Montemanni, R., Casagrande, N.: Time dependent vehicle routing problem with a multi ant colony system. Eur. J. Oper. Res. **185**, 1174–1191 (2008)

Zachariadis, E., Tarantills, C., Kiranoudis, C.: A hybrid meta-heuristic algorithm for the vehicle routing problem with simultaneous delivery and pick-up service. Expert Syst. Appl. (2007)

Erdoğan, S., Miller-Hooks, E.: A green vehicle routing problem. Transp. Res. Part E Logistics Transp. Rev. **48**, 100–114 (2012)

Fagerholt, K., Laporte, G., Norstad, I.: Reducing fuel emissions by optimizing speed on shipping routes. J. Oper. Res. Soc. **61**, 523–529 (2010)

Faigle, U., Schrader, R.: On the convergence of stationary distributions in simulated annealing algorithms. Inf. Process. Lett. **27**, 189–194 (1988)

Figliozzi, M.: Vehicle routing problem for emissions minimization. Transp. Res. Rec. J. Transp. Res. Board **2197**, 1–7 (2010)

Fischetti, M., Toth, P., Vigo, D.: A branch-and-bound algorithm for the capacitated vehicle routing problem on directed graphs. Oper. Res. **42**, 846–859 (1994)

Gendreau, M., Hertz, A., Laporte, G.: New insertion and post-optimization procedures for TSP. OR **40**, 1086–1094 (2001)

Haghani, A., Jung, S.: A dynamic vehicle routing problem with time-dependent travel times. Comput. Oper. Res. **32**, 2959–2986 (2005)

Hemmelmayr, V.C., Doerner, K.F., Hartl, R.F.: A variable neighborhood search heuristic for periodic routing problems. Eur. J. Oper. Res. **195**, 791–802 (2009)

Henderson, D., Jacobson, S.H., Johnson, A.W.: The theory and practice of simulated annealing. In: Glover, F., Kochenberger, G.A. (eds.) Handbook of Metaheuristics. International Series in Operations Research & Management Science, vol. 57, pp. 287–319. Springer, Boston (2003). https://doi.org/10.1007/0-306-48056-5_10

Huang, Y., Shi, C., Zhao, L.: A study on carbon reduction in the vehicle routing problem with simultaneous pickups and deliveries. In: 2012 IEEE International Conference on Service Operations and Logistics, and Informatics (SOLI), pp. 302–307. IEEE (2012)

Jabali, O., Woensel, T., De Kok, A.: Analysis of travel times and CO_2 emissions in time-dependent vehicle routing. Prod. Oper. Manag. **21**, 1060–1074 (2012)

Johnson, D.S., Aragon, C.R., McGeoch, L.A.: Optimization by simulated annealing: an experimental evaluation; part I, graph partitioning. Oper. Res. **37**, 865–892 (1989)

Jorgensen, R.M., Larsen, J., Bergvinsdottir, K.B.: Solving the dial-a-ride problem using genetic algorithms. J. Oper. Res. Soc. **58**, 1321–1331 (2007)

Kara, İ., Kara, Bahar Y., Yetis, M.Kadri: Energy minimizing vehicle routing problem. In: Dress, A., Xu, Y., Zhu, B. (eds.) COCOA 2007. LNCS, vol. 4616, pp. 62–71. Springer, Heidelberg (2007). https://doi.org/10.1007/978-3-540-73556-4_9

Kellehauge, B.: Formulations and exact algorithms for the vehicle routing problem with time windows. Comput. Oper. Res. **35**, 2307–2330 (2008)

Lacomme, P., Prins, C., Ramdane-Chérif, W.: A genetic algorithm for the capacitated arc routing problem and its extensions. In: Boers, E.J.W. (ed.) EvoWorkshops 2001. LNCS, vol. 2037, pp. 473–483. Springer, Heidelberg (2001). https://doi.org/10.1007/3-540-45365-2_49

Lahyani, R., Khemakhem, M., Semet, F.: Rich vehicle routing problems: from a taxonomy to a definition. Eur. J. Oper. Res. **241**, 1–14 (2015)

Laporte, G., Nobert, Y.: Exact algorithms for the vehicle routing problem. North-Holland Math. Stud. **132**, 147–184 (1987)

Li, H., Lv, T., Li, Y.: The tractor and semitrailer routing problem with many-to-many demand considering carbon dioxide emissions. Transp. Res. Part D Transp. Environ. **34**, 68–82 (2015)

Li, X., Leung, S.C., Tian, P.: A multistart adaptive memory-based tabu search algorithm for the heterogeneous fixed fleet open vehicle routing problem. Expert Syst. Appl. **39**, 365–374 (2012)

Lin, C., Choy, K.L., Ho, G.T.S., et al.: A genetic algorithm-based optimization model for supporting green transportation operations. Expert Syst. Appl. **41**, 3284–3296 (2014)

Lyon, T.P., Maxwell, J.W.: Corporate social responsibility and the environment: a theoretical perspective. Rev. Environ. Econ. Policy **2**(2), 240–260 (2008)

Martinelli, R., Pecin, D., Poggi, M.: Column generation bounds for the capacitated arc routing problem. XLII SBPO (2010)

Oliveira, P.R.d.C., Mauceri, S., Carroll, P.: A genetic algorithm for a green vehicle routing problem. In: International Network Optimization Conference 2017 (INOC 2017), Lisboa, Portugal, pp. 26–28 (2017)

Ombuki-Berman, B., Hanshar, F.T.: Using genetic algorithms for multi-depot vehicle routing. In: Pereira, F.B., Tavares, J. (eds.) Bio-inspired Algorithms for the Vehicle Routing Problem. SCI, vol. 161, pp. 77–99. Springer, Heidelberg (2009). https://doi.org/10.1007/978-3-540-85152-3_4

Palmer, A.: The development of an integrated routing and carbon dioxide emissions model for goods vehicles (2007)

Paulo, R., Stefano, M., Paula, C., et al.: A Genetic Algorithm for a Green Vehicle Routing Problem. Electron. Notes Discrete Math. **64**, 65–74 (2018)

Polacek, M., Hartl, R.F., Doerner, K.: A variable neighborhood search for the multi depot vehicle routing problem with time windows. J. Heuristics **10**, 613–627 (2004)

Prins, C., Prodhon, C., Ruiz, A.: Solving the capacitated location-routing problem by a cooperative Lagrangean relaxation-granular tabu search heuristic. Transp. Sci. **41**, 470–483 (2007)

Qian, J., Eglese, R.: Fuel emissions optimization in vehicle routing problems with time-varying speeds. Eur. J. Oper. Res. **248**, 840–848 (2016)

Renaud, J., Laporte, G., Boctor, F.F.: A tabu search heuristic for the multi-depot vehicle routing problem. Comput. Oper. Res. **23**, 229–235 (1996)

Singh, G., Deshpande, K.: On fast load partitioning by simulated annealing and heuristic algorithms for general class of problems. Adv. Eng. Softw. **16**, 23–29 (1993)

Soysal, M., Bloemhof-Ruwaard, J.M., Bektaş, T.: The time-dependent two-echelon capacitated vehicle routing problem with environmental considerations. Int. J. Prod. Econ. **164**, 366–378 (2015)

Suzuki, Y.: A new truck-routing approach for reducing fuel consumption and pollutants emission. Transp. Res. Part D Transp. Environ. **16**, 73–77 (2011)

Taha, M., Fors, M.N., Shoukry, A.A.: An exact solution for a class of green vehicle routing problem. In: International Conference on Industrial Engineering and Operations Management, pp. 7–9 (2014)

Thangiah, S.R., Salhi, S.: Genetic clustering: an adaptive heuristic for the multidepot vehicle routing problem. Appl. Artif. Intell. **15**, 361–383 (2001)

Wu, T.-H., Low, C., Bai, J.-W.: Heuristic solutions to multi-depot location-routing problems. Comput. Oper. Res. **29**, 1393–1415 (2002)

Xiao, Y., Zhao, Q., Kaku, I.: Development of a fuel consumption optimization model for the capacitated vehicle routing problem. Comput. Oper. Res. **39**, 1419–1431 (2012)

Yoshiike, N., Takefuji, Y.: Solving vehicle routing problems by maximum neuron model. Adv. Eng. Inform. **16**, 99–105 (2002)

Yu, B., Yang, Z., Xie, J.: A parallel improved ant colony optimization for multi-depot vehicle routing problem. J. Oper. Res. Soc. **62**, 183–188 (2011)

Zhang, J., Zhao, Y., Xue, W.: Vehicle routing problem with fuel consumption and carbon emission. Int. J. Prod. Econ. **170**, 234–242 (2015)

Failure Mode Analysis of Automotive Final Drive Gears

Rajesh Murukesan[(⊠)] and Teshome Dengiso Megiso

Arba Minch University, Arba Minch, Ethiopia
m.rajesh_fac@yahoo.com

Abstract. After repeated complaints from customers about failure, the crown and pinion assembly of the vehicle was analyzed by standard metallurgical methods. Standard material composition of the part was confirmed by chemical analysis. Tooth contact analysis was done to understand the contact and sequence of failure. Micro hardness test was done to understand about the hardness of the specimen. The nature of fracture is studied by subjecting the specimen to micro-structural study. It was found that the effect of combination of low case hardness and improper composition was augmented by improper alignment while assembling caused premature failure of the component.

Keywords: Failure analysis · Material · Testing · Gear

1 Introduction

Life expectancy of any mechanical system dependents on the life of its critical components. In the power train of an automobile, gears are critical components. Gears in power train should carry high loads at high speeds with minimum size and weight. In gears, tooth bending fatigue has been one of the most common fatigue failure modes. Tooth bending fatigue results in progressive damage to gear teeth which ultimately result in complete failure of the gear [1] (Fig. 1).

In this work a pair of crown wheel and pinion, from the final drive of a passenger car, was tested to find out the cause of their failure. The final drive transmits power from the transmission box to the live axles through the differential unit. The crown pinion transmits power from the propeller shaft to the crown wheel which carries the differential assembly in a carrier. Often combinations of two or three types of stresses are applied to a gear tooth [2]. Also, complex phenomena of failure are involved for surface hardened components during their working life; therefore a deeper comprehension of the damaging mechanisms is necessary to prevent the failure [3].

En353 (15 Ni Cr 1 Mo12) [for heavy- duty applications] and En 207 (20Mn Cr1) [for medium applications] are the two common billet materials used to manufacture these gears.

© ICST Institute for Computer Sciences, Social Informatics and Telecommunications Engineering 2019
Published by Springer Nature Switzerland AG 2019. All Rights Reserved
F. A. Zimale et al. (Eds.): ICAST 2018, LNICST 274, pp. 198–205, 2019.
https://doi.org/10.1007/978-3-030-15357-1_16

Fig. 1. Failed crown and pinion

2 Tests and Analysis

2.1 Visual Inspection

From standards, the life expectancy of the failed part should have been between 150000 km and 200000 km. During visual inspection, cold weld on the edge of the broken tooth of the gear were found. There were indications showing that the crown wheel and pinion were relatively new. The pinion had sub case fatigue initiated by fine cracks. Large fragments have been removed from the teeth. The gear also had fatigue beach marks.

The drive members were subjected to macro examination using a stereomicroscope for pitting failure. Gear teeth pitting is characterized by the presence of small pits on the contact surfaces.

En353 (15 Ni Cr 1 Mo12) [for heavy- duty applications] and En 207 (20Mn Cr1) [for medium applications] are the two common billet materials used to manufacture these gears. Though pitting is found to be less, in the components, relatively large pitting on the pinion than on the crown wheel indicates that the failure is premature and not due to pitting.

2.2 Chemical Analysis

Chemical analyses were done at two different locations on the gear. Portions of the specimen, at the damaged portion and at where the surface was good, was cut using abrasive cut off wheel and chemical analysis was carried out. The chemical analysis would help to identify the variation in the basic composition of the material by comparing with the manufacturer standards.

The EDX analysis [5] done on new component and failed component are shown in Figs. 2 and 3 respectively. It was learnt that En353 was used to manufacture the parts. The carbon equivalent (CE) for the failed component was found to be 0.77. From the chemical analysis it was understood that one of the reason of failure was wrong selection of material. Also, the manufacturer had changed the composition by increasing percentage of manganese. This reduced the carbon content which resulted in low core hardness. This modification also contributed to premature failure of components. Tables 1 and 2, respectively, shows chemical analysis result for new and failed components.

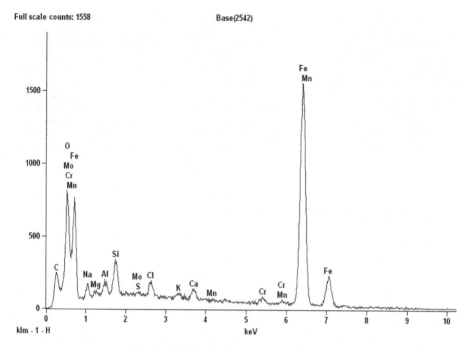

Fig. 2. EDX analysis done on good surface

Table 1. Chemical analysis done on good surface

Element	Net counts	Net counts error	Weight %	Atom %	Formula	Compound %
C	1653	±159	16.71	39.87	C	16.71
O	5423	±663	10.86	19.45	O	10.86
Na	1038	±300	1.76	2.20	Na	1.76
Mg	423	±192	0.35	0.41	Mg	0.35
Al	1210	±363	0.87	0.92	Al	0.87
Si	2763	±390	1.71	1.74	Si	1.71
S	185	±204	0.13	0.11	S	0.13
Cl	1477	±405	1.07	0.87	Cl	1.07
K	417	±183	0.33	0.24	K	0.33
Ca	967	±195	0.85	0.60	Ca	0.85
Cr	547	±177	0.75	0.41	Cr	0.75
Mn	241	±195	0.50	0.26	Mn	0.50
Fe	27135	±879	64.13	32.91	Fe	64.13
Mo	0	0	0	0	0	0
Total			100.00	100.00		100.00

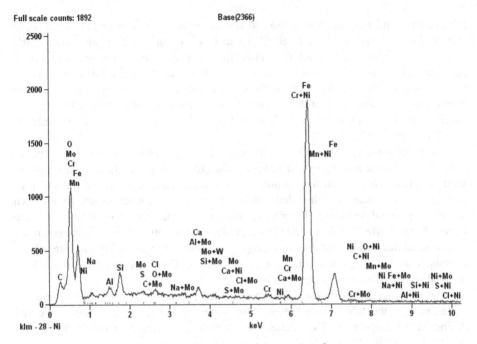

Fig. 3. EDX analysis of damaged surface

Table 2. Chemical analysis done on damaged surface

Element	Net counts	Net counts error	Weight %	Atom %	Formula	Compound %
C	1240	±150	11.05	29.08	C	11.05
O	8142	±684	13.17	26.03	O	13.17
Na	448	±132	0.73	1.00	Na	0.73
Al	666	±165	0.45	0.52	Al	0.45
Si	2037	±204	1.17	1.31	Si	1.17
S	344	±201	0.22	0.21	S	0.22
Cl	538	±198	0.36	0.32	Cl	0.36
Ca	1378	±405	1.09	0.86	Ca	1.09
Cr	458	±189	0.56	0.34	Cr	0.56
Mn	453	±213	0.85	0.49	Mn	0.85
Fe	32623	±969	69.94	39.50	Fe	69.94
Mo	305	0	0	0	0	0
Ni	120	±185	0.41	0.32	Ni	0.41
Total		100.00	100.00		100.00	

2.3 Tooth Contact Studies

Surface contact fatigue is the most common cause of gear failure. It results in damage
to contacting surfaces which can significantly reduce the load-carrying capacity of

components, and may ultimately lead to complete failure of a gear [4]. It has been shown that corrosive wear at tooth fillet can cause pitting, intense localized plastic strain and folds leading to crack formation [6]. The contact and sequence of failure of the gear can be studied by tooth contact study. In this analysis, the failed pinion was revolved on crown wheel by referring the index number given in block cone face of the crown wheel and the shank of the pinion. The gear ratio is 6.1 and the index number of failed teeth of crown wheel is 14, 15, 16 and 26. Table 3 shows tooth contact analysis of crown wheel and pinion.

The failed pinion did not affect all the teeth of crown it mate with. For the failure to occur in all the identified teeth, it is learnt, the crown wheel might have revolved at least six times after the initial failure. The sequence indicates a fairly gradual progression of the damage which ended with the cold weld. The mode of failure of crown wheel is by partial uprooting. The gear teeth have been chipped off from all around the edges of crown wheel. It is revealed that a partial mating between the pinion and crown wheel could have happened due to improper alignment. The misalignment might have developed a high stress between the teeth in contact. This increased load might have resulted in the characteristic teeth chipping.

The sequence in which the failed tooth of the pinion mated with crown wheel is represented in the table given below. Also shown is the level of damage observed during visual inspection. The sequence in which the fracture in crown wheel has occurred is 14, 26, 15, and 16.

Table 3. Tooth contact analysis of crown wheel and pinion

Revolution of crown wheel	Sequence of contact of failed pinion teeth with crown wheel indicating the level of damage						
1	2	8	14 (damaged)	20	26 (damaged)	32	
2	6	12	18	24	30	36	
3	3	9	15 (damaged)	21	27	33	
4	1	7	13	19	25	31	37
5	4	10	16 (damaged)	22	28	34	
6	5	11	17	23	29	36	

2.4 Micro Hardness Test

Micro Vicker's hardness test was done on a sample specimen taken from the crown wheel and the data obtained is shown in Table 4. The hardness values measured from the specimen at varies points are given in the table given below.

Case carburized material has varying hardness from the case to the core. Micro hardness survey gives a better picture on this. For the failed gear, core hardness was measured near the center of base of the damaged tooth. The measured hardness is 276.6 HV, whereas the desired core hardness is between 317 and 401 HV. This means that the failed part had very low case hardness. It can be concluded that the low hardness also contributed to the premature failure (Figs. 4, 5 and 6).

Table 4. The hardness values of crown wheel

S. no	Distance from the surface (mm)	Micro Vickers Hardness (HV 1 kg)
1.	0.1	428.3
2.	0.3	449.8
3.	0.5	453.1
4.	0.7	404.8
5.	0.9	401.3
6.	1.1	439.5
7.	1.3	393.5
8.	1.5	386.1
9.	1.7	382.6
10.	1.9	373.4
11.	2.1	341.5
12.	2.3	340.3
13.	2.4	331.7
14.	2.5	275.7
15.	2.6	293.3
Core hardness	276.6, 283.0, 291.5 HV 1	

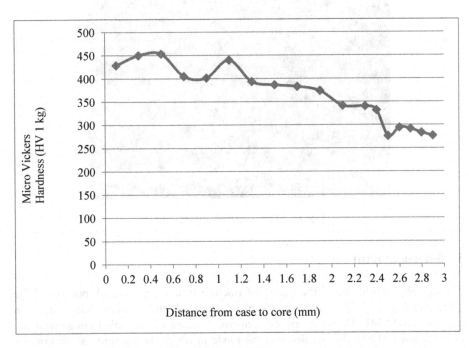

Fig. 4. Micro hardness graph

Fig. 5. SEM image of the failed part

Fig. 6. SEM image of original part

3 Microstructure

Fractography would reveal the nature of fracture in a component. A portion of the failed part was cut and is subjected to micro structural study using scanning electron microscope [SEM]. The case and core micro structure of the failed component are shown below. The study revealed that the mode in which the fracture has occurred is highly brittle in nature. This is evident by the cleavage facets. The SEM images of the specimen are shown in the following figures.

4 Conclusion

The extensive study shows various parameters played their role in different ways causing premature failure of the component. The study implies wrong selection of material as the major cause of failure of the component. Moreover, the manufacturer modification in the selected composition also played an important role. Usage of improper material composition resulted in poor core hardness. Low hardness has resulted in premature failure of the gear. Low case hardness when augmented with misaligned parts assembly has caused severe pitting of the gear teeth.

References

1. Fernandes, P.J.L.: Tooth bending fatigue failures in gears. Eng. Fail. Anal. **3**(3), 219–225 (1996)
2. Alban, L.E.: Systematic Analysis of Gear Failures. ASM International, Russell Township (1985)
3. Boniardi, M., D'Errico, F., Tagliabue, C.: Influence of carburizing and nitriding on failure of gears – a case study. Eng. Fail. Anal. **13**(3), 312–339 (2006)
4. Fernandes, P.J.L., McDuling, C.: Surface contact fatigue failures in gears. Eng. Fail. Anal. **4**(2), 99–107 (1997)
5. Becker, W.T., Shipley, J.R.: Failure Analysis and Prevention. ASM Handbook, vol. 11. ASM International, Russell Township (2002)
6. Abhay, K.J., Diwakar, V.: Metallurgical analysis of failed gear. Eng. Fail. Anal. **9**(3), 359–365 (2002)
7. Fatigue and failures. ASM Handbook, vol. 19 (2002)

Design, Fabrication and Testing of Animal Drawn Multiple Mouldboard Plough

Abebe Firew Guadie[1] and Yonas Mitiku Degu[2(✉)]

[1] Department of Mechanical Engineering, Technology College,
Debre Markos University, Debre Markos, Ethiopia
abe77mulu@gmail.com
[2] Faculty of Mechanical and Industrial Engineering,
Bahir Dar Institute of Technology, Bahir Dar University, Bahir Dar, Ethiopia
yonasm@bdu.edu.et

Abstract. The Ethiopian Ard plough is the most commonly used farm tool in Ethiopia. Nevertheless, using this plough as farm tool is labour intensive, time taking, making shallow depth and narrow cutting width. Thus, this research is initiated to come up with a solution to the aforementioned problems. Therefore, the objectives of this research were to model the basic components of animal drawn multiple mouldboard plough, to fabricate and test the prototype. Eight alternative options were considered for conceptual design among these, without seat to operator, two wheels, two handles and beam attachment design alternative is selected using merit-demerit analysis, pairwise and direct matrix ranking methods. In addition, after the detail design, the prototype is fabricated in Bahir Dar University Institute of Technology Workshop using locally available materials and tested using oxen and horses as draft animals in two most dominant soil types such as Nitrosol and Vertisols at Burie and Gozamin districts of East and West Gojjam Zones of Amhara regional state respectively. The results of the field test reveals that there is a significant difference between Ard plough and the newly designed prototype in time requirements to plough the same plot of land, draft force requirements and cutting width. The newly designed prototype reduces time spent and increasing cutting width during primary tillage. The draft force requirement of both Ard plough and multiple mouldboard plough is higher at Nitrisols than Vertisols. The multiple mouldboard plough cut of width and depth can be adjusted to go along with the available draft animal for optimum field operation performance.

Keywords: Multiple mouldboard plough · Ard plough ·
Merit-demerit analysis · Pairwise comparison · Conceptual design

1 Introduction

The rural population in most developing countries which represents 80–95% are practicing small scale farming. Though the small-scale farming system is of subsistence type, it plays a very important role in the economy of the countries, since the mass of the agricultural production is from this sector. However, agriculture implements used in these countries are inefficient, time consuming and demand a great deal of physical

F. A. Zimale et al. (Eds.): ICAST 2018, LNICST 274, pp. 206–224, 2019.
https://doi.org/10.1007/978-3-030-15357-1_17

strength while putting them in to use. Using these farm implements cannot increase the agriculture productivity unless improved agricultural technologies are used. The history of animal traction in eastern and southern Africa, with the exception of Ethiopia, started with the introduction of ox-plough by the missionaries. In Ethiopia the animal power has been used for thousands of years [1, 2].

The Ethiopian Ard plough called Maresha is using by most of the farmers for seed bed preparation. Maresha is made by wooden parts based on the farmer's experience from locally available wood variety. Pair of ox and horse is the main source of draft animal power in Ethiopia [2] (Fig. 1.).

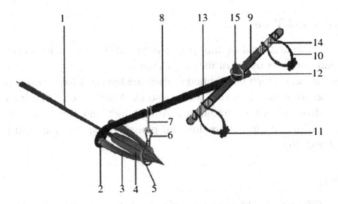

Fig. 1. Parts of Ethiopian Ard plough (Maresha) [5]: (1) handle; (2) wooden pin; (3) side-wing; (4) ploughshare; (5) lower metal loop; (6) upper metal loop; (7) leather stripe or rope (8) beam; (9) yoke; (10) neck holder sticks; (11, 12) leather strap or rope; (13) rubber as washer; (14) leather for safety; (15) centring pin.

Despite, the presence of sufficient livestock population in Ethiopia which can be used as source of draught forces; animal powered technologies are under-utilized due to wrong perception by many decision makers which leads the promotion of animal draught represents being backward. The factors affecting the draught requirements of an animal drawn mouldboard plough are soil type, soil moisture, ploughing speed, depth and width of the furrow slice, mouldboard type, and soil to metal friction characteristics of the soil engaged components [3, 4]. The power requirement of tillage implements is an important design consideration particularly for animal drawn implements, where the power is limited. Several researchers and organizations repeatedly attempted to replace or modify Maresha plough by modern mouldboard plough; farmers rejected the ploughs for its heavy weight, high draft power requirement, difficulty to repair, high cost and, complicated adjustments. Hence they are still using the traditional plough as a farm implement. However, this farm implements are labour intensive, time taking and narrow cutting width. On the contrary, the use of tractors by the peasant farmers is not an economical due to lack of capital, low capability of local industry, lack of skilled personnel, small farm size, and slow industrial development and crop varieties not amendable to tractorization. Thus, it was imperative to modify the present mouldboard plough by increasing the number of mouldboards using light and strong metals to minimize draught power, increase width of slices, enhance speed of operation, and making less labour intensive with minimum cultivation time [5]. Therefore, this study was executed with the objectives of proposing different conceptual design; evaluate, selecting optimum concept, modelling and analysis of the critical components, fabricating and field performance testing of the prototype. For the purpose of validation, comparison of Ard plough and the mould-board plough prototype.

2 Materials and Methods

2.1 Materials and Tools

A pair of ox and horse is used as draft power in the field experiment because of its vast availability and common usage in the study areas.

A pocket balancer which is modified to measure the draft force was prepared in the workshop, in addition ruler and stop watch also used in the field experiment (Fig. 18).

Moreover, two full set of traditional Ard plough and the newly designed and fabricated animal drawn multiple moldboard plough is used on the field performance test (Figs. 19 and 20).

2.2 Methods

In this study, different possible concepts of animal drawn multiple moldboard plough were proposed with its working principles. The proposed alternatives were evaluated against selection parameters. Based on pairwise ranking, the selection parameters prioritized and relative weights were set. Each proposed concepts was evaluated to choose the optimum design by measure its overall performance. Concepts which scored higher total points (sum of the product of the relative weight and scored value out of eleven) are selected and the detail analysis carried out. The analyses end with by providing the geometric dimension of multiple moldboard plough with all mountings and accessories. Then the prototype was fabricated and assembled and floor test was carried out in the workshop. After that, it is brought in to actual field for in-situ test. Once the shop tests are completed it will go for further testing to the actual field test. The experimental sites are East and West Gojjam Zones, Amhara Regional State, Ethiopia dominantly Nitrisols and Vertisoils soil. Finally the test results were recorded and analyzed.

3 Conceptual Design

Conceptual design is the method of developing different ideas by considering the working mechanism and structure of the product. It is also a description of the proposed system in terms of, a set of integrated ideas and concepts, about which a design must do, behave, and accomplish the stated requirements and to be understandable by the users in a way it is applicable [6].

3.1   Animal Drawn Multiple Mouldboard Plough Alternative Design

Four arrangements of multiple mouldboard plough were conceptually proposed depending on; hitch attachments, number of wheels and number of handle and position of operator. Besides each arrangement has two options for the position of the operator (with seat and without seat); number of wheels (one wheel and two wheels); number of handles (one handle and two handles) and for the plough and yoke attachment there are also two options (beam or chain). In relation to the four arrangements twelve options were obtained. However, having seat for the operator on the top of the implement has no relationship with number of handling and one wheel. Therefore eight alternatives were considered for further conceptual development and selection. The proposed conceptual design alternatives were modelled for further understanding of the abstraction as depicted from Figs. 2, 3, 4, 5, 6, 7, 8 and 9.

1. Seat to operator, two wheels and beam attachment (Fig. 2)
2. Seat to operator, two wheels and chain attachment (Fig. 3)
3. Without seat to operator, one wheel, one handle and beam attachment (Fig. 4)
4. Without seat to operator, two wheels, one handle and chain attachment (Fig. 5)
5. Without seat to operator, two wheels, two handles and chain attachment (Fig. 6)
6. Without seat to operator, two wheels, two handles and beam attachment (Fig. 7)
7. Without seat to operator, two wheels, one handle and chain attachment (Fig. 8)
8. Without seat to operator, one wheel, one handle and beam attachment (Fig. 9).

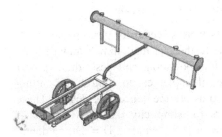

Fig. 2. 1st alternative (conceptual design)

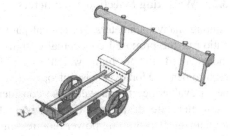

Fig. 3. 2nd alternative (conceptual design)

Fig. 4. 3rd alternative (conceptual design)

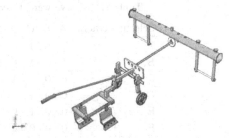

Fig. 5. 4th alternative (conceptual design)

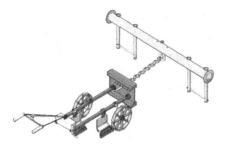

Fig. 6. 5th alternative (conceptual design)

Fig. 7. 6th alternative (conceptual design)

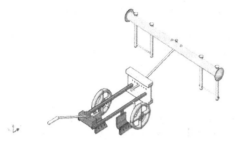

Fig. 8. 7th alternative (conceptual design)

Fig. 9. 8th alternative (conceptual design)

3.2   Weighting Selection Parameters by Pairwise Comparison

Among many parameters, six critical parameters were selected for performance evaluation of the proposed conceptual designs. Due to the fact that animal drawn implements need to be light weight, ease for transportation and less draft power requirements. Moreover ease of operation, ease of implement to control and cutting depth evaluating criteria were also considered to assess the conceptual design. These parameters are designated by alphabetic letters for simplicity (A-F) (A = mass of implement, B = drafting power requirement, C = ease of operation, D = cutting depth, E = ease of implement control and F = ease of transportation).

Table 1. Relative weight assigning by pairwise comparison

Selection criteria	A	B	C	D	E	F	Row total	Relative weight
A	-	0	1	1	1	1	4	4/15 **(0.270)**
B	1	-	1	1	1	1	5	5/15 **(0.330)**
C	0	0	-	0	0	1	1	1/15 **(0.067)**
D	0	0	1	-	0	0	1	1/15 **(0.067)**
E	0	0	1	1	-	1	3	3/15 **(0.200)**
F	0	0	0	1	0	-	1	1/15 **(0.067)**
Total							15	1

Pairwise comparison of the conceptual design selection criteria indicated in Table 1, drafting power requirement with relative weight of (0.330) followed by mass of implement (0.270) and easy of implement control (0.2). Ease of operation, easy of transportation and cutting depth having equal relative weight of (0.067).

3.3   Selection Among Alternative Conceptual Design

Selection of evaluation scheme is important to select the optimum conceptual design. Eleven point scales were chosen to measure the overall performance of the proposed alternative conceptual designs.

Table 2. Selection of variants

Selection criteria	Relative weight	Alternative conceptual design							
		1	2	3	4	5	6	7	8
A	0.2670	3 (0.80)	2 (0.53)	5 (1.34)	5 (1.34)	4 (1.07)	5 (1.35)	6 (1.60)	5 (1.34)
B	0.3300	4 (1.32)	4 (1.32)	4 (1.32)	6 (1.98)	6 (1.98)	7 (2.31)	7 (2.31)	7 (2.31)
C	0.0667	5 (0.34)	6 (0.40)	8 (0.53)	7 (0.47)	7 (0.47)	7 (0.47)	7 (0.46)	6 (0.40)
D	0.0667	10 (0.67)	10 (0.67)	4 (0.27)	6 (0.40)	7 (0.47)	9 (0.60)	7 (0.47)	7 (0.47)
E	0.2000	9 (1.80)	9 (1.80)	3 (0.60)	3 (0.60)	4 (0.80)	5 (1.00)	4 (0.80)	4 (0.80)
F	0.0667	2 (0.13)	3 (0.20)	8 (0.53)	7 (0.47)	6 (0.40)	6 (0.40)	6 (0.40)	6 (0.40)
Total		5.057	4.921	4.59	5.249	5.182	6.112	6.046	5.317
Rank		6th	7th	8th	4th	5th	1st	2nd	3rd

Note: - Numbers outside the parenthesis written in the bold indicate that the given value out of 11 point and those inside the parenthesis is obtained by multiplying the relative weight of each criterion with 11 point scored value.

From the proposed alternative conceptual designs, alternative 6th is selected based on the highest point scored (Table 2), i.e. without seat to operator, two wheels, two handles and beam attachment (Fig. 7).

3.4   Working Principles of the Selected Conceptual Design

From the proposed alternative conceptual design, alternative 6 were selected because of higher scoring result when it is evaluated against the six measuring parameters. The implement working principle is similar to traditional Ard plough, except some parts of implement which are having cut adjustment in depth and width to fit for types of soil, types of land preparation and drafting force requirement (Fig. 10).

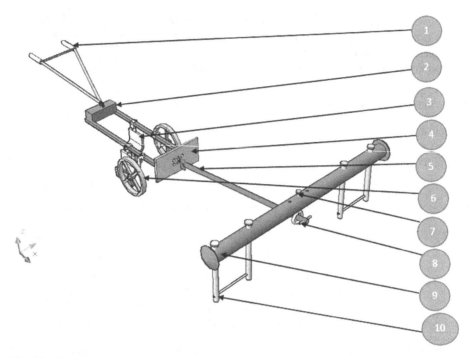

Fig. 10. Features of selected multiple mouldboard plough: (1) handling; (2) handling attachment; (3) mouldboard plough; (4) hitch; (5) beam; (6) wheel; (7) centring pin; (8) beam nose; (9) yoke; (10) neck holder.

4 Detail Design

The detail analysis of all the components and joint were done by taking in to consideration of the following conditions:-

- Pair of ox draft force (F_d) 870 N
- Operator force (F_o) 100–250 N
- The average working speed of ox is 0.63 m/s
- Soil moisture content 0–15%
- Rake angle 20^0
- Wood tensile strength along the grain 5.5 MPa and bearing strength of 2.2 MPa.

4.1 Design of Beam

A beam is a long wooden or metal piece, which connects the main body of the plough to the yoke. The material used as a beam in this research wood because of its light weight and low cost and locally available. Two common types of yokes are head yoke and neck yoke. The neck yoke is the commonly used by Ethiopian farmers.

Force Analysis Between Yoke and Beam

The pulling angle α_1 and α_2 are considered equal ($\alpha_1 = \alpha_2 = \alpha$) and the two animals pulling force F_1 and F_2 are also assumed to be equal ($F_1 = F_2 = F$). The pulling force F_b on the beam can be calculated from condition of equilibrium forces (Fig. 11).

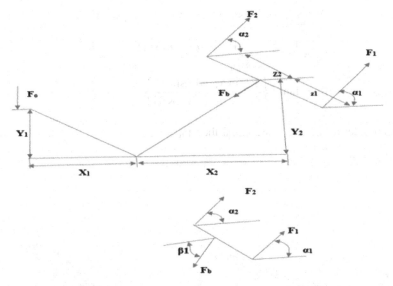

Fig. 11. Free body diagram of force analysis between yoke and beam

It is found from literature review and filed observation the height of animal's and traditional Ard plough beam length is between 1.0 m to 1.4 m and 2.5 m to 3.0 m, respectively. The average animal height of 1.2 m and the smallest beam length of 2.5 m were used for the design (Fig. 12). Using sine law (Eq. 1) the calculated angle is 15°.

$$\frac{\sin 90}{2500} = \frac{\sin \beta_1}{1200 - 550}$$
$$\beta_1 = \sin^{-1}(0.26) = 15° \tag{1}$$

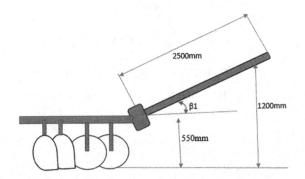

Fig. 12. Dimensions and layout of the beam attachments

The transferred pulling force from the two draught animals to the beam F_b and its angle of action β_1 can be given by Eqs. (2) and (3)

$$\sum F_x = F_1 \cos \alpha_1 + F_2 \cos \alpha_2 = F_b \cos \beta_1 \tag{2}$$

$$\sum F_y = F_1 \sin \alpha_1 + F_2 \sin \alpha_2 = F_B \sin \beta_1 \tag{3}$$

$$F_b = \frac{F_1 \cos \alpha_1 + F_2 \cos \alpha_2}{\cos \beta_1} = \frac{F_1 \sin \alpha_1 + F_2 \sin \alpha_2}{\sin \beta_1}$$

$$\beta_1 = \tan^{-1} \left\{ \frac{F_1 \sin \alpha_1 + F_2 \sin \alpha_2}{F_1 \cos \alpha_1 + F_2 \cos \alpha_2} \right\} \tag{4}$$

By considering β_1 and α are equal then F_b

$$F_d = F_b * \cos \beta_1 \tag{5}$$

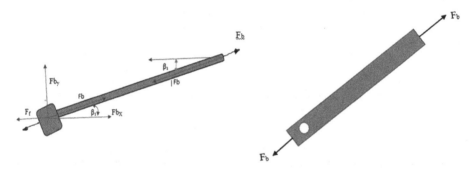

Fig. 13. Free body diagram of beam force

Where, $\beta_1 =$ angle of the beam from the horizontal (Fig. 13).

$$F_d = F_b \cos \beta_1$$
$$F_b = \mathbf{900\,N}$$

$$\sum F_y = F_{by} = F_b \sin \beta_1 = 0 \tag{6}$$

$$\sum F_x = F_{bx} = F_b \cos \beta_1 - F_f = 0$$
$$F_f = \mathbf{900\,N} \tag{7}$$

Stress Analysis of Beam

1. *Tensile stress (σ_t)*

   When a body is subjected to two equal and opposite axial pulls (also called tensile load) then the stress induced at any section of the beam can be calculated as:

$$\sigma_t = F_b/A \tag{8}$$

Where, A = Cross-sectional area of the beam

$$A = \pi \frac{D^2}{4} - D * d = \frac{0.06^2}{4} - 0.06 * 0.01$$
$$A = 0.00223 \, \text{m}^2$$
$$\sigma_t = 403587.4 \, \text{N/m}^2 = 0.4036 \, \text{MPa}$$

The tensile stress induced (0.4036 MPa) on the beam due to the applied force is much less than that the material strength (5.5 MPa), hence the beam is safe for the tensile force acting on it.

Fig. 14. Beam and its cross-sectional area

2. *Bearing stress (σ_b)*

   The induced bearing stress is a localised compressive stress at the surface of contact of the joint between the bolt and the sheet metal and calculated by Eq. 9.

$$\sigma_b = F_b/2td \tag{9}$$

Where t = thickens of sheet metal = 0.004 m

$$d = \text{diameter of bolt} = 0.01 \, \text{m}$$
$$\sigma_b = \frac{900 \, \text{N}}{2 * 0.004 * 0.01} = 1.2125 \, \text{MPa}$$

The bearing stress induce on the beam joint is less that 5.5 MPa, hence the beam is safe for the bearing force acting on it (Fig. 14).

4.2 Design of Hitch

A hitch part which connect the beam and the frame, for this research steel (Fe E 220) IS: 1570 (Part I)-1978 (Reaffirmed 1993) with ultimate tensile strength of 290 MPa and yield strength of 170 MPa is selected due to its low cost, availability and ease to carry the fabrication process (Fig. 15).

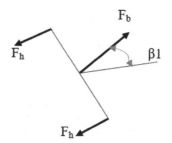

Fig. 15. Free body diagram of hitch

Force Analysis of the Hitch (F_h)

$$\sum F_y = F_b \sin \beta_1 = 0 \tag{10}$$

$$\sum F_z = F_b \cos \beta_1 - 2F_h = 0$$
$$2F_h = F_b \cos \beta_1 = 900\,N \cos 15 = 870\,N \tag{11}$$
$$F_h = 435\,N$$

Stress Analysis of Hitch

1. *Tensile stress (σ_t)*

$$\sigma_t = F_h/A$$
$$A = 4 * t * b = 4 * 0.04\,m * 0.06\,m = 1.6 * 10^{-4}\,m^2$$
$$\sigma_t = 435/1.6 * 10^{-4} = 2.72\,MPa$$

2. *Shear stress (τ)*
   The hitch is connected with the frame by two bolts; hence it should withstand the developed shear stress.

$$\tau = \frac{F_h}{2A} \tag{12}$$

Where diameter of bolt 'd' is 0.01 m

$$A = \frac{\pi d^2}{4} = 7.86 * 10^{-5} \text{m}^2$$
$$\tau = 435/(2 * 7.86 * 10^{-5}) = \mathbf{2.77\,MPa}$$

3. *Bearing stress* (σ_b)

$$\sigma_b = \frac{F_h}{2td}$$
$$\sigma_b = \frac{435}{2 * 0.004 * 0.01} = \mathbf{5.44\,MPa}$$

The tensile stress, shear stress and bearing stress induce on the hitch are lower than the allowable stress limits, hence the hitch is safe to operate.

4.3   Design of Frame

Frame is connecting the wheels, hitch, handling and plough body. The frame is made of steel (Fe E 220) IS: 1570 (Part I)-1978 (Reaffirmed 1993) with ultimate tensile strength of 290 MPa and yield strength of 220 MPa.

Force Analysis of Frame
In order to calculate the force acting on the frame (Fig. 16), it is necessary to consider beam, yoke and hitch forces.

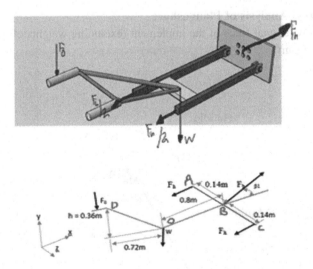

Fig. 16. Free body diagram and force analysis of the frame

The horizontal and vertical components of reaction force and moment on the frame and handle caused by the bolt at sections A, B, C and D were determined by considering equilibrium conditions.

$$\sum F_y = -2F_h + F_b \sin \beta_1 = 0 \qquad (13)$$

From the above calculation F_b and β_1 are known then F_o is:-

$$\sum Mo = -F_o * 0.72 + 2F_h * 0.14 = 0$$

$$F_o = \frac{2Fh * 0.14}{0.72} = \frac{2 * 435 * 0.14}{0.72} = \mathbf{169.2\,N} \qquad (14)$$

Tensile stress

$$\sigma_t = F_h / A$$

$$A = 4 * t * b = 4 * 0.04 * 0.06 = 1.6 * 10^{-4} m^2$$

$$\sigma_t = 435 / 1.6 * 10^{-4} = \mathbf{2.72\,MPa}$$

The tensile stress which is 2.72 MPa is less than the yield strength (170 MPa) of the material, so the frame structure is safe.

4.4   Design of Ploughshare

The share is attached to the frog by welding. It cuts a slice of soil horizontally and starts lifting it to the mouldboard. In ploughshare different forces and stresses are developed then it needs to have hard materials, high strength, and corrosion and wear resistant materials.

Force and Stress Analysis of Ploughshare
Where, V is gravitational force of the implement (excluding weights of the yoke and $\frac{1}{3}$ weights of the beam)

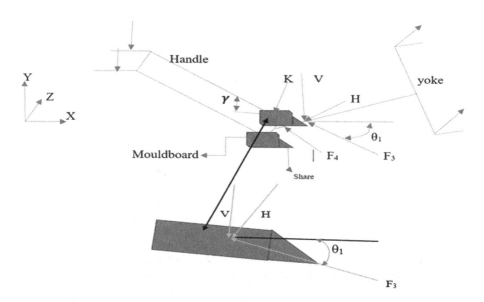

Fig. 17. Free body diagram of ploughshare

H is normal interfacial force of the ploughshare

F_3 is tangential interfacial force of the ploughshare.

From the free body diagram (Fig. 17) H is calculated by taking mass of implement 34 kg and gravitational force of the implement 333 N.

$$\sum F_y = 0 \tag{15}$$

$2F \sin \alpha - F_o - H \sin(90 - \theta_1) + F_3 \sin \theta_1 - V = 0$

$H \sin(90 - \theta_1) = H \cos \theta_1$ \hfill (16)

$$H = \frac{(2F \sin \alpha - Fo + F3 \sin \theta 1 - V)}{\cos \theta 1}$$

$$\sum F_x = 0 \tag{17}$$

$2F \cos \alpha - F_3 \cos \theta_1 - H \cos(90 - \theta_1) = 0$

$$H = \frac{2F \cos \alpha - F_3 \cos \theta_1}{\sin \theta 1} \tag{18}$$

F_3 can be calculated as:

$$\frac{2F \sin \alpha - F_o + F_3 \sin \theta_1 - V}{\cos \theta_1} = \frac{2F \cos \alpha - F3 \cos \theta_1}{\sin \theta_1}$$

$$F_3 = \frac{2F(\cos \alpha \cos \theta_1 - \sin \alpha \sin \theta_1) + V \sin \theta_1 + F_o \sin \theta_1}{\cos^2 \theta 1 + \sin^2 \theta 1} \tag{19}$$

$F_3 = 900(\cos 15 \cos 20 - \sin 15 \sin 20) + 333 \sin 20 + 169.2 \sin 20$

$F_3 = 737.24 + 113.9 + 57.87 = 909 \, N$

Normal interfacial force of the ploughshare can be calculated as:

$$H = \frac{2 * 450 \cos 15 - 909 \cos 20}{\sin 20}$$

$$H = 44.30 \, N$$

Area of penetration of ploughshare at the end of share 4 mm * 2 mm

$$A = 8 * 10^{-6} m^2$$

Force of penetration (F_3) 909 N

$$\sigma = F_3/A = 113.62 \, MPa$$

The stress induced due to the penetration force on the ploughshare is less than the allowable limit; hence the part withstands the stress generated.

5   Results and Discussion

For the selected conceptual design of animal drawn multiple mouldboard plough, a detail design and analysis were performed and based on the result the prototype was fabricated for further test and modification. A prototype multiple mouldboard plough was fabricated at Bahir Dar Institute of Technology, Bahir Dar University (BIT-BDU) Mechanical Engineering workshops. The implement were tested in Burie and Gozamn districts at Nitosols and Vertisols in different soil moister content for primary tillage.

5.1   Results of Field Performance Test

In this research traditional Ard plough and multiple moldboard plough draft force requirement for the primary tillage was measured by modifying pocket balance to act as spring dynamometer.

Fig. 18. Multiple mouldboard plough spring dynamometer setup [Photo by the authors]

The field test was done on two types of plot (Nitosols and Vertisol) and the following result was found and tabulated in Tables 3 and 4.

5.2   Discussion

The conceptual design was made considering six important parameters (weight of implement, drafting power, ease of operation, cutting depth, implement control and transportation) and its relative weight of importance were prioritized by using pairwise ranking method. From the eight proposed alternative design options, the optimum design (Without seat to operator, two wheels, two handles and beam attachment) is selected fabrication and field test. The detail analysis of the selected concept was done and the parts are fabricated and assembled. Preliminary test was made on the farmer's

Fig. 19. Ard plough spring dynamometer setup [Photo by the authors]

Table 3. Ard (Maresha) plough primary tillage filed performance test result

Types of soils	Cutting depth [cm]	Cutting width [cm]	Draft [N]
Nitosols	14	16–18	883–922
Vertisols	15	18–19	883–902

Table 4. Multiple mouldboard plough primary tillage filed performance test result on Nitosols and Vertisol

Cutting depth [cm]	Soil types			
	Nitrosol		Vertisol	
	Cutting width [cm]	Draft [N]	Cutting width [cm]	Draft [N]
12	28	687–706	28	667–706
14	28	755–785	28	726–765
16	28	863–883	28	863–883
18	28	Difficult to pull	28	981

plot and necessary modification was carried out from the test result and the farmers' opinion. Further, field performance was studied on the new implement.

The test was performed on five plot of land for both Ard and multiple mouldboard plough for primary tillage. The data are recorded and analyzed. The results obtained during the test are depicted from Table 5, 6, 7 and 8. The farmers' opinion towards, the implement was positive with respect to its simplicity of harnessing, adjustment and operation. The newly modified farm implement at Nitosols and Vertisols, which showed satisfactory and good results, respectively.

Fig. 20. Multiple mouldboard plough filed performance test setup [Photo by the authors]

Also it is found that the mass of the multiple mouldboard plough is greater than the traditional Ard plough, but this does not affect the field performance due to the fact that the mass will be supported by the two wheels. The wheels also allow moving easily; hence the farmer could harness and pull by animals from home to the field yard.

The draft power requirement of primary tillage at Nitrisols of the multiple mouldboard plough was found less by 17.9% than the Ard plough, even though, the width of cut of the multiple mould board plough was wider by 65% (Table 5). Similarly, at Vertisols the draft force requirement for the multiple mouldboard plough was reduced by 19.7% than the Ard plough, though the width of cut was increased by 55.6% (Table 6). The draft force requirement of both Ard plough and multiple mouldboard plough is higher by 1.1% and 2.7% respectively at Nitrisols than Vertisols. The power requirement for both the ard plough and multiple mouldboard plough was slightly larger at Nitrisols than Vertisols (Tables 7 and 8). Multiple mouldboard plough width of cut and depth of cut can be adjusted to go well with the available draft animal for optimum field operation performance.

Table 5. Comparison of cutting width, depth, draft force of Ard plough and multiple mouldboard plough at Nitrisols

Types of plough	Cutting depth [cm]	Cutting width [cm]	Draft [N]
Ard plough	14	17	902
Multiple mouldboard plough	14	28	765

Table 6. Comparison of cutting width, depth, draft force of Ard plough and multiple mouldboard plough at Vertisols

Types of plough	Cutting depth [cm]	Cutting width [cm]	Draft [N]
Ard plough	14	18	892
Multiple mouldboard plough	14	28	745

Table 7. Comparison of drafting power requirement for Ard plough with multiple mouldboard plough in Nitosols

Types of plough	Draft [N]	Power [w]	Mass [kg]
Ard plough	883–912	0.92	27.5
Multiple mouldboard plough	755–785	0.78	33.8

Table 8. Comparison of drafting power requirement for Ard plough with multiple mouldboard plough in Vertisols

Types of plough	Draft [N]	Power [w]	Mass [kg]
Ard plough	883–902	0.91	27.5
Multiple mouldboard plough	755–785	0.76	33.8

6 Conclusions

The mass of the complete set of newly designed plough was found 33.8 kg and the Ard plough having an average of 27.5 kg. Though the newly designed mouldboard plough having larger mass but, due to the fact that the mass is not totally carried by the draft animal. The effects of the wheels also reduce the magnitude of the sliding friction. Hence multiple mouldboard plough demonstrated higher field operation performance than the Ard plough.

The field test result showed that, while comparing the Ard plough with multiple mouldboard plough at Nitrisols soil, the multiple mouldboard plough reduced the ploughing time by 39.3% in same cutting depth. While comparing Ard plough with that of multiple mouldboard plough at Vertisols soil fror primary tillage, the multiple mouldboard plough reduced the ploughing time by 35.7%. Multiple mouldboard plough also reduced drafting power 15.2% in Nitrisols and 16.5% Vertisols compared to Ard plough. The draft force requirement of Ard plough and multiple mouldboard plough was found higher by 1.1% and 2.7% respectively at Nitrisols than Vertisols. The newly designed multiple mouldboard plough, cut of width and depth can be adjusted to go well with the available draft animal for optimum field operation performance.

References

1. Solomon, G., et al.: Animal drawn tillage, the Ethiopian ard plough, maresha. a review. soil and tillage Res. **89**, 129–143 (2005)
2. Solomon, G., et al.: Design of the ethiopian ard plough using structural analysis validated with finite element analysis. J. Biosyst. Eng. **97**, 27–39 (2007)
3. Smolders, S.: Measurement of draught requirement of ard plough working in vertisol of Ethiopian highlands. Thesis for: Master of Science in bio-systems engineering (2006)
4. Loukanov, I.A., Uziak, J., Michálek, J.: Draught requirements of enamel coated animal drawn mouldboard plough. J. Res. Agri. Eng. **51**(2), 56–62 (2005)
5. Astatke, A., Mohammed-Saleem, M.A.: Experience with the use of a single ox for cultivation in the Ethiopian highlands. In: Animal Traction Network for Eastern and Southern Africa Workshop, Lusaka, Zambia (1992)
6. Hurst, K.: Engineering Design Principles, 1st edn. Elsevier, Amsterdam (1999)

Design, Construction and Testing of Hybrid Solar-Biomass Cook Stove

Bisrat Yilma Mekonnen[1]([⊠]) and Abdulkadir Aman Hassen[2]

[1] Faculty of Mechanical and Industrial Engineering,
Bahir Dar Institute of Technology, Bahir Dar University, Bahir Dar, Ethiopia
bisratyilma20@gmail.com
[2] Faculty of Mechanical and Industrial Engineering,
Addis Ababa Institute of Technology, Addis Ababa University,
Addis Ababa, Ethiopia
abdiaman2004@yahoo.com

Abstract. Many investigations have been conducted in biomass stoves to improve performances and minimize unfavorable effect on both human health and global climate. Solar cookers are also great area of investigation which can cook food without burning any wood. But a solar cooker cannot replace the traditional energy source completely; even in the sunniest regions there will be days and hours the sun doesn't provide enough power to cook meal. Recent researches and investigations are focused on improving the efficiency of existing only biomass or only solar cookers and there is a research gap in combining solar and biomass for cooking. A combined cook stove is another research dimension for intervention with an intention of using the benefit of the free solar energy to save biomass fuel. In this work, design, fabrication, and testing of portable solar-biomass combined cook stove have been done. The test was done by using only biomass, only solar and combined energy sources for cooking. The results show that the biomass stove with reflectors under the sun gives a 5% thermal efficiency rise and 6 g/L reduction in fuel consumption when compared to the only biomass stove. When only solar box oven used the first figure of merit was found to be 0.12 and second figure of merit found to be 0.55.

Keywords: Solar-biomass combined cook stove · Water boiling test · Figure of merit

1 Introduction

Traditional and inefficient ways of cooking using biomass have harsh effect on both human health and global climate. Also too much dependence on biomass energy minimize agricultural productivity, crop residues and animal wastes which can supplement soil nutrition. Similarly, scarcities of wood has become more serious; rural household who depend on collecting free wood have to travel long distances to obtain wood fuel which causes loss of human availability for productive work. Especially, in regions where biomass is scarce, time and effort spent to gather firewood can be a significant burden on households, particularly children and women. Furthermore, wood fuel depletion will promote deforestation and lead to a general degradation. The energy

© ICST Institute for Computer Sciences, Social Informatics and Telecommunications Engineering 2019
Published by Springer Nature Switzerland AG 2019. All Rights Reserved
F. A. Zimale et al. (Eds.): ICAST 2018, LNICST 274, pp. 225–238, 2019.
https://doi.org/10.1007/978-3-030-15357-1_18

problem in Ethiopia is not much use of non-renewable energy sources; instead the problem is one form of energy reliance which is on wood fuel being consumed at an unsustainable rate. People in developing countries like Ethiopia burn biomass fuel to meet home energy needs for heating and cooking. In Ethiopia majority of the population cooks their food and bake the most popular food called Injera on an open fire inside or outside of their homes by burning various forms of biomass such as wood, charcoal, crop residues and dung. Burning each of these biomass fuels emits dangerous chemicals and large amounts of particulates, which have adverse effect on human health, global climate and regional ecosystems [1].

The government and non-governmental organizations have been struggling to provide people with cleaner and more efficient cook stoves as an alternative to traditional cooking methods. Great improvements have been made in cook stove technology. Examples of such improvements include reducing fuel usage of the stove by increasing thermal or heat transfer efficiency and reducing harmful particulate matters by increasing the combustion efficiency. All these improvements have allowed stove designers and manufacturers to provide more effective improved cook stoves to the people who need them. Despite, these considerable and appreciable improvements in cook stove performance many households in developing countries like Ethiopia still rely on inefficient stoves and procedures to cook their food because they cannot afford an improved stove imported. An effective way to provide people with better cooking options is designing cooking technologies that are appropriate for local socioeconomic conditions and cooking culture and seeking an opportunity to transform them into valuable assets.

Improved cook stoves can be designed and constructed depending on the local conditions. A comprehensive review of 50 different cook stove models tested by MacCarty, and found that, the fuel use was reduced by 33%, in comparison to the three-stone fire [2]. Other different studies conducted to assess the performance and use of household biomass cook stoves under field conditions in Africa, Asia and southern America [3–6]. Generally current investigations are intended to improve combustion and heat transfer to the pot, with the aim of improving stove efficiency and reducing pollutant emissions [7]. Solar cookers can be an alternative for the limitations of biomass cookers which is a device that cooks food using only sun energy in the form of solar radiation without consuming fuels or heating up the kitchen. However, the sale and distribution of solar cookers seems did not get off the ground because of its limitation. Different studies conducted to evaluate the performance and usability of solar cookers [8–12].

This study was motivated to use both the benefit of biomass stove and solar reflectors to add up their gain through combined performance and use interchangeably when appropriate to use only biomass or only solar energy. Current researches are focused on improving efficiency of existing cook stoves. A combined cooking system is another research dimension for intervention. In this study the basic features of solar box and biomass cooker investigated to combine them for cooking, which will enable to save dry fuel by using the benefit of the free solar energy.

2 Methodology

2.1 Design Considerations

Design considerations include size, material cost, durability, fuel efficiency, ease of use, cost to customer, marketability, approximate cooking time, indoor air pollution, assembly, safety, maintenance, availability of materials, solar energy potential, optical properties of the reflecting material, cooking power or overall efficiency, daily cooking time, amount of food to be cooked and type of use.

2.2 Sizing Methodology

The stove is designed to meet the cooking energy requirement of a family of six members. The stove size was estimated as follows.

Step 1: Estimation of energy needed which refers to the amount of heat that needs to be supplied by the stove to cook.
Step 2: Estimation of energy Input which indicates the amount of energy given in terms of fuel to be fed into the stove.
Step 3: Estimation of the size based on the energy requirement.

From the estimation maximum of 3600 kJ/h energy is needed for one time use of the cooker. The amount of energy needed in terms of fuel to be fed into the stove is found to be 0.5 kg biomass per hour. Next step is estimating the size of the combustion chamber which should be enough to take an enough amount of wood needed for cooking. The combustion chamber size is a function of a number of variables such as the required time to operate the burning, the burning rate and the density of biomass wood. The diameter and height of the combustion chamber or the furnace is found to be 0.12 m and 0.2 m respectively.

2.3 Material Selection Methodology

The combined stove was constructed from different materials in which number of criteria was considered for the selection of construction materials. The criterion includes affordability, strength, availability, weight, machinability, heat resistance, melting point of the material, reflectivity. For selection a numeric decision matrix is used to compare solution variants or candidate materials against one another using specific criteria that were mentioned above. Based on decision matrix, mild steel sheet is selected to construct the combined stove's body. Portland cement is selected to construct the combustion chamber insulation, and aluminum is selected for a reflector. Mild steel is also selected for fuel grate and glass wool for solar box insulation.

2.4 Combustion Air Requirement

The quantity of air to be supplied for the combustion process is determined by the chemical composition of eucalyptus tree. For an actual air supply which is 20% in excess of stoichiometry, actual air-fuel ratio is found to be 6.96 kg air/kg fuel. The area of air opening of the stove for combustion air inlet was checked.

2.5 Design Description

The stove has one opening and the fuel is putted over the grate, after cooking ash can be collected under the grate. The biomass stove is circular consisting of combustion chamber in which surrounded by insulating material to prevents heat losses (Fig. 1).

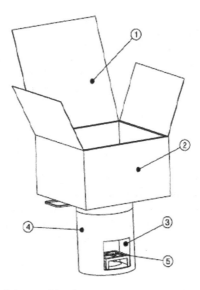

Fig. 1. Pictorial drawing of the combined stove (1- Reflector, 2- Box, 3- Combustion chamber insulation, 4 - Stove body, 5 - Fuel grate)

When the biomass is used fully the reflector can be dropped down to each sides. But the box is used to retain some heat.

2.6 Heat Transfer

It is known that huge amount of heat is lost to the ambient environment conduction, convection, and radiation. Therefore, to minimize the losses and maximize the useful heat transfer to the cooking vessel a careful analysis of heat transfer mechanisms is very important to predict the losses and to minimize the losses through modifications. Each heat transfer modes have losses and gains. The losses are associated with heat that is transferred into the stove body or out to ambient while the gains are associated with heat that is transferred to the cooking vessel. Heat Transfer contribution with losses and gains quantified and Summarizes in Fig. 2.

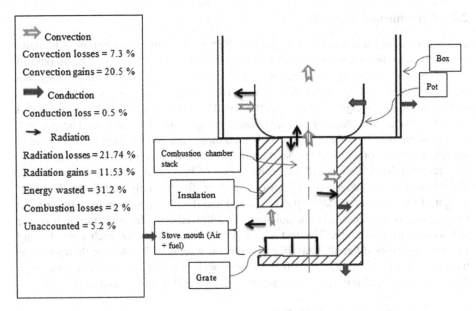

Fig. 2. Schematic of stove cross-section with heat transfer modes contribution.

2.7   Method of Fabrication

The following steps were implemented to construct the combined stove.

- Dimensions were specified for all components and material selected according to the function as it was discussed in the material selection.
- Parts/components were fabricated separately in metal shop.
- Parts were assembled in the way that disassembly is possible.
- Painting and other esthetic was completed.

Table 1. Process and tool required to construct the combined stove

Process	Tooling required
Shearing bulk stock to size	Sheet metal shearing press
Blanking of inlets/fuel opening	Sheet metal blanking press
Rolling into tube form	Sheet metal bend roller
Seaming of edges to form finished tube	Sheet metal vertical seaming machine
Permanent attachment	Welding machine
Attachment of top box to the stove	Force fit and Rivet Gun
Attachment of reflectors to the box	Hinge and lock
Painting	Spray

2.8   Experimental Methods

The water boiling test was done to measure performance metrics when only biomass was used and when biomass is used with the reflectors under sunshine. The amount of same type fuel wood was weighed for each series of tests. The cooking vessel and thermocouple were weighed before a measured amount of water was poured to the pot to determine the final weight of the water after test. The weighed fuel wood was introduced into the combustion chamber and kerosene was sprinkled for ignition. The pot was placed on the stove and the time, the ambient temperature and the initial temperature of the water were recorded. The temperature of the water was recorded at intervals of five minutes until the water reached the boiling point of Bahir Dar which is around 94 °C. The pot was then removed from the stove, and the fire instantly putted out. The final weight of the remaining water, charcoal, wood and the final temperature of water were then measured and recorded. The hot start test followed after the cold start high power test with same procedure. The test was repeated three times for each case. During experimental work different measuring instruments were used like K-type thermocouple (accuracy ± 1.0 °C, resolutions 1.0 °C), digital weight measuring device, contact type thermometer, digital infrared thermometer and stopwatch (Table 1 and Figs. 3, 4).

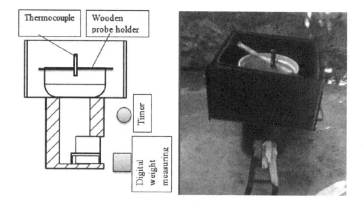

Fig. 3. Water boiling test set up without reflectors (only biomass)

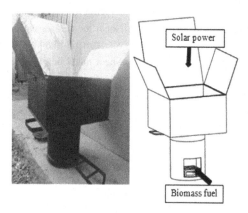

Fig. 4. Water boiling test with reflector

3 Result and Discussion

Variables that are directly measured

f_{hi}	Weight of fuel before test (grams)
P_{hi}	Weight of Pot with water before test (grams)
T_{hi}	Water temperature before test (°C)
t_{hi}	Time at start of test (min)
f_{hf}	Weight of wood after test (grams)
c_h	Weight of charcoal and container after test
p_{hf}	Weight of Pot with water after test (grams)
T_{hf}	Water temperature after test (°C)
t_{hf}	Time at end of test (min)

Variables that are calculated are listed below [7].

Temperature adjusted time to boil pot

$$\Delta t_h^T = (t_{hf} - t_{hi}) \times \frac{75}{(T_{hf} - T_{hi})} \tag{1}$$

Thermal efficiency

$$h_h = \frac{4.186 \times (p_{hi} - p) \times (T_{hf} - T_{hi}) + 2260 \times (w_{hv})}{f_{hd} \times LHV} \tag{2}$$

Burning rate (grams/min)

$$r_{hb} = \frac{f_{hd}}{t_{hi} - t_{hf}} \tag{3}$$

Specific fuel consumption (grams/grams water)

$$sc_h = \frac{f_{hd}}{p_{hf} - p} \tag{4}$$

Temperature corrected specific consumption

$$sc_h^T = \frac{f_{hd}}{p_{hf} - p} \times \frac{75}{(T_{hf} - T_{hi})} \tag{5}$$

Firepower (W)

$$FP_h = \frac{f_{hd} \times LHV}{60 \times (t_{hi} - t_{hf})} \tag{6}$$

Where, LHV is net calorific value (dry wood) (MJ/kg), P is dry weight of empty pot (grams), w_{hv} Water vaporized (grams), f_{hd} is equivalent dry wood consumed (grams).

3.1 Performance Merit Tests When Biomass Is Used with and Without Solar Reflector

The average test results of the stove when only biomass is used is shown in Table 2 and both biomass and solar used with the help of a reflectors is shown in Table 3. The results show that the biomass stove has an average thermal efficiency of 36.9%, temperature corrected specific energy consumption of 886 kJ/L and temperature corrected specific fuel consumption of 47 g/L in cold start high power water boiling test when only biomass is used.

Table 2. Summary of average boiling test results when only biomass is used.

Test phase	Unit	Cold start average	Hot start average
High power WBT			
Time to boil pot	min	18	17
Temp-corrected time to boil	min	19	18
Burning rate	g/min	7	7
Thermal efficiency	%	36.9	39
Specific fuel consumption	g/liter	46	42
Temp-corrected specific fuel consumption	g/liter	47	44
Temp-corrected specific energy cons.	KJ/liter	886	835
Firepower	Watts	2126.4	2083

Table 3. Summary of average water boiling test results when biomass is used with the help of solar reflectors.

Test phase	Unit	Cold start average	Hot start average
High power WBT			
Time to boil Pot	min	17	15
Temp-corrected time to boil	min	18	16
Burning rate	g/min	6	7
Thermal efficiency	%	41.9	43
Specific fuel consumption	g/liter	40	38
Temp-corrected specific fuel consumption	g/liter	41	40
Temp-corrected specific energy cons.	KJ/liter	772	751

The water boiling tests was done by raising the reflector under sunshine intended to measure performance metrics and compares it with previous water boiling test when biomass is only used. The results show in Table 3 that the biomass stove with reflector under sun has an average thermal efficiency of 41.9%, temperature corrected specific energy consumption of 772 kJ/L and temperature corrected specific fuel consumption of 41 g/L in cold start water boiling test. This indicates 5% rise in thermal efficiency and average 6 g/L fuel consumption saving when compared to when only biomass is used separately.

The performance test of the constructed box type solar cooker was tested using two major testing standards for evaluating a solar cooker throughout the world. Which are American Society of Agricultural Engineering Standard and the Bureau of Indian Standard [13]. Bureau of Indian Standard highlighted two methods of test: a stagnation test (test without load), and a load test [14]. Stagnation temperature and the rise in temperature inside the cooker were recorded without load. The stagnation temperature, ambient temperature and absorber plate temperature were measured for different time of the day. The tests with load were done by placing a water-filled vessel in the cooker. The absorber plate temperature, ambient temperature, water temperature, solar radiations were measured.

3.2   Performance Measures

The performance evaluation of the solar box cooker involve estimation of the following parameters: First figure of merit (F_1), Second figure of merit (F_2) and cooker's efficiency. The first figure of merit (F_1) of a solar box cooker is defined as the ratio of optical efficiency and the overall heat loss coefficient (U_L).

$$F_1 = \frac{\eta_0}{U_L} \qquad (7)$$

Experimentally,

$$F_1 = \frac{T_{PS} - T_{as}}{H_S} \qquad (8)$$

Where T_{ps}, T_{as} and H_s are stagnation temperature, average ambient temperature and solar radiation intensity respectively.

The second figure of merit (F_2) is evaluated under full load condition and can be expressed by the expression as follows:

$$F_2 = \frac{F_1(m_w C_w)}{A_t} \ln\left\{\frac{1 - \frac{1}{F_1}\left(\frac{T_{w1} - T_a}{H}\right)}{1 - \frac{1}{F_1}\left(\frac{T_{w2} - T_a}{H}\right)}\right\} \qquad (9)$$

Where F_1 is first figure of merit (Km^2w^{-1}), m_w is the mass of water as load (kg), C_w is the specific heat capacity of water (J/kg°C), T_a is the average ambient temperature (°C), H is the average solar radiation incident on the aperture of the cooker (W/m^2), T_{w1} is the initial water temperature (°C), T_{w2} is the final water temperature (°C), A is the aperture area (m^2) and t is the time difference between T_{w1} and T_{w2} (s).

3.3   Cooker Efficiency

The overall thermal efficiency of the solar box cooker is found mathematically as follows:

$$\eta_U = \frac{m_w Cw \Delta T}{I_{av} A_{c\Delta t}} \tag{10}$$

Where η_u denotes the overall thermal efficiency of the solar cooker; m_w, mass of water (kg); C_w, Specific heat of water (J/kg/°C); ΔT, the change in temperature between the maximum temperature of the cooking fluid and the ambient air temperature; Ac, the aperture area (m^2) of the cooker; Δt, time required to achieve the maximum temperature of the cooking fluid; I_{av}, the average solar intensity (W/m²) during time interval Δt (Fig. 5).

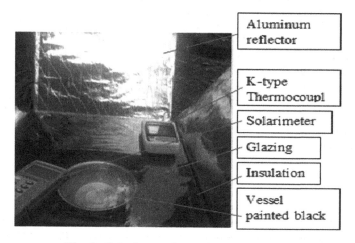

Fig. 5. Solar box cooker performance set up

Stagnation temperature tests, thermal load test or heat up condition test and cooking power estimation was performed based on procedure for testing the solar cookers developed by American Society of Agricultural Engineering (ASAE) Standard S580 and the Bureau of Indian Standard [13]. The stagnation temperature, ambient temperature and absorber plate temperature were measured from different time of the day. The box-type solar cooker was placed in the open sun without load; Type "k" thermocouples were attached to the solar cooker to measure both the cooker and ambient temperatures consecutively at a given interval until the stagnation condition was gotten. Intensity of total solar radiation on horizontal surface was measured, and recorded at a regular interval using digital radiation solarimeter. Also loading test was done by placing a water-filled pot in the cooker. The absorber plate temperature, ambient temperature, water temperature, solar radiations were measured.

3.4   Stagnation Temperature Test

The stagnation temperature test was conducted to evaluate the first figure of merit (F_1) of solar cooker. The test was started at 10:00 a.m. local time until the maximum plate temperature (128 °C), which occurred at 1:00 pm as shown in the Fig. 6. F_1 is calculated to be 0.12 where this value should be greater than 0.12 to be marked as A-Grade solar cooker [15]. The lower value of first figure of merit is because of convection and radiation losses from the bottom side of the cooker and leakage between the single glazing and ambient.

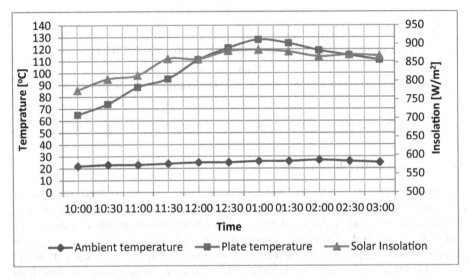

Fig. 6. Stagnation temperature test result of solar cooker.

3.5   Thermal Load Test or Heat up Condition Test

The thermal load test was conducted to determine the second figure of merit F_2 and evaluated under full-load condition. The solar box cooker was loaded with 2 kg of water which can be used for small cookers in an aluminum cooking vessel painted black; the water temperature was initially above the ambient temperature. Results are shown in the Fig. 7. It is clearly seen that the water temperature increases towards the noon period, then decreases towards evening. The figure shows that the maximum water temperature (reaches the boiling point) was achieved during mid-day around 1:30 PM. The variation of temperature throughout the day is due to the fact that the solar radiation is not constant throughout the day and reaching maximum at noon.

Second figure of merit was calculated using Eq. 9 for the water temperature between $T_{w1} = 65$ °C and $T_{w2} = 95$ °C; average solar insolation found is 839 W/m^2 and the average ambient temperature was 25.5 °C. Second figure of merit was computed to be 0.55 which is greater than recommended standard value of 0.40 [7]. It shows that there is a good heat transfer to the contents in the vessel.

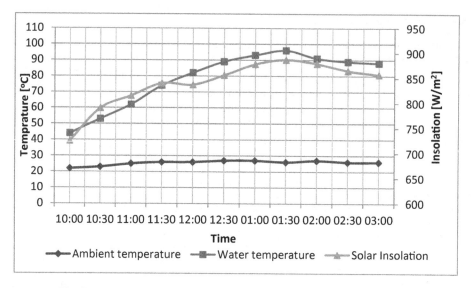

Fig. 7. Water heat up test of solar cooker for second figure of merit (F_2)

3.6   Cooking Power Estimation

The Cooking power experiment was conducted based on international standard of American Society of Agricultural Engineers (ASAE) procedure. Experiment was conducted for the load of 2.0 kg of water. The average cooking power P is the rate of useful energy available during heating period. It may be determined as a product of the change in water temperature for each interval and mass and specific heat capacity of the water. Dividing the product by the time (10-min intervals according to American Society of Agricultural Engineers) contained in a periodic interval yields the cooking power in Watts:

$$P = \frac{(mC_w)(T_2 - T_1)}{600} \tag{11}$$

Where P is interval cooking power (W), T_1 is initial water temperature (°C), T_2 is final water temperature (°C), M is mass of water (kg), and C_w is specific heat capacity (4186 J/kgK).

To determine the standardizing cooking power, P_s, from the cooking power, P, each interval is corrected to a standard insolation of 700 W/m²:

$$P_S = \frac{P \times 700}{I_S} \tag{12}$$

Where Ps is standardized cooking power (W), P is interval cooking power (W), and I_s is interval average solar insolation (W/m²).

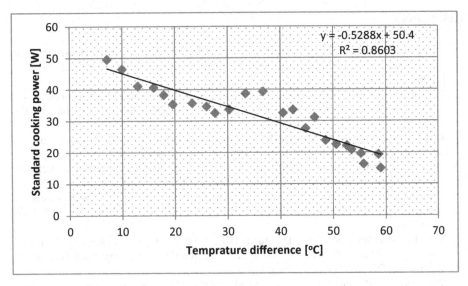

Fig. 8. Standard cooking power plotted over temperature difference.

The Solar cooker was exposed to the sun at 10:00 a.m. to 2:00 p.m., initial and final temperature of water, ambient temperature, and solar insolation were recorded at 10 min interval. Standard cooking power (P_s) is plotted against the difference between water temperature and ambient temperature (T_d) as shown in Fig. 8. The value of the coefficient of determination (R^2) of the regression equation is 0.86 which is greater than the recommended standard value 0.75. The cooking power at 50 °C temperature difference was calculated using the regression equation, P_{50} is to be 24 W.

3.7   Over All Cooker Thermal Efficiency

The overall thermal efficiency of the solar box cooker was calculated to be 34.6% (m_w, mass of water is 2 kg; C_w, Specific heat of water is 4186 J/kg^{0}C; ΔT, temperature difference between the maximum temperature of the cooking fluid and the ambient air temperature is 68.5 °C; A_c, the aperture area is 0.16 m^2; Δt, time required to achieve the maximum temperature of the cooking fluid is 12,600 s; I_{av}, the average solar intensity is 828.5 W/m^2 during time interval Δt.

4   Conclusion

The study shows that the solar- biomass combination system for cooking promotes lower daily fuel consumption by using the benefit of the free solar energy and season independent cooking since biomass can act when the solar is not enough. The biomass stove with reflector under the sun gives a 5% thermal efficiency rise. Improving the existing model and modifications could be made in the future studies.

References

1. Rehfuess, E., Mehta, S., Prüss-Üstun, A.: Assessing household solid fuel use: multiple implications for the millennium development goals. Environ. Health Perspect. **3**, 373–387 (2006)
2. MacCarty, N., Still, D., Ogle, D.: Fuel use and emissions performance of fifty cooking stoves in the laboratory and related benchmarks of performance. Energy. Sustain. Dev. **14**, 161–171 (2010)
3. Berrueta, V., Edwards, R., Masera, O.: Energy performance of wood-burning cook stoves in Michoacan, Mexico. Renewable Energy **33**(5), 859–870 (2008)
4. Sutar, K.B., Kohli, S., Ravi, M.R., Ray, A.: Biomass cook stoves: a review of technical aspects. Renew. Sustain. Energy Rev. **41**, 1128–1166 (2015)
5. Kshirsagar, M.P., Kalamkar, V.R.: A comprehensive review on biomass cookstoves and a systematic approach for modern cookstove design. Renew. Sustain. Energy Rev. **30**, 580–603 (2014)
6. Still, D., MacCarty, N., Ogle, D., Bond, B.T., Bryden, M.: Test Results of Cookstove Performance. Cottage Grove, OR: Aprovecho Research Center, London: Shell Foundation; Washington DC: U.S. Environmental Protection Agency (2011)
7. Winiarski, L.: Design Principles for Wood Burning Cook Stoves. Aprovecho Research Center, Partnership for Clean Indoor Air, Shell Foundation (2005)
8. Gebray, B.: Theoretical Modeling and Experimental Analysis of Box Solar Cooker. M.Sc. Thesis, Department of Mechanical Engineering, EiT – M, Mekelle University (2012)
9. Testing and Reporting Solar Cooker Performance, ASAE S580 JAN03. http://solarcooking. org/asae_test_std.pdf. Accessed May 2017
10. Sethi, V.P., Pal, D.S., Sumathy, K.: performance evaluation and solar radiation capture of optimally inclined box type solar cooker with parallelepiped cooking vessel design. Energy Convers. Manag. **81**, 231–241 (2014)
11. Cuce, E., Cuce, P.M.: A comprehensive review on solar cookers. Appl. Energy **87**, 1399–1421 (2013)
12. Rikoto, I.I., Garba, I.: Comparative analysis on solar cooking using box type solar cooker with finned cooking pot. Int. J. Mod. Eng. Res. **3**(3), 1290–1294 (2013)
13. Mirdha, U.S., Dhariwal, S.R.: Design optimization of solar cooker. Renewable Energy **33**, 530–544 (2008)
14. Ayoola, M.A., Sunmonu, L.A., Bashiru, M.I., Jegede, O.O.: Measurement of net all-wave radiation at a tropical location, Ile-Ife, Nigeria. Atmósfera **27**(3), 305–315 (2014)
15. Mullick, S.C., et al.: Testing of box-type solar cooker: second figure of merit F2 and its variation with load and number of pots. Sol. Energy **57**, 409–413 (1999)

Design and Analysis of Low-Transition Address Generator

Sivasankaran Saravanan[1]([✉]), Mikias Hailu[2], G. Mohammed Gouse[3],
Mohan Lavanya[4], and R. Vijaysai[4]

[1] College of Engineering, Debre Berhan University, Debre Berhan, Ethiopia
saran@dbu.edu.et
[2] Electrical and Computer Engineering Department, Debre Berhan University,
Debre Berhan, Ethiopia
hailumikias@dbu.edu.et
[3] College of Computing, Debre Berhan University, Debre Berhan, Ethiopia
galety.143@dbu.edu.et
[4] School of Computing, SASTRA Deemed University,
Thanjavur, Tamilnadu, India
m_lavanyass@ict.sastra.edu, vijaysai@it.sastra.edu

Abstract. In high-speed Nano-scale VLSI designs, memory plays a vital role of operation. Built-In Self-Test (BIST) for memory is an essential element of the system-on-chip (SoC). Investigating memory with low power techniques have been emerging in the market. Address generators to access memory cores consecutively should have low transition. This paper, attempted to put forward a proposed architecture of address generator with low-transition. In this novel technique, the address generator is constructed by a blend of modulo-counter and binary to gray code convertor with a bit-reversal block. Efficient employment of this architecture has cut-down the switching activity considerably. This proposed work compared the switching activity with conventional Linear Feedback Shift Register (LFSR), Bit-Swapping LFSR (BS-LFSR) and gray-code generator. Simulated and synthesized of the proposed architecture was done by Xilinx tool. The final result shows more than 95% reduction on dynamic power consumption related to the traditional LFSR.

Keywords: Address generator · Gray code counter ·
Memory built in self-test (MBIST) · Low power switching ·
Linear Feedback Shift Register (LFSR)

1 Introduction

Low-power designs, especially microprocessors, have received a large amount of attention recently in portable and wireless related applications. Also, even the highest performance design power has become an issue. In high performance devices extremely high frequencies are attained, there by leading to greater power consumption and higher heat dissipation. To overcome this problem, heat sinks are used, resulting in higher costs and potential reliability problems. It is evident that a system consumes power twice more in testing mode when compared to usual mode. This is because of

F. A. Zimale et al. (Eds.): ICAST 2018, LNICST 274, pp. 239–247, 2019.
https://doi.org/10.1007/978-3-030-15357-1_19

applying parallel testing, wherein multiple embedded memories will be tested simultaneously while few memories are accessed during the normal mode. If the power consumed during the testing mode exceeds the power constraint of the chip, then the chip may become structurally degraded and may be damaged [1].

According to the state of system operation, power dissipation is classified into two major types. They are Static and Dynamic power. In static power, it is the power consumed while there is no circuit activity. In dynamic power, it is the power consumed while the inputs are in change or active. It is the major component of the total chip power consumption. Short- circuit and leakage power are the other two minor components and they can be minimized only at the stage of fabrication process. Charging and discharging of capacitive loads at the output of gates result in dynamic power consumption. Wiring capacitance, junction capacitance, and the input or gate capacitance of the fan-out gates contribute capacitive loads that results dynamic power. Hence, this paper considers dynamic power dissipation, which is determined by the equation

$P_{avg} = \alpha T C_{load} V_{dd}^2 f_{clk}$
αT = Switching activity f actor of gate
C_{load} = Total load capacitance
V_{dd} = Supply voltage
f_{clk} = Operating frequency

In the above equation, the average power is in direct proportion to the T. Therefore, the power dissipation can be scaled down by managing the switching activity when the system is in testing mode. The progress in submicron manufacturing technology and SoC design methodology has resulted in abnormal number of cores, particularly the memory cores included in a single chip. It is forecasted that by the year of 2014, memory cores may use 94% area of a typical SOC [2]. Memory thus plays a significant role in SoC based design. As the prospect of memory flaws is largely contrasted with other kind of defects in a circuit, that are necessary for testing of memory. Anyhow, on account of the existence of a minimum number of I/O pins in a circuit, BIST for Memory (MBIST) is employed as a key to this vexed issue [3]. Thus, this paper focuses on low transition address generator to reduce unnecessary switching in memory access process.

Hierarchy of address generators start with a normal binary up-down counter that produce sequence of addresses. When area and power are concerned, binary up-down counters occupy more area and also consumes more power. It is significant that the address generator plays an imperative role in MBIST. The blueprint of address generator is the foremost intricate problem in MBIST in view of its mammoth area and speed limit [4]. Reducing the switching activity in the address decoder using the Single Bit Change (SBC) instead of using the normal counter was proposed in [5]. This technique minimizes the switching activity in the address bus but it entails large overhead in the hardware area since a modified counter is used. Another technique was based on generating new march sequences with low switching activity by reordering the test sequences using genetic algorithm in [6]. This reordering reduces the switching activity in the data bus whereas it remains the same in the address bus.

To overcome the area problem, linear feedback shift registers (LFSRs) were introduced. It succeeded in scaling down the area occupied by address generators. But it failed to answer the power consumption caused by switching activity. Several algorithms were later introduced to cut down the switching in LFSR. In Bit-swapping LFSR [7] comprise traditional LFSR and 2:1 multiplexers. To overcome power consumption problem, diverse kinds of address generators are found employed for MBIST. In a programmable MBIST, two counters and multiplexer combination are employed as an address generator [8, 20]. A new reseeding technique with a considerable scan power reduction was proposed earlier [18]. The reseeding is applied on general LFSR and modified LFSR in two ways. These generated patterns are sent to a XOR network which will generate an output. A new LFSR reseeding technique for efficient reduction of test pattern was proposed in [19]. A new encoding technique to reduce the size of the test data was proposed in this study. Size of the test data was reduced by clock in LFSR which is in the state of inactive for several clock cycles after the seed is given to the input. Thus, reduction in test data volume is achieved by storing the data only when the clock is in active state. All the remaining test vectors was derived with in the reduced clock.

Linear Feedback Shift Register (LFSR) which is a combination of Bit Swapping LFSR (BS-LFSR) and Dual Speed LFSR (DS-LFSR) has been proposed early [10, 17, 21]. In this paper the modified Dual Speed LFSR (MDSLFSR) consists of two BS-LFSRs, one is the slow speed BS-LFSR and another is the normal speed BS-LFSR each has independent clock rates. The modified DS LFSR lowers the transition density at the input side. Thus, it reduces overall switching activity. In SoC environment, significant changes in testing methods are to be done for memory arrays. Built-In-Self-Test for optimized memory repair analyzer which works with optimal repair rate for memory arrays in [11]. Single test is required for this method even for worst case. The Must-Repair-Analysis (MRA) technique is done on fly during test, it stores faulty addresses and final analysis is done to find a solution to eliminate the analyzed faults. It executes an efficient redundancy analysis algorithm to generate repair solutions. A new method for generating configurations for application dependent testing of a SRAM-based FPGA interconnect was proposed in [12]. This method connects an activating input to multiple nets, thus generating activating test vectors for detecting stuck-at open, and bridging faults. A new technique for reduced switching activity in the address bus when testing SRAM of personal devices has been proposed in previous works [13]. Even though these algorithms deal with power minimization, the power reduction is an endless requirement of modern VLSI world. In certain other cases, Binary up-down counter and Gray code Counters are employed as address generators [9]. In paper [22] shows improved low transition test pattern generator method and targeted to low power application. With a concern to still decrease the switching activity, in our work, we have developed and executed a new address generator which uses bit reversal technique along with a modulo counter and grey code convertor.

2 Proposed Architecture

Linear Feedback Shift Registers (LFSR) or counters generally employed as address generators for memory locations, need to be investigated for flaws. The traditional LFSR is incapable of producing the entire zero patterns because when all the flip-flop output becomes zero then the XOR output is also zero hence the feedbacks to the 1st flip-flop input are also zero. Hence the LFSR becomes stuck at zero stage. To overcome this problem, a complete memory address generator (CLFSR) [15] was proposed in previous works. But power consumption is considerably high when traditional architectures are employed as address generators. To overcome the power consumption problem, a novel architecture is proposed in Fig. 1.

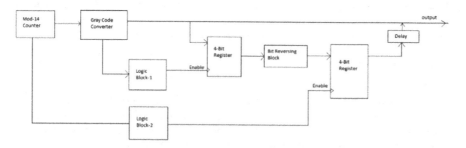

Fig. 1. Proposed block diagram

The architecture of address generator proposed in this paper is a blend of modulo counter and gray code convertor with a blend of bit reversal block. This paper focuses mainly on utilizing the reversible bit patterns. That is when we look at the patterns, we come across certain patterns which can be reversible. For example, 0000000001 is a pattern which is reversible. When certain pattern is reversed, the other address or pattern, 1000000000 can be obtained. Thus, an n-bit length pattern a $(0 \rightarrow n - 1)$ is said to be reversible if

$$a (0 \rightarrow n - 1) \neq a (n - 1 \rightarrow 0)$$

There exist certain other patterns which cannot be reversed. For example, 1000000001 or 1001001001 are some patterns which results in the same pattern even if we reverse them. Thus, an n-bit length pattern a $(0 \rightarrow n - 1)$ is said to be irreversible if

$$a (0 \rightarrow n - 1) = a (n - 1 \rightarrow 0)$$

So, in this paper we tried to make use of one such pattern which is the final outcome from gray code counter. In our observation, the final sequence of a gray code can be generated from the respective reversible pattern which is already generated prior to the final sequence. In this proposed architecture, two logic blocks along with the counter and gray code generator are used.

Algorithm 1 Logic Block-1
Require: Enable = (G0⊕G3) ∧ (G1 ↓ G2)
Repeat while B [3:0] ≠ 1111 do
if Enable=1 then
G [3:0] → G[0 : 3]
else G[3:0] → G[3:0]
end if
end while
until B[3:0] = 1110

Algorithm 2 Logic Block-2
Require: Enable = (B0∧B1∧B2) ∧ (-B3)
Repeat while B[3 : 0] ≠ 1110 do
if Enable=1 then
G[0:3] delayed OUTPUTBUS
else G[3:0] → OUTPUTBUS
end if
end while
until G[3:0] = 1000

The logic block-1 is used to detect the reversible pattern from which the reversed sequence can be generated. The logic block-1 for 4 bit, is designed in such a way to execute the logic as shown in the Algorithm 1. Thus, the detected reversible sequence is given to bit reversing block for reversing the sequence to generate new bit sequence. This reversed sequence has to be inserted in the respective place that is at the end of modulo sequence. The end sequence of modulo gray code counter will be 1110. We use logic block-2 (Algorithm 2) to detect this sequence. The reversed bit stream has to be inserted in output with some delay when the logic block-2 detects the appropriate position.

3 Results and Comparison

The complete block diagram embedded with the two logic blocks included is shown in the Fig. 1. This block diagram consists of a modulo gray code counter which is a combination of modulo counter and gray code converter. It can be implemented for any size of addresses with respective changes in logic blocks. The test outcomes of the proposed method are furnished below. The novel design is simulated and synthesized in Xilinx tool. The simulation-based outcomes and switching activity of the parallel existing methods are contrasted below. The Table 1 furnish comparison between total and dynamic power consumption in the recent methodologies for a 4-bit address. Thus, the proposed technique offered 98.19% saving of dynamic power and 92.28% saving of total power consumption, which offers the low power design of address generator at the cost of 0.031 W of power.

Table 1. Comparison between switching activity with various method

Address generator	Total dynamic power (W)	Saving (%)	Total power (W)	Saving (%)
LFSR [7]	0.222	–	0.402	–
BS-LFSR [7]	0.199	10.36	0.378	5.97
DC-LFSR [14]	0.012	94.59	0.179	55.47
Proposed method	0.004	98.19	0.031	92.28

The Table 2 furnish the details of bit transition and comparison with novel technique. By examining both the tables we can find that the switching activity undergoes considerable alteration which is encouraging outcome to achieve low power design of address generator.

Table 2. Comparison of bit-transition with proposed method

LFSR [7]	BS-LFSR [7]	Gray code [9]	Proposed
1111	1111	0000	0000
0101	0101	0001	0001
1011	1011	0011	0011
0111	0111	0010	0010
1111	1111	0110	0110
1110	1110	0111	0111
1100	1100	0101	0101
1000	0100	0100	0100
0001	0001	1100	1100
0010	0010	1101	1101
0100	1000	1111	1111
1001	1001	1110	1110
0011	0011	1010	1010
0110	1010	1011	1011
1101	1101	1001	1001
1010	0110	1000	
Bit transition values in each weight			
(8)(7)(8)(7)	(9)(4)(8)(7)	(1)(2)(4)(8)	(1)(2)(4)(7)

The Table 3 furnish the switching activity of proposed technique and percentage of saving with the conventional address generator for bit length N = 5 and N = 10 in comparison with several existing methods. The simulation resulted in reduction of switching activity up to 64.70% for a N = 5-bit address generator and 80.08% reduction in N = 10-bit address compared to the conventional LFSR. Here by it is evident that this value may increase when we go for higher bit length address generators. The comparison is also made with the existing methodology [14, 16], which resulted in almost 10% decrease in switching activity. Figure 2 shows Xilinx simulation report of device utilization summary. Figure 3 shows power report of proposed method in Xilinx simulation.

Table 3. Comparison between power consumption

Method	Switching activity			
	Bit length N = 5	Saving (%)	Bit length N = 10	Saving (%)
LFSR [14]	85	–	5130	–
BS-LFSR [7]	69	19	4106	20
DS-LFSR [17]	70	18	2904	43
Bipartite LFSR [16]	45	47	2462	52
BS-DS LFSR [14]	64	25	2376	54
DC LFSR [14]	36	57.65	1783	65.24
Proposed method	30	64.70	1022	80.08

Device Utilization Summary			
Logic Utilization	Used	Available	Utilization
Number of Slice Flip Flops	4	1,536	1%
Number of 4 input LUTs	7	1,536	1%
Number of occupied Slices	4	768	1%
Number of Slices containing only related logic	4	4	100%
Number of Slices containing unrelated logic	0	4	0%
Total Number of 4 input LUTs	7	1,536	1%
Number of bonded IOBs	6	63	9%
Number of BUFGMUXs	1	8	12%
Average Fanout of Non-Clock Nets	2.80		

Fig. 2. Device utilization summary from Xilinx simulation

	Total	Dynamic	Quiescent
Supply Power (W)	0.031	0.004	0.027

Fig. 3. Xilinx simulation power report

4 Conclusion

This paper attempted to introduce an efficient VLSI architecture for a low power address generator based on modulo counter which is having low dynamic power. It is achieved by decreasing the switching activity of the output address provoked. In this architecture, address generator consumes less area and less power consumption. Tradeoff between power and area is minimal in proportion. Proposed method's dynamic power dissipation reduces 90% when compared to traditional LFSR and BS-LFSR. It also 20% superior when compared to conventional gray code generator. The proposed address generator can be employed for MBIST by devising an appropriate MBIST controller. With the proficient employment of this Low power address generator, the entire MBIST unit can be adapted to taste the test patterns with less power consumption.

References

1. Abuissa, A.S., Quigleyr, S.F.: LTPRPG: power minimization technique for test-per-scan BIST. In: International Conference on Design and Technology of Integrated Systems in Nanoscale Era, pp. 1–5 (2008)
2. Marinissen, E.J., Prince, B., Keitel-Schulz, D., Zorian, Y.: Challenges in embedded memory design and test. In: Proceedings of Design Automation Test in Europe, vol. 52, pp. 722–727 (2005)
3. Noor, N.Q., Yusof, Y., Sparon, A.: Low area FSM-based memory BIST for synchronous SRAM. In: Proceedings of the International Colloquium of Signal Processing and Its Application, pp. 409–412 (2009)
4. Van de Goor A.D.J., Kukner, H., Hamdioui, S.: Optimizing memory BIST address generator implementations. In: 6th International Conference on Design & Technology of Integrated Systems in Nanoscale Era, pp. 1–6 (2011)
5. Wang, L.T., Stroud, C.E., Toubam, N.A.: System On Chip Test Architectures, pp. 308–339. Morgan Kaufmann, Los Altos (2008)
6. Gayathri, C.V., Kayalvizhi, N., Malligadevi, M.: Generation of new march tests with low test power and high fault coverage by test sequence reordering using genetic algorithm. In: International Conference on Advances in Recent Technologies in Communication and Computing, pp. 699–703 (2009)
7. Reddy, C.R., Zilani, S., Sumalatha, V.: Low power, low-transition random pattern generator. Int. J. Eng. Res. Technol. (IJERT) 1(5), 1–6 (2012)
8. Park, Y., Park, J., Han, T., Kang, S.: An effective programmable memory BIST for embedded memory. IEICE Trans. Inf. Syst. 92(12), 808–818 (2009)
9. Yarmolik, S.V., Yarmolik, V.N.: Modified gray and counter sequences for memory test address generation. In: Proceedings of International Conference, pp. 572–576 (2006)
10. Chandrakala, S., Banupriya, C.: A low power built in repair analyzer for word-oriented memories with optimal repair rate. In: Green Computing Communication and Electrical Engineering (ICGCCEE), pp. 1–5 (2014)
11. Ohler, P., Bosio, A., Di Natale, G., Hellebrand, S.: A modular memory BIST for optimized memory repair. In: 14th IEEE International on-line Testing (2008)
12. Kumar, T.N., Lombardi, F.: A novel heuristic method for application-dependent testing of a SRAM-based FPGA interconnect. IEEE Trans. Comput. 62(1), 163–172 (2013)

13. Awad, A.N., Abu-Issa, A.S.: Low power address generator for memory built-in self-test. Res. Bull. Jordan ACM **III**(II), 52–56 (2007)
14. Krishna, K.M., Sailaja, M.: Low power memory built in self-test address generator using clock controlled linear feedback shift registers. J. Electron. Test. **30**, 77–85 (2014)
15. Wang, W.-L., Lee, K.J.: A complete memory address generator for scan-based march algorithms. In: Proceedings of the I.E. International Workshop on Memory Technology, Design, and Testing (MTDT05), p. 83–88 (2005)
16. Tehranipoor, M., Nourani, M., Ahmed, N.: Low transition LFSR for BIST-based applications. In: Proceedings of the 14th Asian Test Symposium, pp. 138–143 (2005)
17. Wang, S., Gupta, S.K.: DS-LFSR: a BIST TPG for Low switching activity. IEEE Trans. Comput. Aided Design Integr. Circuit Syst. **21**(7), 842–851 (2002)
18. Sowmiya, G., Premalatha, P., Rajaram, A., Saravanan, S., Vijay Sai, R.: Design and analysis of scan power reduction based on linear feedback shift register reseeding. In: IEEE Conference on Information and Communication Technologies, pp. 638–641 (2013)
19. Saravanan, S., Upadhyay, H.N.: Effective LFSR reseeding technique for achieving reduced test pattern. Res. J. Appl. Sci. Eng. Technol. **4**(22), 4783–4786 (2012)
20. Kumar, S., Manimegalai, R.: Efficient memory built in self-test address generator implementation. Int. J. Appl. Eng. Res. **10**(7), 16797–16813 (2015)
21. Hussain, S., Priya, P.: Test pattern generator (TPG) for low power logic built in self-test (BIST). Int. J. Adv. Res. Electr. Electron. Instrum. Eng. **2**(4), 1634–1640 (2013)
22. Vellingiri, G., Jayabalan, R.: An Improved low transition test pattern generator for low power application. Design Autom. Embedded Syst. **21**(3–4), 247–263 (2017)

Modeling of Induction Heating Inverter Using System Identification

Mulugeta Debebe[1], Endalew Ayenew[1], Beza Neqatibeb[1],
and Venkata Lakshmi Narayana Komanapalli[2(✉)]

[1] College of Electrical and Mechanical Engineering,
Addis Ababa Science and Technology University, Addis Ababa, Ethiopia
muludeb@gmail.com, end_enday@yahoo.com,
bezanek@gmail.com
[2] School of Electrical Engineering and Computing,
Adama Science and Technology University, Adama, Ethiopia
kvlnarayana@yahoo.co.in

Abstract. In this paper, Auto Regressive eXogenous input (ARX), Auto Regressive Moving Average eXogenous input (ARMAX), Output error and BJ models of class D voltage-source half-bridge series-resonant inverter used for induction heating are identified and studied based on prior knowledge and measured data from PSIM simulation Environment. The output data are generated by applying Pseudo-Random-Binary-sequence (PRBS) as an input through the inverter MOSFET gate in the PSIM software. PRBS signal is generated using standard components such as flip-flops or XOR gates to approximate the white noise in the PSIM software. The generated output and input data are loaded in the MATLAB to identify the unknown system parameters of induction heating inverter by using MATLAB system identification toolbox. Estimation of models with pre-selected structures can be performed using system identification toolbox. To validate the models and their limitations, the fitness properties of the models based on percentage best fit and their resonant frequencies are examined.

Keywords: System identification · Induction heating inverter · PRBS

1 Introduction

Recently a class D voltage-source half-bridge series-resonant inverter has become very popular and become more and more widely used in various applications, especially in the applications where small-size electric appliances are required as a main purpose. They are, for example; electronic ballasts, induction heaters and induction cookers, etc. Depending on the position of the load with respect to the elements of the resonant circuit, the converters of class D may be divided into series resonant converters, parallel resonant converters, and series–parallel (hybrid) converters [1]. The characteristics of the induction heating converter must be identified as much as possible accurately to control the efficient transfer of energy from the source. There are many simple analytical methods to obtain the mathematical model of a converter. However, to have a

© ICST Institute for Computer Sciences, Social Informatics and Telecommunications Engineering 2019
Published by Springer Nature Switzerland AG 2019. All Rights Reserved
F. A. Zimale et al. (Eds.): ICAST 2018, LNICST 274, pp. 248–257, 2019.
https://doi.org/10.1007/978-3-030-15357-1_20

good understanding on the correct behavior of the converter, it is necessary to utilize advanced technique to achieve accurate model that resemble the converter. In [2], a PSpice software is used to obtain a simple mathematical model for the series-parallel resonant topology with a capacitor as output filter. A generalized state space averaging model for LCL resonant inductive power transfer is constructed to transform the nonlinear model into a linear approximation model [3]. In this work, the authors mainly consider the running frequency and load parameter uncertainty to detached the uncertain system model from the system model by using the linear fractional transformation method. A good review of analytical methods for IH can be found in [4].

System identification can be used in a wide range of applications, including mechanical engineering, biology, physiology, meteorology, economics, and model-based control design [5]. Among different system identification technique, least square method is probably the most popular and numerically simple, in which error is appropriately defined. However, the least square method suffers if the model order is not sufficiently high and cause accuracy problems if the noise level increases [6]. Moreover, if the model structure is not linear in the parameters, this approach may be invalid [7]. To identify the parameters in nonlinear model structure, the modern optimization techniques such as genetic algorithm and particle swarm optimization algorithms seem to be a more hopeful approach and provide a powerful means. [8] proposed a methodology to find optimal system parameters and optimal control parameters using adaptive particle swarm optimization for nonlinear system. In [9], an overview of the basic principles and results and the problem areas in the practical side of how to approach and solve a real problem have been extensively studied. Nonlinear system on-line identification via dynamic neural networks is studied in [10]. The main contribution of the paper is that the passivity approach is applied to access several new stable properties of neuro identification.

The main concern of the paper is to obtain the linear discrete model of medium frequency induction heating by using system identification technique. This paper is organized as follows. Section 2 proposes a family of different linear model formulations and identification. In Sect. 3, a Class D voltage-source half-bridge series-resonant inverter PSIM data measurement results are presented. Section 4 reports model validation and comparison. Finally, the paper is concluded in Sect. 5.

2 Linear Model Formulation and Identification

The two most common techniques to estimate models that represent linear time-invariant systems are nonparametric estimation and parametric estimation. In this paper, the nonparametric estimation approach has been proposed to obtain the models. Consider the general stochastic model shown in Eq. (1).

$$y(t) = q^{-k} G(q^{-1}, \theta) u(t) + H(q^{-1}, \theta) e(t) \tag{1}$$

Where $u(t)$, $y(t)$, $e(t)$, $G(q^{-1}, \theta)$, $H(q^{-1}, \theta)$, θ are the input, output, zero-mean white noise (the disturbance of the system), transfer function of the deterministic part of the system, transfer function of the stochastic part of the system, the set of model parameters respectively. $G(q^{-1}, \theta)$, $H(q^{-1}, \theta)$ are rational polynomials as defined by the following equations [11].

$$G(q^{-1}, \theta) = \frac{B(q, \theta)}{A(q, \theta)F(q, \theta)} \qquad (2a)$$

$$H(q^{-1}, \theta) = \frac{C(q, \theta)}{A(q, \theta)D(q, \theta)} \qquad (2b)$$

In this section, discrete linear system model formulations are introduced from the general stochastic model by Setting one or more of $A(q, \theta)$, $C(q, \theta)$, $D(q, \theta)$, and $F(q, \theta)$ equal to one. The ARX model of a system is given by setting $C(q)$, $D(q)$, and $F(q)$ equal to one.

$$A(q)y(t) = B(q)u(t) + e(t) \qquad (3)$$

The e(t), residual or equation error, is used to account for the fitting error. The major drawback of the ARX model is lack of adequate freedom in describing the properties of disturbance term. An important properties of the equation error as moving average of the white noise is described in ARMAX model. When $D(q, \theta)$, and $F(q, \theta)$ equal to one.

$$A(q)y(t) = B(q)u(t) + C(q)e(t) \qquad (4)$$

The output error model and Box-Jenkins (BJ) model structures in a more compact form are shown in Eqs. (5) and (6) respectively.

$$y(t) = \frac{B(q)}{F(q)}u(t) + e(t) \qquad (5)$$

$$y(t) = \frac{B(q)}{F(q)}u(t) + \frac{C(q)}{D(q)}e(t) \qquad (6)$$

The issue of system identification technique has been addressed by many authors in several books and survey articles where many different identification methodologies have been exploited. For instance, the authors of [12] obtained the ARX model for billet induction heating process with the help of Matlab system identification toolbox and the result shows the model has high prediction accuracy. In [13], on-line parameter estimation method has been proposed to obtain the model of a 3-phase induction heating. The approach uses PSIM simulation and experimental results to study its impedance matrix for control application.

3 Data Measurement

In practice, most often test signals are added to the inputs of the system to move the output up and down around a working point. For theoretical analysis purpose, white noise is used as test input in system identification since white noise has autocorrelation that is impulse response function at the origin and a wide (theoretically infinite) frequency range. It can therefore excite the process over a wide frequency range. In practice, it is impossible to generate a pure white noise so that we need to approximate the white noise signals by PRBS. This type of noise has a periodic autocorrelation function and it can be easily generated by using a feedback shift register. The different properties of PRBS including its autocorrelation, its realizations and its similarities with white noise is clearly explained in the literature [5]. In this work, we generate PRBS signal using standard components such as flip-flops and XOR gates to approximate the white noise in the PSIM software. This type of signal, $u(t)$, has a periodic autocorrelation function and given by (7).

$$\phi_{uu}(\tau) = \frac{1}{T} \int_0^T u(\lambda)u(\tau + \lambda)d\lambda \tag{7}$$

Pseudo random binary signal was generated by a shift register with 4 stages shown in the Fig. 1. The maximum length of the signal (maximum period) sequence is $N = 2^n - 1 = 15$, where n is the number of D flip flop used in the circuit. As follows from the figure shown in the Fig. 1, the clock frequency of PRBS is $\frac{1}{\Delta} = 100$ kHz. As we know, PRBS is a deterministic signal and its autocorrelation function can resemble the autocorrelation function of a white random noise if the length of signal is large. From Eq. (7), the autocorrelation of PRBS has been found in Eq. (8).

$$\phi_{uu}(\tau) = \begin{cases} 1, & \text{for } \tau = 0, T, 2T, 3T, 4T\ldots \\ \frac{-1}{15\Delta} & \text{elsewhere} \end{cases} \tag{8}$$

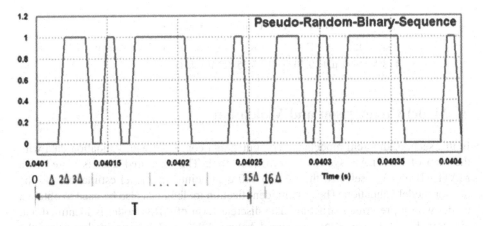

Fig. 1. PRBS waveform

In this paper, a Class D voltage-source half-bridge series-resonant inverter topology shown in Fig. 2 has been proposed to identify the model of induction heating converter by collecting a time varying data in PSIM simulation software. The converter is excited by Pseudo-Random-Binary-Sequence (PRBS) input in the gate of MOSFET and a valuable data is obtained by measuring the output current through the load. L_{eq}, R_{eq}, C_r are the equivalent load inductance, equivalent load resistance and resonant capacitor respectively. For simulation purpose, the load parameters are taken from [14]. Table 1 gives a summary of the PSIM simulation parameters. A total of 20,000 input/output data pairs were collected with a clock frequency of 100 kHz and transferred to MATLAB to estimate a linear discrete model of the system from the measured data. As shown in Fig. 2, the inverter is excited by a 4-stage PRBS at the gate side of the MOSFET and output current data is observed through the load.

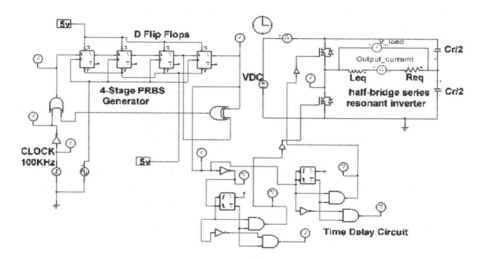

Fig. 2. The complete induction heating PSIM mode

Table 1. PSIM simulation parameters

V_{DC}	L_{eq}	C_r	R_{eq}	Flip-flop clock frequency
198 V	82.4 μH	0.3024 μF	3.55 Ω	100 kHz

4   Model Comparison and Validation

In this section, different models are computed and compared with validation data with the help of MATLAB system identification tool. The measured data is stored in a MATLAB file. We selected the first 13,000 data points for model estimation and the rest for model validation. The system identification toolbox can also be used to obtain a model with a prescribed structure. The discrete form of ARX model is identified and given in Eqs. (9a) and (9b). As stated before ARX model lacks in describing the

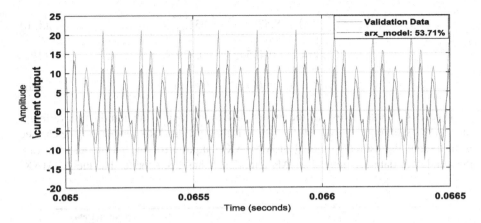

Fig. 3. ARX model simulated response vs. validation data output

properties of disturbance, the data fit is only 53.71 shown in Fig. 3. This reveals that the information in the measured data has not adequately captured by the estimated ARX model. In other word, the model is not rich enough to explain all the information in the measured data of induction heating. By increasing the order of the system, we can get an accurate ARX model that fits the data. However, this increases the complexity of the system. Accordingly, there is a need for improving the fitness value with minimum system order and complexity. Therefore, based on the collected data, the discrete form of ARMAX model is obtained as (10a, 10b and 10c).

$$A(z) = 1 - 1.1328z^{-1} + 0.7323z^{-2} \tag{9a}$$

$$B(z) = 6.946z^{-1} - 6.77z^{-2} \tag{9b}$$

$$A(z) = 1 - 1.422z^{-1} + 0.7602z^{-2} \tag{10a}$$

$$B(z) = 8.334z^{-1} - 8.366z^{-2} \tag{10b}$$

$$C(z) = 1 - 0.7716z^{-1} - 0.2176z^{-2} \tag{10c}$$

Similarly, the discrete form of output error model and BJ model have been found to be in Eqs. (11a and 11b) and (12a, 12b, 12c and 12d) respectively.

$$F(z) = 1 - 1.409z^{-1} + 0.7488z^{-2} \tag{11a}$$

$$B(z) = 9.188z^{-1} - 9.329z^{-2} \tag{11b}$$

$$F(z) = 1 - 1.432z^{-1} + 0.7688z^{-2} \tag{12a}$$

$$B(z) = 8.599z^{-1} - 8.631z^{-2} \tag{12b}$$

$$C(z) = 1 - 0.4554z^{-1} - 0.5293z^{-2} \tag{12c}$$

$$D(z) = 1 - 1.076z^{-1} - 0.5244z^{-2} \tag{12d}$$

Figures 4, 5 and 6 illustrate the model validation using validation data for different models by assuming the order of the system is the same as ARX model. As one can see from figures, the estimated model of ARMAX, Output error and BJ model are fitting the validation data set more than ARX model. It has been found that the ARMAX,

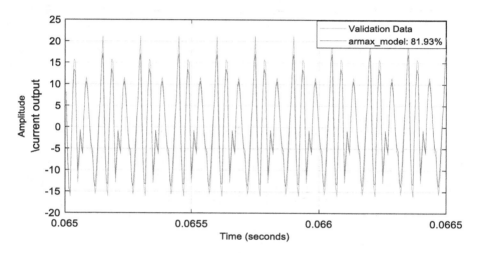

Fig. 4. ARMAX model simulated response vs validation data output

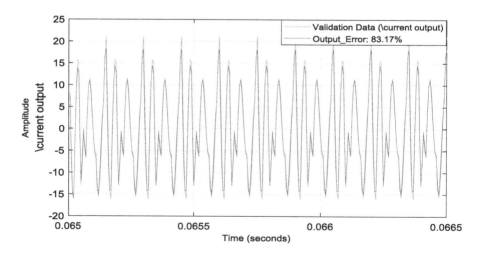

Fig. 5. Output error model simulated response vs validation data output

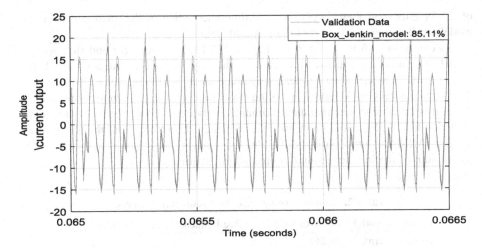

Fig. 6. BJ model simulated response vs validation data output

Output error and BJ model fits to measured data are identified as 81.93%, 83.17%, 85.11% respectively. It can be observed here that the validation agreement is very good, and the models are rich enough to explain most of the information in the measured data of induction heating.

To evaluate the estimated models' quality in frequency domain, we simulate the bode plot and observe the behavior of the models near to the resonance frequency of the induction heating. The simulation result is depicted in Fig. 7. The simulation result shows that the estimated models are very close to each other near to working frequency

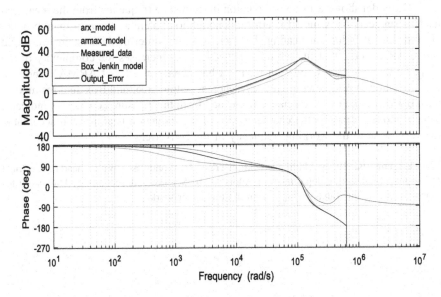

Fig. 7. Bode plot of estimated models

of the inverter, and there is also a clear difference between the measured data and models while moving away from the resonant frequency.

As can be seen from Table 2 and Fig. 7, ARMAX, output error and Box-Jenkins models give a peak magnitude very close to the load resonant frequency (20.3 kHz). Whereas, ARX model shows a peak magnitude away from load resonant frequency. The ARX-model is not so good due to the bias caused by the non-white equation error noise. It is valuable to note that the maximum energy transferred from the source to the induction heating load is at the resonance frequency. Therefore, from the above result suggests ARMAX output error and Box-Jenkins models captures most of the frequency band width of the inverter around the resonance frequency.

Table 2. Response of the models at resonance frequency

Estimated models	Approximated resonance frequency (Hz)	Magnitude (dB)
BJ output error	20,212	31.8
Output error	20,212	31.7
ARMAX	20,053	31.3
ARX	22,600	28.7

5   Conclusion

This paper described the application of model identification technique for medium frequency class D series-resonant inverter used for induction heating based on measured data from PSIM simulation environment. A second order ARX, ARMAX, output error and Box-Jenkins models are obtained, and the result is compared with validation data. ARX model shows a 11.33% deviation in resonance frequency from the measured data. This suggests ARX model is not rich enough to explain all the information in the measured data of induction heating. By increasing the order of the system, we might improve ARX model that fits the data. However, this increases the complexity of the system. From bode plot simulation result, it has been noticed that ARMAX shows a 1.22% deviation in resonance frequency, whereas output error and Box-Jenkins models show a 0.43% deviation in resonance frequency from the measured data. This indicates that these models describe the characteristics of the induction heating with acceptable value very close to the working frequency of the converter.

Acknowledgements. We would like to acknowledge Mr. Wondwesen Wubu, head of Electrical and Computer Engineering department of Addis Ababa Science and Technology University for his encouragement and valuable support during this paper work.

References

1. Skvarenina, T.L.: The Power Electronics Handbook, 1st edn. CRC Press, Purdue University, Boca Raton (2002)
2. Martín-Ramos, J.A., Pernía, A.M., Díaz, J., Nuño, F., Alonso, J.M.: A circuit for the large and small signal dynamic modeling of the PRC-LCC resonant topology with a capacitor as output filter. In: IEEE (2005)
3. Dai, X., Zou, Y., Sun, Y.: Uncertainty modeling and robust control for LCL resonant inductive power transfer system. J. Power Electron. **13**(5), 814–828 (2013)
4. Kennedy, M., Akhtar, S., Bakken, J., Aune, R.: Review of classical design methods as applied to aluminum billet heating with induction coils. In: Proceedings of EPD Congress, San Diego, USA (2011)
5. LabVIEW System Identification Tool Box User Manual, National Instruments, 1st edn. Part Number 371001B-01, September 2004. https://www.ni.com
6. Zhu, Y.: Multivariable System Identification for Process Control, 1st edn. Elsevier Science & Technology Books, New York (2001)
7. Astrom, K.J., Wittenmark, B.: Adaptive Control, 1st edn. Addison-Wesley, Massachusetts (1995)
8. Alfi, A., Modares, H.: System identification and control using adaptive particle swarm optimization. Appl. Math. Model. **35**, 1210–1221 (2011)
9. Ljung, L.: Perspectives on System Identification, Division of Automatic Control. Linköpings universitet, Linköping (2008)
10. Yu, W., Li, X.: Some new results on system identification with dynamic neural networks. IEEE Trans. Neural Networks **12**(2), 412–417 (2001)
11. Ljung, L.: System Identification: Theory for the User, 1st edn. Prentice Hall, Englewood Cliffs (1987)
12. Zhe, X., Xulong, C., Bishi, H., Yaguang, K., Anke, X.: Model identification of the continuous casting billet induction heating process for hot rolling. In: Third International Conference on Intelligent System Design and Engineering Applications (2013)
13. Nguyen, B.A., Phan, Q.D., Nguyen, D.M., Nguyen, K.L., Durrieu, O., Maussion, P.: Parameter identification method for a 3-phase induction heating system. In: IEEE Industrial Application Society Annual Meeting (2014)
14. Koertzent, H.W., van Wyk, J.D., Ferreira, J.A.: Design of the half-bridge, series resonant converter for induction cooking. In: IEEE, pp. 729–735 (1995)

Development of Low Cost Gemstone Polishing Cum Cutting Machine

Fetene Teshome⬤ and Kishor Purushottam Kolhe$^{(\boxtimes)}$⬤

Bahir Dar Institute of Technology-Bahir Dar University, Bahir Dar, Ethiopia
{fetenet,kishorp}@bdu.edu.et

Abstract. Ethiopia has many types of natural resources that can be exported and brought high foreign currency; which can help to improve the financial status of this country. However; one of these resources is gemstone minerals, which is mostly preferred for jewelry purpose globally; due to its unique attraction, properties and natural behavior. Moreover; very expensive gemstone like opals, emerald, ruby, sapphire, etc. are available in this country in a huge quantity. However; these natural resources exported in raw form without post processing to the other developed countries to bring high foreign currency. Nevertheless; due the export presently we are not getting good returns on this export. By considering this fact gemstones processing jobs has been started in Amhara region of Ethiopia to add values and to increase the selling price of it. Hence present study focuses on the "Development of low cost Gemstone polishing cum cutting machine for further value addition of gemstone mineral. Mostly the available machines for gemstone processing globally are very expensive; therefore in the present study the efforts are taken to use the indigenous materials as alternatives to develop the low cost gemstone processing technology. This development work endorsed the dramatic cost reduction of the machine imported from abroad by saving more than 50% total cost.

Keywords: Gemstone · Cutting and polishing · Opal · Lapidary

1 Introduction

A gemstone or gem is a piece of attractive mineral, which is used to make jewelry or other adornments; when cut and polished. Mostly; gemstones are hard, but some soft minerals are used in Jewelry because of their luster or other physical properties that have aesthetic value. The most obvious and attractive feature of gemstones is their color. In general, stones like ruby, sapphire, emerald, and opal are gemstones where Amhara region (Particularly Delanta, Wegel Tena, Mezezo, Debre Brehan etc.) is known to have opal in ample quantity. Opal's mineral chemical name is hydrated silicon dioxide where the most essential feature of opal is its color, clarity and carat weight. The varieties of opal base color include chocolate, white, yellow, orange, dark red, root beer, and caramel [8]. There is a major shortages and importance of gemstone cutting and polishing machine over the years in Amhara region, Ethiopia in particular, and other parts of the country. Where the production of the gemstone jewelers normally takes place has necessitated the need to save foreign currency and modify upon the

F. A. Zimale et al. (Eds.): ICAST 2018, LNICST 274, pp. 258–266, 2019.
https://doi.org/10.1007/978-3-030-15357-1_21

design of the machine. The most important of the components of the machine that can be modified and produced is coolant pumping mechanism. By doing so, there will be enhancement in the productivity, efficiency, ergonomics and safety of handling the machine in order to achieve its cost effectiveness and conducive and environmentally friendly conditions. These conditions will also attract the lapidaries who produce the jewelers for exportations and this will go a long way in contributing to the economy of the countries where large mining of gemstone takes place. Gemstone jewelers' production has been a target for small and large scale investors, and to follow the trend and encourage mass and qualitative production of the gemstone jewelries by trained lapidaries, there is the need to modify the design and manufacture of the existing gemstone cutting and polishing machine that will save high foreign currency. The developments steps of Gemstone polishing cum cutting machines were carried out as per engineering product development cycle [1–9]. As stated earlier, gemstone is used by the jewelry industry. Processed products of Ethiopian gemstones are mainly exported to Europe, America and Asia. In Ethiopia, there is a number of gemstone processing and exporting firms including Ethio-gemstone and Rift valley Gemstone although a complete list of firms engaged in the sector could not be documented [10]. The grading of Opal Gemstone is shown in Fig. 2(a–d).

(a)

(b)

(c)

(d)

Fig. 1. (a): The opal typically fills spaces between pieces of volcanic rock debris, acting as cement. The black areas in this sample also consist of opal, together with Ba-Mn oxides. Photo by Mazzero [15]. (b) The carved wooden pick used by some of these miners to extract the rough opal at Wegel Tena. Photo by Mazzero [15]. (c) The carved wooden pick used by some of these miners to extract the rough opal at Wegel Tena. Photo by Mazzero [15]. (d) Rough opals before polishing [15]. (e) Rough opals before polishing [15].

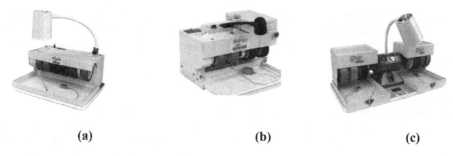

(a)   **(b)**   **(c)**

Fig. 2. (a) Pixie gem maker machine, (b) Bigfoot gem maker machine (c) Genie gem maker

The process of cutting and polishing gems is called gem cutting or lapidary, while a person who cuts and polishes gems is called a gem cutter or a lapidary (sometimes lapidarist). Gemstone material that has not been extensively cut and polished is referred to generally as rough. Rough material that has been lightly hammered to knock off brittle, fractured material is said to have been cobbed [2–5] (Fig. 1).

All gems are cut and polished by progressive abrasion using finer and finer grits of harder substances. Diamond, the hardest naturally occurring substance, has a Mohs hardness of 10 and is used as an abrasive to cut and polish a wide variety of materials, including diamond itself. Silicon carbide, a manmade compound of silicon and carbon with a Mohs hardness of 9.5, is also widely used for cutting softer gemstones. Other compounds, such as cerium oxide, tin oxide, chromium oxide, and aluminum oxide, are frequently used in polishing gemstones [1] (Figs. 3 and 4).

Fig. 3. (a) Titan the biggest gem maker. (b) Sample price of imported gemstone trimming saw machine

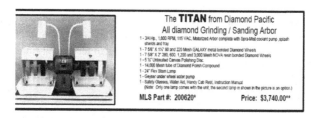

Fig. 4. Sample price of imported gemstone grinding machine.

The price of above machine is 3,740 dollar (about 63,580 birr) without considering the shipping cost. This price is very expensive to purchase the machine for Ethiopian graduate lapidaries; therefore it was decided to develop low cost polishing cum cutting machine to alleviate the problems and to save foreign currency [7].

2 Methodology

The "reverse engineering" methods was used to develop the product. Reverse engineering is a systematic approach for analyzing the design of existing devices or systems. Initial steps in the redesign process during reverse engineering process are: (1) Observe and assess the mechanisms that make the device work. (2) Dissect and study the inner workings of a mechanical device and (3) Compare the actual device to your observations and suggest improvements. Reverse engineering initiates the redesign process, wherein a product is observed, disassembled, analyzed, tested, "experienced", and documented in terms of its functionality, form, physical principles, manufacturability, and ability to be assembled. The intent of the reverse engineering process is to fully understand and represent the current instantiation of a product [10]. The primary objective of reverse engineering is the development of unrestricted technical data, adequate for competitive procurement, through engineering evaluations of existing hardware [15].

The process of the use of local and available materials in the near market and available machine in the near manufacturing area to fabricate the original imported machine which is less in cost and competitive in performance with imported machine is said to be indigenization.

2.1 Study and Value Engineering of the Imported Gemstone Cabbing Machine

The water pan, hood of the machine is manufactured from thermosetting plastics. The base of the machine is manufactured from laminated wood and Formica. It may absorb water and damage easily. It needs extra working table.

2.2 Selection of Materials for the Components of the Machine

The criteria for material selection of the materials for the various components of the machine is based on the type of force that will be acting on them, the work they are expected to perform, the environmental condition in which they will function, their useful physical and mechanical properties, the cost and their availability in the local market or the environment [11]. Since our task is reverse engineering and indigenization of the imported gemstone machine, materials for each component is selected by using experiences familiarities and know ledges with the available materials of properties, fabrication methods, functional requirements, cost and others. After studying and knowing the nature and functional requirement of indigenous engineering materials, the following materials are selected for the basic components of the machine. The most critical machine elements that need design analysis in the reversed gem stone cabbing machine are shaft, pulley, belt, bearing and air pump [12–14]. The material used for the designed components of polishing cum cutting machine for gemstone is as given below in Table 1.

Table 1. Selected materials for the components of the machine

S n	Machine part	Selected materials	Selection criteria
1	Shaft	Medium carbon steel	Easy machinability, local availability cheap in cost relatively and its strength
2	Pulley	Aluminum	Material selected is aluminum since it is deep affordable, resistant to heat and wear, light in weight, and easily machineable
3	Nut	Aluminum	
4	Spacer	Aluminum	Material selected is aluminum since it is cheap and affordable, light in weight resistant to heat and wear, and easily machineable
5	Machine bodies (table, hood bowel and others)	Carbon steel (C20)	Cheap, affordable, easy fabrication and is of high carrying capacity
6	Eccentric circular CAM Piston (follower)	Medium carbon steel	Strength, wear resistant and easy fabrication
7	Piston housing	Medium carbon steel	Strength, wear resistant and easy fabrication
8	Piston housing	Medium carbon steel	Strength, wear resistant and easy Fabrication
9	Air pump top and bottom covers	Aluminum	Material selected is aluminum since it is cheap and affordable, light in weight and easily machineable

3   Results and Discussion

The designed prototype Gemstone polishing cum cutting machine by using reverse engineering techniques is presented in Fig. 5.

Figure 5 present the exploded drawing of gemstone cutting cum polishing machine, the various designed components of Gemstone polishing cum cutting machine are briefly described as follows.

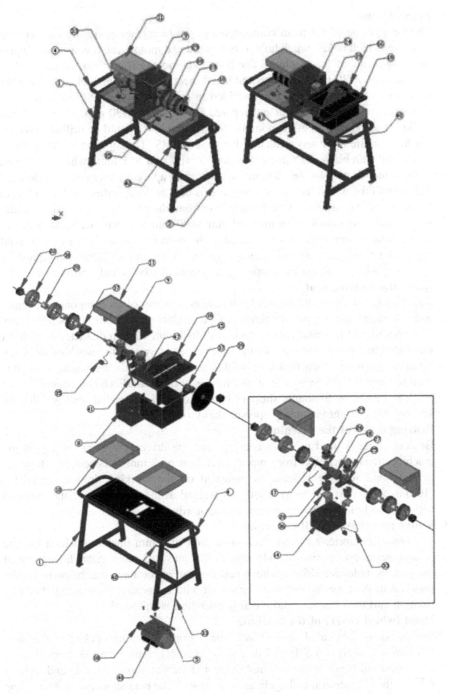

Fig. 5. Parts of the designed gemstone polishing cum cutting machine

1. **Machine base**

   The base is one of the main components of the Gemstone polishing cum cutting machine, which holds switch holder, belt guard and motor seat. It is used to support all components of the machine. The base is fabricated from SHS (square hollow steel 30 mm × 30 mm × 2 mm) and black sheet iron = 3 mm thickness. The SHS is cut to legs and rails to size as specified in the working drawing and assembled with welding. The base foot is prepared from flat iron 30 mm width × 2 mm thickness × 60 mm length and at one end 10 mm hole should be drilled to fix the machine on the floor and welded at the foot of SHS. The top part of the frame is assembled with black sheet iron (1000 mm × 400 mm × 3 mm), which is notched at the center to pass the belt towards to motor, by applying intermittent welding.

   The round tube which has 30 mm diameter is bent at the specified profile and weld to the frame that helps to move the machine from place to place. The switch holder is fabricated from black sheet iron (80 mm × 80 mm × 2 mm) which is drilled at center with 16 mm drill bit and welded at the right top corner of the base to hold the machine switch. The tool kit, motor seat and belt guard are fabricated separately and fixed with the frame by temporary fasteners like bolts and screws.

2. **Shaft and bearing seat**

   This part has a shape of rectangular box after welding of its component together and fabricated from 6 mm thickness of plate (200 mm × 240 mm × 150 mm). The bottom part has four holes which is drilled with 12 mm diameter of drill bit that helps to fix with the base of the machine as shown in the working drawing. Similarly the top part has four holes of diameter 12 mm to fix the bearing on it. It is used to support the bearing and all assemblies of the shaft. Each components of the part can be cut by hydraulic shear or cutter disc and assembled with welding by keeping the straightness and perpendicularity of the part.

3. **Bearing cover of the machine**

   Bearing cover is used to cover bearings and the driven pulley at the top of the machine. It is fabricated from black sheet iron of 2 mm thickness by shearing, bending and welding process as indicated on the working drawing and SHS (10 mm × 10 mm × 1 mm) is cut and welded at the top edges of the cover to support and hold trimmed gemstones temporarily.

4. **Water pan (bowel) of the machine**

   The bowel is fabricated from black sheet iron of 3 mm thickness which has the pattern development size of (445 mm × 420 mm × 3 mm). After laying out of the pattern, holes are drilled with 7 mm drill bit at the back that helps to fix the hood on it. And the lay out line is grooved with cutter disc to minimize bending strength and then bending and welding operation is followed.

5. **Hood (wheel cover) of the machine**

   The hood is fabricated from black sheet iron of 2 mm thickness, flat iron (30 mm × 2 mm) and SHS (10 mm × 10 mm × 1 mm). First the sheet metal is cut in size and bends to the required shape and the flat iron is cut, drill and weld as the specified dimension and again assembled with the bent sheet metal. Finally the SHS is cut in size and weld at the top edges of the hood to hold gemstones temporarily during cutting and grinding process and a plastic mirror is cut to the desired shape by band saw and assembled at the left and right side of the hood for safety and to observe the rotation condition.

6. **Trim saw body**

   The trim saw body is an assembly of stand, trimming table and blade guard. This body is attached to the bowel with screw temporarily during trimming operations. After trimming enough pieces of gemstone the attachment is disassembled and substitute grinding wheels with trim saw blade. The stand and the table is fabricated from 3 mm of black sheet iron by cutting and bending operations. The table has a long slot to run the trim saw blade which is slotted by cutter grinding disc. The curved blade guard is fixed with screw at the back edge of the table.

7. **Shaft of the machine**

   This shaft is fabricated from mild steel of 0.26% carbon content (BS07m26). The actual length of the shaft is 750 mm with stepped profile. But for machining process, 40 mm diameter of steel which has 800 mm length is cut. First of all, the cutting tool and lathe machine should be set up as required. Then steady rest or follower rest should be attached to the lathe bed to support the shaft during machine operation. At the first time the shaft end should be faced accurately and center drilling should be followed to support one end with revolving (live) center. Each section of the shaft should be turned to the specified dimension and allowable tolerance. Produce fine series left and right v-form thread at 16 mm diameter and finish the trim saw blade place. Consequently, cut the required size of the shaft using parting tool and go to cylindrical grinding machine to bring the specified dimension and surface finish. Finally drill a hole on the shaft for pulley and eccentric cam assembling with 5 mm drill bit and produce a v-form thread by using M6x1 thread tap.

8. **Pulley of the machine**

   The two pulleys are fabricated from aluminum materials with the calculated diameters, groove angles and other parameters. It is used to transmit power from one section to the work section.

9. **Spacer of the machine**

   Spacers are fabricated from aluminum ingot and it is used to guide and space the grinding wheel on the shaft.

10. **Nuts of the machine**

    Nuts are fabricated from aluminum ingot and are used to tight and guide the grinding wheel on the shaft.

11. **Air pump of the machine**

    Air pump is an assembly of eccentric cam, piston, piston housing, check valves and cover with seal. It is used to suck air from the surrounding with inlet check valve and the compressed air is displaced to the hose by out let check valve with high pressure to spread water from the bowel through the gather to the grinding wheel.

12. **Painting of the machine**

    To prevent surface corrosion and for aesthetic purposes, first of all the surface of the component of the machine should be polished with wire cup to remove corrosion and other dusts. It is also filled by metal body filler if deformed or irregular surface is observed and is polished by fine sand paper (No. 80, No. 120) to make the surface leveled and smooth. Finally the parts should be painted with antirust by using compressor and consequently, it should be painted with the user desire color repeatedly until getting uniform feature and beauty.

4 Conclusions

The reversed gemstone machine is fabricated from indigenous materials by considering scientific engineering principles and manufacturing processes. This machine is a combination of trim saw and cabbing machine. Therefore it can be used to trim and polish gemstones by exchanging the trim saw blade and gemstone grinding wheels. The critical parts of this machine (shaft, pulley, belt, bearing, pump etc.) are analyzed to ensure the functionality of the machine as expected. The reversed gemstone cabbing machine is manufactured cost effectively which reduces about 60% of the existing machine cost and any lapidarist can afford 26,261.75 birr to buy and to use easily.

Generally, the reversed gemstone cabbing machine are analyzed and manufactured by following the reverse engineering principle and procedures to make it robust, long service life, efficient and effective, cost effective, ergonomically convenient and environment friendly. The reverse engineering and manufacturing of this machine is to provide significant of it manufacturing for, to solve the problem stated in these literature as a whole and to attain the objectives stated.

References

1. Sinkankas, J.: Gemstone and Mineral Data Book, 2nd edn. Winchester Press, New York (1985)
2. Ingle, K.A.: Reverse Engineering. McGrow-Hill, New York (1994)
3. US ARMY Report: Reverse engineering handbook guidelines and procedures (1987)
4. Suresh, S.: Fatigue of Materials, 2nd edn. Cambridge University Press, Cambridge (1998)
5. ASM Handbook: Properties and Selection: Irons, Steels, and High-Performance Alloys. ASM Handbook Committee, vol. 1, pp. 673–688 (1978)
6. Kolhe, K.P.: Design and development of tractor mounted hydraulic lifter for harvesting spraying and pruning of horticultural fruit trees. Int. J. Agric. Eng. 2, 170–175 (2009)
7. Maleev, V., Hartman, J.B.: Machine Design, 3rd edn. CBS Publishers and Distributors, New Delhi (2003)
8. Kolhe, K.P.: Testing of tractor mounted and self propelled coconut climber for coconut harvesting. World J. Eng. 12(4), 399–406 (2015)
9. Kolhe, K.P.: Testing of tractor mounted hydraulic elevator by using digital load shell. World J. Eng. 12(5), 479–488 (2015)
10. Shigley, J.E., Mischke, C.R.: Mechanical Engineering Design, 5th edn. McGraw-Hill Publication, New York (1988)
11. Cornish, E.H.: Materials and the Designer, pp. 28–29. Cambridge University Press, Cambridge (1991)
12. National report on mining from Ministry of Mines and Energy: Federal Democratic Republic of Ethiopia, Addis Ababa, November 2009
13. Awny, M.M.: Technology transfer and implementation processes in developing countries. Int. J. Technol. Manag. 32, 213–220 (2005)
14. Salmon, S.C.: Modern Grinding Process Technology. McGraw-Hill Inc., New York (1992)

Kinetic Modeling and Gas Composition Analysis During Sawdust Pyrolysis

Tesfaye Alamirew[(✉)] and Solomon W. Fanta

Faculty of Chemical and Food Engineering, Bahir Dar Institute of Technology,
Bahir Dar University, Bahir Dar, Ethiopia
jaliniezeco@hotmail.com, Solworkneh@gmail.com

Abstract. This research paper deals about kinetic modeling and gas composition analysis of sawdust pyrolysis. The thermal degradation of sawdust at
lower (10 °C/min), medium (20 °C/min) and higher (50 °C/min) heating rates
were conducted using Beijing Henven Thermo Gravimetric (TG) analyzer. The
sawdust pyrolysis gave 98% gas and 2% char, 80% gas and 20% char, and 70%
gas and 30% char for lower, medium and higher heating rates. The Flynn-Wall
Ozwa (FWO) model free method and the Arrhenius equation was used to
estimate kinetic parameters and rate of this pyrolysis process. The rate equation
was 93% fit with the medium heating pyrolysis data, which was better fit than
the other heating rates. The Thermo Gravimetric analyzer and Jesco 6600
Fourier Transform Infrared (FTIR) analyzer were connected and the released
gases at medium heating were investigated. Using TG-FTIR analysis carbon
monoxide, carbon dioxide, water, hydrogen and char were released during
pyrolysis of sawdust at medium heating rate.

Keywords: Sawdust · Pyrolysis · Kinetic modeling · Gas composition analysis

1 Introduction

Biomass is any organic matter, typically plant-based matter that is available on a
renewable or recurring basis. Biomass resources include forest and mill residues,
agricultural crops and wastes, wood and wood wastes, animal wastes, livestock
operation residues, aquatic plants, fast-growing trees and plants, and municipal and
industrial wastes. Biomass can be used in its solid form or gasified for heating applications or electricity generation, or it can be converted into liquid or gaseous fuels [1].

The process usually begins with drying process, and then followed by pyrolysis.
The pyrolysis process leads to breaking down of the biomass, into solid matter
(charcoal) gaseous mixture (mainly CO_2, CO, CH_4 and H_2) and liquid matter (tar) [2].

Biomass contains cellulose, hemicelluloses and lignin, during the heating biomasses
decomposes and releases the volatiles. Volatile generates due to the presence of cellulose
and hemicelluloses and remaining char generates due to the lignin. Biomass decompositions started at temperature range 250–300 °C and volatile release at 300–350 °C
temperature and complete decomposition carried out above 500 °C. In present work,
kinetics study and the gas composition analysis of sawdust pyrolysis were carried out.

© ICST Institute for Computer Sciences, Social Informatics and Telecommunications Engineering 2019
Published by Springer Nature Switzerland AG 2019. All Rights Reserved
F. A. Zimale et al. (Eds.): ICAST 2018, LNICST 274, pp. 267–273, 2019.
https://doi.org/10.1007/978-3-030-15357-1_22

2 Materials and Methods

The pine sawdust obtained from furniture manufacturing companies in Bahir Dar city, Ethiopia. This sawdust was ground in the laboratory ball mill and then sieved into an average size less than one mm.

2.1 Thermo Gravimetric Analysis

The non-isothermal experiments were performed in atmospheric pressure under nitrogen environment with a flow rate of 36 mL/min from room temperature to 960 °C. Pyrolysis was carried out at 10 °C/min, 20 °C/min and 50 °C/min, the particle size of less than 1 mm and initial weight of 16.6 mg sample was used. Weight losses occurring in correspondence to temperature rises were continuously recorded with a computer fitted in Beijing Henven TGA instrument. In this study, all the experiments were replicated twice with an uncertainty of less than 3% [2–4].

2.2 FTIR Analysis

Chemical compounds and functional groups identified from wood saw dust sample by using FTIR analyzer. A TGA device was coupled with JASCO FT/IR 6600 infrared spectrometer through 10 cm gas cell. The gas flow rate through the transfer line and gas cell was kept constant. Infrared spectra over the range of 4000 to 650 cm^{-1} were collected every 15 s at a resolution of 4 cm^{-1}. The absorption bands of each spectrum collected are simultaneously integrated over the entire spectral range. Gram-Schmidt curves are obtained by plotting this integration from each spectrum as a function of temperature. These curves were used to have an overview of volatile production throughout the test [5–7, 8, 9].

2.3 Kinetic Modeling of Sawdust Pyrolysis

The results obtained from thermo gravimetric analysis were elaborated according to model-free methods to calculate the kinetic parameters. The activation energy (Ea) and pre-exponential factor (A) were obtained using Flynn-Wall-Ozwa (FWO) methods. The FWO method is based on the following equation: [11]

$$ln(B) = ln\left(\frac{AE}{Rg(x)}\right) - 5.331 - 1.052\frac{E}{RT} \qquad (1)$$

Where: B is heating rate, A is exponential factor, R is gas low constant and g(x) is the integral conversion.

Therefore the plot of natural logarithm of heating rates versus 1000/T gives a straight line plot. The slop and y-intercept were used to find the activation energy and the exponential factor parameters. The regression equations and the square of the correlation coefficient (R^2) is also presented. The activation energies (Ea) and pre-exponential factor (A) were derived from the slope and intercept of plotting regression line, respectively.

The rate equation for sawdust decomposition was assumed n^{th} order and percent weight loss with respect to temperature was expressed as follows:

$$R1 = \frac{dx}{dT} = A/B \exp((-E/RT)(1-X)^n) \tag{2}$$

3 Results and Discussion

3.1 Pyrolysis of Sawdust

The weight loss curve in Fig. 1 shows the loss of mass with temperature at different heating rates for Sawdust. As can be seen from the plot, the de volatilization process begins at about 380 K and proceeds rapidly with increasing temperature until about 600 K and then the weight loss decreases slowly to the final temperature. The first weight loss, around 110 °C, corresponds to the moisture loss of the sample. At temperatures below 110 °C, moisture content is reduced by up to 5% of the sample weight. The second weight reduction corresponding to increasing the temperature to 900 °C is attributed to de volatilization and pyrolysis of mainly organic materials. All the volatiles were evolved at below 600 °C for the three heating cases. In this step, the yield of the volatile material is up to 70% for 50 °C/min, 80% for 20 °C/min and 98% for 10 °C/min heating rates respectively.

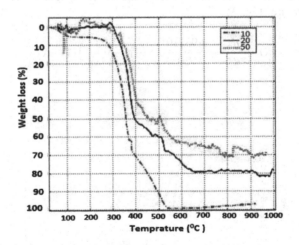

Fig. 1. Sawdust weight loss at different heating rates

It can be seen that the TG curve shifted up as the heating rate increased. As the heating rate increased the char yield increased and the gas release is decreased. At the lower heating rate, fewer char and high gasses are produced. In contrast, at higher heating rate, the de volatilization process occurred sooner due to the increased rate of heat transfer. Faster heating rates give the high amount of char and low gas release.

3.2   Kinetic Modeling of Sawdust Pyrolysis

The parameters obtained from FWO model free method are 5.057 kJ/mol and $8.93 * 10^4\ min^{-1}$ for activation energy (E) and pre-exponential factor (A), respectively. The correlation coefficient (R^2) is 88% (Fig. 2).

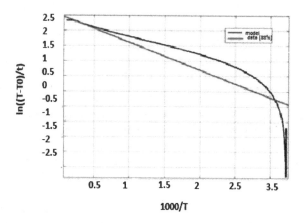

Fig. 2. Logarithm of heating rate with inverse temperature

The reaction assumed is first order and get the following relation for percent weight loss and temperature (Fig. 3).

$$R1 = \frac{dx}{dT} = \frac{8.93x10^4}{20} \exp\left(\frac{-5.057}{8.314xT}\right)(1 - X) \tag{3}$$

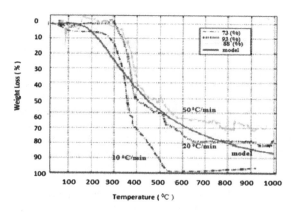

Fig. 3. Model fit with the at different heating rate data

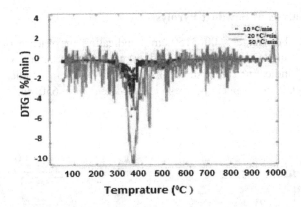

Fig. 4. DTG analysis of Sawdust at different heating rates

When we integrate the above equation, the percent weight loss becomes

$$X = 1 - \exp\left(\frac{-2715.84}{T}\right) exp\left(\frac{-0.61}{T}\right) \tag{4}$$

The Flynn model fits 73% with higher heating rate (50 °C/min), 93% with medium heating rate (20 °C) and 88% with lower heating rate (10 °C). Therefore the first order assumption is reasonable for pyrolysis of sawdust at medium heating rate.

3.3   DTG Analysis of Sawdust Pyrolysis

The derivative thermo gravimetric (DTG) curve could assist in explaining the TG curve.

The spread of the decomposition over temperatures of 25–900 °C appears as a relatively broad peak. The area under the peak represents the weight loss during the reaction. Thus, relative mass losses may be compared. When initial slow decompositions are followed by fast decompositions above 200 °C then a second slow decomposition initiates at 380 °C, there is a gradient change in the DTG curve. This information is used in this study to distinguish the different stages of each process and their gas evolution.

Higher heating rate has given maximum weight change per time compared to the medium and lower heating rates. The DTG curve indicates that different gases released during pyrolysis of sawdust at different temperature. These peaks are important to estimate amount and type of gases released.

3.4 FTIR Analysis of Sawdust Pyrolysis

In the wave number range 3600–3150 cm^{-1} indicating the release of H2O, 3000–2730 cm^{-1} indicating H2 is released, 2400–2160 cm^{-1} indicating the existence of CO2, 2260–1990 cm^{-1} indicating the existence of CO, 1900–1650 cm^{-1} indicating aldehydes released, 1500–950 cm^{-1} phenols/ethers released and 900–650 cm^{-1} hydrocarbons released [12].

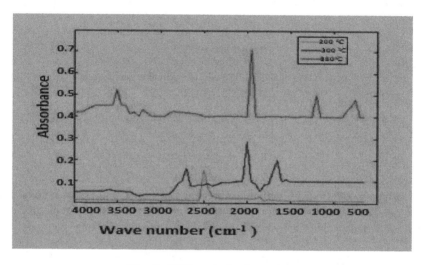

Fig. 5. FTIR analysis of saw dust

At the first stage of the temperatures between 100 and 420 °C, the curves of evolved gases (Figs. 5 and 4) revealed the presence of CO2, H2 and CO, as well as small amounts of some organic volatile compounds such as aldehydes and acids. The first peak at approximately 100 °C represents the water vapor release. The second complex peak confirms the release of volatiles in two steps during active pyrolysis. Individual compounds identified are carbon dioxide, carbon monoxide, hydrogen and char. From DTG & FTIR curve there are many peaks that correspond to functional groups, but major peaks are considered in this work. The progress of released volatile peaks and the temperature interval of their evolution are similar to that observed in this work. The results of sawdust pyrolysis were published by Gu et al. [12]. The pyrolysis process was divided into the following three steps: below 250 °C production of the water vapor. Carbon dioxide, carbon monoxide and hydrogen are produced in the range of 250–500 °C. Above 500 °C char formation process is resulted. Speculative path ways for the mechanism of cellulose, hemicellulose and lignin pyrolysis also presented. The first carbon dioxide signal was detected at approximately 250 °C, reach maximum peak of at 320 °C and decreased up to 450 °C is agreement with the results obtained in this study. However based on the results presented in this study carbon dioxide and hydrogen are released at slightly higher temperatures.

4   Conclusion

The mass loss of sawdust sample during pyrolysis was model using Flynn-Wall-Ozwa model free method. The model was compared with the TG data and 93% of fit was achieved for medium heating rate. The differential analysis shows that higher heating rate has given maximum weight change per time compared to the medium and lower heating rates. The higher heating rate also gives maximum char conversion and low gas release. The DTG & FTIR curve peaks were revealed that for gas release of CO_2, H_2 and CO, as well as small amounts of some organic volatile compounds such as aldehydes and acids.

Acknowledgements. We wish to thank Bahir Dar University Research Center for support of this research fund and Mr. Addisu Wondimu for his cooperation during experimental analysis.

References

1. Raveendran, K., Ganesh, A., Khilar, K.C.: Pyrolysis characteristics of biomass and biomass components. Fuel **75**, 987–998 (1996)
2. Sundaram, E.G., Natarajan, E.: Pyrolysis of coconut shell: an experimental investigation. J. Eng. Res. **6**(2), 33 (2009)
3. Di Blasi, C., Branca, C.: Kinetics of primary product formation from wood pyrolysis. Ind. Eng. Chem. Res. **40**, 5547 (2001)
4. Saddawi, A., Jones, J., Williams, A., Wojtowicz, M.: Kinetics of the thermal decomposition of biomass. Energy Fuels **24**, 1274 (2010)
5. Amutio, M., Lopez, G., Aguado, R., Artetxe, M., Bilbao, J., Olazar, M.: Kinetic study of lignocellulosic biomass oxidative pyrolysis. Fuel **95**, 305 (2012)
6. Varhegyi, G., Gronli, M., Di Blasi, C.: Effect of sample origin, extraction, and hot-water washing on the devolatilization kinetics of chestnut wood. Ind. Eng. Chem. Res. **43**, 2356 (2004)
7. Amutio, M., Lopez, G., Aguado, R., Artetxe, M., Bilbao, J., Olazar, M.: Effect of vacuum on lignocellulosic biomass flash pyrolysis in a conical spouted bed reactor. Energy Fuels **25**, 3950 (2011)
8. Koufopanos, C.A., Papayannanos, N., Maschio, G., Lucchesi, A.: Modelling of the pyrolysis of biomass particles. Studies on kinetics, thermal and heat transfer effects. Can. J. Chem. Eng. **69**, 907 (1991)
9. Prakash, N., Karunanithi, T.: Kinetic modelling in biomass pyrolysis review. J. Appl. Sci. Res. **4**(12), 1627 (2008)
10. Kapoor, L., Chaurasia, A.S.: Products yields and kinetics of pyrolysis of sawdust and bagasse particles. Energy Educ. Sci. Technol. Part A **29**(1), 419 (2012)
11. Babu, B.V., Chaurasia, A.S.: Modeling, simulation and estimation of optimum parameters in pyrolysis of biomass. Energy Convers. Manag. **44**, 2135 (2003)
12. Gu, X., et al.: Pyrolysis of polar wood sawdust by TG-FTIR and Py-GC/MS. J. Anal. Appl. Pyrol. **102**, 16 (2013)

Evaluating the Role of Runoff and Soil Erosion on Nutrient Loss in the Chenetale Watershed, Upper Blue Nile Basin, Ethiopia

Alemsha G. Bogale[1,2]([⊠]), Dessalew W. Aynalem[2],
Anwar A. Adem[2,3] [iD], Wolde Mekuria[4], and Seifu A. Tilahun[2]

[1] Department of Water Technology, Bahir Dar Polytechnic College,
Bahir Dar, Ethiopia
galemsha35@gmail.com
[2] Faculty of Civil and Water Resources Engineering,
Bahir Dar University, Bahir Dar, Ethiopia
workudessu@gmail.com, satadm86@gmail.com
[3] Department of Natural Resource Management, Bahir Dar University,
Bahir Dar, Ethiopia
anwarasefa@gmail.com
[4] International Water Management Institute (IWMI), Addis Ababa, Ethiopia
w.bori@cgiar.org

Abstract. The non-point source pollution of agricultural nutrients (P and N) by surface water is not well quantified in the Ethiopia highlands. The objective of this study was to quantify soil nutrients (N and P) from an agricultural uplands area in upper Blue Nile basin. A small watershed (104.6 ha) and nested gully catchment were gauged for data collection. Two years (2015 and 2016) data of runoff, sediment, sediment-associated and dissolved soil nutrients loss were collected from two gagging stations. Both dissolved and sediment associated nutrients were computed for 2015 and 2016 rainy seasons. The result indicated that sediment associated nutrient loss was significantly higher than the dissolved nutrient loss. In 2015, the nutrients loss was 8.93 kg ha^{-1}yr^{-1} N and 0.3 kg ha^{-1}yr^{-1} P at the outlet of W-1 and 3.04 kg ha^{-1}yr^{-1} N and 0.14 kg ha^{-1}yr^{-1} P at the outlet of W-2. In 2016, 7.67 kg ha^{-1}yr^{-1} N and 0.24 kg ha^{-1}yr^{-1} P were lost at the outlet of W-1 and 8.44 kg ha^{-1}yr^{-1} N and 0.57 kg ha^{-1}yr^{-1} P were lost at the outlet of W-2. Nutrients losses with sediment were 91.3% and 45.6% of N and P, respectively. High amount of nitrogen was lost with sediment than in dissolved form indicating that soil erosion is an important process for soil nutrients losses in the highland. Therefore, soil and water conservation practices are practically significant to control soil nutrients loss.

Keywords: Nutrient loss · Runoff · Erosion · Ethiopia

© ICST Institute for Computer Sciences, Social Informatics and Telecommunications Engineering 2019
Published by Springer Nature Switzerland AG 2019. All Rights Reserved
F. A. Zimale et al. (Eds.): ICAST 2018, LNICST 274, pp. 274–287, 2019.
https://doi.org/10.1007/978-3-030-15357-1_23

1 Introduction

The transport of nutrient from agricultural watersheds has been a worldwide environmental concern due to its sensitivity to reduce productivity and surface water pollution [1]. Nutrients carried with surface runoff and eroded sediment can accelerate the eutrophication in lakes and ponds [2]. The primary surface-water pollutants from agricultural lands are sediments, nutrients and herbicides, which need the management practices to minimize their losses from agricultural watersheds [3–5]. Various studies in the globe have provided critical analysis of the processes involved in the release, transport, and biological availability of soil nutrient [6, 7], and the specific impacts of agricultural nutrients on surface water bodies [8–12].

Agriculture is the major source of livelihood for more than 80% of Ethiopian population [13]. However, the agricultural sector, the major livelihood source of farmers, is under continuous threat from the effects of land degradation mainly caused by water-related soil erosion and soil nutrient depletion [14–17]. Land degradation in the Ethiopian highlands has been one of the most prominent problems for the last few decades. Ethiopia has been described as one of the most serious soil erosion prone areas in the world [18]. But it is important to consider further the impact of runoff and erosion on nutrient losses.

The non-point source pollution of agricultural nutrients (P and N) by surface water are not well quantified in the Ethiopian highlands [3]. Only few studies have been conducted on role of soil erosion to nutrient loss in Ethiopia [19–21]. Nutrient losses from agricultural land also imply an economic loss to the farmer by both reduction of crop yield and increasing the replacement cost of soil nutrients [22]. Moreover, nutrient losses can also contribute to water pollution in downstream water bodies [23].

Given the severity of land degradation in Ethiopia, government and development organizations invested huge amount of resources to combat the soil erosion problem [24, 25]. Promotion of sustainable land management (SLM) technologies such as soil bunds has been suggested as a key strategy to reduce land degradation and increase crop production [15]. As stated by [26] "One of the main issues facing the establishment of effective non-point source management controls is the development of economically and environmentally sound P and N management systems and the balancing of productivity with environmental values". Not surprisingly, the problems are most severe in areas where water movement from soil to surface water is greatest and where soil P and N levels are highest.

This paper therefore, has quantified the nutrient loss from soil erosion and runoff in the upland agricultural watershed of the upper Blue Nile Basin, Ethiopia. Such as assessment of relative contribution of nutrient from soil loss and runoff is of critical importance to prevent environmental pollution and helps to formulate appropriate type of conservation practices in the Ethiopian highlands.

2   Materials and Methods

2.1   Description of Study Area

Chenetale watershed is located in the Ethiopian high lands, in the Blue Nile Basin. It is about 140 km from Bahir Dar to South, in Guagussa-Shigudad Woreda, in Awi Zone, and 10 km from the Woreda capital Tillile. The climatic condition of the watershed is sub-humid and the elevation ranges from 2200 to 2700 meters above sea level. As shown in Fig. 1, the watershed lies between $10°$ $79'76''$ and $10°$ $78'29''$ North and $37°$ $05'59''$ and $37°$ $06'74''$ East. It receives annual rainfall between 1400 mm and 1700 mm. The average minimum and maximum annual temperature vary between 18 °C and 25 °C. The upper part of the watershed is steeper slope which is about 57% while the bottom part of the watershed towards the outlet is gentle slope and about 3%. The total area of the watershed covers about 483.6 ha; only 104.6 ha of the watershed

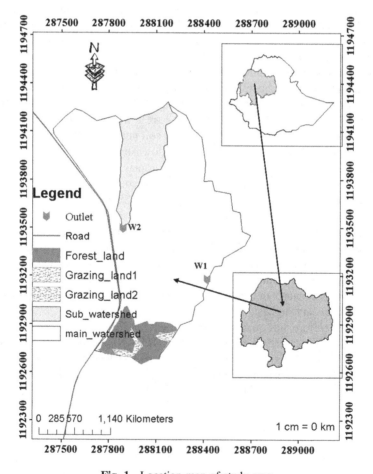

Fig. 1. Location map of study area

is selected for the experimental design. The area is characterized by intensive agri-culture with an average land holding of 0.65 hectares per household.

The watershed is dominated by cultivated land. The most common type of crop is wheat, pea, bean, barley and teff. The major part of the study area (91%) is crop land and small part is covered with forest (juniper tree) (8%) and the remaining is covered with grazing (1%) in the main watershed (Fig. 1). The soils in the watershed are classified as Nitosols and Vertic-Nitosols. Nitosols which are found in the upper part of the water-shed is rich in deep red clay soil. The Vertic-Nitosols also located in down part of the watershed near to the outlet. It is reddish-brown which has a capability to drain and hold water when it gets wet and dry, respectively. It is mostly suitable for teff crop.

2.2 Data and Methodology

Hydro-Meteorological Data. Rainfall and flow measurement were carried out in 2015 and 2016 rainy seasons. One manual plastic rain gauge was installed to collect rainfall data. Rain fall data was collected from June to November 2015 and from May to October 2016. The missed data of May 2015 and early May 2016 were taken from the Bure meteorological station which is 6 km away from the watershed to the south. The rainfall data of Bure meteorological station was collected from the Bahir Dar national meteorological station (Fig. 2).

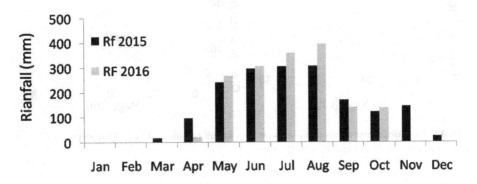

Fig. 2. Monthly rainfall distribution

Two stone masonry weirs were constructed to measure stream flow at the outlets. Weir-1 (W-1) was installed at the outlet of the watershed and weir 2 (W-2) was installed at the outlet of a gully as nested watershed. In 2015 rainy season, flow depth and surface velocity of the runoff using a floating method were collected in 20 min intervals during storm runoff. In 2016 rainy period, the runoff data at W-2 were collected at every 15 min interval but at W-1 measuring interval was continued as 20 min. The change in W-2 was due to the small size of the catchment and to capture all peaks. Surface velocity was measured by dropping a floater at 15 m upstream of the weir and the travel time to reach the weir was recorded using hand watch. The calculated flow velocity at the surface was multiplied by two-third to get average velocity [27]. The flow rate was calculated by multiplying the mean velocity with cross sectional area of the weir at measured depth. Rating curve was developed for each weir from the scatter plotting of depth vs. discharge (Figs. 3 and 4). A power function was as shown in Figs. 3 and 4. The daily average runoff depth was computed by dividing total discharge in the day by contributing area of the watershed.

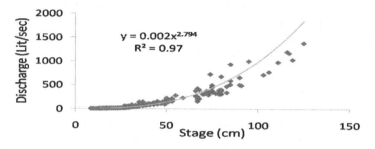

Fig. 3. Stage discharge relationship at weir 1

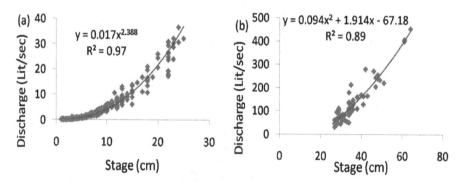

Fig. 4. Stage-discharge relationship at weir 2 (x in the equation indicated the depth of flow in the weir, a, x <= 25 cm and b, x > 25 cm)

Sediment concentration was computed from 1 L of sample collected at weirs (W-1 and W-2) during storm runoff events in 2015 and 2016. The sampling periods were from June 27, 2015 to November 21, 2015 and from May 21, 2016 to October 14, 2016, when there was the surface runoff. From the collected runoff water samples the suspended sediment was estimated by using gravimetric method. The instant sediment yield was calculated by multiplying sediment concentration with calibrated discharge and summed up over the season to estimate the total loss from the watershed.

Nutrient Loss. Atotal of 104 and 105 runoff water and sediment samples were collected in 2015 and 2016, respectively to analyze the nutrients loss by erosion. Filtered water samples from each storm events were composited and samples of 100 ml were collected and preserved by 2 ml of HCL until the collected samples are analyzed at Bahir Dar University, Bahir Dar Technology Institute, Hydrology Laboratory. From the samples dissolved phosphorous (P) and dissolved nitrogen (N) were analyzed using palintest photometer. The total nutrient lost from the watershed was computed by multiplying the nutrient concentration with total instant discharge. The Palintest Nitratest method provided a simple test for nitrate nitrogen within the threshold level of 1 mg/l N and the Palintest Phosphate LR test also measure phosphate levels within the threshold limit of 1.3 mg/l P. The test was however be extended to analyze the nutrient concentration of the sample over the threshold range of the palintest by a simple dilution technique. The diluted concentration of the sample read from the photometer was multiplied by the dilution factor to get the original concentration.

For sediment associated nutrients (N and P) analysis, sediment from two weeks filtered storms runoff samples were composited to meet the minimum requirement of sample size for analysis. The samples were analyzed at Amhara Design and Supervision Works soil laboratory for particulate nutrient lost.

Kjeldahl method was used to determine total nitrogen associated with particulates [28]. The phosphorus concentration was determined using Olsen et al. method [29]. Thus, total soil nutrient lost was the sum of dissolved and sediment-associated laboratory results. The nutrient losses were calculated as following:

$$\text{Nutrient loss (kg)} = \text{concentration of nutrients lost } (\text{mg } l^{-1}) \times \text{runoff } (m^3) \times 10^3 \tag{1}$$

$$\text{Available Phosphorus (Av.P) loss (kg)} = \text{Sediment yield (kg)} \times \text{Av.P (ppm)} \times 10^{-6} \tag{2}$$

$$\text{Total Nitrogen (TN) loss (kg)} = \text{Sediment yield (kg)} \times (\text{TN (\%)}/100) \tag{3}$$

3   Result and Discussion

3.1   Runoff

A total of 213 mm and 268 mm runoff from W-1 and 102 mm and 229 mm runoff from W-2 were recorded in the 2015 and 2016 rainy phases, respectively. The runoff generated from the rainfall was low at the beginning of the rainy season and increased in August. To compare runoff among the sub-watersheds, a runoff coefficient (the quotient of runoff to rainfall volume) was calculated for each month that data was available for each outlet. June had the lowest runoff coefficient in 2016 indicated that most of the rainfall was infiltrated. The increasing trend of runoff coefficient from June to September was observed. The runoff coefficient at W-1 for the month of September was 0.27 in 2015 and 0.4 in 2016. Greater runoff coefficient in 2016 was because of the higher rainfall amount in the season. The runoff coefficient at the outlet of W-1 was higher than the runoff coefficient at the outlet of W-2 in 2015 because higher fraction of rainfall was infiltrated at the upper part of the watershed and contributed by subsurface flow. The difference in runoff coefficients between the two recording years was that the rainfall in 2015 was relatively small in magnitude and uniformly distribute through the year while the rainfall in 2016 was concentrated during the rainy season (Fig. 5).

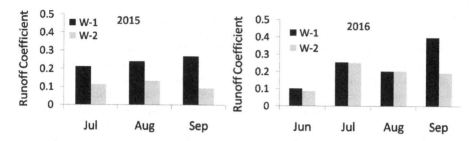

Fig. 5. Runoff coefficients at the outlets in 2015 and 2016

3.2   Sediment Concentration and Load at the Two Gauging Weirs

The sediment concentration and load of the two weirs were monitored at the gauging weirs during two consecutive rainy seasons. it was observed that the sediment concentration from the storm runoff was higher than the sediment concentration during the non-rainy time. This was because of the dilution from base flow. The sediment concentration from storm runoff was very slightly higher in August at the outlet of W-1 and in July at the outlet of W-2 in 2015. In 2016 rainy season, the sediment concentration was higher in July at both gauging stations (Fig. 6). Most of the time high sediment concentration was observed in the month of July. This could be most likely due to the peak agricultural practices and difference in distribution and amount of rainfall in the two rainfall years.

The total sediment lost from whole watershed and nested gully catchment in 2015 was 6.43-ton ha^{-1} yr^{-1} and 2-ton ha^{-1} yr^{-1}, respectively and in 2016, it was 7-ton $ha^{-1}yr^{-1}$ and 9-ton ha^{-1} yr^{-1}, respectively. Less sediment yield and concentration at W-1 than W-2 in 2016 indicated that high rainfall likely raised the perched groundwater table and as a result increased the slumping of gully banks and gullies become source of sediment [30].

3.3   Dissolved Nutrients Loss

The research results indicated that average concentration of dissolved nutrients at the outlet of sub watershed and nested watershed (gully catchment) in 2015 was 1.49 mg l^{-1} and 1 mg l^{-1} N, and 0.272 mg l^{-1} and 0.31 mg l^{-1} P, respectively. In 2016, the average concentration of dissolved N and P was 2.34 and 0.25 mg l^{-1} at the outlet of the sub watershed and 1.61 and 0.62 mg l^{-1} at the nested watershed, respectively. The figures indicated that the difference in the concentration among the experimental watersheds was not significant for P but significant for N in 2015. Nevertheless, there is significantly higher difference among the watersheds for P concentration and vice-versa for N in 2016 (Table 1). This indicated that the highest accumulation of clay has strong relation with P because of the preferential loss of P with finer clay sized particle. High concentration of nutrients lost was significant in low depth and long duration of rainfall and runoff (See Fig. 7).

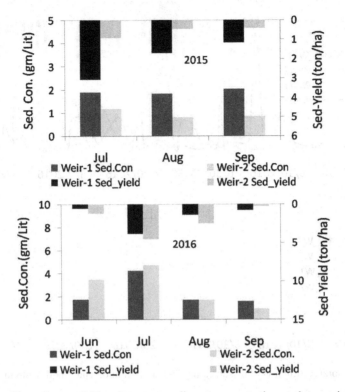

Fig. 6. Monthly sediment yield and average sediment concentration at the gauging outlets in 2015 and 2016

Table 1. Statistical test (ANOVA single factor) at 5% significance level was carried out to compare the nutrients concentration among the watersheds.

Variables	P-value between watersheds	
	2015	2016
N	0.005	0.146
P	0.436	0.0027

The monthly dissolved nutrient losses in experimental watersheds showed that dissolved nutrient losses were low at the beginning of the rainy season and increased progressively throughout the rainy season (Fig. 8). Nutrient transport with in runoff tends to increase with increasing runoff. The total dissolved nutrients lost from W-1 and W-2 in 2015 monsoon period was 0.5 and 0.34 kg ha^{-1}yr^{-1} N, and 0.14 and 0.09 kg ha^{-1}yr^{-1} P, respectively. The amount of nutrients lost from the experimental catchments during 2016 rainy season was estimated, about 0.67 and 0.94 kg ha^{-1}yr^{-1} of N, and 0.08 and 0.37 kg ha^{-1}yr^{-1} of P from W-1 and W-2, respectively. The result of nutrients analysis from storm runoff leaving the study watershed indicated that

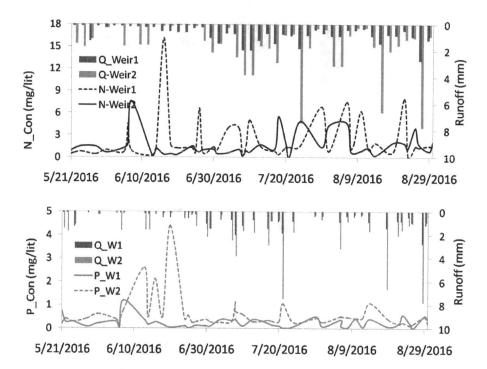

Fig. 7. Temporal distribution of dissolved nutrient concentration and runoff depth in 2016 rainy season

surface runoff is an important component to export dissolved nutrients from agricultural watersheds and runoff should be considered while developing management strategies to minimize nutrients loss from the agricultural lands (Table 2).

3.4   Sediment Associated Nutrients Loss

The analyses of total soil nutrients loss from the experimental catchments were carried out in 2015 and 2016 rainy season. The average amount of loss of total N (8.36 kg ha^{-1}y^{-1}) and P (0.25 kg ha^{-1}y^{-1}) recorded at the outlet of the sub watershed (W-1) were higher than the average amount of loss of N (2.69 kg ha^{-1}y^{-1}), and P (0.054 kg ha^{-1}y^{-1}) observed at the nested gully catchment (W-2) in 2015 rainy period. The sediment associated soil nutrients loss in 2016 rainy period was 6.8 and 7.42 kg ha^{-1}y^{-1} of N and 0.162 and 0.198 kg ha^{-1}y^{-1} of P from W-1 and W-2, respectively. The change in quantity between the years was due to the change in amount and distribution of rainfall that affected the sediment and runoff generated from the catchments.

The monthly loss of N is directly proportional to the estimated soil loss in both rainy seasons. In 2015, unlikely to N, P is highest in August at W-1 than other period which is likely due to saturation of the bottom lands dominated by vertic nitosols and increasing in sediment concentration from the gully banks (Fig. 9). Nutrients eroded or

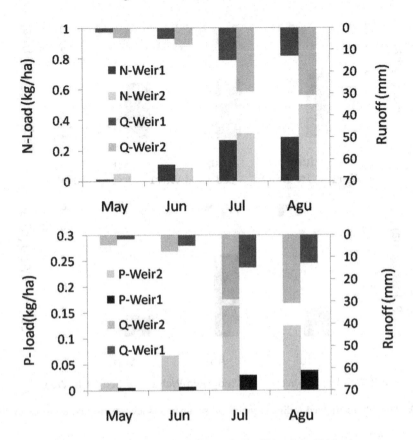

Fig. 8. Monthly dissolved nutrients lost and runoff depth in 2016 rainy season

leached from soil are also subjected to the rate of uptake by the crops as they stay in the soil. In the study watershed, most of the crops were sown from mid of June to end of July when fertilizer is frequently applied. The result indicated that the nutrients loss was significantly high starting from July (mostly at the time of full application of fertilizer) and gets reduced to the next months (Figs. 9 and 10). When tillage is reduced or eliminated, particulate nutrient loss in surface runoff usually declines. Timing and methods of application of fertilizer are more important to control nutrients transported in runoff because nutrients transport with soil tends to increase with increasing nutrient concentration at the soil surface and increasing soil losses [31]. Agricultural practices that reduce nutrient concentrations in the soil surface and reduce surface runoff, therefore, are most effective in controlling nutrient transport.

A statistical test (F-test) at 5% significance level was carried out to compare the particulate and dissolved nutrient loss. The nitrogen loss at W-1 was significantly different among dissolved and particulate nutrient loss. Phosphorus was not statistically different between the particulate and dissolved nutrient loss at both outlets. This indicates that phosphorus is considerably leached by surface runoff.

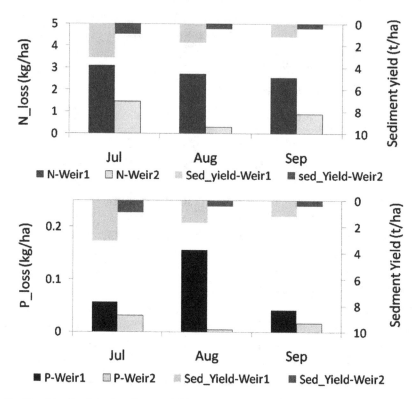

Fig. 9. Monthly distributed sediment yield and sediment associated soil nutrients loss in 2015

Few studies are available on nutrient losses in Ethiopia. The study [21] found that annual average national nutrient losses of N and P in Ethiopia were 79 kg ha^{-1}y^{-1} and 5 kg ha^{-1}y^{-1}, respectively. However, [32] reported smaller losses (35 and 0.2 kg ha^{-1} y^{-1}) of N and P, respectively from the cultivated lands of Tigray (northern Ethiopia). In other studies conducted in Dapo, Mizewa and Meja watersheds in Blue Nile basin, the average nutrients loss for N was 14, 2.1 and 9.7 kg ha^{-1} y^{-1}, respectively. Whereas, 6.8, 1.9 and 4.7 kg ha^{-1} y^{-1} of P was lost, respectively [33]. Further studies were conducted on nutrient loss in sub-Saharan Africa. The alarming annual average nutrient loss for sub-Saharan Africa was 22 kg N ha^{-1} y^{-1}and 2.5 kg P ha^{-1} y^{-1} in 1982–84, and 26 kg N ha^{-1} y^{-1} and 3 kg P ha^{-1} y^{-1} in 2000 [20]. According to the report by [34] the estimated TN and P export from the watersheds in the Mid-Atlantic region is 9.0 kg ha^{-1} y^{-1} and 0.68 kg ha^{-1} y^{-1} respectively. In this study, the N and P lost is still lower than the above mentioned watersheds except Mizewa and Meja watersheds [33] for N lost and [32] studies for P. The extent of soil erosion, rainfall characteristic, watershed size, management practice, fertility status and other variables could be mentioned as causes for variation of nutrient loss in the country.

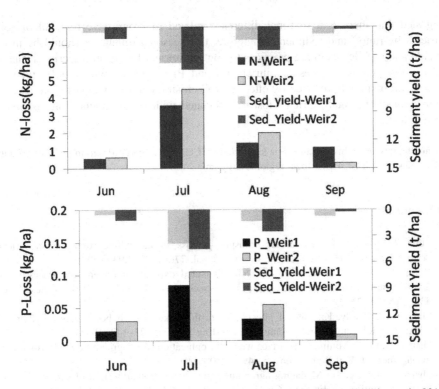

Fig. 10. Monthly distributed sediment load and sediment associated nutrients losses in 2016

Table 2. Statistical comparison of variables among particulate and dissolved nutrient loss using 5% significance level

Variable	Dissolved vs particulate soil nutrients loss	
	Outlet	Nested
N	0.0039	0.011
P	0.165	0.387

4   Conclusion

Dissolved nutrients (N and P) lost in surface runoff were low for each of the two study years than sediment associated nutrient lost. There is statistically significance difference among particulate and dissolved N lost in both outlets, because of agricultural area extent difference while there was no significant difference for P. Dissolved soil nutrients (N and P) lost in runoff was usually small at the beginning of the cropping season and increased progressively throughout the rainy season. Sediment associated soil nutrients (N and P) were usually highest at the beginning of cropping time and decreased progressively throughout the rainy season. Nutrient transport by runoff tends to increase with increasing amount of rainfall and runoff due to leaching. The study suggested that there is a seasonal difference related to progressive removal of soil nutrients by runoff and sediment. Therefore, this seasonal difference should be in to consideration while designing practices to control nutrient losses during critical runoff and erosion periods. Losses of nutrient (N and P) associated with runoff and soil erosion can be greatly reduced by effective soil erosion control practices since a large component of the total nutrients lost is associated with the sediment than dissolved nutrient lost.

Acknowledgment. This research was supported by CGIAR Research Program on Water, Land and Ecosystem's East Africa focal regional program.

References

1. Sims, J., Simard, R., Joern, B.: Phosphorus loss in agricultural drainage: historical perspective and current research. J. Environ. Qual. **27**(2), 277–293 (1998)
2. Haijin, Z., Jie, Y., Hongjiang, Z.: Field simulated experiment on erosion processes of different farm roads under a heavy rain in red soil region. Trans. Chin. Soc. Agric. Mach. **43**(9), 85–90 (2012)
3. Flaig, E.G., Reddy, K.: Fate of phosphorus in the Lake Okeechobee watershed, Florida, USA: overview and recommendations. Ecol. Eng. **5**(2–3), 127–142 (1995)
4. Daniel, T., et al.: Minimizing surface water eutrophication from agriculture by phosphorous management. J. Soil Water Conserv. **49**(2), 30 (1994)
5. Sharpley, A.N., et al.: Managing agricultural phosphorus for protection of surface waters: Issues and options. J. Environ. Qual. **23**(3), 437–451 (1994)
6. Sonzogni, W., et al.: Bioavailability of phosphorus inputs to lakes. J. Environ. Qual. **11**(4), 555–563 (1982)
7. Logan, T.J.: Mechanisms for release of sediment-bound phosphate to water and the effects of agricultural land management on fluvial transport of particulate and dissolved phosphate. In: Sly, P.G. (ed.) Sediment/Freshwater Interaction. DIHY, vol. 9, pp. 519–530. Springer, Dordrecht (1982). https://doi.org/10.1007/978-94-009-8009-9_50
8. Carpenter, S.R., et al.: Nonpoint pollution of surface waters with phosphorus and nitrogen. Ecol. Appl. **8**(3), 559–568 (1998)
9. Correll, D.L.: The role of phosphorus in the eutrophication of receiving waters: a review. J. Environ. Qual. **27**(2), 261–266 (1998)
10. Sharpley, A., Menzel, R.: The impact of soil and fertilizer phosphorus on the environment. Adv. Agron. **41**, 297–324 (1987)
11. Sharpley, A., Tiessen, H., Cole, C.: Soil phosphorus forms extracted by soil tests as a function of pedogenesis. Soil Sci. Soc. Am. J. **51**(2), 362–365 (1987)
12. Taylor, A., Kilmer, V.: Agricultural phosphorus in the environment. In: The Role of Phosphorus in Agriculture, (Theroleofphosph), pp. 545–557 (1980)
13. Brown, C., Miller, S.: The impacts of local markets: a review of research on farmers markets and community supported agriculture (CSA). Am. J. Agric. Econ. **90**(5), 1298–1302 (2008)
14. Hurni, H.: Applied soil conservation research in Ethiopia (1989)
15. Shiferaw, B., Holden, S.T.: Resource degradation and adoption of land conservation technologies in the Ethiopian highlands: a case study in Andit Tid, North Shewa. Agric. Econ. **18**(3), 233–247 (1998)
16. Nyssen, J., et al.: Érosion et conservation des sols en montagne sahélienne: le cas de l 'Éthiopie du Nord. Science et changements planétaires/Sécheresse **15**(1), 33–39 (2004)

17. Descheemaeker, K., et al.: Litter production and organic matter accumulation in exclosures of the Tigray highlands, Ethiopia. For. Ecol. Manag. 233(1), 21–35 (2006)
18. Hurni, H.: Land degradation, famine, and land resource scenarios in Ethiopia. In: World Soil Erosion and Conservation (1993)
19. Stoorvogel, J.J., Smaling, E.M.A.: Assessment of soil nutrient depletion in Sub-Saharan Africa: 1983-2000. Vol. 2: nutrient balances per crop and per land use systems. In: ISRIC (1990)
20. Stoorvogel, J., Smaling, E.A., Janssen, B.: Calculating soil nutrient balances in Africa at different scales. Fertil. Res. 35(3), 227–235 (1993)
21. Haileselassie, T., Skogsmyr, I.: Effects of nutrient level on maternal choice and siring success in Cucumis sativus (Cucurbitaceae). Evol. Ecol. 19(3), 275–288 (2005)
22. Yirga, C., Hassan, R.M.: Social costs and incentives for optimal control of soil nutrient depletion in the central highlands of Ethiopia. Agric. Syst. 103(3), 153–160 (2010)
23. Pimentel, D., et al.: Environmental and economic costs of soil erosion and conservation benefits. Science 267(5201), 1117–1122 (1995). AAAS-Weekly Paper Edition
24. Hoben, A.: Paradigms and politics: the cultural construction of environmental policy in Ethiopia. World Dev. 23(6), 1007–1021 (1995)
25. Nyssen, J., et al.: Soil and water conservation in Tigray (Northern Ethiopia): the traditional technique and its integration with introduced techniques. Land Degrad. Dev. 11, 199–208 (2000)
26. Sharpley, A., Meyer, M.: Minimizing agricultural nonpoint-source impacts: a symposium overview. J. Environ. Qual. 23(1), 1–3 (1994)
27. Tilahun, S.A., et al.: Revisiting storm runoff processes in the upper Blue Nile basin: the Debre Mawi watershed. Catena 143, 47–56 (2016)
28. Hach, C.C., Brayton, S.V., Kopelove, A.B.: A powerful Kjeldahl nitrogen method using peroxymonosulfuric acid. J. Agric. Food Chem. 33(6), 1117–1123 (1985)
29. Olsen, S.R.: Estimation of available phosphorus in soils by extraction with sodium bicarbonate. United States Department of Agriculture, Washington (1954)
30. Tebebu, T., et al.: Surface and subsurface flow effect on permanent gully formation and upland erosion near Lake Tana in the northern highlands of Ethiopia. Hydrol. Earth Syst. Sci. 14(11), 2207–2217 (2010)
31. Sharpley, A.N., et al.: Agricultural phosphorus and eutrophication. US Department of Agriculture, Agricultural Research Service, ARS–149, p. 44 (2003)
32. Girmay, G., et al.: Runoff and sediment-associated nutrient losses under different land uses in Tigray, Northern Ethiopia. J. Hydrol. 376, 70–80 (2009)
33. Erkossa, T., et al.: Linking soil erosion to on-site financial cost: lessons from watersheds in the Blue Nile basin. Solid Earth 6(2), 765–774 (2015)
34. Smith, R.A., Alexander, R.B.: Sources of Nutrients in the Nation's Watersheds. US Geological Survey (2000)

Adaptive Cloudlet Scheduling Algorithm Using Three Phase Optimization Technique

Mohan Lavanya[1], B. Santhi[1], and Sivasankaran Saravanan[2(✉)]

[1] School of Computing, SASTRA Deemed University,
Thanjavur, Tamilnadu, India
m_lavanyass@ict.sastra.edu, shanthi@cse.sastra.edu
[2] College of Engineering, Debre Berhan University, Debre Berhan, Ethiopia
saran@dbu.edu.et

Abstract. The purpose of cloud computing is to give suitable access to the remote scattered resources. This is achieved through virtualization, which separates the physical computing resources into multiple virtual resources. The other technologies like grid, utility and distributed computing are the backbone of cloud computing. The scheduler plays important role because the user has to pay for the resource based on the time consumed during their usage. Currently, cloudlets and the virtual machines are scheduled according to FCFS and round robin which has higher latency. In order to reduce the latency and to have uniform distribution in scheduling the cloudlets to the Virtual Machines, this paper introduces called ACS3O algorithm which consists of 3 phases of optimization techniques using gang and dedicated processor scheduling to schedule the cloudlets. The proposed cloudlet scheduling algorithm optimizes few basic parameters like waiting time and makespan which have significant impact in the performance. Simulation is done in a Cloudsim environment to evaluate the proposed algorithm.

Keywords: Scheduling · Virtual machine · Adaptive approach · Cloudsim

1 Introduction

Cloud computing is an On-Demand service that provides infrastructure, software, platform as services, which is evolved from grid, utility and distributed computing. The cloud computing gives access to the remote scattered resources, which is achieved by Virtualization through virtual machine [4]. The Virtual Machine scheduler implements a suitable scheduling algorithm for executing various tasks [6] in an effective manner. Cloudlet Scheduler plays a crucial role because user has to pay for the resource based on the time consumed during their usage. In the existing cloudlet scheduling algorithm [5], there are various challenges in optimizing the parameters like waiting time, turnaround time, latency, and cost and load distribution. This proposed algorithm optimizes the parameters like waiting time and load distribution, resulting in reduced latency and cost in an effective manner.

F. A. Zimale et al. (Eds.): ICAST 2018, LNICST 274, pp. 288–297, 2019.
https://doi.org/10.1007/978-3-030-15357-1_24

In our paper, we proposed the Adaptive Cloudlet Scheduling with 3 Phase Optimization algorithm. The algorithm schedules the taskset based on categorization of the virtual machines and allocates the tasks to the VM with threshold value. We have calculated the waiting time and turnaround time. We observed the results of various dataset simulations and concluded that the proposed algorithm gives better result. Existing algorithm called RB2B performance compared with the proposed algorithm to shows the advantages of proposed method.

2 Existing System

Scheduling the cloudlet is mainly concerned in distributing the cloudlets to all the available VM, so that the cloud service is provided to user in a faster and effective manner. Thus, the scheduling plays a major role in cloud computing. Here a few existing scheduling algorithms are taken into account to analyze their performances and to compare with the proposed algorithm.

- FCFS
  This a static scheduling algorithm [1], in which the cloudlets are collected and queued until the VM are available and once the VM are free, cloudlet is assigned based on the arrival time. This is a simple scheduling algorithm. Certain smaller cloudlet waits for longer intervals.
- MIN-MIN
  This is a heuristic based scheduling algorithm [8] in which the smallest cloudlet is selected and assigned to a VM which gives the minimum completion time. In this, the longest cloudlet waits until the smaller cloudlets are scheduled.
- MAX-MIN
  It is also a heuristic based scheduling algorithm [2] in which the longest cloudlet is scheduled to the VM based on the minimum completion time. Here the smaller cloudlets starve, anyways it has a better makespan and throughput than the min-min algorithm.
- THROTTLED LOAD BALANCING ALGORITHM
  In this algorithm [7], an index table of VM and their states are maintained whenever a cloudlet arrives as it scans the index table to find a suitable VM. In this algorithm, every VM maintains a separate queue. Because of the queuing and scanning, the index table results in the increase in waiting time.
- SEQUENCE OPTIMISATION
  Here the cloudlets are scheduled, based on their arrival time in sequences. When a cloudlet arrives, it is allocated to be available VM in sequence. In each VM, the in and out parameters are calculated which are the arrival and burst time of that cloudlet. If the VM is busy, then the arriving cloudlet waits until the earlier cloudlet is scheduled, here time parameter is considered as waiting time of that cloudlet. In this, larger cloudlet may be allocated to lower MIPS VM and vice versa [3].

- RANGE WISE BUSY 2-WAY BALANCED ALGORTIHM

  In this algorithm [9], the VM are categorized based on the incoming cloudlet size. Whenever a cloudlet arrives, it checks whether a target VM is free, then the cloudlet is allocated to the target VM. Otherwise, VM is selected based on minimum finish time for that cloudlet. When the chosen VM is busy, the cloudlet is queued in the local queue. In case if the local queue gets filled, the cloudlet is queued to the global queue. Here the VM with higher MIPS gets overloaded with the cloudlets, while the VM with lower MIPS remains idle, resulting in poor resource utilization and waiting time is also increased.

- SLA-MCT ALGORITHM

  In this algorithm [10], single phase service level agreement-based algorithm proposed by authors. Whenever the cloudlet enters from broker system it will be taken for scheduling based on the agreement. If client request for maximum efficiency the tasks allocated to high speed machine. If the budget is mentioned the system which gives less rental are allocated. After allocation of the cloudlet to VM is over, the load of current load is added with the current execution time of VM. In paper [11] proposes the SLA-MCT algorithm for multi-cloud environment.

3   Proposed Architecture

The VM are categorized based on the cloudlet size and their load values are calculated. When a cloudlet arrives, it checks whether the target VM is free, if it is free cloudlet is allocated to that VM, otherwise it checks the load value. If the load value is minimum then it follows dedicated scheduling algorithm, otherwise it follows the gang scheduling algorithm to schedule the cloudlets. The VM is chosen based on the earliest finish time. If the chosen VM has maximum load value then the cloudlet is not allocated to that VM. It has the same time if chosen VM has the load value less than maximum threshold, its load value is calculated for that cloudlet. If the load value of chosen VM reaches the maximum load threshold then the cloudlet is not allocated to the chosen VM and it waits for the target VM. Otherwise, the cloudlet is allocated to the chosen VM. The proposed algorithm consists of three phases namely, (i) VM Categorization (ii) load calculation and (iii) adaptive scheduling. Based on the load values an adaptive approach is implemented in scheduling. The workflow of adaptive scheduling is described as follows: The VM are initialized, allotted to the hosts and are arranged in ascending order of processing speed. The incoming cloudlets from the global queue are sent to the datacentre broker. In the datacentre broker, the proposed scheduling algorithm is implemented. Initially the datacentre broker measures the cloudlet length and accordingly chooses a target VM for that cloudlet. If the target VM is available then the cloudlet is allocated to the VM, Otherwise the load value of VM is checked to determine which type of scheduling should be followed.

VM Categorization Phase

Here the VM are categorized based on the cloudlet acceptability range value. The initial stage involves in choosing a target VM for the arriving cloudlet based on their length. Datacentres broker defines the cloudlet acceptance range for each VM. The range value is obtained through a formula:

d = (cmax-cmin)/total mips
cmax = size of the largest cloudlet
cmin = size of the smallest cloudlet
total mips = $\sum_0^n speed\ of\ vm$i $0 < i < = n$

The cloudlet acceptance range for each VM consists of two values: one is lower limit and another one is upper limit.

Lower limit = cmin + S0d + S1d + ……. + Sm-1d + 1.
Upper Limit = cmin + S0d + S1d + ……. + Smd.

The datacentre broker matches the incoming cloudlet to its targeted VM based on their length.

Load Calculation Phase

This phase is crucial in this algorithm. The cloudlets are distributed to the various VM based on the calculated load values of the VM. This ensures that the VM with a higher speed (MIPS) is not overloaded. Hence their guaranteed utilization of resources properly. This phase involves,

(a) Calculate the load values for all the VM based on the cloudlets targeted at them.
(b) The datacentre broker checks whether the target VM is busy or not. If the target VM is not busy then the cloudlet is allocated to it, otherwise it checks the load value of the targeted VM. After the load calculation of all the VM, we determine the maximum load values as a maximum threshold and minimum load value as minimum threshold.

Adaptive Scheduling Phase

In adaptive scheduling the load value determines the type of scheduling that has to be implemented. If the load value is equal to minimum threshold then dedicated scheduling algorithm is used otherwise gang scheduling is followed. The workflow of the algorithm is as follows: If the targeted VM is busy then the load value is checked equal to minimum threshold, if it is so then the corresponding cloudlet is queued in the targeted VM. Otherwise the next best VM is searched based on the earliest finish time for that cloudlet. As a result, we find a chosen VM for that cloudlet. For the chosen VM the load value is again calculated for that cloudlet. If the calculated load value exceeds the maximum threshold then the cloudlet is queued in the target VM. The calculated load value of a VM is less than the maximum threshold then the cloudlet is queued in the chosen VM.

Flow chart for proposed method

Various conditions and its related paraments were shown in Fig. 1.

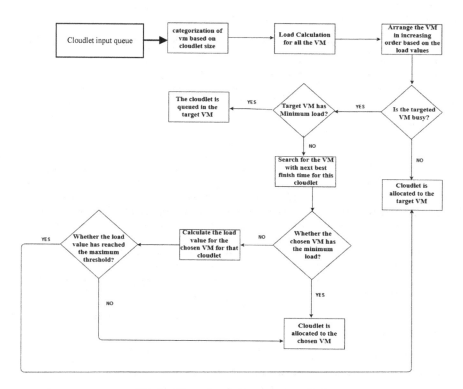

Fig. 1. Flow chart of proposed method

Algorithm steps for proposed method

The proposed algorithm consists of N cloudlets and M number of VM.

INPUT: Cloudlet set $(C_0, C_1, \ldots, C_n)$, N number of cloudlets, $VM(VM_0, \ldots, VM_m)$, Speed of the VM, size of the cloudlets and their arrival time.

1. Arrange the VM in increasing order of their speeds.
2. Calculate the total speed (MIPS).
3. Find the Maximum Size Cloudlet.
4. Find the Minimum Size Cloudlet.
5. Calculate the Interval, d = (cmax-cmin)/total mips.
6. Calculate the upper and lower limit acceptance range values for all VM.
7. Find the target VM for each cloudlet
8. Calculate the Load Values for all the VM
9. Find the Maximum and Minimum threshold load valued VM.
10.   For all the cloudlets,
    10.1 If Target VM is free
    10.1.1   Cloudlet is allocated to that VM
    10.2 Else
        10.2.1   If Load value of target VM==min threshold load   then,
               The cloudlet is queued in the target VM
        10.2.2 Else
               Next best VM is chosen based on earliest finish time for that cloudlet.
               10.2.2.1 If chosen VM has minimum threshold then
                      The cloudlet is queued in the chosen VM
               10.2.2.2 Else
                      Calculate the load for the chosen VM
                      If calc load value>=max threshold then
                      Cloudlet is queued in the target VM
                      Else
                      Cloudlet is queued in the chosen VM.

4   Experimental Result

The proposed adaptive scheduling algorithm is simulated in cloudsim and a small dataset has been taken into account for illustration as shown in Table 1. Due to space constraints, we consider only 10 cloudlets and 3 VM. The cloudlets and VM are considered with the minimum length and their processing speeds. Cloudsim configuration is given in Table 2.

Table 1. Reference VM and cloudlets

Arrival time	C0	C1	C2	C3	C4	C5	C6	C7	C8	C9
	0	1	1	2	2	3	5	6	8	9
Size (MI)	100	10	50	30	90	20	20	40	80	10
	VM0	VM1	VM2							
Processing speed (MIPS)	1	2	3							

Table 2. Cloudsim configuration

Elements	Parameters
Virtual machines	Image size = 1000 (MB), (VM memory) RAM = 512, Speed = x (MIPS), Bandwidth = 1000, Number of CPU's = 1, VMM name = "Xen"
Host	No of hosts and their host ID (Host memory) RAM = 2048 (MB), Storage = 1000000, Bandwidth = 10000
Cloudlets	Length = 1000 (MI), Input and Output File Size, No. of processing elements = 1
Data centre	System architecture = "x86" Operating system = "Linux" VMM = "Xen", Time zone = 10.0 Cost Per Memory = 0.05, Cost Per Storage = 0.001

VM Categorization:

cmax = maximum size cloudlet = 100

cmin = minimum size cloudlet = 10

total mips = (1 + 2 + 3) = 6

d = (cmax-cmin)/total mips = (100 − 10)/6 = 15

Cloudlet acceptance range

VM0 lower limit = 10, upper limit = 25(10 + d)

VM1 lower limit = 25 + 1 = 26, upper limit = 55(25 + 2d)

VM2 lower limit = 55 + 1 = 56, upper limit = 100(55 + 3d)

Load Calculation:

VM0 = C1, C5, C6, C9

VM1 = C2, C3, C7

VM2 = C0, C4, C8

Calculation of load values for each VM

VM0 = (10 + 20 + 20 + 10)/1 = 60

VM1 = (50 + 30 + 40)/2 = 60

VM2 = (100 + 90 + 80)/3 = 89.9

Max threshold load = 89.9 and Min threshold load = 60

Adaptive Scheduling:

Co arrives → Allocated to VM2 (sinceVM2 is free)

C1 arrives → Allocated to VM0 (sinceVM0 is free)

C2 arrives → Allocated to VM1 (sinceVM1 is free)

C3 arrives → Actual targeted VM is VM1 (since VM1 is busy)

Check Load value of VM1 = = min threshold load

Follow dedicated scheduling (i.e.) C3 is queued to VM1

C4 arrives → Actual targeted VM is VM2 (since VM2 is busy)

Check load value of VM2 = = max threshold load

Calculate the expected earlier finish time for C4 in all VM

VM0 - (10 + 90)/1 = 100, VM1 - (80 + 90)/2 = 85, VM2 - (100 + 90)/3 = 63.33
So, C4 is queued to VM2.
C5 arrives → Actual targeted VM is VM0 (since VM0 is busy)
Check Load value of VM0 = = min threshold load

```
cloudlet0allocated to vm:2
cloudlet1allocated to vm:0
cloudlet2allocated to vm:1
cloudlet3allocated to vm:0
cloudlet4allocated to vm:2
cloudlet5allocated to vm:1
cloudlet6allocated to vm:2
cloudlet7allocated to vm:2
cloudlet8allocated to vm:2
cloudlet9allocated to vm:2
999.4333333333334: Broker: Cloudlet 0 received
999.4333333333334: Broker: Cloudlet 4 received
999.4333333333334: Broker: Cloudlet 8 received
1498.9333333333334: Broker: Cloudlet 2 received
1498.9333333333334: Broker: Cloudlet 3 received
1498.9333333333334: Broker: Cloudlet 7 received
3998.9333333333334: Broker: Cloudlet 1 received
3998.9333333333334: Broker: Cloudlet 5 received
3998.9333333333334: Broker: Cloudlet 6 received
3998.9333333333334: Broker: Cloudlet 9 received
Simulation: No more future events
CloudInformationService: Notify all CloudSim entities for shutting down.
Datacenter_0 is shutting down...
Broker is shutting down...
Simulation completed.
Simulation completed.
```

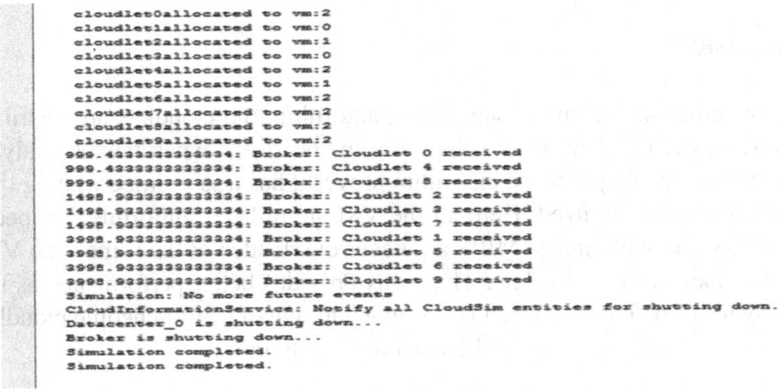

Fig. 2. Cloudlet output results

Table 3. Experimental results

Algorithms	Average wait time	Total execution time
In paper [1]	15.34	90
Adaptive (proposed model)	14.34	89.9

Follow dedicated scheduling (i.e.) C5 is queued to VM0
C6 arrives → Actual targeted VM is VM0 (since VM0 is busy)
Check Load value of VM0 = = min threshold load
Follow dedicated scheduling (i.e.) C6 is queued to VM0
C7 arrives → Actual targeted VM is VM1 (since VM1 is busy)
Check load value of VM1 = = min threshold load
Follow dedicated scheduling (i.e.) so, C7 is queued to VM1
C8 arrives → Actual targeted VM is VM2 (since VM2 is busy)
Check load value of VM2 = = max threshold load
Calculate the expected earlier finish time for C8 in all VM
VM0 - 30 + 80 = 110, VM1 - (70 + 40) = 110, VM2 - (63.3 + 26.6)/3 = 89.9
So, C8 is queued to VM2.
C9 arrives → Actual targeted VM is VM0 (since VM0 is busy)
Check Load value of VM0 = = min threshold load,
C9 is queued to VM0.

Figure 2 shows cloudlet output results for the given data. Table 3 illustrates the inference made is that the proposed adaptive scheduling algorithm has minimum average waiting time than that of existing [1] algorithm. The cloudlets are uniformly distributed and the VM with the higher MIPS is not overloaded, hence load balancing is achieved.

5   Conclusion

In the above proposed Adaptive scheduling algorithm, the cloudlets are distributed to all the VM based on their load values. From the deep experimental analysis and comparative survey, the proposed algorithm proves it has less average waiting time and resources are properly utilized. Here all the VM are utilized uniformly irrespective of their speed, so VM with higher MIPS are never overloaded at the same time VM with lower MIPS does not remains idle. Thus, this provides better performance as the VM are properly utilized. This work can be extended to dynamically schedule cloudlets and updating the load values of the VM by learning techniques.

References

1. Roy, S., Banerjee, S., Chowdhury, K.R., Biswas, U.: Development and analysis of a three-phase cloudlet allocation algorithm. J. King Saud Univ. Comput. Inf. Sci. **29**(4), 473–483 (2017)
2. Lavanya, M., Sahana, V., Swathi Rekha, K., Vaithiyanathan, V.: Adaptive load balancing algorithm using modified resource allocation strategies on infrastructure as a service cloud systems. ARPN J. Eng. Appl. Sci. **10**(10), 4522–4526 (2015)
3. Agarwal, A., Jain, S.: Efficient optimal algorithm of task scheduling in cloud computing environment. Int. J. Comput. Trends Technol. (IJCTT) **9**(7), 344–349 (2014)
4. Bhavani, B.H., Guruprasad, H.S.: Resource provisioning techniques in cloud computing environment: a survey. Int. J. Res. Comput. Commun. Technol. **3**(3), 395–401 (2014)
5. Chawla, Y., Bhonsle, M.: A study on scheduling methods in cloud computing. Int. J. Emerg. Trends Technol. Comput. Sci. **1**(3), 12–17 (2012)
6. Mathew, T., Sekaran, K.C., Jose, J.: Study and analysis of various task scheduling algorithms in the cloud computing environment. In: International Conference on Advances in Computing, Communications and Informatics (ICACCI) (2014)
7. Tohidirad, Y., Abdezadeh, S., Soltani Aliabadi, Z., Azizi, A., Moradi, M.: Virtual machine scheduling in cloud computing environment. Int. J. Manag. Public Sect. Inf. Commun. Technol. **6**(4), 1–6 (2015)
8. Liu, G., Li, J., Xu, J.: An improved min-min algorithm in cloud computing. In: Du, Z. (ed.) Proceedings of the 2012 International Conference of Modern Computer Science and Applications. AISC, vol. 191, pp. 47–52. Springer, Heidelberg (2013). https://doi.org/10.1007/978-3-642-33030-8_8

9. Mao, Y., Chen, X., Li, X.: Max–min task scheduling algorithm for load balance in cloud computing. In: Patnaik, S., Li, X. (eds.) Proceedings of International Conference on Computer Science and Information Technology. AISC, vol. 255, pp. 457–465. Springer, New Delhi (2014). https://doi.org/10.1007/978-81-322-1759-6_53

10. Domanai, S.G., Reddy, G.R.M.: Load balancing in cloud computing using modified throttled algorithm. In: IEEE International Conference on Cloud Computing in Emerging Markets (CCEM) (2013)

11. Teyeb, H.: Integrated optimization in cloud environment, Networking and Internet architecture. Université Paris-saclay (2017)

Design and Development of Household Gasifier Cooking Stoves: Natural Versus Forced Draft

Eshetu Getahun[1,3(✉)], Dawit Tessema[2], and Nigus Gabbiye[3]

[1] Bahir Dar Energy Center, Bahir Dar Institute of Technology,
Bahir Dar University, Bahir Dar, Ethiopia
[2] Ethiopian Textile and Fashion Design Institute,
Bahir Dar University, Bahir Dar, Ethiopia
[3] Chemical Engineering Department, Bahir Dar Institute of Technology,
Bahir Dar University, Bahir Dar, Ethiopia
eshetu201384@gmail.com

Abstract. In recent years, there has been renewed interest on renewable biomass based energies. This is due to the growing environmental stringent regulation, energy security concern and spiraling price of fossil fuel. More than 80% of the Ethiopian population who reside in the rural depend on biomass energy for their cooking and lighting. Traditionally, food cooking and *Injera* baking are carried out using an open fire/three stone/system in the rural areas. Despite the substantial effort made by Ethiopian government to disseminate improved biomass cooking stove technologies such as *Mirt, Lakech, Tikikil,* and *Gonzie,* the end of pipe technological use strategy is very minimal. In this study rigorous natural and forced draft gasifiers stove design were performed based on energy consumption load for cooking and solid waste management purposes. Standard water boiling test (WBT) and controlled cooking test (CCT) were used to determine the performance of the stove. The WBT showed that the gasifier stove had thermal efficiency of 22.7% and 25% for natural draft and forced draft respectively. Moreover, the CCT indicated that the performance of the gasifier stove were 84% and 72% for natural draft and forced draft as compared to the traditional open fire three stone stove. The burning time using 0.8 kg of fuel was 65 min and 40 min for natural and forced draft gasifier stoves respectively.

Keywords: Gasifier stove · Natural and forced draft · WBT and CCT

1 Introduction

1.1 Background

Now a day there are a huge interests in the developing countries to utilize renewable energy resources so as to reduce, fuel price, energy security and global warming concerns associated with fossil fuels [1]. Among those renewable energies, biomass is the oldest source of energy and currently accounts for about 15% of the world's primary energy consumption and about 38% of the primary energy consumption in developing countries [1]. In particular, biomass energy accounts for more than 90% of the total rural energy supplies in Ethiopia. Abundant biomass is available throughout the world which

F. A. Zimale et al. (Eds.): ICAST 2018, LNICST 274, pp. 298–314, 2019.
https://doi.org/10.1007/978-3-030-15357-1_25

can be converted into useful energy forms. Biomass is traditionally available in the form of solid state such as crops residues, forest waste, animal waste, municipal waste, food waste, and plant waste. Biomass is the general term which includes phyto-mass or plant biomass and zoo-mass or animal biomass/cattle excreta [2]. Biomass can be used for the production of power, chemicals, fuels and fertilizer [3].

At global scale more than 3 billion people (nearly half of world human) are deprived of access to modern energy alternatives. Most of these people live in developing countries and depend on traditional biomass resources to meet their basic energy need [4]. Traditional cook stoves consume too much fuel, leading to longer time for fuel collection and deforestation. Subsequent indoor air pollution also results in mortality due to acute respiratory infection and chronic obstructive pulmonary disease [5]. Ethiopia has aimed at shifting from use of high-cost and environmental polluting fossil fuels to cost-effective renewable energies that can be sourced from renewable resources such as biomass, hydro, and wind, geothermal and solar energies.

Major challenge in Ethiopia's energy sector is aligning national energy supply with socio-cultural and economic developmental needs. However, energy crisis in the country is reflected in its overreliance on indigenously sourced biomass fuel. As compared to other energy sources, biomass can be used for production of fuel with diverse and wider uses like cooking, lighting, heating, and power generation. Almost all of the rural societies of Ethiopia depend on biomass energy for their cooking and lighting. Furthermore there is lack of well elaborated study on strategies and efficient cooking technologies for biomass based energies in the country. In Ethiopia, a common type of cooking and unique mode of baking (*injera* baking) requires the bulk of domestic energy demand. Obviously, food cooking and *injera* baking are carried out using an open fire/three stone/system in every households. As it is known this technique is inefficient and resource wasteful. To address this problem, many efforts have been and are being made by the government and non-government organizations since the early 1990s. The development of '*Mirt*' *Injera* stove, '*Lakech*' charcoal stove, *tikikil* and currently '*Gonzie*' biomass *injera* and pot stove are some of the results of these efforts in the country. Now a day, *mirt* stove is being widely promoted throughout the country due to the fact that it can achieve fuel saving efficiency up to 50% as compared to the open fire system. It can also improve the kitchen environment by reducing indoor air pollution and other problems such as burn and exposure to excessive heat [4, 6].

The dominant utilization of traditional fuels coupled with use of technologies of low efficiency contributes to the environmental degradation and prevalence of health problems due to indoor air pollution. Direct burning of biomass significantly contributes to CO_2 as well as black carbon emissions, which intensify greenhouse gas in the atmosphere. When there is a complete combustion of biomass, the resultant products are carbon dioxide and water vapor, which are not harmful at all, whereas incomplete combustion releases health damaging pollutants (CO, N_2O, and CH4) and GHG [7]. Traditional biomass stoves are very inconvenient for utilization. They are difficult to ignite and produce a lot of smoke, especially during the start-up time. The existing cooking technologies such as open fire three stone, *mirt, gonze, tikikil* and *lakech* stoves are direct combustion technology and hence they have less thermal efficiency. Moreover, these combustion cooking technologies pollute the environment by emitting carbon dioxide and other gases. Therefore, the development of improved cook stoves has been employed to improve indoor air quality in developing countries like Ethiopia whose populations depend primarily on biomass fuels. Overuse of these fuels depletes resources and degrades local environments, multiplies the time needed to collect fuel, and creates indoor air pollution that threatens the wellbeing of the members of households [8].

Biomass can be converted into heat and power by adopting appropriate conversion technologies. Digestion, gasification, incineration and combustion are some of the available processes for the conversion of biomass into useful energy forms [9]. However, due to its thermo-chemical conversion efficiencies, less area per unit output and the compatibility of the gas for all combustion engines and utilization of gas for cooking purpose, gasification is comparatively effective conversion alternative amongst the other biomass conversion technologies. Biomass gasifier cook stoves are based on an improved combustion technology, which is different from other common "improved" stoves, like rocket stoves and other rocket-type wood stoves [5]. Gasification is a process that converts carbonaceous materials into carbon monoxide, hydrogen, carbon dioxide, and methane. This is achieved by reacting the material at high temperatures (>700 °C) and a limited amount of oxygen and/or steam. The resulting gas mixture is called syngas or producer gas and is itself a fuel. In terms of volume, syngas of wood gasification contains approximately 15–21% H_2, 10–20% CO, 11–13% CO_2 and 1–5% of CH_4, plus N [10]. All of these gases are combustible except nitrogen which is not combustible. The general reaction for biomass gasification is: Biomass + air (or H_2O) → CO, CO_2, H_2O, H_2, CH_4 and N + tars + particulates.

Reports indicated that fuel moisture content, particle size and air fuel ratio have great impact on the performance of gasifier cooking stove [5].

The aims of this study are (1) to investigate appropriate design parameter such as reactor diameter, height, air fuel ratio, amount of fuel that fit the household energy demand; (2) to determine the temperature distribution and performance of gasifier cooking stove; (3) to compare the performance of the gasifier stove with the existing cooking stove.

2 Materials and Methods

2.1 Materials

Solid waste biomass feed stocks such as rice husk; coffee husk and saw dust were collected and analyzed for their particle size in the range of 0.5 mm and 2.4 mm. Sheet metal used for manufacturing gasifier stove with thickness of 1.6 mm was purchased from suppliers. Fan/blower with power rate of 30 W were purchased from local market for supplying of air to the gasifier. Pipes, fittings, and valves, different types of steel bars, cooking utensils such as *mitad* and pan were obtained from local supplier.

2.2   Methods

The complete household level gasifier stoves were manufactured in pilot scale and the following procedures were implemented. First, preliminary design loads were determined. Moreover, based on the load different parts of gasifier stoves were designed using appropriate software and then according to the design, the natural and forced draft gasifier stoves were manufactured by consulting appropriate manufacturing enterprises. After this, different types of feed stocks were burned. Finally, the pilot scale gasifier stoves performance were characterized for their efficiency, fuel consumption, burning time, heating value. The design parameters were determined using Belonio [11] methodologies.

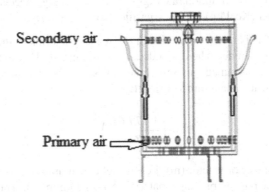

Fig. 1. Schematic sketch of the gasifier cooking stove

The natural and forced-draft gasifier stove tested in this study has two metal walls without thermal insulation material between the walls (Fig. 1). In this gasification process primary and secondary air is taken in at the bottom and the top respectively, and the gas started to burn at the top of the burner. The biomass moves counter to the gas flow and passes successively through drying, pyrolization, reduction, and hearth zones. The temperature distribution of the gasifier stove were measured using K-type thermocouple. The updraft gasifier could be designed to work under a natural and forced draft. For this study cooking energy load and size of gasifier stove for every household in Ethiopia, was investigated based on rice food cooking by taking 2 kg of rice within 20 min cooking time.

Design Parameters: All the appropriate gasifier stove design parameters of the gasifier stove were determined as follow.

Energy Needed. This is the amount of heat that needs to be supplied by the stove which can be determined based on the amount of food to be cooked and/or water to be boiled in a household and their corresponding specific energy. The amount of energy needed to cook this food was determined using Eq. 1.

$$Qn = \frac{Mf * Es}{T} \tag{1}$$

Where Qn - Energy needed (Kcal/h), Mf - Mass of rice to be cooked (Kg), T - Cooking time (h). Es - Specific energy of rice (330.43 kcal/Kg) [11].

Energy Input or Fuel Consumption rate (FCR). This is the amount of energy needed in terms of fuel to be fed into the stove. This was computed using Eq. 2.

$$FCR = \frac{Qn}{Hvf * \eta g} \tag{2}$$

Where, FCR - fuel consumption rate (kg/h), Qn - heat energy needed (Kcal/h), HVf - heating value of fuel (Kcal/kg) and ηg - gasifier stove efficiency (22–25%).

Reactor Diameter. This refers to the size of the reactor in terms of the diameter of the cross-section of the cylinder where woods are being burned. This is a function of the amount of the fuel consumed per unit time (FCR) to the specific gasification rate (SGR) of wood and it is determined using Eq. 3.

$$D = \left(\frac{1.27\,FCR}{SGR}\right)^{0.5} \tag{3}$$

Where, D - Diameter of reactor (m), FCR - fuel consumption rate (kg/h) and SGR - specific gasification rate of biomass material (50–210 kg/m²-h). The specific gasification rate of different biomass materials are in the range of 40–210 kg/m²-h [9]. For this study, the specific gasification rate and density of the fuel were selected as 43 kg/m²-h and 129 kg/m³ respectively.

Time to Consume Wood. This is the total time required to completely gasify the wood inside the reactor. This can be computed using Eq. 4.

$$T = \frac{\rho * Vr}{FCR} \tag{4}$$

Where, T - Time required consuming the wood (h), Vr - volume of the reactor (m³), ρ - Wood density (kg/m³) and FCR is rate of consumption of wood (kg/h).

Height of the Reactor. This is the total distance from the top and the bottom end of the reactor and determines how long the stove would be operated in one loading of fuel. The height of the reactor can be computed using Eq. 5.

$$H = \frac{SGR * T}{\rho} \tag{5}$$

Where, H - Length of the reactor, (m), SGR-specific gasification rate of wood, (kg/m²-h), T - Time required consuming wood (h) and ρ - Wood density (kg/m³).

Amount of Air Needed for Gasification. This is the rate of flow of air needed to gasify biomass. This is very important in determining the size of the fan or of the blower needed for the reactor in gasifying wood. This can be computed using Eq. 6.

$$AFR = \frac{\varepsilon * FCR * SA}{\rho a} \tag{6}$$

Where, AFR - air flow rate (m^3/h), ε - Equivalence ratio of wood, mostly in the range of 0.1–0.38, FCR - rate of consumption of wood (kg/h), SA - stoichiometric air of wood, 6.1 kg air per kg wood and ρa - air density (1.25 kg/m^3). The equivalent ratio of wood biomass is in the range of 0.1–0.38 and stoichiometric of air is also about 6.1 kg air per kg of wood biomass [11]. To determine air flow rate 0.3 equivalent ratio of wood (saw dust) fuel was taken.

Superficial Air Velocity. This is the speed of the air flow in the fuel bed. The velocity of air in the bed of woods will cause channel formation, which may greatly affect gasification and depends on the diameter of the reactor (D) and the airflow rate (AFR). This can be computed using Eq. 7.

$$Vs = \frac{4\,AFR}{\Pi * (D)^2} \tag{7}$$

Where, Vs - Superficial air velocity (m/s), AFR - air flow rate (m^3/h) and D - Diameter of reactor (m).

Resistance to Airflow. This is the amount of resistance exerted by the fuel and by the char inside the reactor during gasification. This is important in determining whether a fan or a blower is needed for the reactor. The height of the fuel column (Hf) and the specific resistance (Sr) of wood (saw dust) will give enough information for the total resistance needed for the fan or the blower. This can be computed using Eq. 8.

$$Rf = Hf * Sr \tag{8}$$

Where, Rf - resistance of fuel (cm of H_2O), Hf - height of the reactor (m) and Sr - specific resistance, which is 0.65 cm of water/m of fuel.

Characterization of the Gasifier Stove

Ultimate Analysis: The elemental compositions of fuel wood were obtained from the database PHYLLIS2 [12].

Proximate Analysis: the sample was milled and sieved to a particle size of 400 µm. To this end moisture content, volatile material, ash and fixed carbon were analyzed according to international standard ASTM D 1762-84.

Moisture Content-after drying the crucible in the muffle, two grams of the sieved sample was put in the crucible and then dried in the oven at 105 °C for two hours. The weight was recorded until constant mass was obtained. Then the moisture content was determined using Eq. 9.

$$Mc = \frac{Wi - Wf}{Wi} * 100 \tag{9}$$

Where, Mc - moisture content (%), Wi - initial mass of the sample before drying (g) and Wf - final mass of the sample after dried (g).

Volatile Material: the value of the volatile material was determine by placing the sample weight that was obtained after subjected to 105 °C in the crucible with cap and then putting it in the muffle at 950 °C. Finally the volatile material was determined using Eq. 10.

$$Vm = \frac{Ws - Wv}{Ws} * 100 \tag{10}$$

Where, Vm - volatile material (%), Ws - Weight of the sample after subjected to 105 °C (g) and Wv - weight of the sample after subjected to 950 °C (g).

Ash Content: the sample mass was put in the crucible without cap and then this sample mass was put in the muffle furnace at 750 °C for six hours to reach the total incineration of the sample. The ash content was determined using Eq. 11.

$$A = \frac{Pa}{Ps} * 100 \tag{11}$$

Where, A - ash content (%), Pa - Weight of the ash (g) and Ps - weight of the sample after subjected to 950 °C (g).

Fixed Carbon: to determine the fixed carbon in content dry base, volatile material and ash content were subtracted to 100 [13] as shown in Eq. 12.

$$Fc = 100 - (Vm + A) \tag{12}$$

Calorific Value: the calorific value was analyzed using the bomb calorie meter.

Performance of Gasifier Stove

Water Boiling Test (WBT): The percentage of thermal efficiency is the ratio of mass of product in the cook pot, heat capacity and temperature change plus the evaporated water mass and latent heat of evaporation versus fuel mass and fuel energy. First of all the fuel and pot to be used in the test were separately weighed. And then the pot was partially filled up with two liter of water and weighed again. To this end the initial temperature of water was recorded before the stove was ignited to initiate heating of the pot. Moreover, boiling temperature of water was recorded. When the burning of the fuel was completed, the weight of water left on the pot was recorded and the thermal efficiency was determined using Eq. 13.

$$\eta = \frac{Mn * Cp * (Tb - To) + Me * L}{Mf * Hv} \qquad (13)$$

Where, η - Thermal efficiency (%), Mn - mass of water in the pan (kg), Cp - specific heat of water (kj/kg/°C), To - starting temperature of the water (°C) and Tb - boiling temperature of the water (°C), Me - mass of water evaporated (kg), L - latent heat of evaporation (kj/kg), Mf - weight of fuel burnt (0.8 kg) and Hv - heating value of the fuel (kj/kg).

Charcoal Yield: At the end of the gasification process the charcoal weight was recorded and the charcoal yield was determined using Eq. 14.

$$Yield = \frac{Charcoal\ weight}{Feed\ stock\ weight} * 100 \qquad (14)$$

Controlled Cooking Test (CCT): The controlled cooking test is an intermediate test between simple water boiling test and the kitchen performance test. It is used to compare the fuel consumed, residual charcoal content and the time spent in cooking a meal on different stoves. In this test, locally available saw dust fuel was used for the cooking. Locally well-known food, *shiro wot*, was selected as cooking meal. All the tests were determined based the VITA [14] methodology in order to compare the fuel saving efficiency of the new technology with the traditional three stone stove. The test was repeated three times for each stove type. Different measurements also included to determine the moisture content of fuel wood, ambient temperature, time needed to cook the dish, time needed to light the fire, initial and final meal mass, initial and final fuel wood mass and the residual charcoal content. For this test, the initial meal and fuel mass were 2.46 kg and 0.8 kg respectively.

3 Results and Discussions

The designed prototype gasifier stove is shown in Fig. 2. The gasifier stove has the gas burner and the pot support on the top. Moreover, this biomass-fired gasifier stove consists of the reaction chamber, primary and secondary air inlet and three legs which support the gasifier stoves. To minimize the heat losses, the gasifier stoves have air gap as an insulation material between the outer and inner diameter of the reactors. In the case of forced draft gasifier stove, 24 V DC supply fan was used to supply primary and secondary airs for the gasifier stove.

3.1 Design Parameters

All the calculated size of natural and forced draft gasifier stove design parameters are summarized in Table 1. As it can be observed in Table 1, the optimal energy demand to cook the food, rice, was 1982.58 kcal/h. The appropriate size of the natural and forced draft gasifier stove diameter and height were 0.29 m and 0.36 mm respectively based on the energy demand and cooking time.

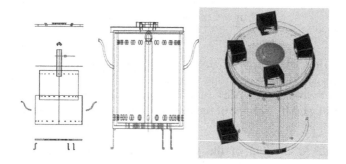

Fig. 2. Designed prototype gasifier stove

Table 1. Design parameters

Parameters	Unit	Natural gasifier stove	Forced gasifier stove
Energy needed	Kcal/h	1982.58	1982.58
Fuel consumption rate	Kg/h	2.33	2.8
Reactor diameter	m	0.29	0.29
Height of the reactor	m	0.36	0.36
Burning time	h	1.086	0.67
Gasification air flow rate	M^3/h	-	3.4
Superficial air velocity	M/s	-	1.77
Resistance to air flow	Cm of H_2O	-	0.234

The amount of air needed for forced draft gasification was 3.4 m^3/h. However, it was visualized that as the amount of air increased, more smoke was released which indicated gasification process was shifted to combustion process. It was also observed from the design size that the superficial air velocity of the forced draft gasification process was 1.77 m/s. Parikh et al. [15] reported that when the superficial air velocity increases, the fuel/air equivalence ratio significantly reduced. In the other way higher air superficial velocity also led to higher fuel consumption rate and consequently there is higher gasification temperature. If the superficial air velocity increases beyond the limit, the velocity of the gas phase increase and it has a convective cooling effect resulting extinction of the process.

Effect of Particle Size on Bio-Char Yield: Selection of natural and forced draft gasification process depends on the nature of the biomass particle size.

In Fig. 3, it was observed that as the particle size of the biomass became small, char yields reduced which signified that of the heat and mass transfer were more effective since the ratio of surface area/volume was increased resulting increase of gas yield and gas heating values. However, as the biomass particle size became very fine and powdered, it was difficult for the movement of air and in this case driving force, like fan, was used to circulate the primary air [16].

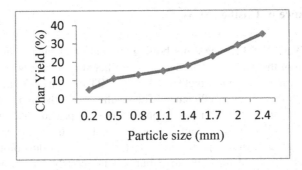

Fig. 3. Effect of particle size on char yield

3.2   Characterization of the Gasifier Stove

Fuel Feedstock Characterization: Different proximate and ultimate analyses were conducted on sawdust and coffee husk. The results of the proximate, ultimate and calorific value analysis carried out on the sawdust and coffee husk are presented in Table 2. The percentage moisture content of sawdust and coffee husk were 10% and 9.9% as shown in Table 2. From the proximate analysis it can be observed that sawdust has higher volatile content than coffee husk. The two feed stocks which have been considered in this study have low moisture and ash contents. The low ash content signified that it reduced problems associated with residual disposal, equipment cleaning and other operational aspects [17]. The result revealed that the moisture contents can be easily reduced by sun drying and the feed stocks have significant biomass energy potentials for gasification process in Ethiopia. Moreover, the ultimate analysis indicated that the percentage of hydrogen, nitrogen, and Sulphur were to some extent similar for the two feed stocks. From this ultimate analysis it was observed that the two feed stocks were relatively rich in carbon and oxygen composition contents.

Table 2. Proximate, ultimate and calorific values of sawdust and coffee husk (dry base)

Element	Proximate analysis		Element	Ultimate analysis	
	Sawdust	Coffee husk		Sawdust	Coffee husk
Moisture content (wt%)	10	9.9	C (%)	47.54	42.1
Volatile material (wt%)	78.30	64.6	H (%)	5.8	4.6
Fixed carbon (wt%)	18.9	31.3	N (%)	0.61	1.53
Ash content (wt%)	2.80	4.1	S (%)	0.00	0.10
HHV (MJ/Kg)	15.59	14.58	O (%)	43.23	47.57

3.3   Performance of Gasifier Stove

Water Boiling Test (WBT): The water boiling test was conducted as shown in Fig. 4. The performance of the natural and forced draft gasifier stoves have been carried out as per the standard water boiling test method (WBT). WBT only measure the heat transfer efficiency rather than the actual efficiency. The gasifier stove thermal efficiency of the fire was evaluated during the high power phase (cooking period). The gasifier stoves were ignited from top and gave combustible gas and a blue flame was established within 6 min of ignition. In this performance test, 0.8 kg of sawdust biomass fuel was used. It has been observed that the stove burnt continuously for about 65 min and 40 min in the natural and forced draft gasifier stove respectively for this amount of fuel.

Fig. 4. Testing of manufactured gasifier stove

The performance parameters of the gasifier stove were presented in Table 3. As it can be seen in Table 3, the thermal efficiency of natural and forced draft gasifier stove were 22.7% and 25% respectively and it is almost similar to the studies reported by Panwar and Rathore [18]. The charcoal contents were 33.3% for natural gasifier stove and 28% for forced gasifier stove.

Table 3. Thermal efficiency determination of gasifier stoves through WBT

Parameter	Unit	Natural draft	Forced draft
Fuel per batch	Kg	1.2	1.2
Time to start up	Min	24	2
Initial water mass	kg	2	2
Mass of water evaporated	kg	1.6	1.9
Time to boil water	Min	16	10
Initial temperature	°C	25	25
Boiling temperature	°C	98	98

(*continued*)

Table 3. (*continued*)

Parameter	Unit	Natural draft	Forced draft
Burning time	Min	65	40
Latent heat of evaporation	kj/kg	2258	2258
Specific heat of water	Kj/kg.°C	4.19	4.19
Maximum stove body temperature	°C	254	260
Maximum flame temperature	°C	700	850
Char yield	%	33.3	28
Thermal efficiency	%	22.7	25

Temperature Distribution: The temperature distribution of natural and forced draft gasifier stoves were plotted in Figs. 5 and 6 respectively. These temperatures were obtained by inserting five thermocouples in the oxidation, reduction, pyrolysis, drying and syngas zones. From this study the highest temperature records were found to be 700 °C and 850 °C in the oxidation zone of the gasifier for the natural and forced draft gasifier stoves respectively. Moreover, the highest temperature was recorded in the forced draft gasifier stove due to the high mass flow rate. The temperature profile were decreased in the order of oxidation, reduction, pyrolysis, drying and syngas of the gasifier reactor chamber as shown in Figs. 5 and 6. From these figures, it can be observed that in the syngas, drying and pyrolysis zones it took a longer time to reach high temperature level than the reduction and oxidation zones.

Ojolo et al. [19] explained that the gasifier has high thermal inertia in the syngas, drying and pyrolysis zones and hence temperature will not be raised to a high level until the thermal inertia is overcome. On the other hand, the thermal inertia helped the gasifierstove to keep a steady temperature level after the whole temperature was raised.

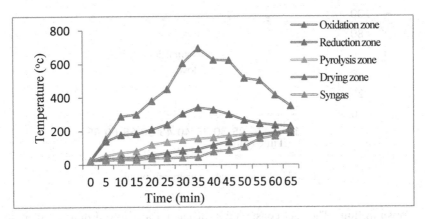

Fig. 5. Temperature distribution in natural gasifier stove

As it can be seen in Figs. 5 and 6, the highest temperature in oxidation zone is due to the combustion of volatile materials in the biomass. As time was gone the char content increased and this char was converted to syngas by endothermic reaction and the temperature was increased gradually and then declined when the char content decreased.

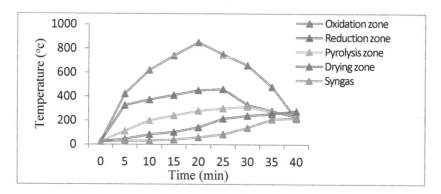

Fig. 6. Temperature distribution in forced gasifier

Water Boiling Test: The water boiling test was conducted by using WBT protocol. The test water was boiled within 10 min of time in the forced gasifier stove and it took about 15 min for the natural gasifier stove. Beyond 20 min, the boiling points were become constant for both gasifier stoves as shown in Fig. 7.

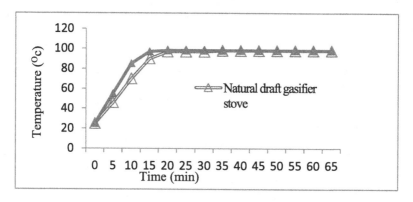

Fig. 7. Boiling water temperature profile

Fuel Consumption: The fuel consumption of natural and forced draft gasifier stove were plotted in Fig. 8. As shown in Fig. 8, it was observed that biomass fuel rapidly consumed in the forced gasifier stove as compared to the natural draft gasifier stove. The slope of the curve gives the mass loss rate of the gasifier stoves.

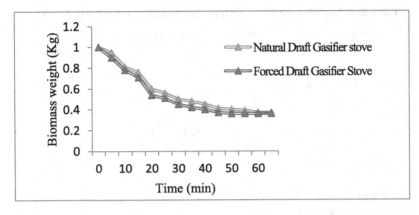

Fig. 8. Burning rate of fuel mass

Controlled Cooking Test (CCT): It is the test of efficacy to evaluate cook stove performance in a controlled environment, using locally available biomass fuels, pots and prevailing cooking practices in the community. This test determines the quantity of fuel used, while the real cook process using a common meal on the stove. It measures the fuel saving efficiency of the stove compared with three stone stove. The fuel saving

Table 4. Comparison of natural draft gasifier and three stone stoves by CCT

Sn.	Test parameters	Units	Test numbers				
			Test 1	Test 2	Test 3	Mean	St Dev
1	**Stove 1: Three stone stove**						
	Total weight of food cooked	g	2,460	2,464	2,468	2,464	4
	Weight of char remaining	g	170	171	172	171	1
	Saw dust consumed	g	221	202	227	217	13
	Specific fuel consumption	g_{-fuel}/kg_{-food}	90	82	92	88	5
	Total cooking time	min	28	30	29	29	1
2	**Stove 2: Gasifier stove**						
	Total weight of food cooked	g	1,560	1,564	1,572	1,565	6
	Weight of char remaining	g	160	161	162	161	1
	Saw dust consumed	g	24	27	17	23	5
	Specific fuel consumption	g_{-fuel}/kg_{-food}	15	17	11	14	3
	Total cooking time	min	18	20	19	19	1
3	**Comparison of Stove 1 and Stove 2**		% difference		T-test	Sig @ 95%?	
	Specific fuel consumption	g_{-fuel}/kg_{-food}	84%		20.62	YES	
	Total cooking time	**min**	34%		12.25	YES	

Table 5. Comparison of forced draft gasifier and three stone stoves by CCT

Sn.	Test parameters	Units	Test numbers				
			Test 1	Test 2	Test 3	Mean	St Dev
1	**Stove 1: Three stone stove**						
	Total weight of food cooked	g	2,460	2,464	2,468	2,464	4
	Weight of char remaining	g	170	171	172	171	1
	Saw dust consumed	g	221	202	227	217	13
	Specific fuel consumption	g_{-fuel}/kg_{-food}	90	82	92	88	5
	Total cooking time	min	28	30	29	29	1
2	**Stove 2: Gasifier stove**						
	Total weight of food cooked	g	1,560	1,816	1,824	1,733	150
	Weight of char remaining	g	160	126	124	137	20
	Saw dust consumed	g	9	87	36	44	40
	Specific fuel consumption	g/kg	6	48	20	25	21
	Total cooking time	min	18	16	17	17	1
3	**Comparison of Stove 1 and Stove 2**		**% difference**		**T-test**	**Sig @ 95%?**	
	Specific fuel consumption	**g/kg**	**72%**		**4.98**	**YES**	
	Total cooking time	**min**	**41%**		**14.70**	**YES**	

comparison of natural draft gasifier and three stone stoves are portrayed in Table 4. As it can be seen in Table 4, the fuel and time saving efficiency of natural draft gasifier stove were 84% and 34% respectively when compared to the three stone stoves. The three stone stoves consumed more fuel than the natural draft gasifier stoves. It was also observed that the fuel and time saving efficiencies of forced draft gasifier stove were 72% and 41% respectively as compared to the three stone stoves as shown in Table 5.

Table 6. Comparison of gasifier stove with existing stoves in terms of efficiency

Sn.	Stove type	Thermal efficiency (%)	Fuel saving efficiency (%)
1	**Conventional stove (existing stove)**		
	Three stone	5–10	-
	Lakech	19–21	25
	Mirt	16–21	40–50
	Gonze	23	42–54
	Tikikil	28	50
2	**New innovation stove (gasifier stove)**		
	Natural draft gasifier	22	84
	Forced draft gasifier	25.7	72

The comparison showed that the natural draft gasifier stove was more efficient than the forced draft gasifier stove in terms of fuel saving efficiency. However, it has less efficiency in terms of cooking time.

Comparison of Existing Stoves with the Gasifier Stoves: The fuels saving efficiency of the conventional stove in Ethiopia are shown in Table 6. As it can be seen from this table, the fuel saving efficiency of the current cooking technologies such as *lakech, gonze, mirte, and tikikil* range between 25–50% as compared to the open fire three stone stoves [20]. The new innovation, gasifier stoves, fuel saving efficiencies were in the range of 72–84% which were more efficient than the existing cooking technologies. Moreover, the thermal efficiency of the gasifier stoves was higher than the three stone, *lakech* and *mirt* stoves efficiency. But it had a similar tendency to *tikiki*l (rocket) and *gonze* stove efficiencies.

4 Conclusions

A laboratory scale updraft natural and forced draft gasifier stoves were rigorously designed and fabricated and evaluated its performance. Solid waste biomass such as saw dust, coffee husk, rice husk and wood were used as feed stock. The performance of the gasifier stove was determined using standard WBT and CCT methods using saw dust as feedstock. The height and diameter of the designed gasifier stove were 0.36 m and 0.29 m respectively. The thermal efficiency of the natural and forced draft gasifier stoves were 22.7% and 25% respectively. Moreover, the fuel saving efficiency were 84% and 72% for natural and forced draft gasifier stove respectively which were higher than the conventional stove (mirt, gonze, lakech, tikikil) efficiency that are ranged between 25–50%.The highest oxidation temperature of natural and forced draft gasifier stoves were 700 °C and 850 °C respectively. The char yields were 33.3% for natural and 28% for forced draft gasifier stove. The burning time of biomass was 65 min for natural and 40 min for forced draft gasifier stoves which can be enough for full cooking process in the household in Ethiopia. Rigorous mathematical model is under way to elucidate the interplay of hydrodynamics with mass and heat transfer for the gasification process.

Acknowledgement. The research fund was granted from Bahir Dar Energy Center, Bahir Dar Institute of technology, Bahir Dar University, Ethiopia.

References

1. Bhattacharya, S.C., Abdul Salam, P.: Low greenhouse gas biomass options for cooking in the developing countries. Biomass Bioenergy **22**(4), 305–317 (2002)
2. Balat, M., Ayar, G.: Biomass energy in the world, use of biomass and potential trends. Energy Sources **27**, 931–940 (2005)
3. Ozokwelu, D., Zhang, S., Okafor, O.C., Cheng, W., Litombe, N.: Biomass utilization. In: Novel Catalytic and Separation Processes Based on Ionic Liquids, pp. 203–220 (2017)

4. Guta, D.D.: Assessment of biomass fuel resource potential and utilization in Ethiopia: sourcing strategies for renewable energies. Int. J. Renew. Energy Res. **2**(1), 132–139 (2012)

5. Huangfu, Y., Li, H., Chen, X., Xue, C., Chen, C., Liu, G.: Effects of moisture content in fuel on thermal performance and emission of biomass semi-gasified cookstove. Energy. Sustain. Dev. **21**(1), 60–65 (2014)

6. Merklein, K., Fong, S.S., Deng, Y.: Biomass Utilization. In: Biotechnology for Biofuel Production and Optimization, pp. 291–324 (2016)

7. Panwar, N.L.: Design and performance evaluation of energy efficient biomass gasifier based cookstove on multi fuels. Mitig. Adapt. Strateg. Glob. Chang. **14**(7), 627–633 (2009)

8. SERI - Solar Energy Research Institute: Gasifier designs. In: Handbook of Biomass Downdraft Gasifier Engine Systems, pp. 30–47 (1988)

9. Chauchan, D., Srivastava, S.: Energy sources. In: Non-Conventional Energy Resources, pp. 1–17 (2000)

10. Dayton, D.: Review of the Literature on Catalytic Biomass Tar Destruction: Milestone Completion Report, December 2002

11. Belonio, A.T.: Rice Husk Gas Stove Handbook. Bioenergylists.Org (2005)

12. Pottmaier, D., Costa, M., Oliveira, A.A.M., Snape, C.: The profiles of mass and heat transfer during pinewood conversion. Phys. Procedia **66**, 285–288 (2015)

13. Berrueta, V.M., Edwards, R.D., Masera, O.R.: Energy performance of wood-burning cookstoves in Michoacan, Mexico. Renew. Energy **33**(5), 859–870 (2008)

14. Baldwin, S., Geller, H., Dutt, G., Ravindranath, N.: Improved woodbunning cookstoves: signs of success. Ambio **14**(4), 280–287 (1985)

15. Parikh, J., Channiwala, S.A., Ghosal, G.K.: A correlation for calculating elemental composition from proximate analysis of biomass materials. Fuel **86**(12–13), 1710–1719 (2007)

16. Worley, M., Yale, J.: Biomass Gasification Technology Assessment - Consolidated Report. Ind. Eng. Chem. Res., 358, November 2012

17. Hernández, J.J., Aranda-Almansa, G., Bula, A.: Gasification of biomass wastes in an entrained flow gasifier: effect of the particle size and the residence time. Fuel Process. Technol. **91**(6), 681–692 (2010)

18. Guo, F., Dong, Y., Dong, L., Guo, C.: Effect of design and operating parameters on the gasification process of biomass in a downdraft fixed bed: an experimental study. Int. J. Hydrog. Energy **39**(11), 5625–5633 (2014)

19. Ojolo, S.J., Abolarin, S.M., Adegbenro, O.: Development of a laboratory scale updraft gasifier. Int. J. Manuf. Syst. **2**(2), 21–42 (2012)

20. Dresen, E., DeVries, B., Herold, M., Verchot, L., Müller, R.: Fuelwood savings and carbon emission reductions by the use of improved cooking stoves in an Afromontane Forest, Ethiopia. Land **3**(3), 1137–1157 (2014)

PSNR and Robustness Comparison Between DCT and SVD Based Digital Image Watermarking Against Different Noise and Attacks

Tarun Rathi[1]([⊠]), Rudra P. Maheshwari[2], Manoj Tripathy[3], and Vikas Chaudhary[4]

[1] Department of Electrical and Computer Engineering, Maddawalabu University, Bale Robe, Ethiopia
rathi.tarun@gmail.com
[2] Raj Kumar Goel Institute of Technology, Ghaziabad, India
rpmaheshwari@hotmail.com
[3] Department of Electrical Engineering, Indian Institute of Technology Roorkee, Roorkee, India
tripathy.manoj@gmail.com
[4] Department of Computer Science and Engineering, KIET Ghaziabad, Ghaziabad, India
Vikas.chaudhary@kiet.edu

Abstract. This paper presents a comparison of extracted watermark image quality and robustness between DCT and SVD based digital watermarking techniques. Here two transform domain DCT and SVD based watermarking algorithms are implemented. For better comparison purpose original host image and watermark image are kept same in both algorithms. Before extracting watermark, different image processing attacks and noise are inserted in watermarked image then DCT and SVD based watermark extraction are performed to check PSNR and robustness against those image processing attacks and noise. Obtained experimental results show that between these two algorithms, robustness, and quality of extracted watermark images are better in SVD based watermarking method.

Keywords: Discrete cosine transform (DCT) ·
Singular value decomposition (SVD) ·
Pseudo random noise sequence (PN sequence) ·
Peak signal to noise ratio (PSNR) · Normalized correlation (NC)

1 Introduction

With the rapid growth of multimedia and internet technology the data communication has been very fast [1]. But these also create the problems of data copyright protection and data security. In order to overcome these issues digital image watermarking is used [2]. Earlier spatial domain based watermarking algorithms were having the problems like quality, security and robustness of extracted watermark. The new transform based

F. A. Zimale et al. (Eds.): ICAST 2018, LNICST 274, pp. 315–321, 2019.
https://doi.org/10.1007/978-3-030-15357-1_26

algorithms are being introduced to reduce the impact of these problems. The transform domain watermarking method is much better than the spatial domain algorithms with respect to different features of watermarking algorithm. In these techniques the message bits are inserted after transforming the host image by using transform based method like discrete cosine transform (DCT), and singular value decomposing (SVD) based algorithm. It is very difficult to detect the hidden contents from the watermarked image in transform based algorithm. If the coefficients of large values are taken to embed the message bits than extracted watermark image will be more robust [3].

There are many features of digital image watermarking like security, capacity, imperceptibility, robustness, etc. but there is a trade-off between three features imperceptibility capacity, and robustness. In recent years more work has been done to find the best tradeoff between the imperceptibility, capacity and robustness [4].

2 Evaluation Parameters

PSNR is peak signal to noise ratio, which represents the quality of the watermark image. Mean square error (MSE) is to be evaluated to compute the PSNR between extracted and original watermark image [5]. PSNR and mean square error (MSE) can be expressed as follows.

$$PSNR = 10 \times \log(\frac{255^2}{MSE}) \tag{1}$$

$$MSE = \frac{1}{M \times N} \sum_{i=1}^{N} \sum_{i=2}^{M} [I(i,j) - I^*(i,j)]^2 \tag{2}$$

Where I(i, j) and I*(i, j) respectively are the pixel values of the original images and watermarked images. Image matrix size is denoted by M × N [6]. Robustness is the ability of the watermark image to preserve the information even after different noise and malicious attacks. This is measured by the normalized correlation (NC) used for similarity measurement between the original watermark and extracted watermark. Normalized correlation (NC) can be expressed as follows.

$$NC = \frac{\sum\limits_{i} w_i w_i^*}{\sum\limits_{i} w_i^2} \tag{3}$$

Here w_i is the original watermark and w_i^* is the extracted watermark [7]. Bigger the NC value means better similarity between two images.

3 Transform Domain Algorithm

3.1 DCT Based Digital Image Watermarking

This is a transform based algorithm which is more robust than spatial domain method. A discrete cosine transform (DCT) changes the host image in terms of a sum of cosine function oscillating at different frequencies [8]. In blind DCT watermarking the host image is segmented into blocks of same size [9]. DCT based algorithm transforms every block into its transformed coefficients. For single image embedding two coefficients are modified. For better result, we choose mid frequencies because higher frequency coefficients are highly sensitive to different image processing attacks and low frequency coefficients are having the feature of visual effect so mid frequency coefficients are selected for inserting the watermark message which improves the robustness of extracted watermark. Selected particular coefficients work as secret key at extracting algorithm [10]. Without knowing this watermark extraction can not be done. After changing coefficients the inverse DCT is taken and combining all blocks to produce the watermarked image.

3.2 SVD Based Digital Image Watermarking

Singular value decomposition is an algorithm to analyze the image matrix. It converts image in to three different metrics [11]. It is a kind of orthogonal transform used for matrix analysis. The SVD of image Im can be described as

$$\text{Im} = \text{HSVT} \tag{4}$$

$$\text{Im} = \text{I}_m = \begin{bmatrix} h1 & h2 & \cdots & hN \end{bmatrix} \begin{bmatrix} s1 & & & \\ & s2 & & \\ & & \ddots & \\ & & & sN \end{bmatrix} \begin{bmatrix} v1 \\ v2 \\ \vdots \\ vN \end{bmatrix}^T \tag{5}$$

Im is the image matrix. H and V are two M × 1 and 1 × N unitary orthogonal matrices, and S is an N × N diagonal matrix [12]. Where the horizontal detail component of image Im is represented by H matrix and vertical detail component of the image Im is represented by V. Both H and V are orthogonal matrices and S is a singular matrix which consists of singular values. Singular values in S matrix are arranged diagonally and in decreasing order. The important feature of SVD is stability, which means small changes in the singular values do not affect the watermark image [13]. This makes the SVD algorithm more robust than other transform based algorithm. After dividing the host image into blocks, each block of host image is transformed using the SVD based algorithm. Singular values of diagonal matrix are modified according to the message bits. Two pseudo random sequences for two binary digits '1' and '0' are added to singular values with a gain factor. After changing singular values we take the inverse process of the SVD to produce a watermarked image. At the extraction algorithm correlation between stored singular value and changed singular values are found. Using this, message bits are recovered, and then reshaped into the watermark image.

4   Experimental Results

To compare both algorithms (discussed above) we extract the watermark from the noisy/attacked watermarked image. For this purpose different noise like Salt and Pepper, Gaussian, Poisson, Speckle, Median filter noise and different geometrical attacks like image rotation and cropping are inserted in the watermarked image before extraction then with the help of DCT and SVD extraction process watermark is extracted. Values of PSNR and normalized correlation of each extracted watermark are measured in DCT and SVD based algorithms and written on watermark images which

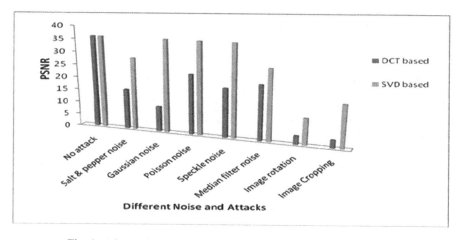

Fig. 1. PSNR of watermark images with respect of different attacks

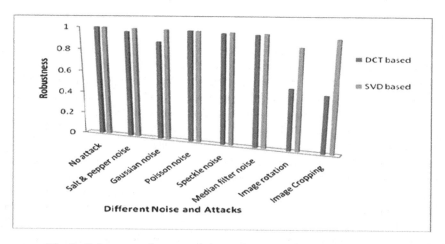

Fig. 2. Robustness of watermark images with respect of different attacks

are shown in Table 1. In two watermarking algorithm, variation in PSNR and robustness against different noise and attacks are shown by the chart in Figs. 1 and 2 respectively where it is clearly visible that extracted watermark image from the SVD based algorithm is of higher PSNR and better robustness then the DCT based algorithm.

Table 1. Comparison of extracted watermark image

SN	Type of noise/attack	DCT based watermarking	SVD based watermarking
1.	No attack		
2.	Salt & Pepper attack		
3.	Gaussian noise		
4.	Poisson noise		

(*continued*)

Table 1. (*continued*)

SN	Type of noise/attack	DCT based watermarking	SVD based watermarking
5.	Speckle noise	watermarked image psnr=23.97 recovered watermark nc=0.99, psnr=19.13 **TAR**	watermarked image psnr=23.47 recovered watermark nc=1.00, psnr=36.12 **TAR**
6.	Median filter noise	watermarked image psnr=32.85 recovered watermark nc=0.99, psnr=21.50 **TAR**	watermarked image psnr=32.05 recovered watermark nc=1.00, psnr=27.67 **TAR**
7.	Image rotation	watermarked image psnr=9.47 recovered watermark nc=0.55, psnr=3.39	watermarked image psnr=9.43 recovered watermark nc=0.90, psnr=10.31 **TAR**
8.	Image cropping	watermarked image psnr=11.78 recovered watermark nc=0.51, psnr=3.10	watermarked image psnr=11.66 recovered watermark nc=0.98, psnr=16.53 **TAR**

5 Conclusions

In this paper, DCT and SVD based digital image watermarking algorithms are implemented using MATLAB. Host and watermark image are kept same for comparison purpose. These algorithms are examined after inserting the different types of noise and attacks in watermarked image at extraction algorithm. SVD based algorithm extracts more robust and better quality watermark image than DCT based algorithm which can be seen through charts in Figs. 1 and 2 respectively. In case of geometric attacks like image cropping and rotation, SVD algorithm is also able to extract watermark image unlike DCT algorithms as shown in Table 1. This is because of the stability, flipping and transpose etc. properties of SVD. A hybrid algorithm using SVD and other transform based watermarking algorithm can also be used to extract much better watermark image.

References

1. Potdar, V.M., Han, S., Chang, E.: A survey of digital image watermarking techniques. In: Proceedings of the IEEE International Conference on Industrial Informatics, pp. 709–716 (2005)
2. Lu, Z.-M., Zheng, H.-Y., Huang, J.-W.: A digital watermarking scheme based on DCT and SVD. In: Proceeding of IIHMSP 2007 Conference, Kaohsiung, pp. 241–244 (2007)
3. Xiao, M.M., Yu, L.X., Liu, C.J.: A comparative research of robustness for image watermarking. In: IEEE International Conference on Computer Science and Software Engineering, pp. 700–703 (2008)
4. Lee, G.-J., Yoon, E.-J., Yoo, K.-Y.: A new LSB based digital watermarking scheme with random mapping function. In: IEEE International Conference on Ubiquitous Multimedia Computing, pp. 130–134 (2008)
5. Na, W., Yunjin, W., Xia, L.: A novel robust watermarking algorithm based on DWT and DCT. In: International Conference on Computational Intelligence and Security, vol. 1, pp. 437–441 (2009)
6. Himanshu, H., Rawat, S., Raman, B., Bhatnagar, G.: DCT and SVD based new watermarking scheme. In: 3rd International Conference on Emerging Trends in Engineering and Technology, pp. 146–151 (2010)
7. Rafigh, M., Moghaddam, M.E.: A robust evolutionary based digital image watermarking technique in DCT domain. In: Proceedings of IEEE Seventh International Conference on Computer Graphics, Imaging and Visualization, pp. 105–109 (2010)
8. Dehkordi, A.B., Esfahani, S.N., Avanaki, N.: Robust LSB watermarking optimized for local structural similarity. In: 19th Iranian IEEE International Conference on Electrical Engineering (ICEE), pp. 1–6 (2011)
9. Run, R.-S., Horng, S.-J., Lai, J.-L., Kao, T.-W., Chen, R.-J.: An improved SVD-based watermarking technique for copyright protection. Expert Syst. Appl. **39**(1), 673–689 (2012)
10. Parashar, P., Singh, R.K.: A survey : digital image watermarking. In: 3rd IEEE International Conference on Industrial Informatics Techniques, pp. 111–124 (2014)
11. Furqan, A., Kumar, M.: Study and analysis of robust DWT-SVD domain based digital image watermarking technique using MATLAB. In: IEEE International Conference on Computational Intelligence & Communication Technology, pp. 638–644 (2015)
12. Bhuyan, T., Srivastava, V.K., Thakkar, F.: Shuffled SVD based robust and secure digital image watermarking. In: International Conference on Electrical, Electronics, and Optimization Techniques, ICEEOT, pp. 1229–1233 (2016)
13. Nana, Z.: Watermarking algorithm of spatial domain image based on SVD. In: ICALIP International Conference on Audio, Language and Image Processing – Proceedings, no. 4, pp. 361–365 (2017)

Multi-font Printed Amharic Character Image Recognition: Deep Learning Techniques

Birhanu Hailu Belay[1](✉), Gebeyehu Belay[1], Tewodros Amberbir Hebtegebrial[2], and Didier Stricker[2]

[1] Bahir Dar Institute of Technology, Bahir Dar, Ethiopia
birhanu.hailub@gmail.com, ge.be09@yahoo.com
[2] DFKI, Technical University of Kaiserslautern, Kaiserslautern, Germany
tedyhabtegebrial@gmail.com, didier.stricker@dfki.de

Abstract. In this paper, we propose a technique to recognize multi-font printed Amharic character images using deep convolutional neural network (DCNN) which is one of the recent techniques adopted from the deep learning community. Experiments were done on 86,715 Amharic character images with different level of degradation and multiple font types. The proposed method has fewer pre-processing steps and outperforms the standard approach used in classical machine learning techniques. We systematically evaluated the performance of the recognition model and achieved 96.02% of character recognition accuracy.

Keywords: Amharic script · Deep convolutional neural network · Deep learning · Printed Amharic character · Pattern recognition · OCR · OCRopus · Visual Geometry Group

1 Introduction

Amharic is Ethiopian widely used language, which is spoken in most federal states of the country. Most histories of the societies and governments has been written and documented in this language. The sample script for Amharic language is depicted below (see Fig. 1). Nowadays, Ethiopian national archive and library agency tries to collect historical Amharic and Ge'ez documents so as to make them available for public. However, Amharic script scanned image documentation and retrieval process is time taking and also is not easy to distribute it for users. Changing this scanned image into full and editable document is an additional technical challenge. Hence, adoption of existing tools and algorithms in the area of OCR to account for Amharic scripts are paramount. An effective OCR model has been developed for other languages, including Latin and non-Latin scripts [6–10]. For Amharic OCR, many researchers attempted using different traditional and statistical machine learning techniques [1–4] which needs further experimentation with state-of-the-art techniques.

© ICST Institute for Computer Sciences, Social Informatics and Telecommunications Engineering 2019
Published by Springer Nature Switzerland AG 2019. All Rights Reserved
F. A. Zimale et al. (Eds.): ICAST 2018, LNICST 274, pp. 322–331, 2019.
https://doi.org/10.1007/978-3-030-15357-1_27

Optical Character Recognition (OCR) is a process that allows printed or hand-written text to be recognized optically and converted into machine-readable code that can be accepted by a computer for further processing and can be electronically edited, searched, stored more compactly, displayed on-line, and used in machine processes such as machine translation, text-to-speech, key data and text mining [1, 2, 8, 12, 16]. It is a systematic approach used for Amharic character recognition by segmenting input image into lines, characters and feature extraction. The extracted features used as an input for a classifier which causes recognition lattice [6, 7] and also need more time and techniques to pre-process and extract feature from the image as well.

To optimize OCR and efficient text image extraction, we propose deep learning techniques. It is an advanced and dynamic tool for multi-font text image recognition. So as to minimize the number of steps and computational resources used for statistical feature extraction, a modified version of Visual Geometric Group (VGG) net is selected [7, 8, 19]. Deep learning takes GPU-days of computation to train on large scale data sets and it also used for character recognition [6, 20], numerals recognition [22] and large-scale image recognition [23].

In VGG net, the convolutional layers enable to automatically extract the salient features which are invariant, a certain degree of shift and shape distortions of the input characters [6, 17]. In addition, shared weight and the same filter are used for each input in the layer. Using sharing weight across CNN layers, reduces the number of parameter and improves performance [6]. On the other hand, different traditional machine learning algorithms applied, in recognition of text images, on a small private database of handwritten and printed character images encountered many challenges, which leads to a collection of multi-font character image and different level of degradation [1–3, 6].

Furthermore, to make Amharic script documents available in the format of electronic text as opposed to page image, we develop an Amharic OCR system which is capable to recognize documents written in Amharic script with multiple fonts and different level of degradation. It is a systematic approach to develop a character image recognition model for printed real-life Amharic documents. In this research work, deep convolutional neural network called VGG net is applied to design the recognition model.

The goal of this paper is to use a synthetic training Amharic character dataset with a printed testing dataset and then to apply deep learning algorithms with different architectures rigorously so as to achieve very low error rates compared to other standard systems and methods. Therefore, in this paper, we apply a modified VGG net architecture using both synthetic and printed Amharic data sets and achieved state-of-the-art performance.

2 Related Works

Various methods have been proposed for character recognition and high recognition rates are reported for different Latin and non-Latin scripts such as the OCR of English [6, 7, 25], Fraktur [8], Arabic [9], Devanagari [11], Malayalam [12] and

Chinese [13–15]. For the last two decades [1–5] many researchers attempted to address problems in Amharic character recognition.

Dereje [1] proposed Binary Morphological filtering algorithm for OCR of Amharic typewritten text. He recommended that adopting recognition algorithms which are not very sensitive to the features of the writing styles of characters helps to enhance recognition rate of Amharic OCR.

Million [2], conducted research to investigate and extract the attributes of Amharic characters written in different fonts and then generalize previously adopted recognition algorithms. Using different test case, 49.38%, 26.04% and 15.75% recognition accuracy were registered for WashRa, Agafari and Visual Geez fonts respectively. In addition, Yaregal [3] noted that, font variation is also a problem in designing OCR system for printed Ethiopic documents.

Hailu et al. [24], attempted to develop a CNN based model so as to recognize Amharic character images with different level of degradation and achieved 92.71% testing accuracy. Wondowsen [4], attempted to develop OCR engine for special type of handwritten Amharic text, which is traditionally called "Yekum Tsehuf" using multilayer perceptron with backpropagation and also Nigussie [5], presented a Neural Network (NN) architecture for a recognition of handwritten Amharic characters of bank cheque.

On the other hand, Shatnawi and Abdallah [18] model a real distortion in Arabic script using real handwritten character examples to recognize characters. They used these distortion models to synthesize handwritten examples that are more realistic and achieved 73.4% recognition accuracy. Zhao et al. [19], proposed a deep learning method based on the convolutional neural networks to recognize scanned characters from real life with the characteristics of illumination variance, cluttered backgrounds, geometry distortion and achieved promising result.

In summary, the above studies noted that written style of characters including font variation, size and level of degradation are important factor for developing OCR model [1–3,18]. And also preprocessing, feature extraction and classification algorithms were the major steps for constructing an effective recognition model [2,3,19].

In addition, to best of the researchers' knowledge, not attempts has been made for Amharic character recognition using deep learning techniques due to scarcity of training dataset. Even though, many researchers have been attempted to recognize a small set of Amharic character image employing hand crafted features which is usually not robust and are computationally intensive.

Therefore, there is still room for improvement of the printed Amharic character recognition using state-of-the-art techniques that can reduce preprocessing steps and computational resource as well.

3   Materials and Methods

This study is concerned with the development of multi-font Printed Amharic character image recognition using deep learning techniques. For experimentation, two datasets; one synthetically generated dataset and the other is scanned image of printed Amharic document, were used.

በቁንጵ መናገር የማሰብ ነገነትንና ሰብዓዊ ፍጥረትን ይበልጥ የሚያገላና ቁንቁን ጨምሮ በሶስት
ነገሮች ማለትም ቁንቁና በሀሳን አሁን ካለበት ወደ ተሻለ ደረጃ ለማሳደግ እንደሚያስፈልጋቸው
ለመረዳት ተችፈል፡፡በበዓሉም የማስተማር ቁንቁ ተግዳሮቶች፣ የትርጉም ስራ አስፈላጊነት ፣
የአስተርሚነት ሙያ እና የብቃት አሰጣጥ በኢትዮጵያንዲሁም የቁንቁ ልማት ስራ
በሀገራችን ያለበትን ደረጃና የወደሬት ሁኔታ በሚሉት ዙሪያ የሚያጠነጥኑ ጥናታዊ
ጽሁፎችቀርበው በተሳታፊዎች ውይይት ተደርጎበቸዋል፡

Fig. 1. Sample Amharic script.

All experiments were performed on a desktop computer with an 8 GB of
NVIDIA GPU memory and LUNIX operating system. During experimentation,
we have used 80,000 synthetically generated Amharic character images and 6715
scanned character images of printed Amharic documents. The synthetic dataset
used in our experimentation were prepared by Hailu et al. [24]. And we prepared
the printed character image data sets using Kyocera TASKalfa 5501i flatbed
scanner at a resolution of 300 DPI. Preprocessing steps including binarization,
skew detection and correction, noise reduction and character image segmentation has been done using the OCRopus [21]. Once we segmented each scanned
Amharic document in to character images, we manually labeled a ground truth
set of each character image in a text file. In addition, VGG net takes the character images as an input and then multiple convolutional layers have been adopted
to extract automatic discriminating features.

3.1   Visual Geometry Group (VGG) Network

For recognition, we use a VGG net architecture. The advanced architecture of
this network may consist stacks of sixteen and nineteen convolutional layers followed by max-pooling layers followed by fully connected and soft-max layer [22].
    In this architecture, the three convolutional layers are used consecutively
with a rectified linear unit (ReLU) as activation function formulated as follows:

$$f(X) = max(0, X) \tag{1}$$

Where X is the input. We did experiments with different architectures of convolutional neural network and the result reported, in this paper, employed a
modified version of the VGG net architecture depicted as follows (see Fig. 2)
and the pseudocode of the proposed model is presented in Algorithm 1 below.
    In each block, the outputs of each convolutional layers pass through an acti-
vation function followed by single 2 × 2 pixel window called max-pooling layer
and illustrated as below (see Fig. 3). And then two fully connected layers with
2048 neurons of each were used at the final layer. The 3 × 3 convolutional filters

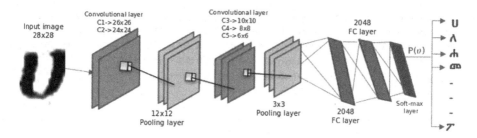

Fig. 2. The proposed VGG network architecture for Amharic character image recognition.

Algorithm 1. Pseudocode for training the proposed model

1: *Input*: Model, T, t // Model= Keras sequential model, T=training dataset, t=test dataset
2: *Output*:Trained model
3: *Start* : // adding convolutional and pooling layers (in this paper, in every
       //three consecutive convolutional layers we apply max-pooling
       Model.add(xConvy), // x= number of filter, y= kernel, Conv=convolution
       Model.add(xPy)//x= is pooling size, y= stride, P=pooling layer
       //here adding the convolutional and pooling layers as many as we want
       Model.add(xFC)//x=number of neurons, FC= fully connected layer
       Model.add(NC)//NC=number of class
       Model.add(softmax)
       Model.compile(Optimizer, accuracy measure)
       Model.fit(T, epochs, validation-split)
4: *Stop*:

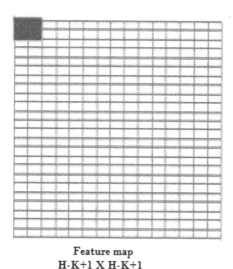

Feature map
H-K+1 X H-K+1

max-pooling
(H-K+1)/2 X (H-K+1)/2

Fig. 3. Pooling process on the feature map that produce a new feature map.

with stride 1 was applied for performing filtering and sub-sampling operations [22]. The total number of parameters used during training the VGG net can be computed as:

$$P = L^2 \times (F^2 \times C^2) \tag{2}$$

Where P is number of parameters, L is the number of consecutive convolutional layers, F is number of filter and C is channel of the image. We considered an input size of 28×28 pixel Amharic character images. The output of each convolutional block is computed using:

$$O = (\frac{W - F + 2 \times P}{S}) + 1 \tag{3}$$

Where O is output of each convolutional block, W is input volume, F is kernel size, P is zero padding and S is number of strides. And then the output of each block is fed to the next network block until the probability of the last layer is calculated. The general process of convolutional layer is depicted in (Fig. 4).

The final output of the model is determined by a Soft-max function, which tells the probability that any of the classes are true, is defined as follows:

$$f(z_j) = \frac{e^{z_j}}{\sum_{k=1}^{K} e^{z_k}} \tag{4}$$

Where z is the vector of the inputs for output layer and j is the indexes which runs from 1 to K and K is output label. To train the proposed network model, we used mini-batches size of 128 and 0.001 learning rate. A dropout rate of 0.25 was used to regularize the network parameters. The ADAM optimizer was used as the optimizing function whereas categorical cross entropy is used to calculate the loss and then found the parameter of connected layers that minimize the prediction loss.

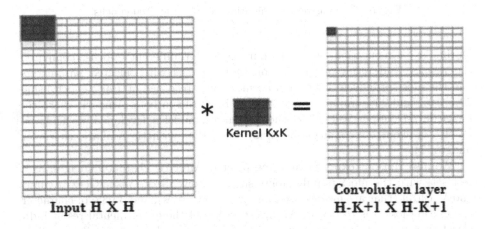

Fig. 4. Illustration of convolutional process.

4   Experimental Results

The implementation is based on deep learning framework using python pro-
graming on Keras Application Program Interface (API) along with TensorFlow
backend. Experiments were run following the network architecture and system
settings introduced in Sect. 3. In this paper, we only consider the 231 basic
Amharic character sets and the results observed during experimentation are
reported as follows (see Figs. 5 and 6).

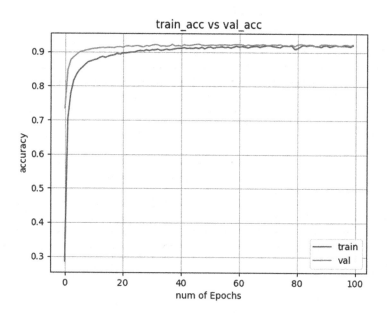

Fig. 5. Training versus validation accuracy for 100 epochs.

During experimentation, we train our model for different epochs, compared
the results, and rerun our model on more epochs with selected parameters
and the most promising validation accuracy was recorded at 100th epoch using
70%, 10% and 20% training, validation and test of synthetic Amharic character
image dataset respectively. Once the recognition model is developed, we achieved
92.71% of average recognition accuracy using the synthetic Amharic character
images [24].

We also run our experiment using printed Amharic character images, as a
test set, with the most popular fonts such as PowerGeez, VisualGeez, Agafari
and WashRa (that are mostly used for typing purposes), and 3.98% of character
recognition loss was recorded. An investigation of the experimental result indicated that some characters were incorrectly recognized due to similarity while
the others were incorrectly recognized even with no similarity between them.

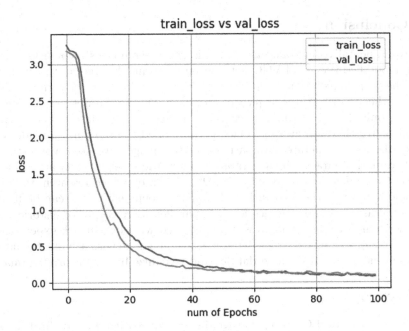

Fig. 6. Training versus validation loss for Amharic character images.

5   Performance Comparison

To the best of the researchers' knowledge, there is no any publicly available dataset for Amharic script recognition and all researchers have been done experiments by preparing their own dataset. Therefore, it is sometimes hard to compare, because previous work has not experimented with large database. However, in order to show the progress of Amharic character image recognition, the result of the current Amharic character recognition model, and the results of previous researches [1–3,24] are shown in Table 1.

Table 1. Performance comparison of related works.

Researchers	Dataset size	Classifier	Accuracy (100%)
Dereje [1]	5172-character images	ANN	61%
Million [2]	7680-character images	SVM	90.37%
Yaregal [3]	1010-character images	ANN	73.18%
Hailu et al. [24]	80,000-character images	CNN	92.71%
Our method	86,715-character images	CNN	96.02%

6   Conclusion

We experimentally developed an Amharic character images recognition model using a modified version of VGG net that outperforms the state-of-the-art methods. The deep convolutional neural network tends to work better with raw input pixels rather than features or part of an image. During dataset preparation we consider only 231 basic Amharic character images. In our dataset each character exists 376 times on average. Once we developed the recognition model with the synthetically generated Amharic character images, we used a printed test set of Amharic character images (about 10% of the total dataset) and achieved an average recognition accuracy of 96.02%. As an extended research, the OCR technology towards the recognition of Amharic document image can be further referenced as word and sentence level, in parallel, large corpus of historical and hand-written document images will be prepared with benchmark experimental result. In addition, an extensive experiment will be done with a syntactic data so as to solve shortage of training dataset and recognize better for printed images.

References

1. Dereje T.: Optical Character Recognition of Typewritten Amharic Text. Master thesis, School of Information studies for Africa, Addis Ababa University, Addis Ababa, Ethiopia (1999)
2. Million, M.: A Generalized Approach to Optical Character Recognition of Amharic Texts. Master thesis, School of Information studies for Africa, Addis Ababa University, Addis Ababa, Ethiopia (2000)
3. Yaregal, A.: Optical Character Recognition of Amharic Text: An Integrated Approach. Master thesis, School of Information studies for Africa, Addis Ababa University, Addis Ababa, Ethiopia (2002)
4. Wondwossen, M.: Optical Character Recognition for Special Type of Handwritten Amharic Text ("Yekum Tsifet"): Neural Network Approach. M.Sc. thesis, School of Information Studies for Africa, Addis Ababa University, Addis Ababa, Ethiopia (2004)
5. Negussie, T.: Handwritten Amharic Text Recognition Applied to the Processing of Bank Cheques. Master thesis, School of Information studies for Africa, Addis Ababa University, Addis Ababa, Ethiopia (2000)
6. Bai, J., Chen, Z., Feng, B., Xu, B.: Image character recognition using deep convolutional neural network learned from different languages. In: 2014 IEEE International Conference on Image Processing (ICIP), pp. 2560–2564. IEEE (2014)
7. Yuan, A., Bai, G., Jiao, L., Liu, Y.: Offline handwritten English character recognition based on convolutional neural network. In: 2012 10th IAPR International Workshop on Document Analysis Systems (DAS), pp. 125–129. IEEE (2012)
8. Breuel, T.M., Ul-Hasan, A., Al-Azawi, M.A., Shafait, F.: High-performance OCR for printed English and Fraktur using LSTM networks. In: 2013 12th In ternational Conference on Document Analysis and Recognition (ICDAR), pp. 683–687. IEEE (2013)
9. ElAdel, A., Ejbali, R., Zaied, M., Amar, C.B.: Dyadic multi-resolution analysis-based deep learning for Arabic handwritten character classification. In: 2015 IEEE 27th International Conference on Tools with Artificial Intelligence (ICTAI), pp. 807–812. IEEE (2015)

10. Shaw, B., Parui, S.K., Shridhar, M.: Offline handwritten deanagari word recognition: a holistic approach based on directional chain code feature and HMM. In: International Conference on Information Technology, ICIT 2008, pp. 203–208. IEEE (2008)
11. Ghosh, D., Dube, T., Shivaprasad, A.: Script recognition-a review. IEEE Trans. Pattern Anal. Mach. Intell. **32**(12), 2142–2161 (2010)
12. Anil, R., Manjusha, K., Kumar, S.S., Soman, K.P.: Convolutional neural networks for the recognition of Malayalam characters. In: Proceedings of the 2015 13th International Conference on Document Analysis and Recognition (ICDAR), pp. 1041–1045 (2015)
13. Yang, W., Jin, L., Xie, Z., Feng, Z.: Improved deep convolutional neural network for online handwritten Chinese character recognition using domain-specific knowledge. In: Proceedings of the 2015 13th International Conference on Document Analysis and Recognition (ICDAR), pp. 551–555 (2015)
14. He, M., Zhang, S., Mao, H., Jin, L.: Recognition confidence analysis of handwritten Chinese character with CNN. In: Proceedings of the 2015 13th International Conference on Document Analysis and Recognition (ICDAR), pp. 61–65 (2015)
15. Zhong, Z., Jin, L., Xie, Z.: High performance offline handwritten Chinese character recognition using GoogLeNet and directional feature maps. In: Proceedings of the 2015 13th International Conference on Document Analysis and Recognition (ICDAR), pp. 846–850 (2015)
16. Baird, H.S., Tombre, K.: The evolution of document image analysis. In: Doermann, D., Tombre, K. (eds.) Handbook of Document Image Processing and Recognition, pp. 63–71. Springer, London (2014). https://doi.org/10.1007/978-0-85729-859-1_43
17. Shin, H.C., et al.: Deep convolutional neural networks for computer-aided detection: CNN architectures, dataset characteristics and transfer learning. IEEE Trans. Med. Imaging **35**, 1285–1298 (2016)
18. Shatnawi, M., Abdallah, S.: Improving handwritten Arabic character recognition by modeling human handwriting distortions. ACM Trans. Asian Low Resour. Lang. Inf. Process. **15**, 1–12 (2015)
19. Zhao, H., Hu, Y., Zhang, J.: Character recognition via a compact convolutional neural network. In: 2017 International Conference on Digital Image Computing: Techniques and Applications (DICTA), 29 November –1 December. IEEE (2017)
20. Lavin, A., Gray, S.: Fast algorithms for convolutional neural networks. In: 2016 IEEE Conference on Computer Vision and Pattern Recognition (CVPR), 27–30 June 2016
21. Breuel, T.M.: The OCRopus open source OCR system. In: Document Recognition and Retrieval XV, vol. 6815, p. 68150F. International Society for Optics and Photonics (2008)
22. Ashiquzzaman, A., Tushar, A.K.: Handwritten Arabic numeral recognition using deep learning neural networks. IEEE (2017)
23. Simonyan, K., Zisserman, A.: Very deep convolutional networks for large-scale image recognition. arXiv preprint arXiv:1409.1556 (2014)
24. Hailu, B., Amberbir, T., Stricker, D.: Amharic character image recognition. In: 18th IEEE International Conference on Communication Technology, 8–11 October 2018. (Accepted for Publication)
25. Tkachenko, I., Gomez, P.: Robustness of character recognition techniques to double printed and scanned documents. In: 14th IEEE International Conference on Document Analysis and Recognition (2017)

Modeling and Control of Electro-Hydraulic Actuator

Beza Nekatibeb[1], Venkata Lakshmi Narayana Komanapalli[2(✉)],
Mulugeta Debebe[1], and Endalew Ayenew[1]

[1] College of Electrical and Mechanical Engineering,
Addis Ababa Science and Technology University, Addis Ababa, Ethiopia
bezanek@gmail.com, muludeb@gmail.com,
end_enday@yahoo.com
[2] School of Electrical Engineering and Computing,
Adama Science and Technology University, Adama, Ethiopia
kvlnarayana@yahoo.co.in

Abstract. Modeling and position control of an Electro-Hydraulic Actuator
(EHA) system is investigated in this paper. Linear ARX EHA system model is
identified by taking the experimental data using system identification toolbox in
the MATLAB/Simulink. From the identified models the best fit ARX 331 model
is used to design a controller using fuzzy logic and Particle swarm optimization
(PSO) methods. In the self-tuning Fuzzy PID controller, the controller parameters K_P, K_I, and K_D are tuned by the fuzzy controller depending on the two
inputs: error and derivatives of the error. In the PSO optimized PID controller,
the sum of the time-weighted absolute error objective function is minimized and
optimized controller parameters are tuned using PSO algorithms. The results are
simulated in the MATLAB/Simulink and compared among conventional
Ziegler-Nichols (Z-N), Fuzzy, and PSO PIDs. The results indicate that the self-
tuning fuzzy PID and PSO optimized PID give better performance than the
Z-N PID controller and the PSO-optimized PID controller demonstrates superior
performance in terms of percentage overshot and speed of response with 5%
overshoot, 0.02 s rise time and 0.15 s settling time.

Keywords: System identification · Electro-Hydraulic Actuator ·
Fuzzy self-tuning PID · PSO optimized PID

1 Introduction

Electro-Hydraulic Actuators (EHA) due to high power, fast and smooth response
characteristics and good positioning capability are becoming famous in many applications like manufacturing systems, mining, automotive, robotics, flight simulation,
ships and marine engineering etc. [1]. However, the nonlinear nature of such actuators
characterizes a great challenge in designing the best possible controller for EHA [2, 3].
Difficulties in identifying an accurate model of inherently nonlinear to its equivalent
linear model, and time-varying dynamics make controller design more complicated and
challenging [4, 5]. A number of studies have been conducted to minimize the impact of
nonlinearity and uncertainty in the model [6–9]. Many researchers have also used

© ICST Institute for Computer Sciences, Social Informatics and Telecommunications Engineering 2019
Published by Springer Nature Switzerland AG 2019. All Rights Reserved
F. A. Zimale et al. (Eds.): ICAST 2018, LNICST 274, pp. 332–342, 2019.
https://doi.org/10.1007/978-3-030-15357-1_28

advanced control strategies to improve the system performance mainly in tracking control and motion controllability [7–13]. In the literatures, various Fuzzy controller structures have been proposed and extensively studied [1, 2, 4–6].

Proper modeling of a given system is a decisive step before designing any control strategy. There are number of approaches that can be used to identify the model of a given system. To get the required model, two main approaches are used. The first principle based on physical and chemical laws and system identification based on input-output data [14, 15]. Physical modeling using fundamental physical laws require high level of understanding about EHA system to derive the mathematical model. In such models, it is hard to capture and insight unmodeled dynamics and uncertainties in the model. Unlike first principle method, system identification approaches able to insight and capture unmodeled dynamics and uncertainties [10, 11, 13, 15, 16].

2 Model Estimation

The most costly procedure in system identification is obtaining experimental data. Data are raw input for identification. Here, model estimation is investigated using experimental input-output data on Matlab/Simulink system identification tool box. The EHA system used in paper is single rod hydraulic cylinder driven by a direct servo valve with 40-L/min flow rate at 70 bars. The dimension of the hydraulic cylinder is 63/30/300 mm. Piston position is measured by using a 300 mm draw wire sensor with an input-output data recorder. The input to the system is the sum of sinusoidal voltage as seen in (1), which ranges from −5 V to 5 V, is used to generate an output displacement of EHA.

$$Sum\,of\,sine\,input \; = \; 2sin2t_s k + sin6t_s k + 2sin0.3t_s k \tag{1}$$

The input and output signals are shown in Fig. 1.

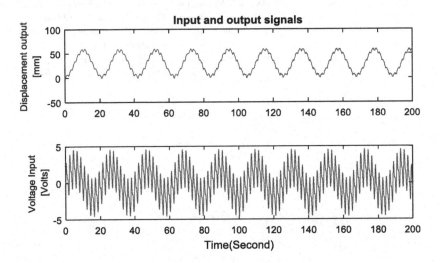

Fig. 1. Electrohydraulic model training and validation

Number of data generated for training and validation are 4000 with sampling time 50 ms. In order to estimate and validate the model, the data have been divided into two parts. The first sample (1 to 200) and the second sample (2001 to 4000) data have been used to estimate and validate the model.

One of the objectives of this paper is to find a linear EHA model with adequate accuracy to design a controller that will drive the output in the desired manner. Taking this into considerations, linear discrete-time ARX model structure is selected. As displayed in Table 1, second-order and third-order ARX models are estimated with best fit more than 85%. From the results, the ARX331 model has better performance with 92.35% percentage model fit, 0.258×10^{-4} final prediction error (FPE) and 0.2565×10^{-4} mean square error (MSE). The model validation for result of ARX331 using validation data is illustrated in Fig. 2.

The selected ARX 331 model used to design controller is represented as:

$$A(z)y(t) = B(z)u(t) + e(t). \tag{2}$$

Where $A(z) = 1 - 0.9458z^{-1} - 0.3192z^{-2} + 0.2652z^{-3}$ and $B(z) = 0.23z^{-1}$
$-0.1753z^{-2} - 0.3144z^{-3}$. Assuming zero initial conditions, the transfer function can be represented as shown in (3).

$$\frac{Y(z)}{U(z)} = \frac{0.23z^{-1} - 0.1753z^{-2} - 0.3144z^{-3}}{1 - 0.9458z^{-1} - 0.3192z^{-2} + 0.2652z^{-3}} \tag{3}$$

Table 1. ARX model representation with best fit criteria

S. No.	Model structure	Best fit (%)	FPE $\times 10^{-4}$	MSE $\times 10^{-4}$	ARX model
1	ARX211	87.54	0.2902	0.2967	$A(z) = 1 - 0.798z - 1 + 0.3985z^{-2}$, $B(z) = 0.2438z^{-1}$
2	Arx331	92.35	0.258	0.2565	$A(z) = 1 - 0.9458z^{-1} - 0.3192z^{-2} + 0.2652$, $B(z) = 0.23z^{-1} - 0.1753z^{-2} + 0.3144z^{-3}$
3	Arx321	92.13	0.2616	0.2603	$A(z) = 1 - 0.925z^{-1} + 0.4978z^{-2} - 0.2923z^{-3}$ $B(z) = -0.03458z^{-1} + 0.364z^{-2}$
4	Arx332	88.5	0.2576	0.2566	$A(z) = 1 - 0.95419z^{-1} + 0.455z^{-2} - 0.336z^{-3}$, $B(z) = 0.4714z^{-2} - 0.3379z^{-1} + 0.2366z^{-4}$

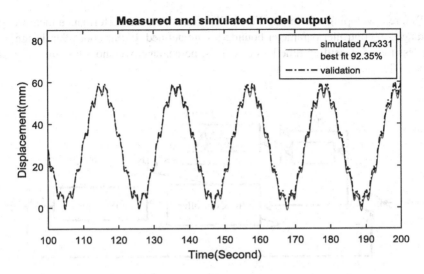

Fig. 2. Model validation curve (ARX331)

3 Self-tuning Fuzzy PID Controller

In this section of the paper, development of a self-tuning fuzzy PID controller for controlling the position variation of EHA is presented. In classical tuning methods, PID controller cannot give satisfactory response for system with nonlinearity and unpredictable parameters variations [2, 3]. Hence, the self-tuning controller, which is a combination of a classical PID and a fuzzy controller, is proposed. The general discrete PID structure shown in (4) is modified and used in combination with Fuzzy logic controller.

$$PID = K_P\left(1 + \frac{T_S}{\tau_I(z-1)} + \frac{\tau_D(z-1)}{T_s z}\right) \tag{4}$$

where K_P is proportional gain, τ_I, and τ_D are integral and derivative time constants respectively and T_s is sampling time.

The proposed structure of the self-tuning fuzzy PID controller shown in Fig. 3 has two inputs to the fuzzy logic inference engine; the feedback error $e(t)$ and the derivative of error $de(t)/dt$. The PID parameters are tuned by using fuzzy inference. This provides a nonlinear mapping from the error and derivative of error to parameters (K_P', K_I', K_D'). The rules are designed to tune the controller parameters to get the required response characteristics of the EHA. The fuzzy reasoning of fuzzy sets of output is gained by aggregation operation of fuzzy sets inputs and the designed fuzzy rules. The aggregation and defuzzification methods are used respectively max-min and centroid method.

Before developing self-tuning Fuzzy PID controller, the performance measure and the ranges of controller parameter boundaries are defined. In this controller design, rise time less than 5 s, settling time less than 10 s, percentage overshoot less than 15% are taken as the performance measure.

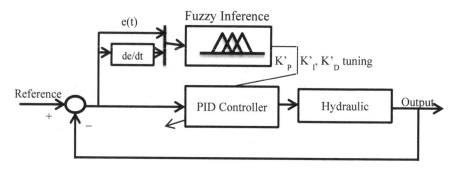

Fig. 3. Structure of self-tuning fuzzy PID Controller [1]

The upper and lower boundaries of gain values of Fuzzy PID parameters are determined simulating Z-N PID parameters ranges from stability limit with large time constants to that of near instability. This results in the ranges of each parameters, i.e., $K_P \in [1, 10]$; $K_I \in [0, 1]$; $K_D \in [0, 0.5]$. Hence, the output parameters from fuzzy tuner can be calibrated over the interval [0, 1] and, therefore, the designed discrete-PID controller has the form as shown in (5).

$$PID = (9K'_P + 1) + \frac{K'_I}{(z - 1)} + 0.5K'_D \frac{(z - 1)}{z} \qquad (5)$$

Thus, the PID controller parameters have a relation $Kp = 9K'_P + 1$, $K_I = K'_I$ and $K_D = 0.5K'_D$.

The universe discourse of the fuzzy membership function designed for the error, change of error and the outputs are Gaussian. The input membership functions for error and change of error is designed within the range [−0.1, 0.3] and [−0.1, 0.1] respectively. The output parameters K'_P, K'_I and K'_D with Gaussian membership function within the range [1, 10], [0, 1], and [0, 0.5] are taken. The linguistic values of the error and change of error are designed with 5 linguistic terms for each input: negative big (NB), negative small (NM), zero (Z), positive small (PS), and positive big (PB). For the output 5 linguistic terms small(S), medium small (MS), Medium (M), medium big (MB), and big(B) are designed. Since there are five linguistic variables that have been set, thus, 25 fuzzy rules are applied in the system. Centroid method of defuzzification is used to get the definite values that are sent to PID controller.

4 Particle Swarm Optimization (PSO) PID

In PSO-PID control design process, the objective is to minimize the objective function defined as Sum of time weighted absolute error, which determines the performance of criteria in terms of rise time, percentage overshoot and settling time. In this PSO optimized PID controller design, the objective function is modified as seen in (6)

$$f(k) = \sum_{k=1}^{N} |e(k)| * k \qquad (6)$$

Figure 4 illustrates the implementation structure of PSO optimized PID controller. The optimal values of the controller parameters (K'_P, K'_I, and K'_D) are selected using PSO algorithm based on sum of time weight absolute error performance index.

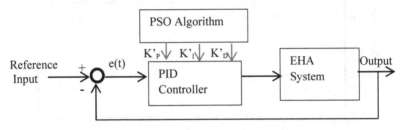

Fig. 4. PSO optimized PID control structure

For implementing the PSO algorithm the following parameters are chosen. The population number be 50, maximum iteration 100, variable size 3, damping weighting inertial maximum 0.99 to minimum 0.75, personal and social cognitive coefficients are 2. By taking Z-N PID simulation as reference, the lower and upper bounds of the PID parameters are defined within the stability ranges. The lower and the upper bounds K'_P, K'_I and K'_D are chosen from 1 to 5, 0 to 0.2 and 0 to 0.05 respectively. Then the PID controller structure has the form:

$$PID = (1 * K'_P + 3) + \frac{(K'_I + 0.019)}{(z-1)} + (K'_D + 0.01)\frac{(z-1)}{z} \qquad (7)$$

5 Results and Discussion

5.1 Self-tuning Fuzzy PID

The results are simulated in the MATLAB/Simulink simulation environment. Square wave and step input test signals have been used to show the tacking and transient performance of the Fuzzy PID controller respectively. The results are illustrated in Figs. 5 and 6.

Figure 5 shows the performance of the self-tuning fuzzy PID controller with respect to step reference input signal. It achieves better response characteristics as compared to the defined design criterion with fast rise time of 0.05 s and settling time of 0.2 s. As can be seen from Fig. 5, the response demonstrates good tracking performance for the square wave test signal. However the response of the proposed system looks satisfied, it needs to develop by including disturbance and any others nonlinearity and uncertainties in the design with various frequencies in reference input signals.

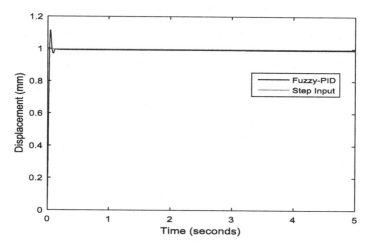

Fig. 5. Output signal of self tuning – fuzzy PID with step input

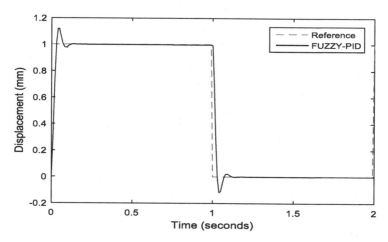

Fig. 6. Output signal of fuzzy PID with square input

5.2   PSO Optimized PID

The PSO PID algorithm is implemented in the MATLAB assuming the size of the swarm to be 50, maximum iterations 100, damping weighting inertial 0.99 max to 0.75 min, personal and social cognitive coefficients 2. The lower and the upper bounds of K'_P, K'_I and K'_D from 0.5 to 1, 0 to 0.2 and 0 to 0.05 respectively are taken. The simulation result shows that after 100 iterations the best cost that is the minimum of performance measure sum of time-weighted absolute error is 1.2752×10^{-09} with coefficient positions of K'_P, K'_I and K'_D at 0.0115, 0.0011, and 0.0642 respectively.

Figures 7 and 8 demonstrate the response of PSO-optimized PID controller with step input and square reference input. The step response shows the PSO optimized PID control has better performance with 6% overshoot, 2 ms rise time and 17 ms settling

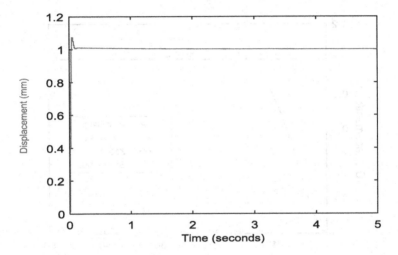

Fig. 7. Step response of PSO-PID system

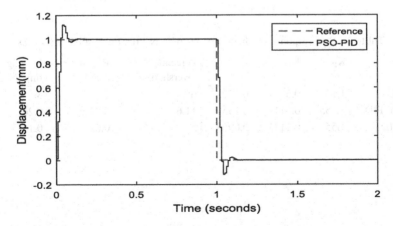

Fig. 8. Response of PSO-Optimized PID with square wave input

time with respect to the design performance criteria. From Fig. 8 it can be observed that the PSO-PID controller can track the square wave reference input with fast response and less overshoot.

5.3 Comparison of the Results

Figure 9 and Table 2 show a comparison of the step response performances of the proposed controllers with respect to the conventional Z-N PID. It can be observed that as compared to Z-NPID controller, self-tuning fuzzy PID and PSO optimized PID have better performance in terms of speed of response. However, less overshoot the classical Z-N PID demonstrates very slow response as compared to the two proposed controllers with rise time of 7 s and settling time of 30 s.

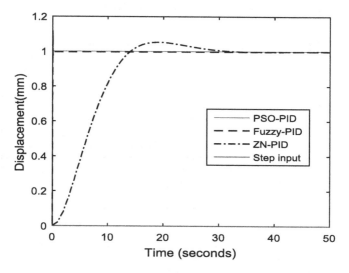

Fig. 9. PSO–PID, FUZZY–PID, and Z-N PID step response

Table 2. Step response of characteristics of Z-N-PID, Fuzzy-PID, PSO-PID

	K_P	K_I	K_D	Percentage-Overshoot	Rise time (sec.)	Settling time (sec.)
Z-NPID	1.72	0.5	0.772	6	7	30
FUZZY PID	3.855	0.311	0.1559	11.6	0.05	0.20
PSO-PID	1.55	0.1171	0.0957	5	0.02	0.15

6 Conclusion

System Identification technique has been used to get the linear model of the EHA system. Three low order ARX models are estimated and ARX331 with best fit of 92.35% is used for controller design. Self-tuning fuzzy and PSO optimized PID controllers are proposed to tune the value of K_P, K_I, and K_D of the PID controller. The responses self-tuning fuzzy PID controller and PSO optimized PID controller show that the performance of the EHA system is improved and satisfied as compare to the Z-N PID controller and the defined designed criteria. From the results, it can be observed that PSO-optimized PID controller demonstrates superior performance in terms of percentage overshot and speed of response with 5% overshoot, 0.02 s rise time and 0.15 s settling time.

Acknowledgment. The authors would like to acknowledge Mr. Habib Mohammed and Dr. Dawit Burussie for their valuable comments.

References

1. Zulfatman, Rahmat, M.F.: Application of self-tuning fuzzy PID controller on industrial hydraulic actuator using system identification approach. Int. J. Smart Sens. Intell. Syst. **2**(2), 246–261 (2009)
2. Ha, Q.P., Nguyen, Q.H., Rye, D.C., Durrant-Whyte, H.F.: Impedance control of a hydraulically actuated robotic excavator. Autom. Constr. **9**(5–6), 421–435 (2000)
3. Ishak, N., Tajjudin, M., Adnan, R., Ismail, H.: System identification and model validation of electro-hydraulic actuator for quarter car system. WSEAS Trans. Adv. Eng. Educ. **4**, 27–35 (2017)
4. Qiao, W.Z., Mizumoto, M.: PID type fuzzy controller and parameters adaptive method. Fuzzy Sets Syst. **78**, 23–35 (1996)
5. Güzelkaya, M., Eksin, I., Yesil, E.: Self-tuning of PID-type fuzzy logic controller coefficients via relative rate observer. Eng. Appl. Artif. Intell. **16**, 227–236 (2003)
6. Woo, Z.-W., Chung, H.-Y., Lin, J.-J.: A PID type fuzzy controller with self-tuning scaling factors. Fuzzy Sets Syst. **115**, 321–326 (2000)
7. Chen, H.M., Renn, J.-C., Su, J.P.: Sliding mode control with varying boundary layers for an electro-hydraulic position servo system. Int. J. Adv. Manuf. Technol. **26**, 117–123 (2005)
8. Ghazali, R., Sam, Y.M., Rahmat, M.F., Hashim, A.W.I.M., Zulfatman, M.: Sliding mode control with PID sliding surface of an electro-hydraulic servo system. Aust. J. Basic Appl. Sci. **4**(10), 4749–4759 (2010)
9. Daniel, M., Wonohadidjojo, G.K., Mohammed, H.: Using fuzzy logic controller optimized by particle swarm optimization. Int. J. Autom. Comput. **3**, 181–193 (2013)
10. Guan, C., Pan, S.: Nonlinear adaptive robust control of single-rod electro-hydraulic actuator with unknown nonlinear parameters. IEEE Trans. Control Syst. Technol. **16**(3), 434–446 (2008)
11. Ling, T.G., Rahmat, M.F., Husain, R.: A comparative study of linear ARX and nonlinear ANFIS modeling of an electrohydraulic actuator system, vol. 5, pp. 1–8 (2014)
12. Siu, L., Yao, B.: Indirect adaptive robust control of electro-hydraulic systems driven by single-rod hydraulic actuator. In: Proceedings of the IEEE/ASME International Conference on Advanced Intelligent Mechatronics, pp. 296–301 (2005)

13. Sohl, G.A., Bobrow, J.E.: Experiments and simulations on the nonlinear control of a hydraulic servosystem. IEEE Trans. Control Syst. Technol. **7**(2), 238–247 (1999)
14. Ljung, L.: System Identification Theory for User, 2nd edn. Prentice Hall, Englewood Cliffs (1987). Linkoping University Sweden
15. Keesman, K.J.: System Identification: An Introduction. Springer, London (2011). https://doi.org/10.1007/978-0-85729-522-4
16. Ling, T.G., Rahmat, M.F., Husain, R.: System identification and control of an electro-hydraulic actuator system. In: 2012 IEEE 8th International Colloquium on Signal Processing and its Applications, pp. 85–88 (2012)

Wind Energy Conversion System Model Identification and Validation

Endalew Ayenew[1](✉), Mulugeta Debebe[1], Beza Nekatibeb[1],
and Venkata Lakshmi Narayana Komanapalli[2]

[1] College of Electrical and Mechanical Engineering,
Addis Ababa Science and Technology University, Addis Ababa, Ethiopia
end_enday@yahoo.com, muludeb@gmail.com,
bezanek@gmail.com
[2] School of Electrical Engineering and Computing,
Adama Science and Technology University, Adama, Ethiopia
kvlnarayana@yahoo.co.in

Abstract. Wind energy conversion system (WECS) is complex because of wind speed varies in time and space. Model identification is required to represent its dynamics for real-time implementation. In this paper a doubly-fed induction generator (DFIG) WECS is used. Different model structures are generated and simulated using MATLAB/SIMULINK. The models are generated using both nonlinear and linear system identification tool boxes. Linear system identification toolbox generates both model structure and model parameters; whereas the nonlinear system identification tool generates only the system model structures. From linear models, the BJ33221 model has better performance with best fit of 74.78%, final prediction error (FPE) value of 0.0445 and mean square error (MSE) is 0.04265. ARX211 model structure provides best fit of 74.39%, FPE of 0.0453, and MSE is 0.04465. This study shows as model order increases, the best fit value too, but the system become more complex. The nonlinear models have better performance than the linear models. The nlarx121 model structure provides the best fit of 96.43% and MSE of 0.0322, with other technique for its model parameters estimation. The output residuals are within the confident range (0.2 to −0.2), indicating the model structure was validated.

Keywords: WECS · Model identification · BJ33221 · nlarx121

1 Introduction

Wind energy conversion system (WECS) is a stochastic system, since wind speed varies in time and space. Therefore identification of the model is required to represent its dynamics which is used for real-time implementation. In a doubly-fed induction generator (DFIG) WECS, power and speed are the outputs for system, require regulation by controlling the torque and pitch angle. The WECS mathematical model representation requires multi structural input-output model identification. It is known as the Nonlinear Auto Regressive Moving Average with exogenous inputs model (NARMAX) [1, 2]. NARMAX was represented by Auto Regressive Moving Average with exogenous inputs model (ARMAX) model by interpolating between a set of

© ICST Institute for Computer Sciences, Social Informatics and Telecommunications Engineering 2019
Published by Springer Nature Switzerland AG 2019. All Rights Reserved
F. A. Zimale et al. (Eds.): ICAST 2018, LNICST 274, pp. 343–353, 2019.
https://doi.org/10.1007/978-3-030-15357-1_29

ARMAX models [3]. An alternative representation for fitting NARMAX models was given based on the radial basis function [4]. The NARMAX model was also expressed as ARMAX model of single-input single-output linear systems [5]. This because of simplicity of ARMAX than NARMAX and even in MATLAB its function is not available. In this paper the other models such as Output Error (OE), Box Jenkins (BJ) and Nonlinear Auto Regressive with exogenous inputs (NLARX) were also generated and discussed. Single input single output system is considered and different model structures are generated and simulated using MATLAB/SIMULINK. The models fit criterions and simplicities are compared. The best model was selected. Actually, the models are generated using both nonlinear and linear system identification tool boxes. Linear system identification toolbox generates both model structure and model parameters; whereas the nonlinear system identification tool generates only the system model structures. For this purpose best fit percentage, FPE and MSE values were used as criterions. In [6, 7] MSE was well defined and used for measure of error introduced in neural network during its training and analysis for model selection.

2 Model Estimation

The most costly procedure in system identification is obtaining experimental data. The quality of final model depends on quality of data; hence great care must be taken to generate data. Model estimation of the wind energy conversion system experimental input-output data on Matlab/simulink system identification tool box is used. The general procedure was pre-processing the data, model structure selection, parameter estimation and model validation. Data preprocessing and examination is done by adjusting the experimental data to be loaded into Matlab in order to get good data which is suitable for system identification. Model structure is selected based on prior knowledge and taking into consideration model complexity. Validation is done to validate the estimated model output compare to the real output from the experiments. The model validation can be accepted if it satisfies the percentage of best fit and other criterions.

The accuracies of model of WECS is highly affects overall performances of the system. For instance, it has been shown that a very common 5% modeling error in the optimal tip speed ratio-λ alone can cause an energy loss of around 1%–3% [8–10] during the wind turbine operates below rated speed. This is a significant loss. Consider a 324 MW installed capacity wind farm (Ethiopia wind farm case), which is operating with a reasonable 32% capacity factor can produce about 908.237 GWh of energy per year. If the cost of energy is $0.09 per kWh, 1% loss of energy on this wind farm is equivalent to a loss of $817413 per year. To overcome this inaccuracy, system model validation is one of the first important steps.

The input to the system is wind speed (random) with mean value of 12 m/s and variance equal to one is used to drive turbine and then generator at different speed. The input and output signals are shown in Fig. 1 below. Number of data generated for training and validation is 2000 with sampling time 0.1 s. In order to estimate and validate the model, the data is divided into two parts. The first part, which is (1–1000) data sets are used to determine the model of the systems. The second (1001–2000) data sets are used to validate the model. All procedures to estimate the model is done by using System Identification Toolbox in Matlab/Simulink.

The objective of this paper is to find the model for wind energy conversion system which can be used for controller design. Both linear and nonlinear identification process were applied, but in the nonlinear identification only the model structure are determine since the model parameters are not identified by the matlab tools for nonlinear case. The discrete time ARX and ARMAX model structures were selected because both the structure and parameters of the model are available. The input data shown in Fig. 1 was applied into the WECS simulink model shown in Fig. 2 so that the output on Fig. 1 was measured at the out port of the model. Figure 2 is the inter connection of aerodynamic, wind turbine, and electric generator subsystem in the WECS. All these subsystems have their components as shown in Figs. 3, 4, 5 and 6. For system identification purpose, the wind speed was used as input to simulator and the generator speed is considered as output of generator. Figure 3 is the model for the simulation of turbine blade pitch angle simulation diagram. In this diagram the relation of wind speed, generator speed, attack angle and blade radius to the pitch angle is represented. The disturbance due wind speed variation can be regulated by this block. The mathematical equations for aerodynamic to mechanical energy conversion by DFIG type wind turbine are described in Figs. 3, 4 and 5 using matlab/simulink subsystem simulation representation. For instance from Fig. 4 the wind turbine rotor instantaneous torque and power can be relate by

$$T_t = 0.5 \rho A u^3 C_p(\lambda, \beta) / \omega_t \qquad (1)$$

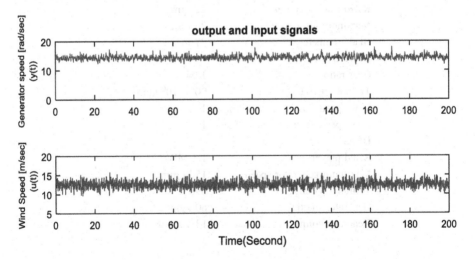

Fig. 1. WECS model identification and validation data

where, ρ is air density, A is area swept by turbine blade and u is the instantaneous wind speed and $C_p(\lambda, \beta)$ is wind power to mechanical power conversion efficiency as a function of the turbine's tip-speed ratio-λ and rotor blade Pitch angle-β and ω_t is wind turbine rotor rotational.

Figure 4 is the representation Simulation Model of aerodynamics energy conversion to mechanical energy through wind turbine. This model includes wind speed, area swept by wind turbine blade and power conversion efficiency. The mechanical power generated by turbine is divided by turbine and gives turbine torque. Figure 5 is simulation model of wind turbine blade tip speed ratio, which depends on wind speed, blade rotational speed, and percents of blade radius starting from hub to blade tip. The model for aerodynamics power to mechanical power conversion efficiency is required. The efficiency is highly depends on the blade pitch angle and tip speed ratio.

Table 1. Wind turbine plant rating and specifications

Specifications	Values
Wind turbine and rotor	
Number of blades	3
Cut in speed	3.5 m/s
Cut out speed	25 m/s
Rated speed	9.5 m/s
Air density ρ	1.25 kg/m
Optimum tip speed ratio λ	8
Power coefficient Cp	0.49
Rated rotor speed ω	22 rpm
Maximum rotor speed	23 rpm
Blade diameter	77 m
Drive train	
Gear ratio	1:94
Turbine inertia	90×10^6 kgm^2
Low speed shaft torsion stiffness	160×10^6 Nm/rad
Low speed shaft torsion stiffness	10×10^6 Nm/rad
DFIG	
Rated power	1.5 MW
Maximum generator speed	1500 rpm
Terminal Voltage	690 ± 5% v
Generator inertia	60 kgm^2
Generator torque	13.4 k Nm

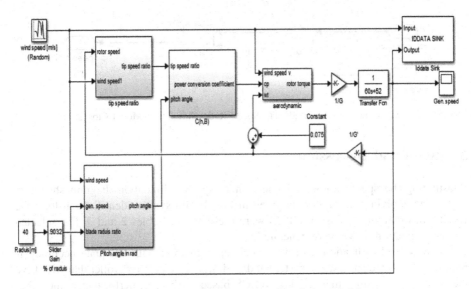

Fig. 2. Wind Turbine Generator Simulation Model

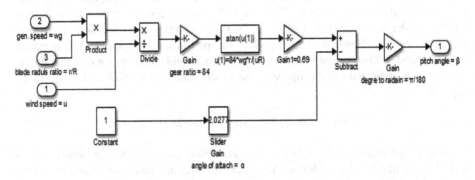

Fig. 3. Wind Turbine blade pitch angle Simulation model subsystem

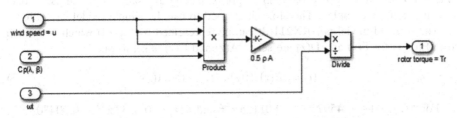

Fig. 4. Aerodynamics to wind turbine torque conversion Simulation Model subsystem

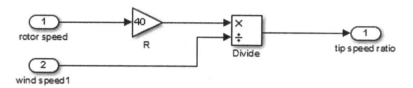

Fig. 5. Wind Turbine Blade Tip Speed Ratio Simulation Model subsystem

3   Result and Discussion

Substituting the specification in Table 1 in to system simutation diagram shown in Fig. 2 and applying the input data given in Fig. 1 with system identification tool, the results for different models of WECS were presented in Tables 2 and 3. For selected models validation curve were generated.

In system identification process model representation with adequate accuracy is required in order to analyse the system and/or design a suitable controller that will drive the output in a desired manner. For WECS based on best fit performance and other criteria like model simplicity, the appropriate system model can be selected from the lists in the Table 2. As instance BJ33221 is the best model to represent the system. From the results shown in Table 2, the BJ33221 model has better performance with 74.78% model best fit, 0.0445 final prediction error and 0.04265 mean square error. In this table, as it is shown next to BJ33221, the performance of armax2321 is better. Figures 6 and 7 illustrate the model validation using validation data for different model structures as indicated on the figures. The model structure of BJ33221 is given by Eq. (2).

$$y(t) = [B(z)/F(z)]u(t) + [C(t)/D(t)]e(t) \qquad (2)$$

For sample time is 0.1 s. Where y(t) is generator speed, u(t) is wind speed, e(t) is disturbances like wind turbulence. All these variables are functions of discrete time. B(z), F(z), C(z) and D(z) as given in Table 2 for sample time is 0.1 s. When the performance of BJ is compared with that of ARX211 (best fit = 74.39%, FPE = 0.0453, and MSE = 0.04465), approximately the same, but the BJ model structure is more complex. Therefore, it is good to use the simple model structure.

The selected model is ARX211. It can be represented by Eq. (3) which is derived from Eq. (1) for F(z) and D(z) are set to A(z) and C(z) is set to one.

$$y(t) = [B(z)/A(z)]u(t) + e(t)/A(z) \qquad (3)$$

For $A(z) = 1 - 0.4597\,z^{-1} + 0.01125\,z^{-2}$ and $B(z) = 0.6333\,z^{-1} - 0.004303\,z^{-2}$.

The nonlinear model structures shown in the Table 3 have better fit criteria than the linear model structures given in Table 2. These nonlinear model structures are generated by using the nonlinear system identification toolbox and system which was shown by Fig. 2 with input data in Fig. 1. The tool box gives only model structure, and

Table 2. Different linear model structure and model representation with best fit criteria

No.	Model structure	Best fit (%)	FPE	MSE	Linear model representation
1	ARX211	74.39	0.0453	0.04465	$A(z) = 1 - 0.4597\,z^{-1} + 0.01125\,z^{-2}$ $B(z) = 0.6333\,z^{-1} - 0.004303z^{-2}$
2	ARX231	74.44	0.0451	0.04422	$A(z) = 1 - 0.5285\,z^{-1} + 0.03795\,z^{-2}$ $B(z) = 0.6369\,z^{-1} - 0.0452\,z^{-2} - 0.01058\,z^{-3}$
3	ARX321	74.46	0.0451	0.04424	$A(z) = 1 - 0.5272\,z^{-1} + 0.04451\,z^{-2} + 0.004223\,z^{-3}$ $B(z) = 0.638\,z^{-1} - 0.04329\,z^{-2}$
4	ARX331	74.40	0.0451	0.04409	$A(z) = 1 - 0.5271\,z^{-1} + 0.00683\,z^{-2} + 0.01614\,z^{-3}$ $B(z) = 0.6385\,z^{-1} - 0.04337\,z^{-2} - 0.02961\,z^{-3}$
5	ARMAX2221	74.44	0.0447	0.04351	$A(z) = 1 - 0.3926\,z^{-1} - 0.008379\,z^{-2}$ $B(z) = 0.64\,z^{-1} + 0.04316\,z^{-2}$ $C(z) = 1 + 0.1342\,z^{-1} + 0.1393\,z^{-2}$
6	ARMAX2321	74.73	0.0449	0.04346	$A(z) = 1 + 0.2827\,z^{-1} - 0.3044\,z^{-2}$ $B(z) = 0.6372\,z^{-1} + 0.4713\,z^{-2} + 0.007185\,z^{-3}$ $C(z) = 1 + 0.8055\,z^{-1} + 0.1576\,z^{-2}$
7	ARMAX3321	74.45	0.0451	0.04342	$A(z) = 1 + 0.09438\,z^{-1} - 0.2034\,z^{-2} - 0.005598\,z^{-3}$ $B(z) = 0.6383\,z^{-1} + 0.3528\,z^{-2} + 0.01862\,z^{-3}$ $C(z) = 1 + 0.6171\,z^{-1} + 0.1817\,z^{-2}$
8	ARMAX3331	74.45	0.0451	0.04327	$A(z) = 1 + 0.4487\,z^{-1} - 0.3563\,z^{-2} - 0.005191\,z^{-3}$ $B(z) = 0.6383\,z^{-1} + 0.58\,z^{-2} + 0.02187\,z^{-3}$ $C(z) = 1 + 0.9782\,z^{-1} + 0.2333\,z^{-2} + 0.08585\,z^{-3}$
9	ARMAX3441	74.71	0.0445	0.04233	$A(z) = 1 - 0.628\,z^{-1} - 0.7424\,z^{-2} + 0.3976\,z^{-3}$ $B(z) = 0.6508\,z^{-1} - 0.09641\,z^{-2} - 0.5359\,z^{-3} + 0.01264\,z^{-4}$ $C(z) = 1 - 0.1184\,z^{-1} - 0.7337\,z^{-2} - 0.08582\,z^{-3} - 0.05154\,z^{-4}$
10	ARMAX4441	74.71	0.0447	0.04234	$A(z) = 1 - 0.6248\,z^{-1} - 0.7481\,z^{-2} + 0.4007\,z^{-3} - 0.0005654\,z^{-4}$ $B(z) = 0.6508\,z^{-1} - 0.09429\,z^{-2} - 0.5387\,z^{-3} + 0.01343\,z^{-4}$ $C(z) = 1 - 0.1151\,z^{-1} - 0.738\,z^{-2} - 0.0833\,z^{-3} - 0.05301\,z^{-4}$
11	BJ22221	74.47	0.0449	0.04334	$B(z) = 0.6401\,z^{-1} - 0.03059\,z^{-2}$ $C(z) = 1 + 0.5496\,z^{-1} + 0.1425\,z^{-2}$ $D(z) = 1 + 0.02626\,z^{-1} - 0.2208\,z^{-2}$ $F(z) = 1 - 0.5082\,z^{-1} + 0.04257\,z^{-2}$
12	BJ33221	74.78	0.0445	0.04265	$B(z) = 0.6511\,z^{-1} + 0.6379\,z^{-2} + 0.0003357\,z^{-3}$ $C(z) = 1 - 0.7787\,z^{-1} - 0.04604\,z^{-2} - 0.1752\,z^{-3}$ $D(z) = 1 - 1.3\,z^{-1} + 0.3001\,z^{-2}$ $F(z) = 1 + 0.5014\,z^{-1} - 0.459\,z^{-2}$
13	OE221	74.47	0.0625	0.06128	$B(z) = 0.6308\,z^{-1} + 0.05367\,z^{-2}$ $F(z) = 1 - 0.3841\,z^{-1} - 0.01572\,z^{-2}$

not able to generates model parameters. It requires other techniques for parameters estimation as it is indicated by [11–13].

Any appropriate nonlinear model structure listed in Table 3 can be selected for WECS representation. The result in Table 3 shows that specific model structure has different performance criteria for different nonlinearity types such as tree partition, wavenet and sigmoidnet. The nlarx121 provides the best fit (96.43%) and small MSE (0.0322). This is when the nonlinearity type is tree partition and was represented by Eq. (4).

$$y(t) = f(y(t-1), u(t-1), u(t-2)) + e(t) \qquad (4)$$

Where $f(.)$ is some polynomial or rational nonlinear function with known model structure.

Table 3. Nonlinear model structures and model representation with best fit criteria

No.	Nonlinear model structure	Best fit (%)	FPE	MSE	Nonlinear model structures regresses representation
1	NLARX121	96.43	NA	0.0322	**Nonlinearity: tree partition** $y(t) = f(y(t-1), u(t-1), u(t-2)) + e(t)$
2	NLARX221	89.50	0.01125	0.04564	**Nonlinearity: wavenet** $y(t) = f(y(t-1), y(t-2), u(t-1), u(t-2)) + e(t)$
3	NLARX221	93.48	NA	0.01535	**Nonlinearity: tree partition** $y(t) = f(y(t-1), y(t-2), u(t-1), u(t-2)) + e(t)$
4	NLARX221	89.64	0.00440	0.00573	**Nonlinearity: sigmoidnet** $y(t) = f(y(t-1), y(t-2), u(t-1), u(t-2)) + e(t)$
5	NLARX341	81.93	0.04211	0.08438	**Nonlinearity: wavenet** $y(t) = f(y(t-1), y(t-2), y(t-3), u(t-1), u(t-2),$ $u(t-3), u(t-4)) + e(t)$
6	NLARX341	85.73	0.02100	0.2277	**Nonlinearity: wavenet** $y(t) = f(y(t-1), y(t-2), y(t-3), u(t-1), u(t-2),$ $u(t-3), u(t-4)) + e(t)$
7	NLARX341	83.13	NA	0.05202	**Nonlinearity: wavenet** $y(t) = f(y(t-1), y(t-2), y(t-3), u(t-1), u(t-2),$ $u(t-3), u(t-4)) + e(t)$
8	NLARX231	81.53	0.03340	0.07163	**Nonlinearity: wavenet** $y(t) = f(y(t-1), y(t-2), u(t-1), u(t-2),$ $u(t-3)) + e(t)$
9	NLARX321	83.66	0.02680	0.06309	**Nonlinearity: wavenet** $y(t) = f(y(t-1), y(t-2), y(t-3), u(t-1),$ $u(t-2)) + e(t)$
10	NLARX441	81.34	0.04080	0.09058	**Nonlinearity: wavenet** $y(t) = f(y(t-1), y(t-2), y(t-3), y(t-4), u(t-1),$ $u(t-2), u(t-3), u(t-4)) + e(t)$

4 Model Validation Test

For linear system identification, as it was shown in the simulation Figs. 6 and 7 and results in Table 2, the curve fit is almost 74%. This indicates linear model for wind energy conversion less validate. But based on the result in Table 3 and in Fig. 9 the best fit is in the range of 81% to 96.43%, according to the selected corresponding nonlinear model structure. This shows the nonlinear model the best validate structure.

The other important result is the *whiteness* criterion was indicated in Fig. 9. A good model has the output autocorrelation function inside the confidence interval of the corresponding estimates, indicating that the outputs are uncorrelated. Typically Fig. 9 is the autocorrelation of the output, and cross correlation between output and input of the nlarx121 model of wind energy conversion system. On both correlations graphs, the output residuals are within the confident range (0.2 to −0.2). This indicates that residual of outputs are not correlated and independent from past inputs for the desired model structure which proves the model structure is validated (Fig. 8).

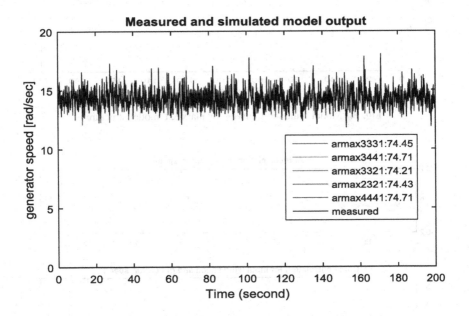

Fig. 6. Model validation curves (ARMAX....)

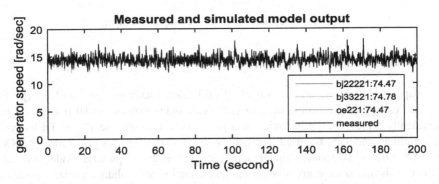

Fig. 7. Model validation curves for BJ22221, BJ33221 and OE221

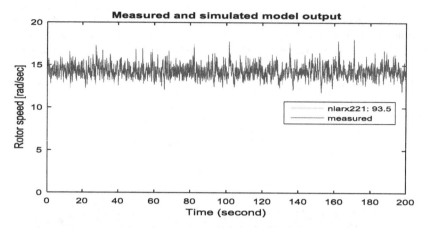

Fig. 8. Model validation curves for nlarx221 model structure

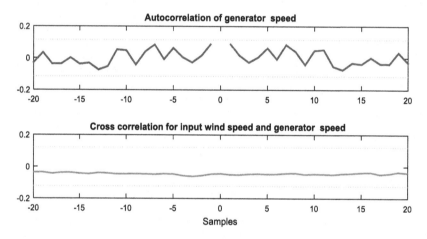

Fig. 9. Correlation curves of the output and input.

5 Conclusion

This paper has focused on the model identification technique for wind energy to electrical energy conversion system to select best mathematical model that would be equivalently represents the behavior of a physical system specifically for DFIG type wind turbine and can be used for analysis and controller design. Among ARX, ARMAX, OE and BJ model structures, it seems reasonable to pick BJ model structure as a better choice; since it gives better model estimation and validation than the others. Its best fit is 74.78%. It also observed that except OE, all linear model structures have FPE and MSE less than 0.04600, passing model validation test under output (generator speed) residual analysis. On the other hand, BJ model structure increases model complexity due to increase in system order. This indicates there is a contradiction between system order and percentage of model best fit. Therefore to overcome the model complexity of BJ, ARX211 model structure can be used. Because it has almost the same best fit with simplest model. Comparing the best fit of linear model structures with that of the nonlinear model structures, it has lower value. For illustration nlarx121 has best fit of 96.43%. This is due to the nonlinear behaviour of the wind energy plant. The nonlinear system identification toolbox gives only model structure without model parameters. As illustrated, the output residuals are within the confident range (0.2 to −0.2). This indicates that residual of outputs are not correlated and independent from past inputs for the desired model structure which proves that the selected model structure is validated.

Acknowledgment. We would like to acknowledge Mr. Wondwesen Wubu, head of Electrical and Computer Engineering department of Addis Ababa Science and Technology University for his encouragement and valuable support during this paper work.

References

1. Bidyadhar, S., Pedda, S.: Non-linear autoregressive moving average with exogenous input model-based adaptive control of a wind energy conversion system. J. Eng. **2016**, 218–226 (2016)
2. Billings, S.A., Chen, S., Korenberg, M.J.: Identification of MIMO non-linear systems using a forward-regression orthogonal estimator. Int. J. Control **49**, 2158–2159 (1989)
3. Johansen, T.A., Foss, B.: Constructing NARMAX models using ARMAX models. Int. J. Control **58**, 1126–1142 (2007)
4. Chen, S., Billings, S.A., Cowan, C.F.N., Grant, P.M.: Practical identification of NARMAX models using radial basis functions. Int. J. Control **52**, 1328–1330 (2007)
5. Leontaritis, I.J., Billings, S.A.: Input-output parametric models for non-linear systems part II: stochastic non-linear systems. Int. J. Control **41**, 343 (2007)
6. Perez-Llera, C., Fernadez-Baizan, M.C., Feito, J.L., Gonzalez del Valle, V.: Local short-term prediction of wind speed: a neural network analysis. In: International Congress on Environmental and Software, p. 126 (2002)
7. Cadenas, E., Rivera, W.: Wind speed forecasting in three different regions of Mexico, using a hybrid ARIMA-ANN model. J. Renew. Energy **35**, 2737 (2010)
8. Johnson, K.E., Pao, L.Y., Balas, M.J., Fingersh, L.J.: Control of variable speed wind turbine: standard and adaptive techniques for maximizing energy capture. IEEE Control Syst. Mag. **26**, 74–75 (2006)
9. Pao, L.: A tutorial on the dynamics and control of wind turbines and wind farms. In: Proceedings of the American Control Conference, St. Louis, MO, USA, pp. 18 & 32 (2009)
10. Keesman, K.J.: System Identification: An Introduction, pp. 156–158. Springer, London (2011). https://doi.org/10.1007/978-0-85729-522-4
11. Asma, A., Saida, B., Kamel, A.: System identification: parameter and time-delay estimation for wiener nonlinear systems with delayed input. Trans. Inst. Meas. Control **40**, 1035–1044 (2018)
12. Wang, C., Zhu, L.: Parameter identification of a class of nonlinear systems based on the multi-innovation identification theory. J. Franklin Inst. **352**, 4625–4635 (2015)
13. Chen, S., Billings, S.A., Luo, W.: Orthogonal least squares methods and their applications to nonlinear system identification. Int. J. Control **50**, 1873–1896 (1989)

Evolutionary Based Clustering Protocol for Wireless Sensor Networks

Melaku Tamene[1(✉)], Kuda Nageswara[2], and Ravuri Daniel[3]

[1] Department of Electrical and Computer Engineering,
Wollo University, Dessie, Ethiopia
melakutam2013@gmail.com
[2] Department of Computer Science and Systems Engineering,
Andhra University, Visakhapatnam, India
knraoauce@gmail.com
[3] Department of Computer Science,
Debre Tabor University, Debre Tabor, Ethiopia
danielravuri@gmail.com

Abstract. Many cluster based routing protocols have been developed in order to enhance the network lifetime, but the potency of clustering in energy management highly relies on the optimality of clusters. Optimal cluster formation is the chief source of challenges in clustering protocols. In this paper, new approach has been introduced to formulate the optimization problem in the partition of networks into optimal organization of clusters. The optimization problem consists of finding optimal configuration of clusters such that the distance of cluster heads from the pre-computed cluster centers, communication cost of nodes to transport data and the expected energy dissipation of the network per the residual energy of cluster heads are minimized. The solution to the devised nonlinear clustering problem is found using the genetic algorithm. The genetic algorithm toolbox is developed in C++ and integrated with OMNeT++ simulation platform to implement the protocol. The experimental results verify that the proposed protocol extends the network lifetime compared to the prominent LEACH, LEACH-C and CHEF protocols.

Keywords: Clustering protocol · Wireless sensor networks · Routing protocol

1 Introduction

Wireless sensor networks (WSNs) are primarily designed to furnish the user with the required information in an interest zone ranging from less infrastructure region to physically challenging environment. The integrations of different disciplines such as microelectronics, wireless communication, signal processing and network protocols make the realization of these micro-sensor devices. The architecture of sensor node typically consists of sensing, processing, communication and power supply modules. As the military forces evolved from mechanization to information, sensor networks supply the necessary information for commander of an army to have military dominance through detection of biological, nuclear and chemical attacks in the battlefield. Target tracking and conflict zone inspection are also the potential applications of sensor

© ICST Institute for Computer Sciences, Social Informatics and Telecommunications Engineering 2019
Published by Springer Nature Switzerland AG 2019. All Rights Reserved
F. A. Zimale et al. (Eds.): ICAST 2018, LNICST 274, pp. 354–365, 2019.
https://doi.org/10.1007/978-3-030-15357-1_30

networks in military surveillance [1, 2]. Medical doctors can easily give persistent treatment and follow up the physiological status of their patients at far distance if the customers are equipped with wireless medical sensors [3]. Nuclear emission detection in nuclear power plant, active volcano recognition and forest fire detection are some of the applications of sensor networks in environmental monitoring and control [4]. Nowadays, even buildings are equipped with wireless sensors to reduce the energy wastage by regulating the air conditioning, temperature, ventilation, and humidity of rooms [5].

Wireless sensor networks are somehow similar to other distributed systems. But, it has its own unique challenges and constraints which initiate the system designers to develop new hardware architectures, network protocols and algorithms that are well suited for WSN applications [6–8]. Considering that nodes are left unattended after deployment, they are exposed to malicious attack and intrusions [9, 10]. Generally, self-adaptation, healing, protection and organization are the main challenges in sensor network design. Clustering is one of the methods broadly used to reduce the energy consumption of network and effectively utilizing the channel bandwidth [11–13]. In clustering, leaders are selected and the rest of nodes send their data to the respective cluster leaders so as to reduce the communication distance. The data collected per cluster is highly correlated that the cluster leaders aggregate the received packets from their members before forwarding the data to the base station.

In this paper, we propose Evolutionary based Clustering Protocol, termed ECP to build efficient clusters in wireless sensor networks. The distance of cluster leaders from the pre-computed centroid of clusters, the communication cost of nodes to transport data and the expected energy of dissipation of networks per the remaining energy of cluster leaders are the optimization parameters in the formulated clustering problem. Of the parameters used in optimal configuration of clusters, the distance of candidate Cluster Heads (CHs) from the centroid of clusters can be computed by finding the center points of data points (spatial position of nodes) using the Fuzzy C-Means (FCM) clustering algorithm. The problem of finding cluster centers from the set of geographical position of nodes is formulated as nonlinear constrained optimization problem. The FCM and genetic algorithm (GA) toolboxes are developed in C++ and integrated with OMNeT++ simulation environment to implement the protocol. The experimental results prove that ECP outperforms LEACH, LEACH-C and CHEF protocols.

2 Related Work

In [14], Low Energy Adaptive Clustering Hierarchy (LEACH) protocol has been presented. The data gathering period in LEACH has cluster setup and steady state phases. In cluster setup phase, nodes are randomly configured as cluster head based on the set threshold model, $T(n)$ and their corresponding cluster members will be recognized. Nodes randomly choose any number between 0 and 1 among which those that are able to take a number less than the value of $T(n)$ is selected as cluster head.

$$T(n) = \begin{cases} \frac{p}{1-p\left(r \bmod \frac{1}{p}\right)} & , if \ n \varepsilon \ G \\ 0 & , otherwise \end{cases} \qquad (1)$$

The symbols p, r and G respectively define the desired percentage of cluster leaders, current round number and the set of nodes which are not designated as cluster leader in previous $1/p$ rounds. The cluster heads announce their presence using Carrier Sense Multiple Access (CSMA) Medium Access Control (MAC) protocol so as to identify the cluster members. Then, the cluster heads assign Time Division Multiple Access (TDMA) slots to their children. During steady state phase, the cluster heads receive data from their members, aggregate correlated data and forward it to the base station by making the use of spreading codes and CSMA MAC protocol. The random configuration of clusters in LEACH not only affects the number but also distribution of cluster heads. Regardless of their energy, all nodes are equally probable to act as cluster leader in LEACH that will most likely reduce the lifetime of lower energy nodes in the course of protocol operation. Unlike the distributed cluster formation in LEACH, the paper in [15] describes centralized version of LEACH (LEACH-C) protocol that will initially build clusters at the base station and then announce the details of network back to nodes. LEACH-C protocol configures the clusters such that the communication distance within the cluster is minimized. The protocol applies Simulated Annealing (SA) algorithm to minimize the sum of the square of Euclidean distance between regular nodes and cluster leaders.

The authors in [16] present Fuzzy logic based Cluster Head Election system, termed CHEF. The residual energy and the sum of Euclidean distance of a node from its neighbors are the input variables of the fuzzy system. Each node randomly takes any number between 0 and 1 to construct clusters and asserts itself as a candidate cluster head whenever the generated number is less than the pre-set threshold value.

The authors in [17] present instantaneous clustering protocol for WSNs. The authors design a clustering scheme that is not only able to minimize the time required to setup the clusters but also increase the energy efficiency networks. Instead of using vote in clustering, the authors use the pre-assigned chance of being cluster head so as to accelerate the selection process. The regular nodes in existing methods use acknowledgments (ACKs) to verify the reception of ID of the cluster head. However, concurrent ACKs from multiple nodes within the cluster lead to signal collision. For that reason, the authors avoid ACKs mechanism in clustering. Instead, only the cluster heads are allowed to contend and broadcast their presence during the given period. In order to assure the delivery of ID of the cluster head without collision, the authors formulate the optimal number of time slots adequate for each cluster head.

3 Modelling Energy Consumption of Wireless Sensor Node

The simplified model has been used for radio hardware energy dissipation. The free space and multipath channel models [18] have been used for the experiments in this paper. The power amplifier is adjusted such that the desired output power is delivered to antenna interface to compensate for the path loss during electromagnetic radiation.

Let the energy consumed in the transceiver to receive and transmit data over a distance d be ERx and ETx respectively. Then, the energy consumption in the radio hardware to transmit or receive l bits of data can be computed via the following equations.

$$ETx = \begin{cases} l * Eelc + l * efs * d^2, & d < do \\ l * Eelc + l * emp * d^4, & d \geq do \end{cases} \tag{2}$$

$$ERx = l * Eelc \tag{3}$$

$$do = \sqrt{\frac{efs}{emp}} \tag{4}$$

The constant $Eelc$ refers to per-bit energy consumption of the transmitter or receiver electronics. The coefficients efs and emp are energy dissipation factors in the power amplifier for free space and multipath channel models respectively.

4 Proposed Protocol Design

4.1 Problem Formulation

Consider a WSN with the set of nodes that are randomly placed within the domain of an interest region. At the beginning of every cluster setup phase, nodes send their energy and geographical position parameters to the base station so as to trigger clustering of nodes. Given a network of sensors with known clustering parameters, the problem consists of finding the set of nodes that can be configured as cluster heads to minimize the overall data transmission cost in the network. The base station considers the spatial position of node as a data point to make up dataset pool based on which the pending cluster analysis starts. Data points in the dataset pool will be grouped into clusters such that the similarity of data points measured in terms of Euclidean distance is strong within the cluster. Each cluster is known for its cluster center (centroid) from which the sum of squared distance of data points within cluster is minimized. The analogy is that nodes very near to the cluster centers should be elected with high probability as the potential cluster leaders in order to minimize intra-cluster communication cost provide that they have sufficient amount of residual energy. Given N number of nodes in WSN area, let the desired number of clusters is k. Consider the data point matrix $\mathbf{Z}$ that consists of vectors $zi, i = 1, \ldots, N$ in its column where the vectors are actually (x, y) coordinates of nodes. Similarly, let the vector of cluster centers is represented as follows.

$$\mathbf{C} = [\mathbf{c}1 , \mathbf{c}2 , \ldots , \mathbf{c}k] \tag{5}$$

The fuzzy clustering has been used for assignment of data points into clusters. Unlike the traditional or hard clustering techniques for which the data point totally belongs to one of the clusters, the fuzzy clustering enables natural grouping of data where the given data point belongs to many clusters with different membership degrees. Let the degree of membership of node i to cluster j is represented as uij and m is the fuzzy control parameter. The optimization problem is to find the feasible set of clusters so that the sum of Euclidean norm of the given data points to the cluster centers is minimized. Hence, the problem of grouping data points to clusters is based on minimization of the following objective function.

$$Jc = \sum_{i=1}^{N} \sum_{j=1}^{k} (uij)^{m} \|\mathbf{z}i - \mathbf{c}j\|^{2} \quad 1 \leq m < \infty \tag{6}$$

$$s.t \begin{cases} uij \in [0,1], & 1 \leq i \leq N, \ 1 \leq j \leq k \\ \sum_{j=1}^{k} uij = 1, & i = 1, 2, \cdots, N \\ 0 < \sum_{i=1}^{N} uij < N, & 1 \leq j \leq k \end{cases}$$

The minimization of the above objective function is nonlinear constrained optimization problem that can be solved by a range of methods among which the fuzzy c-means clustering algorithm has been used. The fuzzy c-means clustering algorithm finds the solution through iteratively updating the membership degrees and cluster centers as follows until the algorithm converges.

$$uij = \frac{1}{\sum_{l=1}^{k} \left(\frac{\|\mathbf{z}i - \mathbf{c}j\|}{\|\mathbf{z}i - \mathbf{c}l\|} \right)^{\frac{2}{m-1}}}, \quad 1 \leq i \leq N, \ 1 \leq j \leq k \tag{7}$$

$$\mathbf{c}j = \frac{\sum_{i=1}^{N} (uij)^{m} \mathbf{z}i}{\sum_{i=1}^{N} (uij)^{m}}, \quad 1 \leq j \leq k \tag{8}$$

Let $\mathbf{U}f$ defines the fuzzy partition matrix that consists of *vectors of* membership degree of nodes to the given clusters and represented by $N \times k$ matrix as follows.

$$\mathbf{U}f = \begin{bmatrix} u11 & u12 & \cdots & u1k \\ u21 & u22 & \cdots & u2k \\ \vdots & \vdots & \vdots & \vdots \\ uN1 & uN2 & \cdots & uNk \end{bmatrix} \tag{9}$$

The pseudocode of the fuzzy c-means clustering algorithm is shown in Algorithm 1. The algorithm iteratively computes the fuzzy partition matrix and the termination criteria is when the difference between current and previously computed partition matrix resides below the predefined threshold value ε, as shown in the following equation.

$$\left\| Uf^{now} - Uf^{previous} \right\| < \varepsilon \tag{10}$$

Algorithm 1: Fuzzy C-Means (FCM)

Input: spatial position of nodes
Output: vector of cluster centers
begin
    initialize Uf

    repeat
        for cluster $j = 1$ to k **do**
            $c_j \leftarrow$ compute the cluster center
        end for
        update Uf
    until the algorithm converges

    return $\{C\}$
end

When the fuzzy c-means clustering algorithm converges, the set of cluster centers for the given coordinates of nodes in WSN field will be identified and then it can be used as one of the input parameters in genetic algorithm based computation. Let the set of cluster heads and regular nodes are stored in the variables H and R respectively such that $H \cup R = N$. Let dij represents the distance between node i and j. Suppose $CTij$ defines the cost of transferring data from node i to j and ϕj is the amount of data node j must send. In addition to minimizing the communication cost, the remaining energy of cluster leaders per expected dissipation of energy should be increased in order to extend the network lifetime. Suppose the residual energy of node i is represented as ei. Hence, the problem of optimal network clustering is a combinatorial optimization problem that consists of finding the possible combination of cluster heads so that the following objective function is minimized

$$fobj = \begin{cases} \sum_{i \in N} si * dij, \ j = \arg \min_h \{ dih, \ h \in C \} + \sum_{i \in H} \left(\sum_{j \in R} qij\, CTji + CTibs \right) + \\[2ex] \dfrac{\sum_{i \in H} \left(\left(\sum_{j \in R} qij\, \phi j\, Eelc \right) + \phi i\, Eelc + \varepsilon a\, dibs^m \right)}{\sum_{i \in H} ei} \end{cases} \tag{11}$$

The symbol εa in the above equation refers the amplifier coefficient and the constant m defines the path loss exponent. Consider the parameter Tx^j that defines the transmission range of node j. The symbols si and qij are the decision variables and can be represented as follows.

$$si = \begin{cases} 1 & \text{if node } i \text{ configured as } CH \\ 0 & \text{otherwise} \end{cases}$$

$$qij = \begin{cases} 1 & \text{if } \|dij\| \leq Tx^j \\ 0 & \text{otherwise} \end{cases}$$

4.2 Solution Finding Based on Genetic Algorithm

The genetic algorithm starts with initial population $(Pt \mid t = 0)$ of chromosomes which are generated randomly as preliminary solutions to the problem but through iterative randomization and guided search mechanisms, the solutions are transformed to finer results. The best chromosome (*Cbest*) in history of population generations is the basis for cluster configuration. The WSN nodes are represented by sequence of bits in binary encoded chromosome structure. Hence, the size (length) of a chromosome is equivalent to the dimension of network which is prescribed as the number of nodes in WSN area. The content of a chromosome is uniquely identified by *gene index* and *gene value* pair in which the *gene value* and *gene index* are the state of node to act as cluster leader and ID of node respectively. Consider the *gene value* of a chromosome at *gene index* i is represented as $g(i) \ \forall \ i \in \{1, 2, \ldots, N\}$. Then, it can be mathematically expressed as follows.

$$g(i) = \begin{cases} 1 & \text{if node } i \text{ configured as cluster leader} \\ 0 & \text{otherwise} \end{cases} \tag{12}$$

Suppose r defines the size of population which is fixed to the same value over generations and let *len* symbolizes the length of a chromosome, then the chromosomes of population in each generation can be designated as follows.

$$Cr^g = \left\{ Cr_j^g \ \middle| \ 1 \leq j \leq r, \ Cr_j^g = (g(1), g(2), \ldots, g(i), \ldots, g(n)), \ n \leftarrow len \right\} \tag{13}$$

The initial population of chromosomes are evolved to future generations through the genetic recombination and mutation of those individuals which are allowed to breed based on the given selection strategy. In our algorithm, chromosomes are selected for mating based on Roulette-Wheel selection scheme where the selection probability of an individual increases with the rank (fitness value) of a chromosome. A single point *crossover* is applied to chromosomes in the mating pool in which a point (crossover site) is selected at random over the span of chromosome and the *gene value* of parts of parent chromosomes are exchanged to produce a pair of child chromosomes. In order to alleviate the premature convergence for which the solution tends to stick into local optimum, the *mutation* operator is applied to child chromosomes. The fact that *mutation* adds variation to generation allows the algorithm to go through a wide range of search space in an attempt to achieve the global optimum. Since *mutation* is a divergence operation, it should happen less frequently than the *crossover* operation in order to speed up the convergence rate. The pseudocode of genetic algorithm is shown in Algorithm 2. In the late stages of data gathering periods, some nodes may run out of energy for which the base station must update the history of those nodes in the chromosome structure. Hence, at end of population *initialization, crossover* and *mutation* operations, the *gene value* of such nodes should be updated using *chromosome repair* operation to avoid them from possible inclusion in the cluster leaders list. The evolution operators are applied repeatedly till the algorithm is terminated in the late evolving periods at which the solutions are no longer changed.

Algorithm 2: Genetic Algorithm

---
begin

    $t \leftarrow 0 \{\text{generation counter}\}$

    $Pt \leftarrow$ generate initial population

    while $t <$ max generation count**do**

        $Ft \leftarrow evaluate\ (Pt)$

        $C_{best} \leftarrow update\_best\ (Pt, Ft)$

        $Pt' \leftarrow genetic\_operation\ (Pt)$

        $Pt'' \leftarrow chromosome\_repair\ (Pt')$

        $Pt \leftarrow Pt''$

        $t \leftarrow t+1$

    end while

end

4.3   Network Configuration

Due to the stochastic nature of genetic algorithm, there is an appearance of spike in the number of clusters. Hence, upon the convergence of the GA computation, the cluster maintenance module takes the GA suggested clusters and find out those that will create fair distribution of clusters in WSN field. Normally, good distribution of clusters can be obtained if the cluster leaders are at significant distance to each other so that the average of regular nodes can easily reside within the minimum transmission diameter of cluster leaders. As it is stated in the previous section, the desired number of clusters is k. The cluster maintenance module takes k cluster leaders randomly from the pool of GA suggested clusters. Then, it will find out those that are able to maximize the spatial distance between cluster leaders so as to preserve good distribution of clusters in WSN region. Hence, the problem of finding k cluster leaders from the GA suggested clusters is based on maximization of the following objective function.

$$fobj = \sum_{i \in \mathbf{CL}} \left(\sum_{j \in \mathbf{CL}, j \neq i} \| dij \| \right) \tag{14}$$

The parameter d_{ij} represents the distance between cluster leaders i and j. The GA suggested cluster leaders are stored in vector **CL**. Once the clusters are configured, the base station announces the details of network configuration back to nodes. The configuration consists of selected cluster heads and the time schedule (TDMA slot) of regular nodes. The nature of steady state data transmission phase is much similar to LEACH protocol and for this reason the detail is omitted here.

5   Performance Evaluation

5.1   Simulation Environment

The experiment is done using Objective Modular Network Test-bed (OMNeT++) simulation platform. The networks of 100 sensor nodes are uniformly deployed across $100 \, \text{m} \times 100 \, \text{m}$ WSN area. The configuration parameters used in the simulation are initial energy = 2 J, base station location = (175, 50) m, control packet size = 25 bytes, data packet size = 500 bytes, $Eelc$ = 50 nJ/bit, energy consumed for data aggregation (Eda) = 5 nJ/bit/signal, efs = 10 pJ/bit/m2, emp = 0.0013 pJ/bit/m4 and TDMA frames per round = 6. The GA parameters used in the experiment are population size = 50, mutation rate = 0.001, crossover rate = 0.8 and generations count = 2000.

5.2   Experimental Results and Analysis

The base station iteratively executes the genetic algorithm till the convergence criterion is achieved. The plot in Fig. 1 depicts the minimum and maximum fitness of chromosome per each generation and the highest fitness recorded in the history of generations for randomly taken data gathering round. Initially, the fitness tends to get better quickly and as the iteration proceeds to the convergence point, the algorithm hardly shows improvement in the value of fitness. The simulation result shows that the algorithm converges after 1000 generations are gone for the selected data gathering round.

Owing to the presence of duplicate data in network, the death of a few nodes does not severely affect the quality of network except being a good indication of the kick-off of quality degradation. From this perspective, the time elapsed till 50% of nodes die (HND) is thus an acceptable metric to numerically measure the network lifetime compared to other metrics, viz. the time at which the first node runs out of energy (FND) and the time at which the last node dies (LND). For most application of WSNs, the network is considered non-functional right after HND. Figure 2 describes the number of functional nodes versus time. The simulation result shows ECP improves the network lifetime by 42.96%, 7.71% and 5.01% compared to LEACH, LEACH-C and CHEF protocols respectively. The substantial rate of premature death of nodes in LEACH is due to random configuration of clusters in which incapable nodes (nodes having lower energy) are not blocked to act as cluster head. The delayed death of nodes in ECP is the manifestation of fair distribution of load among sensors. Nodes drain energy nearly at the same rate in ECP than its counterparts. Owing to this fact, higher death rate and steeper gradient appear following the death of the first node in ECP than

LEACH, LEACH-C and CHEF protocols. ECP also dominates LEACH, LEACH-C and CHEF protocols in terms of FND, HND and LND metrics. After the death of first node, the network is mostly considered unstable even if the quality is not quickly diminished at high rate. Hence, the proposed protocol has higher network stability than LEACH, LEACH-C and CHEF protocols.

One of the root causes of premature death of nodes in WSN region is unbalanced load distribution in the network. Unbalanced load hastens the power consumption rate of the particular set of nodes. Due to aforementioned problem, the variance of energy expenditure among nodes shall be reduced to extend the system lifetime. The standard deviation of the residual energy of nodes in each simulation round is depicted in Fig. 3. The simulation result shows that ECP improves the degree of energy equilibrium among nodes compared to LEACH, LEACH-C and CHEF protocols. LEACH-C dominates LEACH and CHEF protocols in terms of load balance since the clusters are configured at the base station. In addition to load balance, the overall energy consumption of nodes per each round must be reduced to maximize the residual energy of the network. Figure 4 shows the network energy consumption in each round for the four protocols. The result proves ECP has reduced energy usage than LEACH, LEACH-C and CHEF protocols. The average energy consumption of nodes is also examined for randomly taken simulation rounds.

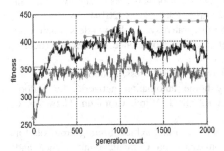

Fig. 1. Fitness of chromosome per each generation

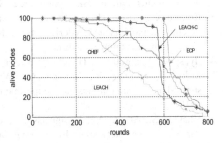

Fig. 2. Number of functional nodes versus time

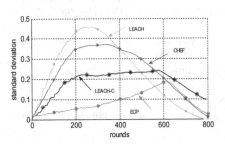

Fig. 3. Standard deviation of residual energy of nodes

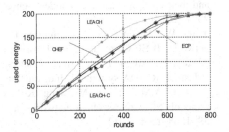

Fig. 4. Consumed energy of network over time

6 Conclusion

Wireless sensor networks are typically characterized by inherent shortage of energy. Unlike the traditional computer networks, energy conservation is the prominent and critical issue in design of sensor networks in which other parameters such as delay, reliability and throughput are treated as secondary requirements. Effective use of channel bandwidth, data aggregation and reduced consumption of energy are the typical benefits of cluster based protocols. In this paper, we present optimization of cluster formation based on the computational models of evolutionary algorithm. Considering that the exhaustive search methods do not find optimal solutions to NP-Hard problems within polynomial bounded time, the genetic algorithm has been applied to find optimal or suboptimal solution at reduced computational time. In cluster setup phase, the base station configures the cluster heads and nodes are then informed about the details of configuration to begin data dissemination. The simulation results prove that the proposed protocol dominates LEACH, LEACH-C and CHEF protocols.

References

1. Akyildiz, I., Su, W., Sankarasubramaniam, Y., et al.: A survey on sensor networks. IEEE Commun. Mag. **40**, 102–114 (2002)
2. Priyanka, R., Kamal, D., Hakima, C., et al.: Wireless sensor networks: a survey on recent developments and potential synergies. J. Supercomput. **68**(1), 1–48 (2014)
3. Rotariu, C., Costin, H., Andruseac, G., et al.: An integrated system for wireless monitoring of chronic patients and elderly people. In: International Conference on System Theory, Control and Computing (2011)
4. Ilyas, M., Mahgoub, I.: Handbook of Sensor Networks. CRC Press, London (2005)
5. Milo, S., Stefano, S., Monica, N.: Wireless home automation networks for indoor surveillance; technologies and experiments. EURASIP J. Wirel. Commun. Netw., p. 6 (2014)
6. Vhatkar, S., Atique, M.: Design issues and challenges in hierarchical routing protocols for wireless sensor networks. In: International Conference on Computational Science and Computational Intelligence (2014)
7. Shaikh, F.K., Zeadally, S.: Energy harvesting in wireless sensor networks: a comprehensive review. Renew. Sustain. Energy Rev. **55**, 1041–1054 (2016)
8. Bharat, B., Gadadhar, S.: Recent advances in attacks, technical challenges, vulnerabilities and their countermeasure in wireless sensor networks. Wirel. Pers. Commun. **98**(2), 2037–2077 (2018)
9. Yong, W., Attebury, G., Ramamurthy, B.: A survey of security issues in wireless sensor networks. IEEE Commun. Surv. Tutorials **8**(2), 2–23 (2016)
10. Alexey, F., Anton, F.: Information attacks and security in wireless sensor networks of industrial SCADA systems. J. Ind. Inf. Integr. **5**, 6–16 (2017)
11. Zungeru, A.M., Ang, L.-M., Seng, K.P.: Classical and swarm intelligence based routing protocols for wireless sensor networks: a survey and comparison. J. Netw. Comput. Appl. **35**, 1508–1536 (2012)

12. Yang, S.-S., Shim, J.-S., Jang, Y.-H., Ju, Y.-W., Park, S.-C.: Design of clustering algorithm for efficient energy management in wireless sensor network environments. In: Park, J., Chen, S.-C., Raymond Choo, K.-K. (eds.) MUE/FutureTech -2017. LNEE, vol. 448, pp. 607–612. Springer, Singapore (2017). https://doi.org/10.1007/978-981-10-5041-1_96

13. Rostami, A.S., Badkoobe, M., Mohanna, F., et al.: A survey on clustering in heterogeneous and homogenous wireless sensor networks. J. Supercomput. **74**(1), 277–323 (2018)

14. Heinzelman, W., Chandrakasan, A., Balakrishnan, H.: Energy-efficient communication protocol for wireless microsensor networks. In: International Conference System Sciences (2000)

15. Heinzelman, W., Chandrakasan, A., Balakrishnan, H.: An application specific protocol architecture for wireless microsensor networks. IEEE Trans. Wirel. Commun. **1**, 660–670 (2002)

16. Kim, J-M., Park, S-H., Han, Y-J., Chung, T-M.: CHEF: cluster head election mechanism using fuzzy logic in wireless sensor. In: International Conference Advanced Communication Technology (2008)

17. Kong, L., Xiang, Q., et al.: ICP: instantaneous clustering protocol for wireless sensor networks. Comput. Netw. **101**, 144–157 (2016)

18. Rappaport, T.S.: Wireless Communications: Principles and Practice. Prentice-Hall, Englewood Cliffs (1996)

SMS Based Agricultural Information System for Rural Farmers

Alemu Kumilachew Tegegnie[(✉)], Tekeste Demessie Dagne,
and Tamir Anteneh Alemu

Faculty of Computing, Bahirdar institute of Technology (BiT),
Bahirdar University, Bahirdar, Ethiopia
alemupilatose@gmail.com, lolteke@gmail.com,
tamirat.1216@gmail.com

Abstract. Agriculture is the back bone of Ethiopia's economy. Despite the strength and volume of agriculture related information and training available through Ethiopia's vast public extension system, ensuring farmers receive up-to-date data and knowledge in a timely, complete and quality manner remains a great challenge. The existing practice for delivering agricultural information through agricultural extension officers, farmer-to-farmer visit and mass Medias couldn't satisfy the information needs of rural farmers. This is attributed by few numbers of extension officers, budget bottle neck and absence of electricity and network. This paper presents a SMS based agricultural information system (SMSbAIS) aimed to solve such challenges in agricultural sector. The SMSbAIS was developed based on a conceptual framework, developed during the course of this research, is used as a platform where rural farmers and agricultural extension officers can get agricultural knowledge service, request agricultural information and supply any information that demands the intervention of higher agricultural officers. It helps users not only to request for agricultural information; it also used to deliver such information to the hands of users via their mobile phones. The system is developed using Rapid Application Development (RAD) methodology with a series of iterative development and testing is done based on System Usability Scale (SUS) method. Testing and evaluation is targeted the systems usability, accuracy and performance. Therefore, it was found that on the SUS scale that ranges from 0 to 100, the system scored 87.6 with feedback from 20 users. The Query Understanding engine (QUE) accurately translated 90% of all incoming user requests. The mean average response system time is found to be 3.34 s. These results show that problem of lack of appropriate and easily accessible agricultural information can be solved using a system like the one developed in this research based on a framework that seeks solutions to challenges faced in accessing agricultural information in rural community.

Keywords: Agricultural information · Agricultural knowledge service · SMS · SMS based agricultural information system · Rural farmer · Usability

© ICST Institute for Computer Sciences, Social Informatics and Telecommunications Engineering 2019
Published by Springer Nature Switzerland AG 2019. All Rights Reserved
F. A. Zimale et al. (Eds.): ICAST 2018, LNICST 274, pp. 366–379, 2019.
https://doi.org/10.1007/978-3-030-15357-1_31

1 Introduction

Agriculture is the back bone of Ethiopia's Economy. More than 80% of the country's Population employed in this sector [1]. Agriculture constitutes products of the major key resources such as land, livestock, plants, water and minerals. The sector is dominated by agrarian society (largely small-scale farmers).

Accelerating agricultural growth in Ethiopia has wide-ranging impacts beyond smallholder farmers and rural development. Little has been done to transform the peasants' in Ethiopian agriculture information system [2, 3]. Despite the strength and volume of agriculture related information and training available through Ethiopia's vast public extension system, ensuring farmers receive up-to-date data and knowledge in a timely manner remains a great challenge.

ICT in Ethiopia is acknowledged as having the potential to accelerate the socio-economic development of the country. However, the area is dominated by traditional practice of agricultural information system such as farmer-to-farmer visit, meetings, broadcasting special programs via mass media, etc., along with insufficient budget and little modern practices that lead to a tremendous bottle neck in the area. One of the perceived benefits of modern ICT is greater access to information on farm related information which has an impact in improving the capability of farmers for effective cultivation and reduction farm related disease.

Agricultural information system can facilitate an effective knowledge service for supporting the farmers in problem-solving, decision making, and early warning through the application of mobile phones. They are an essential tool for sustainable economic development in the area of agriculture thorough providing effective communication in the areas of travel, harvesting, productivity, and understanding of market analysis [4–6]. Providing real-time agricultural information using SMS (Short Message Service) text messaging via mobile phones can be used to deliver shorter often time critical messages. SMS is a better way for giving knowledge service, especially automatic interchange of short text messages, by providing the information from an automatic agricultural information system. A system for the bulk distribution of these text messages can be send to targeted farmers to notify important weather, proactive alerts, seasonal agriculture information and other farm cultivation tips. Besides the agricultural knowledge service, the system shall notify farmers with the possible occurrence of a plant and crop disease, pest, sudden flood, unseasonal rain, wind, drought, crop harvestation, preparedness, and other warning notifications.

In an effort to address the aforementioned issues, this research project is aimed investigate the possibilities and evaluation of designing and developing SMS based agricultural information system platform that enables the stakeholders of the agricultural sector share agricultural information.

2 Related Work

2.1 Overview of Mobile (SMS) Based Information System

The Short Message Service (SMS) allows text-based messages to be sent to and from Mobile phones on a GSM network. The applications of SMS based systems are getting a prior choice in Africa due to the fact that there is poor and inadequate telecom infrastructure that does not entertain voice and IP services [7]. Unlike voice and IP services, SMS is a 'best effort service' in which a message can get through even when the 'network is busy' for hours or when there is not enough free capacity in the network.

SMS based systems can be applied for services that require instant messaging to the consumer which have varied set of objectives from providing market price information for national planning to government institutions to providing information for monitoring of household livelihoods to donors funding various interventions. Such systems has been becoming increasingly popular in developed countries and some of African countries in which the information system content management is done in local language via SMS on mobile phones. Various applications developed showed that SMS messaging has shown great potential in Africa. FAMIS in COMESA region; RATIN in East Africa; ESOKO in Ghana and MFARM in Kenya [7, 8] are some of the mentioned mobile (SMS) based applications.

2.2 SMS Based Systems in the Case of Ethiopia

Mobile phones have recently started being used in Ethiopia for sending SMS-based information through a mobile phone. It has been used by organization for promotion, announcement, collecting funds, and sending comments [9]. Full-fledged mobile (SMS) based systems are rare except a little effort by Commercial Bank of Ethiopia (CBE) and Ethiopian Agricultural Transformation Agency (ATA).

SMS (USSD) Banking, Commercial Bank of Ethiopia (CBE). The recently started CBE's Mobile Banking (MB) services enable you to access your bank accounts, make fund transfers, payments and balance inquiries as well as get instant notifications on all your accounts linked with MB services-using the SMS, XHTML and DOWN-LOADABLE application channels.

8028- Hotline IVR System by Agricultural Transformation Agency (ATA). To ensure farmers receive up-to-date data and agricultural knowledge service in real time, ATA is initiated and developed an Interactive Voice Response (IVR) platform to deliver information directly to farmers through mobile phones [10]. However, significant calls and callers has been becoming increasing after the service is launched, the delivery of the service content is still a bottleneck. The usability issue of the system is also in question for several reasons. First, long list procedure of user registration process and selection of menus to get a customized content delivery is also tiresome. Second, a farmer is just only forced to listen to the computer voice (one way communication, no way to speak back). Third, it is not possible to get the service offline. Currently a computer voice is not downloaded into your handset and won't be able to play back.

Even if, we can provide a record-and-play back service, it is not suitable for all kinds of mobile handsets. Lastly, even though, the system can provide different statistics (e.g. the number of callers), it is impossible to evaluate its usability and satisfaction of the user, i.e. critical input to extend/improve the services. This study used the 8028 hotline IVR system as an initial bench mark to design and develop the system.

3 Design of the Study

3.1 Research Methodology

Population. The population included mobile service provider (Ethio telecom), farmers, extension officers, agricultural and system experts. This choice has been made as it affects the objective of the study and this group of people was interviewed for data collection.

Sampling Size and Technique. As a research comprises farmers and extension officers, system and agricultural experts, a purposely selected 20 participants of which (ten rural farmers, two agricultural knowledge experts, five agricultural extension officers, and three system experts) are included in this study. The selection is influenced by the knowledge and experience they had and the accessibility of those people by the researcher.

Data Source. The data source constituted ethio-telecom, software companies, agricultural research institutes, Agricultural Bureau and ministry of Agriculture.

Data Collection Methods. The relevant data is collected using interview and questionnaire method. The questions that respondents were asked (or tried to filled) were based on SUS (System Usability Scale) method developed by Brooke in 1986 [11]. Queries sent in and responses sent out were recorded in the database are collected and used for data analysis.

Experimental Setup and Evaluation Procedures. The development process of a prototype system is passed through a series of iteration. Different version of a system is produced at each level of iteration and usability testing is made for each version by technical and end users using SUS method. They were interviewed and their responses used to fill a System Usability Scale (SUS) as shown in Table 1. Individual SUS score is determined from each individual response using SUS method as shown in Eq. 1. The sum of the whole respondents SUS value is used for average SUS value calculation using Eq. 2. Meanwhile, the conceptual design (architecture) of the system is re-designed at each iteration and a final version is drawn.

To calculate the SUS score, first sum the score contributions from each item. Each item's score contribution will range from 0 to 4. For items 1, 3, 5, 7 and 9 the score contribution is the scale position minus 1. For items 2, 4, 6, 8 and 10, the contribution is 5 minus the scale position. Next, the summation is multiplied by 2.5. This raises the possible values from 0, to 40 to a new scale of 0, to 100.

Table 1. System Usability Scale (SUS)

		Strongly disagree			Strongly agree	
		1	2	3	4	5
1	I think that I would like to use the system frequently					
2	I found the system unnecessarily complex					
3	I thought the system was easy to use					
4	I think that I would need the support of a technical person to be able to use this system					
5	I found the various functions in this system were well integrated					
6	I thought there was too much inconsistency in this system					
7	I would imagine that most people would learn to use this system very quickly					
8	I found the system very cumbersome to use					
9	I felt very confident using the system					
10	I needed to learn a lot of things before I could get going with this system					

SUS method for one respondent

$$2.5 \sum \left(\left(\times^{+ve} - 1 \right) + \left(5 - \times^{-ve} \right) \right) \tag{1}$$

SUS value for the whole respondent,

$$\frac{\sum_{n=1}^{n} 2.5 \sum \left(\left(\times^{+ve} - 1 \right) + \left(5 - \times^{-ve} \right) \right)}{n} \tag{2}$$

Determining the accuracy of the system is done by measuring how many of queries sent by users are correctly understood by the Query Understanding Engine (QUE) and correct responses are sent to the user, as follows.

$$Accuracy = \frac{the\ number\ of\ correct\ responses\ determined\ by\ the\ system}{the\ number\ of\ expected\ responses\ stored\ in\ the\ database} \tag{3}$$

In the other hand, system performance testing is done for functional and non-functional system modules and speed. Functional and non-functional performance testing is done in the lab by the researcher together with system experts. Whereas, speed testing is evaluated by measuring the amount of time taken by the system to process user queries (inputs) and corresponding responses sent to the user. The response time is recorded for each user interacting in three of the system modules. Since users interacted with a system a number of times, different time statistics is measured. Hence, average of the maximum registered time, average of the minimum registered time, and the average of these two are computed and used as a system's response time. The minimum (mt) and maximum (Mt) response time is labeled by the researcher after computing mean average response time (at) as follows.

$$min.time\,(mt) = any\,time\,(T) < Avg.Res.time\,(at)$$
$$Max.time\,(Mt) = any\,time\,(T) \geq Avg.Res.time\,(at)$$

$$(4)$$

Development Tool and Methodology. The system was developed using Rapid Application Development (RAD) methodology with iterative development and testing done. Choosing RAD as opposed to other methodologies is due to the fact that it is fast and less error prone. GlassFish server and Java Programming Language are selected for programming tool due to its familiarity with the researchers.

3.2   Design of the System

Overview. In going about this research project, a systematic approach was followed. To achieve the research objectives, applications which are accessed and run on the user mobile were considered and studied comparatively. Together with this, the major impediments to achieving a usable, affordable and accessible system were analyzed. To design and develop the system, a conceptual framework that guides the development of the system is developed considering major impediments.

The developed system consisted of key functional modules which include Query Understanding Engine (QUE), SMS gateway, database and web interface. The system is attempted to handle five major activities within this module: user registration, message broadcasting, Broadcast message to multiple users, handle system driven AIS services, maintain incoming SMS into database, and perform Automatic Request Response (ARR) as shown in Fig. 1.

Testing and Evaluation was done at each series (version) of the development and final version of the prototype system using two methods: using M-choice SMS/USSD simulator software and temporarily hosting a final version on Ethio-Telecom server. M-choice similar is used for functional test; whereas, the later is used for practical testing and evaluation of the system's usability, accuracy and performance (speed) using standard mobiles and smart phones.

Design of the Interaction. The system involves the key system functional modules, system functions and actors who use these functions as shown in Fig. 2.

Conceptual Framework. In order to addresses the challenges mentioned in earlier sections, a conceptual framework was formulated that guides the design and development of SMSbAIS. Pictorial representation of the framework is shown in Fig. 3.

Accessibility entails the availability of ubiquitous media in which rural farmers in Ethiopia to have reach of systems that avail agricultural information to them. Agricultural services should be tailored to local languages where majority of the population speaks. This framework prioritizes a more flexible syntax where users can send in SMS using a preset syntax or using a natural question asking format. Such kinds of systems

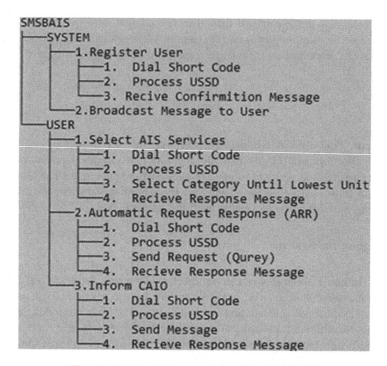

Fig. 1. Functional decomposition of the SMSbAIS

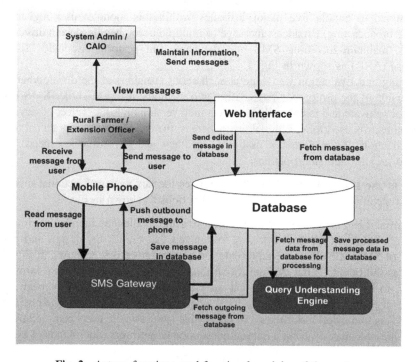

Fig. 2. Actors, functions, and functional modules of the system

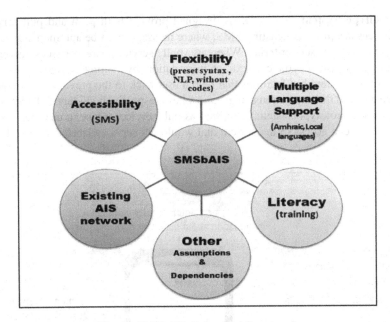

Fig. 3. SMSbAIS Conceptual framework

require basic literacy skills: reading and writing in their own languages. The framework assumed the existing AIS model rural community in Ethiopia.

Architectural Design of the System. An agricultural information system can be constructed based on a mobile platform to send and receive short agricultural messages and also receive expert advice through agriculture expert knowledgebase. Figure 4 depicts the proposed architectural for SMS based Agricultural information system.

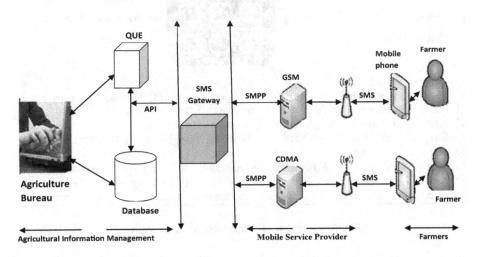

Fig. 4. Architectural design for SMS based Agricultural Information System (SMSbAIS)

The Prototype System. SMSbAIS is designed provide both push and pull services. Push services are just broadcasting SMS, where messages will be automatically sent to you based on pre-set criteria. Whereas, pull services are services given on demand/request, where you can extract information by texting us the codes. Each function of the system has facilities that help a user back to the previous option and/or automatically end the interaction using * and # keys respectively. Figure 5 depicts major services of the prototype system, identified as pull services. Once, a user has got registered, he/she can access to the system and would get services labeled 2, 3 & 4.

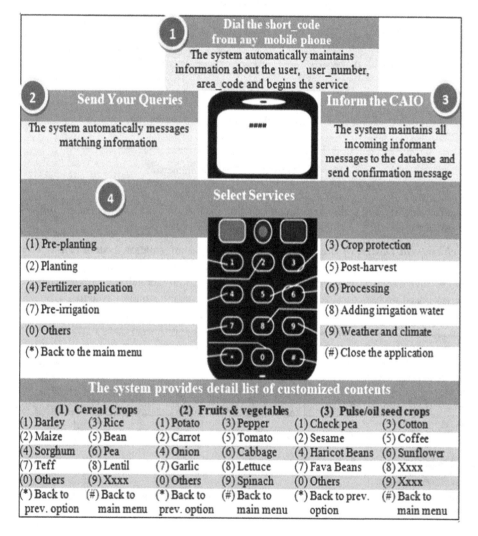

Fig. 5. Overview of SMSbAIS service structure

4   Results and Discussions

Attainment of the objectives set in this research was measured by analyzing data collected using the questionnaire and data generated from the database. The evaluation is made via testing the system based on its usability, accuracy, performance and meeting its research objectives.

4.1   Usability Testing

The collected data is analyzed using the standard SUS formula as shown in Eqs. (1 & 2). Use of the SUS for analyzing usability encompasses all aspects of the system that determined usability performance such as effectiveness, efficiency, user satisfaction, user perception and overall ease of use. Figure 6 shows average SUS score obtained during each iteration of the prototype system from a total of 20 respondents involved in a total of 8 iterations. This gives a total of 200 responses in a single iteration, i.e. 1600 responses in all iterations. The average SUS score is found to be optimal (87.6) during the 5th iteration. Then after, these values have shown a very slight difference because of the fact that the respondents didn't find significant differences and believed to feel the same level of satisfaction and ease of use during the interaction; and because of these they have given the same rating as that of the fifth iteration.

As can be seen from Fig. 6, different version of the system is obtained. The fifth iteration scored the highest SUS score value. In addition, this version of the prototype system gained the highest level of user during the experiment. Because of this fact the system experts and the researchers selected the 5th version as a final version system.

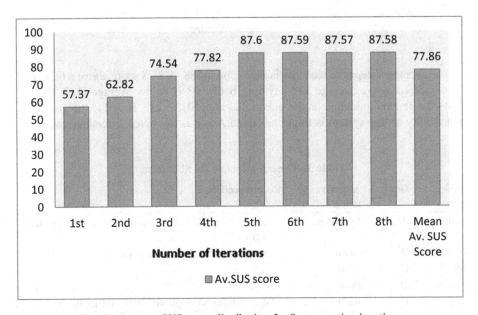

Fig. 6. Average SUS score distribution for 8 consecutive iterations

The remaining measurements done in this experiment was done using this version. Table 2 below shows detail SUS results of the final version.

Table 2. Detail results of SUS score for 20 participants

Participant	Q1	Q2	Q3	Q4	Q5	Q6	Q7	Q8	Q9	Q10	SUS score
p1	5	1	5	1	5	1	3	1	4	1	92.5
p2	4	1	5	2	5	1	4	1	3	2	85.0
p3	5	1	4	1	4	1	5	1	5	3	90.0
p4	5	2	5	1	5	2	5	2	4	1	90.0
p5	5	1	5	1	5	1	4	2	5	2	92.5
p6	4	1	5	1	4	1	5	1	4	2	90.0
p7	5	3	4	1	3	2	4	1	5	2	80.0
p8	5	1	5	1	5	1	5	2	5	1	97.5
p9	5	1	5	2	4	2	4	1	4	1	87.5
p10	4	2	5	1	5	2	5	1	5	2	90.0
p11	5	1	5	2	5	3	5	1	4	1	90.0
p12	4	2	4	1	3	1	4	1	3	2	77.5
p13	5	1	5	2	5	2	4	1	4	1	90.0
p14	4	1	4	1	4	1	4	2	5	2	85.0
p15	5	2	4	2	5	1	5	1	4	1	90.0
p16	4	1	5	1	4	2	4	2	5	3	82.5
p17	5	2	4	1	3	1	5	1	4	1	87.5
p18	5	1	5	2	4	2	4	1	3	1	85.0
p19	4	2	5	1	5	1	3	1	4	1	87.5
p20	5	1	5	2	3	2	5	1	3	2	82.5
									Avg. SUS score		**87.6**

The average acceptable usability is SUS score of 68. A SUS score above a 68 would be considered above average and anything below 68 is below average [12]. Table 3 shows the general guideline on the interpretation of SUS score. Based to the guideline, the usability of this system is found be Grade A and is has given 'excellent' rate.

Table 3. General guideline for SUS score

SUS score	Grade	Adjective rating	Recommendation
>80.3	A	Excellent	Users are more likely to be recommending the product to a friend
68–80.3	B	Good	You're doing OK but could improve
68	C	Okay	
51–68	D	Poor	
<51	F	Awful	Make usability your priority now and fix this fast

4.2 Accuracy

Analyzing for accuracy of system in understanding queries was done by comparing responses of the system to expected responses. For a total of 150 messages, the system accurately responded to 135 messages. The other 15 messages were not accurately understood, it requires human touch.

$$Accuracy = \frac{135}{150} \times 100\% = 90\%$$

4.3 Performance Testing

An interaction log file that involves that amount of time taken by the system (server) is generated and used to analyze the performance (speed) of the system with respect to users' request. Testing involves for all three of the system modules (services). Table 4 shows the time statistics (generated based on Eq. 4) used by the system during interaction with the user for the given services. Hence, the average response time for 20 participants is found to be 3.09, 3.26 and 3.65 s for Inform CAIO, AIS services and ARR respectively. The average response time for ARR services is significantly higher than the other services since the ARR undergoes further transactions and process that require searching and matching.

As it can be shown from Table 4, each test contains average maximum or minimum response time for each system service from which mean average response time (more representative time) is calculated. These values are collected from a minimum of 15 transactions of the first 20 users in the database for the period of three weeks.

Figure 7 below shows the distribution of mean average response time for each system service. It re-assured that ARR service take more time to respond to user requests for the explained reason. The mean average response time value is taken as the

Table 4. The average response time for each functional module

Test	Inform CAIO			AIS services			ARR		
	Avg. Max Res. Time	Avg. Min Res. Time	Mean Avg.	Avg. Max Res. Time	Avg. Min Res. Time	Mean Avg.	Avg. Max Res. Time	Avg. Min Res. Time	Mean Avg.
p1	3.27	2.64	2.96	3.11	2.96	3.04	4.23	3.06	3.65
p2	3.46	2.71	3.09	3.65	2.89	3.27	4.06	3.65	3.86
p3	4.23	3.01	3.62	3.21	2.69	2.95	3.97	3.06	3.52
p4	3.59	2.41	3.00	4.09	3.12	3.61	3.85	2.89	3.37
p5	3.78	2.35	3.07	4.23	3.01	3.62	4.12	3.25	3.69
p6	3.47	2.01	2.74	3.62	3	3.31	3.76	3.09	3.43
p7	4.09	3.21	3.65	3.99	2.36	3.18	4.23	3.69	3.96
p8	3.21	2.09	2.65	4.03	2.45	3.24	3.96	3.16	3.56

(*continued*)

Table 4. (*continued*)

Test	Inform CAIO			AIS services			ARR		
	Avg. Max Res. Time	Avg. Min Res. Time	Mean Avg.	Avg. Max Res. Time	Avg. Min Res. Time	Mean Avg.	Avg. Max Res. Time	Avg. Min Res. Time	Mean Avg.
p9	3.98	2.13	3.06	3.21	2.17	2.69	4.02	3.57	3.80
p10	4.06	3.34	3.70	3.69	2.36	3.03	4.96	3.89	4.43
p11	3.07	2.46	2.77	3.98	2.26	3.12	4.75	3.21	3.98
p12	3.56	2.94	3.25	3.96	2.65	3.31	3.65	2.79	3.22
p13	3.49	2.67	3.08	4.03	3.01	3.52	3.76	2.86	3.31
p14	3.67	2.46	3.07	3.67	2.99	3.33	3.94	3.01	3.48
p15	4.03	2.79	3.41	3.94	2.98	3.46	3.12	2.56	2.84
p16	3.26	2.54	2.90	3.91	3.21	3.56	3.73	2.79	3.26
p17	3.04	2.06	2.55	3.64	3.01	3.33	4.67	3.67	4.17
p18	3.40	2.41	2.91	4.79	2.09	3.44	4.79	3.29	4.04
p19	3.58	2.34	2.96	4.35	2.04	3.20	3.65	2.79	3.22
p20	3.73	3.01	3.37	3.86	2.17	3.02	4.89	3.77	4.33
Avg	**3.60**	**2.56**	**3.09**	**3.85**	**2.67**	**3.26**	**4.11**	**3.20**	**3.65**

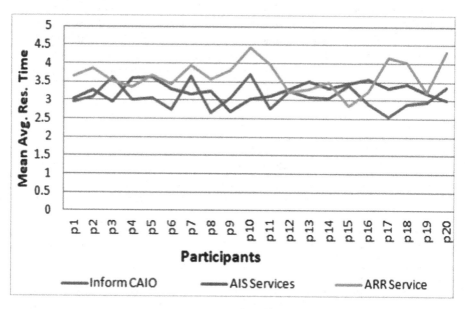

Fig. 7. Mean average response time distribution for system services among 20 users

performance (speed) of the system, which is calculated from the final mean average response time value of the three services (3.09, 3.26 & 3.65 respectively). Therefore, the results found to be 3.34 and it is promising. With further optimization, the system could perform even better.

5 Conclusion and Recommendation

Mobile SMS is a potential solution in that to get the information flow faster and correctly; deliver the right information to the right user; and address effective information with minimum cost and effort. An SMS based agricultural information system built using a framework (developed during the course of this research) that addressed specific challenges faced by rural farmers is possible and meet its objectives. The results of the experimentation show that problem of lack of appropriate and easily accessible agricultural information can be solved using a system like the one developed in this research by following a framework that targets solutions to challenges faced in accessing agricultural information in rural community. The researcher highly recommended future researchers in areas of inclusion of additional languages, enhancement of query understanding engine and learning. Accepting user replies (inputs) using a natural language (e.g. speech) for ARR and Inform CAIO services are also recommended for further work.

References

1. Emmanuel Development Association (EDA) and KOPIN (Koperazzjoni Internazzjonali): A review of Ethiopian agriculture: roles, policy and small-scale farming systems, December 2010. http://www.edaethiopia.org, http://www.kopin.org
2. ATA Annual Report. Transforming Agriculture in Ethiopia, 2013/14
3. ATA Annual Report: Agricultural Transformation Agenda, 2016/17
4. Zhang, G., et al.: Study and design of an agricultural SMS system based on a GSM modem. N. Z. J. Agric. Res. (2010)
5. Mittal, S., Mehar, M.: How mobile phones contribute to growth of small farmers? Evidence from India. Q. J. Int. Agric. **51**(3), 227–244 (2012)
6. Fafchamps, M., Minten, B.: Impact of SMS-based agricultural information on Indian farmers, September 2011
7. Chemweno, K.: SMS based rural agricultural markets monitoring information system in Kenya. Master's thesis in Computer Science, University of Nairobi, Kenya (2012)
8. Jaiswal, P.K.: SMS based information systems. Master's thesis, University of Eastern Finland, September 2011
9. Ethio-Telecom Annual Report (2017). https://www.budde.com.au/Research/Ethiopia-Telecoms-Mobile-and-Broadband-Statistics-and-Analyses. Accessed Jan 2018
10. Ethiopian Agricultural Transformation Agency (ATA). http://www.ata.gov.et. Accessed Dec 2017
11. Brooke, J.: SUS - a quick and dirty usability scale. Redhatch Consulting Ltd., 12 Beaconsfield Way, Earley, READING RG6 2UX, United Kingdom. email: john.brooke@redhatch.co.uk
12. Measuring Usability With The System Usability Scale (SUS) Jeff Sauro, 2 February 2011

Review on Dynamic Stall Control in Airfoils

Abraham Adera[✉] and Siva Ramakrishnan

Department of Mechanical Engineering, Bahir Dar Institute of Technology,
Bahir Dar University, Bahir Dar, Ethiopia
abraham1928adera@gmail.com, abrahama@bdu.edu.et,
vsmp1967@yahoo.com

Abstract. Dynamic stall is a process that occurs when the angle of attack of airfoils exceeds the critical value which leads to fluctuation of aerodynamic loads and loss of performance of streamlined bodies like wind turbines and helicopters as a result of boundary layer separation. This review presents dynamic stall control methods in the oscillating airfoil. Airfoil shape modification and momentum blowing on a boundary layer were the focus of this paper. From the review, it was found that making the leading edge of an airfoil to change its shape dynamically, can help to alleviate dynamic stall in different flow conditions. Similarly, energizing the boundary layer of the flow by momentum blowing both steadily and unsteadily was found to be effective in dynamic stall control while the latter was superior. From the review, it was shown that whatever methods were applied to control dynamic stall, the effectiveness of those methods depend on other parameters too like reduced frequency.

Keywords: Airfoil shape · Angle of attack · Boundary layer · Dynamic stall · Momentum blowing

1 Introduction

Dynamic stall is a phenomenon which occurred when the angle of attack exceeds the critical value which leads aerodynamic loads to sharply vary as the boundary layer dynamically separates from the suction surface [1]. When AOA increases its value more than the static stall angle, an unsteady nonlinear phenomenon of dynamic stall occurs leading to shedding of flow separation at the airfoil surface followed by a higher loss of lift force and moment [2] as well as high - level noise [3]. It is characterized by series of fluid flow separations and reattachments which yield suction-side boundary layer separation and subsequent roll-up into a leading edge vortex, which is responsible to massive structural vibrations, lower efficiency, and unwanted noise [4]. This situation can occur on any lifting surface including but not limited to helicopters, highly maneuverable fighter jets and modern wind turbines as their angle of attack being above their normal static stall angle forcing to undergo pitching, flapping, and plunging or vertical translating movements series [5].

In helicopter forward flight, the normal velocity component with respect to ambient air at rest varies while the rotor covers one full revolution. Since there is high velocity (M = 0.9) at the tip of the blade, there will be a significant pressure difference between advancing and retreating blades as there is only very low velocity on the latter blade.

© ICST Institute for Computer Sciences, Social Informatics and Telecommunications Engineering 2019
Published by Springer Nature Switzerland AG 2019. All Rights Reserved
F. A. Zimale et al. (Eds.): ICAST 2018, LNICST 274, pp. 380–400, 2019.
https://doi.org/10.1007/978-3-030-15357-1_32

The sinusoidal pitching motion of retreating blade so as to bring the two pressure differences equal, makes the AOA to continually vary. This unsteady flow situation observed in helicopters causes vortices to develop at the leading edge which then shed in to wake. This causes flow separation that severely limits the flight envelop [6]. It is a function of airfoil geometry, the amplitude of oscillation, reduced frequency, Reynolds number, and the Mach number. Its overall stages are LEV at slightly higher AOA above static stall, full stall during shedding and flow reattachment [5, 7, 8].

The angle of attack variation in wind turbines is due to many reasons such as atmospheric turbulence, the earth boundary layer, the wakes of wind turbines located further upstream, tower shadow effects, yaw misalignment, wind shear and tower passage [9]. In VAWT, the blade velocity magnitude and direction, as well as the azimuthal angle of attack change continuously at low tip speed ratio due to complex flow regime created by the above - listed effects. To understand clearly why the angle of attack varies in wind turbines, let's refer to Fig. 1 adapted from [1] based on sinusoidal rotating HAWT. As shown in Fig. 1(a) in the absence of any wind gust, the wind speed is perpendicular to the rotor disc and is constant. In this case, the AOA will be constant. However, this is not the situation observed in the real operation of wind turbines. Wind gust causes the wind speed to increase and thus both AOA, and relative wind speed will vary from previous values, specifically increase, see Fig. 1(b). In yawed operation, the wind speed is not totally perpendicular to the rotor disc. When the blade moves towards the wind, Fig. 1(c), relative wind speed increment and AOA decrement happen and the opposite will happen when the wind moves away from the blade, Fig. 1(d). This causes the variation in AOA. The airfoil then will undergo an oscillatory motion with a turbine rotation frequency. This frequency, in most of the literature, given in terms of reduced frequency as, $Kred = \omega C/U\infty$. The sole effect of this situation in dynamic stall perspective is a LEV to develop and flow separation to shed on creating an additional vortex as it retreats to the trailing edge [1].

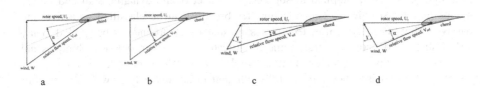

a   b   c   d

Fig. 1. Angle of attack variation in HAWT [1]

The variation of the angle of attack as the airfoil rotates can be obtained by referring Fig. 2 from [9]. Where VW = V∞ = free stream velocity, CN = normal force coefficient, θ = azimuth angle which will be zero when the blade becomes parallel and faces to the wind, CF = tangential force coefficient.

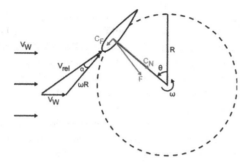

Fig. 2. Angle of attack variation in VAWT [9]

Vrel is the relative velocity induced as a result of blade rotation

$$Vrel = \left((R\omega)^2 + V\infty^2\right)^2 \tag{1}$$

$$Vrel = \sqrt{\left[(TSR + cos\theta)^2 + sin^2\theta\right]} \, [9] \tag{2}$$

The variation of AOA as azimuthally angle varies is given as

$$AOA = tan^{-1}\left(\frac{sin\theta}{TSR + cos\theta}\right)[10] \tag{3}$$

Having an understanding of the detrimental consequences of dynamic stall, many research works have been done on alleviating these negative effects. There are many techniques that can be applied to suppress the onset of the dynamic stall and totally reduce its adverse effects. These techniques broadly can be classified as active and passive techniques. Active flow techniques are state of the art and can be applied to any airfoil shape and geometry after some modification. However, active techniques are expensive and their implementation is cumbersome. While passive techniques are simple and cost wise, they are not fully efficient in an unsteady flow condition. For example, [10] applied three passive methods to control dynamic stall of the NACA0021 airfoil. Their control strategies were Leading - edge vortex generators to create counter-rotating stream wise-oriented vortices by using delta type leading edge vortex generators, generating counter-rotating span wise-oriented vortices by elevated wire and applying a cavity at the quarter-chord of the airfoil to act as a sink to the upstream moving vortex. However, all methods were found to delay the onset of vortex only at lower pitch rate. Additionally, vortex generators have a drag penalty while they can improve aerodynamic forces to some extent [11]. Due to this reason, this review paper will focus on active methods to control dynamic stall.

Amongst the many active methods seen in the literature, [1, 12] applied to a momentum fluid to energize the boundary layer so as to delay boundary layer separation and enhance the aerodynamic performance. In both of these studies, it was found that blowing in an unsteady manner that follows the sinusoidal variation of the AOA was effective than constant blowing, especially at higher reduced frequencies. [6] applied navel concept of variably dropping the leading edge of the airfoil so as to improve the pressure distribution that causes flow separation and hence dynamic stall. Many other researchers worked on dynamically dropping the leading edge with the aim as that of [6]. Periodic surface morphing of the airfoil has also found to be the most effective way in reducing dynamic stall as per from [11].

Addition of free stream turbulence [13–15] on a flowing fluid in order to balance the internal turbulence of the fluid by external turbulence was found to be effective in reducing the fluctuations of aerodynamic loads. Energizing the boundary layer [9, 12] by giving high suction pressure in order to prevent flow separation which is the result of adverse pressure gradient was also ideal for suppression of dynamic stall. Redesigning methods, [6, 11], to get higher radius at the leading edge so as to delay separation by making it to travel more distance were also found to be an effective way of suppressing dynamic stall.

Wondering the unreserved efforts on studying dynamic stall control by using active techniques from previous researchers, from the knowledge of the authors, there has not been an attempt to review those active dynamic stall alleviating mechanisms as a single study except that performed by [16] on periodic excitation. Thus, the aim of the present paper is to study dynamic stall control techniques so as to separately study effects of different dynamic stall determining parameters like Reynolds number, reduced frequency, free stream velocity, Mach number, and turbulence effects. Since some authors focus on low Reynolds numbers while others on high, similarly the inconsistency of selecting the reduced frequency and Mach number among many researchers, the aim of this review paper is to bring those different parameters into one so that a reader can get many notes at various parameters in a single document. As a final note this review will focus on only momentum blowing and leading edge modification. Therefore, the reader should not be confused as the lists in the review were considered as the only active control methods.

The flow of this review paper is as follows. The paper starts with defining mathematically the adverse pressure gradient that is responsible for flow separation and then a review has been made on the overall dynamic stall process. Detailed discussions on airfoil shape modifications and the addition of momentum fluid as a means to control dynamic stall follow and then the conclusion has made.

2   Results and Discussion

2.1   Pressure Gradient and Lift

Pressure gradient: When the air moves aft from lower static pressure to trailing edge, adverse pressure gradient develops which causes flow transition from laminar to turbulent and the lower boundary layer to separate from the surface. This causes lift loss due to the loss of suction pressure along the chord by the airfoil. This is the sole effect observed in the dynamic stall. The pressure gradient as a function of tip speed ratio can be determined from [13].

Motion equation

$$\frac{Vr\partial Vr}{\partial r} = r\omega^2 - \frac{\partial P}{\rho \partial r} \tag{4}$$

In the above equation, r is the distance from the hub (in the case of the wind turbine), Vr is radial velocity (assumed to be constant), ω is angular velocity of blades and ρ is density. Rewriting the pressure term in terms of the coefficient of pressure, we can get the relation

$$\frac{Vr\partial Vr}{\partial r} = r\omega^2(1 - Cp - (v^2\partial Cp)2\partial r \tag{5}$$

Assume Cp (pressure coefficient) is constant in the radial direction,

$$v^2\left(\frac{\partial Cp}{2\partial r}\right) = 0, \text{thus, } Vr = r\omega^2\sqrt{(1 - Cp)}$$

For totally stalled condition, Cp is of the order of -1 and hence $Vr = \sqrt{2r\omega}$

Therefore, $\left(\sqrt{2r\omega}\right)\partial\frac{\sqrt{2r\omega}}{\partial r} = r\omega^2 - r\omega^2 - \frac{\partial P}{\rho\partial r}$ and thus, the pressure gradient will be $\frac{\partial P}{\rho\partial\theta} = 2Vr\omega$

In terms of tip speed ratio, TSR, and radial position on the blade,

$$\frac{\partial Cp}{r\partial\theta} = \left(4\sqrt{2}\right)r^{0.5}\left(1 + \left(\left(\frac{R}{r}\right)TSR\right)^2\right)[14] \tag{6}$$

Lift: Since the angle of attack is continually changing in a dynamic stall situation, the lift gain and loss during the entire upstroke and downstroke motion are totally different and it is time-dependent. [17] conducted a dynamic stall model to determine wind turbine lift coefficient employing time delay fully attached and separated flow conditions with LE separation vortex and pressure peak contributions. According to them, lift starts dimensioning as TEV counteracts LEV and this dimensioning effect can be described by the following first order differential equation.

$$CL, v(t) + \omega 4Cl, v(t) = \left\{\begin{array}{l} \Delta Cl(t), for\ \alpha > 0\ and\ \alpha < 0 \\ 0\ for\ other\ conditions \end{array}\right\}[18] \tag{7}$$

Here CLv(t) is the actual value of the induced lift after the initiation of dimensioning effect and $\omega 4$ is a parameter that controls the dimensioning effect of vortex lift and α is the maximum angle of attack (Fig. 3).

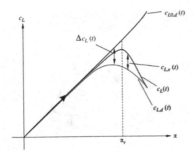

Fig. 3. lift versus angle of attack [17]

2.2   Overall Dynamic Stall Situation

[5] were able to show the whole dynamic stall process while simulating of NACA 0012 pitching airfoil at a Reynolds number of 105 as shown in Fig. 4. Formation and shedding of LEV which has low - pressure wave on the suction surface of the airfoil is a characteristic of the deep dynamic stall.

Upstroke motion: fluid flow is attached to the airfoil until it passes through some important angles of attack. This situation is shown from [−5°, 10°] by [5] until the creation of the LSB at 15.7° which then converted to LEV at about 20.6° causing thick reverse separation flow. Sudden lift increase observed from [5] at 22.5° which remained up to 23.86° where LEV gets peak by covering the whole airfoil surface. According to [18], LEV breaks down into two small counter - rotating vortices, showing LE boundary layer is unstable. However, this breakdown doesn't affect the attachment. TEV formed as LEV departs from the airfoil surface while traveling downstream. The situation is shown at 24.7° upstream from [5]. The creation of TEV is so as to satisfy Kelvin's circulation theorem, i.e. a TEV rotating in anti-clockwise fashion created in order to satisfy the conservation of circulation.

An airfoil at a high angle of attack creates an adverse pressure gradient on the upper surface that is too strong for the kinetic energy in the boundary layer to overcome. A Stall occurs when the boundary layer does not adhere to the surface near the leading edge. This occurs beyond Clmax AOA which causes a significant decrease in Cl. From [5] this can be observed at 25° up, where LEV becomes severe as it rolled on the upper surface which makes extraordinary complex flow on the upper surface. [19] were able to show the aerodynamic lift coefficient curve trend in a dynamic stall at K = 0.026 & Re = 106. Even if they employed high Reynolds number of 106 which can be considered turbulent region, their result will not affect description of flow topology of [5] who employed 105 Reynolds number. The reason is Reynolds number will not independently affect the flow and additionally, both laminar and turbulent flows have an almost the same aerodynamic trend. They compare their simulation result of the S809 airfoil at a reduced frequency of 0.026 to prior experimental and numerical works of their reference. They concluded that all trend of lift coefficient curve of the stationary airfoil is almost the same to the oscillating airfoil.

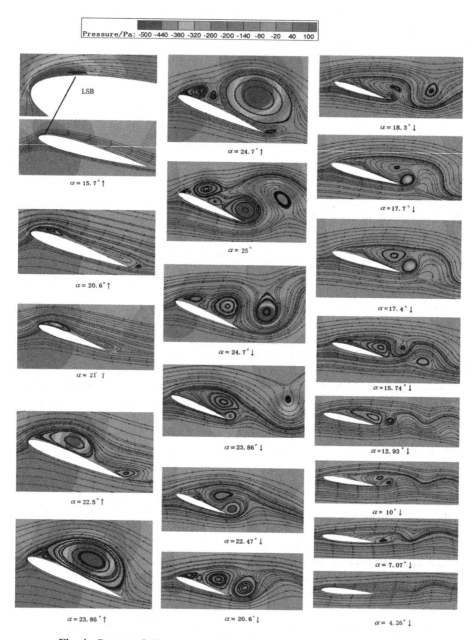

Fig. 4. Pressure field superimposed on the instantaneous streamlines [18]

Downstroke: it is during downstroke motion that small vortices created and merged to form a large vortex. [5] showed this at 24.7° down. After the shedding of the rolling up vortex, according to [14], higher magnitude induced re-circulated flow increases from TE in this downstroke motion causing TEV to push one big vortex obtained by merging of smaller vortices at 23.86° [14]. TEV detaches exactly after passing 18.3° and after 15.74° onwards, merging of the upper surface vortex into one and then rolling of detached TEV continue to happen until 7.707° where flow reattachment occurs [5]. Generally, as we seen above, flow reverses from trailing edge and moves upstream towards leading edge and hence dynamic stall vortex formed when the shear layer lifts up as a result of the reversed flow.

3 Dynamic Stall Control

We can reduce the detrimental effect of the dynamic stall by carried out different strategies. Broadly speaking, dynamic stall suppression methods can be classified as active and passive methods. As we tried to discuss at the beginning, passive control techniques are simple and cost-effective yet they fail in alleviating dynamic stall for all components at all flow conditions. As per the literature we found from [11], passive control methods like trips and vortex generators are only effective in limited flow conditions i.e. they can improve aerodynamic coefficients at some conditions but they will bring drag penalty at other conditions. Also, boundary layer trips were found effective only if the flow separation point is fixed which is not always possible in unsteady flow situation. Based on this, in this paper, active flow control methods are discussed.

3.1 Airfoil Shape Modification

The shape of an airfoil has its own meaning in terms of aerodynamic performance of a helicopter or aircraft. Sharp leading edge of an airfoil can make air flow to accelerate on the upper surface. According to [20] the movement of air from stagnation point towards the suction peak at the upper surface downstream of the nose causes the flow to accelerate and this effect is enhanced by the sharp leading edge of the airfoil. This high acceleration can lead to local supersonic flow that will generate shock. Additionally, due to the relationships among pressure, force and acceleration, there will be a high adverse pressure gradient. Both of these effects can cause flow separation and dynamic stall. According to [6] local shape of the airfoil near the leading edge plays a major roll on the development of dynamic stall formation which helps us to consider changing the airfoil leading edge to reduce dynamic stall without affecting the lift generation. According to [21], increased leading edge radius can alleviate peak suction pressure and the adverse pressure gradient can be reduced by distributing low - pressure region to the airfoil upper surface by making the leading edge to have more rounded shape. Thus, modifying the shape of the leading edge can help to suppress of dynamic stall on the airfoil.

[20] provide a clear and detailed process of designing a dynamically deforming airfoil. The aim was to get an airfoil that adapts the dynamically changing flow situation observed in unsteady flow environment, especially for a helicopter airfoil. It is called dynamically deforming leading edge airfoil, DDLE. The airfoil was designed and manufactured from a 0.001- inch thick fiberglass inside and carbon fiber outside. 20% of its leading edge i.e. the distance from leading edge up to 0.2 C of the airfoil

was made from fiberglass. The disadvantage of metals of being yielded, too thin sheets, residual stress, and chemical milling forced him to use composite material for his work. The airfoil's leading edge deformation accomplished by a mandrel sandwiched between inner and outer surfaces. There was software driven motor equipped with an encoder and assisted by a PDI to record digital display of DDLE deformation. The synchronization among drive system, motion controller and drum camera of PDI were made by the sinusoidal oscillations of the airfoil and DDLE shape changes at different rates from various AOA. The DDLE airfoil deformation images were taken by PDI image plane and it is then traced to give new airfoil profiles. Each 0.003 in rearward leading edge displacement from the previous position gives a new single airfoil shape. The new generated airfoil shape given numbers with 0 means no change in shape. The details of designing and fabricating DDLE can be found in [20]. In [21] a dynamic shape adaptation method was applied experimentally for controlling dynamic stall at Mach number $M = 0.3, Kred = 0.0503$ for a NACA 0012 airfoil oscillating at $\alpha = \alpha o + 10 \sin \omega t$. The manufacturing and all working conditions were the same as seen above on [20]. The designed DDLE airfoil was alternately named SAP (shape adapting while pitching) and the results were validated against a fixed shape 8.5 airfoil. From the interferograms recorded using PDI (not shown), the flow fully attached for shape 2 and shape 7.5 until AOA reaches 16° which was much better than that of the NACA 0012 airfoil that shows the onset of dynamic stall earlier at 14° as the same Mach number of 0.3 revealing the advantage of dynamic shape changing. The result was the same for a fixed 8.5 shape airfoil too. A small number of fringes observed for shape 7.5 at 14 AOA indicate the dropping of peak suction though the flow remains attached to its leading edge. This was seen after a trailing edge separation occurred from AOA of 17° to 19° for shape 7. The reduction in peak suction has also observed in down stroke motion at 18 and 19 AOA for shape 7 followed by a light dynamic stall at AOA of 16° which has low severity for a full dynamic stall.

Figure 5 gives the change effects on vorticity flux though NACA 0012 airfoil did not include in Fig. 5 as it already stalls at 14° and complicated flow separation has occurred at 16°. As shown in Fig. 5, dynamically adapting SAP airfoil shows better vorticity distribution at AOA of 15° than that of the fixed 8.5 shape airfoil. However, the peak vorticity flux of SAP goes upstream from X/C = 0.08 to 0.05 and its value was not exceeding that of fixed 8.5airfoil. At further increase in AOA of 20°, the vorticity flux of the fixed 8.5 shape airfoil doubles that of SAP at X/C = 0.05 showing no dynamic stall vortex seen in the deforming case. During downstroke motion, SAP experiences slightly higher vortices than fixed 8.5 shapes. However, this slight increase in vorticity can give higher circulation that can add lift improvement. Having the decent conclusions and analysis from the work of [21], we don't notice at what shape types (how much displacement of the leading edge) of the SAP airfoil the improvements in Fig. 5 reached.

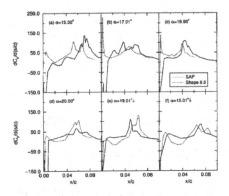

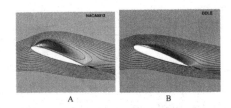

Fig. 5. Effect of shape change on vorticity flux development [21]

Fig. 6. Vortex distribution, AOA = 19.3° [22]

In [22], applying 2D Navier Stokes solver to define moving boundaries, they alleviated dynamic stall of NACA 0012 airfoil as compared from the surface pressure distribution and load hysteresis loops for NACA0012 or baseline airfoil. Curvilinear body fitted grid which is a system of interconnected springs from a 2D Navier Stoke solver was applied. The grid line was a tension spring connecting two consecutive grid points. The system worked such that the motion of the airfoil determines the motion of grid nodes. The magnitude of grid motion was determined by the spring stiffness value.

As shown on Fig. 6a, due to the leading edge vortex there was separation and recirculation on the upper surface of NACA 0012 airfoil at 19.43° upstroke. However, the smaller separation thickness of DDLE implied the suppression of LEV. This LEV sheds at 20° upstroke giving a decrease of the suction peak that is a sign of lift loss. However, the DDLE airfoil will start dynamic stall at this time. The DDLE airfoil gradually attaches to the boundary layer and its separation point moves to TE. In contrast the NACA0012airfoil, DDLE airfoil experiences a secondary vortex shedding which differentiates the two airfoils during down stroke. Keeping the other parameters same, at higher Mach number of 0.4, shock-induced flow separation found to cause the dynamically changing airfoil to experience dynamic stall during upstroke and a secondary vortex during down stroke. Thus, the DDLE airfoil will not good at high Ma.

Another interesting research on dynamic stall study using a deformable leading-edge concept was done by [6]. In this work, the start of deformation was designated by φ, the phase angle of pitch motion in cyclic pitch such that the leading edge starts to drop at point A where phase angle increases to φdef. The maximum drop amplitude corresponds to the maximum value of overall AOA at point B as φ further increases to $\frac{\pi}{2}$. Further moving of φ to the right leads the beginning of the rise of the leading edge

Fig. 7. VDLE airfoil [6]

Fig. 8. VDLE mechanism [6]

until the airfoil recovers its shape at which the deformation ends and the rigid airfoil continues to pitch, see Figs. 7 and 8.

The process of dropping the leading edge in the region between A & c was defined a half period of sinusoidal wave given as

$$\omega def = \omega(\pi/(\pi - 2\varphi def))$$

Thus for one period of airfoil pitching motion, each point on the first quarter chord of the deforming edge is

$$\delta(x,t) = \left\{ \begin{array}{c} -A(x) \sin\left[\omega def\left(t - \frac{\varphi def}{\omega}\right)\right], \frac{\varphi def}{\omega} < t < \frac{\pi - \varphi def}{\omega} \\ 0, otherwise \end{array} \right\}, [6] \qquad (8)$$

Where, $A(x) = Al * \frac{C}{4} X^n$ and $X = |x|/\left(\frac{c}{4}\right)$, X is non dimensionalized x coordinate. Control parameters were Al, n, and φ which determine respectively amplitude of drop of leading edge, the closeness of deformation to the leading edge point and how long the drop will take to begin. Thus, for mode 1 Al varies from 0.01, 0.5, to 0.1, n from 1.5 to 5 and φ from 0.2π, 0.3π, 0.35π to 0.4π and the test cases for mode two were a range of φ from 0.2π, 0.3π to 0.35π; and a special case of stationary leading edge.

Figure 9 shows how VDLE improves the lift, drag and moment coefficients by 61%, 69%, and 81% respectively for three different droop amplitudes at 0.2π. Additionally, we can easily observe that keeping π constant, increasing droop amplitude means improving the hysteresis loops of lift and drag. This can be seen by comparing Fig. 9B which shows attached flow with no vortex of the VDLE airfoil to that of

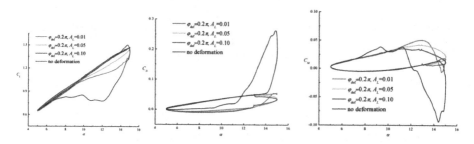

Fig. 9. Aerodynamic coefficients [6] at $\varphi def = 0.2\pi$

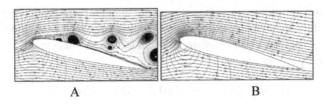

Fig. 10. Flow field improvement at a = 13.42 down stroke A. baseline B. VDLE at $\varphi def = 0.2\pi, Al = 0.05, n = 1.5$[6]

baseline at Fig. 9A. The same situation was observed for 3π except flow separation and instability of flow as Al is bigger (Fig. 10).

Changing n from 1.5 to 5 (making the distribution of deformation more to the leading edge) at the same deformation location improves aerodynamic loads and delays flow separation. This is because in an airfoils pitching motion dynamic stall and flow separation mostly happen from the leading edge which then distributes to the remaining part. From Fig. 11 we can observe that increasing the value of Al has the same meaning as increasing n as the concentration of droop deformation and amplitude of droop really

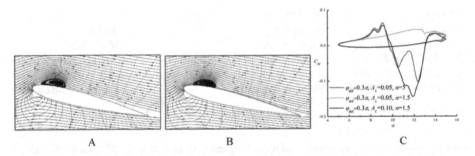

Fig. 11. A and B streamline and pressure counters at 13.42 AOA downstream A. $\varphi def = 0.3\pi, Al = 0.05, n = 5$, B. $\varphi def = 0.3\pi, Al = 0.1, n = 1.5$ C. pitching moment [6]

matter on dynamic stall control. However, this situation brings a bigger nose-down pitching moment that is a limitation for this assumption, see Fig. 11c.

To this end, we have seen two - dimensional airfoils in dynamic stall control. However, very few researches have been carried out to show how dynamic stall looks like in three - dimensional shape of the airfoil. [23] performed a dynamic stall control method that combines both two dimensional and three - dimensional effects. In their work, they used both the CFD method and a new optimal or Sequential Quadratic Programming (SQP) method with a new linear search strategy. In the numerical method, they generated a C O topology 3D rotor blade which employs geometric conservation law in order to prevent errors due to the deformed grid. The aim of using SQP was to reduce the computational cost of aerodynamic load simulation by working with many constraints at a time. Constraint optimization problem and design functions are respectively given as

$$\{\min f(x)\,ands.tci(x) \geq 0, i = 1, 2, \ldots, m\}, [24] \tag{9}$$

$$x^{new} = x + tsd, [24] \tag{10}$$

Where $x = x1, x2, \ldots, xn$ are design variable obtained from airfoil parameters used to design the new airfoil, $d = d1, d2, \ldots, dn$ is search direction, ts is step size.

Their optimization procedure employs 12 design variables so as to fit the geometry of the airfoil based on OA209 airfoil and the final shape of the optimized airfoil is shown in fig below with blue color which has larger leading edge radius as compared to the original OA 209 airfoil.

Rotor airfoil in its forward flight situation experiences dynamic stall on its retreating side between 0.7R to 1.0R. This shows that a helicopter rotor airfoil works

Table 1. Design points of [23]

2D case		3D case	
Design point 1	Design point 2	Forward flight	Hover
$M = 0.3$	$M = 0.4$	Advance ratio = 0.344	$M = 0.626$
$K = 0.07$	$K = 0.05$	Cyclic pitch,	Advance ratio = 0
$\alpha = 10 \pm 6$	$\alpha = 8 \pm 6$	$\theta = 12.55° + 1.92 \cos \omega t - 6.94 \sin \omega t$	Pitch angle
		Flapping angle,	$\alpha = 12 - 6 \sin \omega t$
		$\beta = 2.85° - 0.14 \cos \omega t + 0.34 \sin \omega t$	

under various Mach numbers, reduced frequencies, and angles of attack. So as to account these working conditions, [23] select two design points as given on the Table 1.

Based on the design point 1, time-varying aerodynamic loads are compared between the optimized and baseline airfoil in Fig. 12. The hysteresis loop of Cl of OA209 airfoil was found wider than that of the optimized airfoil which means flow

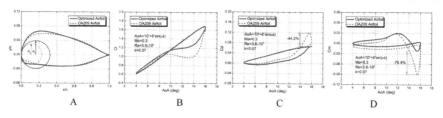

Fig. 12. A. Optimized vs. baseline airfoil, B, C, and D aerodynamic force improvement under design point 2 [23]

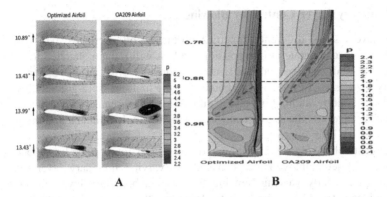

Fig. 13. Comparisons on A. Vortex development, B. nondimensional pressure in hover [23]

reattachment was achieved at very small AOA during the downstroke and thus light stall occurs. See Fig. 12B, C, D.

Under design point 2, Fig. 13A shows the alleviation of the dynamic stall as the vortex was already shed at 13.99° upstroke for the baseline, while it remains small at the same AOA and streamlines are almost attached to the boundary for the optimized cases. Figure 12B also shows the non-dimensional pressure distribution at 270° phase angle the region from 0.68R to 0.85R in the case of baseline airfoil and from 0.8R to 0.9R which is very narrow for optimized are affected by the LEV.

Under design point three - dimensional rotor condition, a new rectangular rotor based on SA349/2 helicopter rotor was designed with $Ma = 0.626$, $\alpha = 12 - 6\sin\omega t$ at a 0.75R location.

Figure 14 shows the pressure coefficients at different azimuth angles at 0.7R of the two airfoils. As shown in Fig. 14A and B, the adverse pressure gradient of the optimized airfoil was found lower than baseline OA209 airfoil. In Fig. 14C even if the

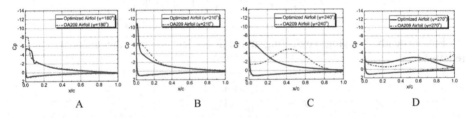

Fig. 14. Pressure coefficient in forward flight [23]

adverse pressure gradient of the optimized airfoil leads the baseline near the leading edge, it is less disturbed and comes to smaller value at 270°.

3.2 Boundary Layer Control by Blowing

Viscous layers show different properties as the airfoil oscillates. This causes the boundary layer to separate at one position while it will remain attached to the other.

Dynamic stall can be reduced and consequently lift can be increased if the boundary layer is energized so as to counteract the high-pressure gradient. Energizing can be carried out by adding high momentum fluid to the boundary layer. This will help the boundary layer to adhere to the airfoil at a higher angle of attack and the process is called boundary layer control.

In tangential blowing steady applying of the jet was found to be less effective since the amount of jet employed was constant for varying boundary layer interaction. However, periodically varying blowing follows the boundary layer movement and hence the idea is to add a strong jet to the boundary that tends to separate and weak jet to that less susceptible to separation. Both steady and unsteady blowing techniques were studied in [12] and are summarized in this review.

Boundary conditions and assumptions were; the jet nozzle is convergent, 1D and isentropic slot exit.

At the inflow boundary, the velocity components and temperature were specified as free stream conditions while the pressure is extrapolated from the interior. At the outflow boundary, the pressure was set equal to the free-stream static pressure and the velocity and temperature were extrapolated from the interior. Along the grid cut-line, periodic boundary conditions were enforced. On the airfoil surface (except for the slot exit), adiabatic, impermeable wall and no-slip boundary conditions were applied.

With these assumptions and for a given jet total pressure, Pt, and temperature, Tt, assuming known pressure at the slot exit, Pi, other quantities found as:

$$Tj = Tt \left[\frac{Pj}{Pt} \right]^{(\gamma-1)/\gamma}, [13] \tag{11}$$

$$Uj = \frac{\sqrt{2\gamma R}}{(\gamma - 1)} Tt \left[1 - \left(\frac{Pj}{Pt} \right)^{\frac{\gamma-1}{\gamma}} \right], [13] \tag{12}$$

For unsteady blowing neglecting dynamic inflow effects, the equation can be redefined as

$$Tj = Tt(t) \left[\frac{Pj(t)}{Pr(t)} \right]^{(\gamma-1)/\gamma}, [13] \tag{13}$$

$$Uj = \frac{\sqrt{2\gamma R}}{(\gamma - 1)} Tt(t) [1 - \left(\frac{Pj(t)}{Pr(t)} \right)^{\frac{\gamma-1}{\gamma}}, [13] \tag{14}$$

And unsteady total pressure,

$$Pt = Pts + \Delta Pt + \Delta Ptcos(\omega t + \phi) [13] \tag{15}$$

Where Tj and Uj are free stream temperature and velocity of the jet at slot exit inlet, Pj is pressure obtained by extrapolation of the flow pressure near the slot exit. The instantaneous total pressure Pr (t), total temperature Tt (t) and exit pressure (t) are used in the above formulas. A jet momentum coefficient was defined as:

$$C\mu = \frac{mVjet}{\frac{1}{2}\rho\infty V\infty^2 C}, [13] \tag{16}$$

Where $m = \rho jUjh$, h = slot hight and Vj is reference velocity of the jet assumed to flow isentropically to the free stream. For unsteady blowing, the momentum coefficient

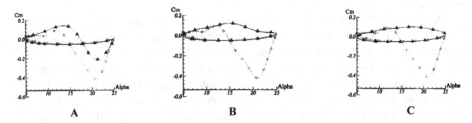

Fig. 15. Moment coefficient for NACA0012 at steady blowing in k = 0.25, momentum coefficient at (A. 0.05, B. 0.07, C. 0.09) [12]

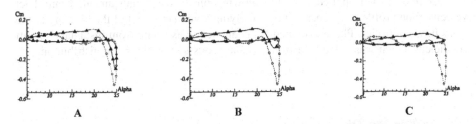

Fig. 16. Moment coefficient for NACA0012 at steady blowing in k = 0.15, momentum coefficient at (A. 0.05, B. 0.07, C. 0.09), O baseline, △ blowing [12]

variation was defined as

$$C\mu - \Delta C\mu \le C\mu \le C\mu + \Delta C\mu \tag{17}$$

The specification is: airfoil NACA0012 pitching at its quarter chord, motion $15° + 10° sin\,\omega$, $Re = 10^6$, $M = 0.2$, $K = 0.15, K = 0.25$, where $K = \frac{\frac{1}{2}\omega C}{V\infty}$

On Fig. 15 the effect of steady blowing is shown in terms of pitch moment coefficients. From the fig, it is shown that steady blowing was effectively suppressed nose down pitch moment especially at high momentum coefficients. On Fig. 16 for k = 0.15, until momentum coefficient reaches 0.09, the effect of blowing was not significant as there are pitching moment bouncing though a little reduction in the hysteresis loop was revealed. However, at 0.09, the positive impact of steady blowing on reducing nose down pitching moments was very satisfactory as those obtained at 0.07,0.09 at K = 0.25. Hence, in addition to the comparison of blowing at higher momentum coefficients, it can be understood that higher reducing frequency tends to suppress undesired moment coefficients. Other aerodynamic coefficients were also shown similar improvement at [12]. Additionally, as per flow structures (not shown here), blowing at higher momentum coefficient brings dynamic stall suppression except at 0.05 at which the improvement was not satisfactory.

Unsteady Blowing. The idea is varying the blowing strength following the AOA variation. The motion of the airfoil was kept the same as that used for steady blowing for comparison purpose.

The unsteady Pt was controlled to maintain the change in momentum coefficient a value 0.015%. Unsteady blowing was found to be effective as it gives very satisfactory result in suppressing flow separation from the airfoil. Flowing at an average Cμ of 0.05 (not shown) was comparable to steady blowing at Cμ = 0.07 showing effectiveness of the periodically varying blowing. The cases at higher average Cu (not shown) are also well noticed in improving dynamic stall better than constant blowing. Figure 17 elaborates this illustration more clearly at a phase shift of [−30, 30] at k = 0.25 at which the control was not satisfactory in other phases. Though the control was less effective relative to that at higher k, k = 0.15 also gives better control result than steady blowing [12].

Just like [1, 12] applied unsteady blowing on an oscillating airfoil. Control jet velocity-time profile was generated by supplying a voltage signal of the blowing to the mass flow controller. Phase-averaged lift coefficient was found from instantaneous lift coefficient which was calculated from instantaneous surface pressure distribution.

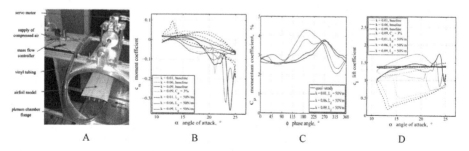

Fig. 17. Adaptive blowing (A), phase averaged lift and moment coefficients (B&C), momentum coefficient (D) [1]

$$Cl(\emptyset) = \frac{1}{N} \sum_{i=1}^{N} Cli(\emptyset), [1] \tag{18}$$

Mass flow controller regulates control jet speed to yield timed variation of $C\mu$. A compressed air at a temperature range of [295.5, 298] was supplied to a pressure vessel to give constant pressure upstream of the mass flow controller which was connected to leading edge plenum chamber, see Fig. 17 A. $C\mu$ was found from phase averaged wind tunnel speed $U\infty(\emptyset)$ and control jet speed $Uj(\emptyset)$. Phase averaged control jet speed $Uj(\emptyset)$ can be found from instantaneous volume flow rate $v(\phi)$.

$$Uj(\phi) = Uj, v = v(\phi)/sh[1] \tag{19}$$

This value is then normalized by the ratio of average jet speed to average phase averaged jet speed. The aim was to get the appropriate relationship between minimum lift per unit span and control jet momentum flux. The base for load control in adaptive blowing was a quasi-steady state. From the quasi-steady blowing, it was found that steady blowing at Cu of 2% has given a change in lift coefficient of 0.5 between AOA of 11 and 25° respectively. Based on this, an adaptive blowing was applied where finding minimum Cl was possible. This situation was found at momentum coefficient of 0.5% and 0.8% for an angle of attacks of 11° & 18° and 25° respectively. First $\alpha(\phi)$ and $U\infty(\emptyset)$ were found and then lift coefficient as a function of momentum coefficient were found by interpolating experimental results by phase. From the lift coefficient, the lift per unit span $Ld(\phi)$ can be found which can be better used for calculating steady state phase averaged momentum coefficient time profiles as an input for adaptive blowing. As shown on Fig. 17, steady blowing at momentum coefficient of 3% was effective in eliminating dynamic stall vortex. Having this, varying momentum coefficient to adapt a constant lift per unit span of 50 N/m was carried out at various reduced frequencies especially at k = 0.09 which is very close to the value for wind turbines at a corresponding momentum coefficient profile that, Fig. 17D.

4 Nomenclature

Latin symbols

2D	two dimensional
3D	three dimensional
Al	amplitude of deformation
AOA	angle of attack
CFD	computational fluid dynamics
DDLE	dynamically deformed the leading - edge
HAWT	horizontal axis wind turbine
LEV	leading-edge vortex
NACA	national advisory committee for aeronautics
SAP	shape changing while pitching
SQP	sequential quadratic programming

TEV	trailing edge vortex
TSR	tip speed ratio
VAWT	vertical axis wind turbine
VDLE	variable drop leading edge
C	chord
$C\mu$	momentum coefficient
Cl	lift coefficient
CLd(t)	dimensioned lift
CLv(t)	actual value of induced lift after dimensioning
$Cl(\emptyset)$	phase averaged lift coefficient
$Cli(\emptyset)$	instantaneous lift coefficient
Cd	drag coefficient
CF	tangential force coefficient
Cm	moment coefficient
CN	normal force coefficient
Cp	pressure coefficient
d	search direction
h	slot height
K	reduced frequency

Greek symbols

ω	angular speed of the blade
$\omega_4 a$	parameter that controls the dimensioning effect of vortex lift
α	angle of attack
αv	critical angle at which the leading edge vortex detaches from the leading edge
$\emptyset$	phase angle
θ	pitch angle
ψ	phase angle
ρ	density
λ	tip speed ratio
φ def	starting point of deformation
Tj	free stream temperature of the jet at slot exit inlet
ts	step size
Tt	jet total temperature
$U\infty$	free stream speed
$U\infty(\emptyset)$	phase averaged wind tunnel speed
Uj	free stream velocity of jet at slot exit inlet
$Uj(\emptyset)$	control jet speed
$v(\phi)$	volume flow rate
Vi	reference velocity
Vr	radial velocity
Vrel	induced relative velocity
X	design variable
X/C	location from leading edge

Ld	lift per unit span
m	meter
M	mach number
Ma	mach number
N	Newton
P	Pressure
Pi	pressure at the slot exit
Pj	the extrapolated pressure at the slot exit
Pt	jet total pressure
R	radius
r	radial distance from hub
Re	Reynolds number
t	time

5 Conclusion

Dynamic stall control in oscillating airfoils was discussed. Airfoil shape modification especially at the leading edge and energizing the boundary layer by adding momentum fluid were the focus of this review. In order to make any modifications on an airfoil it is better to make attached flow as a basis. This can help us to reconsider the different arrangement of design parameters like Reynolds number, Mach number, and free stream velocity so that we will be able to arrive at the selection of best strategies that help us to suppress dynamic stall at a different angle of attack. Hover motion with both pitching and flapping motion, the effect of varying rate of change of airfoil deformation in dynamic stall control and further studying in reducing negative pitch down moment in VDLE might be the objective of the future researcher. In momentum blowing, the instability caused by increasing deformation amplitude and φ def at the same time and the combined use of constant and periodic momentum at a higher reduced frequencies and higher Mach numbers might also be a future idea.

Acknowledgment. This work acknowledged professor Siva & Dr. Shoeb for giving their helpful comments.

References

1. Müller-Vahl, H.F., Nayeri, C.N., Paschereit, C.O., Greenblatt, D.: Dynamic stall control via adaptive blowing. Renew. Energy **97**, 47–64 (2016)
2. Almohammadi, K.M., Ingham, D.B., Ma, L., Pourkashanian, M.: Modeling dynamic stall of a straight blade vertical axis wind turbine. J. Fluids Struct. **57**, 144–158 (2015)
3. Laratro, A., Arjomandi, M., Kelso, R., Cazzolato, B.: A discussion of wind turbine interaction and stall contributions to wind farm noise. J. Wind Eng. **127**, 1–10 (2014)
4. Buchner, A., Lohry, M.W., Martinelli, L., Soria, J., Smits, A.J.: Dynamic stall in vertical axis wind turbines: comparing experiments and computations. J. Wind Eng. **146**, 163–171 (2015)
5. Wang, S., Ingham, D.B., Ma, L., Pourkashanian, M., Tao, Z.: Turbulence modeling of deep dynamic stall at relatively low Reynolds number. J. Fluids Struct. **33**, 191–209 (2012)

6. Niu, J., Lei, J., Lu, T.: Numerical research on the effect of variable droop leading-edge on oscillating NACA 0012 airfoil dynamic stall. Aerosp. Sci. Technol. **72**, 476–485 (2018)
7. Li, Q., Maeda, T., Kamada, Y., Hiromori, Y., Nakai, A., Kasuya, T.: Study on stall behavior of a straight-bladed vertical axis wind turbine with numerical and experimental investigations. J. Wind Eng. **164**, 1–12 (2017)
8. Geissler, W., van der Wall, B.G.: Dynamic stall control on flapping wing airfoils. Aerosp. Sci. Technol. **62**, 1–10 (2017)
9. Yen, J., Ahmed, N.A.: Enhancing vertical axis wind turbine by dynamic stall control using synthetic jets. J. Wind Eng. Ind. Aerodyn. **114**, 12–17 (2013)
10. Choudhry, A., Arjomandi, M., Kelso, R.: Methods to control dynamic stall for wind turbine applications. Renew. Energy **86**, 26–37 (2016)
11. Jones, G., Santer, M., Debiasi, M., Papadakis, G., Debiasi, M., Papadakis, G.: Control of flow separation around an airfoil at low Reynolds numbers using periodic surface morphing. J. Fluids Struct. **76**, 536–557 (2018)
12. Sun, M., Sheikh, S.R.: Dynamic stall suppression on an oscillating airfoil by steady and unsteady tangential blowing. Aerosp. Sci. Technol. **3**(6), 355–366 (1999)
13. Sicot, C., Devinant, P., Loyer, S., Hureau, J.: Rotational and turbulence effects on a wind turbine blade. Investigation of the stall mechanisms. J. Wind Eng. Ind. Aerodyn. **96**(8–9), 1320–1331 (2008)
14. Hand, B., Kelly, G., Cashman, A.: Numerical simulation of a vertical axis wind turbine airfoil experiencing dynamic stall at high Reynolds numbers. Comput. Fluids **149**, 12–30 (2017)
15. Kim, Y., Xie, Z.-T.: Modelling the effect of freestream turbulence on dynamic stall of wind turbine blades. Comput. Fluids **129**, 53–66 (2016)
16. Greenblatt, D., Wygnanski, I.J.: The control of flow separation by periodic excitation, vol. 36 (2016)
17. Larsen, J.W., Nielsen, S.R.K., Krenk, S.: Dynamic stall model for wind turbine airfoils. J. Fluids Struct. **23**(7), 959–982 (2007)
18. Wang, S., Ingham, D.B., Ma, L., Pourkashanian, M., Tao, Z.: Numerical investigations on dynamic stall of low Reynolds number flow around oscillating airfoils. Comput. Fluids **39** (9), 1529–1541 (2010)
19. Gharali, K., Johnson, D.A.: Dynamic stall simulation of a pitching airfoil under unsteady freestream velocity. J. Fluids Struct. **42**, 228–244 (2013)
20. Chandrasekhara, M.S., Carr, L.W., Wilder, M.C., Paulson, G.N.: Design and development of a dynamically deforming leading edge airfoil for unsteady flow control
21. Chandrasekhara, M.S., Wilder, M.C., Carr, L.W.: Compressible dynamic stall control using dynamic shape adaptation. AIAA J. **39**(10), 2021–2024 (2001)
22. Sahin, M., Sankar, L.N., Chandrasekhara, M.S., Tung, C.: Dynamic stall alleviation using a deformable leading edge concept-a numerical study. J. Aircr. **40**(1), 77–85 (2003)
23. Wang, Q., Zhao, Q.: Rotor airfoil profile optimization for alleviating dynamic stall characteristics. Aerosp. Sci. Technol. **72**, 502–515 (2018)

Simulation Study of Inventory Performance Improvement in Consumer Products Trade Business Unit Using System Dynamic Approach

Maseresha Agumas[1], Jeyaraju Jayaprakash[2]($\boxtimes$) (iD),
and Melkamu Teshome[2]

[1] ETBC Consumer Products Trading Business Unit (AlleBjmela),
Po. box-29, Bahir Dar, Ethiopia
masreshaagumas@gmail.com
[2] Faculty, Department of Mechanical and Industrial Engineering,
Bahir Dar Institute of Technology, Bahir Dar, Ethiopia
profjaya@gmail.com

Abstract. This paper focused optimal inventory study on multi-product, multi-period, perishable products replenishment quantity in consumer product trade business unit (CPTBU) warehouse in Bahir Dar city. We proposed system dynamics method to improve optimal replenishment quantity of expired and stock-out products and saved the total operation cost such as loss of sale, expired cost, holding cost and ordering cost using vensim software. This study proposed 34.7% improved replenishment quantity of expired products, 32.2% replenishment quantity of stock-out products and totally this proposal saved 43,000US$ (1.2 million birr) of operational cost per year.

Keywords: Stock and flow diagram · Inventory replenishment · Simulation · System dynamics

1 Introduction

Inventory replenishment of multi-product, multi-period, perishable consumer goods is highly complex nature. Vermore and Joannes (2012) proposed mathematical model for inventory operation problem. They optimized replenishment quantity and total cost of inventory operation cost of stock-out and expired products.

Inventory management comprises various actions taken by the management to reduce cost, maintain production, continuous supply with optimal quantity and reduce loss according to Saleemi (2009); Nyabwanga and Ojera (2012). Many fast moving distribution companies such as whole sale and retailer have been giving due to attention to compute in global market by delivering quality product and service according to Ballou (2000). Distribution company have the responsibility to deliver quality products and service by good inventory management because of the cost of inventory and discontinuous supply with non-optimal quantity have the impact of profitability and customer satisfaction. Numerous tools and techniques have been developed for

F. A. Zimale et al. (Eds.): ICAST 2018, LNICST 274, pp. 401–409, 2019.
https://doi.org/10.1007/978-3-030-15357-1_33

designing optimal inventory parameter for transfer, order and storage to reduce the cost of operation and optimal quantity replenishment due to this increase company profitability and customer satisfaction of distribution system chain. But replenishment quantity and the operation cost of inventory have variations in the planned replenishment quantity by 25%, inventory operation cost by more than 890000 birr from the actual replenishment quantity and cost of inventory operation in consumer product business unit. This is because most of tools taken to solve this problem in distribution companies are not effective enough to reducing the inventory operation cost and replenishment quantity. In consumer product business trade unit, the common nonconforming or damage product and shortage quantity which are occurring in replenishment products that result loss products as expired and stock-out; operation inventory cost occurred due to expired cost, lost sale cost, ordering cost and holding cost. The high inventory replenishment quantity fluctuation and inventory cost in CPTBU occurred due to poor of replenishment quantity products and poor inventory operation.

Application of mathematics, statistics and a system dynamics process has contributed to the development of many models, which has real life applications. Also separate set of models has been developed for the determination of optimal re-order size for perishable products such as vegetables, fruits, eatables, and drugs. Proceeding below is few of the literature related to the models under study. Fast changing competitive world, companies are losing their significant number of customer not because of the price they offered to those products but the quality of the product or not delivering quality service. Inventory management comprises various actions taken by the management to reduce cost, maintain production, continuous supply according to Nyabwanga and Ojera (2012). System Dynamics is an integrated methodology that combined system scientific theory with Computer simulation, believing that the internal structure is the determination of the behavior model and features of a system according to Zhong et al. (2013). The structure of a system in inventory system dynamics methodology is exhibited by causal-loop diagram (CLD) and stock and flow diagram.

System dynamics (SD) is an approach to understanding the nonlinear inventory of complex systems over time using stocks, flows, internal feedback loops, and time delays. System dynamics is a methodology and mathematical modeling technique to frame, understand, and discuss complex issues and problems. Managing a company's perishable inventory stock based on demand and supply is important in different firms and Business such as food, chemical, parametrical warehouse and stores. Without a proper perishable inventory stock management sys-tem in warehouse, stores and retailer long-term profits can be affected, as more inefficiency is likely to occur Bai and Zong (2008).

Simulation of system dynamics approach has been used to improve the performance of fast moving consuming goods and optimize the replenishment quantity, ordering quantity using casual loop and stock and flow diagram.

2 Methodology

Different literatures from various journal and related to inventory simulation and performance and improper replenishment quantity and inventory operation costs are reviewed in writing this article. Both primary and secondary data were collected using questionnaire, face to face interview, observation and NAV report in case company, Consumer Product Trade Business Unit (CPTBU) AlleBejmila, (Government of Ethiopia, warehouse) Bahir Dar Branch. Collected data such as quantity of transferring product, quantity of expire product, quantity of shortage and demand the customers and other data were collected from different and concerned department. At the time working in this case company and have been seen such problem in working process and operation at the time of replenishment products, operation of storage and dispatching products and sale of products to customer. The collected data through the means of interviews, observation and NAV report analyzed by using table, figures and theoretically interpreted from system dynamics vensim software.

Many of the systems and problems can be built as models on a computer. System dynamics is an approach to present and analyze the inventory of a complex system in order to have a well understanding of what is exactly going on within the process according to Zhong et al. (2013).

System dynamics takes advantage of the fact that a computer model can be of much greater complexity and carry out more simultaneous calculations than the mental model in the human mind. Manetsch and Park (1982) lists six steps to solve a problem with system dynamics:

- Identifies a problem
- Develops a dynamic hypothesis explaining the cause of the problem
- Builds a computer simulation model of the system at the root of the problem
- Tests the model to be certain that it reproduces the behavior seen in the real world
- Devises and tests in the model alternative policies that alleviate the problem

A. Mathematical model for perishable products

Total expired cost = (Expired quantity of a product M at period T (EVMT)) (Expiry cost of a unit product type M at period T(WEM)) plus (Inventory level of product M with j periods of lifetime remaining at the end of period T (LJMIT))(Cost of discount remaining life product Mat period T(CSMT)) plus Cost of replenishment near expiry product M at period (RGMT) plus Disposal cost product M (DOM)

$$(1)$$

Total loss of sales cost due to shortage = (Shortage of quantity of products M at period T (OMTD)) (Price per unit(UMT) Stock out day(yMT)) + Cost of consequence(AMT)

$$(2)$$

Total holding cost (AT)= (holding cost rate) unit cost of inventory) or (IO)(CI) that by ordering Q units every time we order, we will have to place D/Q orders per year

$$(3)$$

Total ordering cost = (number of order/year)(cost/order) or ((KM/T)/QMT)(CO)   (4)

Minimization total cost = $\sum$ CMT. QMT + $\sum$ AT. QMT + $\sum$ HMT.IJMT + $\sum$ LMt.Omt + ($\sum$ WEM.EVMt + $\sum$ + WEM.IJMT + $\sum$ DOM + $\sum$ RGMT

(5)

From mathematical Eq. 1 calculate total expired cost, Eq. 2 calculate total loss of sales due to shortage items, Eq. 3 calculate total holding cost, Eq. 4 calculate total ordering cost and Eq. 5 minimize total cosy. After model of expired, stock-out and total cost products as shown in Fig. 1, output of replenishment quantity and others factor related to operation cost such as cost of disposal, cost of reaming life, day stock-out quantity, average inventory level and cost of order are calculated. Figures 2 and 3 shown the simulation model of annual percentage improvement in both expired and shortage items. Finally Fig. 4 calculate model of expired and total cost simultaneously using casual loop and stock and flow diagram engineering tools with vensim software.

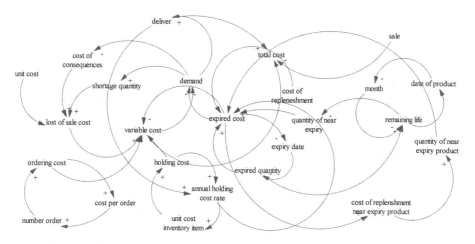

Fig. 1. Simulation model of shortage, expiry and total cost in casual loop diagram

B. Minimization of total inventory cost by stock and flow diagram.

Total expired cost = quantity of unsold * cost of expire product quantity of remaining life product * cost of discount remaining life product total cost of near expiry replenishment disposal cost.

Total loss of sale cost = Shortage quantity * price per unit * out of stock day cost of consequences.

Total holding cost = average inventory level * unit cost holding.

Total ordering cost = unit of cost per order * number order.

Variable cost = INTEG (total expired cost total holding cost total loss of sale cost + total ordering cost, 0).

Total cost = INTEG (variable cost, 0).

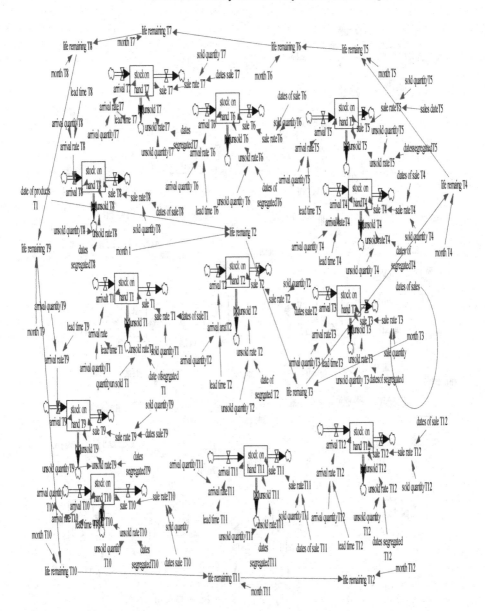

Fig. 2. Annual percentage improvement of expired replenishment quantity in stock and flow diagram

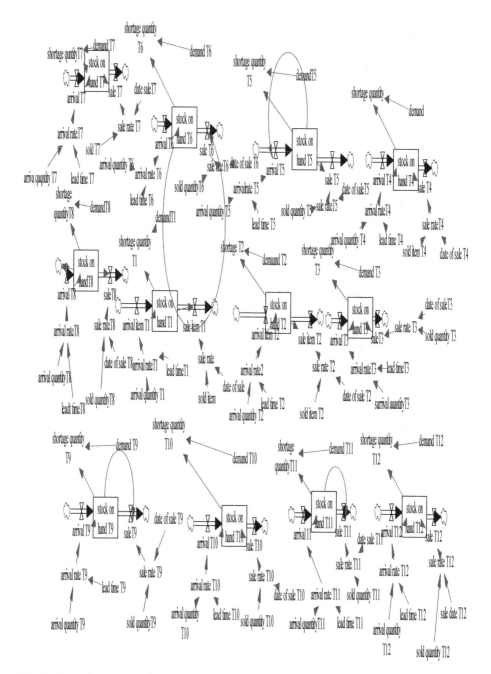

Fig. 3. Annual percentage improvement of shortage replenishment quantity in stock and flow diagram

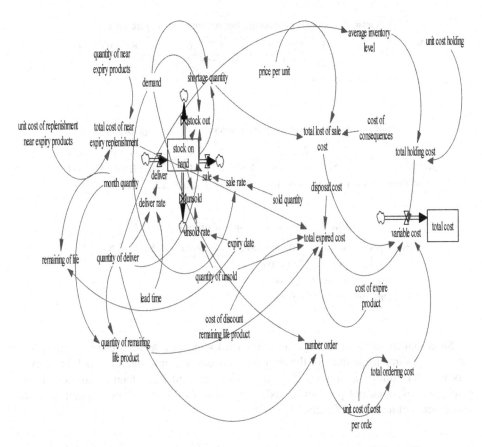

Fig. 4. Simulation model of expired cost and total cost by stock and flow diagram

3   Result and Discussion

Expired and shortage products in our case company warehouse was affected total inventory cost. In this article casual loop and stock & flow diagrams with different parameters were considered in each expired and shortage products separately. The dynamic nature of the business, affects inventory performances such as replenishment quantity, remaining of life, customer demand and other factors. Incorporated expired, loss of sale and cost operation in 12 months for 10 expired and 10 stocks out products.

Expired quantity of each product in each month has been changed by their replenishment quantity in the proposed system dynamic model. Expired products with RI number for model of stock and flow diagram reduced the percentage of expired products by considering factors of replenishment quantity, remaining life of products and date of sales as shown in Table 1. Improved percentage of shortage products in Table 2 and total inventory operational cost in Table 3.

Table 1. Annual percentage improvement of expire cost

No	1	2	3	4	5	6	7	8	9	10
RI	241	245	186	500	252	320	325	326	338	732
% of improvement	3.92	4.6	2.1	3.37	2.7	3.69	3.8	4.1	4	2.4

Table 2. Annual percentage improvement of shortage products

No	1	2	3	4	5	6	7	8	9	10
RI	521	320	964	1011	385	343	750	185	342	351
% of improvement	24.5	14.6	11	9.9	10.1	10.3	12.5	11	10.9	18.3

Table 3. Total cost saving of proposed model

No	Types of cost	Amount saved in birr/year (1US$ = 27.8 Birr)
1	Expired cost	751410.6
2	Loss of sale cost	457886.1
3	Ordering cost	457886.1

Stock-out quantity of each product in each month has been reduced by changing their replenishment quantity in the proposed system dynamic model. Stock-out products with RI number in the Table 1 model of stock and flow diagram improved the percentage of stock-out products considering factors of replenishment quantity, customer demand and date of sales.

4   Conclusion

In this work, system simulation study was carried out in consumer product trade business unit warehouse inventory management in Bahir Dar-Ethiopia. Every year, huge amount of items was expired due to fluctuation of market demand and some items were stock-out within short period due to high demand. This work was pro-posed optimal inventory replenishment quantity of both expired and stock-out items using system dynamic simulation method. After detail investigation of all existing items transfer process, we have selected 10 most expired items and 10 high demand items in this case study. Framed mathematical model of both expired items & their costs and shortage items & their cost with all the variables related to replenishment. Simulated expired, shortage and total operational cost items separate system dynamics model. We optimized transfer replenishment quantity of expired products and stock-out products for saved in total inventory operation cost using casual loop and stock and flow diagram.

Acknowledgment. We wish to thank Dr. Essay Kebede, Department of Statistics and Dr. Tadel Yalew, given suggestions during my course of research. We specially thanks to Mr. Aby Melese, Manager, AlleBejmila, Bahir Dar Branch and Mr. Adane Alemu, General Manager, AlleBejmila, Addis Ababa H.O Ethiopia, given permission, guidelines and support. Also I grateful to consumer products trading business unit company employees for providing desired information during data collection and technical support.

References

AlleBejimilla: Overview and history of AlleBejimilla, Technical report (2016)

Bai, L., Zhong, Y.: Improving inventory management in small business. Master thesis in International Logistics and Supply Chain Management (2008)

Ballou, H.: Evaluation inventory management performance using turnover curve. Int. J. Phys. Distrib. Logistics Manag. (2000)

Manetsch, T.J., Park, G.L.: Systems analysis and simulation with applications to eco-nomic and social systems. Department of Electrical Engineering and System Science, Michigan State University, USA (1982)

Nyabwanga, R.N., Ojera, P.: Inventory management practices and business performance for small-scale enterprises in Kenya. J. Bus. Manag. 1(4), 11–28 (2012)

Vermorel, J.: Economic Order Quantity (EOQ), Definition and Formula (2012). Accessed 14 April 2015

Zhong, Y., Jia, X., Qian, Y.: System Dynamics. Science, Beijing (2013)

Optimized Secure Scan Flip Flop to Thwart Side Channel Attack in Crypto-Chip

Sivasankaran Saravanan[1]([⊠]), Mikias Hailu[2], G. Mohammed Gouse[3], Mohan Lavanya[4], and R. Vijaysai[4]

[1] College of Engineering, Debre Berhan University, Debre Berhan, Ethiopia
saran@dbu.edu.et
[2] Electrical and Computer Engineering Department,
Debre Berhan University, Debre Berhan, Ethiopia
hailumikias@dbu.edu.et
[3] College of Computing, Debre Berhan University, Debre Berhan, Ethiopia
galety.143@dbu.edu.et
[4] School of Computing, SASTRA Deemed University,
Thanjavur, Tamilnadu, India
m_lavanyass@ict.sastra.edu, vijaysai@it.sastra.edu

Abstract. Present crypto based smart systems very popular for secure application. But all this system was targeted by various threats, malfunctions, hacking and side channel attack. Cryptography algorithm will try to give secure in data encryption and decryption but failed in direct hardware implementation. This paper provides an optimized secure testing method against side channel attack in crypto chips. This proposed system reduces the switching activity in latches and also reduces the power consumption in architecture. It avoids unwanted latches to obtain optimization in area by random insertion of scan chain design. This optimized architecture was targeted to RSA crypto algorithm to show the effectiveness of the proposed method over various existing methods.

Keywords: Cryptography algorithms · Side channel attack · Secure testing · Crypto chips

1 Introduction

Crypto-devices like Smartcards, Credit cards, SIM cards had a rapid growth in usage [1], similarly threats on reliability of such devices has raised concern due to side channel attack. LSI (Large Scale Integration) in Crypto-devices exhibit a secure architecture to achieve a user-friendly communication. Hence security can be obtained by use of cryptography algorithm such as Advanced Encryption Standard (AES), Data Encryption Standard (DES), RSA, Elliptic Curve Cryptography (ECC) to encrypt/ decrypt important data. AES and DES are Symmetric key crypto-systems which make use of the same secret key in encryption and decryption. However, it may be difficult to securely share the same secret key while in communication. RSA and ECC Public-key cryptosystem, on the other hand, make use of different keys to encrypt and decrypt so

© ICST Institute for Computer Sciences, Social Informatics and Telecommunications Engineering 2019
Published by Springer Nature Switzerland AG 2019. All Rights Reserved
F. A. Zimale et al. (Eds.): ICAST 2018, LNICST 274, pp. 410–417, 2019.
https://doi.org/10.1007/978-3-030-15357-1_34

that it solves the key sharing problem. Still we cannot able to implement cryptography technique directly onto an LSI itself.

It may be applicable along with memories, processors, I/O's, and control circuits. Then it's quite possible that a scan path includes random elements caused by memories, processors, I/O's, and control circuits other than registers of cryptography circuits storing the intermediate values. Although cryptographic algorithm is used, there is a threat on LSI chip to deciphered a secret key from crypto-devices. Scan-based attack is a method to retrieve a secret key from the scanned data obtained from the scan path in the cryptography LSI chip. Therefore, without any compromise in testing and security it is necessary to develop secure scan architecture against scan-based attack. Testing in LSI circuit can be take place by two types BIST (Built In Self-Test) and DFT (Design For Testability). BIST is more secure because it does not require visible scan chains, but BIST incurs more overhead and yields less fault coverage when compared to scan-based DFT. It has high fault coverage and least hardware overhead. However, scan chains are open and visible to use. Hence, this paper focuses on crypto-chip testing by DFT. Already crypto-chip have been hacked by Scan-based Attacks against Cryptography LSIs and their Counter-measure [2].

2 Existing System

Few papers had been proposed with secure design against side channel attack, in this some of the proposed methods make scan path unusable for attackers by limiting scan path control. Side Channel Attack on Dedicated Hardware Implementations of DES was discussed in paper [3], by loading pairs of known plaintexts with one-bit difference in the normal mode and then scanning out the internal state in the test mode, which determine the position of all scan elements in the scan chain. In paper [4], scan-based attack against ECC was elaborated. In paper [5], instead of secret key, test key is used in test mode to prevent scan-based attack. However, by doing this will limit the test application, which is because it doesn't support at-speed online testing. In paper [6], an inverter is placed randomly to scan chain and test controller limit the use of scan chain by comparing scan in with the pre-set value when the circuit is designed.

To reduce the test timing and volume of test data we follow the circular scan method [7]. This method increases scan chain count exponentially in the circuit while retaining the original scan input pin count. Hence no necessity for high cost Automatic Test Equipment (ATEs). Output is given to Multi-Input Signature Register (MISR) were only the varying bits of a test slice in the new scan chains is updated for each shift cycle. In paper [8], Secure Scan and Secure chip technique is introduced for DFT were the comparison scan chain cannot perform directly for retrieving the secret key but this method uses large amount of electronic component in terms of multipliers and flip flops. Robust Secure Scan Design Against Scan-Based Differential Cryptanalysis [9], efficient spatial dependency method but has a drawback in internal scan structure still able to hack by using reset-based scan or flush test. In paper [10], Design-for-Secure-Test for Crypto Cores by adding a stimulus launched flip-flop into the traditional scan flip-flop to maintain the high-test quality without compromising the security but result in hardware overhead. In paper [12, 14] discussed about side channel attack in SM9 method. Cache based side channel attack was elaborated in paper [13]. In paper [18], bit level power consistency analysis in hardware Trojan was discussed. A hardware Trojan attack on FPGA based cryptographic key generation was explained in paper [19].

In paper [11], secure scan architecture against scan-based attack by using SDSFF (State Dependent Scan Flip-Flop) is proposed as in Fig. 1. In SDSFF, an XOR and a latch are integrated into a traditional scan FF to increase the security of scan chain. The latch memorizing a past state of the scan FF can change a scan FF output. According to the load signal, the value of the latch could be updated. By doing this, the structure of scan chain could be dynamically changed even after it is designed. Hacker cannot know the value updated in latch, so that the SDSFF can't be operated by attackers. Hence our proposed Optimized Scan Flip Flop (OSFF) will reduce the switching activity in latches which leads us to reduce the power consumption in architecture, by reducing the unwanted latches we can obtain optimization in area. Hence latches should insert randomly to scan chain design. The optimized architecture was emulated on RSA to show the effectiveness of the proposed method.

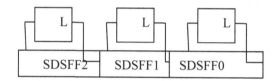

Fig. 1. Block diagram of existing system [11]

3 Proposed Architecture

Optimized architecture design is to encrypt and decrypt data in scan chain were hacker cannot able to observe the working functionality of flip flops. Hence its complicated for unintended user to find the difference between pair of plaintext. The proposed architecture OSFF design is shown in Fig. 2. Along with traditional flip flop, in addition it contains Single Latch and XOR Gate. As it contains two working mode, normal mode and test mode. In normal mode, its act like a general flip flop were the input and output value are same but differ in clock pulse. In test mode its act like OSFF flip flop output is depend upon latch value.

Fig. 2. Proposed block diagram

Example: Scan chain model which consists of OSFFs in the first position shown in Figs. 3 and 4. Table 1 shows the changes in scan output data where it depends upon latches. Here test vector of Scan In data is taken as SI = S3, S2, S1, S0 and DI = D3, D2, D1, D0, all this four bit vector produce Scan Out depends upon Latch Enable. If EN is 0 then the scan chain performs as normal mode else its act in test mode.

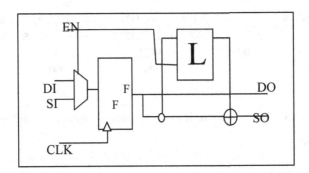

Fig. 3. Basic block of the proposed method

The latch (L) is always presented in the test-mode. The output in test-mode depends upon the number of latch presented in that scan chain. If total number of latches inserted to scan chain is even then input is equal to output otherwise output was inverted from the applied input. Selection between the mode is take place by Enable (En), which is also load signal for latch. By doing this we can able to operate the latch only at test-mode. Here, latch is inserted randomly to scan structure no need to replace a flip flop with OSFF. Assume that latch is attached in j^{th} flip flop of scan chain, then j^{th} flip flop is called as OSFF flip flop. All existing system, have need to replace the flip flop in scan chain but our proposed system not required the replacement which give us additional advantage. Now apply a test vector to the optimized architecture as,

Test Vector $V = (V_{N-1}, V_{N-2}, \ldots V_2, V_1, V_0)$.
Response $R = (R_{N-1}, R_{N-2}, \ldots R_2, R_1, R_0)$.
Scan In $SI = (SI_{N-1}, SI_{N-2} \ldots SI_2, SI_1, SI_0)$.
Scan Out $SO = (SO_{N-1}, SO_{N-2} \ldots SO_2, SO_1, SO_0)$.

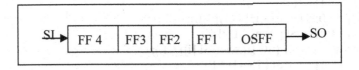

Fig. 4. Scan chain with OSFFs

Table 1. Changes in scan out

Scan in		Scan out	
		EN = 0	EN = 1
SI	DI	DO	SO
S3, S2, S1, S0	D3, D2, D1, D0	D3, D2, D1, D0	S3′, S2′, S1′, S0′
S3, S2, S1, S0	D3, D2′, D2, D1	D3, D2′, D2, D1	S3′, S2′, S1′, S0
0010	0001	0001	1101
1111	000	000	0000

Hence $SO_{[i]}$ will depends latch, if latch is enabled otherwise, latch is disabled.

Pseudo code:
```
If  ~ (EN)
{   DO [ i ] = DI [ i ] ;
    DO [ i + 1] = DI [ i+1]; ......
    DO [ i + (n-1)] = DI[i + ( n-1 )]; // i = LSB
    DO [ i + n] = DI [ i + n];        // n = MSB
} Else
{   N = 1                  // i = Current Flip Flop Position
  For (i =0; i<j;i= i+1)        // j=Total no of Flip Flop
    N = N+1;        // N = Total number of  Latches
    If (N % 2 == 0) then {
    if (L == ' 0 ' and  i == ' 0 ' ) then  process State 1
    else if (L ==' 1 ' and  i == ' 0 ' )then process State2
    else if (L ==' 0 ' and  i == ' 1 ' )then process State1
    else (L ==' 1 'and  i == ' 1 ' )then process State2 }
    else {
    if (L == ' 0 ' and  i == ' 0 ' ) then  process State 2
    else if ( L ==' 1 ' and  i == ' 0 ' )then process State1
    else if ( L ==' 0 ' and  i == ' 0 ' )then process State2
    else (L ==' 1 ' and  i == ' 1 ' )then process State1}
    Process (State 1) {SO [i] = ((SI [i]) ^ L);
    SO [ i + 1] = ((SI [ i + 1]) ^ L);
    SO [ i + (n-1)] = (SI [i+( n-1)] ^ L);
    SO [ i + n] = (SI [i + n] ^ L);}
    Process (State 2) {SO [i] = ~ ((SI [i]) ^ L);
    SO [ i + 1] = ~ ((SI [ i + 1]) ^ L);
    SO [ i + (n-1)] = ~ (SI [i+( n-1)] ^ L);
    SO [ i + n] = ~ (SI [ i + n] ^ L);}
    L = Value of Latch either 0 or 1,were Value of  Latch  L = SI [Previous Bit Value
].
```

In SDSFF, Total number of Flip Flop is always equal to Total number of Latch. In SDSFF Scan Out $SO[i] = SI[i] \wedge L[i] \wedge L[i-1] \wedge L[i-2] \ldots\ldots$ (Untill i = 0). OSFF Scan Out: $SO[i] = SI[i] \wedge L[i]$. To increase the security level we can increase the latch randomly to the scan chain, but this would not affect the test time because in SDSFF we want add the N numbers of content in N latches to the value of flip flop, for finding the output of Nth flip flop which take large amount of time and operation [11]. But in our proposed method, were the scan chain containing N number of Latches for M numbers of flip flop (were N is always less than M), We count the total number of latches N, if N modulus of 2 is equal to 0 then output is equal to input else output is equal to inverse of input. In normal mode, DI is given as input and output DO is produced as same as input working like general flip flop.

In test mode, SI is given as input and output SO is produced based on value of Latch. Total number of latch is even then, SO = SI if its add SO = $\sim$ SI were SI is XOR ed with LATCH L. The existing state dependent scan flip flop method uses N number of latch for N number of flip-flops. However, our proposed optimized method uses random number of latch for N number of flip flops were shown in Fig. 3. Hence total number of transaction to compute scan out in proposed method is very less when compared to state dependent flip flop. This help us to reduce the consumption of power. Total number of latches used to compute output in state dependent flip flop is high. Overall usage of number of latch in proposed system is less, hence total area is reduced in our LSI circuit.

4 Experimental Result

The optimized architecture was implemented on 512-bit RSA. It was simulated, synthesis using VHDL and targeted to SPARTAN 3 on Xilinx software. Result report was tabulated on Tables 2 and 3. RSA cryptographic processor architecture is based on Montgomery Algorithm. This architecture made the processing time faster and used for comparatively smaller amount of area space in the FPGA [15–17].

Table 2. Scan chain of single SDSFF and OSFF

Components utilization	Slices	Flip flops	4 input LUTs
Basic RSA (512-bit)	11090	8132	19748
SDSFF [11]	11170	8244	19860
Proposed OSFF	11170	8228	19844

Table 3. Scan chain of multiple SDSFF and OSFF

Scan-chain content	Total number of latches	Overhead [%]	Delay [%]
Proposed OSFF	4/16/32	0	4.83
SDSFF	4	0.135	4.83
SDSFF	16	0.274	4.83
SDSFF	32	0.551	4.83

Proposed method targets to optimized architecture design for both the functions of encrypt and decrypt data in scan chain. It promises to complicate the user to find the changes between pair of plaintext information. The proposed architecture OSFF, designed along with basic flip flop latch and xor logic. To implement our proposed method, inserting the latch at the fourth position was observed and synthesis report is generated. Similarly, now replace fourth position flip flop with SDSFF and report is taken which show the overhead of flip flop and LUTs in Table 2.

Table 3 show the result of SDSFF overhead comparison with OSFF when the scan chain containing 4, 16, 32 SDFF and OSFF. Overall critical path delay is same, hence the test time will remain same in both the method. Analyzing the security for OSFF based design were the possibility to discover a secret key through scan chains using known scan-based attack is to know the number of OSFFs. The random positions of inserted latch were the data in latches changes from time to time. However, all of these are not known to attackers which make impossible or at least very difficult for them to discover through scan operations.

5 Conclusion

Crypto-chips are very popular in secure applications but it also targeted for various attacks. Side channel attack is one of the attack which focuses in this paper. Proposed work provides an efficient secure to prevent side channel attack, which is caused by various parameters. This proposed system saves power by reduces unnecessary switching. Area optimization is also achieved in this method. Experimental results show that proposed method is very useful for reduced area optimization without compromising time. Thus, this method will be well fit to prevent side channel attack with efficient area. Using this method along with high speed design is recommended for future research work.

References

1. Thomasson, J.P., Baldi, L.: Smartcards: portable security. In: Innovative Systems in Silicon Conference, pp. 259–265. IEEE (1997)
2. Ryuta, N.: Scan-based attacks against cryptography LSIs and their countermeasure, ICSLABS (2011)
3. Yang, B., Wu, K., Karri, R.: Scan based side channel attack on dedicated hardware implementations of data encryption standard. In: ITC International Test Conference (2004)
4. Nara, R., Togawa, N., Yanagisawa, M., Ohtsuki, T.: Scan-Based Attack Against Elliptic Curve Cryptosystems, IEEE Conference (2010)
5. Yang, B., Wu, K., Karri, R.: Secure scan: a design-for-test architecture for crypto chips. IEEE Trans. Comput. Aided Des. Integr. Circ. Syst. 25(10), 2287–2293 (2006)
6. Sengar, G., Mukhopadhyay, D., Chowdhury, D.R.: Secured flipped scan-chain model for crypto-architecture. IEEE Trans. Comput. Aided Des. Integr. Circ. Syst. 26(11), 2080–2084 (2007)

7. Arslan, B., Orailoglu, A.: Circular scan: a scan architecture for test cost reduction. In: Proceedings of the Design, Automation and Test in Europe Conference and Exhibition. IEEE (2004)
8. Hely, D., Flottes, M.L., Bancel, F., Rouzeyre, B., Berard, N., Renovell, M.: Scan design and secure chip. In: Proceedings of the 10th IEEE International On-Line Testing Symposium (IOLTS 2004) (2004)
9. Shi, Y., Togawa, N., Yanagisawa, M., Ohtsuki, T.: Robust secure scan design against scan-based differential cryptanalysis. IEEE Trans. Very Large Scale Integr. (VLSI) Syst. **20**(1), 176–181 (2012)
10. Shi, Y., Togawa, N., Yanagisawa, M., Ohtsuki, T.: Design-For-Secure-Test for Crypto Cores, International Test Conference (2009)
11. Atobet, Y., Shi, Y., Yanagisawa, M., Togawat, N.: Dynamically Changeable Secure Scan Architecture Against Scan-Based Side Channel Attack, IEEE Conference (2012)
12. Zhang, Q., et al.: Side channel attacks and countermeasures for identity based cryptographic algorithm SM9, Security and communication networks (2018)
13. Yarom, Y., Falkner, K.: FLUSH + RELOAD: a high resolution, low noise, L3 cache side channel attack. In: USENIX Security Symposium (2014)
14. Yuan, F., Cheng, Z.: Overview on SM9 identity-based cryptographic algorithm. J. Inf. Secur. Res. **2**, 1008–1027 (2016)
15. Anand, A., Praveen, P.: Implementation of RSA algorithm on FPGA. Int. J. Eng. Res. Technol. (IJERT) **1**(5), 1–5 (2012)
16. Sahu, S.K., Pradhan, M.: FPGA implementation of RSA encryption system. Int. J. Comput. Appl. **19**(9), 10–12 (2011)
17. Ibrahimy, M.I., Reaz, M.B.I., Asaduzzaman, K., Hussain, S.: FPGA implementation of RSA encryption engine with flexible key size. Int. J. Commun. **3**(1), 107–113 (2007)
18. Zhang, Y., Quan, H., Li, X., Chen, K.: Golden free processor hardware Trojan detection using bit power consistency analysis. J. Electron. Test. **34**(3), 305–312 (2018)
19. Govindan, V., Chakraborty, R.S., Santikellur, P., Chandhary, A.K.: A hardware Trojan attack on FPGA based cryptographic key generation: impact and detection. J. Hardw. Syst. Secur. **2**, 225–239 (2018)

Inbound Multi-echelon Inventory Supply Network Model in Ethiopian Leather Industry: A Simulation Study

Robel Negussie[(✉)] and Jeyaraju Jayaprakash

Faculty of Mechanical and Industrial Engineering,
Bahir Dar Institute of Technology, Bahir Dar University, Bahir Dar, Ethiopia
robelneg@gmail.com, profjaya@gmail.com

Abstract. Leather processing companies are highly affected due to irregular availability of raw hide and skin by trends of globalization and dynamic behaviour of meat usage in Ethiopia. Maintaining optimal inventory stock in inbound multi-echelon supply networks is more complex in nature due to high fluctuation of raw materials availability. This paper presents a deterministic optimal procurement inventory policy among four designed inventory replenishment strategies in the tanning industries to avoid fluctuation raw materials. We proposed simulation model for these four different procurement strategies of raw materials in each inbound multi-echelon supply network. After running the trial simulation, a significant method of controlling the inventory level in the tanneries while keeping the operating performance in a reasonable level is achieved. The outputs are analyzed using ARENA simulation inventory stock information in every tier of the supply chain network. Finally simulated outputs of these strategies in each level are compared with performance using analytic hierarchy process (AHP) a multi-criteria decision model.

Keywords: Discrete event simulation · Multi-echelon inventory ·
Multi-criteria decision · Supply chain

1 Introduction

Ethiopia possesses one of the largest populations of livestock in Africa and 7th–9th in the world. Ethiopian hides and skins are having very good reputations in the international leather market for their unique natural substance of fitness, cleanness, and compactness of texture, thickness, flexibility and strength.

Acute shortage and poor quality of raw hides and skins are the major problems faced by Ethiopian tanning industries and force them to operate under capacity. According to Tolossa (2013) there are 22 tanneries operating in the country with annual tanning capacity of 2.2 million hides, 25.9 million sheep skins and 13.7 million goat skins. But the annual potential of purchase of these tanneries is 1.7 million hides, 7.7 million sheep skins and 8 million goat skins. This illustrates that the tanneries are utilizing only 77.3%, 29.7% and 58.4% of their tanning potential respectively due to the shortage of raw material. On the other side collecting hides and skins with

© ICST Institute for Computer Sciences, Social Informatics and Telecommunications Engineering 2019
Published by Springer Nature Switzerland AG 2019. All Rights Reserved
F. A. Zimale et al. (Eds.): ICAST 2018, LNICST 274, pp. 418–428, 2019.
https://doi.org/10.1007/978-3-030-15357-1_35

acceptable quality grade is becoming a challenge due to poor husbandry, storage and transport mechanism.

The potential supply of hides and skins depend of the scale of meat production, not on the size of livestock population. Thus availability of hides and skins depends on the need of meat usage rate. In Ethiopia the raw hides and skins have very high fluctuation which depends on festivals and fasting periods. High volatility of raw hide and skin may considerably impact on the profit margin and production capacity of leather manufacturing industries.

In this research maintaining optimal inventory stock in inbound multi-echelon supply network is considered as an alternative solution for this dynamic market by taking one tanning industry as a case which is located in Addis Ababa, Ethiopia. Modelling and simulation of inbound multi-echelon supply network with four different scenarios on the inventory replenishment strategies using ARENA simulation software is proposed to address this issue. Etraja and Jayaprakash (2016) proposed Analytic Hierarchical Process (AHP), a multi criteria decision model is employed to evaluate the alternative results of the simulation model.

2 Literature Review

In this research, literature review has been conducted in three stages. First identification of list of journals published with more priority in simulation and modelling of supply chain methodology and then identification of most influenced operational performance criteria and finally identification of research gap & performance analysis on different aspects of supply chain with respect to case company problems.

Nearly more than thirty research articles have been reviewed in simulation of logistics and supply chain management with decision support system from various e-resources from 2001 to 2018.

2.1 SCM Network Operational Performance Indicators

Beamon (1998) classified performance measures of supply chain design and analysis into qualitative and quantitative categories. Agarwal and Shankar (2005) evaluated qualitative measures include customer satisfaction, flexibility, information and material flow integration, effective risk management and supplier performance. Quantitative measures include measures based on cost and measures based on customer responsiveness etc. These performance criteria are mainly depends on the supply chain network structure, its complexity and the product/service type that is flowing in the chain. Mobini et al. (2013), who reviewed simulation model for the design and analysis of wood pallet supply chain selects cost, energy consumption and carbon dioxide emission as the key performance indicators. Jansen et al. (2000) identified satisfaction of customer and lead time in their catering supply chain simulation model. Noche and Elhasia (2013) introduced strategies in cement industries, Carvalho et al. (2011), Li et al. (2010), Cannella and Ciancimino (2008) and Cigolini et al. (2013), proposed simulation supply network. Simic et al. (2015) proposed hybrid GA inbound network, Fengli et al. (2009) simulated bio-mass supply chain, Klimov and Merkuryev (2008) considered the resilience and reliability of the supply chain network when there is something that interrupts the chain and Datta and Christopher (2011) simulated uncertainty in supply chains.

We have identified eight different performance indicators of supply chain network with related to the Ethiopian leather context from the literature review. The identified supply chain performance evaluation criteria are quality of goods, lead time, operational cost, risk mitigation strategy, flexibility to survive uncertain environments, access to the required quantity, service level and inventory level.

During the article review process in addition to the eight supply chain performance indicators we prepared five other evaluation criteria to identify literature gap. These are number of sources of raw material or sub assembled items, variety of goods, number of echelons, resource constraint (whether the model is developed with limited or unlimited resource) and the type of simulation software used to model the supply chain. Wan et al. (2005) considered single source of input and single echelon. Nikolopoulov and Ierapetritov (2012) and Zhang and Zhang (2006) considered two source of input with two echelons. These assumptions are mostly unpractical in the global world in which companies extend their supply up to thousands of sources to survive in the market by mitigating risk factors and uncertainties in the supply. The number of the variety of inputs also significantly affects the performance of the chain. Most of the articles consider the variety of inputs as one or two which is also rare in real world. A supply chain also should have to react for limited resources which cannot be found when needed like hide and skin. The number of echelons/tiers is also directly related with the performance of supply chains.

2.2 Research Gap

From the review of SCM inbound logistic distribution network, Persson and Olhager (2002) has considered quality of good/service criteria and rest of the researchers neglected it. But in our case leather industry suffering with more second grade quality of raw hide and skin and significantly it affects the performance of leather production. Even though all the eight key performance indicators of the supply chain are necessary to measure the performance of Ethiopian leather industry, according to a survey conducted in the industry quantity, quality, cost and lead time and tanneries capacity utilization are identified in the order of seriousness by keeping in mind the uncertain environment in different scenarios.

The other basic element in supply chain network is the availability of the required raw material/resource in sufficient amount for production. Umeda and Zhang (2001), Jie and Cong (2009), Chan and Prakash (2011), Mishra and Chan (2011), Wan and Zhao (2009), Patil et al. (2011) and Persson and Olhager (2002) consider inventory level criteria. Nikolopoulov and Ierapetritov (2012) and Mobini et al. (2013) considered limitation of resources in the supply chain network. In this research work source of raw materials is limited.

No research articles were found to interlink between the supply quantity and the inventory level for perishable goods. In this case, we made an attempt with case Ethiopian leather company, simulation study of interlink supply quality and inventory in supply chain with either fresh or salted hides and skins are considered. The unsalted fresh hides and skins should never been stored for more than a single day and fifteen days on average after salt is applied.

Even though there are millions of hide and skin producers, thousands of small collectors and hundreds of hide and skin traders, the tanneries are suffering from shortage of raw hide and skin. None of the researches indicate seasonal and dynamic supply of raw materials like the Ethiopian hide and skin. In addition no research addresses the by-product nature of supplied goods and lacks integration with the original product. To overcome these limitations and other challenges there should be a balance between the amount of on hand inventory and the quantity of the raw material received per unit time by considering the daily demand of the tanneries while keeping the limitation of the resource (not found in the required quantity when required) under consideration.

This research is basically focuses on handling this situation by developing a validated simulation model with the help of Arena software and testing different scenarios/experiments to see the operating performance of the tanneries with a reasonable amount of raw hides and skins in their stocks. This is done by developing four scenarios by varying the time between consecutive orders and the quantity of shipment per unit order.

2.3   Supply Chain Network Problem Associate with Case Company

This study focused four echelon supply chain in which two nodes in two of the echelons in Addis Ababa (capital of Ethiopia) and regional small traders of hides and skins, Dire Hide and Skin Procurement and Collection Centre (DHSPCC), regional big suppliers and the case company. The general framework of the supply chain under study is depicted in Fig. 1 below. Dire Hide and Skin Procurement and Collection Center (DHSPCC) received raw hide and skins from small producers located in Addis Ababa, some other regional small traders and Addis Ababa municipality abattoir by participating on a bid which is held monthly. DHSPCC then send shipment of 1000 sheep skins/order to the tannery after receiving order.

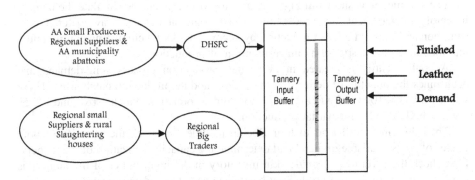

Fig. 1. General framework of the supply chain under study

The Regional Big Suppliers (RBS) of Dire tannery are a lot which are distributed all over the country. Some of the major suppliers come from Sellalie, Jimma, Gojam and Wollo regions in Ethiopia. These regional big traders will receive collected skins and hides from the small ones and rural slaughtering houses on daily basis without quantity restriction. Those regional big suppliers of hide and skin will ship a full truck load of 4000 sheep skins on average after receiving order from the tannery if and only if they have inventory on hand. If the inventory level of the RBS is less than the economic order quantity (EOQ) of the tannery the order will wait until the stock is replenished.

The case company, Tannery have strived to fulfil their daily demand with first grade quality of raw hides and skins to operate with its full installed capacity. If there is any difference in the supply of first quality the case company would be forced to operate with second grade quality or partial/under capacity or stop production/starved.

3 Simulation of Inbound Supply Chain Network

Discrete event system simulation and modelling methodology accommodate more realistic characteristic study in different supply chain environments, like stochastic, dynamic, and distributed environments and allow the supply chain decision makers can make quick decisions related to various critical conditions. In this study we divided the case company supply network model in to eight different logically interlinked sub-models from various suppliers, distribution, case company warehouse, work-in-process inventory, finished goods inventory and finally simulate these sub models distribution with real data for a year. The simulation is done in varying the time between consecutive orders and the amount of skins required by the tannery.

One year daily data is collected for the case company supply chain and provided in the developed simulation model to conduct experiment. The developed sub-models in the main research are inventory management segment for regional small suppliers, Addis Ababa suppliers, Addis Ababa – DHSPCC suppliers, regional big suppliers, DHSPCC, Inventory replenishment control strategy of the tannery and production inventory management of work-in-process tannery. The latter is indicated in Fig. 2 below.

The sub-model as shown in Fig. 2, work-in-process inventory simulate the tannery inventory management and production control segment manages raw-material consumption and finished goods production by keeping track of a circulating control entity that modulates the suspension and resumption of production.

A control entity is created in every day production process skin demand and determines the quantity of demand in the assign module production batch sizes. These values are "5e+003 + EXPO (505)" for full production batch size and "2.5e +003 + EXPO(253)" for partial production.

Then the entity will lead to four Decide modules to check the quantity of both grades of skins available on hand and determine the capacity utilization of the tannery. First check the level of first grade skin inventory in the input buffer of the tannery is greater or equal to the full production batch size and if not check second graded skin inventory. The tannery gives first priority to run the company to full production capacity with either first or second grade of skins. Second check the level of inventory fulfils minimum requirement for partial production for both quality grade skins. Finally

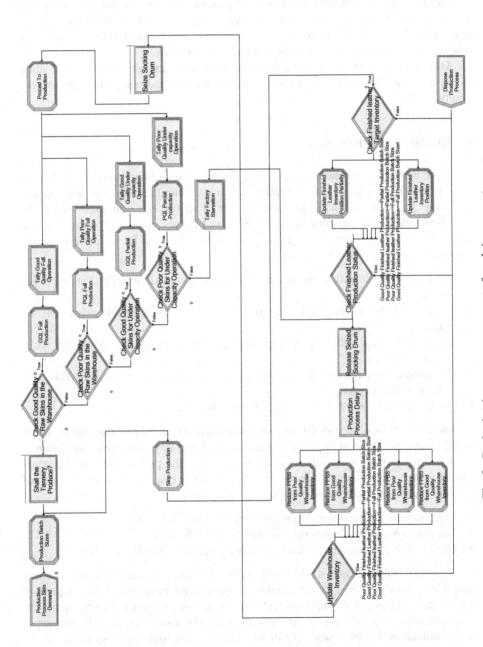

Fig. 2. Production inventory management of work-in-process tannery

the tannery faces with more scarcity of the raw material and inventory level reduced less than partial production then factory will be starved.

Another sub-model developed is finished goods inventory. For this case study it is taken as the daily demand of the finished product exceeds the daily production. At the same time the finished leather target stock is assumed to be 100,000 to abandon production termination due to excess finished product stock.

After validating the conceptual framework by company experts, the simulation model is verified by comparing the simulation result with the real performance of the supply chain.

4 Result and Discussion

The basic performance measurement criteria for this system under study is the factory status of tanning operation (four operations and a starvation) and the daily average and maximum inventory available in each suppliers and tannery warehouse stock. As described earlier the more time the skins are stored the less quality of skins. The five status of tanning operation are the primary measurement criteria for the performance of the supply chain system under study are:

- The number of days that the tannery processes first grade quality skins with full capacity.
- The number of days that the tannery processes second grade quality skins with full capacity.
- The number of days that the tannery processes first grade quality skins with under installed capacity.
- The number of days that the tannery processes second grade quality skins with under installed capacity.
- The number of days that the tannery is fully starved.

These conditions are varied based on the availability of the raw material on hand. These all are measured in days out of the operating 365 days (one year simulation).

The other output of the simulation that is used as the performance measurement criteria for the supply chain system under study is the average and maximum value of on hand inventory under stock in each echelons. These are

- The average and maximum skins inventory in DHSPCC stock
- The average and maximum skins inventory in RBS stock
- The average and maximum skins inventory in tannery warehouse stock.

This is selected because of the skins quality deterioration when stocked for more than fifteen days as well as to know and share information between echelons regarding the inventory status in each suppliers and customers. Based on this regard below are the four basic scenarios and cases under each scenario to be tested and the analyzed output of the simulation model. These four different strategically developed scenarios are

- Place the order with fixed time interval and fixed quantity of hide and skin
- Place the order with fixed time interval and variable quantity of hide and skin

- Place the order with variable time interval and fixed quantity of hide and skin
- Place the order with variable time interval and variable quantity of hide and skin.

This order placement is done by the tannery for its immediate suppliers. The simulation result of all developed scenario are listed in Table 1 below.

Table 1. Criteria comparison with various scenarios

Scenario	Number of days factory running				
	Full capacity with first grade quality	Full capacity with second grade quality	Under capacity with first grade quality	Under capacity with second grade quality	Factory starved
S-1	117	2	159	26	46
S-2	261	14	65	6	4
S-3	323	19	8	0	0
S-4	297	17	33	2	1

5   Optimal Inventory Decision Using AHP Method

After the completion of simulation results, each scenario has different working days with different levels of production capacities. Consider these mixed combination simulation results to evaluate optimal inventory level scenario using multi-criteria decision model. Multi-criteria decision using AHP model problem has three element parts. First level: to improve the production capacity of leather plant without shortage and surplus of inventory of raw hide and skin. Second level: selection of important criteria which influences the first level. These are

- Full capacity with first grade quality of raw material (FCFQ).
- Full capacity with second grade quality of raw material (FCSQ).
- Partial capacity with first grade quality of raw material (PCFQ).
- Partial capacity with second grade quality of raw material (PCSQ).
- Factory starved (FS).

Third level: contains the options of finalize the alternatives of this problem. The alternatives are fired the Inventory order to Factory warehouse, DHSPCC and RBS in the following scenario.

- Fixed time and fixed economic order quantity (FTFQ).
- Fixed time and variable economic order quantity (FTVQ).
- Variable time and fixed economic order quantity (VTFQ).
- Variable time and variable economic order quantity (VTVQ).

In a final step after weighing and scoring, the option scores are combined with the criterion weights to calculate an overall score for each option. Then evaluate all the options satisfy the criteria based on weightage according to the relative importance of the criteria. This is done by simple weighted summation. Finally, after judgments have

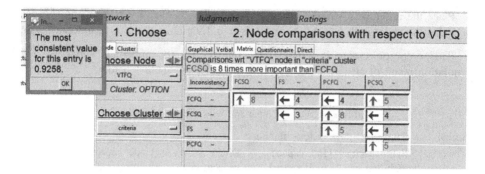

Fig. 3. Multi-criteria decisions for order placed with variable time and fixed quaintly

been made on the impact of all the elements and priorities have been computed for the hierarchy as a whole. Order placed with variable time and fixed quantity has arrived maximum consist value of 0.9258 as shown in Fig. 3.

Therefore, by observing all those parameters the tannery decision makers are able to make decisions based on the tested results so that they are able to make decisions based on facts rather than assumptions. Based on the executed data it can be simply observed that scenario 3 is found the better strategy for replenishing the tannery raw material warehouse.

6 Conclusion

Among the evaluation schemas identified for the article revision a big ignorance has been found for the two basic parameters that has an immense point while modelling and simulation. These evaluation parameters are the quality of goods in and out in the supply chain and the availability of the resources in the supply chain while the Ethiopian leather industries, particularly the tanneries are suffering from the shortage of raw material (hides and skins) as well as its quality problem.

This study paved the way to create a balance between the two conflicting objectives of tanning industries while keeping the operating performance of the tannery to the optimum level. After developing a four echelon verified simulation model four different scenarios (Inventory Replenishment Strategies) are designed by varying the time between two consecutive orders and the quantity of shipment per unit order. These scenarios are tested in the model for one year simulation run time with three replications to evaluate the tannery operating performance and the amount of on-hand inventory accumulated. But the simulation result has given mixed composition of full and partial number of tannery working days with both first grade and second grade quality raw skins. So we adapted AHP multi criteria decision method to rank these strategies. Hence, scenario three (Placing order to the suppliers with variable time interval and fixed quantity of skins in a shipment) result in the best operating performance of the tannery by keeping both capacity utilization and amount of raw material inventory in a reasonable quantity. Therefore, tanneries and other related sectors have a possibility to make decisions based on facts rather than assumptions in such uncertain environment.

References

Nikolopoulov, A., Ierapetritou, M.G.: Hybrid simulation based optimization approach for supply chain management. J. Comput. Chem. Eng. **47**, 183–193 (2012)

Agarwal, A., Shankar, R.: Modeling supply chain performance variables. Asian Acad. Manag. J. **10**(2), 47–68 (2005)

Beamon, B.M.: Supply chain design and analysis, models and methods. Int. J. Prod. Econ. **55**(3), 281–294 (1998)

Noche, B., Elhasia, T.: Approach to innovative supply chain strategies in cement industry; Analysis and Model simulation. Procedia Soc. Behav. Sci. **75**, 359–369 (2013)

Zhang, C., Zhang, C.: Design and simulation of demand information sharing in a supply chain. J. Simul. Model. Pract. Theory **15**, 32–46 (2006)

Jansen, D.R., Van Weert, A., Beulens, A.J.M., Huirne, R.B.M.: Simulation model of multi compartment distribution in the catering supply chain. Eur. J. Oper. Res. **133**, 210–224 (2000)

Simic, D., Svircevic, V., Simic, S.: A hybrid evolutionary model for supplier assessment and selection in inbound logistics. J. Appl. Log. **13**(2), 38–147 (2015)

Bottani, E., Montanari, R.: Supply chain design and cost analysis through simulation. Int. J. Prod. Res. **48**(10), 2859–2886 (2009)

Etraja, P., Jayaprakash, J.: An integrated fuzzy AHP and fuzzy DEMATEL approach in green supplier selection for green supply chain management. Int. J. Control. Theory Appl. **9**(52) (2016)

Chan, F.T.S., Prakash, A.: Inventory management in a lateral collaborative manufacturing supply chain: a simulation study. Int. J. Prod. Res. **50**(16), 4670–4685 (2011)

Zhang, F., Johnson, D.M., Johnson, M.A.: Development of a simulation model of biomass supply chain for bio-fuel production. Renew. Energy **44**, 380–391 (2012)

Persson, F., Olhager, J.: Performance simulation of supply chain designs. Int. J. Prod. Econ. **77**, 231–245 (2002)

Carvalho, H., Barroso, A.P., Machado, V.H., Azevedo, S., Cruz-Machado, V.: Supply chain redesign for resilience using simulation. J. Comput. Ind. Eng. **62**, 329–341 (2011)

Li, J., Sheng, Z., Liu, H.: Multi-agent simulation for the dominant players' behavior in supply chains. J. Simul. Model. Pract. Theory **18**, 850–859 (2010)

Patil, K., Jin, K., Li, H.: Arena simulation model for multi echelon inventory system in supply chain management. In: Proceedings of the 2011 IEEE IEEM (2011)

Mishra, M., Chan, F.T.S.: Impact evaluation of supply chain initiatives: a system simulation methodology. Int. J. Prod. Res. **50**(6), 1554–1567 (2011)

Mobini, M., Sowlati, T., Sokhansanj, S.: A simulation model for the design and analysis of wood pellet supply chains. J. Appl. Energy **11**, 1239–1249 (2013)

Gottfried, O., De Clercq, D., Blair, E., Weng, X., Wang, C.: SWOT-AHP-TOWS analysis of private investment behavior in the Chinese biogas sector. J. Clean. Prod. **184**, 632–647 (2018)

Datta, P., Christopher, M.: Information sharing and coordination mechanism for managing uncertainty in supply chains: a simulation study. Int. J. Prod. Res. **49**(3), 765–803 (2011)

Byrne, P.J., Heavey, C.: Simulation, a framework for analyzing SME supply chains. In: Proceedings of the 2004 Winter Simulation Conference (2004)

Sirisawat, P., Kiatcharoenpol, T.: Fuzzy AHP-TOPSIS approaches to prioritizing solutions for reverse logistics barriers. Comput. Ind. Eng. **117**, 303–318 (2018)

Cigolini, R., Pero, M., Rossi, T., Sianesi, A.: Linking supply chain configuration to supply chain performance: a discrete event simulation model. J. Simul. Model. Pract. Theory **40**, 1–11 (2013)

Klimov, R., Merkuryev, Y.: Simulation model for supply chain reliability evaluation. Technol. Econ. Dev. Econ. **14**(3), 300–311 (2008)

Umeda, S., Zhang, F.: Supply chain simulation: generic models and application examples. J. Prod. Plan. Control **17**(2), 155–166 (2007)

Cannella, S., Ciancimino, E.: Capacity constrained supply chains: a simulation study. Int. J. Simul. Process Modell. **4**(2), 139–147 (2008)

Wan, J., Zhao, C.: Simulation research on multi-echelon inventory system in supply chain based on arena. In: The 1st International Conference on Information Science and Engineering (2009)

Wan, X., Pekny, J.F., Reklaitis, G.V.: Simulation-based optimization with surrogate models— Application to supply chain management. J. Comput. Chem. Eng. **29**, 1317–1328 (2005)

Tolossa, Y.H.: Skin defects in small ruminates and their nature and economic importance: the case of Ethiopia. Global Veterinaria **11**(5), 552–559 (2013)

Efficient FPGA Implementation of an Integrated Bilateral Key Confirmation Scheme for Pair-Wise Key-Establishment and Authenticated Encryption

Abiy Tadesse Abebe[1(✉)], Yalemzewd Negash Shiferaw[1],
Workineh Gebeye Abera[1], and P. G. V. Suresh Kumar[2]

[1] Addis Ababa Institute of Technology, AAU, Addis Ababa, Ethiopia
abiytds@yahoo.com, yalemzewdn@yahoo.com,
workinehgebeye@yahoo.com
[2] Ambo University, Ambo, Ethiopia
pendemsuresh@gmail.com

Abstract. The purpose of this paper is to propose a bilateral key confirmation scheme which provides a trustworthy key establishment between two communicating parties. There are various cryptographic schemes proposed based on unilateral key confirmation. But, such schemes do not confirm the equality of the common secret information computed independently by each communicating party, and do not consider whether the other end is the intended owner of the shared secret. However, exchanging of the secret information blindly without verifying that both of the ends have computed the same common secret information and without ensuring the identity of the other end with whom they are communicating, can create security risks since attackers can impersonate acting as a claimed sender or recipient. The proposed work provides bilateral key confirmation for pair-wise key-establishment based on FPGA by integrating a key agreement protocol and an authenticated encryption scheme. The implementation outcomes show the proposed scheme's reasonable hardware complexity and enhanced performance compared to existing similar works.

Keywords: Authenticated encryption · FPGA · Hybrid cryptography · Key agreement · Key confirmation

1 Introduction

In cryptography, establishment of secret keying material between communicating ends can be done electronically based on public key methods such as key-agreement protocols for key exchange [1, 2], or key transport for secure key distribution [3, 4]. When establishing a pair-wise key-agreement, the secret keying material will not directly be sent from one end to another. But, the two ends exchange only the required information from which both of them can compute a shared secret independently. Therefore, this method requires selection and exchange of valid domain parameters before performing the computation of the secret information for key establishment. In case of

© ICST Institute for Computer Sciences, Social Informatics and Telecommunications Engineering 2019
Published by Springer Nature Switzerland AG 2019. All Rights Reserved
F. A. Zimale et al. (Eds.): ICAST 2018, LNICST 274, pp. 429–438, 2019.
https://doi.org/10.1007/978-3-030-15357-1_36

key-transport, the secret keying material which is selected by the sender is wrapped with a key-wrapping algorithm being encrypted by the public key of the recipient and then transported to the other end. The recipient then unwraps the encrypted key using the same algorithm and the corresponding private key. Various hybrid cryptosystems have been proposed by different researchers to effectively utilize the advantages of symmetric and asymmetric key methods [4–6]. The well-known integrated encryption schemes such as Diffie-Hellman Integrated Encryption Scheme (DHIES) and Elliptic Curve Integrated Encryption Scheme (ECIES) are also hybrid cryptosystems which compose a public key key-agreement schemes, namely, Diffie-Hellman (DH) key exchange and Elliptic Curve Diffie-Hellman (ECDH) key exchange algorithms respectively, a hash function, a Key Derivation Function (KDF) or Hash-based Message Authentication Code (HMAC)-based KDF (HKDF), a symmetric key encryption algorithm, a Message Authentication Code (MAC) algorithm, and digital signature schemes [7–9]. Though they integrate different crypto mechanisms together, the objective is to provide better security by combining their advantages. The advantages can be described in terms of performance and security. Performance in this case means to utilize fast symmetric key algorithms for large data encryption and decryption instead of using public key algorithms for this purpose which are considered slower. On the other hand, security refers to utilizing the public key algorithms for secret key distribution to be used by symmetric key schemes, as well as for signature generation and verification. The key derivation function (KDF) in DHIES and ECIES is used for generation of one or more suitable secret keys from the exchanged shared secret for encryption (ENK key) and for Message Authentication Code (MAC) generation (MAC key) [7–9]. KDF or HKDF can be used to obtain keys of a required format from the result of a DH or ECDH key exchange suitable for the selected symmetric key algorithm such as AES. Keyed cryptographic hash functions are commonly used to construct Hash-based Message Authentication Code (HMAC) for key derivation in HKDF [10].

The integrated encryption schemes (DHIES and ECIES) have used unilateral key confirmation. However, bilateral key confirmation [10] is important since key agreement algorithms exchange secret information which are required for computation of common shared secret between two communicating ends. Without confirmation of the equality of the shared secrets created at both ends, and without verifying the identification of the entity communicating at the other end, exchanging secret information blindly can create security risks. In this paper, a pair-wise key-establishment method with bilateral key confirmation capability is presented by integrating a key agreement and an authenticated encryption schemes for authenticated encryption/decryption and authenticated key distribution.

The rest of the paper is organized as follows: Sect. 2 presents related works. The proposed work is explained in Sect. 3. Implementation approaches are discussed in Sect. 4. Section 5 summarizes the results. Finally, Sect. 6 concludes the paper.

2 Related Works

Various research works have been proposed based on the combination of public key and symmetric key algorithms to provide authenticated key agreement and encryption. Hybrid cryptosystems based on the combinations of public key and symmetric key algorithms can be found in [4–6]. Hybrid cryptosystems based on integrated encryption schemes such as DHIES and ECIES can also be found in [7–9]. In such systems only unilateral key confirmation is considered. Figure 1 depicts the DHIES presented in [7]. In this figure, M stands for plaintext, g is generator of cyclic group. Public keys of two communicating parties are represented by g^u and g^v respectively. Private keys of the two ends are represented as u and v respectively. Also, in the figure, E represents a symmetric key algorithm, H represents a hash function, and T stands for Message Authentication Code (MAC) generation function.

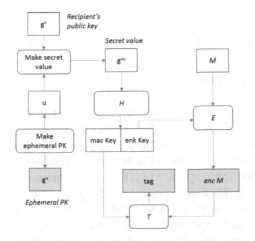

Fig. 1. DHIES functional diagram (Source: [7])

Similarly, Fig. 2 represents the ECIES functional diagram at the sender end [8, 9]. The working principle of the DHIES and ECIES are similar, but the former uses DH key exchange method, and the later uses ECDH key exchange method based on elliptic curve cryptography for key agreement. But, in both cases, a unilateral key confirmation approach has been followed. In DHIES and ECIES, the hash function and the KDF generate a MAC key and an ENC key which are the keys used for authentication and encryption respectively. The important issue here is that the MAC tag and the encrypted message are sent together to the other end without ensuring whether same shared secret is generated at the other end, and even without exactly knowing who the owner of the common secret information is at the other end.

The bilateral key confirmation scheme proposed in this work allows both of the communicating ends to ensure that they have generated equal secret key and also helps to confirm with whom the secret information sharing is done creating a trustworthy key establishment.

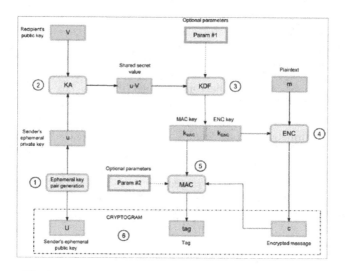

Fig. 2. ECIES encryption functional diagram (Source: [8, 9])

3   The Proposed Method

The proposed method integrates the Diffie-Hellman (DH) key agreement and Advanced Encryption Standard-Galois Counter Mode (AES-GCM) authenticated encryption [11] schemes for bilateral key confirmation and authenticated encryption as shown in Figs. 3, 4 and 5. Unlike the DHIES and ECIES, the output of the KDF is used for ENC key and *IV*, instead of ENC key and MAC key. This is because the MAC is generated using the hash sub-key (*H*) which is computed using the ENC key itself as part of the AES-GCM process such that: $H = AES (ENC\ key,\ 0^{128})$. This is computed at both ends to generate and exchange MAC tags which are related to the encrypted identification data of party A and party B (ID_A and ID_B) used for authentication and verifying that the same secret key is generated at both communicating ends. The proposed method is presented based on the following four major steps (see Sects. 3.1 to 3.4) and also depicted in Figs. 3, 4 and 5.

3.1   Key Exchange

In the first step, the following main tasks are performed by the communicating parties.

(i)   sharing of authentic public parameters which are used for generation of public keys
(ii)   selection of private key, and then, computation and exchange of public keys
(iii)   computation of shared secret and generation of secret key and *IV*
(iv)   exchange of encrypted identities for key confirmation.

Before starting of the key exchange process, both communicating ends (the sender and recipient) first share authentic public parameters. These public parameters and randomly selected private keys at each end will be computed to produce the respective

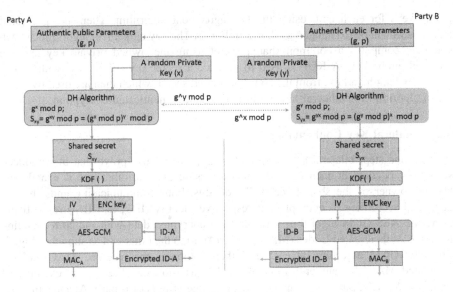

Fig. 3. Authenticated key agreement

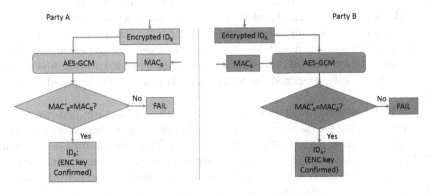

Fig. 4. Bilateral key confirmation

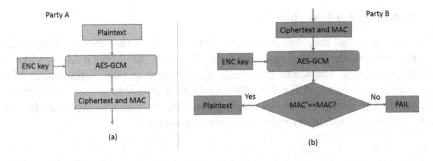

Fig. 5. Encryption and Decryption: (a) authenticated encryption; (b) authenticated decryption

public keys for each end, using the key agreement algorithm. Then, the generated public keys will be exchanged as shown in Fig. 3. The key agreement algorithm at each end then computes a common shared secret using the owned private key and the received public key. A KDF is used to produce a secret key (ENK key) with appropriate key length and *IV*, from the common shared secret, which then are used by AES-GCM algorithm for bilateral key confirmation and authenticated encryption.

3.2 Bilateral Key Confirmation

As a second step, bilateral key confirmation is performed to prove that the produced secret key is equal at each end, and also to assure that the other end is exactly the claimed owner of the shared secret. To do this, both communicating ends use the generated secret key to encrypt their respective identity (ID_A, and ID_B) respectively using the AES-GCM algorithm, and send the encrypted data with the corresponding Message Authenticated Codes (MAC_A and MAC_B) to the other end as shown in Fig. 3. The AES-GCM algorithm at each end then compares the received MAC and the calculated MAC′ for authentication of the IDs as shown in Fig. 4. For example, if $MAC_A = MAC'_A$, party B ensures that the message originator is party A; and similarly, if $MAC_B = MAC'_B$, then, party A confirms that the message originator is party B. It is only after the MACs are verified true that decryption of the encrypted message will follow. By decrypting the encrypted ID of the other end, then both ends confirm that the secret key is equal at both ends, and the other end is the claimed owner of the secret key, meeting the requirement of bilateral key confirmation. The computed ENC key is not directly used for encryption of the sensitive data without knowing first that the other end has exactly generated the same secret key and is the intended owner of that key.

Even if the two ends trust each other, it is important to confirm first that both of them have generated the same secret key and authenticate each other before encrypting and sending sensitive data blindly to the other end. This protects man-in-the-middle (MITM) not to establish a shared secret between the sender and recipient. Using the bilateral key confirmation scheme, the sender will not trust and accept the attacker's shared secret as a true recipient's secret information, and also the recipient will not trust and accept the attacker's shared key as a trusted sender's shared key.

3.3 Authenticated Encryption

In the third step, authenticated encryption is performed by the sender. After bilateral key confirmation, the sender uses the secret key and the AES-GCM algorithm to encrypt the message. The sender then sends the ciphertext and the corresponding MAC to the recipient as shown in Fig. 5(a). The AES-GCM algorithm is used here since it is fast compared to public key algorithms and can provide confidentiality, data integrity check, and authentication crypto services simultaneously.

3.4 Authenticated Decryption

The last step is authenticated decryption process performed at the receiving end. At the receiving end, the AES-GCM algorithm, first, validates the authenticity of the message by comparing the received MAC and the calculated MAC' as shown in Fig. 5(b). If the MAC values are equal, then the message will be decrypted and utilized. But, if the MAC values are not equal, then the message will be discarded. Therefore, using the proposed method, authenticated key exchange along with bilateral key confirmation and authenticated encryption/decryption are possible.

4 Implementation

In this work, the integrated scheme using Diffie-Hellman key-agreement protocol and AES-GCM algorithm is implemented on FPGA. VHDL is used as a hardware description language. Xilinx ISE 14.5 is used for synthesis, and the integrated simulator, ISIM, is used for simulation. Xilinx Virtex 5 FPGA device is used as a target implementation platform. It is assumed that the public parameters are authentic and shared between the two communicating ends before starting secure communication. Also, it is assumed that the two ends have exchanged the generated public keys at each end, using a chosen trusted method. The computed shared secret at both ends was made to produce 224 bits length value using SHA-224 [12] to produce 96 bits IV and 128 bits secret key which are suitable for AES-GCM algorithm. For bilateral key confirmation, the IDs of the respective ends were encrypted using the generated secret key so that both ends could assure that the secret key was equal, and the other end was the claimed owner of that key whose ID was sent with the corresponding MAC. After creating a trusted communication based on bilateral key confirmation, a message was encrypted using AES-GCM, and the ciphertext and the corresponding MAC were sent to the other end. The AES-GCM at the receiving end first compared the calculated MAC and the received MAC to verify the authentication and data integrity, and decrypted the message after verification. A Fully Pipelined AES [13] algorithm and bit-parallel Galois Hash (GHASH) have been implemented for AES-GCM [14]. In pipelining architecture, registers have been placed at each step/round to construct the pipeline as shown in Fig. 6. The depth of the pipeline, K, determines how many data blocks can be processed concurrently. The architecture is fully pipelined when K equals the total number of rounds. The area and the latency of the pipelined architecture are proportional to K. Pipelining can increase the encryption speed by processing multiple blocks of data simultaneously. The GHASH core has been implemented using the Mastrovito bit parallel multiplier [15]. The Mastrovito multiplier performs the finite field multiplication with parallel inputs and outputs with no clock cycle latency. The Mastrovito multiplier uses a Matrix Vector Product (MVP) which can compute a modulo reduced result in a single step [15]. Figure 7 shows the structure of the GHASH core.

For implementation of Diffie-Hellman key agreement algorithm, Montgomery multiplier [16] has been used to perform the modular multiplication which is used to

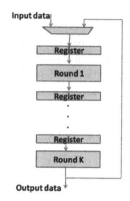

Fig. 6. Pipeline architecture

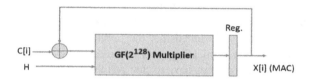

Fig. 7. Bit-parallel GHASH multiplier

speed up the process. The public parameters selected for implementation of the DH protocol are: p = 991 bits and q = 503 bits.

5 Results

The proposed cryptosystem has been implemented on Virtex 5 FPGA device. The implementation results and the performance comparisons with existing works are shown in Table 1, in terms of utilization of FPGA resources, maximum frequency, and the achieved throughput. As shown in Table 1, less number of Virtex 5 FPGA slices: 3533, 2478, and 3836 were utilized in the works presented by [17], [18] and [19] respectively, as they implemented only AES-GCM algorithm with no hybrid technique. However, 40, 41, and 50 BRAMs were utilized by [17], [18] and [19] respectively. Also, in [20], totally, 21194 slices and 20 BRAMs were used on Virtex II demonstrating the ECIES implementation. The hybrid scheme proposed in this work utilized 7886 FPGA slices, and 18 BRAMs as it is expected from the nature of the hybrid schemes. But concerning the throughput, the present work achieved 39.4 Gbps, which is an enhanced performance compared to the existing works with the same BRAM based optimization and single core AES-GCM implementation on the same implementation platform. Unlike the existing works where the implementations were restricted to performance enhancement and utilization of reasonable FPGA resources, but shared secret issue of AES-GCM has remained unresolved, the contributions of this work include authenticated encryption and authenticated key distribution with bilateral key confirmation offering strong security with more crypto security services in addition to performance enhancement and reasonable FPGA resources utilization. The simulation wave form of the proposed scheme is shown by Fig. 8.

Table 1. Performance comparison

Author	Target device	Design	Slices	BRAM	Freq. (MHz)	Thrpt. (Gbps)
This work	Virtex 5	Hybrid	7886	18	308.2	39.4
[17]	Virtex 5	AES-GCM	3533	41	314	16.9
[18]	Virtex 5	AES-GCM	2478	40	242	30.9
[19]	Virtex 5	AES-GCM	3836	50	273.4	32.46
[20]	Virtex II	ECIES	21194	20	-	-

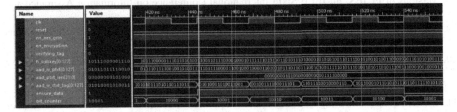

Fig. 8. Simulation waveform of the hybrid cryptosystem

6 Conclusions

An integrated scheme using DH algorithm for key agreement and AES-GCM for authenticated encryption of sensitive data has been implemented on Xilinx Virtex 5 FPGA platform offering bilateral key confirmation and authenticated encryption. Compared to the traditional hybrid cryptosystems which provided only one sided key confirmation, bilateral key confirmation allows both communicating ends to create a trustworthy communication. The proposed method saves extra resource requirement and key management by reducing the use of separate MAC algorithm compared to DHIES/ECIES schemes, and provides authenticated key distribution which is not addressed by existing FPGA based AES-GCM implementations. The implementation outcomes show that the proposed hybrid system has consumed reasonable amounts of FPGA resources with better throughput achievement which we can further improve by applying better optimization techniques.

References

1. Diffie, W., Hellman, M.: New directions in cryptography. IEEE Trans. Inf. Theory **22**(6), 644–654 (1976)
2. Boneh, D., Shparlinski, I.E.: On the unpredictability of bits of the elliptic curve Diffie-Hellman scheme. In: Kilian, J. (ed.) CRYPTO 2001. LNCS, vol. 2139, pp. 201–212. Springer, Heidelberg (2001). https://doi.org/10.1007/3-540-44647-8_12

3. Rivest, R., Shamir, A., Adleman, L.: A method for obtaining digital signatures and public-key cryptosystems. ACM Trans. Commun **21**, 120–126 (1978)
4. Gutub, A.A., Khan, F.A.: Hybrid crypto hardware utilizing symmetric-key & public-key cryptosystems. In: IEEE International Conference on Advanced Computer Science Applications and Technologies (ACSAT), pp. 116–121 (2013)
5. Nadjia, A., Mohamed, A.: AES IP for hybrid cryptosystem RSA-AES. In: IEEE 12th International Multi-Conference on Systems, Signals & Devices (SSD 2015), pp. 1–6 (2015)
6. Kapur, R.K., Khatri, S.K.: Secure data transfer in MANET using symmetric and asymmetric cryptography. In: IEEE International Conference on Reliability, Infocom Technologies and Optimization (ICRITO) (Trends and Future Directions), pp. 1–5 (2015)
7. Abdalla, M., Bellare, M., Rogaway, P.: The oracle Diffie-Hellman assumptions and an analysis of DHIES. In: Naccache, D. (ed.) CT-RSA 2001. LNCS, vol. 2020, pp. 143–158. Springer, Heidelberg (2001). https://doi.org/10.1007/3-540-45353-9_12
8. Martínez, V.G., Alvarez, F.H., Encinas, L.H., Ávila, C.S..: A comparison of the standardized versions of ECIES. In: IEEE Sixth International Conference on Information Assurance and Security (2010)
9. Martínez, V.G., Álvarez, F.H., Encinas, L. H.: Analysis of ECIES and other cryptosystems based on elliptic curves. CSIC Digital (2013)
10. Barker, E., Chen, L., Roginsky, A., Vassilev, A., Davis, R.: Recommendation for Pair-Wise Key-Establishment Schemes Using Discrete Logarithm Cryptography. NIST Special Publication 800-56A Revision 3, April 2018
11. Dworkin, M.: NIST Special Publication 800-38D: Recommendation for Block Cipher Modes of Operation: Galois/Counter Mode (GCM) and GMAC (2007)
12. Federal Information Processing Standards (FIPS) Publication 180-4,: Secure Hash Standard (SHS), vol. 4 (2015)
13. Satoh, A., Sugawara, T., Aoki, T.: High-speed pipelined hardware architecture for Galois counter mode. In: Garay, J.A., Lenstra, A.K., Mambo, M., Peralta, R. (eds.) ISC 2007. LNCS, vol. 4779, pp. 118–129. Springer, Heidelberg (2007). https://doi.org/10.1007/978-3-540-75496-1_8
14. Wang, J., Shou, G., Hu, Y., Guo, Z.: High-speed architectures for GHASH based on efficient bit-parallel multipliers. In: IEEE International Conference on Wireless Communications, Networking and Information Security (WCNIS), pp. 582–586 (2010)
15. Mastrovito, E.D.: VLSI architectures for computations in Galois fields. Ph.D. thesis, Linköping University, Department of Electrical Engineering, Linköping, Sweden (1991)
16. Montgomery, P.: Modular multiplication without trial division. Math. Comput. **44**, 519–521 (1985)
17. Zhou, G., Michalik, H., Hinsenkamp, L.: Improving throughput of AES-GCM with pipelined karatsuba multipliers on FPGAs. In: Becker, J., Woods, R., Athanas, P., Morgan, F. (eds.) ARC 2009. LNCS, vol. 5453, pp. 193–203. Springer, Heidelberg (2009). https://doi.org/10.1007/978-3-642-00641-8_20
18. Abdellatif, K.M., Chotin-Avot, R., Mehrez, H.: Authenticated encryption on FPGAs from the static part to the reconfigurable part. Microprocess. Microsyst. **38**(6), 526–538 (2014)
19. Abdellatif, K.M., Chotin-Avot, R., Mehrez, H.: AES-GCM and AEGIS: efficient and high speed hardware implementations. J. Signal Process. Syst. **88**(1), 1–12 (2017)
20. Sandoval, M.M., Uribe, C.F.: A hardware architecture for elliptic curve cryptography and lossless data compression. In: IEEE International Conference on Electronics, Communications and Computers, pp. 113–118 (2005)

Spatial Analysis of Groundwater Potential Using GIS Based Multi Criteria Decision Analysis Method in Lake Tana Basin, Ethiopia

Agumase T. Kindie[1,2(✉)], Temesegen Enku[2], Mamaru A. Moges[2],
Berhanu S. Geremew[1,2], and Haimanot B. Atinkut[3]

[1] Department of Hydraulic and Water Resource Engineering,
Gondar Institute of Technology, University of Gondar,
P.O. Box 196, Gondar, Ethiopia
agumasekt2006@gmail.com
[2] Department of Hydraulic and Water Resource, Engineering,
Faculty of Civil and Water Resource Engineering, Bahir Dar University,
P.O. Box 79, Bahir Dar, Ethiopia
[3] Colleges of Agriculture and Rural Transformation, University of Gondar,
P.O. Box 196, Gondar, Ethiopia

Abstract. Groundwater resource development for various uses is increasing in the Lake Tana basin, as surface water became limited in quantity and quality. Assessment of the groundwater potential (GWP) in the basin is crucial for sustainable use of water resources. This study aims at assessing the GWP in the basin using remote sensing and GIS-based Multi Criteria Decision Analysis (MCDA). Seven factors (lithology, lineaments, drainage density, rainfall, slope, land use/land cover and soils) that affect groundwater distribution were considered. Analytical Hierarchy Process (AHP) approach were used to compute each layer weight. Thematic weighted layers were overlaid in ArcGIS to identify GWP are-as in the basin. The result indicated that, 15% (1765 km^2) classified as "very high", 26.5% (3151 km^2) as "high", 31% (3592 km^2) as "medium", and 27.5% (3224 km^2) were classified as "low" GWP zones in the basin. The GWP map was validated using observed borehole and springs data in the basin, and it indicated that 76% of agreement. It was found that GWP was highly sensitive to lithology and rainfall with mean variation index of 2.7% and 2.0%, respectively. High GWP is available at the southern and eastern side of the Lake Tana.

Keywords: Groundwater · GIS and RS · Lake Tana · Blue Nile · Ethiopia

1 Introduction

Groundwater resource is an important natural resource for its use in agriculture, industries and domestic purposes. It is unevenly distributed both spatially and temporally all over the world. In northern Ethiopia, where rainfall is scarce and unevenly distributed; groundwater is the main source to meet various water demands [4]. The demand for groundwater in Lake Tana basin (LTB) has been increasing over the years [48]. Development of groundwater resources is essential to satisfy the increasing

© ICST Institute for Computer Sciences, Social Informatics and Telecommunications Engineering 2019
Published by Springer Nature Switzerland AG 2019. All Rights Reserved
F. A. Zimale et al. (Eds.): ICAST 2018, LNICST 274, pp. 439–456, 2019.
https://doi.org/10.1007/978-3-030-15357-1_37

demand [47]. In this area, groundwater recharge varies significantly in space and time due to the difference in distribution and amount of rainfall, permeability of rocks, geomorphology and availability of surface water bodies close to major unconfined and semi-confined aquifers that feed the groundwater [4–37].

There are several conventional methods, used to assess groundwater potential, some are: Ground surveys, Geophysical Methods such as resistivity, and ground penetrating radar; Probabilistic Models like Logistic Regression Methods [3] are unreliable and time consuming. There are also various statistical methods that were adopted for groundwater potential mapping such as frequency ratio [13–27], multi-criteria decision evaluation [16–43], weights-of-evidence model [29]; random forest model [24] maximum entropy model [30] boosted regression tree, classification and regression tree [24]. Remote sensing and Geographic Information System (GIS) techniques have become an easier, effective and time efficient in the assessment, monitoring and conservation of groundwater resources [45]. These days a number of researchers, [2, 10, 15, 19, 28] applied remote sensing and GIS through Analytical Hierarchy Process (AHP) for the assessment of groundwater potential.

Even though the importance of the groundwater resources is essential for development, limited groundwater studies have been carried out in the basin. The potential is not well defined. However, the government of Ethiopia has declared the Lake Tana – Beles as a growth corridor. Therefore, the objective of this study is to assess the groundwater potential in Lake Tana basin using Geographical Information System (GIS) and Remote Sensing (RS) based MCDA techniques, and to produce a groundwater potential map.

2   Methods and Materials

2.1   Description of the Study Area

Lake Tana basin is located in northwestern Ethiopia (Fig. 1), which feed to the Blue Nile River. Geographically, it is located between $10°57'–12°47'N$ and $36°38'–38°14'E$. The basin landscape is part of the western plateau of Ethiopia and includes the escarpments of Gondar and Gojjam, the lower plains surrounding the lake that forms extensive wetlands of Dembiya, Fogera, and Kunzila plains located in the north, east, and southwest of the lake, respectively. The basin has a total area of 15,320 km^2.

2.2   Data Collection and Preparation

In this study eight thematic layers (drainage density, rainfall, slope steepness, land cover/use, lineaments, soil and lithology) were used. The rainfall map was prepared using Inverse Distance Weighting (IDW) interpolation from 26 stations long term mean annual rainfall data. The lithology, soil, and land use are collected from Ethiopian Geological survey. These thematic layers were prepared using Arc GIS 10.1 platform. The drainage and lineament density maps have been prepared using the line density analysis tool in Arc GIS 10.1. The slope and drainage density were derived from

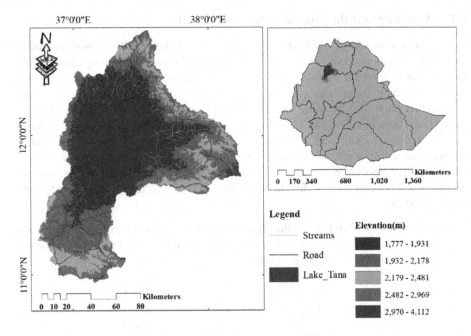

Fig. 1. Location map of Lake Tana basin

Shuttle Radar Terrain Mapping Digital Elevation Model (STRM DEM) of 30 m resolution. Arc Hydro tool was used to generate stream network and drainage density was calculated in Arc GIS 10.1 using Eq. 1 [12].

$$DD = \Sigma Li/A \tag{1}$$

Where, DD is drainage density; Li denotes the total length of streams (L) and A denotes the unit area.

Cloud free Landsat 8 Operational Land Imager (OLI) images (Row 52/Path 169, Row 51/Path 170, and Row 52/Path 170), dated June 17 and 24, 2017 were downloaded from USGS website (https://earthexplorer.usgs.gov) for lineament extraction. After applying principal component analysis (PCA) technique using ENVI 5.1 to produce uncorrelated output bands, to segregate noise components, and to reduce the dimensionality of data sets [25–43], lineaments were extracted automatically using PCI Geomatica 2017 trial version from Landsat 8 [23]. Lineament density was calculated in Arc GIS 10.1 using Eq. 2 [13].

$$LD = \Sigma Li/A \tag{2}$$

Where, LD is lineament density; Li is denotes the total length of lineaments (L) and A is denotes the unit area.

2.3 Weighting and Ranking of Each Layers (AHP)

Because all parameters do not have equal effect on groundwater distribution, ranking of each parameter is needed. Weighting each factor and a pair-wise comparison matrix were prepared for each map based on [34]. The rate/rank for classes in a layer and weights for each factor was assigned and a pair-wise comparison matrix has been prepared for each map by using Multi Criteria Decision Analysis technique based on Analytical Hierarchy Process (AHP) [35] by considering seven factors (lithology, lineament density, soil, and drainage, rainfall, slope and land use/cover). Square matrices are constructed, where each criterion is compared with the other criteria, relative to its importance, on Saaty's scale from 1 to 9 (Table 2). The rate/rank for classes in a layer and weights for thematic layers of each factor was calculated as the following steps:

1. Square matrix A = aij (Eq. 3) the element of row i column j was produced and the lower triangular matrix was Completed by taking the reciprocal values of the upper diagonal using the formula aij = 1/aij

$$A = \begin{pmatrix} \frac{p1}{P1} & \cdots & \cdots & \frac{P1}{Pj} & \cdots & \cdots & \frac{P1}{pn} \\ \frac{pi}{P1} & \cdots & \cdots & 1 & \cdots & \cdots & \frac{Pi}{pn} \\ \frac{pn}{P1} & \cdots & \cdots & \frac{Pn}{Pj} & \cdots & \cdots & 1\frac{Pn}{Pn} \end{pmatrix} \qquad (3)$$

2. Summation of all columns j matrix from (Eq. 3) using (Eq. 4)

$$\frac{p1}{Pi} + \ldots \frac{Pi}{Pj} + \ldots \frac{Pn}{Pn} = \left(\sum_{i=1}^{n} Pi\right)/Pi \qquad (4)$$

3. Divide each element of matrix aij = pi/pj (Eq. 3) by (Eq. 4) to get normalized relative weight (Eq. 5)

$$\frac{\frac{Pi}{Pj}}{\left(\sum_{i=1}^{n} Pi\right)/Pj} = \frac{Pi}{Pj} * \frac{Pj}{\sum_{i=1}^{n} Pi} = \frac{Pi}{\sum_{i=1}^{n} Pi} \qquad (5)$$

4. Averaging across the rows (Eq. 6) to get the normalized principal Eigen vector (priority vector) i.e. Rate (Ri) or weight of row 'i'(Wi). Since it is normalized, the sum of all elements in priority vector should be one.

$$W_i/R_{i=} \left(\frac{Pi}{\sum_{i=1}^{n} Pi} + \ldots + \frac{Pi}{\sum_{i=1}^{n} Pi}\right) * 1/n \qquad (6)$$

The judgments of the pair-wise comparison within each thematic layer were checked by the consistency ratio [35]. The consistency ratio (CR) is a measure of consistency of the pair-wise comparison matrix. Scholars [21–35] recommended that for matrices with CR rating greater than 0.1, the process is repeated until the desired value of CR < 0.1 is achieved. The value of CR is computed as (Eq. 7)

$$CR = CI/R \qquad (7)$$

where, RI is Saaty's ratio index; CI is Consistency index.

Consistency index is a measure of consistency or degree of consistency of the judgment [21–34] and computed using (Eq. 8).

$$CI = (\lambda max - n)/(n - 1) \qquad (8)$$

where, n is the number criterion, the value of RI for n criteria as indicated in Table 1.

Table 1. Random consistency index (RI)

Numbers of criteria (n)	Saaty's ratio index (RI)
1	0
2	0
3	0.58
4	0.9
5	1.12
6	1.24
7	1.32
8	1.41
9	1.45

To compute λmax, first multiply the normalized value by the respective Weight (Eq. 6) and then, the values of the product are added together to get λmax (Eq. 9)

$$\lambda max = \sum_{i=1}^{n} (Wi * (Pi / \sum_{i=1}^{n} Pi)) \qquad (9)$$

where, λmax, the largest Eigen value of the pair wise comparison matrix. Pi is the priority of the alternative and wi is the assigned rate/weight.

Table 2. Scale of preference between two parameters in AHP [34]

Scale	Degree of preference	Explanation
1	Equally	Two activities contribute equally to the objective
3	Moderately	The judgment slightly-to-moderately favor one activity
5	Strongly	The judgment strongly or essentially favor one activity
7	Very strongly	Very strong preference or importance
9	Extremely	Quite preferred or quite important
2, 4, 6, 8	Intermediate values	Preferences between the preferences in weights 1, 3, 5, 7 and 9

2.4   Overlay Analysis

After assigning the rates for classes in a layer and weights for thematic layers each factors the final map (Fig. 9) was obtained by overlaying all thematic maps using weighted overlay methods [19–21], using the spatial analysis tool in are G.I.S 10.1 as shown (Eq. 10)

$$GWP = \sum_{i=1}^{n} Wi * Ri \tag{10}$$

Where, GWP is groundwater potential zone; Wi is weight for each thematic layer and Ri; rates for the classes within a thematic layer derived from AHP.

2.5   Sensitivity Analysis

The map-removal sensitivity analysis was used to examine the impacts of removing one of the thematic layers in the computation of the GWP distribution map. The map removal sensitivity analyses [5–17] were used to identify the factors that affect the groundwater potential, details are shown in Table 4. In this method, each of the thematic layers are removed, and a new GWP map is obtained each time for the remaining layers overlaying each other. Map removal shows the sensitivity of the GWP map to the removal of one of the thematic layers. This analysis is expressed in terms of an index of sensitivity as shown (Eq. 11).

$$S = [((GWP/N) - (GWP'/n))/GWP] * 100 \tag{11}$$

where S is the index of sensitivity associated with the removal of one map; GWP is the groundwater potential index computed using all the thematic layers; GWP' is the groundwater potential index computed by excluding one thematic layer at a time; N and n are the number of thematic layers used to compute GWP and GWP', respectively.

3   Results and Discussion

3.1   Design and Preparation of Thematic Maps

Drainage Density (DD)
Drainage Density is expressed as the total length of all streams or rivers per unit drainage area [12, 13]. In areas where a higher drainage density is dominant, groundwater potential is generally poor, because less time for infiltration. Whereas, areas of low drainage density allow more infiltration to recharge the groundwater system [1–22]. Stream network derived from 30 m DEM, mainly six drainage density categories have been identified and mapped as shown in Fig. 2. The highest drainage density was found in the southern, eastern and northeastern part of the Lake Tana basin. However, moderate and low drainage density concentrates in the southern and central

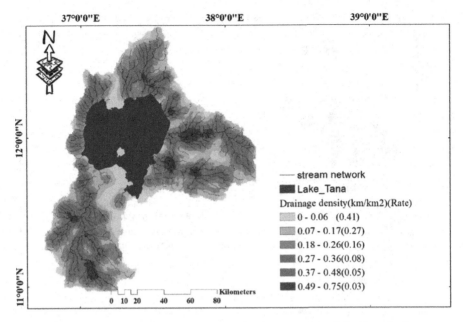

Fig. 2. Stream network and drainage density map of the Lake Tana basin

part of the lake basin. By using pairwise comparison, the rate was set based on groundwater potential for areas with low drainage density were assigned the higher rate, and high drainage density were assigned the lowest rate due to low groundwater potential. The lowest drainage density (0–0.06 km/km^2) were assigned the highest rate (0.41) and areas having higher drainage density 0.35–0.5 and 0.5–0.8 km/km^2 were assigned the lowest rate of 0.05 and 0.03, respectively.

Lineament Density (LD)

Lineaments are the simple and complex linear properties of geological structures like: faults, cleavages, fractures, and various surfaces of discontinuities (terraces and ridges) arranged in a straight line or a slight curve that are identified by remote sensing [25]. Lineaments were extracted automatically using Geomatica module, which is extracted from a single image of principal component analysis (PCA) and record the output as polyline with vector segment. Due to multispectral imaging bands are often highly correlated; Principal Components used to produce uncorrelated output bands, to segregate noise components, and to reduce the dimensionality of data sets [23–25]. This is done by finding a new set of orthogonal axes that have their origin at the data mean and that are rotated so the data variance is maximized. After applying Principal component analysis of Landsat images eight-bit gray scale lineaments are extracted automatically (Fig. 3). Areas with high lineament density are assumed good for groundwater potential [10–41]. From the result, the highest lineament density was observed in the North Eastern escarpments and South tip of the basin. As shown in Fig. 3, the highest lineament density (0.63–1.10 km/km^2) was assigned the maximum rank (0.39) and the lowest rate/rank (0.02) was assigned to the lineament density class of 0–0.083.

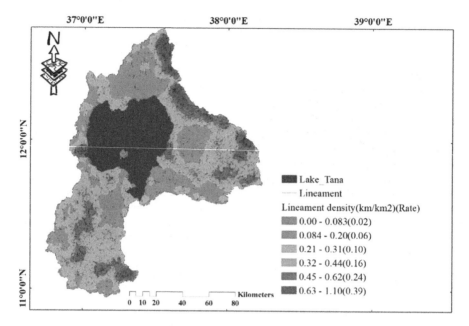

Fig. 3. Lineament density map

Slope

Slope defines the variation of elevation in a particular area which influences the runoff [24]. In gentle slopes, the movement of water is generally slow, which allows more infiltration. Whereas, in steep slopes runoff is favored and lower infiltration. Slope map has been derived from 30 m resolution DEM (Fig. 4). Slope varies from 0 to 72.8° and classified based on natural break classification method [26]. It classified in to six classes viz., 0–2.6, 2.6–6.7, 6.7–12.6, 12.6–19.4, 19.4–28.3, and 28.3–72.8. The highest rate (0.39) was assigned for the lowest slope gradient which is observed in central parts of the basin surrounding to Lake Tana and the lowest rate (0.02) was assigned for the highest slope gradient which found in northeastern, eastern and northern tip of the basin.

Rainfall

Rainfall is another factor that governs the amount of water that would be available to infiltrate and joins the groundwater zones, and thus it controls groundwater potential [42]. The rainfall map is classified into six classes using equal-interval classes [32]. Long term mean annual rainfall map of the area is prepared using IDW interpolation from 26 meteorological stations (Fig. 5). Based on the mean annual rainfall and its contribution for groundwater recharge; the relative weight (rate) was given for each rainfall classes. The rate was given based on the contribution to groundwater recharge, higher rate was assigned for high rainfall; and low rainfall areas were assigned the lowest rate for low groundwater potential [16]. Mean annual rainfall between 1713–2231 mm were assigned the highest rate (0.41), and 1507–1712 mm rainfall were assigned the next higher rate of 0.25. Areas having mean annual rainfall of 1039–1205 mm and less than 1000 mm mean annual rainfall were assigned the lowest rate as 0.05 and 0.03, respectively.

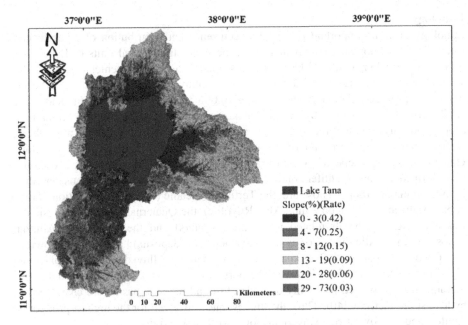

Fig. 4. Slope gradient of Lake Tana basin

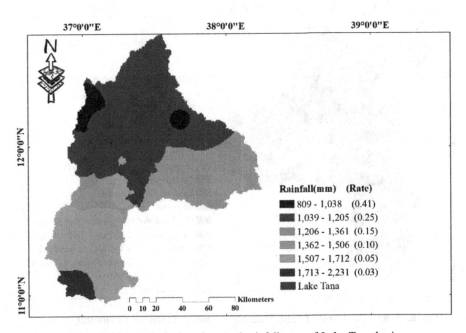

Fig. 5. Meteorological stations and rainfall map of Lake Tana basin

Lithology

Lithology plays an important role in the occurrence and distribution of groundwater. According to Ethiopian Geological survey, the major lithological units of Lake Tana basin are Tarmaber basalts (39.8%), Basalts related to volcanic center (26.5%), alluvium deposit (4.7%), lacustrine deposits (2.3%), colluvium (1.9%), Amba Aiba Basalts (0.07%), Lateriteon Amba Alaji Rhyolite (0.003%), marsh soil (4.7%), and Lake (20%). The basin covered by Basalts related to volcanic center mainly containing scoriaceous basalt widely found at southern part and the Tarmaber Basalts at northern, western and the southern end of the basin (6–7). The lowland covered by a thick Quaternary alluvial deposit (clay to gravel grain size), lacustrine deposits and Colluvium formed the major aquifer zones. Based on their age, the aquifer systems classified in to three major groups. Those are: the Tertiary Volcanic (Tarmaber formation, Amba Aiba Basalts and Lateriteon Amba Alaji Rhyolite), the Quaternary Fractured Vesicular Basalt (quaternary basalt related to volcanic centers) and the Quaternary Alluvial deposits such as Alluvium, Colluvium and Lacustrine deposits) [39, 40]. As shown as Fig. 6 the south part with Quaternary Basalt overlain by Alluvial Deposit displays the highest productive aquifer. However, the northern, southern and eastern mountainous regions, mostly covered by highly degraded tuff and massive basalt, are characterized by lowest productivity [40]. Thus, the highest rate was given for the highest productive aquifer, and the lowest rate was given for lowest productivity.

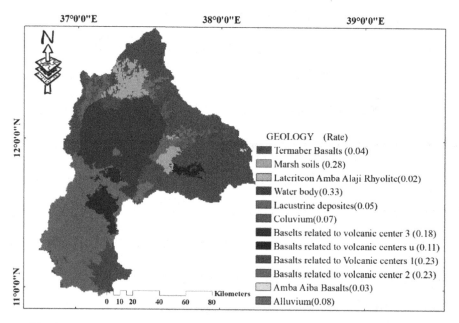

Fig. 6. Lithological map of Lake Tana basin (source: Ethiopian Geological survey)

Land Use/Land Cover

Land use cover significantly affects hydrological processes; i.e. interception, infiltration capacity of soil, runoff generation mechanism, are affected by the land use/land cover type. This in turn affect groundwater recharge and discharge [33]. Most of the study area is covered by cropland with sparse woodlands while only few limited areas of highlands are forested (less than 1% of the basin). The major land cover types are cropland 45%, wood land 18%, water body (20%), Grass land (13%), and bare land (2%) Forest (1%), and urban and built 0.2% [47]. As shown in Fig. 7 forests were assigned the highest rank due to less runoff because leaves and trees slow down the rain before it hits the ground, giving plant root's time to infiltrate and join into the groundwater system. From the pair-wise comparison, the rate was given based on contributions for groundwater recharge [38]. Highest rates were assigned for areas cover with water bodies (0.26) and swampy (0.19). Whereas, the lowest rates were given for cultivated (0.02) and urban areas (0.01).

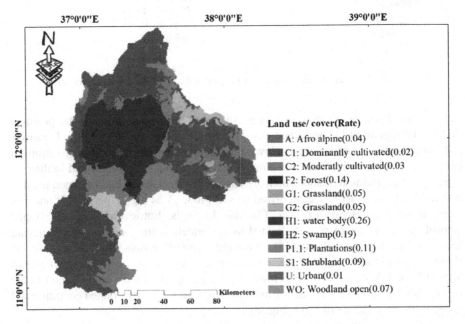

Fig. 7. Land use/land cover map of Lake Tana basin

Soil Group

Soil is an important factor for delineating the groundwater potential areas. Soil characteristics invariably control rates of infiltration; percolation and permeability [38–44]. Tana basin is covered by a wide range of soil groups. As shown Fig. 8, the major soils are: Haplic Luvisols which covers (26%), Chromic Luvisols (20%), Eutric Leptosols (16%), Eutric Vertisols (15%), Eutric Fluvisols (12%), Haplic Alisols (6%), Lithic Leptosols (3%), Haplic Nitisols as medium portion, and Eutric Regosols and Eutric Cambisols less than 1% of the basin. The southern part is covered by Hablic Luvisols

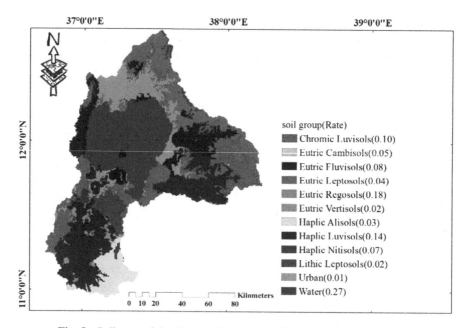

Fig. 8. Soil map of the Tana basin (source: Ethiopian Geological Survey)

and Chromic Livisols which have higher infiltration infers high groundwater potential [8]. The floodplain to the north and east of Lake Tana is covered by Eutric Leptosols and Eutric Vertisols which have the lowest infiltration rate. The major soil properties of Lake Tana basin are classified based on its texture, drainage condition and infiltration capacity. Thus, Eutric Regisols which are characterized by sandy loam to loam texture; It excessively drain and are categorized as soil group A as highly permeable and soil group B such as: Haplic Livisols, Chromic Livosols, Eutric Fluvisols and Haplic Nitosols are characterize as well drained to moderately drain condition due to having textural class of clay to silt clay [8]. Therefore, Eutric Regosols, Hablic Luvisols and chromic Livisols which have higher infiltration were given the relative weight (rate) of 0.18, 0.14 and 0.10, respectively. However, soil group like Eutric vertisols and Lithic Leptosols which contain clay texture and characterized by poorly drained condition and assigned the lowest rate of 0.02 (Fig. 8).

3.2   Combination of Thematic Layers

Since for all layers, the value of consistency ratio (CR) is less than 0.1 and, hence, the judgments of the pair-wise comparison within each thematic layer (Table 3) were acceptable [35]. Therefore, groundwater potential areas were obtained by the combination of all layers using overlay analysis method in Arc GIS 10.1 [22] using Eq. (12).

$$GWPZ = 0.38 * LT + 0.24 * LD + 0.16 * Soil + 0.10 * SL + 0.06 * DD + 0.04 \\ * RF + 0.02 * LU/C \tag{12}$$

Table 3. Pair-wise comparison matrix between all thematic layers (CR = 0.03)

Classes	GEO	LD	GM	SOIL	SL	DD	RF	LU	W
LT	1								0.38
LD	1/2	1							0.24
SOIL	1/4	1/2	1/2	1					0.16
SL	1/5	1/3	1/3	1/2	1				0.10
DD	1/6	1/5	1/4	1/2	1/2	1			0.06
RF	1/7	1/6	1/5	1/3	1/2	1/2	1		0.04
LU/C	1/9	1/7	1/6	1/5	1/4	1/3	1/2	1	0.02

where, W = Weight, LT = lithology, LD = lineament
density, SL = slope, DD = drainage density, RF = rainfall,
LU/C = land use/cover

As shown in Fig. 9, the southern and eastern part of the basin shows very high groundwater potential zones due to presence of Quaternary basalts related to volcanic centers which are highly productive, alluvial plain and gentle slope. Similar studies have been reported [18 36 & 38]. The least groundwater potential areas are found in south eastern and northern escarpments (tips) of study area. The result indicated that, about 15% (1765 km^2) classified as "very high," 26.5% (3151 km^2) as "high," 31% (3592 km^2) as "medium," and 27.5% (3224 km^2) were classified as "low" groundwater potential areas in the basin.

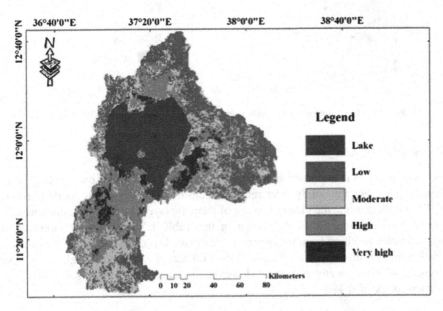

Fig. 9. Groundwater potential map of Lake Tana basin

3.3   Validation of Groundwater Potential Map

Validation of the groundwater potential zones were conducted using existing groundwater yield data of hand dug wells and/or bore holes and springs [9]. The groundwater potential map was verified with 195 existing boreholes and springs data (Fig. 10). Out of 195 existing water points (boreholes and springs) in which 149 (76%) were matched with its corresponding classes of groundwater potential zones (GWPZ). This indicates that, the groundwater potential map and actual borehole data shows good agreement.

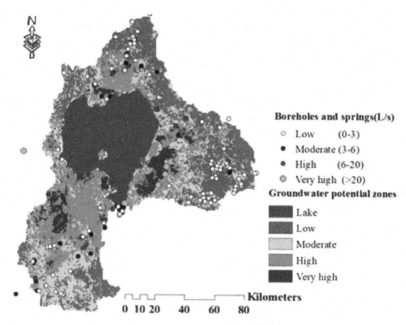

Fig. 10. Distribution of boreholes and springs with its yield in GWP zone

3.4   Sensitivity Analysis

Sensitivity analysis is important to know the influence of each factor on a ground-water potential map. For this study map removal, sensitivity analysis was used based on [5–17]. It indicates that the index variation of thematic layers by removing one thematic layer at a time using Eq. 6. As shown in the Table 4, the statistical summary of variation index resulting from removing each thematic layer was identified. The highest variation index with mean 2.65% associated to lithology, which is the highest sensitive parameter of groundwater potential. However, it is less sensitive to soil with mean variation index of 0.44%.

Table 4. Statistics of map removal sensitive analysis

Layer removed	Variation index (%)			
	Min	Max	Mean	SD
LT	0.75	3.14	2.70	3.79
LD	0.00	0.41	1.92	1.61
SOIL	0.40	0.45	0.44	0.46
SL	1.33	1.65	1.61	1.70
DD	0.00	0.77	0.89	2.99
RF	0.30	2.43	2.01	2.98
LU/C	1.53	1.58	1.53	1.52

where, Max = maximum,
Min = minimum, SD = standard
deviation, LT = lithology,
LD = lineament density,
GM = geomorphology, SL = slope,
DD = drainage density, RF = rainfall,
LU = land use/cover

4   Conclusions

The result of this study indicated that from the total area of the basin; about 27.5% (3224 km^2) classified as: "low", 30.6% (3592 km^2) "moderate", 26.9% (3151 km^2) "high", and 15% (1765 km^2) "very high" groundwater potential zones, excluding the lake area. Out of 195 existing (borehole and springs) data for validation; 149 (76.4%) were agreed with corresponding groundwater potential classes. High ground-water potential was found at the southern and eastern side of Lake Tana. Groundwater can be exploited in these areas. On the other side, the least potential areas were found in northern, eastern and southern escarpments (tips) of the basin, respectively. This was because of the characterization by high gradient mountains, steep slope, high drainage density, hills, and hard-rock formation, which contribute high run off and less infiltration. Hence, in order to meet the increasing demand, new well fields may be formed in high groundwater potential zones, especially in the southern and eastern part of Lake Tana basin. But, in low groundwater areas, soil and water conservation measures and integrated watershed management should be applied to improve groundwater recharge. Future detail geophysical survey investigation in the basin is required for better results.

Acknowledgments. The authors would like to thank three anonymous reviewers for their constructive and insightful comments and suggestions which contributed improve the manuscript. The first author would like to provide his gratitude to: Bahir Dar University, Institute of Technology, University of Gondar and Ethiopian Road Authority (ERA) for sponsorship, Abay Basin Authority (ABA) and Amhara Design Works and Supervision Enterprise (ADWSE) are acknowledged for providing data.

References

1. Agarwal, E., Agarwal, R., Garg, R.D., Garg, P.K.: Delineation of groundwater potential zone: an AHP/ANP approach. J. Earth Syst. Sci. **122**(3), 887–898 (2013)
2. Al-Abadi, A.M., Al-Shamma'a, A.: Groundwater potential mapping of the major aquifer in Northeastern Missan Governorate, South of Iraq by using analytical hierarchy process and GIS. J. Environ. Earth Sci. **10**, 125–149 (2014)
3. Alemayehu, T.: Groundwater Occurrence in Ethiopia, p. 107. Addis Ababa University, Addis Ababa (2006)
4. Al-Ruzouq, R., Shanableh, A., Merabtene, T.: Geomatics for mapping of ground-water potential zones in northern part of the United Arab Emiratis - Sharjah City. In: ISPRS - International Archives of the Photogrammetry, Remote Sensing and Spatial Information Sciences, XL-7/W3, pp. 581–586 (2015). https://doi.org/10.5194/isprsarchives-xl-7-w3-581-2015
5. Babiker, I.S., Mohamed, M.A., Hiyama, T., Kato, K.: A GIS-based DRASTIC model for assessing aquifer vulnerability in Kakamigahara Heights, Gifu Prefecture, central Japan. Sci. Total Environ. **345**(1), 127–140 (2005)
6. BCEOM: Abbay River Basin Integrated Development Master plan Project, Part-2, Hydrology (1998)
7. Chorowicz, J., Collet, B., Bonavia, F.F., Mohr, P., Parrot, J.F., Korme, T.: The Tana basin, Ethiopia: intra-plateau uplift, rifting and subsidence. Tectonophysics **295**(3), 351–367 (1998)
8. Daniel, Y.: Remote sensing based assessment of water resource potential for Lake Tana Basin. M. Sc. thesis, Addis Ababa University (2007)
9. Fashae, O.A., Tijani, M.N., Talabi, A.O., Adedeji, O.I.: Delineation of groundwater potential zones in the crystalline basement terrain of SW-Nigeria: an integrated GIS and remote sensing approach. Appl. Water Sci. **4**(1), 19–38 (2014)
10. Fenta, A.A.: Spatial analysis of groundwater potential using remote sensing and GIS-based multi-criteria evaluation in Raya Valley. Hydrogeol. J. (2014). https://doi.org/10.1007/s10040-014-1198-x
11. Thannoun, R.G.: Automatic extraction and geospatial analysis of lineaments and their tectonic significance in some areas of Northern Iraq using remote sensing techniques and GIS. Int. J. Enhanc. Res. Sci. Technol. Eng. Bull. **2** (2013)
12. Greenbaum, D.: Review of remote sensing applications to groundwater exploration in basement and regolith (1985)
13. Guru, B., Seshan, K., Bera, S.: Frequency ratio model for groundwater potential mapping and its sustainable management in cold desert, India. J. King Saud Univ. Sci. **29**(3), 333–347 (2017)
14. Horton, R.E.: Drainage-basin characteristics. Eos Trans. Am. Geo Phys. Union **13**(1), 350–361 (1932)
15. Jaiswal, R.K., Mukherjee, S., Krishnamurthy, J., Saxena, R.: Role of remote sensing and GIS techniques for generation of groundwater prospect zones towards rural development–an approach. Int. J. Remote Sens. **24**(5), 993–1008 (2003)
16. Kumar, T., Gautam, A.K., Kumar, T.: Appraising the accuracy of GIS-based multi-criteria decision making technique for delineation of groundwater potential zones. Water Resour. Manage **28**(13), 4449–4466 (2014)
17. Lodwick, W.A., Monson, W., Svoboda, L.: Attribute error and sensitivity analysis of map operations in geographical information systems: suitability analysis. Int. J. Geogr. Inf. Syst. **4**(4), 413–428 (1990)

18. MacDonald, A.M., Calow, R.C., Nicol, A.L., Hope, B., Robins, N.S.: Ethiopia: water security and drought (2001)
19. Magesh, N.S., Chandrasekar, N., Soundranayagam, J.P.: Delineation of groundwater potential zones in Theni district, Tamil Nadu, using remote sensing, GIS and MIF techniques. Geosci. Front. **3**(2), 189–196 (2012)
20. Malczewski, J.: GIS and Multicriteria Decision Analysis. Wiley, New York (1999)
21. Malczewski, J.: GIS-based multicriteria decision analysis: a survey of the literature. Int. J. Geogr. Inf. Sci. **20**(7), 703–726 (2006)
22. Murasingh, S.: Analysis of groundwater potential zones using electrical resistivity, RS & GIS techniques in a typical mine area of Odisha (2014)
23. Hassan, M.A., Adhab, S.S.: Lineament automatic extraction analysis for Galal Badra river basin using Landsat 8 satellite image. Iraqi J. Phys. **12**(25), 44–55 (2014)
24. Naghibi, S.A., Pourghasemi, H.R., Dixon, B.: GIS-based groundwater potential mapping using boosted regression tree, classification and regression tree, and random forest machine learning models in Iran. Environ. Monit. Assess. **188**(1), 44 (2016)
25. O'Leary, D.W., Friedman, J.D., Pohn, H.A.: Lineament, linear, lineation: some pro-posed new standards for old terms. Geol. Soc. Am. Bull. **87**(10), 1463–1469 (1976)
26. Osaragi, T.: Classification methods for spatial data representation (2002)
27. Ozdemir, A.: GIS-based groundwater spring potential mapping in the Sultan Mountains (Konya, Turkey) using frequency ratio, weights of evidence and logistic regression methods and their comparison. J. Hydrol. **411**(3), 290–308 (2011)
28. Pinto, D., Shrestha, S., Babel, M.S., Ninsawat, S.: Delineation of groundwater potential zones in the Comoro watershed, Timor Leste using GIS, remote sensing and analytic hierarchy process (AHP) technique. Appl. Water Sci. **7**(1), 503–519 (2017)
29. Pourghasemi, H.R., Beheshtirad, M.: Assessment of a data-driven evidential belief function model and GIS for groundwater potential mapping in the Koohrang Watershed, Iran. Geocarto Int. **30**(6), 662–685 (2015)
30. Rahmati, O., Pourghasemi, H.R., Melesse, A.M.: Application of GIS-based data driven random forest and maximum entropy models for groundwater potential mapping: a case study at Mehran Region, Iran. Catena **137**, 360–372 (2016)
31. Richards, J.A.: Remote Sensing Digital Image Analysis: An Introduction, p. 240. Springer, Berlin (1999). https://doi.org/10.1007/978-3-642-30062-2
32. Rose, R.S.S., Krishnan, N.: Spatial analysis of groundwater potential using remote sensing and GIS in the Kanyakumari and Nambiyar basins, India. J. Indian Soc. Remote Sens. **37**(4), 681–692 (2009)
33. Roy, S., Sahu, A.S.: Investigation for potential groundwater recharge area over the Kunur river basin, Eastern India: an integrated approach with geosciences. J. Geomat. **9**(2), 165–177 (2015)
34. Saaty, T.L.: The Analytic Hierarchy Process: Planning, Priority Setting, Resource Allocation, p. 287. MacGraw-Hill, New York International Book Company, New York (1980)
35. Saaty, T.L.: How to make a decision: the analytic hierarchy process. Eur. J. Oper. Res. **48**(1), 9–26 (1990)
36. Sedrette, R.: Automatic extraction of lineaments from Landsat Etm+ images and their structural interpretation: case Study in Nefza region (North West of Tunisia). J. Res. Environ. Earth Sci. **04**(2016), 139–145 (2016)
37. Seifu, K.: Groundwater in Ethiopia. Springer Hydrogeology. Springer, Heidelberg (2013). https://doi.org/10.1007/978-3-642-30391-3_2
38. Sisay, L.: Application of Remote Sensing and GIS for Groundwater Potential Zone Mapping in Northern Ada'a Plain (Modjo Catchment) (2007)

39. SMEC, IP.: Hydrological Study of The Tana-Beles Sub-Basins, part 1. Sub-basins Groundwater Investigation report (2007)

40. SOGREAH: Consulting service for detailed groundwater investigation & monitoring in tana and Beles sub-basins stage 1 final report (unpublished), Volume II - Part 6: Hydrogeological Survey (2013)

41. Subagunasekar, M., Sashikkumar, M.C.: GIS for the assessment of the groundwater recharge potential zone in Karunkulam block, Thoothukudi district, Tamil Nadu, India. Int. J. Curr. Sci. **15**, 159–162 (2012)

42. Terzer, S., Wassenaar, L.I., Araguás-Araguás, L.J., Aggarwal, P.K.: Global isoscapes for [delta] 18O and [delta] 2H in precipitation: improved prediction using regionalized climatic regression models. Hydrol. Earth Syst. Sci. **17**(11), 4713 (2013)

43. Thannoun, R.G.: Automatic extraction and geospatial analysis of lineaments and their tectonic significance in some areas of Northern Iraq using remote sensing techniques and GIS. Int. J. Enhanc. Res. Sci. Technol. Eng. Bull. **2** (2013)

44. Thapa, R., Gupta, S., Guin, S., Kaur, H.: Assessment of groundwater potential zones using multi-influencing factor (MIF) and GIS: a case study from Birbhum district, West Bengal. Appl. Water Sci. **7**, 4117–4131 (2017)

45. Tiwari, A.K., Lavy, M., Amanzio, G., De Maio, M., Singh, P.K., Mahato, M.K.: Identification of artificial groundwater recharging zone using a GIS-based fuzzy logic approach: a case study in a coal mine area of the Damodar Valley, India. Appl. Water Sci. **7**, 4513–4524 (2017)

46. Waikar, M.L., Nilawar, A.P.: Identification of groundwater potential zone using remote sensing and GIS technique. Int. J. Innov. Res. Sci. Eng. Technol. **3**(5), 1264–1274 (2014)

47. Wale, A.: Hydrological Balance of Lake Tana Upper Blue Nile Basin, Ethiopia (2008)

48. Worqlul, A.W., Collick, A.S., Rossiter, D.G., Langan, S., Steenhuis, T.S.: Assessment of surface water irrigation potential in the Ethiopian highlands: The Lake Tana Basin. CATENA **129**, 76–85 (2015)

Hydrothermal Synthesis of Na-P$_1$ Zeolite from Pumice to Enhance Moisture Content and Water Retention Capacity of Sandy Soil

Yonas Desta[1($\boxtimes$)], Nigus Gabbiye[2], and Agegnehu Alemu[2]

[1] Department of Chemical Engineering,
Kombolcha Institute of Technology, Kombolcha, Ethiopia
yonasdesta27@gmail.com
[2] Department of Chemical and Food Engineering, Bahir dar Institute
of Technology, Bahir Dar University, Bahir Dar, Ethiopia
nigushabtu@gmail.com, agegnehua@gmail.com

Abstract. In this study, pumice as a precursor from Semen Shoa, Minjar Shenkora Woreda was used in synthesis of Na-P$_1$ zeolite. Hydrothermal treatment was performed with sodium hydroxide at different ratio of pumice to NaOH pellets (1:1.2, 1:1.5 and 1:1.8) at varying temperatures of 60, 80 and 100 °C and reaction time of 70,100 and 130 min. Effect of pumice to NaOH ratio, reaction temperature and reaction time on Si/Al ratio of synthesized zeolite was studied. Optimal silica to alumna ratio of 2.5 was obtained at temperature of 100 °C, reaction time of 100 min and pumice to NaOH ratio of 1:1.5. Na-P$_1$ zeolite obtained at optimum operating conditions was used for other characterizations such as FTIR, XRD and surface area analysis and for the moisture testing & pressure plate extractor testing. The surface area for this zeolite was found to be 56.04 m^2/g. The XRD patterns of the synthesized material after formation of zeolite Na-P$_1$ was observed through reflections on 2θ = 19.31°, 23.44°, 28.32°, 32.43°, 33.5° and 49.10°. The synthesized zeolite showed the most prominent reflection peak at 32.43°. Effects of different dozes of the synthesized zeolite on sandy soil moisture content and water retention capacity were studied. As the dose of zeolite increased from 0 g/kg to 20 g/kg, the rate of moisture loss from sandy soil decreased. The results showed that application of zeolite to the sandy soil significantly increased the moisture content in the mixtures of soil-zeolite. The water holding capacity of the amended soil was tested using pressure plate extractor at 1, 3, 5 and 15 bars. At 0 bars, all soil samples were observed to have the same water content since at the beginning all soil samples had been moistened with water (70% by weight. Then at 1 bar sandy soil without zeolite had a moisture content about 12% whereas sandy soil with 10 g/kg had 15.65%. As the amount of zeolite added increased from 10 g/kg to 15 g/kg and to 20 g/kg, it was observed that adding zeolite on the sandy soil increases the water retention capacity of the soil.

Keywords: Pumice · Na-P$_1$ zeolites · Hydrothermal synthesis · Moisture content · Water holding capacity · Pressure plate extractor

© ICST Institute for Computer Sciences, Social Informatics and Telecommunications Engineering 2019
Published by Springer Nature Switzerland AG 2019. All Rights Reserved
F. A. Zimale et al. (Eds.): ICAST 2018, LNICST 274, pp. 457–472, 2019.
https://doi.org/10.1007/978-3-030-15357-1_38

1 Introduction

An understanding of the nature of soils in natural and human influence ecosystems is essential [1]. Soil water retention is a major soil hydraulic property that governs soil functioning in ecosystems and greatly affects soil management. Extensive research has shown that water retention is a complex function of soil structure and composition [2, 3]. Soil organic matter content and composition affect both soil structure and adsorption properties; therefore, water retention may be affected by changes in soil organic matter that occur because of both climate change and modifications of management practices. Thus, effects of organic matter on soil water retention should be understood and quantified [4].

Basically the soil particle size, the soil particle size distribution, and the structure of the soil determine the moisture characteristics (soil water relationships). Soil particles are basically composed of sands, silt, clays and organic matter [5]. Soil texture and structure greatly influence water infiltration, permeability, and water-holding capacity [6]. Soil texture refers to the composition of the soil in terms of the proportion of small, medium, and large particles (clay, silt, and sand, respectively) in a specific soil mass [7]. The contents of particle size classes (sand, 2.0–0.05 mm; silt, 0.05–0.002 mm; and clay, <0.002 mm) are presented according to the FAO/USDA classification system [2]. Soils with smaller particles (silt and clay) have a larger surface area than those with larger sand particles, and a large surface area allows a soil to hold more water [8]. Sand has large particles which take up a lot of physical space. Also, as sand particles do not bind water, a lot of water will drain out of the sand due to gravity before field capacity is reached. For these two reasons, sand has much lower maximum and minimum water content than a clay soil does. The low content of clay in sandy soils usually limits humus accumulation, nutrients, and water availability as well as buffering capacity, which is a reason why many of these soils become acidified [9].

Contrary to most other African soils, the majority of Ethiopian highlands soils remain relatively fertile at depth [10]. All over Ethiopia there are varied rates of soil degradation due to climate, soil types, biological conditions, and plant life and farming systems. The soil is not getting the nutrients that it needs to grow vegetation. Salinization and acidification is seriously affecting crop yield and agriculture productivity [11].

The best sandy soil amendments are ones that increase the ability of the sandy soil to retain water and increase the nutrients in the soil as well [12]. One of the measures considered highly effective, biologically justified and environmentally safe, especially on degraded and other soils having unfavorable productive traits for crop cultivation, is the use of zeolite mineral [13]. Zeolites can be successfully used in cultivating different crops such as cereals, forage crops, vegetables, vine and fruit crops [14]. Their use in crop production stems primarily from high nutrient-exchange capacities, which allow them to absorb and release plant nutrients and moisture without any change in the nature of the zeolite [15]. In addition, zeolite adds a permanent water reservoir, providing prolonged moisture holding power during dry periods and it promotes rapid re-wetting and improved lateral spread of water in the root zone during irrigation [16].

Taking into account problem of sandy soils, it was found an immediate concern and essential to treat sandy soil with synthetic zeolite in order to keep moisture content of sandy for longer period. Therefore, this study, based on pot experiment, was aimed at synthesize of Na-P$_1$ from pumice, locally available rock, and analyzing moisture content and testing water retention capacity of sandy soils.

2 Materials and Methods

2.1 Chemicals

NaOH was used to activate raw pumice before slurry preparation. Sulfuric acid (98%) was used for pH adjusting until a gel is formed. Analytical grade aluminium sulphate $Al_2(SO_4)_3$ and bentonite ($Al_2O_34SiO_2H_2O$) were used as a precursor for the standard solution preparation. Sodium hexametaphosphate was used as dispersing agent during soil texture analysis. Sandy soil was collected from Wollo farm land since it is the nearest when compared with others. And also clay, other type of soil that was collected from farm land (around Bahir dar) and used as control sample.

2.2 Instruments and Equipment

Electric furnace (Nabertherm B180, Germany) was used to activate the mixture of sodium hydroxide. Digital autoclave (Lx-B50L) which was available in environmental laboratory was used for crystallization of gel to get crystalline zeolite. All the above instruments were available in Bahir Dar Institute of Technology. After synthesis of zeolite different characterization techniques such as X-ray Diffraction, Induced Coupled Plasma-Optical Emission Spectroscopy Horiba Scientific and Fourier Transformed Infrared Radiation were used. Characterization of XRD and FTIR were conducted at Addis Ababa University, Faculty of Science whereas elemental analysis using ICP-EOS and surface area measurement using analytical methods (UV-VIS) were conducted at Bahir Dar Institute of Technology Research Grade Lab. Hydrometer (152H) was used for soil texture analysis. Pressure plate extractor (1500F215) was used to analyze the water-holding capacity of soil samples throughout the pressure range of interest. All soil testing materials and equipment were available at Bahir Dar Institute of Technology Soil Laboratory.

2.3 Experimental Procedure

Pumice Collection and Preparation

The main material used in this work was pumice grain and it was collected from Debrebirhan, Shenkora wereda, around Arerti town (coordinate 097°, 90′ 36″N, 054°, 69′15″E) which is 150 km away from Addis Ababa. The pumice was dried at room temperature and ground using jaw crusher and sieved using 75 μm pore size. In order to determine the optimum amount of NaOH that can be used for zeolitization process, different ratio of pumice to NaOH were used. In this Na-P$_1$ zeolite synthesis pumice powder was mixed with different amount of NaOH (ratio of pumice to NaOH (g/g), 1:1.2, 1:1.5 and 1:1.8) [17] and activated at 600 °C in furnace.

Activating Raw Pumice Using Sodium Hydroxide

Fixed amount of pumice (14 g) was weighed and mixed with different amount of NaOH (ratio of pumice to NaOH (g/g), 1:1.2, 1:1.5 and 1:1.8) to see the effect of sodium hydroxide on zeolitezation process. Hence, for the first ratio 16.8 g of NaOH pellet was mixed to the 14 g pumice powder (1:1.2), and put into the furnace using crucible for activation. Then the furnace was adjusted to 600 °C for 1 h. After withdrawal of the sample from furnace, it was again grounded to fine particles. Similarly for the 2nd ratio (1:1.5), 21 g of NaOH pellet was weighed and added to the 14 g pumice and put to the furnace with same activation temperature and duration. Similarly, the third ratio of pumice to sodium hydroxide (1:1.8) was also activated.

The Formation of Aluminosilicate Gel as Zeolite Precursor

After preparation of the required pumice to sodium hydroxide ratio, the fused product was dissolved in appropriate amount of distilled water (with a ratio of fused product to volume of distilled water to be 1/4.9 g/ml) [18]. In this step, the slurry was heated on a magnetic stirrer hot plate under vigorous stirring at temperatures of 60, 80 and 100 °C and stirring time of 70, 100 and 130 min. The filtered solution was taken and adjusted its pH to be less than 10 by using H_2SO_4.

Crystallization of Zeolite

After white amorphous gel formation, the resulting gel was then transferred into a beaker. The beaker was placed into autoclave and left for crystallization for 2 days at 180 °C under autogenous pressure. Then, the zeolite products were separated from the solution and recovered by filtration followed by washing the zeolite crystals with distilled water several times until pH of 9-10 of the filtrate was achieved. The zeolites products were then dried in an oven for 24 h at 110 °C. For calcinations, the dried powder was heated to 80 °C and kept at this temperature for 2 h. After that, the product was milled to convert it to a fine powder, which was sieved to a particles size ≤ 75 μm for further analysis.

2.4   Determination of Surface Area of Na-P$_1$ Zeolite Using Methylene Blue Adsorption

The surface area of zeolite was determined by using methylene blue solution. It was done through three steps. The first step was determination of λmax of absorption. This step was done by measurement of absorbance of the methylene blue solution 2.0 mg/L with ranges of wave length from 500–700 nm [19]. Secondly, using the maximum wave length, the calibration curve of methylene blue was done by measuring the absorbance of methylene blue in the variation of concentration (1, 2, 3, 4 and 5 mg/L). The data obtained was used to make the calibration curve. Then 3 g of Na-P$_1$ zeolite was added to 1000 ml methylene blue having 50 mg/L concentration. The amounts of methylene blue were contacted with the zeolite in variation of time (30, 40, 50, 60 and 70 min). Absorbance of the methylene blue remained in each contact time are used to substitute y value of the regression equation and therefore the x-values of the equation could be calculated. Amounts of adsorbed methylene blue were difference between the initial concentrations (50 mg/L) with amounts of remnant. The result of calculation was used to draw a curve: number of adsorbed methylene blue (x) per gram of adsorbent

(m) versus time of contact. The optimum amount of methylene blue adsorbed could be used to calculate the surface area of adsorbent by using equation [20]:

$$S_A = \frac{Wm*N*A}{M} \qquad (1)$$

Where; Wm = Methylene blue (mg) adsorbed per gram of Na-P$_1$ zeolite
N = Avogadro's number (6.022 * 10^{23} mol)
A = surface area of one mole of methylene blue (197 * 10^{-20} m^2/g)
M = Mass of 1 mol methylene blue (320.5 g/mole)

2.5   Effect of Na-P$_1$ Zeolite on Sandy Soil Moisture Content and Water Retention Capacity

Sandy soil was collected from Meket Woreda (in Wollo) to 30 cm depth in an agricultural field (coordinate 11°, 12' 10"N, 38°, 56' 36"E) which is 130 km away from Bahir Dar. Clay soil was collected from farm land (around Bahir dar). After collection, the soil was put in oven at 80 °C for 2 h and allowed to pass through a 5 mm sieve before analysis. But before investigating the effect of zeolite onto sandy soil moisture content and water retention capacity, the soil has to be checked that it was sandy soil using hydrometer analysis.

Effect of Na-P$_1$ Zeolite on Sandy Soil Moisture Content
In sandy soil treatments, 0, 10, 15 and 20 g/kg of Na-P$_1$ zeolite were used with duplication. For all treatments 1000 g of sandy soil was placed in a plastic container. And also 1000 g of clay soil without zeolite was taken as a control. Then, zeolite was added to the sandy soil and mixed well. Then all soil and zeolite mixtures were moistened with tap water to a water content of 40% (w/w). All treatments were then treated under identical conditions. The plastic containers were weighed every 2 h interval for 20 h to determine the soil moisture content using the following formula.

$$\text{Moisture content } (\%) = \frac{W_t}{m_i} \times 100 \qquad (2)$$

Where: $w_t = m_i\text{-}m_f$ = Mass of water with container after certain time interval (g)
m_i = Mass of soil with container after moistened with water to 40% (w/w)
m_f = Mass of soil with container after certain time interval (g)

Effect of Na-P$_1$ Zeolite on Sandy Soil Water Holding Capacity
Sandy soil preparation for water holding capacity measurement was similar to that of moisture content measuring. For this 50 g of sandy soil was mixed with 10, 15 and 20 g zeolite and moistened with tap water to a water content of 70% by weight. Then the mixture was packed into brass rings. Thereafter, a pressure plate extractor was used to measure water retention at matric potentials of 1, 3, 5 and 15 bars. Water retention was measured in a constant room temperature to minimize changing temperature effects on soil water characteristics.

Measuring Moisture at Different Pressures

Two 1 bar ceramic plates were submerged in water for 24 h to saturate. Then plates were placed on a workbench. The brass rings containing 50 g dried sandy soils with 0, 10, 15 and 20 g/kg and clay soil that were moistened with tap water to a water content of 70% by weight were placed on the plate. The triangular support was placed in the extractor vessel on the bottom. Then the plastic spaces should be placed between plates. In order to collect the extracted water, outflow tubes were connected. The extractor was closed and tightened, ensuring that the "O" ring is in place and all nuts were uniformly tightened. Then a pressure of 1.0 bar was applied. A beaker was placed to collect water from the outflow tubes. Pressure was maintained until no more water was being released for 24 h. Pressure from extractor was released. Finally the extractor was opened and the water collected in beaker was measured. A similar fashion was followed to measure water retention capacity of sandy soil at 3, 5 and 15 bars as it was followed for 1.0 bar. The only difference was the pressure supplied. The pressures applied were 3, 5 & 15 bars and after pressure was released from extractor the corresponding water collected in a beaker was measured.

3 Results and Discussions

3.1 Characterization of Pumice and Na-P$_1$ Zeolite

Determination of Si to Al ratio of Na-P$_1$ Zeolite

The results of elemental composition for major elements (Si and Al) in ICP-EOS were expressed in mg/l. The concentrations of all the analysis solutions were determined on the basis of the calibration points. The obtained result is in agreement with the Si/Al ratio of Na-P$_1$ zeolite reported elsewhere [21] which is in the range of 2 to 3. At low value of pumice to NaOH ratio, reaction temperature and reaction time the obtained Si to Al ratio was low. The gel obtained at these low operation conditions requires longer aging period and longer hydrothermal treatment to obtain very crystalline zeolite. Hence, at lower operating conditions the obtained zeolite cannot be selected as optimal Si/Al ratio. Therefore the optimum operating conditions at pumice to sodium hydroxide, reaction temperature and reaction time were 1:1.5, 100 °C and 100 min respectively. Na-P$_1$ zeolite obtained at these operating conditions was used for other characterizations such as FTIR, XRD and surface area analysis.

FTIR Analysis of Pumice and Na-P1 Zeolite

Comparison of IR spectra of raw pumice and zeolite Na-P$_1$ is shown in Figs. 1 and 2 respectively. Pumice showed a band at 3588 cm^{-1}, which is attributed to free OH stretching vibration. An absorption band at 1663 and 1473 cm^{-1} is due to the bending vibration of adsorbed water molecule.

Vibration bands in a region of TO$_4$ tetrahedral units of pumice at about 1,000 cm^{-1}, 799 cm^{-1}, 663 cm^{-1} and 472 cm^{-1} are asymmetric stretching (internal vibration of (Si, Al)–O), symmetric stretching (internal vibration of (Si, Al)–O), double ring and T-O bending vibration (bending mode of Si–O–Al vibration) respectively. Na-P$_1$ zeolite showed Al-O-H vibration stretching bands around (3601–3355) cm^{-1}. A strong

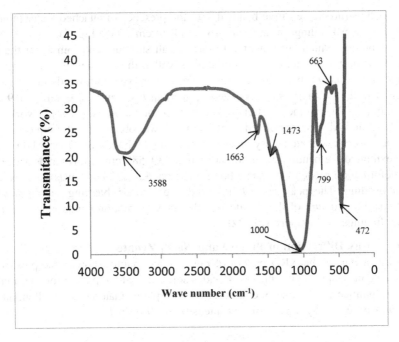

Fig. 1. FIR spectra of raw pumice

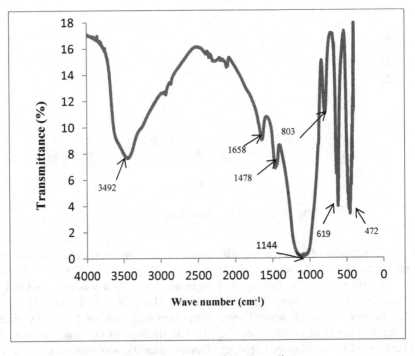

Fig. 2. IR spectra of Na-P$_1$ zeolite

characteristic structure sensitive bands due to the presence of attached water molecule indicates a water bending vibration at (1658, 1478) cm^{-1} (see Fig. 2).

The vibration which are sensitive to the overall structure and joining of the individual tetrahedral in secondary structural unit as well as their existence in the large pore openings are of second types of vibrations. These were vibration bands in a region of TO$_4$ tetrahedral (T = Si or Al) units of zeolite at about 1144 cm^{-1}, 803 cm^{-1}, 619 cm^{-1} and 472 cm^{-1}. The symmetric stretching vibrations of zeolite Na-P$_1$ framework structure of Si–O and Al–O were noticed at, 803 cm^{-1}. It was observed that, frequencies near 1144 cm^{-1} were ascribed to asymmetric stretching of bonds Si–O or Al–O. Na-P$_1$ zeolite exhibited the bending vibration at around 430–580 cm^{-1}, this bands are related to the deformation mode of the same bonds. The band at 472 cm^{-1} was assigned to be O-Si-O bending. The peak at 619 cm^{-1} indicates the double ring vibration which constitutes the structure of the zeolite. All the above vibration bands were consistent with the findings of Sudaporn [21, 22].

Powder X-Ray Diffraction of Pumice and Na-P$_1$ Zeolite

As shown in Fig. 3, the XRD pattern of raw pumice mainly showed the presence of crystalline quartz and mullite phases. Besides some crystalline phases (quartz, mullite, hematite), pumice was primarily composed of amorphous material. A small amount of quartz was observed by a peak of low intensity at 2θ = 26.7°.

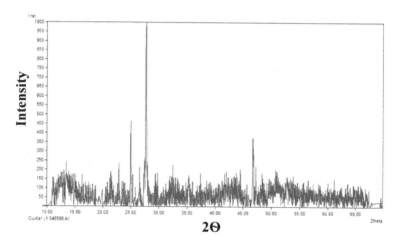

Fig. 3. X-ray diffraction (XRD) of pumice

In XRD patterns of pumice impurities such as mullite, hematite were observed through reflections on two theta values (2θ = 12.48°, 17.66°, 21.89°, 28.29° and 33.4°). This was consistent with the findings of Chigondo et al. which was observed to have reflections on two theta values (2θ = 12.4°, 17.7°, 21.8°, 28.2° and 33.5°) [23].

After pumice treatment, several sharp diffraction peaks of great intensity emerge confirming formation of zeolites (see Fig. 4). The findings of this study showed that XRD patterns of the synthesized product obtained after the zeolitization process from pumice, the formation of zeolite Na-P$_1$ was observed through reflections on 2θ = 19.31°, 23.44°, 28.32°, 32.43°, 33.5° and 49.10° which was consistent with data from other study by Hildebrandoa et al. [24]. According to Hildebrandoa et al., the formation of Na-P$_1$ zeolite was observed through reflections on 2θ = 12.4°, 17.7°, 21.8°, 28.2° and 33.5° [24]. A similar peak reflections result was also observed elsewhere (Rodrigues [25]) in which Na-P$_1$ zeolite was synthesized from coal fly ash. According to Rodrigues, the X-ray diffraction analysis showed the presence of Na-P$_1$ zeolite in the synthesized sample as evidenced from reflections near 2θ = 12.4°, 17.8°, 21.7°, 28.2°, 33.3°, 35.76°, 38.01°, 42.20° and 44.18° [25]. It can be said in general that, the material synthesized showed the most prominent reflection peak at 32.43° indicating highly crystalline of the material. While the peaks positioned in 34.88°, 41.09° and 47.39° may be zeolite A or 35.05°, 38.94° and 44.12° zeolite Y and this result was also consistent with finding presented by Rodrigues [25]. The result obtained in this study showed that almost complete transformation of pumice into Na-P$_1$ zeolite of high purity.

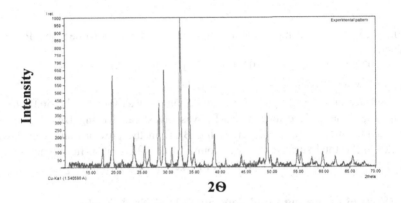

Fig. 4. X-Ray diffraction (XRD) of Na-P$_1$ Zeolite

Determination of Surface Area of Na-P$_1$ Zeolite Using Methylene Blue Adsorption
Based on the spectra, the λmax of the methylene blue was 660 nm. The linear regression equation was y = 0.144x − 0.052 with R^2 = 0.9972. This equation would be used to measure the remains concentration of the methylene blue that was unable adsorbed by the zeolite matrices. The absorbance measurement of the remnant of 50 mg/L of 1000 ml methylene blue after adsorption with 3 g Na-P$_1$ zeolite with time was.

The methylene blue adsorbed by zeolite matrices was used to interpret the surface area of the zeolite. The result of calculation of number of adsorbed methylene blue (x) per gram of adsorbent (m) versus time of contact (30, 40, 50, 60 and 70 min) was shown in Fig. 5. Data reported in Fig. 5 indicate that the optimum time of contact was 60 min (at 15 mg of methylene blue per gram adsorbent (Na-P$_1$ zeolite). The optimum amount of methylene blue adsorbed (15 mg/g) could be used to calculate the surface area of adsorbent by using Eq. 3.

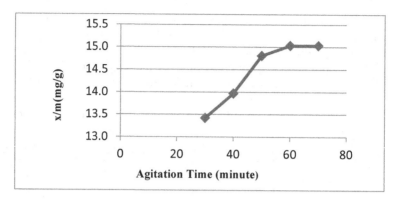

Fig. 5. Methylene blue adsorbed by Na-P$_1$ zeolite

$$S_A = \frac{Wm*N*A}{M} \qquad (3)$$

Wm = 15 mg/g or 15 mg of methylene blue per gram of adsorbent (Na-P$_1$ zeolite). Where:

N = 6.022 * 10^{23} mol A = 197 * 10^{-20} m^2/g; M = 320.5 g/mole

$S_A = \frac{15*10^{-3}*6.022*10^{23}*197*10^{-20}}{320.5} = 56.04$ m^2/g.

The surface area for the prepared zeolite material was found to be 56.04 m^2/g. In other findings, the surface area of Na-P$_1$ was investigated using Brunauer-Emmett-Teller (BET), Surface area analyzer. Using BET, in the previous study by Dwivedi et al. (2016) the total surface area was found to be 60.36 m^2/g. In another study, by Gitari et al. [26], total surface area for Na-P$_1$ zeolite was 67.63 m^2/g.

3.2 Effects of Operating Conditions on Si/Al of Na-P$_1$ Zeolite

Effect of temperature on Si/Al ratio of Na-P$_1$ Zeolite

Increasing the reaction temperature leads to an increase in ratio of Si to Al (see Fig. 6).

This is because during zeolite synthesis, an increase in temperature results in an increase in silicon (Si) dissolution compared to aluminium (Al) dissolution from pumice [27]. Due to this Si/Al increases. But this increment continuous until no more silicon and aluminium present in the slurry. In this zeolite synthesis; 60, 80 and 100 °C and ratio of pumice to NaOH (1:1.2, 1:1.5, 1:1.8) were the factors. The outcomes showed that when the temperature increases from 60 °C to 80 °C and then to 100 °C, keeping other parameters constant (at reaction time of 70 min and ratio of pumice to NaOH 1:1.2), the ratios of Si to Al were in between 1.77 and 2.00. Similarly, for the same temperature variation and keeping other parametres constant (at reaction time of 100 min and ratio of pumice to NaOH of 1:1.2), the ratios of Si to Al were in between 1.80 and 2.18. This indicate that the increment of Si/Al ratios with variation of reaction temperature and at constant reaction time and ratio of pumice to sodium hydroxide is low (1.77–2.00) and (1.80–2.18). And even by increasing the reaction time but keeping the other the two parametres constant the Si/Al values were in range of 1.77 to 2.18

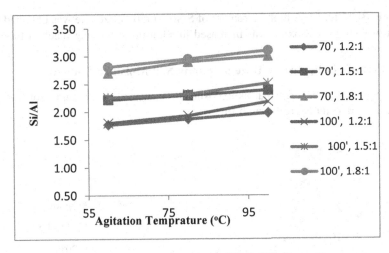

Fig. 6. Effect of temperature on Si/Al of Na-P$_1$ zeolite

which was also a small increment of Si/Al. This pointed out that varying reaction temperature and keeping the other two parameters constant, there was a small increase on the ratio of Si to Al. This implies that Si to Al ratio of zeolite obtained was highly affected by amount of sodium hydroxide when compared to effect of reaction temperature (Fig. 6).

Effect of Pumice to Sodium Hydroxide Ratio on Si/Al of Na-P$_1$ Zeolite

Increasing amount of sodium hydroxide also results an increase in ratio of Si to Al. Sodium hydroxide fusion decomposes silicon and aluminum from pumice and also acts as a mineralising agent, which depolymerises the silicon (Si) feedstock and forces the reactants into solution [28] and hence an increase in silicon. When the ratio of sodium hydroxide to pumice increase from 1.2:1 to 1.8:1 but at reaction temperature of 60 °C and reaction time of 70 min, the ratios of Si to Al increase from 1.77 to the values of 2.71. Similarly when reaction temperature increased to 100 °C but keeping reaction time at 70 min the Si/Al values were in range of 1.98 to 3.01. When the reaction time increased to 100 min at temperature of 60 °C, the ratios of Si to Al is found to be in between 1.8 and 2.82 (see Fig. 6). This implies that higher amount of sodium hydroxide were more likely to increase Si/Al than higher temperatures and longer reaction time.

Effect of Agitation Time on Si/Al of Na-P$_1$ Zeolite

Similar to the other parameters, increasing the reaction time leads to an increase in ratio of Si to Al. However, similar to that of reaction temperature, the rate of increase in ratio of Si to Al was slow when it was compared to an increase due to amount of NaOH (see Fig. 6). When the reaction time increases from 70 to 100 and then to 130 min, keeping other parameters constant (at reaction temperature of 60 °C and ratio of pumice to sodium hydroxide oxide of 1:1.2), the ratios of Si to Al were in between 1.77 and 1.85. These values (Si/Al) are close to each other. This implies that varying reaction time and keeping the other two parameters constant, there was no a large increase in values of Si to Al ratio (see Fig. 6). A high increment of Si to Al ratio of zeolite was obtained when amount of sodium hydroxide was increased in addition to varying reaction time.

3.3   Effect of Na-P$_1$ Zeolite Doze on Sandy Soil Moisture Content

From Fig. 7, it can be seen that as exposure time increased, all sandy soil treatment samples lost their moisture through time.

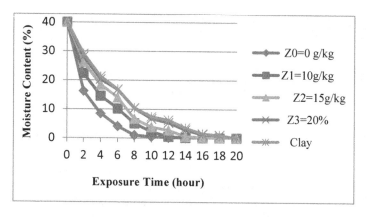

Fig. 7. Moisture content on sandy soil of particle size

However their rate of moisture loss was different depending on the amount of zeolite added to them. The results showed that as the dose of zeolite increased from 0 g/kg to 20 g/kg, the rate of moisture loss from sandy soil decreased. After 10 h, sandy soil without zeolite had mean moisture content of 0.45% and sandy soil with 10, 15 and 20 g/kg zeolite had mean moisture content of 2.04%, 3.58% and 6.48% respectively (see Fig. 7). The result obtained verified that greatest increase in moisture content in sandy soil was observed when 20 g/kg zeolite was used compared to the control other soil sample. In this study, effect of zeolite on sandy soil was in line with the findings of Tallai [29] that was aimed to compare effect of natural zeolite and bentonite on moisture content of sandy soil. The finding of Tallai stated that bentonite and zeolite have good water adsorption property [29]. It was, however, difficult to compare the findings of this paper with (Tallai [29]) since it used field experiment to test effect of zeolite on sandy soil whereas this paper was based on pot experiment. In this pot experiment, amount of zeolite was in g/kg in contrast the field experiment, zeolite was measured t/ha (amount of zeolite in ton per hectare). Due to this inconsistency of units, it was difficult to compare the findings of Tallai [29] quantitatively. Tallai [29] used natural zeolite to test moisture whereas this paper was based on Na-P$_1$ zeolite. Nevertheless, both this study and the finding of Tallai [29] showed that treatment of sandy soil with zeolite maintained higher soil water level than the control. According to Tallai, in small pot experiment the quantity of the available nutrients was increased by the two natural amendments. Since amount of nutrient in the soil depends on moisture content, this confirms that application of zeolite onto soil increases the moisture content.

Another research on the effect of clinoptilolite zeolite on typical agricultural soils of the U.S. Pacific Northwest was examined by Ippolito [30]. In this study, the effect of banding or fully mixing zeolite with N fertilizer on soil moisture content was investigated during a period of 6 weeks. The amount of zeolite added was measured in terms of Mg ha^{-1} [30] where as in the present study, the amount of zeolite is measured in terms of g/kg and the duration was 20 h. Even though the units used to measure zeolite and the duration time is different for the two studies are different, there is an increment of moisture in sandy soil in both studies. According to Ippolito [30], mixing zeolite into a sand soil at 44.8 Mg ha^{-1} increased soil moisture by 2.6% and 2.1% (by weight) as compared with a band application of 44.8 Mg ha^{-1} or a control, respectively. In the present study, during 20 h, mean moisture content of the sandy soil for 20 g/kg was increased by 6% when compared to the control.

3.4   Effect of Doze of Na-P$_1$ Zeolite on Sandy Soil Water Retention Capacity

Effect of increasing zeolite dosage on water retention capacity of sandy soil was shown in Fig. 8. It can be seen that, using pressure plate extractor and applying 1, 3, 5 and 15 bars, as pressure increased, the water remained in the soil decreased.

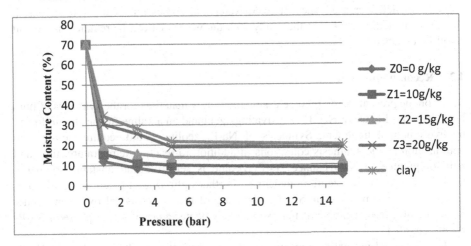

Fig. 8. Water retention capacity of sandy soil with zeolite at different bar

This implies that the water that was extracted from the soil increased as pressure increases. However, by adding zeolite onto sandy soil the water that can be retained in the soil could be increased. At 0 bar, all soil samples were observed to have the same water content. Then at 1 bar sandy soil without zeolite had a moisture content about 12% whereas sandy soil with 10 g/kg had 15.65%. As the amount of zeolite added increased from 10 g/kg to 15 g/kg and to 20 g/kg, moisture content in the soil increased from 15.65% to 19.90% and to 30.47% respectively. Again at 1 bar sandy soil with zeolite 20 g/kg had moisture content 30.47% which had no significant difference with clay soil (34.5%).

4 Conclusion and Recommendations

4.1 Conclusion

In summary, pure zeolite Na-P$_1$ has been successfully prepared from pumice. The silica to aluminium ratio of Na-P$_1$ zeolite obtained at reaction temperature of 100 °C, reaction time of 100 min and ratio of pumice to NaOH of 1:1.5 was 2.5. The FTIR analysis of pumice and Na-P$_1$ zeolite indicate the four vibration bands were found to be in ranges of expected vibrational wave number (cm^{-1}). During pumice treatment there was disappearance of some mullite and quartz peaks as well as emergence of new peaks. The formation of Na-P$_1$ zeolite was observed through reflections on $2\theta = 19.31°$, 23.44°, 28.32°, 32.43°, 33.5° and 49.10°. The surface area of Na-P$_1$ zeolite was 56.04 m^2/g.

After synthesis and characterization, Na-P$_1$ zeolite was applied on to sandy soil to investigate moisture content and water retention capacity. Rate of moisture loss from soil samples decreased from soil samples due to the presence of zeolite. During water retention testing, applying 1 bar to the packed sandy soil without zeolite, moisture content about 12% was obtained whereas sandy soil with 10 g/kg had 15.65%. As zeolite dose increased from 10 g/kg to 15 g/kg and to 20 g/kg, moisture content in the soil increased from 15.65% to 19.90% and to 30.47% respectively. In general, as pressure applied increased, the extracted water that comes out of the soil increased. However, by adding zeolite to the sandy soil, the water that can be retained in the soil could be enhanced.

4.2 Recommendations

Based on the present study, pumice is suitable as raw materials for the synthesis of pure Na-P$_1$ type zeolite using NaOH as activating agent and an alkaline fusion step followed by hydrothermal treatment. Synthesis of Na-P$_1$ zeolite would require step-by-step optimization of the synthesis conditions in addition to reaction temperature, time and ratio of pumice to NaOH since Na-P$_1$ zeolite is sensitive and unstable so that it transforms into another zeolite (analcime). Further optimization of the synthesis conditions and adjustment of the Si/Al molar ratio of the synthesis gel by adding either SiO$_2$ or Al$_2$O$_3$ from a supplementary source may be necessary if a pure phase of Na-P$_1$ zeolite targeted.

Besides small-pot experiment was used to investigate the effect of doze of Na-P$_1$ zeolite on moisture content of sandy soil. Field experiment has to be conducted to further explain the heterogeneity of the soil as well as to consider the actual environmental condition including the evaporation and transpiration rate of the soil and the plant.

References

1. Dominati, E., Patterson, M., Mackay, A.: A framework for classifying and quantifying the natural capital and ecosystem services of soils. Ecol. Econ. **69**(9), 1858–1868 (2010)
2. Nemes, A., Rawls, W.: Soil texture and particle-size distribution as input to estimate soil hydraulic properties. Dev. Soil Sci. **30**, 47–70 (2004)
3. Wösten, J.H.M., Pachepsky, Ya.A, Rawls, W.J.: Pedotransfer functions: bridging the gap between available basic soil data and missing soil hydraulic characteristics. J. Hydrol. **251**, 123–150 (2001)
4. Rawlsa, W.J., Pachepsky, Y.A., Ritchiea, J.C., Sobeckic, T.M., Bloodworth, H.: Effect of soil organic carbon on soil water retention. Geoderma **116**, 61–76 (2003)
5. Kopec, D.M.: Soil characteristics and how they affect soil moisture, vol. 2(10). University of Arizona Cooperative Extension (1995)
6. Tarboton, D.G.: Soil Properties. Utah State University (2003)
7. Mouat, M., Nes, P.: Soil water content affects the availability of phosphate. In: Proceedings of the New Zealand Grassland Association (1985)
8. Davor, M.D.: Soil Nutrient Management for Maui Country (2016)
9. Croker, J., et al.: Effects of recycled bentonite addition on soil properties, plant growth and nutrient uptake in a tropical sandy soil. Plant Soil **267**(1–2), 155–163 (2004)
10. Tefera, M., et al.: The role of communities in closed area management in Ethiopia. Mt. Res. Dev. **25**(1), 44–50 (2005)
11. AGL, F.: Land and plant nutrition management service: Global network on integrated soil management for sustainable use of salt affected soils (2000)
12. Basso, A.S., et al.: Assessing potential of biochar for increasing water-holding capacity of sandy soils. GCB Bioenergy **5**(2), 132–143 (2013)
13. Polat, E., et al.: Use of natural zeolite (clinoptilolite) in agriculture. J. Fruit Ornamental Plant Res. **12**(1), 183–189 (2004)
14. Treacy, M.M.J., Higgins, J.B.: Collection of simulated XRD powder patterns for zeolites. Published on behalf of the Structure Commission of the International Zeolite Association. p. 203: 204 (2001)
15. Hall, B.: Alternative Soil Amendments: Horticultural Technical Note. ATTRA, July 1998
16. Vassilis, J.A.I.: Natural Mineral Zeolite For Soil Conditioner/Fertilizer Additive (2006)
17. Ozdemir, O.D., Piskin, S.: A Novel Synthesis Method of Zeolite X From Coal Fly Ash: Alkaline Fusion Followed by Ultrasonic-Assisted Synthesis Method. Waste and Biomass Valorization, pp. 1–12 (2017)
18. Ríos, C.A., Williams, C.D., Castellanos, O.M.: Crystallization of low silica Na-A and Na-X zeolites from transformation of kaolin and obsidian by alkaline fusion. Ingeniería y competitividad **14**(2), 125–137 (2012)
19. Ola, P.D., Djami, A.G., Wogo, H.E.: The Use of Activated Natural Zeolite as an Adsorbent on Removing of Rhodamine B from Aqueous Solution (2013)
20. Yukselen, Y., Kaya, A.: Suitability of the methylene blue test for surface area, cation exchange capacity and swell potential determination of clayey soils. Eng. Geol. **102**(1–2), 38–45 (2008)
21. Tangkawanit, M.S.: Synthesis of Zeolites from Perlite and Study of their Ion Exchange Properties. Degree of Doctor of Philosophy in Chemistry, Suranaree University of Technology (2004)
22. Sudaporn, T.: Synthesis and Kinetic Study of Zeolite from Lobburi Perlite (2004)
23. Chigondo, M., et al., Synthesis and characterization of zeolites from coal fly ash (CFA) (2013)

24. Hildebrando, E.A., et al.: Synthesis and characterization of zeolite NaP using kaolin waste as a source of silicon and aluminum. Mater. Res. **17**, 174–179 (2014)
25. Rodrigues, M., Souza, A., Santos, I.: Brazilian kaolin wastes: synthesis of zeolite p at low-temperature. Am. Chem. Sci. J. **12**(4), 1–11 (2016)
26. Gitari, M.W., Petrik, L.F., Musyoka, N.M.: Hydrothermal conversion of south african coal fly ash into pure phase zeolite Na-P1. In: Zeolites-Useful Minerals. InTech (2016)
27. Du Plessis, P.W.: Process design for the up-scale zeolite synthesis from South African coal fly ash. Cape Peninsula University of Technology (2014)
28. Pfenninger, A.: Manufacture and Use of Zeolites for Adsorption Processes, Molecular Sieves, vol. 2. Springer-Verlag, Berlin Heidelberg (1999). https://doi.org/10.1007/3-540-69749-7_6
29. Tallai, M.: Effect of Bentonite and Zeolite on Characteristics and Change Of Microbial Activity of Acidic Humic Sandy Soil, Debrecen (2001)
30. Ippolito, J.A., Tarkalson, D.D., Lehrsch, G.A.: Zeolite soil application method affects inorganic nitrogen, moisture, and corn growth. Soil Sci. **176**(3), 136–142 (2011)

Spectrum Sensing Using Adaptive Threshold Based Energy Detection for LTE Systems

Hiwot Birhanu[1], Yihenew Wondie[2], and Fikreselam Gared[1(✉)]

[1] Faculty of Electrical and Computer Engineering,
BIT, BDU, Bahir Dar, Ethiopia
mylifehiwi7@gmail.com, fikreseafomi@gmail.com
[2] Faculty of Electrical and Computer Engineering, AAIT, AAU,
Addis Ababa, Ethiopia
yihenew.wondie@aait.edu.et

Abstract. The rapid growth of wireless communication system has put pressure on radio spectrum usage. Due to the widely used fixed spectrum access, spectrum utilization is very low. In order to overcome this problem, cognitive radio (CR), which leads the way for dynamic spectrum access capability is necessary. CR listens to the channel and enables to access unused spectrum of the primary user (PU). The detection decision would be done by either a single secondary user (SU) or by multiple SUs cooperating with each other.

Adaptive threshold based energy detection (ED) is the proposed detection technique in which the received signals SNR will be estimated by the SUs using minimum mean square error (MMSE) estimator and if SU is not efficient enough to detect the idleness of the channel due to the reception of weak signal, the SUs will cooperate to detect the PU signal. The simulation results indicate that the proposed system yields much better detection performance both at low and high SNR values.

Keywords: Cognitive radio · Adaptive threshold · Energy detection

1 Introduction

Now a day, the demand for mobile communication has been grown significantly. Due to the growing demand, the development of the design and optimization of radio access technologies and a further evolution of the existing system has laid down the foundation of Long Term Evolution (LTE) which is capable of providing high data rate. This growth in the evolution of a wireless system requires an increased frequency spectrum which leads to misbelieve as most of the spectrum that is the scarce resource has been sufficiently occupied. However, it had been observed that the radio frequency spectrum is inefficiently utilized due to the existing static spectrum allocations and regulatory policies of the governments [1, 2]. Due to this underutilization of the radio frequency spectrum, it had been resulted to the spectrum holes or white spaces which will provide an opportunity for the users without a license to have access to those unused spectrum holes. Based on the interference level, radio frequency spectrum can be a black space that are fully occupied; grey space that are partially occupied and

© ICST Institute for Computer Sciences, Social Informatics and Telecommunications Engineering 2019
Published by Springer Nature Switzerland AG 2019. All Rights Reserved
F. A. Zimale et al. (Eds.): ICAST 2018, LNICST 274, pp. 473–491, 2019.
https://doi.org/10.1007/978-3-030-15357-1_39

white space that are not occupied and have low interference level with the only interference being noise. This white spaces or spectrum holes could be utilized by unlicensed user or secondary users (SUs) [3]. CR that opens a gateway to overcome the inefficient radio frequency spectrum utilization will achieve these. CR has the ability to acquire, measure, sense, learn and be aware of the environment in order to keep track of free and occupied channels so that it can make use of the free spectrum bands [4].

With CR technology, SUs will check continually to know the idleness of a primary user (PU) channel and whenever it gets a free band it will occupy during that free time. However, if there is an incoming signal from the PU, the SU will leave the channel to avoid interference by switching to a different free channel if available or by terminating the transmission if there is no free channel to switch to [5]. When CR detects a free spectrum it will provide an opportunity for the surrounding unlicensed users to occupy it. In doing this task having a smooth integrity between PUs and SUs and also between SUs are necessary not to cause interference for the PU as priority is always given to the licensed owner.

2 Related Works

There have been numerous studies on spectrum detection mechanisms of CR. In order to sense the idleness of the radio frequency spectrum, adaptive spectrum sensing scheme that switches between Eigen values based detection, energy detection (ED) and matched filter detection (MFD) based on the threshold value had been implemented in [6]. In this paper first the availability of prior knowledge about the PU signal will be checked and if it gets a prior information about the PU signal the system will use matched filter detection technique if not it will proceed with estimating the SNR and compare it with the threshold and based on the comparison result the system applies Eigen value for low SNR and ED for high SNR since both does not require a prior knowledge about PU signal. The results found shows that, for low SNR values the ED system suffers from a low detection performance but it has a good performance on higher SNR values. And Eigen value detection gives a much better performance at low SNR values. Hence, whenever there exists a prior knowledge of PU signal the matched filter detection was applied to give a good detection performance, however, when there is no prior information the Eigen value and ED shows a better detection performance at low and high SNR values respectively. Even though the detection probability of Eigen value detection is good and also the system is adaptive there still exists a computational complexity due to the Eigen value detection. A data fusion scheme for cooperative detection was investigated in [7]. In this paper a comparative analysis had been made for hard and soft fusion schemes. From hard fusion schemes, AND and OR fusion rules had been investigated. Also Selection combination (SC), square low combining (SLC) and maximal ratio combining (MRC) had been studied. From the results, cooperative detector with a hard combining scheme of OR fusion rule gives a better performance than the other schemes and MRC gives better performance than SC and SLC but all of them have good detection performance than single detector. However, MRC requires channel state information which is not the case for SC and SLC.

MRC and SC performance had been analyzed over AWGN and Nakagami-m fading channel in [8] and also the authors proposed amplify-and-relay and detect-and-relay cooperative spectrum sensing strategies to improve the detection performance with the help of other eligible SUs so as to quickly vacate the channel to the primary network when the neighboring PUs switch to active state. The simulation result shows MRC has better detection probability than SC scheme and detect-and-relay spectrum sensing scheme gives better performance than amplify-and relay detection scheme. Even if MRC gives better performance it needs channel state information. Cooperative adaptive threshold based matched filter and ED were proposed in [9] to detect the available of PU spectrum. ED had been chosen for its simplicity; however, it is highly affected by noise uncertainty. The authors used an adaptive threshold $\lambda 1$ and $\lambda 2$ with some uncertainty so that if the energy lies in between those threshold values (the uncertainty region), MFD was used and outside the uncertainty region the ED was the detection scheme that had been used with OR fusion rule. The results in this proposed system shows a better detection performance than that of conventional energy and double threshold detection scheme. The presence of MFD makes the system to require prior information about PU in the uncertainty region.

Cooperative spectrum detection based on noise uncertainty estimation using soft decision fusion was the scheme used by the authors in [10]. In this paper the performances of soft detection schemes such as SLC, square low selection (SLS) and MRC had been studied. From the results the detection performance of the proposed detection scheme that takes noise uncertainty into consideration and use two thresholds, was better than that of the conventional soft combination detection schemes. Also from the comparisons of the soft combination schemes MRC provides better result than SLC and SLS schemes. In contrast to the reviewed works, this work uses a single and cooperative energy detection algorithm adaptively to access the unused spectrum band. Single energy detection has low computational complexity but it is prone to hidden node problem. On the other hand cooperative energy detection gives better detection performance within a short period of time at the cost of increased computational complexity and increased bandwidth requirement for the control channel. Combining these two will provide a good detection performance with reduced complexity, bandwidth and sensing time. The spectrum sensor makes a series of measurements and then computes these measurements to make decision.

3   Proposed System Model

ED is one of detection schemes that are capable of detecting the whitespaces without the need of prior knowledge of the PU signal. This makes it an easy detection scheme to implement; however, the huge challenge that is imposed to an ED is that, it is highly prone to shadowing and multipath effects. This leads to hidden terminal problem that caused the SU to be interference for PU. To overcome this problem spectrum detection decision can be made by cooperating multiple SUs. Though cooperative detection provides much better detection performance, increased complexity and overhead are the main challenges it faced. In order to combine the advantages of both the non-cooperative and cooperative ED, threshold based adaptive energy detection scheme that uses both non-cooperative and cooperative detection with SC scheme had been proposed.

In this proposed system, the first task is to estimate the SNR of the received PU signal at SU in order to determine the type of detection scheme to be used as shown in Fig. 1. The selection of detection scheme of weather to share information with others SUs or to make the detection decision by itself would be determined based on the estimated SNR. If the received signals SNR value at SU is strong enough the system will use a non-cooperative detection scheme, that means, each SU will decide the presence or absence of the PU signal by themselves without sharing any information or without cooperating with each other. However, if the received signal SNR value is very low the SUs will cooperate (share information with others) to detect the presence or absence of the PU signal by sending their sensing information to the FC. For FC to perform this task SC is the proposed combination scheme to be used. The reason for choosing SC scheme is because; it is easiest combination scheme to implement and provides a better performance than hard combination scheme. One problem of using SC scheme is requiring a higher bandwidth for the control channel to communicate between SUs and the FC. This problem can be reduced by the system proposed using cooperative and non-cooperative detection adaptively. This does not always need SC implementation due to the presence of non-cooperative detection.

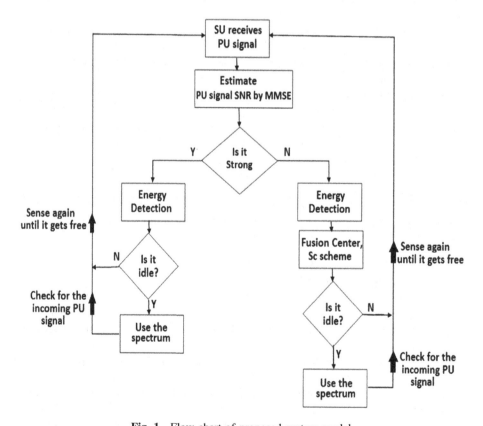

Fig. 1. Flow chart of proposed system model

The system uses cooperative ED scheme at low SNR and non-cooperative energy detection scheme at high SNR. This is due to the fact that, using cooperative detection at low SNR enables to achieve the detection of the free spectrum band without causing an interference for the PU within a minimum period of time. However, this cooperative detection scheme has an increased complexity and traffic overhead which makes it inefficient to apply it all the time. Since non-cooperative ED is capable of providing a good detection performance at high SNR with less complexity it is used at high SNR. Hence, using non-cooperative ED whenever the received signal SNR is high and cooperative ED when the received signal SNR is low enables to achieve good detection performance without causing interference to PU with reduced complexity, low sensing time and less traffic overhead.

3.1 Signal Model

The main task of the proposed system is to explore available free PU bands so that it can be occupied by SU to improve the spectrum utilization efficiency. Here the signal model is a single PU- multiple SU with the existence of k number of cognitive radio users (CRUs), that is one or more CRUs will sense the spectrum of one PU channel. In the case of this work the PU is UHF800 MHz TV band and the CRUs are the LTE 800 MHz mobile communication users. Due to the digitization of television transmissions there exist a lot of free spectrum bands that would be in need of efficient utilization. This channels could be explored and be used by other unlicensed users such as an LTE 800 MHz mobile users. Because of the increased population and demand there might exist congestion on mobile user's network and for such cases the congested network area users can be transferred to other network environment in a temporal manner which can be made possible by CR. For such cases the proposed system gives solution by enabling the unlicensed mobile users' to access the TV band so as to increase the spectrum utilization efficiency. However this can also be extended to other PU channels to be explored by different SUs. The received PU signal at k-number of CRUs is shown in Eq. 1 [11]:

$$y(n)_k = \begin{cases} n(n)_k & : H_0 \\ h_k s(n) + n(n)_k & : H_1 \end{cases} \tag{1}$$

Where n = 1..., N is number of samples, and $n(n), s(n)$ and $y(n)$ are noise, PU signal and the PU signal received at SU respectively. When SU receives the PU signal it always first estimates the SNR of the received PU signal, $y(n)$, using MMSE estimator, which has low complexity and minimum error in estimating the received PU signal, [12] to know the received signal's strength. For the received PU signal y with variance of δ_y^2 the MMSE error estimation for SNR γ is:

$$mmse(y, \gamma) = \frac{\delta_y^2}{1 + \gamma \delta_y^2} \tag{2}$$

The threshold value can be determined based on the estimated MMSE as shown in Eq. 3 [12]:

$$\lambda_{mmse} = \delta_n^2 Q^{-1}(P_f) + \frac{\delta_n^4}{N}(\gamma_{mmse} + 1)^2 \tag{3}$$

where P_f is probability of false alarm. Based on this estimation and threshold, the SU will decide to detect the free band either by itself or by cooperating with surrounding SUs. The detection scheme used in this work is ED that averaged the received PU signal to determine the decision statistics and make the decision as shown in Fig. 2.

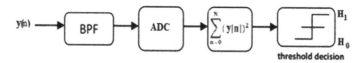

Fig. 2. Block diagram of energy detector [13]

In ED, the received signal is first filtered by a BPF to get the desired signal with one sided power spectral density (PSD) N_{01} [14].

$$H(f) = \begin{cases} \frac{2}{\sqrt{N_{01}}}, & |f - f_c| \leq W \\ 0, & |f - f_c| > W \end{cases} \tag{4}$$

The output of this filter that is shown in Eq. 4 would be squared and accumulated to get the decision statistics for the output of analog to digital converter (ADC), $y(k)$, which is given as [15]:

$$Y = \sum_{k=0}^{N} [y(k)]^2 \tag{5}$$

Under AWGN channel (h = 1) for hypothesis H_0, the normalized decision (test) statistics Y with variance δ_n^2 have a central Chi-square distribution with 2 m degrees of freedom [16].

And for hypothesis H_1, Y with variance of the signal, δ_n^2 have a central Chi-square distribution with 2 m degrees of freedom and non-central parameter 2γ where $\gamma = \frac{\delta_s^2}{\delta_n^2}$ represents the SNR. This decision statistics is given as [14, 15]:

$$Y = \begin{cases} y_{2m}^2 & : H_0 \\ y_{2m}^2(2\gamma) & : H_1 \end{cases} \tag{6}$$

The probability of detection, P_d, and probability of false alarm, P_f, can be obtained from its PDF to give Eqs. 7 and 8 respectively using the marcum Q-function, $Q_m(.)$ and the gamma function $\Gamma(a, b)$ with m = TW [11, 17]:

$$P_d = P[Y > \lambda/H_1] = Q_m(\sqrt{2\gamma}, \sqrt{\lambda}) \tag{7}$$

$$P_f = P[Y > \lambda/H_0] = \frac{\Gamma(m, \frac{\lambda}{2})}{\Gamma(m)} \tag{8}$$

For large number of samples, N, the decision statistics can be rewritten as [15]:

$$Y = \begin{cases} N(\mu_0, \delta_0^2) & : H_0 \\ N(\mu_1, \delta_1^2) & : H_1 \end{cases} \tag{9}$$

where $N(\mu_0, \delta_0^2)$ is Gaussian distribution with $\mu_0 = N\delta_n^2$ and variance $\delta_0^2 = 2N\delta_n^4$ for hypothesis H_0 and mean $\mu_1 = N(\delta_s^2 + \delta_n^2)$ and variance $\delta_1^2 = 2N(\delta_s^2 + \delta_n^2)^2$ for hypothesis H_1. The probability of detection and false alarm for such cases are given by Eqs. 10 and 11 respectively [11, 17]:

$$P_d = Q\left(\frac{\lambda - N(\delta_s^2 + \delta_n^2)}{\sqrt{2N(\delta_s^2 + \delta_n^2)^2}}\right) \tag{10}$$

$$P_f = Q\left(\frac{\lambda - N\delta_n^2}{\sqrt{2N\delta_n^4}}\right) \tag{11}$$

For a signal under Rayleigh fading channel with fading amplitude α, the instantaneous and average SNR per symbol will become $\gamma = \frac{\alpha^2 E_s}{N_0}$ and $\bar{\gamma} = \Omega \frac{E_s}{N_0}$ with $\Omega = \overline{\alpha^2}$ respectively. For such fading channel the SNR follows exponential distribution is given by [15, 18]:

$$f_\gamma(\gamma) = \frac{1}{\gamma} \exp(\frac{-\gamma}{\bar{\gamma}}) \tag{12}$$

The decision statistics under Rayleigh fading channel with exponential distribution $e_2(\gamma^2 + 1)$ and $\alpha = 2(\gamma^2 + 1)$ with central chi-square distribution having $2(N + 1)$ degrees of freedom for parameter α is [15]:

$$Y = \begin{cases} y_{2(N+1)}^2 & : H_0 \\ e_{2(\gamma 2 + 1)} + y_{2N}^2 & : H_1 \end{cases} \tag{13}$$

Using this, the SC scheme enables to determine the probability of detection under Rayleigh fading channel is given in Eq. 14 [15].

$$P_{dRay} = \int_0^\infty Q_m\left(\sqrt{2\gamma}, \sqrt{\lambda}\right) f_\gamma(x)\, dx \tag{14}$$

Noise is random variable with a distribution assumption of perfectly Gaussian which is not the case for the practical implementation as there exist some uncertainty in the distribution. The uncertainty, ρ, affects the detection performance of the ED as it will vary the threshold. The variation of the threshold has the region given in Eq. 15 between $\frac{\delta_n^2}{\rho}$ and $\rho\delta_n^2$. The larger uncertainty will result in higher detection performance degradation given by [19]:

$$\sigma^2 \varepsilon\left[\frac{\delta_n^2}{\rho}, \rho\delta_n^2\right] \tag{15}$$

where $\rho > 1$ is noise uncertainty coefficient. Equations 16 and 17 can obtain the probability of detection and false alarm under this uncertainty respectively [15, 19].

$$P_d = Q\left(\frac{\lambda - N(\frac{1}{\rho}\delta_n^2 + \delta_s^2)}{\sqrt{2N(\frac{1}{\rho}\delta_n^2 + \delta_s^2)^2}}\right) \tag{16}$$

$$P_f = Q\left(\frac{\lambda - N\,\rho\delta_n^2}{\sqrt{2N\rho^2\delta_n^4}}\right) \tag{17}$$

The basic detection task that is performed by the ED is to compare the energy with a certain threshold value given by [15]:

$$\lambda = \sqrt{N\rho^2\delta_n^4}Q^{-1}(P_f) + N\rho\delta_n^2 \tag{18}$$

Based on the comparison the decision of presence or absence of PU signal will be made by each SUs.

When the PU channel state is detected by a cooperative energy detection scheme shown in Fig. 3, the probability of detection and false alarm using SC at the fusion center for AWGN channel is: [8]

$$\begin{cases} Q_{m,sc} = Q_m\left(\sqrt{2\gamma_{sc}}, \sqrt{\lambda}\right) \\ Q_{f,sc} = \frac{\Gamma(m, \frac{\lambda}{2})}{\Gamma(m)} \end{cases} \tag{19}$$

Where: $\gamma_{sc} = \max\left(\gamma_1, \gamma_2, \ldots, \gamma_k\right)$

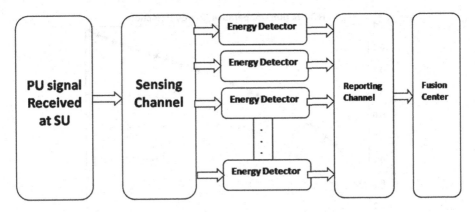

Fig. 3. Cooperative energy detection [15]

Under Rayleigh fading channel for K number of SUs PDF of the maximum SNR from k-number of SUs can be determined as:

$$f_{\gamma max}(\gamma) = \frac{K}{\gamma}\left(\left(1 - e^{\frac{-\gamma}{\bar{\gamma}}}\right)^{(k-1)} e^{\frac{-\gamma}{\bar{\gamma}}}\right) \tag{20}$$

And the detection probability is [11]:

$$Q_{dsc} = \int_{\gamma} Q_m\left(\sqrt{2\gamma_{sc}}, \sqrt{\lambda}\right) f_{\gamma max}(\gamma) d\gamma \tag{21}$$

4   Simulation Results and Discussions

In this section some results of our work are presented. Based on the proposed system model simulation analysis had been done for the case of Rayleigh fading channel to evaluate the detection capability of the system. To do that, various parameters shown in Table 1 had been used.

Table 1. Simulation parameters used for analysis

Simulation parameters	Type and value
Number of PU	1
Number of SU	≥ 1
PU signal	BPSK modulated
Bandwidth	6 MHz
Center frequency	4 MHz
Channel	Rayleigh fading channel
SNR	[−30 dB, 2 dB]
N	100
Probability of false alarm	$\leq 10\%$

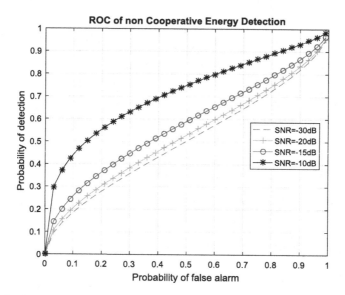

Fig. 4. ROC of non-cooperative energy detection for different SNR values under Rayleigh fading channel

Figure 4 shows the ROC of non-cooperative energy detector under different SNR values. The energy detector capability is highly affected by the strength of the received signal. From the results for the probability of false alarm of 0.5, the probability of detection increases from 0.5 to 0.75 which is a 25% increment achieved by the increase in SNR from −30 dB to −10 dB. Hence, whenever the received signal has higher strength the detection probability will be better.

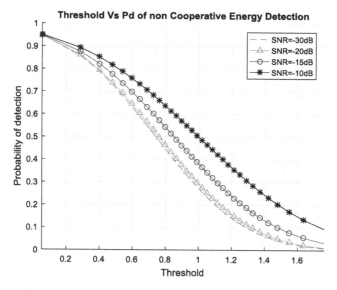

Fig. 5. Threshold Vs Pd of non-cooperative energy detection for different SNR values under Rayleigh fading channel and Pf = 10%

From the result in Fig. 5, it can be seen the increment in the threshold value which is the function of false alarm probability leads to the decrements in the detection probability. If the threshold is set to be higher, it will lead for the detector to make the decision of the PU channel being idle even if there exists a strong PU signal, as it only compares the energy with the threshold. Being low threshold means it can detect the signal even if it has low energy. The detection performance was upgraded by incrementing the SNR, which means, the reception of a signal with high strength leads to improvement in detection performance at the same threshold value.

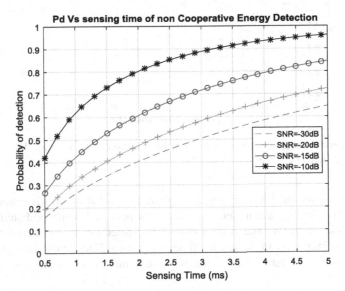

Fig. 6. Pd Vs sensing time of non-cooperative energy detection for different SNR values under Rayleigh fading channel and Pf = 10%

Figure 6 demonstrates the effect of SNR on the time it takes to achieve a better probability of PU signal being detected by SUs. When the received signal is strong, the sensing time needed by SUs to detect a PU signal will be too short.

Figure 7 shows the relationship between SNR to the probability of detection for the cases of cooperative ED scheme. The results shows that for a low SNR value cooperating SUs gives a good detection performance that leads for the SU not to cause interference for the PU transmission. Also in observing the results that gives unity probability of detection, the non-cooperative detection achieves probability of detection of 100% at the SNR of −6 dB; by cooperating two and three SUs the detector achieves this value at SNR of −8 dB and −10 dB respectively. Even if the signal strength is very weak cooperating two and more SUs enables the detectors to detect the PU signal in a better way.

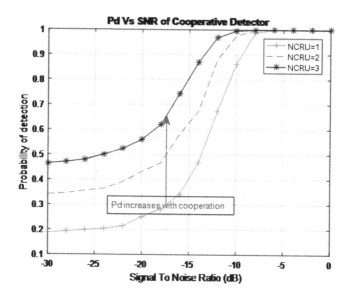

Fig. 7. Cooperative energy detection effect on the detection of signal with different strength under Rayleigh fading channel and Pf = 10%

Figure 8 shows the effect of sensing time on the probability of detection of a PU signal by SU. The increase in sensing time gives better detection probability for the non-cooperation detection and also for cooperative detection as indicated in the result. However, this increment in the sensing time has its own effect on the throughput of the SUs. Whenever SU takes longer sensing time, the data transmission would be

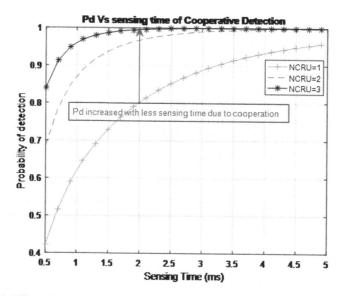

Fig. 8. Probability of detection versus sensing time for cooperative energy detection with SC fusion scheme effect under Rayleigh fading channel for SNR = −10 dB and Pf = 10%

shortened which leads for the decrements in the throughput of the system as it will lead for longer sensing time and shorter transmission time. To reduce this effect, cooperative detection is preferable to achieve optimum detection within short sensing time.

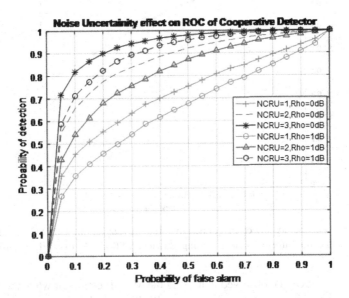

Fig. 9. Noise uncertainty effect in cooperative energy detection with SC fusion rule under Rayleigh fading channel and SNR = −10 dB

The effect of noise uncertainty on the cooperative energy detection with SC fusion rule is illustrated in Fig. 9. The detection probability which takes noise uncertainty factor in to consideration had been improved using cooperative energy detection scheme. But, even if it gives much better performance the noise uncertainty factor has an effect in reducing the performance of both cooperative and non-cooperative detection. Cooperating SUs under uncertainty gives a better detection performance than the non-cooperative detection.

From the result in Fig. 10, the cooperative detection scheme manages to reduce the effect of detection probability with respect to the threshold value. In order to detect the signals of low energy it needs to have a threshold value as small as possible. For the system to achieve a probability of detection of 0.8, the threshold value needed for the case of a single SU detection with considering noise uncertainty is 0.42. And cooperating two and three SUs needs a threshold of 0.53 and 0.7 respectively which is increased due to the cooperation detection that would enable the system to detect signals much better.

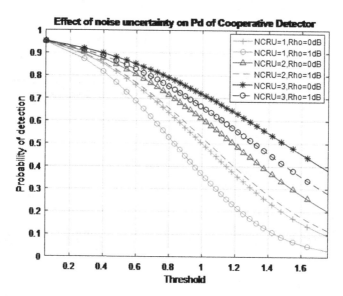

Fig. 10. Noise uncertainty effect in cooperative Energy Detection with SC fusion rule for detection with threshold under Rayleigh fading channel, SNR = −10 dB and Pf = 10%

From Fig. 11 it can be observed that using the MMSE estimator when the threshold of the SNR value had been estimated as −10 dB it will have some performance degradation with the reception of a PU signal with SNR from −10 dB to −7 dB. This degradation was improved when the estimated threshold is −9.2 dB which was further

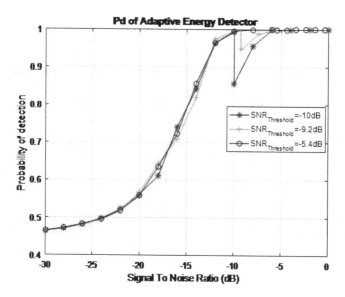

Fig. 11. Detection probability of proposed adaptive Energy Detection under Rayleigh fading channel, Pf = 10%

enhanced while the SNR threshold estimation is −5.4 dB. Hence, better detection probability can be achieved at low and high SNR regions with less complexity and reduced overhead by combining the advantages of both cooperative and non-cooperative energy detection adaptively. Also the results show that the optimal threshold SNR value for the system which provides a good detection performance is −5.4 dB.

As illustrated in Fig. 12, even though the introduction of 1 dB uncertainty reduced the detection performance, still the proposed system gives a better detection both at low and high SNR values. The result demonstrates with the existence of uncertainty, fading and shadowing problems in Rayleigh fading channel, using adaptive threshold based energy detection had can sense and detect PU frequency spectrum even with the reception of weak signals.

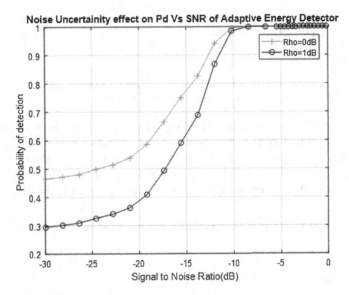

Fig. 12. Detection probability of proposed adaptive Energy Detection under Rayleigh fading channel, Pf = 10% and $\lambda_{\_SNR}$ = −5.4 dB with noise uncertainty

Using the optimal estimated SNR threshold that is −5.4 dB, the proposed system attains an optimum detection probability within short period of sensing time with the existence of 1 dB uncertainty. As shown in Fig. 13 when the SU estimates PU signal strength and find it to be lower than −5.4 dB, the system can achieve 0.95 detection probability within 0.9 ms when there is no uncertainty. However, the introduction of 1 dB uncertainty leads the system to take 1.4 ms time to achieve the same detection probability. If the PU signal's SNR is estimated above −5.4 dB each SU with no uncertainty will take 4.5 ms to achieve 0.95 detection probability this time will be incremented to 5 ms with the introduction of 1 dB uncertainty to achieve the same detection probability. This shows the system needs extra 0.5 ms sensing time to obtain same detection probability due to the uncertainty.

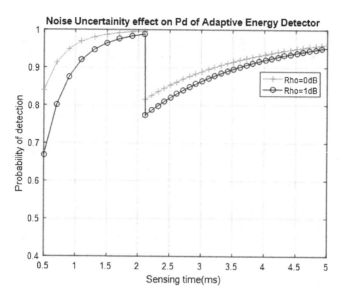

Fig. 13. Pd Vs sensing time of proposed adaptive Energy Detection under Rayleigh fading channel, Pf = 10% & λ_{SNR} = −5.4 dB with noise uncertainty

The result in Fig. 14 depicts the effect of threshold value on the detection performance of the proposed system. With the SNR of PU signal being estimated with a threshold value of less than −5.4 dB, the system works at the energy threshold value up to1 with uncertainty (Rho = 1 dB) and 1.08 with no uncertainty (Rho = 1 dB) cooperating three SUs. And whenever the SUs receive the PU signal with strength above

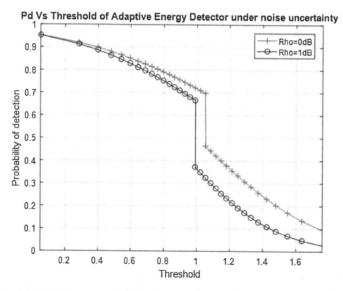

Fig. 14. Threshold Vs Pd of proposed adaptive energy detection under Rayleigh fading channel, Pf = 10% and λ_{SNR} = −5.4 dB with noise uncertainty

−5.4 dB each SUs will have energy threshold value above 1 and 1.08 with no uncertainty and with uncertainty of 1 dB respectively. This shows that, with the reception of weak signal the system gives a good detection having allowed threshold values. Also when the PU receives strong signals the system will adjust its threshold value a bit higher for good detection.

Even if MFD needs a prior knowledge about the PU signal it is one of the robust signal detection schemes capable of providing higher probability of detection. In MFD scheme, the received signal would be passed through a BPF to get the desired signal followed by a matching filter which is capable of minimizing the noise component and maximizing the signal component to maximize SNR. This would enable the MFD to achieve a good detection performance by correlating the two signals (the reference signal and impulse response of the matched filter) to determine the places at which the two signals are the same. This task makes the detector to identify the idleness of the channel in a better way [14].

When the proposed system performance with −5.4 dB threshold SNR value is compared with the conventional ED and the MFD, it gives a better performance on the case of both weak and strong signal reception as shown in Fig. 15.

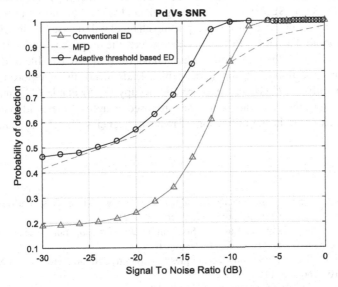

Fig. 15. Pd Vs SNR comparison for conventional ED, MFD and adaptive threshold based ED under Rayleigh fading channel and Pf = 10%

Whenever the SU receives a weak signal or with low SNR it compares the signal with the threshold. If the SNR receives weak PU signal it will share information with the surrounding SUs and make the decision using SC fusion rule to attain the detection performances shown in the above results. But if the SU receives strong PU signal it will make the detection decision by itself without sharing information with other SUs as shown in the figures. This will enable for the system to attain a reliable detection performance even at low SNR values cooperating more than one SU. Also for signals of good strength, the detection was much better using non cooperative detection which is less complex with no overhead.

5 Conclusion

Current static spectrum allocation leads for underutilization. To reduce this problem CR with a dynamic spectrum accessing capability is a good solution.

In this work, threshold based adaptive ED scheme that uses cooperative ED for low SNR values and non-cooperative ED for high SNR values had been proposed and analyzed supported by simulation for various parameters.

The system gives a good detection performance for low SNR regions by cooperating three SUs and non-cooperative detection at high SNR regions. Hence, whenever a SU gets a low SNR it manages to get a good detection performance by detecting it cooperatively that gives the solution for the non-cooperative energy detection problem. And also whenever the SU receives a strong signal the SU can manage to decide the state of the spectrum by themselves that enable to reduce complexity and overhead, as it does not require a central FC. This is due to the reason that, if a system always uses cooperative detection SUs require a reporting channel to send the information about PU signal to the central FC. And also this reporting channel will be used by the FCs to send the decision about the state of PU channel. However, the proposed system needs for the SUs to cooperate with the reception of week signal only and are capable of deciding by themselves in reception of strong signal which leads to not using reporting channels always. Generally the CRUs can explore and occupy the available PU bands without causing an interference by applying the proposed adaptive threshold based ED to achieve improvement in the utilization of radio frequencies for LTE systems.

References

1. Chaudhari, S.: Spectrum Sensing for Cognitive Radios: Algorithms, Performance, and Limitations. Aalto University publication series (2012)
2. Guo, H., Reisi, N., Jiang, W., Luo, W.: Soft combination for cooperative spectrum sensing in fading channels. IEEE Access 5, 975–986 (2017)
3. Salahdine, F.: Spectrum Sensing Techniques for Cognitive Radio Networks", arXiv preprint arXiv:1710.02668 (2017)
4. Mukherjee, T., Nath, A.: Cognitive radio-trends, scope and challenges in radio network technology. IJARCSMS 3(6) (2015)
5. Uma, C.H., Dhana Lakshmi, P., Venkateswarao, N.: Blind spectrum sensing in cognitive radio using BPSK and QPSK modulation techniques. IJEECS 6(6) (2017)
6. Xiao, J., Hu, R.Q., Qian, Y., Gong, L., Wang, B.: Expanding LTE network spectrum with cognitive radios: from concept to implementation. IEEE Wireless Commun. 20(2), 12–19 (2013)
7. Lavanya, S., Sindhuja, B., Bhagyaveni, M.A.: Implementation of an adaptive spectrum sensing technique in cognitive radio networks. In: International Conference on Computing and Communications Technologies (ICCCT), pp. 344–349. IEEE (2015)

8. Teguig, D., Scheers, B., Le Nir, V.: Data fusion schemes for cooperative spectrum sensing in cognitive radio networks. In: Military Communications and Information Systems Conference (MCC), pp. 1–7. IEEE (2012)
9. Mohamad, M.H., Sani, N.M.: Energy detection technique in cognitive radio system. IJET-IJENS **13**(05), 69–73 (2013)
10. Jaglan, R.R., Mustafa, R., Sarowa, S., Agrawal, S.: Performance evaluation of energy detection based cooperative spectrum sensing in cognitive radio network. In: Satapathy, S. C., Das, S. (eds.) Proceedings of First International Conference on Information and Communication Technology for Intelligent Systems: Volume 2. SIST, vol. 51, pp. 585–593. Springer, Cham (2016). https://doi.org/10.1007/978-3-319-30927-9_58
11. Nguyen, T.T., Nguyen, T.M., Dang, K.L., Nguyen, P.H.: Selection combining technique and its real-time FPGA implementation for spectrum sensing efficiency improvement in cognitive radio. In: Zelinka, I., Duy, V.H., Cha, J. (eds.) AETA 2013: Recent Advances in Electrical Engineering and Related Sciences. LNEE, vol. 282, pp. 181–189. Springer, Heidelberg (2014). https://doi.org/10.1007/978-3-642-41968-3_19
12. Guo, D., Wu, Y., Shitz, S.S., Verdu, S.: Estimation in gaussian noise: properties of the minimum mean-square error. IEEE Trans. Inf. Theory **57**(4), 2371–2385 (2011)
13. Zayen, B.: Spectrum Sensing and Resource Allocation Strategies for Cognitive Radio. Doctor of Electronic and Communications, TELECOM Paris Tech (2010)
14. Lavanya, S., Sindhuja, B., Bhagyaveni, M.A.: Implementation of an adaptive spectrum sensing technique in cognitive radio networks. In: IEEE, pp. 344–349 (2015)
15. Abdo-Tuko, M.: Performance evaluation and comparison of different transmitter detection techniques for application in cognitive radio. IJNC **5**(5), 83–96 (2015)
16. Umar, R., Mohammed, F., Deriche, M., Sheikh, A.U.H.: Hybrid cooperative energy detection techniques in cognitive radio networks. In: Handbook of Research on Software-Defined and Cognitive Radio Technologies for Dynamic Spectrum Management, pp. 1–37. IGI Global (2015)
17. Shen, B., Kwak, K.S.: Soft combination schemes for cooperative spectrum sensing in cognitive radio networks. ETRIJ **31**(3), 263–270 (2009)
18. Hailegnaw, B.: SNR Enhancement of Energy Detector Algorithm using Adaptive Wiener Filter in Cognitive Radio. M.Sc thesis, Addis Ababa University (2016)
19. Eerla, V.V.: Performance analysis of energy detection algorithm in cognitive radio. Ph.D. thesis (2011)

Evolving 3D Facial Expressions Using Interactive Genetic Algorithms

Meareg Hailemariam[1,2,3(✉)] [iD], Ben Goertzel[1,2], and Tesfa Yohannes[1,2]

[1] Hanson Robotics, Hong Kong, China
{meareg,tesfa}@hansonrobotics.com, ben@goertzel.org
[2] SingularityNET, Hong Kong, China
{meareg,ben,tesfa}@singularitynet.io
[3] Addis Ababa University, Addis Ababa, Ethiopia

Abstract. Interactive Genetic Algorithms (IGA) are applied in optimization problems where the fitness function is fuzzy or subjective. Its application transcends several domains including photography, fashion, gaming and graphics. This work introduces a novel implementation of Interactive Genetic Algorithm (IGA) for evolving facial animations on a 3D face model. In this paper, an animation of a facial expression represents a chromosome; while genes are equivalent, depending on the crossover method applied, either to a keyframe point information (f-curve) of a facial bone or f-curves of grouped sub-parts such as the head, mouth or eyes. Crossover techniques uniform, cut-and-spice, blend and their hybrids were implemented with a user playing fitness function role. Moreover, in order to maximize user preference and minimize the user fatigue during evolution, sub-parts based elitism was implemented. Subjective measurements of credibility and peculiarity parameters among a given artist animated and evolved expressions were done. For the experiment results here, an average crossover percentage of 85%, a mutation level of 0.01, initial population of 36, and 8 rounds of evolution settings were considered. As detailed in the experiment section, the IGA based evolved facial expressions scored competitive results to the artist-animated ones.

Keywords: Evolutionary algorithms · Interactive genetic algorithms · 3D facial expressions

1 Introduction

People show different facial expressions when expressing different kinds of emotions. Even though the number and type of emotions along with their associated facial expressions differ from person to person, moment to moment, there are six basic set of emotions recognized globally. These six basic emotions are angry, disgust, fear, happiness, sadness, and surprise [1]. However, there are far more set of emotions and associated facial expressions that people are capable of feeling and expressing in their daily life.

© ICST Institute for Computer Sciences, Social Informatics and Telecommunications Engineering 2019
Published by Springer Nature Switzerland AG 2019. All Rights Reserved
F. A. Zimale et al. (Eds.): ICAST 2018, LNICST 274, pp. 492–502, 2019.
https://doi.org/10.1007/978-3-030-15357-1_40

In spite of heterogeneity in the interpretation, facial expressions are globally used by most people as a primary means to express emotions. In the virtual world, animated or virtual character, express emotions via facial expressions. The recent advancement of 3D facial models, avatar bots and humanoid robots which have various applications across multiple domains raise the demand and expectation of users/audiences for more human like facial expressions. Hence, facial expressions are expected to be more expressive, have better subtlety and more variation.

Even if there is a huge interest in generating realistic or novel facial expressions on 3D animation models, creating a new facial animation is not an easy task. This is, partly due to the fact that animation techniques in general tend to follow an ad-hoc and inextensible approach [2]. These factors cause limitation on the performance in generating new and realistic facial animation expressions.

In this work, we explore the application of evolutionary algorithmic approach to achieve partial automation in generating 3D facial expressions. We particularly used one category of evolutionary approach called Interactive Genetic Algorithm (IGA) which is a form of genetic algorithm that demands a human involvement in the evolution loop as a fitness function; a property which compliments the subjective metrics nature of facial expressions.

2 Applications of IGAs

The broad category of IGAs, or Interactive Evolutionary Computation (IEC), in general has application in industrial design, speech processing and synthesis, data mining, image processing, education and in artistic vocations such as graphic arts, animation, music and much more [3]. Specifically, IGAs have been applied in photography, fashion, gaming, virtual reality and facial animation.

In relation to face/body animation or photography, IGAs have been used: (1) to change facial expressions by changing pixel positions, (2) to create animated graphic art by evolving mathematical equations that apply to the pixel attributes, (3) to create animations by evolving the combination of joint angles for arms and legs, (4) for evolving deformations of a 2D body for comical movements, (5) with 2D photos of partial images to compose a facial image for identifying a criminal suspect [4]. Facial animation is also an important research goal in human-computer interaction, as in the quest to build a believable Embodied Conversational Agent (ECA). These agents would be able to communicate complex information with human-like expressiveness. ECAs are becoming popular as front ends to web sites, and as part of many computer applications such as virtual training environments, tutoring systems, storytelling systems, portable personal guides, and entertainment systems [5].

3   Related Work

Kim and Cho [5] used IGA to evolve fashion design clothes. In this scenario IGA-based evolution plays well; as the fashion industry has a changing trend and thus a human fitness function would ideally be able to influence the trajectory of the evolution procedure to get more appealing results. In their approach, they classified parts of a cloth into three parts: neck and body, arm and sleeve, skirt and waistline. Each of these three sub parts include color as their parameter; expanding the search space. These six parameters (three sub parts and their respective colors) are considered as genes which give new cloth results via IGA based combination. They used a population size of 8 and limited the number of maximum generation to 10. They have done convergence and subject tests which measure the fitness value changes and user satisfaction respectively on the generated fashion designs in terms of being cool-looking and splendor clothes criteria; and they achieved encouraging results in both measurements.

A dissertation paper of Smith in [4] applied IGAs to evolve facial expressions and used Neural Networks as a surrogate function to reduce user fatigue. While a chromosome is a face animation of expression, different from our approach, genes are equivalent to key frame sequences (fraction of duration) of a full face animation. Thus, both chromosomes and genes are basically the same except for the time length difference between them. In this type of setting, due to the nature of the genes here, a crossover would mean a mere arrangement of instances (splits of keyframes) of parent facial expressions in order to form new expression. A sample scenario that depicts this for instance would be; given a sad and happy expressions (as two parents)- generating a new facial expression (the child) would then be via crossover between multiple fractions of time/keyframe splits (genes) of the two parent expressions. Logically, the generated child expression is potentially going to be far from realistic as it would be constituted of keyframes sequences (genes) that jump from one type of parent expression/animation to the other back and forth prematurely. However, in our work we used a location/region, on the face of parent expressions, based crossovers instead of based on splices keyframe sequences of parent expressions where a sequence of keyframes from a single point on the face can be splitted into genes as done here.

Similarly, the face image generation system called E-FIT applies Interactive Evolutionary strategy, which is in the broader category of evolutionary algorithms, for parameter optimization [11].

4   IGA Based Facial Animation Evolver

In a typical IGA design there are representations of population, chromosomes and genes. While a chromosome consists of genes, a population is a collection of chromosomes. In order to evolve a new children population, crossover and mutation of the chromosomes must happen in terms of the switching between and mutation of genes found in different chromosomes.

In this implementation, while a chromosome represents an individual facial animation, population is a collection of the different separate facial animations presented. A gene is equivalent either to a single location's keyframe or to keyframes of a group of subparts of the face facial animation depending on the type of crossover used. The 3D facial model used for experiment uses both bone and morph driven animation [8]. The keyframe sequences interpolation was automated with a function of time called FCurve (f-curve) which is similar to bezier curves interpolation technique but with a modification which enforces any specific keyframe location to hold only a single value at a time for the purpose of doing animation/transformation [9]. The keyframe information of is treated as a sub-phenotype input since a 3D facial expression is represented via a set of keyframes while the set of bones that drive the facial morphing to generate expressions are considered the genotypes.

In this work, the crossovers of IGA refer the breeding of bone locations/values, or interchangeably referred here as fcurves, between the corresponding sequence of keyframes of the two parent expressions a new/child expression. In our case, a child expression is generated only from two parents. All used expressions have a duration of 10 s in a 30 keyframes per second rate. This duration uniformity allows crossover operations, between facial bone locations (fcurves), across each corresponding or same-indexed keyframes of both parents. Generated Child generation expressions too have similar keyframes duration and follow the same general rule of breeding. The genetic crossover process to generate a child can be put in a simplified format as:

Child Expression C = Parent Expression A<Crossover Operator>Parent Expression B. Further more this notation can be further decomposed into keyframes level as shown below.

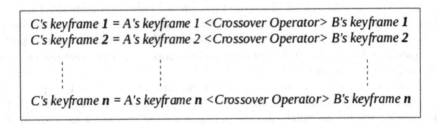

Fig. 1. Abstraction of genes crossover in a parallel keyframes level of parents (A an B) to generate genes in similar keyframes index of expression C (child).

Though in Fig. 1 roughly shows that crossover between parents happen at keyframes level, the exact procedure of generating new locations (fcurve values) for all the facial bones of the child expression depends on the type of the crossover operator used. But it can be put in a generic notation of:

C's Facial Bone's locations at keyframe n = A's Facial Bone's locations at keyframe n<Crossover Operator>B's Facial Bone's locations at keyframe n.

GA has different types of crossover operators. In our case we experimented with the uniform, cut-and-splice, blend and their hybrids. These crossovers are widely applied in many GA and IGA works. Implementation wise, we incorporated elitism to enable partially controlled breeding which helps in evolving sensible facial animations in some cases.

In GA, mutation is applied to weak solution candidates. It helps prevent the population from getting stuck in a local optima by introducing some diversity. In our experiments a default value of 0.01 mutation degree was applied only to facial animations which were rated lowest during the generation process.

4.1   Uniform Crossover

This crossover is based on separate selection mechanism of genes from both parents. One way to do uniform crossover is to randomly select genes from parents. In the case when the gene from the first parent is not selected, the corresponding location value of the facial bone (gene) of the second parent will be inserted into the child instead. Selection of all of the genes (locations of all included facial bones) in a single keyframe is done in a loop of choose either of the corresponding genes in the similarly indexed keyframes of the two parents. This same technique is followed across the rest of keyframes in both parents.

4.2   Cut-and-Splice Crossover

In this case the crossover can be generally assumed as a version of two-point crossover but where there is a fixed point of selection and also where each segment contains location values of more than one facial bones instead of a single bone's. Potentially, this lowers down the possible active exchange of fcurves during a crossover. On the other hand, since the three slicing point segments used are the sub-parts of the face (Head, mouth and eyes areas), this increases the likelihood of generating more human-like expressions due to the fact that these sub-parts are treated as indivisible units (genes) during crossover. This assumption was validated by the experiment.

In order to increase flexibility of generation and increase solution space, six different kinds of choosing combination of the three sub-parts were offered. So it is possible to choose which one the genes or two of the genes we want to be selected from the first parent (the reverse is applied on the other parent automatically). These are 'Head', 'Mouth', 'Eyes', 'Head-Mouth', 'Head-Eyes' and 'Mouth-Eyes'. For example if the 'Head' option is chosen, the child expression will have its head animation from its first parent and, mouth and eyes animations from the other parent. Or if the 'Head-Mouth' option is selected, the child's genetic make up of head and mouth animations will be taken from its first parent and eyes animations from their second parent and so on for the rest of the options. This feature adds the capability of seeing six different kinds of children chromosome population within a single crossover. This approach provides a short cut to explore the search space extensively.

4.3   Blend Operator

This is a crossover type which in general sums two points and returns their average point as an output; a blended output. Each f-curve of a parent facial expression is summed to its corresponding f-curve of the other parent and then summed result is averaged. Thus, the child expression will be comprised of averaged f-curves of its parents.

4.4   Elitism: By Retaining Interesting Facial Animation Sub-parts from the Current Population Members

In IGAs, minimizing the user fatigue involved when generating facial animations is critical. Elitism greatly speeds up and enhances the quality of the overall population by retaining chosen sub-parts from some members' in the current population and to be incorporated in the next generation without the potential loss of them through crossover or mutation. In our implementation we have incorporated a feature that enables selection of one or more sub-parts (head, mouth and eyes) of parent expressions to be transferred to the next generation without potential loss or change due to crossover and mutation.

4.5   Search Space

A search space indicates the number of possible combinations of the different models of genes in a given population. We have sampled initial population of 36 during all the IGA based experiments. During the cut-and-splice, crossover happens in terms of defined sub parts (head, eyes and mouth area) of the face animation. Thus, a gene is equivalent to a head, mouth, or eye animation which themselves are composed of multiple f-curves. There are 9 different models of mouth movements, 22 different models of eye movements and 24 different models of head movement out of 36 total initial chromosome population/facial animations models. Six different kinds of breeding combinations were offered during the cut-and-splice crossover. Thus, the total size of initially accessible search space is $9*22*24*6 = 28{,}512$.

   On the other hand, in case of uniform and blend crossovers, search space is very much larger as a gene is equivalent to single f-curves in a given facial animation. Thus, it is reasonable to imagine that the search space is very big. But in reality, this doesn't mean that it gives exaggerated diversity in evolved facial animations. The main reason for this is mostly the difference of animation between each corresponding f-curves of the different the given facial animations might not always be that big/obvious except for the active facial areas of the given expressions. Corresponding f-curves of another facial animation might not be that big/obvious unless the two facial animations are quite different. These conditions have direct effect on the diversity of newly generated animations despite the deceptively large looking search space.

5   Experiment and Result Summary

As an experiment platform the blender 3D engine [7] was used. It supports python scripting interface which allows programmatic access the graphics objects on the tool. Further more the 3D face model we used for experimentation also provides a python based API which is suitable for extension and modification. User satisfaction based subjective measurement for credibility and peculiarity parameters on the evolved 3D facial expressions, via the different operators discussed, and also on artist animated ones was done. Five subjects were used for rating the provided facial expressions in a specified questionnaire formats. Three of the subjects work in research and technology (computer science) area; the fourth one is an artist level animator while the last one is a registered nurse. The first four are familiar with the goal of the work. All of the candidates were allowed to finish the questionnaire in a period of two weeks in their own pace. The potential inconsistencies of metrics that could be caused due the degree of familiarity of the subjects with technology or the aim of the research or mood changes are not considered.

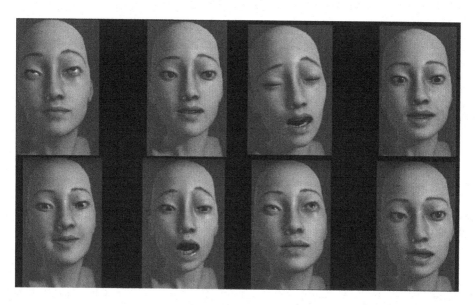

Fig. 2. Some screen captures of IGA based evolved 3D facial expressions of the model used.

5.1   Credibility

The credibility parameter in this experiment refers to the measurement of the facial animations in terms of their degree of acceptance as potential human expression like. Figure 3 shows subjective credibility score for expressions evolved using uniform, cut-and-splice, blend, uniform-blend hybrid and artist animated 3D facial expressions.

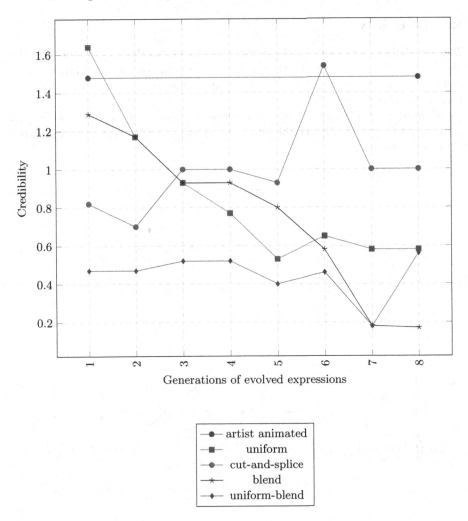

Fig. 3. Credibility score for the different IGA crossovers based evolved and artist-animated expressions.

Overall Average Credibility

Artist-animated	Uniform	Cut-and-Splice	Blend	Uniform-Blend
87%	71.4%	74.9%	68.9%	61%

5.2 Peculiarity

The peculiarity parameter in this experiment refers to the measurement of the facial animations in terms of their degree of uniqueness or distinctiveness. A facial expression despite having a less human-like appeal, it can still have a higher distinctiveness.

Figure 4 shows subjective peculiarity measurement of expressions evolved using uniform, cut-and-splice, blend, uniform-blend hybrid and artist animated 3D facial expressions.

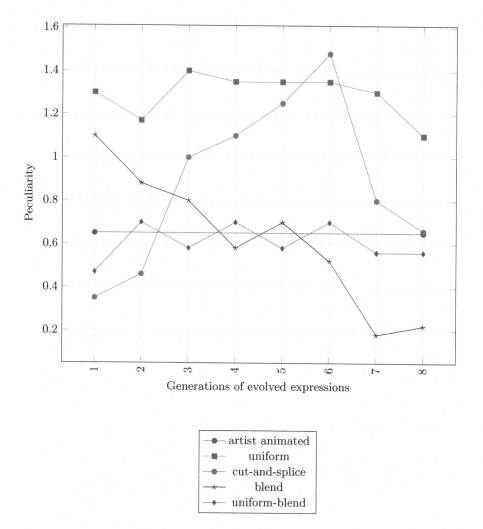

Fig. 4. Peculiarity score for the different IGA crossovers based evolved and artist-animated expressions.

Overall Average Peculiarity

Artist-animated	Uniform	Cut-and-Splice	Blend	Uniform-Blend
66.25%	82.25%	72%	65.5%	65%

5.3 Retain Interesting Sub-parts of Current Parent Expressions During the Next Generation

The sub-parts keeping feature (elitism)used was experimented with the uniform based evolver. All IGA parameters such as probabilities of crossover and mutation were kept to the same level as used during the other pure operators based generation experiments.

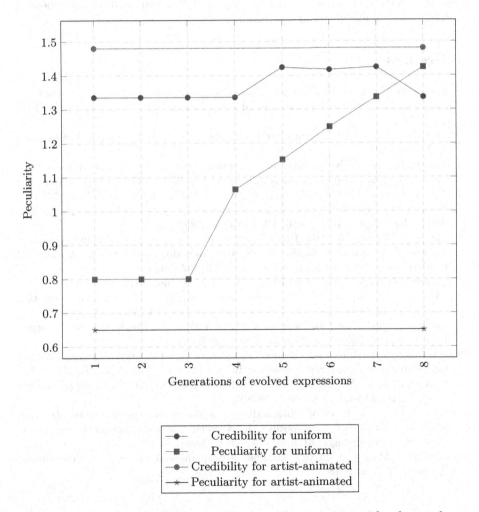

Fig. 5. Credibility and peculiarity score for the uniform operator with sub-parts keeping feature based evolved expressions in comparison to artist-animated expressions.

Figure 5 shows the credibility and peculiarity scores for the elitism based uniform evolver and also artist-animated expressions just for comparison purpose.

This feature of retaining interesting features members of the current population to the next ones resulted in a general quality increase in lesser number of generations. The uniform based breeding with interesting sub-parts keeping feature improved to 84.2% and 76.95% scores for the credibility and peculiarity parameters respectively.

6   Conclusion

This paper has shown that IGAs can be competitively useful in generating credible and quality 3D facial expressions. In particular, it showed the use of keyframe point information (f-curve) as an IGA gene and demonstrated its usefulness in evolving realistic and peculiar expressions.

References

1. Sauter, D.A., Eisner, F., Ekman, P., Scott, S.K.: Cross-cultural recognition of basic emotions through nonverbal emotional vocalizations. Proc. Natl. Acad. Sci. **107**, 2408–2412 (2010)
2. Parke, F., Waters, K.: Computer Facial Animation, 2nd edn. AK Peters Ltd., Wellesley (2008)
3. Takagi, H.: Interactive evolutionary computation: fusion of the capabilities of EC optimization and human evaluation. Proc. IEEE **89**(9), 1275–1296 (2001)
4. Nancy, S.: Evolving Credible Facial Expressions with Interactive GAs (2012)
5. Kim, H.-S., Cho, S.-B.: Application of interactive genetic algorithm to fashion design. Eng. Appl. Artif. Intell. **13**, 635–644 (2000)
6. Mana, N., Pianesi, F.: HMM-based synthesis of emotional facial expressions during speech in synthetic talking heads. In: Proceedings of the 8th International Conference on Multimodal Interfaces, pp. 380–387 (2006)
7. Blender 3D Engine: www.blender.org. Accessed 20 June 2018
8. Chen, L.: An Analysis of the Current and Future State of 3D Facial Animation Techniques and Systems. Communication University of China, B.A. (2009)
9. Farin, G.: Curves and Surfaces for CAGD: A Practical Guide, 5th edn. Morgan Kaufmann Publishers Inc., San Francisco (2002)
10. Kurt, B., et al.: Active appearance model-based facial composite generation with interactive nature-inspired heuristics. In: Gunsel, B., Jain, A.K., Tekalp, A.M., Sankur, B. (eds.) MRCS 2006. LNCS, vol. 4105, pp. 183–190. Springer, Heidelberg (2006). https://doi.org/10.1007/11848035_26
11. George, B., et al.: EFIT-V - interactive evolutionary strategy for the construction of photo-realistic facial composites. In: Genetic and Evolutionary Computation Conference Proceedings, Atlanta, GA, USA (2008)
12. Blender Manual. https://docs.blender.org/manual/en/dev/modeling/curves. Accessed 10 June 2018

Comparative Study of Modulation Techniques for 5G Networks

Getachew H. Geleta[1], Dereje M. Molla[1], and Kinde A. Fante[2(✉)]

[1] Institute of Technology, Hawassa University, 05 Hawassa, Ethiopia
getachewaman21@gmail.com, desperansa@gmail.com
[2] Institute of Technology, Jimma University, 378 Jimma, Ethiopia
Kinde.anlay@ju.edu.et

Abstract. Fifth Generation (5G) communication systems applications are expected to use or require lower latency, higher data rates, and efficient spectrum usage which are impacted by the adopted modulation scheme. Thus, proper selection and usage of efficient modulation scheme is crucial. Orthogonal Frequency Division Multiplexing (OFDM) suffers from high peak to average power ratio, which results in low efficiency of power amplifier and increases the battery consumption. Moreover, the OFDM spectrum has high out of band side lobes or side lobe leakage causing problem of low spectral efficiency. So, to overcome some of these drawbacks new modulation techniques for 5G communication systems such as Generalized Frequency Division Multiplexing (GFDM), filtered – OFDM (f-OFDM), Universal Filtered Multi-Carrier (UFMC), Filter Bank Multi-Carrier (FBMC) are considered. In this paper, we perform the comparative study of UFMC and FBMC in terms of Spectral Efficiency (SE) and Power Spectral Density (PSD). Simulations were done to evaluate the performance variation that can be achieved by varying the parameters of these modulation techniques, such as filter length, burst duration and overlapping factor. Our simulation results show that, FBMC has better SE for large burst durations whereas UFMC is better for small burst durations. In terms of PSD, FBMC has lower side lobe than UFMC. This implies that FBMC is more preferable to minimize the inter symbol interference and inter carrier interference.

Keywords: 5G · FBMC · UFMC

1 Introduction

Wireless communications have become an essential tool for our life. Starting from the First-Generation wireless networks (1G), there has been an exponential growth in number of users and their applications. Fifth generation mobile networks or 5th generation wireless systems are the proposed next telecommunications standards beyond the current Fourth Generation (4G/IMT -Advanced Standard). 5G planning aims at higher capacity than current 4G, allowing a higher density of mobile broadband users, and supporting device-to-device, more reliable, and massive machine communications. 5G research and development also aims at lower latency than 4G equipment and lower battery consumption, for better implementation of the Internet of Things (IoT). In addition to providing simply faster speeds, it is predicted that 5G networks also will

F. A. Zimale et al. (Eds.): ICAST 2018, LNICST 274, pp. 503–518, 2019.
https://doi.org/10.1007/978-3-030-15357-1_41

need to meet new use cases, such as the IoT, as well as broadcast-like services and lifeline communication in times of natural disaster [1].

Owing to a broad range of applications spanning from wireless regional area networks to machine type communications, future wireless networks have challenging objectives such as very high spectral and energy efficiency, very low latency and very high data rate, which require more effective physical layer solutions [1]. In this context, the vision and overall objectives of future wireless networks for 2020 and beyond have been defined by the International Telecommunication Union (ITU); and standardization activities for 5G wireless networks have been started through discussions about scenarios and requirements by Third Generation Partnership Project (3GPP) [2].

Orthogonal Frequency Division Multiplexing (OFDM) is the core of the physical layer of 4G wireless networks and fulfills the requirements and challenges of 4G scenarios. Despite of its proven advantages, OFDM has some shortcomings that make it difficult to address the scenarios foreseen for future 5G wireless networks. In OFDM, every symbol requires a Cyclic Prefix (CP). The insertion of CP reduces the spectral efficiency and prevents obtaining a low latency by shortening the symbols. Furthermore, OFDM is very sensitive to time and frequency synchronization errors and has high Out-of-Band (OOB) emission due to rectangular pulse shaping. Thus, OFDM can fulfill the requirements of 5G wireless networks in a limited way [3].

In recent years, several waveform proposals have been presented to overcome the above limitations of OFDM. These proposals can be categorized into two main classes: Cyclically-Prefixed OFDM (CP-OFDM) and non-CP-OFDM. The proposals in the first class, such as filtered OFDM (f-OFDM) and windowed OFDM (W-OFDM) [3], attempt to resolve the aforementioned problems by keeping the orthogonality. The proposals in the second class initially dismiss orthogonality to obtain better temporal and spectral characteristics, thus, causes a major paradigm shift in the context of waveform design, which may yield some backward compatibility issues [4]. Thus, in order to overcome these drawbacks, new modulation techniques such as f-OFDM, Filter Bank Multicarrier (FBMC), and Universal Filtered Multicarrier (UFMC) were suggested as novel modulation techniques of 5G wireless networks.

The comparative analysis of FBMC with OFDM, and UFMC with OFDM in terms of Power Spectral Density (PSD) and Spectral Efficiency (SE) was done in [5–7]. However, the sensitivity of the performance metrics on the parameters of these modulation techniques was not done so far. In this paper, however, we perform the comparative study of UFMC and FBMC in terms of SE and PSD. We will also analyze the performance of these modulation techniques by varying their parameters. The result of this research will play a significant role in selecting efficient modulation scheme for the upcoming 5G wireless networks.

This paper has two contributions. These are (1) we evaluate the dependency of the performance metrics of FBMC and UFMC on their parameters. We identify the parameters that strongly influences the performance of these modulation techniques. (2) We show the advantage of employing different modulation techniques for different applications to enhance the performance. The characteristics of the communication systems, such as burst duration, can influence the performance of these modulation techniques.

This paper contains four sections. A brief Introduction is given in Sect. 1. UFMC and FBMC system model details are discussed in Sect. 2. Sections 3 and 4 will deal with simulation results and conclusion, respectively.

2 Candidate 5G Modulation Techniques

Various types of modulation techniques have been proposed to address the new challenges that 5G networks are expected to solve, such as pulse shaping, filtering, and pre-coding to reduce the out-of-band (OOB) leakage of OFDM signals. Filtering is the most straightforward approach to reduce the OOB leakage and with a properly designed filter, the leakage over the stop-band can be greatly suppressed. Pulse shaping can be considered as a type of subcarrier-based filtering that reduces overlaps between subcarriers even inside the band of a single user. Thus, FBMC is an example of 5G modulations based on pulse shaping, whereas UFMC is an example of 5G modulations based on sub band filtering.

(1) **Filter Bank Multicarrier (FBMC)**: FBMC is an OFDM-like modulation format wherein subcarriers are passed through filters that suppress signal side lobes, making them eventually strictly band limited. FBMC is usually either coupled with Quadrature Amplitude Modulation (QAM) or with Offset QAM (OQAM) modulation formats. But, to achieve the best spectral efficiency OQAM is usually applied to make FBMC real-domain orthogonal in time and frequency domains. By adding generalized pulse shaping filters, the FBMC technique overcomes the limitations of OFDM which delivers a well localized sub channel in both time and frequency domain. The filter bank used at the transmitter side is called synthesis filter bank and that used in receiver side is called analysis filter bank [8].

As shown in Fig. 1, the input signal is first converted from serial to parallel (S/P) form and then passed through synthesis filter bank and then it is converted back to serial form after coming out of synthesis filter bank. Whereas at the receiver side, Fig. 2, after the signal passes through the channel it is converted to parallel form by serial to parallel converter and passed through analysis filter bank. Finally, when the output signal is obtained it is again converted to serial form by parallel to serial (P/S) converter.

(2) **Universal Filter Multicarrier (UFMC)**: In UFMC, the sub bands are equal in size, and each filter is a shifted version of the same prototype filter. OFDM is applied within a sub band for this modulation. Since the bandwidth of the filter in UFMC is much wider than that of the modulations based on the pulse shaping, the length in time domain is much shorter. Therefore, interference caused by the train of the filter can be easily eliminated by adopting a zero-padding (ZP) prefix with a reasonable length.

The UFMC transmitter and receiver block diagrams are shown below in Figs. 3 and 4, respectively. UFMC employs the full band of subcarriers (N) divided into sub bands. Each sub band has a fixed number of subcarriers and not all sub bands need to be employed for a given transmission. The modulation technique processes these sub bands individually and each sub band consists of fixed number of subcarriers. The narrowband and closely spaced individual sub bands undergoes N-point Inverse Fast Fourier Transform (IFFT) to get time domain of each sub band from Frequency

Domain of each sub band. An N-point IFFT for each sub band is computed, inserting zeros for the unallocated carriers [6].

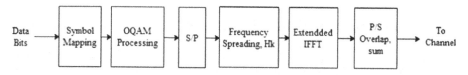

Fig. 1. Filter Bank Multicarrier Transmitter Block Diagram

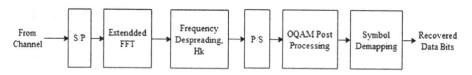

Fig. 2. Filter Bank Multicarrier Receiver Block Diagram

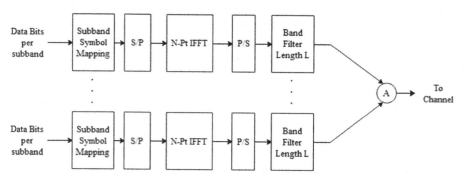

Fig. 3. Universal Filter Multicarrier transmitter block diagram

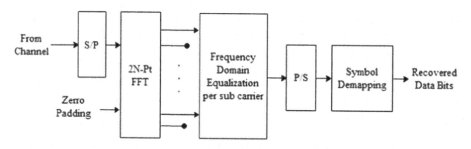

Fig. 4. Univeral Filter Multicarrier receiver block diagram

The UFMC receiver performs 2N point FFT on the data obtained from the channel. A guard interval of zeros is added between successive IFFT symbols. This prevents inter symbol interference (ISI) due to transmitter filter delay. Discard even subcarrier points to get N length frequency domain receive signal. FFT block is used to process the received signal and converts data received in time domain into frequency domain. Equalization detects the transmitted data. The Symbol de mapping is performed to the frequency domain equalization to get the original data bits [6].

3 Performance Analysis

3.1 Comparison of Spectral Efficiency of UFMC and FBMC

The term spectral efficiency is used to describe the rate of information being transmitted over a given bandwidth in specific communication systems. Spectral Efficiency may also be called bandwidth efficiency. Since frequency spectrum is limited, it has to be utilized efficiently. A given bandwidth is said to be used effectively if maximum information can be transmitted over it. The spectral efficiency of UFMC and FBMC modulation schemes is given by [9]:

$$\eta_{UFMC} = \frac{mxN_{FFT}}{N_{FFT} + L - 1} \tag{1}$$

$$\eta_{FBMC} = \frac{mxS}{S + K - \frac{1}{2}} \tag{2}$$

Where: NFFT = number of FFT; S = duration of burst; m = bits per subcarrier; K = Overlapping factor; L = filter length.

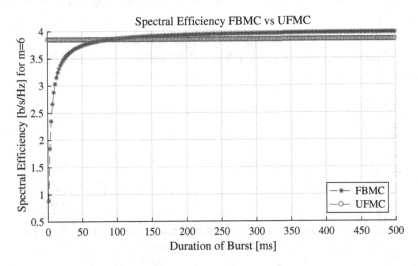

Fig. 5. Spectral Efficiency of FBMC and UFMC with filter length equal to 43.

We now show the spectral efficiency of the UFMC and FBMC for different value of number of FFT (NFFT), duration of burst (s), bits per subcarrier (m), overlapping factor (K), and filter length (L).

Figures 5 and 6 show the spectral efficiency of UFMC and FBMC with number of FFT 1024, bits per subcarrier and overlapping factor equal to four, and with the burst duration of up to 500 ms and with filter length equal to 43 and 23, respectively.

In Fig. 5, the spectral efficiency of UFMC is constant (around 3.85b/s/Hz) throughout the burst duration. Whereas the spectral efficiency of FBMC increases rapidly with burst duration till 70 ms. After around 70 ms, the spectral efficiency of FBMC increases gradually with larger value than UFMC.

Everything being the same, decreasing the filter length from 43 to 23, in Fig. 6, increases the spectral efficiency of both FBMC and UFMC near to 3.95b/s/Hz.

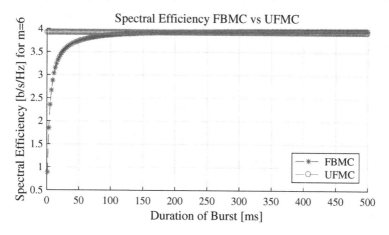

Fig. 6. Spectral efficiency of FBMC and UFMC with filter length equal to 23.

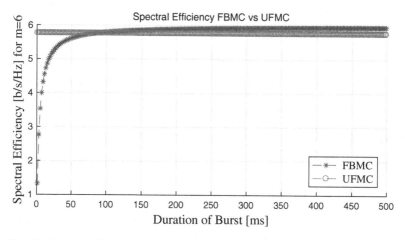

Fig. 7. Spectral efficiency of FBMC and UFMC with bits per subcarrier (m) = 6

Where FBMC still increases gradually beyond this value, showing its efficiency being larger than UFMC.

Figures 7 and 8 show the spectral efficiency of UFMC and FBMC for burst duration of up to 500 ms, overlapping factor equal to four, filter length equal to 43, bits per subcarrier, m = 6 and number of FFT 1024 and 512, respectively.

Increasing the bits per sub carrier from 4, in Figs. 5 and 6, to 6, in Figs. 7 and 8, the spectral efficiency of both FBMC and UFMC increases up to around 5.7b/s/Hz and beyond. As Fig. 7 shows, the spectral efficiency of FBMC is larger than UFMC and continues to increase after burst duration of 100 ms. But, when we decrease the number of FFT value from 1024 to 512 as in Fig. 8, the spectral efficiency of FBMC increases rapidly and copes with UFMC at around 40 ms with an efficiency value of 5.52b/s/Hz. Moreover, the spectral efficiency of UFMC has decreased from 5.7b/s/Hz in Figs. 7, 6 and 5.52b/s/Hz in Fig. 8 with decreasing value of number of FFT. However, the spectral efficiency of FBMC is same, at around 5.7b/s/Hz with decreasing the number of FFT.

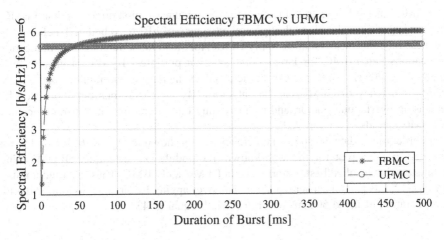

Fig. 8. Spectral efficiency of FBMC and UFMC with number of FFT 512.

Figure 9 is the spectral efficiency of FBMC and UFMC for burst duration of up to 500 ms with number of FFT 512, filter length 43, Bits per subcarrier equal to 6, and with overlapping factor increased to six.

By increasing the overlapping factor from 4 to 6, in Fig. 9, the spectral efficiency of FBMC is lower than 5.7b/s/Hz. Whereas, UFMC has the same spectral efficiency in both cases.

From the output results, shown in Figs. 5, 6, 7, 8 and 9, we see that the spectral efficiency of FBMC increases rapidly for the first few intervals of the burst duration and then, it increases smoothly with the burst duration until it attains the spectral efficiency of UFMC. After that, it looks constant for some range of burst duration like UFMC. Then, it increases beyond this constant value. However, the spectral efficiency of UFMC is constant throughout the burst duration.

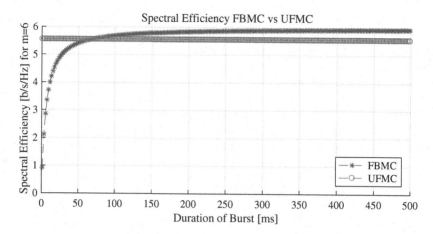

Fig. 9. Spectral efficiency of FBMC and UFMC with overlapping factor = 6

UFMC has better spectral efficiency for small value of burst durations than FBMC. But, for larger burst durations the spectral efficiency of FBMC is better. To effectively use these modulation techniques, apply UFMC for small burst duration communication applications and FBMC for larger burst duration purposes. By decreasing the filter length, by increasing bits per sub carrier, and by increasing the number of FFT the spectral efficiency of UFMC can be enhanced. By increasing bits per subcarrier, by decreasing overlapping factor, and by increasing burst duration the spectral efficiency of FBMC can also be improved.

In order to validate the spectral efficiency results shown in Figs. 5, 6, 7, 8 and 9, we also performed a plot for the well-known 4G-modulation technique, OFDM, using parameters that resulted best performance in UFMC and FBMC. Thus, we used number of FFT 512, bits per subcarrier equal to 6 and overlapping factor equal to four, and with burst duration of up to 500 ms and filter length equal to 43.

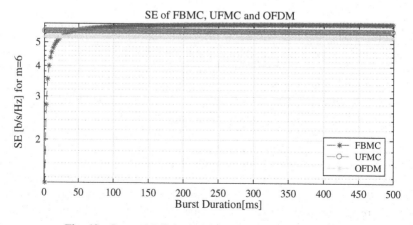

Fig. 10. Spectral Efficiency of FBMC, UFMC and OFDM

As Fig. 10 shows, the spectral efficiency of UFMC and OFDM is constant throughout the burst duration, around 5.7b/s/Hz and 5.2b/s/Hz, respectively. However, the spectral efficiency of FBMC increases rapidly with burst duration till 50 ms. After around 50 ms, the spectral efficiency of FBMC increases gradually with larger value than UFMC and OFDM.

As our result shows OFDM has low spectral efficiency than both UFMC and FBMC. This is due to the wide frequency guards and the cyclic prefix used by OFDM. Unlike OFDM, UFMC and FBMC do not use cyclic prefix, which results in the increase in spectral efficiency. Thus, the spectral efficiency of FBMC and UFMC is very efficient and OFDM is rather inefficient.

3.2   Power Spectral Density of FBMC

To compromise the Bit error rate (BER) and peak-to-average power ratio (PAPR) for both UFMC and FBMC modulation techniques, 15 dB signal-to-noise ratio (SNR) value is considered for comparison and 4QAM is used for FBMC whereas, 16QAM is used for UFMC as a mapping scheme. In addition, the system parameters, as shown in Table 1, are considered initially to simulate the FBMC for the PSD unless and otherwise stated.

Table 1. Simulation Parameters

Parameters	Values
Overlapping symbols K	4
Number of FFT points NFFT	1024
Guard bands on both sides	212
Number of symbols	100
Bits per subcarrier (4QAM)	2
Signal to noise ratio SNR	15 dB

As shown in Fig. 11, the PSD of FBMC occupies its band width within the frequency range of between nearly −0.3 and 0.3. But, the power spectral density outside of this range is not necessary because it is considered as out of bound and leads to inter symbol interference.

Figure 12 shows, the PSD of FBMC with number of FFT decreasing from 1024 to 512.

As shown in Fig. 12, the PSD of FBMC occupies its bandwidth within the frequency range of between nearly −0.1 and 0.1. But, the PSD outside of this range is not necessary because it is considered as out of bound and leads to inter symbol interference. Compared to the result in Fig. 11 with NFFT = 1024, the bandwidth of this spectral density and the power occupied within this bandwidth is smaller. However, out-of-band leakage is lower than that of Fig. 11. Therefore, it has an efficient PSD than with the number of FFT equal to 1024.

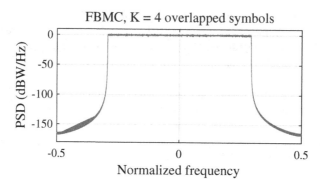

Fig. 11. Power spectral density of FBMC with NFFT = 1024

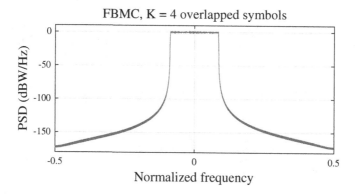

Fig. 12. Power Spectral Density of FBMC (Number of FFT = 512)

Figure 13 shows the PSD of FBMC with number of FFT 512, overlapping symbol equal to four, and with decreasing the guard band from 212 to 112.

As shown in Fig. 13, the PSD of FBMC occupies its band width within the frequency range of between nearly −0.4 and 0.4. The bandwidth and the power occupied within this bandwidth is higher, when we compare with guard band of 212. However, the gap between the graph of the power spectral density outside of this bandwidth range and the normalized is increasing. This shows that it is highly affected by the ISI than with guard band 212. Therefore, it has less efficient PSD than with guard band 212.

The PSD of FBMC with overlapping symbol equal to three is shown in Fig. 14. As shown in Fig. 14, the PSD of FBMC occupies its bandwidth within the frequency range of between nearly −0.3 and 0.3. The bandwidth of this spectral density and the power occupied within this bandwidth is the same with the overlapping symbol equal to four. However, the out-of-band leakage is higher than that of Fig. 13. This shows that it leads to higher ISI than with overlapping symbol equal to four. Therefore, it has less efficient PSD than with overlapping symbol equal to four.

Figure 15 shows the PSD of FBMC with number of FFT equal to 512, guard bands on both sides equal to 212, and overlapping symbol equal to two.

FBMC, K = 4 overlapped symbols

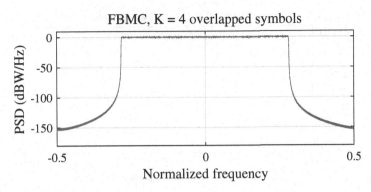

Fig. 13. Power Spectral Density of FBMC with number of FFT = 512 and guard band 112.

FBMC, K = 3 overlapped symbols

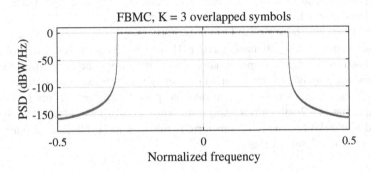

Fig. 14. Power Spectral Density of FBMC with overlapping symbol equal to 3

As shown in Fig. 15, the PSD of FBMC occupies its bandwidth within the frequency range of between nearly −0.1 and 0.1. The bandwidth of this spectral density and the power occupied within this bandwidth is smaller, when we compare it with the overlapping symbol equal to three and four. And also, the out-of-band spectral leakage increases with decreasing overlapping symbol. This shows that it is extremely affected by ISI than with the overlapped symbol equal to three and four. Therefore, it has very less efficient PSD when we compare it with the overlapping symbol equal to three and four. The out-of-band spectral leakage increases, which increases ISI, with decreasing overlapping symbol.

3.3 Power Spectral Density of UFMC

Simulation result of the PSD of UFMC for various values of sub bands and sub-carriers is demonstrated.

Figure 16 shows the PSD of UFMC for 72 subcarriers with 6 sub bands and 12 sub-carriers. Thus, the overall band is divided into 6 sub bands, each sub band having 12 subcarriers with less side lobes. The required bandwidth range is covered between

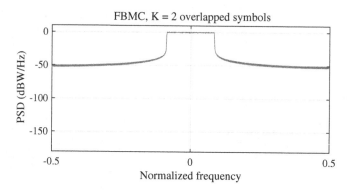

Fig. 15. Power Spectral Density of FBMC with number of FFT = 512

the normalized frequency of −0.1 and 0.1. Outside of this range of frequency is unwanted because it leads to inter symbol interference.

Figure 17 shows the PSD for 162 subcarriers. That is, the overall band is divided into 9 sub bands, each sub band having 18 subcarriers with less side lobes. The required bandwidth range is approximately covered between the normalized frequency of −0.2 and 0.2. Outside of this range of frequency is unwanted because it leads to ISI. This result shows that the bandwidth and the power occupied at this bandwidth is higher than that of 72 sub carries. And also, out-of-band spectral leakage is higher as compared to the UFMC with 72 subcarriers. So, it is more affected to inter symbol interference than 72 sub carries.

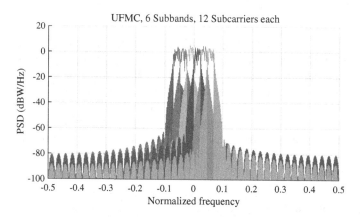

Fig. 16. Power Spectral Density of UFMC with 6 sub bands

Figure 18 shows the power spectral density of UFMC with 15 sub bands and 30 sub-carries.

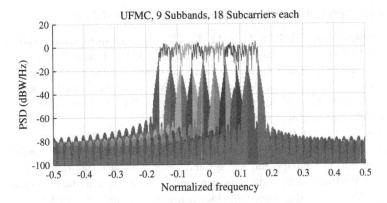

Fig. 17. Power Spectral Density of UFMC with 9 sub bands

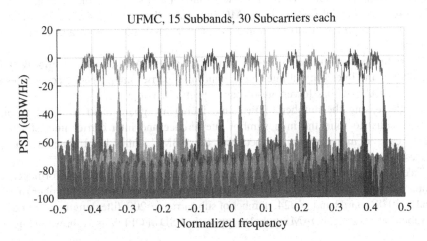

Fig. 18. Power Spectral Density of UFMC with 15 sub bands

Figure 18 shows the PSD of UFMC for 450 subcarriers. The overall band is divided into 15 sub bands, each sub band having 30 subcarriers with less side lobes. The required bandwidth range is approximately covered between the normalized frequency of −0.45 and 0.45. Then, outside of this range of frequency is unwanted because it leads to inter symbol interference. This result shows that the bandwidth and the power occupied at this bandwidth is higher than that of 72 and 162 sub carries. Furthermore, the out-of-band spectral leakage has increased when we compare it with the 72 and 162 sub carries. So, it is more affected by inter symbol interference than 72 and 162 sub carries. Therefore, its power spectral density is less efficient compared to the 72 and 162 sub carriers.

3.4   Power Spectral Density Comparison of UFMC and FBMC

Generally, the PSD of FBMC in Figs. 11, 12, 13, 14 and 15 shows that with decreasing number of FFT, the out-of-band spectral leakage reduces. But, it decreases with the bandwidth. With decreasing the guard bands, the out-of band spectral leakage reduces. The bandwidth also increases. And with decreasing the overlapping factor the out-of-band spectral leakage increases which leads to higher ISI. The bandwidth also reduces with decreasing overlapping symbol.

Figures 16, 17 and 18 shows the PSD of UFMC with increasing number of sub bands and sub carriers. It shows that with increasing the number of sub bands and sub carriers, the out-of-band spectral leakage increases. And also, the range of frequency occupied by the transmitted signal has increased. This shows that, the amount of power within the bandwidth increases with increasing the number of sub bands and sub-carriers.

If the out-of-band spectral leakage is low, the Modulation's spectral density is efficient. From our result, FBMC has lower out-of-band spectral leakage than UFMC. Therefore, the spectral density of FBMC is greater than that of the UFMC. Hence, FBMC is more preferable to minimize the inter symbol interference and inter carrier interference.

By reducing the number of sub carriers, the PSD of UFMC can be improved. In other words, the inter symbol interference and inter carrier interference becomes lesser because, the UFMC has lower out-of-band spectral leakage.

By decreasing the number of FFT and increasing guard band with overlapping symbols equal to four, the inter symbol interference and inter carrier interference of FBMC can be more minimized because, the FBMC out-of-band spectral leakage reduces. The bandwidth occupied by the signal also reduces.

Taking values of the OFDM parameter that results the best PSD performance we compared the output of PSD of UFMC and FBMC with OFDM. The number of FFT equal to 2048, guard band = 924, number of sub carrier = 200, filter length = 43 and bits per subcarrier = 2 (i.e. 4QAM symbol mapper) the PSD of OFDM is as shown in Fig. 19.

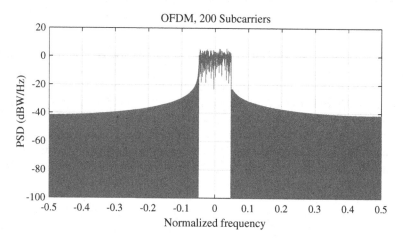

Fig. 19. Power Spectral Density of OFDM with 200 subcarriers

Figure 19 shows the PSD of OFDM for 200 subcarriers. The required bandwidth range is approximately covered between the normalized frequency of −0.05 and 0.05. This result shows that the bandwidth and the power occupied at this bandwidth is lesser than that of UFMC and FBMC with lesser sub carriers and number of FFT. Furthermore, the out-of-band spectral leakage of OFDM is higher when we compare it with the other modulation techniques. So, OFDM is more affected by inter symbol interference making its power spectral density less efficient.

Thus, this drawback of OFDM is addressed by UFMC and FBMC with efficient PSD result as depicted in Sects. 3.2 and 3.3 of this paper.

4 Conclusions

In this paper, we have performed comparison of candidate 5G modulation techniques (UFMC and FBMC) in terms of their spectral efficiency and power spectral density. The results found depicted that both can overcome the limitation of OFDM in its SE and PSD performance to meet the requirement set for 5G. Thus, both can be applied to 5G communication applications. Specifically, since UFMC has better SE for small burst duration than FBMC, it can be applied to applications requiring small burst duration. On the other hand, FBMC can be applied to communication systems where larger burst duration is required.

In terms of their PSD, FBMC has lower out-of band spectral leakage than UFMC, which results the spectral density of FBMC to be greater than that of the UFMC. From these finding we conclude that FBMC is more preferable to minimize the inter symbol interference and inter carrier interference, which are the requirement of 5G systems. Thus, FBMC is more preferable to 5G scenarios than UFMC.

In the future, we will further extend this work by comparing more Modulation techniques such as OFDM, f-OFDM, GFDM. The comparative study can be further extended by considering more parameters such as peak-to-average power ratio, delay and computational complexity of the modulation techniques.

References

1. Wunder, G., et al.: 5G NOW: Non-orthogonal, asynchronous waveforms for future mobile applications. IEEE Commun. **52**, 97–105 (2014)
2. GPP: Study on scenarios and requirements for next generation access technologies. Technical report 38.913, February 2016
3. Abdoli, J., et al.: Filtered OFDM: a new waveform for future wireless systems. In: Signal Processing Advances Wireless Communication, Stockholm, Sweden, June 2015
4. Öztürk, E., Basar, E., Çirpan, H.A.: Generalized Frequency Division Multiplexing With Flexible Index Modulation, Istanbul, Turkey (2017)
5. Kansal, P., Shankhwar, A.K.: FBMC versus OFDM Waveform Contenders for 5G Wireless Communication Systems, India (2017)
6. UFMC: The 5G Modulation Technique. Naga Rani, P., and Dr. Ch. Santhi Rani Machilipatnam, Andhra Pradesh, India (2016)

7. Banelli, P., Buzzi, S., et al.: Modulation Formats and Waveforms for the Physical Layer of 5G Wireless Networks: Who Will BE the Heir of OFDM?', 22 July 2014
8. Cai, Y., Qin, Z., et al.: Modulation and Multiple Access for 5G Networks, China (2017)
9. El Gholb, Y., El Imrani, N., Ghenniouiet, H.: 5G: an idea whose time has come. Int. J. Sci. Eng. Res. **8**(8) (2017)

Phytoremediation Potential of Free Floating Plant Species for Chromium Wastewater: The Case of Duckweed, Water Hyacinth, and Water Lilies

Samuel Gemeda[1]([✉]), Nigus Gabbiye[2], and Agegnehu Alemu[3]

[1] School of Mechanical and Chemical Engineering,
Kombolcha Institute of Technology, Wollo University,
P.O.Box 208, Kombolcha, Ethiopia
samigemeda16@gmail.com
[2] Faculty of Chemical and Food Engineering, Bahir Dar Institute of Technology,
Bahir Dar University, P.O.Box 26, Bahir Dar, Ethiopia
nigus_g@yahoo.com
[3] College of Science, Department of Chemistry, Bahir Dar University,
Bahir Dar, Ethiopia
agegnehua@gmail.com

Abstract. Chromium is the second most toxic metal in groundwater, soil, and sediments. Due to its large scale industrial utilization, it exist in various forms in the environment. The present technologies used to eliminate chromium are too expensive and not eco-friendly. Phytoremediation, which is low cost and eco-friendly technology for wastewater treatment was analyzed via Aquatic free-floating plants. This study was conducted to check the phytoremediation capability of three free-floating aquatic plants: Duckweed, Water lilies, and Water hyacinth for the removal of chromium (III) and (VI) in aqueous solutions. The aquatic plants were put in 15 L solution containing 1, 5, and 10 mg/L of Cr (III) and Cr (VI) for 14 days after two weeks acclimation period. The relative growth, tolerance index and chromium uptake by the three plants were measured. The concentrations of chromium in the samples were analyzed using Inductively Coupled Plasma Optical Emission Spectrometer (ICP-OES). The results showed a significant increase ($P < 0.05$) in accumulation of chromium in the plant's tissues. Maximum total accumulation of 322.57 and 82 mg/kg for plant treated with 10 mg/L for both solution of Cr (III) and Cr (VI) were obtained in Water hyacinth as compared to Duckweed with maximum accumulation of 169.43 and 37.29 mg/kg at 10 mg/L for both Cr (III) and Cr (VI) respectively. Water lilies show a relatively low removal performance with a maximum uptake of 160.82 and 28.78 mg/kg at 5 mg/L for both Cr (III) and Cr (VI) respectively. The relative growth of all plants increase with time but decrease for an increase in concentration of chromium. The study showed that Water hyacinth as an efficient candidate for phytoremediation of chromium compared with Duckweed and Water lilies.

Keywords: Heavy metal · Chromium · Wastewater treatment · Phytoremediation · Water hyacinth · Water lilies · Duckweed

F. A. Zimale et al. (Eds.): ICAST 2018, LNICST 274, pp. 519–535, 2019.
https://doi.org/10.1007/978-3-030-15357-1_42

1 Introduction

The release of untreated sewage and waste into surface water is still a common practice in many countries [1]. All over the world, 80% of used water is not either collected nor treated and is directly released into our water environment [2]. Both organic and inorganic pollutant of water from such action put all marine life and human health at danger and specially intimidate developing region, where between 75 and 90% of their populations are subjected to insecure drinking water [3]. The water contaminant of primary concern are the heavy metals such as lead, arsenic, cadmium, mercury, chromium, and thallium, due to their non-biodegradability and tenacity in the environment [3].

Heavy metals contamination is a primary environmental concern due to their toxicity, non-biodegradability, and high bioaccumulation possibility [4]. Water pollution due to toxic heavy metals and dyes are the major concern for the aquatic environment. Metals and dyes are non-biodegradability and susceptible to form complex, result in very slow degradation [5].

Because of their high degree of toxicity arsenic, mercury, chromium, lead, and cadmium are major concern in term of public health significance [6]. Toxic heavy metals such as As, Pb, Hg, Cd, Cr, Ni, Fe, Cu, Co, and Zn have caused a prevailing water, air, and soil pollution due to industrial and mining activities [7]. Chromium exist mostly in hexavalent and trivalent forms in industrial wastewater [8]. They are used widely in industries such as leather tanning, metallurgical operation, steel production, electroplating, pigment and textile manufacturing, wood preservation, and chromate preparation [9]. Cr (III) and Cr (VI) are the predominate oxidative state found to be stable in an aqueous environment [10]. Cr (VI) is relatively insoluble, carcinogen, and is 500 times more harmful than Cr (III) [11].

Phytoremediation is an economical, no generation of secondary waste, and eco-friendly [12], in that it uses living plants for in situ removal of contaminants from water and soil [3, 13–15]. It depends on the ion uptake mechanism, and the physiological, anatomical and morphological characteristics of each species [16]. Moreover, it allows the restoration of contaminated environments with low costs and minimum collateral impacts [17].

In developing countries, as in Ethiopia and India, the tanning industry is the primary polluting operation. Different research studies shows that chromium is the most toxic heavy metal in these countries. Currently, about 26 tanneries are under operation in Ethiopia [18]. Different concentrations of chromium discharge were reported by different scholars. From Mojo tannery effluent about 32.2 ± 5.7 mg/L were reported, which resulted in a concentration of 2–15 mg/L in downstream [19]. Chromium concentration of about 7.82 mg/L were reported from Sheba Tannery effluent [20] and 3.54 ± 0.55 mg/L from Bahir Dar tannery effluent [21, 22]. The World Health Organization (WHO), set a tolerance limit of 0.1 mg/L Cr (VI) for discharge into inland surface waters and 0.05 mg/L into potable water. For hexavalent chrome, Ethiopian Environmental Protection Authority (EPA) also set a tolerance limit of

0.1 mg/L for industrial effluent [23]. Therefore, removal of chromium from industrial effluents is highly desirable to accord with these legal requirements and to keep the water quality [23].

For removal of heavy metals and organic compounds, different conventional methods are used, such as electrolysis [24], reverse osmosis [25], ion exchange [26], adsorption [27], simultaneous adsorption and bioaccumulation [28], and oxidation-reduction [29]. However, major limitations of such treatments are the production of large amount of sludge and inefficient or expensive processes [30]. Therefore, an effective method to treat Cr contaminated water prior to its discharge is mandatory to address the environmental and public health concerns.

Therefore, the objective of this study was to compare the level of chromium uptake, tolerance index, and relative growth of the plant species in chromium containing aqueous solutions under an ambient air condition.

2 Methodology

2.1 Reagents and Chemicals

All chemicals used were analytical-reagent graded. Diluted stock solutions were used to prepare a hydroponics solution, containing macronutrients and micronutrients for aquatic macrophytes cultivation containing Quarter-strength Hoagland's ($(MgSO_4.7H_2O)$, 246 mg/L; $Ca(NO_3).4H_2O$, 542.8 mg/L; KH_2PO_4, 68 mg/L; KNO_3, 252.25 mg/L)). The final medium was diluted to half strength before use for plant culture [31]. The PH of solution were adjusted by using 1 N HCl and 1 N NaOH [32]. Chromium chloride $CrCl_3.6H_2O$ and chromium oxide $K_2Cr_2O_7$ were used to prepare a stock solutions of Cr (III) and Cr (VI) ions in glass volumetric flasks by dissolving in deionized water respectively.

The standard solutions used for calibration were prepared by diluting a stock solution of 1000 mg/L of the given element and stored in glass volumetric flasks for quantitative analysis. The reagents used for sample digestion were HNO_3 (65%) and H_2O_2 (30%). All solutions and dilutions were prepared in distilled water.

2.2 Instrumentation

All sample containers, glassware, and reagent bottles were washed with 10% v/v nitric acid before rinsing with high amount pure water and drying in the air before use. Analyses of all digested samples extracted by hotplate and water-bath were performed by using Optima inductively coupled plasma-optical emission spectrometer (ICP-OES). The ICP-OES instrumental conditions used for the metals determination is presented in Table 1 below.

Table 1. ICP-OES measurement parameters

Parameter	Reading
Power	1500
Plasma flow	PL1
Sheath flow	G1
Auxiliary flow	0
Nebulizer flow	0.66
Nebulization pressure	1.78
Pump speed	30
Analysis element	Ar

2.3   Experimental Plant

This study was conducted by using Water hyacinths (Eichhornia crassipes), Duckweed (Spirodela polyrrhiza), and Water lilies (Nymphaea spontanea) plant species as shown in Fig. 1. The plants were collected from the Lagoon behind Bahir Dar University, Peda Campus, Lake Tana, and from the Blue Nile River, Bahir Dar city, Ethiopia.

Water hyacinth   **Water lilies**   **Duckweed**

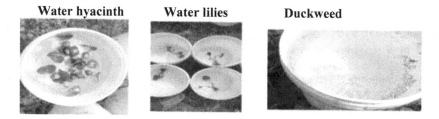

Fig. 1. Free-floating experimental plants

2.4   Experimental Setup and Design

Randomized Block Design were used for the experiment with three factors and three replication, i.e. chromium forms with two level (Cr (III), Cr (VI)), chromium concentrations with three level (1, 5 and 10 mg l^{-1}), and free-floating aquatic plant species with three level (Duckweed, Water hyacinth and Water lilies) with a total of 72 experimental run. The aquatic plants with an equal size and number were treated at different concentration of chromium. The setups were left in the greenhouse undisturbed for 30 days.

2.5   Phytoremediation Study

Phytoextraction study were carried out in a plastic container in the greenhouse. After collection, macrophytes were plentifully cleaned under running tap water to remove any sediment and particles. Healthy plants with equal size and weight were selected and put into a 25-L plastic container containing tap water in a greenhouse for experimental purposes. A two-week acclimation time was allowed to stabilize the collected plant by placing them in a plastic container containing tap water with the addition of nutrient media but not chromium metal to let them adapt to the new environment of the greenhouse. After the suitable acclimation time, plants of similar size and shape were allowed to grow in clean plastic containers containing 15 L solution of chromium metal.

Plastic containers were separated into three groups, Cr (III) contaminated, Cr (VI) contaminated, and control. A control experiment setup with no metal added to half-strength Hoagland nutrient medium were used. Three replicate experiments were set for each test and control. The plastic container was supplemented with tap water, nutrient media, and with the individual addition of 1, 5, and 10 mg l^{-1} chromium metal which was added as their water-soluble salts in the form of their aqueous solutions as waste chemicals. Cr (III) solutions were prepared using $CrCl_3.6H_2O$ while $K_2Cr_2O_7$ was used for Cr (VI).

The experimental concentrations were chosen because they are in the level found in aquatic systems near industrial areas of Bahir Dar Tannery Industry [21]. The plants were left in the greenhouse with an area of 20 m^2 supplemented with tap water, nutrient media, and subjected to chromium metal at 1, 5, and 10 mg l^{-1} concentrations under the conditions of average water temperature ranging between 14 and 26 °C, and with pH of 7.3–7.8. Tap water was added regularly to compensate water losses by plant through transpiration and evaporation to keep the initial volume of water [33]. After two weeks of metal exposure, plants and water sample were collected for metal extraction and analysis.

2.6   Preparation of Sample and Metals Analyses

At the end of the experiment, plants were cut into stems, roots, and leaves and weighed. The element concentrations measured were based on dry weight after correcting for moisture content determined from separate subsamples dried in an oven for 48 h at 60 °C. Digested sample, that could not analyzed immediately were stored at 4 °C until analysis [34]. Triplicate samples (0.5 gm.) of each plant sample variety were accurately weighed in 100 mL conical flasks. About 10 mL of a freshly prepared mixture of concentrated HNO_3–H_2O_2 (2:1, v/v) was added to each flask and kept for 10 min at room temperature. After that, the samples were heated on a hot plate at 80 °C until pure solutions were obtained. Finally, they were evaporated, the semi-dried mass was dissolved in 5 mL 0.2 M HNO_3, filtered through Whatman No.42 filter paper, made up to final volume of 10 mL in volumetric flasks with distilled water, and the metal contents were determined in the diluted solutions by ICP-OES [35]. For metal analysis in water, each collected sample (25 mL) were put in a beaker; 1.25 mL of nitric acid was added and covered with a watch glass. Then, the beakers were placed in a water bath at 90 ± 5 °C for 30 min. After cooling, the digested samples were arranged to a final volume of 25 mL with distilled water. The final suspended mixtures were filtered through 11 μm membrane filter with standard quantitative cellulose filter paper. The samples were then analyzed by inductively coupled plasma optical emission spectrometry (ICP-OES) [34].

2.7   Data Analysis

Translocation Factors

Translocation Factors (TF):- Used to indicate the efficiency of the plant in translocating the accumulated heavy metals from roots to shoots. It is calculated by dividing the concentration of the heavy metal in shoots (leaves or stem) to that in its roots as follows [36, 37].

$$TF = (C\ shoot)/(C\ root) \tag{1}$$

Growth Assessment

Plants growths were studied by measuring the wet weight of the plants at the start and at the end of the experiment. The relative growth of the plants is calculated as- [38].

$$Relative\ growth = (Wf)/(Wi) \tag{2}$$

Where, Wf is the final wet weight of plants after exposure to contaminant and Wi is the initial weight of the plants.

The Tolerance Index

It indicate the ability of plants to grow in the presence of a given concentration of metal.

Ti is calculated as- [39, 40].

$$Ti = \frac{(\text{Dry weight treated plant (gm)})}{(\text{Dry weight control plant (gm)})} * 100\% \tag{3}$$

2.8   Statistical Analysis

The result were analyzed using descriptive statistics (mean and standard deviation). The weight of the plant and metal concentration was given to two decimal places as a means. A significant difference between metal uptake and control was assessed by a one-way analysis of variance (ANOVA). The comparisons of mean using the least significant difference test were calculated for P-values and a value of $P < 0.05$ was considered as significant. Analysis of variance was done by using a statistical package software SPSS, version 20 followed by Turkey's post hoc test between the means of treatments to determine the significant difference.

3   Results and Discussion

3.1   Chromium Accumulation in the Plant

The uptake of chromium ions by Duckweed, Water lilies, and Water hyacinth for different concentrations was analyzed and presented in Figs. 2, 3, and 4 respectively. As can be seen in the Fig. 2, it is clear that chromium uptake by all plant significantly increased (P < 0.05) with an increase in chromium concentration up to 5 mg/L. For Duckweed, at chromium concentration of 1, 5, and 10 mg/L, the chromium accumulation significantly increased to 25.12 and 13.39, 167.99 and 33.38, and 169.43 and 37.29 mg/kg for Cr (III) and Cr (VI) respectively. As indicated in Fig. 4, for Water hyacinth the result obtained were increase in Cr concentration from 3.71 mg/kg to 64.02 and 20.07, 306.56 and 79, and 322.57 and 82 mg/kg for Cr (III) and Cr (VI) at 1, 5 and 10 mg/L respectively. The results indicated maximum accumulation was obtained at 10 mg/L for both Cr (III) and Cr (VI). On the other hand, Water lilies show a low uptake of Cr and a decrease in accumulation for an increase in concentration from 5 to 10 mg/L. The result obtained were increase in Cr accumulation from 0.51 mg/L to 21.57 and 15.3, 160.82 and 28.78, and 123.87 and 16.39 mg/kg for Cr (III) and Cr (VI) at 1, 5 and 10 mg/L, respectively. Maximum accumulation obtained at 5 mg/L for Cr (III) and Cr (VI), as indicated in Fig. 3.

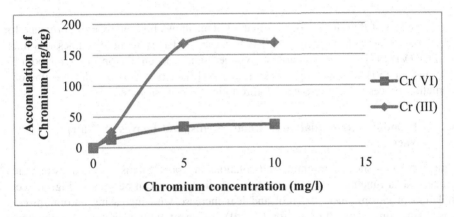

Fig. 2. Accumulation of Chromium in Duckweed

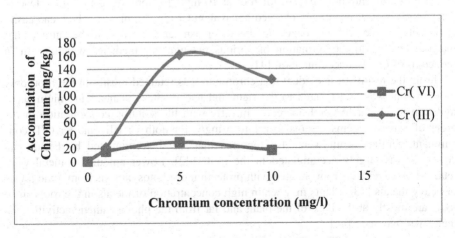

Fig. 3. Accumulation of Chromium in Water lilies

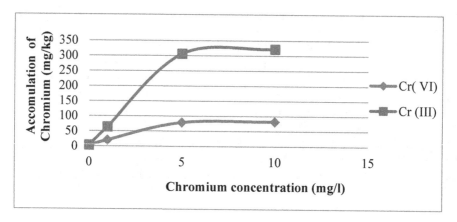

Fig. 4. Accumulation of chromium in Water hyacinth

The result of this study indicates that all plant shows low removal performance for Cr (VI) as compared to Cr (III). This is because Cr (III) is about 300 times less toxic than Cr (VI) [41]. Water hyacinth shows the highest accumulation of Cr for both Cr (III) and Cr (VI) followed by Duckweed, which can be used for effective phytoremediation process in the removal of chromium from wastewater.

3.2   Chromium Accumulation in Roots, Stems, and Leaves of Water Hyacinth

Figures 5 and 6 show chromium accumulations in Roots, Stems, and Leaves of Water hyacinth as a function of chromium concentration. As it can be seen in Fig. 5, accumulation of chromium in the root and leaf increase with increasing chromium concentration from 5 to 10 mg/L for Cr (III) treatment with maximum accumulation obtained in the root at 10 mg/L. For Cr (VI), their accumulation increase with an increase in concentration (except for root at 10 mg/L) as presented in Fig. 6. Due to their toxic effect of negatively charged hexavalent Cr ion complexes, which can easily cross cellular membranes, penetrate the cytoplasm and react with the intracellular material leading to the formation of various reactive intermediates which result in reduction of Cr (VI) accumulation [41].

From the results, it is evident that chromium was retained mostly in the root, only little amount was translocated to the stem and leaf of these plants. Chromium accumulation by Water hyacinth increases linearly with the solution concentration in the order of leaves < stems < roots from1 to 5 mg/L for both Cr (III) and Cr (VI) contaminant. Similar result were also reported that metal accumulated by Eichhornia crassipes was largely accumulated in the roots [42]. Lower amount of metal were retained in leaves than roots related with protection of photosynthesis from toxic levels of heavy metals [43]. Plants may retain high concentration of metals in the roots since roots are mostly at the base of the plant and far from the photosynthetic activities for their own tolerance [44].

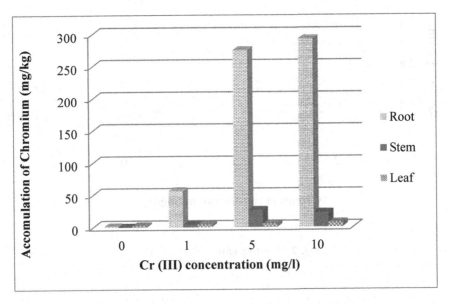

Fig. 5. Accumulation of Cr (III) in Water hyacinth

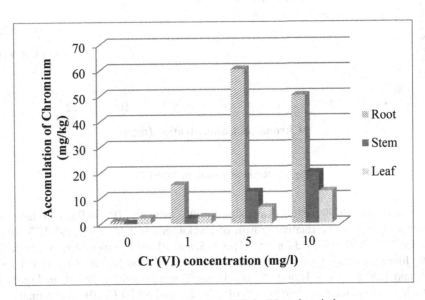

Fig. 6. Accumulation of Cr (VI) in Water hyacinth

3.3   Plant Growth Assessment

Figures 7, 8 and 9 presents the effects of Cr concentration on the relative growth of Duckweed, Water lilies, and Water hyacinth at different Cr concentrations respectively.

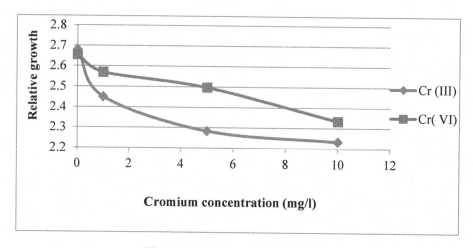

Fig. 7. Relative growth of Duckweed

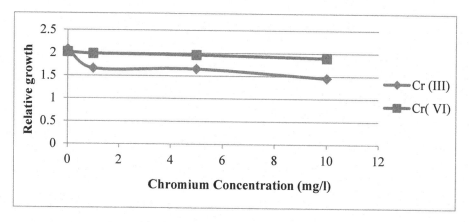

Fig. 8. Relative growth of Water lilies

The relative growth of control plants significantly increased ($P < 0.05$) with time. As presented in Fig. 7, the relative growth of Duckweeds is 2.45, 2.28, and 2.23 for Cr (III) and 2.57, 2.50, and 2.33 for Cr (VI) at 1, 5, and 10 mg/L respectively. Whereas for Water lilies, the relative growth obtained was 1.66, 1.65, and 1.46 for Cr (III) and 1.98, 1.99, and 1.90 for Cr (VI) at 1, 5, and 10 mg/L respectively as shown in Fig. 8. In Water hyacinth plant, a relative growth of 2.36, 2, and 1.85 for Cr (III) contaminant and 2.92, 2.46, and 2 for Cr (VI) were obtained as presented in Fig. 9. The result indicates that Duckweed with the highest relative growth followed by Water hyacinth for both Cr (III) and Cr (VI) contaminant.

With an increase in chromium concentration a decrease in relative growth was observed in all plants, this agree with several other finding [45]. Since, the top leaves of a plant shades the lower leaves and restricting the uptake of nutrients as well as the

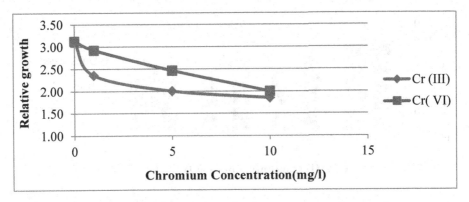

Fig. 9. Relative growth of Water hyacinth

increase of plant and non-photosynthetic biomass (roots and stems) resulting in a decrease of the relative growth rate (RGR) over time. Because, the relative growth of all plants is greater than one, which indicates their ability to accumulate the acceptable amount of chromium and survive in a contaminated condition [37].

3.4 Tolerance Index (TI)

Figures 10 and 11, shows the percentage of Tolerance index (Ti) value for Duckweed, Water lilies, and Water hyacinth after 14 days of treatment in chromium contaminate. The Ti value of all plant shows a decrease with an increase in Cr concentration. As shown in Fig. 10 a decrease in Ti value from 83.6% (in 1 mg/L) to 81.8% (in 5 mg/L), 81.8% (in 5 mg/L) to 79.9% (in 10 mg/L) were obtained for Duckweed when feeding with Cr (III) contaminant. For Water lilies a decrease in Ti value from 82.9% (in 1 mg/L) to 81.1% (in 5 mg/L), 81.1% (in 5 mg/L) to 68.2% (in 10 mg/L) were obtained. For Water hyacinth the Ti value decrease from 72.9% (in 1 mg/L) to 58.5% (in 5 mg/L), 58.5% (in 5 mg/L) to 56.2 (in 10 mg/L). Figure 11 shows decreased in Ti in Cr (VI) contaminant for Duckweed from 77.6% (in 1 mg/L) to 72.4% (in 5 mg/L), 72.54% (in 5 mg/L) to 1.5% (in 10 mg/L). For Water lilies the Ti value decrease from 86.4% (in 1 mg/L) to 82.7% (in 5 mg/L), 82.7% (in 5 mg/L) to 80.2% (in 10 mg/L). Water hyacinth shows a Ti value reduction with increase in Cr (VI) concentration from 91.4% (in 1 mg/L) to 76.5% (in 5 mg/L), 76.5% (in 5 mg/L) to 66.4% (in 10 mg/L). The result shows that, their exist a significant difference ($P < 0.05$) in the Ti value of the plant for an increase in Cr concentration.

Plants tolerance to heavy metal related with the potential of plants to restrict heavy metals movement to the cell walls and activation of antioxidant defense mechanisms [46]. Different plant species develop different system to tolerate excess levels of metals. Plants limit metals uptake or metal transport or develop internal tolerance mechanism to tolerate high concentration of heavy metal as phytochelatins (PCs) in plants produce oligomers of glutathione, which synthase enzyme for Cd detoxification [47].

The result of this study shows that Duckweed has more tolerance to Cr (III) compared to both Water lilies and Water hyacinth. For instance, the Ti vale is 79.9% (in

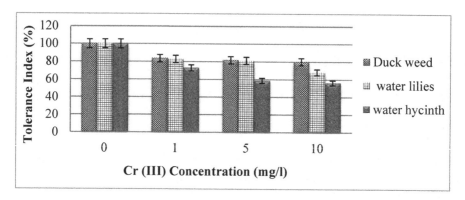

Fig. 10. Tolerance index (Ti) of plants in Cr (III) contaminant

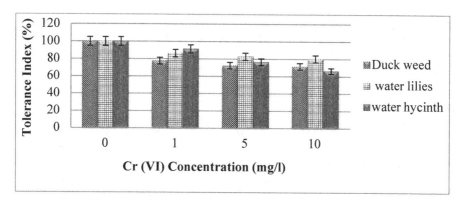

Fig. 11. Tolerance index (Ti) of plants in Cr (VI) contaminant

10 mg/L) for Duckweed, but it is 68.2% and 56.2% in 10 mg/L for Water lilies and Water hyacinth respectively. In contrast to Water hyacinth with Ti value of 58.5% (in 5 mg/L), Water lilies have a good Ti value of 81% (in 5 mg/L). The order of tolerance for Cr (III) contaminant were Duckweed > Water lilies > Water hyacinth. For Cr (VI) contaminant, Water hyacinth has a good Ti value of 91.4% (in 1 mg/L) as compared to Ti value of 86.4 and 77.6% for Water lilies and Duckweed respectively. However, in 5 and 10 mg/L Water lilies have good Ti value to that of Water hyacinth and Duckweed. The order of tolerance follows that Water hyacinth > Duckweed at 5 mg/L and Water hyacinth < Duckweed at 10 mg/L. Generally, plants with high Ti value have a good ability to grow in the presence of a given concentration of chromium.

3.5   Statistical Analysis

The analysis of variance (ANOVA) test was done for the differences in the accumulation of chromium between the experiment (with plants), between chromium type, and between chromium concentration. As shown in Tables 2, 3 and 4, the experiment (with plants) has a significant difference in chromium accumulation for the aquatic plants of Duckweed, Water lilies and Water hyacinth (P-value < 0.05). The accumulations between different concentrations of Cr for the three aquatic plants were proved statistically significant (P < 0.05). As presented in Table 2, there exists a significant difference (P < 0.05) in chromium accumulation for plant type, chromium

Table 2. ANOVA table showing the performance of plants in term of accumulation of chromium metal

Tests of between-subjects effects					
Dependent variable: plant chromium uptake					
Source	Type III Sum of squares	df	Mean square	F	Sig.
Corrected model	125202.071[a]	5	25040.414	8.508	.001
Intercept	158522.036	1	158522.036	53.860	.000
Plant type	24836.087	2	12418.044	4.219	.041
Cr type	59593.027	1	59593.027	20.248	.001
Concentration	40772.956	2	20386.478	6.927	.010
Error	35318.450	12	2943.204		
Total	319042.556	18			
Corrected total	160520.520	17			

a. R Squared = .780 (Adjusted R Squared = .688)

Table 3. Showing pairwise comparisons of plants performance in term of accumulation of chromium metal

Pairwise comparisons						
Dependent variable: plant chromium uptake						
(I) Plant type	(J) Plant type	Mean difference (I-J)	Std. error	P-value	95% confidence interval for difference[b]	
					Lower bound	Upper bound
Duckweed	Water lilies	13.495	31.322	.674	−54.750	81.740
	Water hyacinth	−71.178[a]	31.322	.042	−139.423	−2.934
Water lilies	Duckweed	−13.495	31.322	.674	−81.740	54.750
	Water hyacinth	−84.673[a]	31.322	.019	−152.918	−16.429
Water hyacinth	Duckweed	71.178[a]	31.322	.042	2.934	139.423
	Water lilies	84.673[a]	31.322	.019	16.429	152.918

Based on estimated marginal means
a. The mean difference is significant at the .05 level.
b. Adjustment for multiple comparisons: Least Significant Difference (equivalent to no adjustments).

Table 4. Univariate tests for plants performance in term of chromium accumulation

Univariate tests

Dependent variable: plant chromium uptake

	Sum of squares	df	Mean square	F*	Sig.
Contrast	24836.087	2	12418.044	4.219	.041
Error	35318.450	12	2943.204		

*The F tests the effect of Plant Type. This test is based on the linearly independent pairwise comparisons among the estimated marginal means.

concentration and chromium type between the groups. Table 3 shows the pairwise comparisons of plants performance in term of accumulation of chromium metal. The result indicated that there exists a significant difference ($P < 0.05$) in the accumulation of chromium between Duckweed and Water hyacinth, also within Water lilies and Water hyacinth. However, there exists no significant difference in chromium accumulation between Duckweed and Water lilies. In Table 4, F test for the plan type were given and the result shows that there exists a significant difference ($P < 0.05$) in chromium uptake by the plants.

4 Conclusion

The potential of three living free-floating aquatic plants species, Duckweed, Water lilies, and Water hyacinth for removal chromium from chromium waste solutions was investigated. It was observed that the uptake of chromium by all plant is significantly increased ($P < 0.05$) for an increase in chromium concentration. It was found that, Water hyacinth with higher total accumulation of 322.57 and 82 mg/kg for plant treated with 10 mg/L for both solution of Cr (III) and Cr (VI). In contrast, Water lilies show a relatively low removal performance with the maximum uptake of 160.82 and 28.78 mg/kg at 5 mg/L for both Cr (III) and Cr (VI). However, Water lilies show good tolerance for Cr (VI) for an increase in concentration from that of Water hyacinth and Duckweed.

The highest percentage removal of chromium was 96.7% of Cr (III) at 10 mg/L for Water hyacinth; 92% of Cr (VI) at 5 mg/L for Duckweed; and 96.7% of Cr (VI) at 10 mg/L for Water lilies. The relative growth of all plant, increase with the passage of time but decreases for an increase in chromium concentration. These results indicated that the biomass of the plant is suitable for the development of efficient accumulator for the removal of Cr from wastewater at a lower concentration.

However, Water hyacinth was proven an efficient candidate for removal of chromium metals from contaminated water body with great potential for future applications. This study suggests, the tested living aquatic plants species were found to have a potential for phytoremediation and can be used for removal of chromium metal from industrial effluent.

5 Recommendation

Further studies on the recovery of chromium metals by employing a controlled condition and investigating the **synergic effect** of the different plant species will be useful for large-scale industrial application of laboratory work.

References

1. Ismail, Z., Beddri, A.: Potential of water hyacinth as a removal agent for heavy metals from petroleum refinery effluents. Water Air Soil Pollut. **199**(1–4), 57–65 (2009)
2. Corcoran, E.: Sick water?: the central role of wastewater management in sustainable development: a rapid response assessment. UNEP/Earthprint (2010)
3. Sood, A., et al.: Phytoremediation potential of aquatic macrophyte. Azolla. Ambio **41**(2), 122–137 (2012)
4. Mishra, A., Dubey, A., Shinghal, S.: Biosorption of chromium (VI) from aqueous solutions using waste plant biomass. Int. J. Environ. Sci. Technol. **12**(4), 1415–1426 (2015)
5. Geetha, K.S., Belagali, S.: Removal of heavy metals and dyes using low cost adsorbents from aqueous medium-, a review. IOSR J. Environ. Sci., Toxicol. Food Technol. **4**(3), 56–68 (2013)
6. Machado, M.D., Soares, H.M., Soares, E.V.: Removal of chromium, copper, and nickel from an electroplating effluent using a flocculent brewer's yeast strain of Saccharomyces cerevisiae. Water Air Soil Pollut. **212**(1–4), 199–204 (2010)
7. Choo, T., et al.: Accumulation of chromium (VI) from aqueous solutions using water lilies (Nymphaea spontanea). Chemosphere **62**(6), 961–967 (2006)
8. Bonanno, G., Giudice, R.L.: Heavy metal bioaccumulation by the organs of Phragmites australis (common reed) and their potential use as contamination indicators. Ecol. Ind. **10**(3), 639–645 (2010)
9. Greger, M.: Metal availability and bioconcentration in plants. In: Prasad, M.N.V., Hagemeyer, J. (eds.) Heavy Metal Stress in Plants, pp. 1–27. Springer, Heidelberg (1999). https://doi.org/10.1007/978-3-662-07745-0_1
10. Xia, H., Ma, X.: Phytoremediation of ethion by water hyacinth (Eichhornia crassipes) from water. Biores. Technol. **97**(8), 1050–1054 (2006)
11. Abbasi, T., Abbasi, S.: Factors which facilitate waste water treatment by aquatic weeds–the mechanism of the weeds' purifying action. Int. J. Environ. Stud. **67**(3), 349–371 (2010)
12. Alkorta, I., Garbisu, C.: Phytoremediation of organic contaminants in soils. Biores. Technol. **79**(3), 273–276 (2001)
13. Tatar, Ş.Y., Öbek, E.: Potential of Lemna gibba L. and Lemna minor L. for accumulation of boron from secondary effluents. Ecol. Eng. **70**, 332–336 (2014)
14. Goswami, C., et al.: Arsenic uptake by Lemna minor in hydroponic system. Int. J. Phytorem. **16**(12), 1221–1227 (2014)
15. Sasmaz, M., et al.: The potential of Lemna gibba L. and Lemna minor L. to remove Cu, Pb, Zn, and As in gallery water in a mining area in Keban, Turkey. J. Environ. Manage. **163**, 246–253 (2015)
16. Rahman, M.A., Hasegawa, H.: Aquatic arsenic: phytoremediation using floating macrophytes. Chemosphere **83**(5), 633–646 (2011)
17. Ibañez, S., et al.: Transgenic plants and hairy roots: exploiting the potential of plant species to remediate contaminants. New Biotechnol. **33**(5), 625–635 (2016)

18. Wassie, A.B., Srivastava, V.C.: Teff straw characterization and utilization for chromium removal from wastewater: Kinetics, isotherm and thermodynamic modelling. J. Environ. Chem. Eng. **4**(1), 1117–1125 (2016)

19. Leta, S., Assefa, F., Dalhammar, G.: Characterization of tannery wastewater and assessment of downstream pollution profiles along Modjo River in Ethiopia. Ethiop. J. Biol. Sci. **2**(2), 157–168 (2003)

20. Gebrekidan, A., Gebresellasie, G., Mulugeta, A.: Environmental impacts of Sheba tannery (Ethiopia) effluents on the surrounding water bodies. Bull. Chem. Soc. Ethiop. **23**(2), 269–274 (2009)

21. Wosnie, A., Wondie, A.: Bahir Dar tannery effluent characterization and its impact on the head of Blue Nile River. Afr. J. Environ. Sci. Technol. **8**(6), 312–318 (2014)

22. Alemu, A., Gabbiye, N.: Assessment of chromium contamination in the surface water and soil at the riparian of Abbay River caused by the nearby industries in Bahir Dar city Ethiopia. Water Pract. Technol. **12**(1), 72–79 (2017)

23. Belay, A.A.: Impacts of chromium from tannery effluent and evaluation of alternative treatment options. J. Environ. Prot. **1**(01), 53 (2010)

24. Hamdan, S.S., El-Naas, M.H.: Characterization of the removal of Chromium (VI) from groundwater by electrocoagulation. J. Ind. Eng. Chem. **20**(5), 2775–2781 (2014)

25. Lin, L., et al.: Sorption of metals and metalloids from reverse osmosis concentrate on drinking water treatment solids. Sep. Purif. Technol. **134**, 37–45 (2014)

26. Cavaco, S.A., et al.: Removal of chromium from electroplating industry effluents by ion exchange resins. J. Hazard. Mater. **144**(3), 634–638 (2007)

27. Gupta, A., Balomajumder, C.: Simultaneous adsorption of Cr (VI) and phenol onto tea waste biomass from binary mixture: multicomponent adsorption, thermodynamic and kinetic study. J. Environ. Chem. Eng. **3**(2), 785–796 (2015)

28. Gupta, A., Balomajumder, C.: Simultaneous removal of Cr (VI) and phenol from binary solution using Bacillus sp. immobilized onto tea waste biomass. J. Water Process Eng. **6**, 1–10 (2015)

29. Dittert, I.M., et al.: Integrated reduction/oxidation reactions and sorption processes for Cr (VI) removal from aqueous solutions using Laminaria digitata macro-algae. Chem. Eng. J. **237**, 443–454 (2014)

30. Szczygłowska, M., et al.: Use of brassica plants in the phytoremediation and biofumigation processes. Int. J. Mol. Sci. **12**(11), 7760–7771 (2011)

31. Carvalho, K.M., Martin, D.F.: Removal of aqueous selenium by four aquatic plants. J. Aquatic Plant Manage. **39**, 33–36 (2001)

32. Clark, R.B.: Characterization of phosphatase of intact maize roots. J. Agric. Food Chem. **23**(3), 458–460 (1975)

33. Maine, M.A., et al.: Kinetics of Cr (III) and Cr (VI) removal from water by two floating macrophytes. Int. J. Phytorem. **18**(3), 261–268 (2016)

34. Chand, V., Prasad, S.: ICP-OES assessment of heavy metal contamination in tropical marine sediments: a comparative study of two digestion techniques. Microchem. J. **111**, 53–61 (2013)

35. Camin, F., et al.: Characterisation of authentic Italian extra-virgin olive oils by stable isotope ratios of C, O and H and mineral composition. Food Chem. **118**(4), 901–909 (2010)

36. Padmavathiamma, P.K., Li, L.Y.: Phytoremediation technology: hyper-accumulation metals in plants. Water Air Soil Pollut. **184**(1–4), 105–126 (2007)

37. Adesodun, J.K., et al.: Phytoremediation potentials of sunflowers (Tithonia diversifolia and Helianthus annuus) for metals in soils contaminated with zinc and lead nitrates. Water Air Soil Pollut. **207**(1–4), 195–201 (2010)

38. Lamaia, C., et al.: Toxicity and accumulation of lead and cadmium in the filamentous green alga Cladophora fracta (OF Muller ex Vahl) Kutzing: A laboratory study. Sci. Asia **31**(2), 121–127 (2005)
39. Lux, A., et al.: Differences in structure of adventitious roots in Salix clones with contrasting characteristics of cadmium accumulation and sensitivity. Physiol. Plant. **120**(4), 537–545 (2004)
40. Bianconi, D., et al.: Uptake of Cadmium by Lemna minor, a (hyper?-) accumulator plant involved in phytoremediation applications. In: E3S Web of Conferences. EDP Sciences (2013)
41. Gikas, P., Romanos, P.: Effects of tri-valent (Cr (III)) and hexa-valent (Cr (VI)) chromium on the growth of activated sludge. J. Hazard. Mater. **133**(1), 212–217 (2006)
42. Hammad, D.M.: Cu, Ni and Zn phytoremediation and translocation by water hyacinth plant at different aquatic environments. Aust. J. Basic Appl. Sci. **5**(11), 11–22 (2011)
43. Landberg, T., Greger, M.: Differences in uptake and tolerance to heavy metals in Salix from unpolluted and polluted areas. Appl. Geochem. **11**(1), 175–180 (1996)
44. Kamal, M., et al.: Phytoaccumulation of heavy metals by aquatic plants. Environ. Int. **29**(8), 1029–1039 (2004)
45. Paine, C., et al.: How to fit nonlinear plant growth models and calculate growth rates: an update for ecologists. Methods Ecol. Evol. **3**(2), 245–256 (2012)
46. Sharma, P., Dubey, R.S.: Lead toxicity in plants. Braz. J. Plant. Physiol. **17**(1), 35–52 (2005)
47. Akpor, O., Muchie, M.: Remediation of heavy metals in drinking water and wastewater treatment systems: Processes and applications. Int. J. Phys. Sci. **5**(12), 1807–1817 (2010)

Rainfall-Runoff Process and Groundwater Recharge in the Upper Blue Nile Basin: The Case of Dangishta Watershed

Abdu Yimer Yimam[1]($\boxtimes$), Ayele Mamo Bekele[1], Prossie Nakawuka[2], Petra Schmitter[2], and Seifu Admasu Tilahun[1]

[1] Faculty of Civil and Water Resources Engineering, Bahir Dar University, Bahir Dar, Ethiopia
abdukemer62@gmail.com
[2] International Water Management Institute (IWMI), Addis Ababa, Ethiopia

Abstract. For planning, development and management of water resources, understanding runoff mechanism and groundwater recharge is useful especially to watershed management and groundwater use for domestic and irrigation water supply. During the period of the study, stream flow, groundwater levels, infiltration tests, rainfall and soil moisture measurements were conducted. The result from these measurement showed that saturation excess runoff were dominant in Dangishta watershed while infiltration excess runoff also contributes in some parts of the upslope area. This result was also corroborated by better correlation of ($R^2 = 0.82$) at the main outlet than upstream sub watershed outlet ($R^2 = 0.56$) using SCS runoff equation. The result from groundwater level measurement using water table fluctuations approach showed that the total annual groundwater recharge were found to be 400 mm (i.e. 24% of the total annual rainfall) which is a significant amount likely because of the interflow processes to each well.

Keywords: Dangishta watershed · Rainfall runoff mechanism · Groundwater recharge

1 Introduction

To simulate the transport mechanisms of sediment, nutrient and pollutants basic understanding of storm runoff and its mechanisms in the landscape is useful [24, 26, 27]. Important findings so far in the Ethiopian highlands are that saturation-excess surface runoff is generated in the periodically saturated bottom lands and from the degraded areas on the hill sides [14, 22]. Determination of the mechanism and runoff source areas are an important consideration in understanding where to implement watershed management [8]. The role of understanding runoff mechanism is not only useful to watershed management but also helps to identify areas of infiltration or recharge to groundwater. Any infiltrated water could lead to generation of runoff through subsurface flow either as interflow or groundwater flow to streams or as a return flow to the surface when the subsurface flow encounters a seepage face [5]. This groundwater from underground aquifers can be used for irrigation using deep and shallow wells. There is

F. A. Zimale et al. (Eds.): ICAST 2018, LNICST 274, pp. 536–549, 2019.
https://doi.org/10.1007/978-3-030-15357-1_43

however little information about groundwater recharge and it's potential for irrigation in Ethiopia which is a challenge for its use for wide scale irrigation.

In order to promote an increase in agricultural production and sustainable use of groundwater, location of recharge areas, and quantification of groundwater recharge is needed which is a fundamental component in the water balance of any watershed [2].

Previous efforts to estimate ground water recharge were done in the northern semi-arid Ethiopian highlands by using MODFLOW and soil moisture balance (SMB) [31], and in the Blue Nile basin highlands using different methods such as base flow analysis, BASF model, Hydro chemical analysis (i.e. chloride mass balance) [2].

The recharge to groundwater depends on the infiltration area and overall runoff mechanism [7]. Spatial soil moisture and infiltration capacity measurement is a good indicator to understand the runoff mechanism in the watershed. The soil moisture content in the surface soil layer prior to a rainfall event strongly affects infiltration, and will thus affect the occurrence of runoff [15]. For a rainfall event of high intensity or where soils are less permeable, runoff generation might not depend on the antecedent soil moisture content of the surface soil layer. In this case, infiltration excess overland flow will be predominant. In this case more runoff is generated on the landscape and groundwater recharge is likely by infiltration of the surface runoff [13].

However, when rain storms are less intense and are falling on soils with high permeability, runoff is strongly controlled by the antecedent soil moisture of the surface soil layer [5]. In this case saturation excess overland flow will be the dominant runoff generating mechanism. On shallow depth soils located on hill slopes, rain water infiltrates and drains laterally following deep or short path to valley bottoms and rising the water level of shallow groundwater located on deep soils [22].

In order to strengthen the knowledge of runoff mechanism, runoff source areas, recharge areas and rate of recharge, Dangishta watershed in the Blue Nile Basin was selected since it is one of the location with good potential of shallow groundwater sources. This knowledge can improve identification of land management interventions to implement by locating runoff source areas. Groundwater recharge quantification would foster sustainable use of groundwater by balancing the recharge with the ground water use.

2   Study Area

Dangishta has a watershed size of 5700 ha and is found with in Dangila Woreda which is one of AGP and Feed the Future Woreda in the Amhara Regin (Fig. 1). Dangila Woreda is located in the North West highlands, in Awi zone in the Amhara region. It is located about 80 km south west from Bahir Dar, 36.83° N and 11.25° E and on average 2000 m above sea level. Brantie is located within Blue Nile Basin and drains to Gilgel Abay River that drains to Lake Tana. Brantie River is the river draining the watersheds. The climate of the region is moist subtropical with little annual temperature variation through high diurnal variation. The climate is sub-tropical with average annual rainfall of about 1600 mm but varies between 1180–2000 mm where the rain starts in the middle of June and stops at the beginning of October. The elevation of the watershed is within the range of 2036 to 2440 m a.s.l.

The geology of Dangishta watersheds are predominantly quaternary basalt and trachyte above ecocene oligocene basalts and trachyte including massive, fractured and vescular basalts, weathered basalt regolith overlain by red soils which is more litic and clayey with depth and other superficial materials underlying the flood plain which are often browner in color. The soils in Dangishta watersheds are Regosols accounts for 47%, Alisols for 16% and Nitosols and Vertisols for 13%.

Agricultural land is the main land use in the watershed covering 60% of the area. The main crops produced in the watershed are teff, millet, maize, chat and vegetables. Soil sample taken within the watershed show that the textural classification of soils in Dangishta to be clay and heavy clay. Most of the local people in Dangishta have wells use for irrigation, domestic use and livestock feeding.

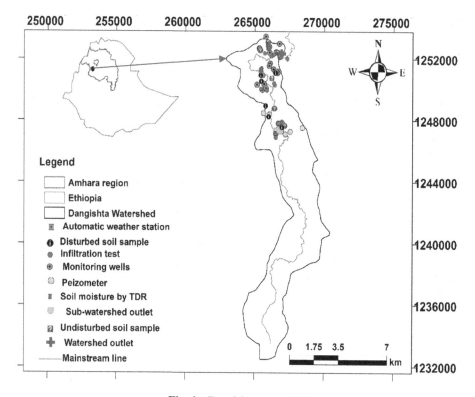

Fig. 1. Dangishta watershed

3   Materials and Methods

3.1   Data and Methodology

Field work as part of the Innovation Lab for Small Scale Irrigation funded by Feed the Future program of USAID was started during December 2014 after the rainy season in Dangishta Watershed. Rainfall, flow depth at sub watershed outlet and total watershed outlet, infiltration tests before and during rainy season, soil moisture by TDR and shallow ground water levels were monitored starting from December 2014 to end of October 2015.

Rainfall Measurement and Effective Rainfall Computation: An automatic weather station was installed in March 2015 to measure climatic parameters at 10 min interval. Effective rainfall was then be computed by subtracting the reference evapotranspiration from the total precipitation [6, 28]. The reference evapotranspiration for the entire watershed was estimated by the Penman- Monteith method [12, 32] using climatic data from the automatic weather station installed in the watershed.

Infiltration Measurement: Soil infiltration rates were measured at 19 different points throughout the watershed using 30 cm diameter single ring infiltrometer before and during rainy season of 2015 respectively. The steady state infiltration rates were then compared with the probability of exceedance of rainfall intensities to evaluate the runoff generation mechanism (Fig. 2).

Table 1. Number of repetition for each land use at different topography during infiltration measurement in the rainy season.

Land use	Upslope	Midslope	Downslope
Maize	3	2	1
millet	1	n.a	1
Teff	2	1	1
Eucalyptus	1	1	1
Vegetable	n.a	n.a	1
Grazing	1	1	1

Soil Moisture Measurement: To support determination of runoff generating mechanism in Dangishta watershed, soil moisture measurements were taken once every week using TDR at the dominant land uses (i.e. maize, millet, teff, eucalyptus and grazing land) at upslope, midslope and downslope topographic locations. For this study, moisture status of the surface soil layer was monitored using 20 cm long TDR roads. The TDR measurements was calibrated by gravimetric method. The soil field capacity is an indicator used in this study to determine how wet or dry the surface soil layer was prior to rainfall events and also throughout the study period.

Stream Flow Measurement and Base Flow Separation: Staff gauges were installed in May 2015 at the watershed outlet to be able to read the water level in the stream.

Stream flow discharge was measured from December 22, 2014 up to November 10, 2015 and the stage discharge relation was developed and finally Bflow base flow filter program (http://swat.tamu.edu/software/baseflow-filter-program/) [1] was used to separate the base flow from the stream flow. In this method, the interflow component is included in the surface runoff.

Runoff Depth and Determination of Runoff Coefficient: The runoff depth in the watershed was computed by dividing the runoff volume by the watershed area. To show the relation between rainfall and runoff for different months in the rainy period, runoff coefficient i.e. ratio of runoff (mm) to rainfall (mm) was determined. The result was compared for the different months in the rainy season.

SCS Runoff Equation: The watershed runoff response for the rainfall events was simulated using SCS runoff equation [20, 23, and 29] to support determination of runoff mechanism using Eq. 3-1.

$$Q = \frac{P_e^2}{P_e + S_e} \tag{3-1}$$

Where, P_e is the effective rainfall in mm and S_e is the available watershed storage after runoff starts in mm. The simulated runoff from Eq. 3-1 using the developed Se value was plotted against the measured runoff and both R^2 and Nash Sutcliff Efficiency (NSE), [17] were used to indicate how well the plot of observed versus simulated data fits the 1:1 line.

Determination of Specific Yield: In this study, specific yield was determined by taking soil samples one from each topographic positions (i.e. Upslope, Midslope and Downslope) using two methods namely: by means of a pressure plate and by means of standing tubes of 10 cm in diameter and 50 cm height and finally average specific yield was taken. The standing tube approach determines the specific yield from the gravimetric moisture content difference of the soil at saturation and the moisture content retained by the soil sample in a standing tube after it was left to drain from saturation for two weeks without evaporation [10, 18]. In the pressure plate approach the moisture content difference between soil at saturation and soil after draining when a pressure of 0.33 bar was applied was taken to determine the specific yield.

Recharge Estimation: The amount of groundwater recharge in the watershed is a function of soil surface characteristics i.e. vegetation cover, soil type, soil surface condition and antecedent soil moisture content [9, 19, 21]. To determine the amount of annual recharge in the watershed groundwater level was monitored daily in the main rainy season of 2015. A total of 36 wells were monitored. Among the various methods used to estimate recharge [19], the water table fluctuation method was used for this study. Wells selected for water table monitoring in Dangishta are in unconfined aquifers. Recharge was calculated as:

$$R = S_y * \frac{dh}{dt} = S_y * \frac{\Delta h}{\Delta t} \tag{3-2}$$

Where S_y is specific yield, h is water table height and t is time. For detail description of the method, [9] can be referred.

4   Results and Discussions

4.1   Runoff Generating Mechanisms Analysis

Infiltration Capacity and Rainfall Intensity: The median and average infiltration rate during dry period was 180 mm/h and 217 mm/h respectively but in the rainy season median and average infiltration rates were 72 mm/h and 86 mm/h respectively. In the valley bottoms where the soils get saturated, lowest infiltration rates of 6 mm/h was observed, which was consistent with similar studies conducted in the Ethiopian highlands where infiltration rates are limited in saturated soils [4, 25]. In general, infiltration rates were lowest in the grass lands. This is due to the compaction in these areas caused by free grazing of animals [16] and saturation from the shallow groundwater levels [26]. The rate of infiltration decreased in the rainy season when compared to the dry season measurements due to the increase in soil moisture in the soil profile that decreases infiltration of water into the soil. The difference in infiltration is similar with the studies conducted in Debre Mawi, Anjeni, Andit Tid, Maybar [6, 14, and 25]. From the rainfall recorded by automatic rain gauge at 10-min interval a total of 606 rainfall events were recorded during 2015 rainy period having a variation in rainfall intensities between 1.2 mm/h and 104 mm/h with an average of 6.8 mm/h. The probability of exceedance of each of the rainfall intensities was computed and plotted with the median infiltration capacity of the soil to compare the rainfall intensities with the infiltration capacity. The median is the most meaningful term to describe infiltration capacity of the watershed [3] (Table 2).

Table 2. Average steady state infiltration during the rainy season for different land use (mm/h).

Land use	Upslope	Midslope	Downslope
Maize	105	180	144
millet	60	Not taken	72
Teff	48	60	192
Eucalyptus	12	90	36
Vegetable	n.a	n.a	72
Grazing	24	6	n.a

As shown Fig. 2, during the rainy period the median infiltration rate was exceeded by the rainfall intensity almost 2.5% of the time. This shows that the most dominant runoff mechanism in the watershed during this period was saturation excess, but there were some portions of the watershed either in the upslope or downslope where the runoff contribution is due to infiltration excess as minimum infiltration rate during wet season was exceeded by rainfall intensity 25% of time.

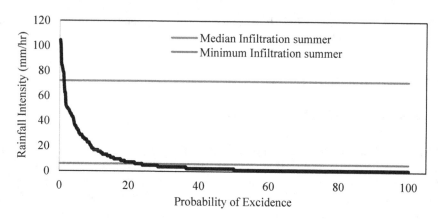

Fig. 2. Plot of the exceedance probability against ten minute rainfall intensity and steady state infiltration capacity

Soil Moisture: The moisture status of the upper 20 cm of soil was measured at different landscapes (upslope, midslope and downslope) portions of the watershed by considering maize, millet, eucalyptus, teff and grazing land as the dominant land uses. The measurement shows that the soil moisture status of the soil was dependent on the type of land use. As shown in Fig. 3, the soil moisture content was closer or below to the field capacity in various land uses in the upslope of the watershed. Rainfall raised the soil moisture content thus reducing space for water to infiltrate hence contributing to surface runoff (i.e. saturation excess flow). Any incoming precipitation on these areas produces runoff fast. In areas were soil moisture content was below field capacity but runoff was observed in the upslope areas, it suggests that infiltration excess was playing a role in runoff generation.

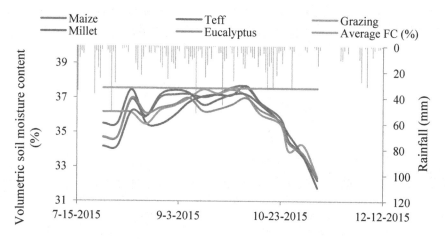

Fig. 3. Plot of soil moisture (vol %) for each of the land uses in the upslope area.

The minimum infiltration rate during rainy season in Fig. 2 showed that, 25% of the time the rainfall rate exceeds the infiltration rate which indicates there were places (for example in the upslope area as seen above) in the watershed which contributes infiltration excess runoff which support the above discussion on runoff generation mechanisms

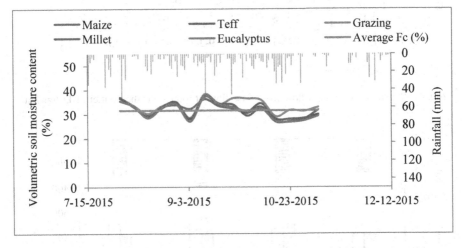

Fig. 4. Plot of soil moisture (vol %) for each of the land uses in the downslope areas.

The moisture status of the soil in the midslope and downslope areas shows similar trends during the rainy season (Fig. 4). The soil moisture content was greater than the field capacity for most of the time indicating that the soil was saturated and the main runoff mechanism for the measured runoff for these topographic positions was saturation excess.

Midslope and downslope areas receive water from both rainfall and both runoff and lateral subsurface flow from upper slopes [26]. As a result soil moisture content in upslope was below field capacity while in the mid and downslope areas, the soil moisture was above field capacity almost throughout the rainy season.

4.2 Base Flow Separation and Runoff Coefficient

During the rainy season both base flow and surface runoff contributes to stream flow which were determined from base flow separation techniques as shown in Fig. 5. Runoff coefficients at two outlets stations were then calculated for rainy period of 2015 for June, July, August and September (Fig. 6). An increase in runoff coefficient in Fig. 6 for the main rainfall season showed the dominance of saturation excess runoff mechanism because the soil surface gets saturated as the rains continues and any further rainfall became runoff as shown by the increasing runoff coefficients for the rest of the months. The result was similar with the findings of [28].

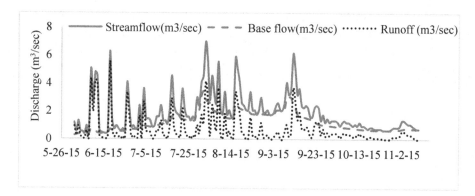

Fig. 5. Separation of stream flow from base flow at total watershed outlet of Dangishta

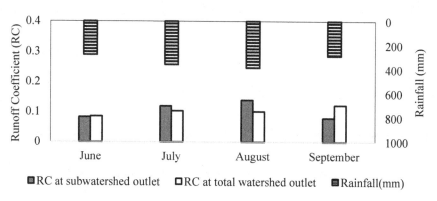

Fig. 6. Runoff coefficient at outlets of Dangishta watershed

4.3   SCS Runoff Equation

The measured runoff was used to calibrate the effective available storage, S_e, for Dangishta watershed. For the SCS runoff Eq. 3-1, weekly effective rainfall was computed as the difference between weekly rainfall and weekly reference evapotranspiration. The value of S_e was adjusted such that the simulated weekly runoff values from Eq. 3-1 have the closest fit to the measured weekly runoff. Better correlation was observed for the watershed at the outlet for effective available watershed, S_e, of 350 mm than upstream sub watershed outlet having effective available watershed, S_e, of 400 mm (Fig. 7).

The sub watershed at the upstream of the watershed loses water by lateral flow to the downstream. As a result the downstream remains saturated during the main rainy season which showed a high Se (i.e. 400 mm) value at sub watershed. Similar finding is reported at Debre Mawi watershed [29]. The better correlation at the total watershed outlet than upstream sub watershed outlet corroborates the fact that saturation excess runoff mechanism dominates while infiltration excess contributes in few cased for the upstream sub watershed.

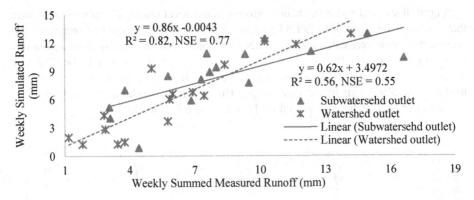

Fig. 7. Plot of measured cumulative runoff vs. cumulative runoff estimated by SCS at watershed outlets.

4.4   Groundwater Recharge

To use the water table fluctuation approach, an estimate of specific yield is important. Disturbed soil sample from three wells, one from each topographic location were taken to determine the average specific yield which is found to be approximately 0.089 which is equivalent with findings of [30] (Tables 3 and 4).

Table 3. Specific yield determination by pressure plate

Soil moisture at saturation (vol %)	Soil moisture at 0.33 bar pressure (vol %)	Specific yield (%)
50	37.5	12.5
51.1	48.6	2.4
56.8	44	12.7
Average		9.2

Table 4. Specific yield determination by standing tube

Soil moisture at saturation (vol %)	Soil moisture after draining (vol %)	Specific yield (%)
51.63	43.37	8.26
54.50	53.63	0.87
55.46	43.37	12.09
60.44	53.63	6.80
61.28	42.25	19.03
57.84	53.64	4.19
Average		8.54

Figure 8 showed a rise in shallow ground water level during the rainy season and that the water level starts to fall when rainfall declined. The amount of recharges for each of the wells were calculated by water table fluctuation method as discussed in the methodology section. The average total annual recharge was found to be 400 mm which is 24% of the annual rainfall. Spatially, there is a recharge of 380.6 mm in the upslope and 501.1 mm in the downslope. This estimate is within the range of 0 to 400 mm per year recharge reported by [11] for the Ethiopian high land.

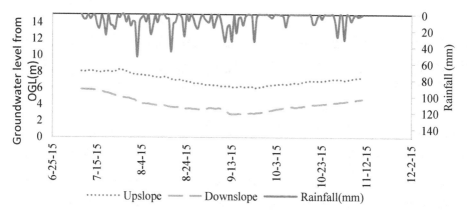

Fig. 8. Trend of average water level fluctuation for monitoring wells located upslope and downslope where the top line is the average of 5 wells and the bottom line is the average of 20 wells.

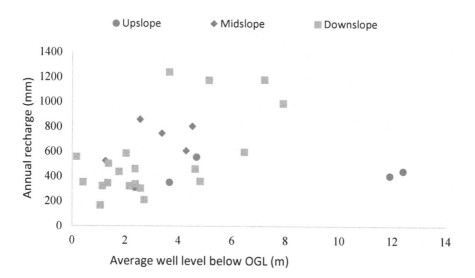

Fig. 9. Annual recharge of all monitoring wells in the watershed where OGL is original ground level

A study conducted by [30] reported a higher recharge amount in Dangishta using water table fluctuation method even if the sampling wells do not represent the spatial distribution in the watershed. This shows that a significant amount of groundwater exists which can be used for small scale farming activities using small scale irrigation technologies. The result also shows the downslope parts of the watershed is a potential area than the upslope part of the watershed to irrigate during dry period from shallow groundwater. As shown in Fig. 9 the maximum and minimum recharge is 1239 mm and 165 mm respectively.

5   Conclusions

Generally the dominant runoff mechanism in Dangishta watershed was found to be saturation excess but it does not mean infiltration excess runoff was not occurring. The minimum infiltration rate and the soil moisture content in the upstream part of the watershed shows that infiltration excess was also occurring in the upslope parts of the watershed. This was supported by the calculated runoff coefficient, SCS runoff equitation and soil moisture measurement. An increase in runoff coefficient and better correlation of measured runoff with SCS at the total watershed outlet supports the findings that saturation excess runoff was the dominating runoff generating mechanism in the watershed.

The total amount of recharge in the watershed was found to be 400 mm which was 24% of the annual rainfall, which is significant groundwater storage for irrigation and domestic water supply during the dry period.

Acknowledgment. The research was funded through the Innovation Laboratory for Small-Scale Irrigation (ILSSI) project (#AID-OAA-A-13-000SS) funded by Feed the Future through the U.S. Agency for International Development. The first author is also thankful for Ethiopian Road Authority (ERA) in providing the graduate study opportunity with Bahir Dar Institute of Technology.

References

1. Arnold, J.G., Allen, P.M., Muttiah, R., Bernhardt, G.: Automated base flow separation and recession analysis techniques. Ground Water 33(6), 1010–1018 (1995)
2. Asmerom, G.H.: Groundwater contribution and recharge estimation in the Upper Blue Nile flows, Ethiopia. ITC MSc thesis, The Netherlands (2008)
3. Bayabil, H.K., Tilahun, S.A., Collick, A.S., Yitaferu, B., Steenhuis, T.S.: Are runoff processes ecologically or topographically driven in the (sub) humid Ethiopian highlands? The case of the Maybar watershed. Ecohydrology 3(4), 457–466 (2010)
4. Bayabil, H.K.: Modeling Rainfall-runoff Relationship and Assessing Impacts of Soil Conservation Research Program Intervention on Soil Physical and Chemical Properties at Maybar Research Unit, Wollo, Ethiopia. Cornell University (2009)
5. Dunne, T., Black, R.D.: An experimental investigation of runoff production in permeable soils. Water Resour. Res. 6(2), 478–490 (1970)

6. Engda, T.A., et al.: Watershed hydrology of the (semi) humid Ethiopian highlands. In: Melesse, A.M. (ed.) Nile River Basin, pp. 145–162. Springer, Dordrecht (2011). https://doi.org/10.1007/978-94-007-0689-7_7

7. Freeze, R.A.: The mechanism of natural ground-water recharge and discharge: 1. One-dimensional, vertical, unsteady, unsaturated flow above a recharging or discharging ground-water flow system. Water Resour. Res. 5(1), 153–171 (1969)

8. Guzmán, G., Quinton, J.N., Nearing, M.A., Mabit, L., Gómez, J.A.: Sediment tracers in water erosion studies: current approaches and challenges. J. Soils Sediments 13(4), 816–833 (2013)

9. Healy, R.W., Cook, P.G.: Using groundwater levels to estimate recharge. Hydrogeol. J. 10 (1), 91–109 (2002)

10. Johnson, A.I.: Specific yield: compilation of specific yields for various materials: US Government Printing Office (1967)

11. Kebede, S.: Groundwater potential, recharge, water balance: vital numbers. In: Groundwater in Ethiopia. Springer Hydrogeology, pp. 221–236. Springer, Heidelberg (2013). https://doi.org/10.1007/978-3-642-30391-3_7

12. Kisi, O.: Comparison of different empirical methods for estimating daily reference evapotranspiration in Mediterranean climate. J. Irrig. Drain. Eng. 140(1), 04013002 (2013)

13. Liang, X., Xie, Z., Huang, M.: A new parameterization for surface and groundwater interactions and its impact on water budgets with the variable infiltration capacity (VIC) land surface model. J. Geophys. Res. Atmos., 108(D16) (2003)

14. Liu, B.M., Collick, A.S., Zeleke, G., Adgo, E., Easton, Z.M., Steenhuis, T.S.: Rainfall-discharge relationships for a monsoonal climate in the Ethiopian highlands. Hydrol. Process. 22(7), 1059–1067 (2008)

15. Merz, B., Plate, E.J.: An analysis of the effects of spatial variability of soil and soil moisture on runoff. Water Resour. Res. 33(12), 2909–2922 (1997)

16. Mwendera, E.J., Saleem, M.A.M.: Infiltration rates, surface runoff, and soil loss as influenced by grazing pressure in the Ethiopian highlands. Soil Manag. 13, 29–35 (1997). https://doi.org/10.1111/j.1475-2743.1997.tb00553.x

17. Nash, J.E., Sutcliffe, J.V.: River flow forecasting through conceptual models part I-A discussion of principles. J. Hydrol. 10(3), 282–290 (1970)

18. Neuman, S.P.: On methods of determining specific yield. Ground Water 25(6), 679–684 (1987)

19. Scanlon, B.R., Healy, R.W., Cook, P.G.: Choosing appropriate techniques for quantifying groundwater recharge. Hydrogeol. J. 10(1), 18–39 (2002)

20. Schneiderman, E.M., et al.: Incorporating variable source area hydrology into a curve number based watershed model. Hydrol. Process. 21(25), 3420–3430 (2007)

21. Sophocleous, M.: Interactions between groundwater and surface water: the state of the science. Hydrogeol. J. 10(1), 52–67 (2002)

22. Steenhuis, T.S., et al.: Predicting discharge and sediment for the Abay (Blue Nile) with a simple model. Hydrol. Process. 23(26), 3728–3737 (2009)

23. Steenhuis, T.S., Winchell, M., Rossing, J., Zollweg, J.A., Walter, M.F.: SCS runoff equation revisited for variable-source runoff areas. J. Irrig. Drain. Eng. 121(3), 234–238 (1995)

24. Tilahun, S.A., et al.: An efficient semi-distributed hillslope erosion model for the subhumid Ethiopian highlands. Hydrol. Earth Syst. Sci. 17(3), 1051–1063 (2013)

25. Tilahun, S.A., et al.: Spatial and temporal patterns of soil erosion in the semi-humid Ethiopian highlands: a case study of Debre Mawi Watershed. In: Melesse, A.M., Abtew, W., Setegn, S.G. (eds.) Nile River Basin, pp. 149–163. Springer, Cham (2014). https://doi.org/10.1007/978-3-319-02720-3_9

26. Tilahun, S.A., et al.: Revisiting storm runoff processes in the upper Blue Nile basin: the Debre Mawi watershed. Catena **143**, 47–56 (2016)
27. Tilahun, S.A., et al.: Distributed discharge and sediment concentration predictions in the sub-humid Ethiopian highlands: the Debre Mawi watershed. Hydrol. Process. **29**(7), 1817–1828 (2015)
28. Tilahun, S.A.: Observations and modeling of erosion from spatially and temporally distributed sources in the (semi) humid Ethiopian highlands. Cornell University (2012)
29. Tilahun, S.A., et al.: A saturation excess erosion model. Trans. ASABE **56**(2), 681–695 (2013)
30. Walker, D., et al.: Insights from a multi-method recharge estimation comparison study. Groundwater (2018)
31. Walraevens, K., et al.: Groundwater recharge and flow in a small mountain catchment in northern Ethiopia. Hydrol. Sci. J. **54**(4), 739–753 (2009)
32. Zotarelli, L., Dukes, M.D., Romero, C.C., Migliaccio, K.W., Morgan, K.T.: Step by step calculation of the Penman-Monteith Evapotranspiration (FAO-56 Method). Institute of Food and Agricultural Sciences. University of Florida (2010)

Testing the Bending Strength of Solid Bamboo and Hollow Bamboo Particleboard

Melak Misganew$^{(\boxtimes)}$ and Nehemiah Peddinti

Faculty of Mechanical and Industrial Engineering,
Bahir Dar Institute of Technology, Bahir Dar University, Bahir Dar, Ethiopia
melakmisganew33@gmail.com, prof.nehemiah@gmail.com

Abstract. The aim of this study is to test experimentally and determine the bending strength of a particleboard made from hollow and solid bamboo chip composition with urea formaldehyde. The particle board is manufactured at Ethiopian Chip Wood And Furniture Share Company in Addis Ababa. The ratio of solid bamboo to hollow bamboo is 75/25, 25/75, and 50/50 respectively with urea formaldehyde. The bending strength of 75% hollow bamboo (HB) and 25% solid bamboo (SB) is 32.13 MPa and eucalyptus particleboard (EPB) bending strength is 30.63 MPa. The bending strength of 75/25 SB/HB is 159 MPa. The bending strength of 50/50 HB/SB is 30.80 MPa and the bending strength of eucalyptus particleboard is 30.63 MPa. The test results show that the bending strength of bamboo particle board is greater than the bending strength of eucalyptus particle board, and these boards can be used instead of eucalyptus particleboards. Based on the result of the study, bamboo can be recommended as a raw material.

Keywords: Solid bamboo · Hollow bamboo · Bending strength · Particle board · Eucalyptus · Urea formaldehyde

1 Introduction

The chip composition products are very important for different types of household service, construction purpose like partition board, ceiling, tables, bed etc. From those chip composition products particle board is the basic product which is manufactured in Ethiopia.

Composite materials are composed of two or more different materials, with the properties of the resultant material being superior to the properties of the individual materials which makes the composite. "Composite materials consist of one or more discontinuous phase embedded in a continuous phase. The discontinuous phase is usually harder and stronger than the continuous. Properties of composites are strongly dependent on the properties of their constituent materials, their distribution, and the interaction among them. The shape of the discontinuous phase (which may be spherical, cylindrical, or rectangular cross-sectioned prisms or platelets), the size and size distribution (which controls the texture of the material) and volume fraction determine the interfacial area, which plays an important role in determining the extent of the interaction between the reinforcement and the matrix. It can be either of random orientation or preferred orientation" [1].

© ICST Institute for Computer Sciences, Social Informatics and Telecommunications Engineering 2019
Published by Springer Nature Switzerland AG 2019. All Rights Reserved
F. A. Zimale et al. (Eds.): ICAST 2018, LNICST 274, pp. 550–561, 2019.
https://doi.org/10.1007/978-3-030-15357-1_44

The raw material that used to manufacture different type of board is eucalyptus tree in Ethiopia. The reason to use it is, its availability in cheap cost. But lowland bamboo particleboard is not studied early in Ethiopia. Lowland bamboo particleboard can use for particleboard purpose. The particleboard made from lowland bamboo (Oxytenanthera Abyssinica) is stronger than eucalyptus tree particle board. As the study result shows, the bending strength of lowland bamboo particleboard in both dry and wet condition is stronger than eucalyptus tree particleboard [2].

The total Ethiopian natural bamboo forest is estimated to cover around 1 million hectare, which is about 7% of the total of the world and 67% of the African bamboo population. The lowland species (Oxytenanthera Abyssinica) covers 85% of the total population bamboo in Ethiopia. The species of the bamboo, which is the lowland bamboo, farmed in Benishagul Gumuz region [3].

It is known that the solid bamboo coverage is more than the hollow bamboo coverage in Ethiopia. This research needs to use the mixed of solid and hollow bamboo particleboard. The reason to use the mixed of sold and hollow bamboo chips is to balance the resource utilization in fifty percent and to keep the advantage of lowland and highland area farmers by supplying the raw materials.

The lack of skill and technological inputs into the production chain, resulting in poor quality products that do not command the attention of potential purchasers, a complete lack of marketing infrastructure to enable products to reach out and find new markets [4].

Urea formaldehyde (UF) resin at solid content can be used as an adhesive. According to the researcher, test result shows that the effect of temperature on the modulus of rupture (MOR) has an inverse relationship and density has a direct relationship with MOR. This test result shows that the screw holding strength becomes low when temperature value was increased in each specific density level [5].

The bamboo age difference has an effect on the bending strength of particleboard. Considering the age of the bamboo is important to determine the strength of the board. The bending strength of one-year-old bamboo fiberboard was the same as that of tallow wood fiberboard and has higher internal bond (IB) strength than tallow wood at 8% resin content [6].

Bamboo waste with urea formaldehyde can use for particleboard. To prepare the board the researcher used urea formaldehyde glue as a binder. Generally, the thickness swelling property and water absorption property are increasing when the time is increased in both planer waste and hammer milled chips [7].

The press temperature has an effect on properties of medium density fiberboard produced from Eucalyptus camaldulensis fibers. The target of the study was to investigate the possibility of MDF production from Eucalyptus camaldulensis wood. The study result show, longer steaming time produced higher MOR but lower modulus of elasticity (MOE) except for press temperature of 190 °C. It can be anticipated that longer steaming time initiated the thermo-hydrolysis of the wood substances especially hemicelluloses and weakens the structure of the wood itself [8].

The particleboard is produced from fonio husk with gum Arabic resin adhesive as a binder. The mechanical tests which a flexural strength tests standards are determined. The study standard was according to ASTM, D-1037. Three samples were tested for each replacement percent level and the average value was determined. After reviewing the above literature it is found that the research work on bending properties of solid and hollow bamboo mixture particleboard was not carried out. This research focuses on studying the bending properties of bamboo particleboard and replacing the eucalyptus particleboard by bamboo particleboard [9].

In the research observation, all chip wood factories are using eucalyptus tree as the raw material for particleboard in Ethiopia. For example Ethiopian Chip wood and Furniture Share Company in Addis Ababa, Maichew particleboard factory in Maichew, Debre Birehan particleboard factory in Debre Birehan and Hawassa chip wood factory in Hawassa are used eucalyptus tree as their raw materials. Till now they use it due to different reasons. As they mention some of the reasons to use eucalyptus are; its availability with less cost, its strength for the product and there is no any other raw material for which, mechanical properties are studied.

Due to the demand, the high land area wide planting of eucalyptus tree has its own negative side effect. From those negative impact, it reduces the crop productivity. The growth of the crop, which germinates near the tree is very less and its productivity is also low [12].

The objective of this research work is to test experimentally and determine the bending strength of a particleboard made from hollow and solid bamboo chip composition with urea formaldehyde and to compare its bending strength with eucalyptus particleboard. Before this time mixing of the solid and hollow bamboo for particleboard is not studied in Ethiopia. So to recommend solid and hollow bamboo plants as the raw materials and to substitute eucalyptus the bending strength of bamboo particleboard should be greater than or equal to the bending strength of eucalyptus particleboard since particleboard application areas are mostly subjected for bending load condition.

2   Methodology and Materials

2.1   Methodology

The processes that are used to manufacture the board are based on the factories manufacturing method to fulfill their manufacturing standard. Tasks in the factory were making boards in different ratios. The ratio of the board was 75/25 for solid bamboo (Oxytenanthera Abyssinica) with hollow bamboo (Yushania Alpina) respectively and the second proportion was reversing the ratio to 25/75 and made respectively to justify which species is more strong. The third proportion was also made the board in one to one (50/50) ratio. The reason to use these mixing ratio is to obtain the optimized result. Generally, there are three types of boards in different ratio. To prepare the board there is an additive which UF and it is used to give strength by making bonds between the smaller particles of chips. Then preparing a specimen for the test from the sample boards.

2.2   Materials

In this work materials such as solid bamboo chips, hollow bamboo chips, and urea formaldehyde as a resin are utilized directly for the board preparation and to carry out the particleboard.

Formaldehyde-Based Binders. The factory uses urea formaldehyde for their product as adhesive material, and also this research carried outs eucalyptus particleboard (EPB) with bamboo particleboard (BPB) by using similar manufacturing method with ECAFCO. The liquid Urea formaldehyde (UF) is shown in Fig. 1.

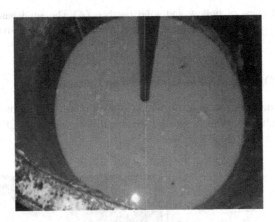

Fig. 1. Urea formaldehyde

Bamboo. Both the solid and hollow type of bamboo is grown either naturally grown or farmed in a farmyard north-west of the countryside of Ethiopia in Awi Zone. In the highland part of the area especially at Enjibara town area, the hollow bamboo or Highland bamboo (Yushania Alpina) species are grown widely. In the lowland part of the area especially at Jawi Woreda, the solid bamboo or lowland bamboo (Oxytenanthera Abyssinica) species are grown.

2.3   Bamboo Board Manufacturing Process and Specimen Preparation

The manufacturing process of the sample board was carried out at Ethiopian Chip wood And Furniture Share Company (ECAFCO). The basic raw materials were lowland bamboo (Oxytenanthera Abyssinica) chips, hollow bamboo (Yushania Alpina) chips, and urea formaldehyde as an adhesive material.

The additive content was 12% urea formaldehyde [10] (UF) in mass and the remaining is bamboo chips. The ratio proportion was the same with ECAFCO eucalyptus particleboard manufacturing ratio.

The particleboard preparation is randomly oriented discontinuous fiber lamina [11]. The three boards were prepared in different size and different proportions. The applied pressing pressure and the temperature was 220 kp/cm^2 and 181 °C respectively and the pressing time was 5 min for 8 mm thickness (Figs. 2, 3 and 4).

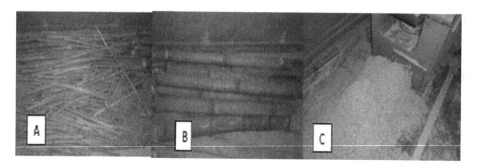

Fig. 2. The shaved chips of hollow and solid bamboo (A) The solid bamboo prepared for shaving (B) hollow bamboo prepared for shaving (C) bamboo chips after shaving at the exit of shaver machine

2.4   Randomly Oriented Discontinuous Fiber Lamina

A thin lamina containing randomly oriented discontinuous fibers in Fig. 3A exhibits planar isotropic behavior. The properties are ideally the same in all directions in the plane of the lamina [11] (Fig. 3).

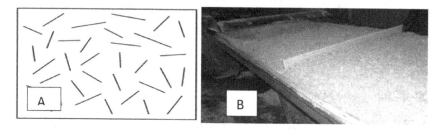

Fig. 3. (A) Randomly oriented discontinuous fiber lamina © [11] (B) Bamboo chips in the mould

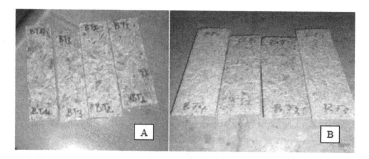

Fig. 4. (A) Specimen of bamboo particleboard, (B) Specimen of eucalyptus particleboard

Bending Strength Test. The flexural specimen is prepared as per the JIS A 5908 standards with a load rate of 10 mm/min and Samples dimension of the flexural test was 200 × 50 × 13 mm of length, width and thickness respectively [2]. Bamboo particle board was at a density of 0.6 g/cm³ which obtained in measurement of mass per volume of the particleboard. But eucalyptus particleboard has a density of 0.596 g/cm³ which measured in the same way of density measurement with bamboo particleboard to compare the two types of particleboards. That means density is mass per volume and the standard was JIS A 5908.

The three-point flexural test is the most common flexural test for composite materials. Specimen deflection was measured by the crosshead position [9].

The maximum fiber stress at a failure on the tension side of a flexural specimen is considered the flexural strength of the material. Thus using a homogeneous beam theory, the flexural strength in a three-point flexural test and the bending load resistance obtained during the test was related to the result of the highest flexural strength (uf) of three point bending calculated values [11].

$$\sigma_{UF} = \frac{3P_{max}L}{2bh^2} \tag{1}$$

Where, P_{max} = maximum load failure, b = specimen width, h = specimen thickness, L = specimen length between the two support points (Fig. 5).

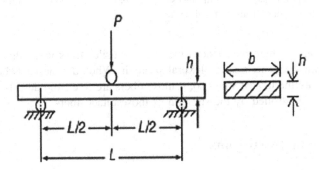

Fig. 5. Flexural test arrangements in three-point bending © [11]

Bending Strength Test Procedure. The test was carried out at Bahir Dar Institute of Technology (BIT) by using YF Zhejiang Tugong PN 0206000031 WAW-1000B Microcomputer controlled universal testing machine. The composition of the board was made from bamboo chips and urea formaldehyde. The bending load setup and failure is shown in Fig. 6.

As shown in Fig. 6B & C, the beam failure is happened due to the applied bending load in the specimen. In the Fig. 6B shown, the lower part is responsible for tensile stress and the upper side is subjected to compressive stress. At the edge of the object on the inside of the bend (concave face), the stress will be at its maximum compressive stress value. At the outside of the bend (convex face), the stress will be at its maximum

Fig. 6. (A) Three-point loading bending test setup (B) Failure of sample board for bending load C) Failure of sample board 1due to bending load

tensile stress value. Then the outsides maximum tensile stress value that can be sustained before the beam fails is its flexural strength. When a material is bent only the extreme fibers are the largest stress so, if those fibers are free from defects, the flexural strength will be controlled by the strength of those intact fibers.

3   Results and Discussions

3.1   Bending Strength Test Results of 75% SB and 25% HB Particleboard

In case of 75%, solid bamboo chips with 25% hollow bamboo chips particle board which has the dimension of 200 mm × 50 mm × 15 mm length, width and thickness, the average flexural strength were 159 MPa. But here the adhesive addition is the constant rate which was 12% in the liquid form of urea formaldehyde. Bamboo particle board which made from 75% solid bamboo chips with 25% hollow bamboo chips is stronger than any other particleboard. The reason to become strong in its bending load resistance is its intimacy between the chips was high.

The eucalyptus particleboard with a dimension of (200 × 50 × 13) mm length, width, and thickness respectively has a bending strength of 51.33 MPa in lengthwise at the dry condition [2] (Tables 1, 2 and 3).

Table 1. Bending strength test applied load on 75% SB and 25% HB

Type of materials	Applied load (kN)			
	Specimen 1	Specimen 2	Specimen 3	Average
Bamboo	12.71	13.13	9.94	11.93
Eucalyptus	0.7	0.65	0.61	0.65

Table 2. Bending strength test results of 75% SB and 25% HB

Type of materials	Specimens strength in MPa				Standard deviation
	Specimen 1	Specimen 2	Specimen 3	Average	
Bamboo	169.45	175	132.56	159	18.84
Eucalyptus	32.82	30.30	28.78	30.63	1.67

Table 3. Deformation of 75% SB and 25% HB due to a bending load

Type of materials	Maximum deformation (mm)				Standard deviation
	Specimen 1	Specimen 2	Specimen 3	Average	
Bamboo	19.026	19.828	16.11	18.32	1.60
Eucalyptus	16.502	13.186	7.474	12.38	3.73

3.2 Bending Strength Test Results of 50% SB and 50% HB

The bending strength test result of 50/50 solid and hollow bamboo chips with UF particleboard (PB) shows that better result obtained than eucalyptus particle board (EPB) bending load resistance. The mode of the graph profile becomes an irregular shape. The reason is in practice, fiber strength is not a unique value, and instead, it follows a statistical distribution. Therefore, it is expected that a few fibers will break at low-stress levels. Although the remaining fibers will carry higher stress, the may not fail simultaneously. The following Tables 4, 5 and 6 show the bending strength of 50% SB and 50% HB.

Table 4. Bending strength test load result of 50% SB and 50% HB

Type of materials	Applied load (kN)			
	Specimen 1	Specimen 2	Specimen 3	Average
Bamboo	0.67	0.64	0.67	0.66

Table 5. Bending strength test results of 50% HB and 50% SB

Type of materials	Specimens strength in MPa				Standard deviation
	Specimen 1	Specimen 2	Specimen 3	Average	
Bamboo	31.31	29.79	31.31	30.80	0.72
Eucalyptus	32.82	30.30	28.78	30.63	1.67

Table 6. Deformation of 50% HB and 50% SB due to a bending load

Type of materials	Maximum deformation (mm)				Standard deviation
	Specimen 1	Specimen 2	Specimen 3	Average	
Bamboo	14.136	16.046	13.928	14.70	0.95
Eucalyptus	16.502	13.186	7.474	12.38	3.73

3.3   Bending Strength Test Result of 75% HB and 25% SB

The bending strength test result of the 75% HB and 25% SB particleboard are shown in Tables 7, 8 and 9.

Table 7. Bending strength test result of 25% SB and 75% HB

Material	Applied load (kN)			
	Specimen 1	Specimen 2	Specimen 3	Average
Bamboo	0.57	0.66	0.83	0.69

Table 8. Bending strength test results of 75% HB and 25% SB

Types of materials	Specimens strength in MPa				Standard deviation
	Specimen 1	Specimen 2	Specimen 3	Average	
Bamboo	26.76	30.80	38.83	32.13	5.02
Eucalyptus	32.82	30.30	28.78	30.63	1.66

Table 9. Deformation of 75% HB and 25% SB due to bending load

Materials	Maximum deformation (mm)				Standard deviation
	Specimen 1	Specimen 2	Specimen 3	Average	
Bamboo	7.92	11.99	15.75	11.88	3.20

The deformation of each type of particleboard is proportional to the amount of load and the resulting stress.

The comparison between [2] test result and this research result, the bending strength of the two type of bamboo mixed particle board has higher strength in the lengthwise direction, and the study's test result was 69.6 MPa at a dry condition. The higher result is obtained in the condition of 75% SB & 25% HB particleboard. The researchers' test also carried out in the widthwise direction and the solid bamboo particleboard bending strength result (21.4 MPa) at dry condition is much lower than the mixed ratio 75/25 SB/HB of the two-species particleboard. That is mixing the two type of bamboo species for particleboard improves the bending strength of the particleboard. Due to this using both type of bamboo for particleboard can makes a profit since the resource is grown in both highland and lowland area in Ethiopia. That means the hollow bamboo is grown in the highland area and the solid bamboo grown in the lowland region. In this case, the farmers can also get benefit by supplying the resource.

The research result shows that the current eucalypts particleboard bending strength is about 30.63 MPa which is accepted in its strength in the market and bamboo particleboard bending strength is outshined (Fig. 7).

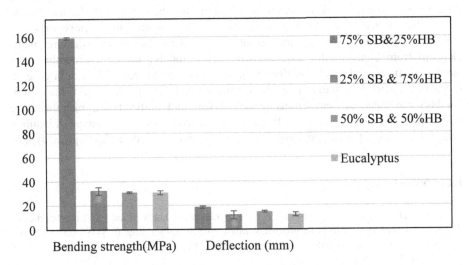

Fig. 7. Combined graph of each proportions deflection and bending strength results

The result which obtained from the bending strength test of solid and hollow bamboo particle board in different production ratio, the bending load resistance of the specimen was higher than the eucalyptus particle board bending load resistance. The deflection of the specimen illustrated in the above deflection Tables (3, 6 and 9) can be expressed in the following formula by considering the specimen as a beam from the center.

$$Dc = \frac{rxL^2}{6d} \tag{2}$$

Where, Dc = the maximum deflection at the center of the specimen in (mm), r = strain, d = depth of the specimen, L = span length between the support.

The reason to have high strength of 75% SB and 25% HB particle board is the natural intimacy of the chip each other was higher than the other chip particleboards and the board is manufactured in a medium density fiberboard mode.

4   Conclusions

In the research work, solid or lowland bamboo (Oxytenanthera Abyssinica) and hollow or highland bamboo (Yushania Alpina) chips are used to make particle board and the bending strengths have been examined. The bending strength of the bamboo particleboard is compared with that of eucalyptus particleboard and bamboo particle board has a greater strength. In addition this bamboo particle board has better smooth surface finish than eucalyptus particleboard in observation. But, the factory uses the machine to polish the surface of eucalyptus particleboard. Due to this, the factory expenses increase in machining, energy and operation cost. If the factory manufactures particleboard from bamboo, this expense will reduce totally, since the smoothness of bamboo particleboard was better than the polished eucalyptus particleboard. In general, if the manufacturing condition can be controlled well, the particleboard made from bamboo can substitute eucalyptus particle board and particleboard manufacturing companies can use bamboo plant. If the farmers teach about the advantage of bamboo and disadvantage of eucalyptus, they can plant bamboo instead of planting eucalyptus.

References

1. Banga, H., Singh, V.S., Choudhary, S.K.: Fabrication and study of mechanical properties of bamboo fiber reinforced bio-composites. Innovative Syst. Des. Eng. **6**, 84–98 (2015). http://citeseerx.ist.psu.edu/viewdoc/download?doi=10.1.1.823.1104&rep=rep1&type=pdf.   ISSN 2222-1727
2. Shimels, H., Eyassu, W.: Particleboard from Ethiopian lowland bamboo (Oxytenanthera Abyssinica). Int. J. Res. Mech. Eng. **2**(1), 33–37 (2014)
3. Embaye, K.: Ecological aspects and resource management of bamboo forests in Ethiopia. Doctoral thesis, Uppsala, Swedish University of Agricultural Sciences, pp. 8–12 (2003). https://pub.epsilon.slu.se/229/. ISSN 1401-6230
4. Kasahun, T.: Review of the bamboo value chain in Ethiopia. Int. J. Afr. Soc. Cult. Tradit. **2** (3), 52–67 (2015). Published by European Centre for Research Training and Development UK
5. Laemlaksakul, V.: Physical and mechanical properties of particleboard from bamboo waste. World Acad. Sci. Eng. Technol. Int. J. Chem. Mol. Nucl. Mater. Metall. Eng. **4**(4), 276–280 (2010).   https://waset.org/publications/10061/physical-and-mechanical-properties-of-particleboard-from-bamboowaste
6. Xiaobo, L.: Physical, chemical and mechanical properties of bamboo and its utilization for fiberboard manufacturing. M.Sc. thesis, submitted to the school of renewable natural resources. Agriculture and Mechanical College, Louisiana State University, pp. 50–62 (2004)
7. Biswas, D., Bose, S.K.: Physical and mechanical properties of urea formaldehyde bonded particleboard made from bamboo waste. Int. J. Adhes. Adhes. **31**(2), 84–87 (2011). Institute of Forestry and Environmental Science, University of Chittagong, Chittagong 4331, Bangladesh
8. Kargarfard, A., Jahan-Latibari, A.: The effect of press temperature on properties of medium density fiberboard produced from Eucalyptus camaldulensis fibers. Int. J. Lignocellul. Prod. **1**(2), 142–150 (2014). Islamic Azad University, Karaj, Iran

9. Ndububa, E.E., Nwobodo, D.C., Okeh, I.M.: Mechanical strength of particleboard produced from Fonio Husk with gum Arabic resin adhesive as binder. Int. J. Eng. Res. Appl. **5**(4), 29–33 (2015). http://ijera.com/papers/Vol5_issue4/Part%20-%205/F504052933.pdf. ISSN: 2248-9622

10. Eroğlu, H., İstek, A., Usta, M.: Medium density fiberboard (MDF) manufacturing from wheat straw (Triticumaestivum L.) and straw wood mixture. J. Eng. Sci. 305–311 (2001). Pamukkale University Engineering College. Zonguldak Karaelmas University, Bartın Forestry Faculty, Department of Forestry Industry Engineer. http://pajes.pau.edu.tr/eng/jvi.asp?pdir=pajes&plng=eng&un=PAJES-25478

11. Mallick, P.K.: Fiber-Reinforced composites materials, manufacturing, and design. Department of Mechanical Engineering University of Michigan-Dearborn, pp. 181–183. Taylor & Francis Group, LLC, Dearborn, Michigan (2007)

12. Alemie, T.C.: The effect of eucalyptus on crop productivity, and soil properties in the Koga Watershed, Western Amhara Region, Ethiopia. A Thesis Presented to the Faculty of the Graduate School of Cornell University in Partial Fulfillment of the Requirements for the Degree of Masters of Professional Studies (2009)

Investigations of the Influence of Fiber Orientation on Strength Properties of Agrostone Composites

Ephrem Zeleke, Mulugeta Eshetu$^{(\boxtimes)}$ (iD), Taye Meheretu,
Mehiret Betemariam, and Samuel Melkamu

Faculty of Mechanical and Industrial Engineering,
Bahir Dar University, Bahir Dar, Ethiopia
karrakorea@gmail.com, mulugetaeshetu88@gmail.com

Abstract. Agrostone is a construction material and a substitute for concrete that used as an exterior wall and interior partition. It is composed of Magnesium Oxide Powder (MgO), Magnesium Chloride ($MgCl_2$), Bagasse, Glass fiber and Pumice. The Agrostone panel has improved damage tolerance, environmental resistance, fire resistance, and recyclability, good strength, lightweight and potential for fast processing. However, the influence of fiber orientation on tensile, compressive and bending strength of agrostone panel is not studies from the previous researchers. The aim of this experimental study is investigate the influence of different fiber orientation arrangements on tensile, compressive and bending strength of agrostone panel. The testing specimens for experimental analysis prepared by hand layup process using a mixing ratio of 1.5 kg Magnesium oxide Powder (MgO) and 2 L Magnesium Chloride ($MgCl_2$). Waste recyclable bagasse 0.15 kg, 0.065 kg Fiber Glass and 0.2 kg of Pumice based on ASTM standard D 3039/D 3039M for tensile testing, D 3410/D 3410M – 03 for Compressive testing and D 790 – 02 for Flexural testing at 0°, 45°, 90°, cross and random arrangement are prepare. From the experiment, the tensile, compressive and bending result of 0° is higher than the other arrangements that has the value of 191.87 MPa, 178 MPa and 181 MPa respectively, therefore it means 0° fiber orientation give a better strength values in general for tensile, compressive and bending loading as compare to others.

Keywords: Agrostone composites · Mechanical properties · Fiber orientation · ASTM standard

1 Introduction

Understood of characterized, statistically based, material property data are essential to an efficient engineering development process; material suppliers, engineering users, and system end-users. Composites used throughout the history back to early 20th century. In 1940, fiberglass was first used to reinforce epoxy. I.e., straw in bricks, metal rod-reinforced concrete and lightweight aerospace structures. Fiber reinforced polymer matrix composite materials are presented in military systems and in the Department of Defense's effort to lighten the force. However, polymer matrix composites have natural

© ICST Institute for Computer Sciences, Social Informatics and Telecommunications Engineering 2019
Published by Springer Nature Switzerland AG 2019. All Rights Reserved
F. A. Zimale et al. (Eds.): ICAST 2018, LNICST 274, pp. 562–573, 2019.
https://doi.org/10.1007/978-3-030-15357-1_45

temperature restriction based on their hydrocarbon structure. The high temperature alternative to high-density metals is ceramics, offering weight savings as well high temperature capability and oxidation resistance [1].

The sustainable construction materials and innovative technology are the main problems of the construction industry in developing countries. Furthermore, the building materials cost has shared about 70% of the construction. Finally, the cost effective local material and construction technology of composite agrostone material is obtainable as a practical workable solution for the building of equitable housing units [2].

A composite material can be express as a combination of two or more macro elements that are vary in nature and organic arrangement and which are insoluble in each other. The two-macro elements are reinforcement and a matrix. That effects in superior properties than the individual components used alone. Composite materials are light in weight, high strength and stiffness compared to the bulk materials. The reinforcing phase materials are better strength and stiffness than the matrix phase materials [3]. Composite materials are classified based on reinforcement shape [4] (Fig. 1).

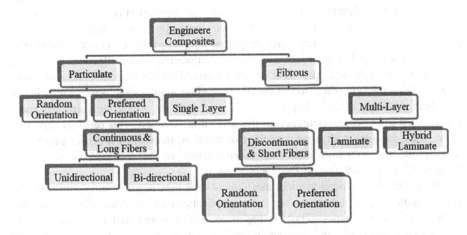

Fig. 1. Classification of composites

Fiber reinforced magnesium matrix composites are the representative of advanced composites, which have important potential in automotive, aviation, aerospace and national defense industries, etc., due to their lightweight, excellent mechanical properties, low thermal expansion coefficient, and high damping capacities. The growing applications of fiber reinforced magnesium matrix composites make it more important to understand and forecast their mechanical properties. Many endeavors have mainly motivated on the effects of the fiber volume fraction and the interfacial adhesion between the fiber and matrix, which guaranteed the effective transfer of stress. However, it was pointed out that the mechanical properties of composites also depended strongly on the fiber direction and fiber aspect ratios [5] (Fig. 2).

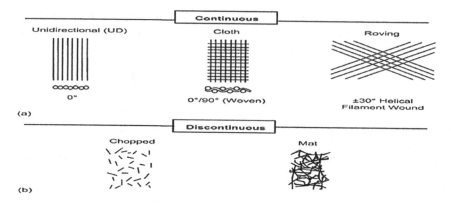

Fig. 2. Typical reinforcement types

The influence of the fiber direction on the mechanical reaction when the samples are stretch along different angles with respect to the orientation of the fiber evaluated using the stress-strain measurements and their respective young modulus and yield point. PVDF fiber morphology and properties are affect by processing parameters including initial polymer solution, solvent evaporation and collection procedure, allowing the collection of random or oriented fibers. This can explained once the force is apply along the same direction of the fibers, leading mainly to an actual stretching of the fibers, contrary to what happens in 45° and 90°, [6] where the force has more influence on the fibers reorientation to the stretching direction. This result is expected, since in the samples with a random fiber orientation, there exist a higher number of fibers along the stretching direction, independently of the direction of stretching, excepting for the stretching of the fibers along 0°.

The effect of fiber location under mechanical stretching is particularly applicable for tissue engineering applications once it has implications for mechanically guided maturation of specific tissues. Thus, it has been demonstrated that the orientation of mesenchymal stem cells and changes in nuclear morphology were PVDF electro spun fiber mats with aligned and randomly oriented fibers were produced and subjected to mechanical stretching along three different directions. 0°, 45° and 90°, relative to the fiber orientation within the fiber mats in order to study the variation in fiber mats morphology and mechanical response. Additionally, there is an increase of the strain value at break when subjected to stretching at the same direction of fibers orientation, but a decrease when the angle between the stretching direction and fiber orientation is 900. These variations must be quantitatively taken into account when the fiber composite mats are used as scaffolds for tissue engineering applications [7].

From the study of [8] Young's modulus of unidirectional glass fiber reinforced polymer (GFRP) composites for wind energy applications were studied using analytical, numerical and experimental methods. In order to explore the effect of fiber orientation angle on the Young's modulus of composites, from the basic theory of elastic mechanics, a procedure which can be applied to evaluate the elastic stiffness matrix of GFRP composite as an analytical function of fiber orientation angle (from 0° to 90°), was developed. The results of the investigation provide some design guideline for the microstructural optimization of the glass fiber reinforced composites and it shows relation between them is nearly linear.

Polymer materials reinforced with glass fiber have received tremendous attention in both scientific and industrial communities due to their extraordinary enhanced properties, such as lower weight, higher toughness and higher strength characteristics. In response to these requirements, research on composites has attracted much attention, which results in numerous publications [9–19]. In order to evaluate the mechanical behaviors of composites materials, different approaches, including experimental investigation, numerical simulations and theoretical modeling, were employed [20–24]. In the present work, theoretical analysis, finite element models as well as experimental investigations used to study the stiffness, i.e. Young's modulus, of glass fiber reinforced composites.

The effect of fiber orientation on Young's modulus for unidirectional GFRP studied by theoretical analysis, finite element numerical simulations as well as experimental investigations. All results indicate that Young's modulus of the composites strongly depends on the fiber orientation angles. A U-shaped dependency of the Young's modulus of composites on the inclined angle of fiber is find. At the same time, there is slight difference among analytical, simulated and experimental results. The difference is that the fiber orientation angle is around 45° when Young's modulus reaches its lowest value for experimental case and the fiber orientation angle is around 60° when Young's modulus reaches its lowest value for numerical and analytical cases. This is cause by:

1. The material properties for analytical, simulations and experiments are not completely the same;
2. For the experimental case, there are many facts affect the results. Nevertheless, for simulation and analysis, the model is simplified and some conditions are ideal.

In addition, analytical results also indicate that the shear modulus Gp has significant effect on the composites Young's modulus. Lower value of Gp led to lower Young's modulus at the same fiber orientation angle and the angle for the least Young's modulus decreases with the smaller Gp. simulated results indicate the relationship between Young's modulus and fiber volume content is nearly linear. The more glass fiber in the composites, the higher Young's modulus of the composites. Use the rule-of-mixture when loading direction alone the fiber axes for fiber-reinforced composites if the fiber/matrix interface is suppose as strong interface.

The effects of SGF and SCF incorporation on the tribological properties of PES composites were also investigated [25]. The incorporation of SGFs results in a monotonic increase of the friction coefficient of the PES composites, and a maximum increase of 48.8% is achieve with the addition of 30% SGFs. However, the friction coefficient of SCF/PES composites decreases with the addition of SCFs, and a maximum drop of 29.8% compared with pure PES is reached with the addition of 20-vol. % SCFs. The wear process of fiber-reinforced composites includes fiber-matrix debonding followed by fiber breakage because of micro cracking, micro cutting, and micro-pulverization due to reciprocating shearing stress [26, 28]. In general, the mechanical property enhancement effectiveness of SCFs is better than that of SGFs for injection molded PES composites. As for the tribological performance, the specific wear rate of PES is significantly reduce by the incorporation of either SGFs or SCFs.

Paper [29] is analysis in ceramic matrix composite materials for investigation on effect of fiber orientation on failure behavior of 3DN C/SiC torque tube. On the study a simplified FEM model is use to analyze failure behaviors. Torsional tests conducted using special attachments to a universal material test machine to obtain the stress strain curves and failure strength. Failure analysis made according to the fracture mopholo-gies of SEM.

In the experiment, torque tubes with fiber orientation of ±45° exhibited a higher torque capacity and modulus than fiber orientation of 0°/90°, it shows good agreement with simulation results. Failure behaviors and changes in predominant failure factors among specimens observed. Both 0°/90° and ±45° fiber orientation belong to tensile failure mode. From the analysis of stress distribution simulation and SEM image, we obtained that the predominant failure factor of M02 torque tube is the failure of the short-cut fiber lamina, and the predominant failure factor of M04 torque tube is the failure of the non-woven fiber lamina. Failure analysis is of great benefit to engineering design, and helps to improve our fabrication process for high property components.

On [30] paper the researcher examine the effect of fiber orientations on surface grinding process of the unidirectional C/SiC composites by diamond grinding wheel conducted and the effect of fiber orientation on grinding force and surface quality discussed. The main effects of cutting conditions (depth of cut, feed speed, cutting speed) on CFCC grinding at the three typical directions (to the reinforced fibers) were systematically analyzed.

The effects of the fiber orientation and fiber aspect ratio on the tensile strength of Csf/Mg composites, several different representative volume units generated by using the random sequential adsorption algorithm. From The research, it showed that the angles between the fiber orientation and applied load played a significant role on the properties improvement of Csf/Mg composites. The tensile strength of Csf/Mg com-posites gradually decreased with the fiber orientation angle increasing from 00 to 600 and slightly increased with the fiber orientation angle increasing from 600 to 900 [31]. Author [32] examined on Influence of Thickness and Fiber Orientation on a Tensile and Flexural Properties of a Hybrid Composite on 300, 450 and 600 fiber orientation of Carbon, S-glass and E-glass fiber reinforced polymer composites. The study conclude that the 300 arrangement gives greater result as compare to others.

From the previous literature the authors considers the influence of 00, 900 and random fiber orientation on the tensile and bending strength of the composite material for natural fiber and some other polymer material. However, the effect of glass fiber orientation on tensile, compressive, bending and other tribological aspects based on different fiber orientations are not that much detail investigated on the previous liter-atures. Nevertheless, the studied of the above listed parts leads for a better finding of new material. Therefore, the aim of this paper is to test and investigate the influence of fiber orientation on mechanical properties of Agrostone at different fiberglass arrangement, prepare an organized document and to recommend an appropriate fiberglass orientation for the advancement of the new agrostone material with better strength and properties.

2   Material and Methodology

2.1   Material

Bagasse, pumice and diatomite are use as fillers. Magnesium Oxychloride Cement (MOC) known as Sorel is used as binder. MOC is a non-hydraulic binder, which is form by mixing Magnesium Oxide (MgO) with Magnesium Chloride (MgCl$_2$).

Factors for the selection of Matrices and Fibers:

- Most matrices materials are locally available
- The majority of agrostone factories used those products
- Mixing ratio of matrices materials

    Advantages of the Matrix material:

- It is the naturally available material in Ethiopia, which are abundant.
- Cost of the material is cheap.
- Utilization of these materials reduces the wastes accumulation and unvalued goods becomes valued.

    Reason for selecting the fiber material

- Fiber strengthens the matrix material.
- The fiber selected for this application are available.
- Cheap cost and abundantly available in Ethiopia.
- It has good strength in normal atmosphere when comparing with other type of fiber materials.

2.2   Mould Preparation

A mould is made up of plastic material with a dimension of ASTM standard is prepared. Casting of the composite materials is done in this mould by hand layup process. Later specimens are cut from the prepared casting according to the ASTM Standards (Fig. 3).

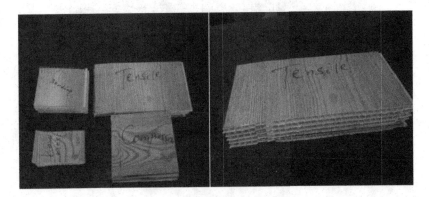

Fig. 3. Finally prepared mold

2.3   Specimen Preparation

Based on the working consistency of Agrostone Production Center mix proportion 1.5 kg of Magnesium Oxide (MgO) powder by weight and 2 L of Magnesium Chloride (MgCl$_2$) were mixed along with 0.2 kg of pumice powder. Estimated quantity of filler, 0.15 kg bagasse and 0.06 kg of fiberglass added until a working consistency of the mix. The mix work done in an open pan type mixer of 4-liter capacity. The casting of the composite made by hand layup process for different fiber orientations such as 0°, 45°, 90°, cross and random, as shown in Fig. 4.

Fig. 4. Hand layup techniques preparation of specimens for testing

The samples for tensile test cut from the molded composite to a size of (250 × 25 × 2.5) mm as per ASTM D-3039 for tensile specimens and (155 × 25 × 3) mm as per ASTM D-3410 for compressive specimens and (127 × 12.7 × 3) mm as per ASTM D-790 for bending specimens. Shown in Fig. 5.

Fig. 5. Slicing specimen of all testes

Testing of Specimens

The experiments conducted on a calibrated universal testing machine (UTM) for tensile, compressive and bending specimens by appropriately changing the grips and the loading procedure. In case of tensile testing, the specimens are placed in the upper and lower grips, and then the computer setting is adjusted according to the specimen dimensions, type of material and grip length. After entering the data related to above parameters, loading is started and continued until the specimen is failed. The result is displayed on the screen of the computer. Loading adjustments for tensile, compressive and bending specimens is shown in Fig. 6.

Fig. 6. Specimens on the UTM

3   Result and Discussion

3.1   Tensile Strength

The average ultimate strength of the Agrostone composite for 0° fiber arrangement is 191.87 MPa. For 45° fibers orientation, the strength value is 144 MPa. For 90° orientation of fiber, the strength value is 146 MPa. For cross fibers, the tensile strength is higher than for the above orientation. Even for random fiber, the strength is less than that of 90° orientations, equal to 145 MPa. It can be noted that maximum strength of composite is obtained only for fibers oriented in the direction of loading and the next better value is obtained for the cross fiber laminate. The strength is reduce for the orientations from 0° to 90° for unidirectional fiber composites. It shows that the full strength of the fibers and the matrix are sharing the load when the loading is inline. The values of ultimate tensile strength of composite with different fiber orientations are present in Fig. 7.

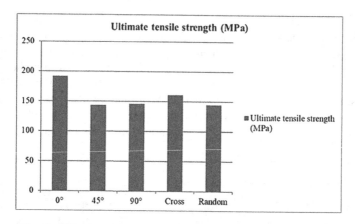

Fig. 7. Ultimate tensile strength and force with fiber arrangement

3.2   Compressive Strength

The highest value of ultimate compressive strength for 00 fibers is 178 MPa and 145 MPa for 45° fibers. For 90° fibers, the strength is 172 MPa and for cross fibers, it is equal to 175 MPa, which is next to that of 0° fibers. For random fibers, the strength is 165 MPa. The pattern of strength is similar to that of tensile loading. The compressive strength values are higher for composites with 90°, cross and random orientation compared to that of tensile strength values. The values of compressive strength for different fiber orientations are shown in Fig. 8.

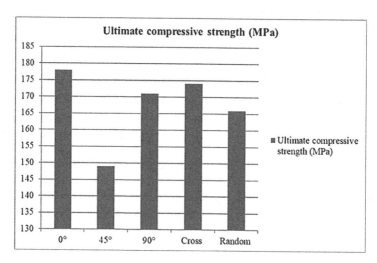

Fig. 8. Ultimate compressive strength and force with fiber arrangement

3.3 Bending Strength

The bending strength for cross fiber orientation is 181 MPa and for random fibers, it is equal to 173 MPa. For 0° fibers, it is equal to 162 MPa and for 45° orientations, it is equal to 153 MPa and for 90°, it is 142 MPa. The values of bending strength for composites with different orientations are shown in Fig. 9. It noted from the results, that the composite has higher bending strength if the fibers are cross and random. The strength is much less for unidirectional composite.

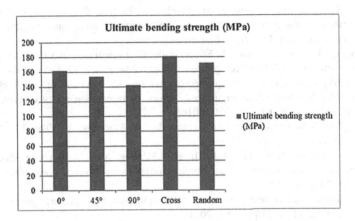

Fig. 9. Ultimate bending strength and force with fiber arrangement

4   Conclusion

The tensile and compressive strength values for 0° fibers is much higher compared to other orientations. The compressive strength values are higher for 90°, cross and random fiber orientation compared to tensile strength values. For 45° orientation, the strength values are minimum in both the cases. It clearly indicates that the strength of composite has higher bearing on the strength of the reinforcing fibers. Especially, it is higher if the loading is in the direction of fiber orientation.

However, in case of bending, the composite has exhibited highest strength for cross fiber composite and next higher value is for random fiber composite. For bending loads, the spreading of fibers in different orientations, in more layers will increase its strength than for composites unidirectional fibers of any orientation.

It can be concluded that 0°, cross and random orientations can be preferred for composites with a general kind of loading compared to other fiber orientation.

References

1. Rowell, R.M.: The State of Art and Future Development of Bio-Based Composite Science and Technology Towards The 21 St Century (1996)
2. Woundimagegnehu, T.: Affordable Houses for Middle and Low Income Group in Ethiopia Self help housing with innovative construction technology, pp. 1–16
3. Elanchezhian, C., Ramnath, B.V., Ramakrishnan, G., Rajendrakumar, M., Naveenkumar, V., Saravanakumar, M.K.: Review on mechanical properties of natural fiber composites. Mater. Today Proc. 5(1), 1785–1790 (2018)
4. Sanjay, M.R., Madhu, P., Jawaid, M., Senthamaraikannan, P., Senthil, S., Pradeep, S.: Characterization and properties of natural fiber polymer composites: a comprehensive review. J. Clean. Prod. 172, 566–581 (2018)
5. Tian, W., Qi, L., Zhou, J., Guan, J.: Effects of the fiber orientation and fiber aspect ratio on the tensile strength of Csf/Mg composites. Comput. Mater. Sci. 89, 6–11 (2014)
6. Pauly, H.M., et al.: Mechanical properties and cellular response of novel electrospun nanofibers for ligament tissue engineering: effects of orientation and geometry. J. Mech. Behav. Biomed. Mater. 61, 258–270 (2016)
7. Maciel, M.M., Ribeiro, S., Ribeiro, C., Francesko, A., Maceiras, A., Vilas, J.L.: "AC SC," Compos. Part B (2018)
8. Wang, H.W., Zhou, H.W., Gui, L.L., Ji, H.W., Zhang, X.C.: Analysis of effect of fiber orientation on Young's modulus for unidirectional fiber reinforced composites. Compos. B Eng. 56, 733–739 (2014)
9. Hui, D., Dutta, P.K.: A new concept of shock mitigation by impedance-graded materials. Compos. B Eng. 42(8), 2181–2184 (2011)
10. Rhee, K.Y., Park, S.J., Hui, D., Qiu, Y.: Effect of oxygen plasma-treated carbon fibers on the tribological behavior of oil-absorbed carbon/epoxy woven composites. Compos. B Eng. 43(5), 2395–2399 (2012)
11. Wosu, S.N., Hui, D., Daniel, L.: Hygrothermal effects on the dynamic compressive properties of graphite/epoxy composite material. Compos. B Eng. 43(3), 841–855 (2012)
12. Liu, Y.G., Zhou, J.Q., Hui, D.: A strain-gradient plasticity theory of bimodal nanocrystalline materials with composite structure. Compos. B Eng. 43(2), 249–254 (2012)
13. Cerbu, C., Curtu, I.: Mechanical characterization of the glass fibres/rubber/resin composite material. Mater. Plast. 48(1), 93–97 (2011)
14. Reis, J.M.L., Coelho, J.L.V., Mattos, H.S.D.: A continuum damage model for glass/epoxy laminates in tension. Compos. B Eng. 52, 114–119 (2013)
15. Chen, Q., et al.: Fabrication and mechanical properties of hybrid multi-scale epoxy composites reinforced with conventional carbon fiber fabrics surface-attached with electrospun carbon nanofiber mats. Compos. B Eng. 44(1), 1–7 (2013)
16. Cavdar, A.: A study on the effects of high temperature on mechanical properties of fiber reinforced cementitious composites. Compos. B Eng. 43(5), 2452–2463 (2012)
17. Ku, H., Wang, H., Pattarachaiyakoop, N., Trada, M.: A review on the tensile properties of natural fiber reinforced polymer composites. Compos. B Eng. 42(4), 856–873 (2011)
18. Liang, J.Z.: Predictions of Young's modulus of short inorganic fiber reinforced polymer composites. Compos. B Eng. 43(4), 1763–1766 (2012)
19. Zhou, H.W., et al.: Compressive damage mechanism of GFRP composites under off-axis loading: experimental and numerical investigations. Compos. B Eng. 55, 119–127 (2013)
20. Dai, L.C., Feng, X., Liu, B., Fang, D.N.: Interfacial slippage of inorganic electronic materials on plastic substrates. Appl. Phys. Lett. 97(22), 221903 (2010)

21. Lei, Z.K., Qiu, W., Kang, Y.L., Gang, L., Yun, H.: Stress transfer of single fiber/microdroplet tensile test studied by micro-Raman spectroscopy. Compos. A Appl. Sci. Manuf. **39**(1), 113–118 (2008)

22. Li, Q., et al.: Deformation mechanisms of carbon nanotube fibres under tensile loading by in situ Raman spectroscopy analysis. Nanotechnology **22**, 225704 (2011)

23. Qiu, W., Kang, Y.L., Lei, Z.K., Qin, Q.H., Li, Q.: A new theoretical model of a carbon nanotube strain sensor. Chin. Phys. Lett. **26**(8), 080701 (2009)

24. Cerbu, C., Curtu, I., Consntinescu, D.M., Miron, M.C.: Aspects concerning the transversal contraction in the case of some composite materials reinforced with glass fabric. Mater. Plast. **48**(4), 341–345 (2011)

25. Zhao, Z., Du, S., Li, F., Xiao, H., Li, Y., Zhang, W.: Mechanical and tribological properties of short glass fiber and short carbon fiber reinforced polyethersulfone composites. Compos. Commun. **8**, 1–6 (2018)

26. Bijwe, J., Awtade, S., Ghosh, A.: Influence of orientation and volume fraction of aramid fabric on abrasive wear performance of polyethersulfone composites. Wear **260**, 401–411 (2006)

27. Sharma, M., Bijwe, J., Mitschang, P.: Abrasive wear studies on composites of PEEK and PES with modified surface of carbon fabric. Tribol. Int. **44**, 81–91 (2011)

28. Sharma, M., Bijwe, J., Singh, K.: Studies for wear property correlation for carbon fabric-reinforced PES composites. Tribol. Lett. **43**, 267 (2011)

29. Zhao, H., Zhang, L., Chen, B., Zhang, J.: The effect of fiber orientation on failure behavior of 3DN C/SiC torque tube. Ceram. Int. **44**, 1–8 (2018)

30. Zhang, L., Ren, C., Ji, C., Wang, Z., Chen, G.: Effect of fiber orientations on surface grinding process of unidirectional C/SiC composites. Appl. Surf. Sci. **366**, 424–431 (2016)

31. Borgaonkar, A.V., Mandale, M.B., Potdar, S.B.: Effect of changes in fiber orientations on modal density of fiberglass composite plates. Mater. Today Proc. **5**, 5783–5791 (2018)

32. Santhosh Kumar, M., Krisna, S.G.G., Rajanna, S.: Study on effect of thickness and fibre orientation on tensile and flexural properties of a hybrid composite. Int. J. Eng. Res. Appl. **4**, 56–66 (2014)

A Comparative Analysis of Watermarked and Watermark Images Using DCT and SVD Based Multiple Image Watermarking

Tarun Rathi[1]([✉]), Rudra P. Maheshwari[2], Manoj Tripathy[3],
Rahul Saraswat[4], and X. Felix Joseph[5]

[1] Department of Electrical and Computer Engineering,
Maddawalabu University, Bale Robe, Ethiopia
rathi.tarun@gmail.com
[2] Raj Kumar Goel Institute of Technology, Ghaziabad, India
rpmaheshwari@hotmail.com
[3] Department of Electrical Engineering, Indian Institute of Technology Roorkee,
Roorkee, India
tripathy.manoj@gmail.com
[4] Department of Electronics and Communication Engineering,
Anand Engineering College, Agra, India
rahulsaraswat.ece@gmail.com
[5] Department of Electrical and Computer Engineering, Bule Hora University,
Hagere Mariam, Ethiopia
felixjoseph75@gmail.com

Abstract. In many applications of digital watermarking, watermarked image of good quality is required. But there is a trade-off between a number of embedded watermark images and quality of watermarked image. This aspect is quite important in the case of multiple digital images watermarking. In this case, multiple images singular value decomposition based watermarking algorithm performs much better than other transform based methods. This paper presents robust multiple digital images watermarking using singular value decomposition (SVD) method. The results are compared with Discrete Cosine Transform (DCT) based multiple images watermarking method. In the case of multiple images DCT watermarking or in other transform based method more coefficients are varied according to the watermark images, which degrade the quality of watermarked image. In the case of SVD image watermarking method only singular values are being varied either in single or multiple images water-marking. This helps in preserving the quality of watermarked image.

Keywords: Singular value decomposition (SVD) ·
Discrete cosine transform (DCT) · Peak signal to noise ratio (PSNR) ·
Normalized correlation (NC) · Accuracy rate (AR) ·
Multiple image watermarking

F. A. Zimale et al. (Eds.): ICAST 2018, LNICST 274, pp. 574–581, 2019.
https://doi.org/10.1007/978-3-030-15357-1_46

1 Introduction

To prevent the illegal copying and tracking of the digital contents and for several other important applications, digital image watermarking is being introduced. This hides the information within the digital document like image, audio, video, [1].

Watermarking methods can be classified in two categories spatial domain and transform domain [2]. In spatial domain changing the pixels of the host image directly embeds the watermark. Due to this, extracting watermark in a noisy channel is very rare in the spatial domain, [3]. So, transform based algorithms like discrete Fourier transform (DFT), discrete cosine transform (DCT), discrete wavelet transform (DWT), are introduced which are more robust than spatial domain but in the case of geometric attacks or noisier channel these algorithms do not perform well, [4]. We have used singular value decomposition (SVD) algorithm for better result.

The multiple images watermarking method is a trade-off between the numbers of embedded watermark images and quality of watermarked image. In the case of transform domain watermarking, quality of watermarked image degrades more due to more changed coefficients. So this paper proposes a method of SVD based multiple images watermarking. In SVD based watermarking the watermarked image does not degrade as much as in other transform based watermarking method because only singular diagonal values are being varied. SVD is having stability, flip and transpose property etc. [5]. This makes SVD based multiple images watermarking robust and secured.

2 Evaluation Parameters

Peak signal to noise ratio represents the quality of the watermark image. Mean square error (MSE) is to be calculated to compute the PSNR between extracted and original watermark image. PSNR and mean square error (MSE) can be expressed as follow:

$$PSNR = 10 * \log\left(\frac{255^2}{MSE}\right) \tag{1}$$

$$MSE = \frac{1}{M * N} \sum_{i=1}^{N} \sum_{i=2}^{M} [I(i,j) - I^*(i,j)]^2 \tag{2}$$

Where $I(i,j)$ and $I^*(i,j)$ are the pixel values of original images and watermarked images respectively. Image matrix size is denoted by $M * N$.

Robustness is the feature of the watermark image to preserve information even after the different noise and malicious attacks [6]. This is measured as normalized correlation (NC) used for similarity measurement between the original watermark and extracted watermark. Normalized correlation (NC) can be expressed as follow.

$$NC = \frac{\sum_i w_i w_i^{*^2}}{\sum_i w_i^2} \tag{3}$$

Here w_i is the original watermark and w_i^* is the extracted watermark. Bigger the NC value means better similarity between two images.

Accuracy rate (AR) is also used to compare original image and processed image. AR increases in proportion to the image quality and it is defined by the following formula.

$$AR = \left(\frac{No.\ of\ pixels\ in\ processed\ image}{No.\ of\ pixels\ in\ original\ image} \right) * 100\%. \tag{4}$$

3 DCT Based Multiple Images Watermarking

DCT is a very useful method for image processing which converts the image into different frequency coefficients. In blind multiple images DCT watermarking; the host image is segmented into multiple blocks of the same size. Then each block is transformed using DCT. The message bits are embedded as a coefficient modification. In the case of more watermarking images, more coefficients are varied. Here four coefficients are modified for two watermark image (see Fig. 1). High-frequency coefficients are more sensitive to image processing attacks and low-frequency coefficients are having visual effect so middle-frequency coefficients are selected for embedding the watermark message. These selected coefficients work as a secret key without knowing that one can not extract the watermark. After modification in coefficients, the inverse DCT is applied to produce the watermarked image. At extraction part, watermarked image is segmented in blocks and DCT is applied to every block. From known coefficients message bits are recovered and reshaped into watermark image.

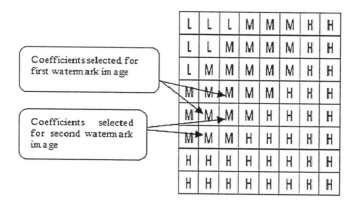

Fig. 1. Coefficients of a DCT block of the host image.

4 SVD Based Multiple Images Watermarking

SVD is very useful for image processing. This is a numerical technique to analyze the image matrix, which converts the image into three different metrics, [7]. The SVD of image I_m can be described as

$$I_m = HSV^T \tag{5}$$

$$I_m = [h_1\, h_2 \ldots h_N] \begin{bmatrix} s_1 & \cdots & \\ \vdots & \ddots & \vdots \\ & \cdots & s_N \end{bmatrix} \begin{bmatrix} v_1 \\ \vdots \\ v_N \end{bmatrix}^T \tag{6}$$

In Eq. (5), I_m is the image matrix, H and V are two $M * N$ and $N * N$ unitary orthogonal matrices, and S is a $N * N$ diagonal matrix, [8]. Where, H represents the horizontal detail component of the image and V represents the vertical detail component of image I. Both H and V are orthogonal matrices and S is a singular matrix, which consists of singular values. Singular values in S-matrix are arranged diagonally and in decreasing order [9]. One of the important properties of SVD is that a little change in the singular values does not affect the quality watermark image. Due to the property of SVD, SVD algorithm produces more robust and secure watermark, [10].

A host image is divided into blocks, and then SVD is applied for each block. Two watermark images are embedded in the form of singular values modification, [11]. For this different random sequence for a different bit of every watermark image is added to singular values with a gain factor. After modifying singular values we take the inverse of the SVD process to produce watermarked image. At extraction part, SVD is applied to watermarked image. From the correlation between stored singular values and modified singular values message bits are recovered and reshaped into watermark image, [12].

5 Experimental Results

5.1 DCT Based Multiple Image Watermarking

For single and multiple images watermarking, different values of accuracy rate (AR), $PSNR$ and normalized correlation (NC) with respect to gain factor K are used (see Table 1 in Appendix). This K is the difference between two coefficients in transformed matrix. This shows that for the same value of K, $PSNR$ of the watermarked image in single image watermarking is more than the $PSNR$ of watermarked image in multiple images watermarking because more coefficients are varied in multiple images watermarking. While $PSNR$ of watermark images depends on the selected coefficients in which watermark bits are being embedded. DCT algorithm based watermarking is applied on images with a constant gain factor (k_1) of 20 (see Fig. 4 in Appendix). $PSNR$ Variations with respect to gain factor K in DCT based algorithm for single and multiple images watermarking are compared (see Fig. 2). The watermarked image-1 of single image DCT watermarking method is having higher PSNR value than the watermarked image-2 of multiple images DCT watermarking method (see Fig. 2).

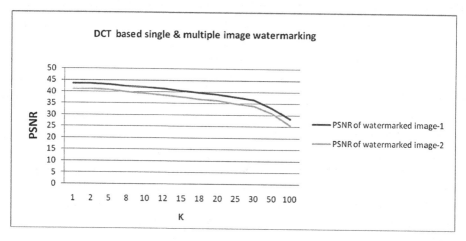

Fig. 2. PSNR variation in DCT single image and multiple image watermarking. (K = Gain factor for DCT based watermarking)

5.2 SVD Based Multiple Image Watermarking

SVD based single and multiple images watermarking is applied with different values of *AR*, *PSNR* and normalized correlation with respect to gain factor *alpha* (see Table 2 in Appendix). For the same value of *alpha*, *PSNR* of the watermarked image in single image watermarking is slightly more than the *PSNR* of watermarked image in multiple

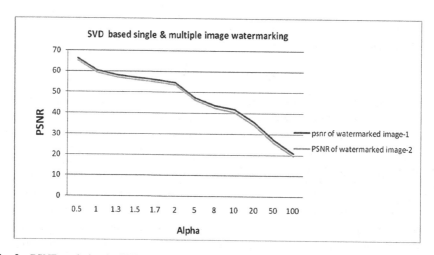

Fig. 3. PSNR variation in SVD single image and multiple image watermarking. (Alpha = Gain factor for SVD based watermarking).

images watermarking unlike in DCT based method because only singular values are varied in multiple images watermarking (see Table 2 in Appendix).

SVD based multiple images watermarking with gain factor *alpha* as 20 is applied to the same image (see Fig. 5 in Appendix). *PSNR* Variations of watermarked images with respect of gain factor *alpha* are compared for image-1 and image-2 (see Fig. 3).

The watermarked image-1 of single image SVD watermarking method is having slightly higher PSNR value than the watermarked image-2 of multiple images SVD watermarking method (see Fig. 3).

6   Conclusions

In this paper, two multiple images digital image watermarking algorithm is implemented using MATLAB which is based on DCT and SVD. Experiment results conclude that SVD based multiple images watermarking algorithm has better watermarked image compared to DCT based multiple images watermarking algorithm.

Two watermarks are extracted in each method and we can see the difference that in DCT based multiple image watermarking two watermarks are having different psnr depending on the different coefficient which we are selected while there is slight change in the psnr of two watermarks in SVD based multiple images watermarking.

Appendix

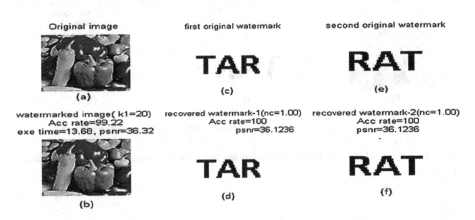

Fig. 4. DCT multiple image watermarking, (a) Host image, (b) Watermarked image, (c) First watermark, (d) First recovered Watermark, (e) Second watermark, (f) Second recovered watermark. ($k1$ = Gain factor for DCT based multiple image watermarking, nc = normalized correlation).

Table 1. DCT single image and multiple image watermarking

Gain factor	DCT single image watermarking					DCT multiple images watermarking							
	Watermarked image		Watermark			Watermarked image		Watermark-1			Watermark-2		
K/K1	AR	PSNR	NC	AR	PSNR	AR	PSNR	NC	AR	PSNR	NC	AR	PSNR
1	100	43.4	0.7	81.2	5.2	100	41.2	0.7	82.8	5.2	0.59	70.3	3.8
2	100	43.3	0.71	81.2	5.3	100	41.2	0.7	79.6	5.2	0.59	70.3	3.8
5	100	43.0	0.79	82.8	6.8	100	40.7	0.8	82.8	7.0	0.61	78.1	4.0
8	99.8	42.3	0.95	95.3	13.5	99.8	40	0.94	95.3	12.5	0.67	76.5	4.7
10	99.4	41.8	0.99	98.4	21.0	99.4	39.3	0.99	100	20.4	0.74	90.6	5.7
12	99.2	41.3	1	100	36.1	99.2	38.6	1	100	36.1	0.83	95.9	7.6
15	98.8	40.4	1	100	36.1	99.2	37.7	1	100	36.1	0.93	96.8	11.9
18	98.8	39.6	1	100	36.1	99.2	36.8	1	100	36.1	1	100	31.3
20	98.8	39	1	100	36.1	98.9	36.3	1	100	36.12	1	100	36.1

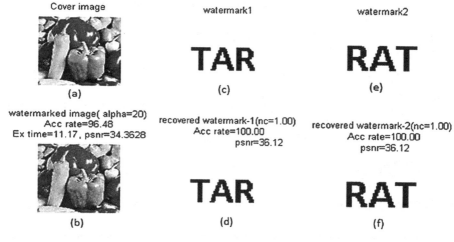

Fig. 5. SVD multiple image watermarking, (a) Host image, (b) Watermarked image, (c) First watermark, (d) First recovered watermark, (e) Second watermark, (f) Second recovered watermark. (alpha = Gain factor for SVD based multiple image watermarking, nc = normalized correlation).

Table 2. SVD single image and multiple images watermarking

Gain factor (alpha)	SVD single image watermarking					SVD multiple images watermarking							
	Watermarked image		Watermark			Watermarked image		Watermark-1			Watermark-2		
	AR	PSNR	NC	AR	PSNR	AR	PSNR	NC	AR	PSNR	NC	AR	PSNR
1	100	60.3	0.04	7.8	0.73	100	59.2	0.05	4.69	0.76	0.07	12.5	0.96
1.3	100	58.2	0.66	71.8	5.1	100	57.0	0.72	79.6	6.03	0.75	75	6.73
1.5	100	57.0	0.97	96.8	15.1	100	55.9	0.98	100	16.7	0.98	96.8	18.7
1.7	100	56.0	1	100	33.1	100	54.8	1	100	36.1	1	100	36.1
2	100	54.6	1	100	36.1	100	53.5	1	100	36.1	1	100	36.1
5	99.4	47.4	1	100	36.1	99.2	46.3	1	100	36.1	1	100	36.1
8	99.2	43.7	1	100	36.1	99.2	42.4	1	100	36.1	1	100	36.1
10	99.0	41.9	1	100	36.1	98.8	40.5	1	100	36.1	1	100	36.1

References

1. Potdar, V.M., Han, S., Chang, E:. A survey of digital image watermarking techniques. In: Proceedings of the IEEE International Conference on Industrial Informatics, pp. 709–716 (2005)
2. Lu, Z.M., Zheng, H.Y., Huang, J.W.: A digital watermarking scheme based on DCT and SVD. In: Proceeding of IIHMSP 2007 Conference, Kaohsiung, pp. 241–244 (2007)
3. Rykaczewski, R.: Comments on "An SVD-based watermarking scheme for protecting rightful ownership". IEEE Trans. Multimedia 9(2), 421–423 (2007)
4. Wang, N., Wang, Y., Li, X.: A novel robust watermarking algorithm based on DWT and DCT. In: International Conference on Computational Intelligence and Security, vol. 1, pp. 437–441 (2009)
5. Rafigh, M., Moghaddam, M.E.: A robust evolutionary based digital image watermarking technique in DCT domain. In: Proceedings of IEEE 7th International Conference on Computer Graphics, Imaging and Visualization, pp. 105–109 (2010)
6. Lai, C.-C., Tsai, C.-C.: Digital image watermarking using discrete wavelet transform and singular value decomposition. IEEE Trans. Instrum. Measur. **59**, 3060–3063 (2010)
7. Run, R.S., Horng, S.J., Lai, J.L., Kao, T.W., Chen, R.J.: An improved SVD-based watermarking technique for copyright protection. Int. J. Expert Syst. Appl. **39**(1), 673–689 (2012)
8. Parashar, P., Singh, R.K.: A survey : digital image watermarking techniques. In: 3rd IEEE International Conference on Industrial Informatics Techniques, pp. 111–124 (2014)
9. Chinchmalatpure, P., Ramteke, K., Dahiwale, P.: Fingerprint authentication by hybrid DWT and SVD based watermarking. In: IEEE International Conference on Innovations in Information, Embedded and Communication Systems, ICIIECS, pp. 0–3 (2015)
10. Rao, R.S.P., Kumar, P.R.: An efficient genetic algorithm based gray scale digital image watermarking for improving the robustness and imperceptibility. In: International Conference on Electrical, Electronics, and Optimization Techniques (ICEEOT), pp. 4568–4571 (2016)
11. Gupta, P., Parmar, G.: Image watermarking using IWT-SVD and its comparative analysis with DWT-SVD. In: 2017 International Conference on Computer, Communications and Electronics, COMPTELIX, pp. 527–531 (2017)
12. Ansari, I.A.: On the security of "block -based SVD image watermarking in spatial and transform domains". In: International Conference on Digital Arts, Media and Technology (ICDAMT), pp. 44–48 (2018)

The Role of Natural Ecosystem in Purifying Municipal Wastewater in Bahir Dar Metropolitan City

Fitfety Melese[1]([✉]), Ayalew Wondie[2], and Nigus Gabye[1]

[1] Faculty of Chemical and Food Engineering,
Bahir Dar Institute of Technology, Bahir Dar, Ethiopia
fitfetymelese@gmail.com
[2] Department of Biology, College of Science,
Bahir Dar University, Bahir Dar, Ethiopia

Abstract. The main purpose of this study was to study the Ecosystem functionality in purifying municipal wastewater. Three drainage lines were selected to determine the efficiency of ecosystem in purifying waste water. The water quality parameters considered for this study were dissolved oxygen, total dissolved solids, biological oxygen demand, pH, conductivity, nitrate, phosphate, and ammonia. Pollutant load concentration flowing along to the three drainage lines and contributions to the Blue Nile river pollution were determined for the months March to May 2018. The load of BOD, TDS, and electrical conductivity, pH, nitrate, phosphate, and ammonia were reduced by 58.10%, 54.33%, 53.50%, 13.55%, 52.28%, and 75.20% respectively. The average concentration load of dissolved oxygen for canals #1 and #2 were enhanced by 70% while for Blue Nile river course it is reduced by 18%. Although the natural ecosystem show significant amount of reduction in chemical pollutants, the concentration in some parameters were still above the standard which requires enhancement of the ecosystem. Most water quality parameters of effluents at the Blue Nile river (Downstream) except BOD and DO were with within levels set by international standards for effluents to be discharged to surface water and FAO maximum permissible level set for waste water to be used for irrigation purposes. To reverse the adverse outcomes of effluents, treating wastes and preservation of the ecosystem is beneficial.

Keywords: Ecosystem · Wetland · Wastewater

1 Introduction

1.1 Background

Liquid waste discharge over water bodies is a daily practice in many developing countries [1, 2]. It is reported that 70% of industries in developing countries disposed their untreated waste in to water bodies and to the environment [3]. In Ethiopia, almost all natural waters are affected by municipal, agricultural, and industrial waste in the form of solids, liquids and hazardous materials [1]. The natural streams and rivers passing through cities such as Bahir Dar and Addis Ababa can be described as sewer

© ICST Institute for Computer Sciences, Social Informatics and Telecommunications Engineering 2019
Published by Springer Nature Switzerland AG 2019. All Rights Reserved
F. A. Zimale et al. (Eds.): ICAST 2018, LNICST 274, pp. 582–598, 2019.
https://doi.org/10.1007/978-3-030-15357-1_47

lines for domestic and industrial waste [4]. Wastewater disposal is a serious problem in Bahir Dar City. Major institutions and industries like Bahir Dar University, Textile and tannery factories, commercial centers, and hotels discharge their effluents directly or indirectly into the natural streams and the municipal drainage system, and finally drained into Blue Nile river and Lake Tana without treatment (personal observation). It is estimated that two-thirds of the community living in Bahir Dar City discharge their domestic waste water in to streets and flood water drainages which ultimately end up to Blue Nile river.

Chemical and physical assessment is widely utilized to evaluate the efficiency of ecosystem in reducing pollutions of water bodies from different point and non-point sources. However, the combination of biological assessment with physio-chemical assessment is the most appropriate means of figure out the role of ecosystem to reduce pollution in aquatic system [1]. Because it can detect cumulative physical, chemical and biological impacts of adverse effect to an aquatic systems [5–7]. In Ethiopia, physio-chemical and biological parameters have been used as stream and river water quality indicators [1]; [8–11]. However information about the role and extent of ecosystem (sediment, macrophytes, planktons, and microbes) in purifying municipal wastewater is limited. Therefore, the objective of this study was to investigate the role of ecosystem to purify municipal wastewater in Bahir Dar City by using water quality parameter as indicators through the following research questions: (1) To what extent the natural ecosystem (vegetation, wetlands and big rivers) purify municipal wastewater in the longitudinal gradient of pollution? (2) To what extent the measured water quality parameters vary as compared to accepted international standard, and (3) How the Blue Nile river affected by the wastewater effluent?

2 Materials and Methods

2.1 Study Areas

Bahir Dar, the capital of Amhara National Regional State is situated on the Southern shore of Lake Tana, the source of the Blue Nile river, around 565 km, Northwest of Addis Ababa. The total population of the Bahir Dar was 220,000 in 2007, and has a population growth rate of 6.6% per year [12], which is more than twice as high as the average population growth rate in Ethiopia [1]. In Bahir Dar City, there are more than five constructed municipal storm water canals and few natural streams and water courses (e.g. Chimbil, Amora Gedel). The constructed drainage lines usually drain towards Southeast while the natural streams drain towards Southwest of the city. The areas studied in this manuscript are: (i) From Gudo Bahir reservoir along the Stadium to Peda, then to Blue Nile river including site numbers 1–7, 13 and 14 (hereinafter named canal #1); (ii) From Gudo Bahir reservoir along the Stadium to Yitamot wetland including site numbers 1–5, 8 and 14 (hereinafter named canal #2). (iii) The main Blue Nile river course from lake Tana to the end of the sampling station including site numbers 9–14 (hereinafter named Blue Nile river course).

2.2   Sampling

A total of 14 sampling sites were selected for testing the difference among the study areas mentioned above. Samples were collected three times between February and May 2018. Three replicates per site and per sampling time were applied. A total of 126 samples were analyzed. (Table 1 and Fig. 1).

Table 1. Description of sampling sites

Site	Description of location
1 (Gudo Bahir)	A reservoir to collect storm water from rural upstream and receive liquid and solid wastes from the surrounding industrial and residential areas. It is surface water in mudflats without buffer zone. It serves as grazing land, illegal garbage disposal. Nearby land is used for grazing and the community used to dump solid and mining of peat soil by the local communities
2 (*Kebele* 16 at the back of telecommunication.)	A natural municipal storm water drainage line/canal/buffered by swampy papyrus vegetation. The buffer is almost 50 m wide covered with 60% papyrus, 30% polygonium and 10% grass species. The storm water move very slowly
3 (*Kebele* 16 near Negde Weyto community)	Natural canal with relatively faster moving storm water. Although filled by garbage the bed is rocky with some grassy buffers. Since the *Negede* community had no sufficient sanitation facilities, they also use the canal as open field toilet
4 (*Kebele* 16 at the back of Fasillo School)	A natural canal with a larger volume since a mix with *kebele 3* drainage line, moderate movement and width, and mud bottom. It contains 70% polygonium and 30% of indigenous grass buffered by eucalyptus plantation
5 (*Kebele* 14 at the back of New Stadium)	A natural canal with large volume, very slow movement /since very gentle slope/ and higher width, and mud bottom. It contains 95% Polygonium and 5% of indigenous grass buffered by eucalyptus plantation
6 (*Kebele* 17 near Livestock market)	A natural canal with increasing volume since a mix with another bigger drainage line from papyrus hotel, though vertical but slow moving and higher width, and mud bottom. It was covered by 75% grasses, 20% polygonium, and 5% papyrus and partly buffered by eucalyptus plantation.. It serves was waste dumping, traditional tanning, and illegal slaughtering sites

(continued)

Table 1. (*continued*)

Site	Description of location
7 (*Kebele* 7 near Peda campus)	A natural canal with mud bottom and buffered by papyrus, and similar canal width to site 6. It was covered by 70% papyrus, 25% polygonium and 5% indigenous grass; then it receives wastewater from the Bahir Dar University and discharges its waste directly to the Blue Nile river
8 (Yitamot wetland)	A wetland open space that receives municipal wastewater from dividing line of site 5 along Silassie church, lower reach of *kebele 14* areas, and partly from peda campus. It is highly encroached by grazing, pollution and illegal settlement as well as open-field slaughtering
9 (Lake Tana in front of Bahir Dar Institute of Technology)	Lake Tana shoreline in front of Bahir Dar Institute of Technology campus. It is rich in papyrus and *Echinochloa sp* (Shafri/Shenkotet)
10 (Blue Nile river at Chere-chera)	A place where the river immediately outflow from the lake before the main Blue Nile river bridge. It was covered by 10% of indigenous grass, 80% *Echinochloa sp.* and 10% papyrus
11 (after Blue Nile bridge)	A place along Blue Nile river after the main Bridge. Car washing is a common practice. It was covered by 20% of indigenous grass, 80% *Echinochloa sp*
12 (After textile factory)	A place along Blue Nile river after the discharge of textile factory. It was covered by 20% of indigenous grass, 80% *Echinochloa sp.*
13 (Blue Nile river at *Teklehymanot* church traditional bridge)	Part of a river after the discharge of site 7 with mud bottom, relatively fast moving, and wider width. It was covered by 75% of papyrus and 20% polygonium 5% indigenous grass
14 (Blue Nile river downstream)	Blue Nile river, downstream of the study area that receives municipal wastewater from Ytemote discharge and from the *Teklehymanot* church wooden bridge. It is highly covered by *Echinochloa sp.*, papyrus and water hyacinth.

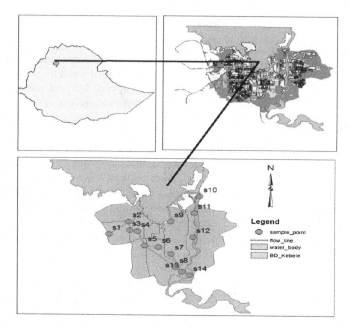

Fig. 1. Sampling sites location along the Bahir Dar municipal wastewater canal and Blue Nile river course.

2.3 Physiochemical Parameters

DO, pH, TDS, and conductivity were measured insitu using YSI 556 MPS Multi-probe field meter and samples for BOD_5 were analyzed according to standard methods (APHA 1998) and ammonia, nitrate, phosphate were analyzed using paqua lab 700 photometer. Water samples for laboratory analysis were collected and stored at 4 °C in polyethylene bottles that had been pre-washed with 10% nitric acid and thoroughly rinsed with de-ionized water [13].

3   Results and Discussion

3.1   Biological Oxygen Demand and Dissolved Oxygen for Canal #1

Table 2 presents values of water quality parameters for Bahir Dar municipal waste water drainage for Canal #1. For comparison purposes, food and agricultural organization (FAO) for irrigation as well as with world Health organization (WHO) maximum limits are included.

In Table 2 and Fig. 2 (**canal #1**); the minimum and maximum average value of BOD (range from 15.7–47 mg/L) and DO (range from 1.75–5.9 mg/L) were recorded at site 14 and 7 respectively. The p-values for BOD and DO parameters show significant variation ($p < 0.05$) in both cases. Even though the minimum BOD record exceeds the maximum allowable limits set by FAO for irrigation as well as with WHO for drinking, there is a significant difference in BOD among sites.

Table 2. Mean ± SE of water quality parameters for Canal sites. #1

Parameters	Site #1	Site #2	Site #3	Site #4	Site #5	Site #6	Site #7	Site #13	Site #14	p-value	FAO*	WHO*
BOD mg/L	36.5 ± 0.5	28.5 ± 0.35	44.99 ± 2	40.1 ± 0.8	34 ± 0.7	43.7 ± 1	47 ± 0.5	20 ± 0.35	15.7 ± .3	p < 0.05	10	<10
DO mg/L	3.32 ± 0.16	4.83 ± 0.1	1.78 ± 0.4	2.17 ± 0.4	3.2 ± 0.1	1.8111	1.75 ± .1	5.1 ± 0.1	5.9 ± .21	p < 0.05	2	>10
IDS mg/L	288.6 ± 3	445 ± 0.1	634 ± 2	529 ± 2.5	556 ± 2	653.5 ± 2	673 ± 2	171 ± 2.6	166 ± 1.5	p < 0.05	1000	300
Conductivity` µs/cm	398.5 ± 2.2	587 ± 1.2	870 ± 1.5	723 ± 1.5	733 ± 3	926 ± 2.7	967 ± 4.6	237 ± 2.5	245 ± 4.4	p < 0.05	350	250
pH	8.45 ± 0.03	8.95 ± 0.1	8.33 ± 0.1	8.23 ± 0.5	8.2 ± .04	8.2 ± 0.1	8.35 ± .6	7.7 ± 0.1	7.48 ± .07	p < 0.05	6.5-8.8	6.5-9.3
NO$_3$ mg/L	16.2 ± 0.3	14.84 ± 0.2	15.7 ± 0.1	17.8 ± 0.3	10.4 ± 0.2	4.8 ± 0.1	7.9 ± 0.1	6.69 ± .1	6.68 ± .1	p < 0.05		
PO$_4$ mg/L	0.5 ± 0.1	7.7 ± 0.02	3.53 ± 0.05	3.9 ± 0.03	2.5 ± .03	2.6 ± 0.05	5.1 ± 0.2	0.46 ± .1	0.35 ± 01	p < 0.05	3	
NH$_3$ mg/L	3.45 ± .1	4.4 ± 0.03	5.8 ± 0.04	4.1 ± 0.03	3.1 ± .06	4 ± .08	5.45 ± .3	.59 ± 0.01	0.44 ± 0.2	p < 0.05		

*: FAO and WHO maximum accepted limits

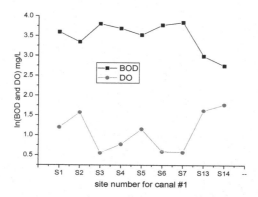

Fig. 2. BOD and DO values for Canal #1.

The maximum value of BOD and drastic reduction of DO at site 7 is mainly by receiving high concentration of organic waste that is biodegradable chemical organic waste from residential and commercial centers along the main canal (including *kebele* 03, 04, 07, 12, 15, and 16) and cultural leather processors and illegal slaughtering activities. Moreover, some residential houses and hotels directly connect their sewage to the municipal drainage lines. Most portion of the canal before site 7 is concrete paved and no option to uptake the waste by aquatic and wetland macrophytes. The drastic BOD reduction and improvement of dissolved oxygen at site 14 is explained by reduction in organic matter through nature based processes (sediment, vegetation, water volume) and ecosystem purification along the drainage canals and dilution effect of the Blue Nile river. A previous study conducted [14] in rainy season also confirms low dissolved oxygen with mean value of 2.4 mg/L in natural waste water canal that discharge to Blue Nile river from Bahir Dar city.

3.2   Total Dissolved Solids and Conductivity Nutrient and PH for Canal #1

In Table 2 and Fig. 3A, the minimum and maximum average values of TDS (range from 166-673 mg/L) and electrical conductivity (range from 237–967 µs/cm) were recorded at site 14 and 7 respectively. The p-value for both parameters show significant variation among the sampling sites ($p < 0.05$) for all cases. The maximum values for both parameters were recorded in site 6 and 7 where higher concentration and volume due to the collected effluents of wastewater from hotels, residents especially from garages.

As previously reported study[1] showed the mean value of TDS during the rain seasons was 738 mg/L. Because of increment of nutrient in rainy season the result is a bit higher than to the result of the current study.

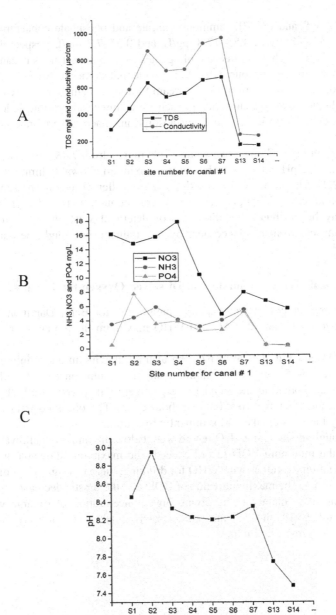

Fig. 3. TDS, conductivity, nutrients and pH variations for different sites of Canal #1.

From Table 2 and Fig. 3B, ammonia, nitrate and phosphate concentration ranges were from 0.44–5.8 mg/L, 4.85–17.8 mg/L, and 0.35–7.7 mg/L, respectively. Recorded nutrients were higher in three sampling sites (3, 4 and 2). This is because of direct effluent mix from various sources such as residential domestic wastewater including organic foods. As it moves from the upstream to downstream along the canal shows a trend of reduction due to many factors such as sediment adsorption, redox chemical reaction, microbial activities, vegetation absorption, macro-invertebrate consumption and dilution.

As shown in Fig. 3C, the mean value of pH ranges from 7.48–8.95 where record at site 14 and 2. The pH values were below the maximum allowable limit set by FAO as well as WHO . The mean value was significantly different among the sampling sites ($p < 0.05$) in all cases. High pH was recorded at site number two. The rising of pH at this site may be attributed the discharge of detergent waste water from *Keble* 16 condominium and from residence near by the drainage line might be contribute for rising of pH.

3.3   Biological Oxygen Demand and Dissolved Oxygen for Canal #2

Table 3 presents values of water quality parameters for Bahir Dar municipal waste water drainage for Canal #2. FAO and WHO maximum limits may be referred from Table 2.

In Table 3 and Fig. 4 (**Canal #2**); the average maximum and minimum concentration of BOD 45–15.7 mg/L and minimum and maximum concentration of DO 1.78–5.9 mg/L were recorded in site 3 and 14, respectively. The p-value for both parameters show significant difference ($p < 0.05$) in both cases. The observed reduction can be explained by biomass uptake and sediment adsorption.

Even though the maximum DO record were below the minimum allowable limit by WHO, and the minimum BOD record exceeds the maximum allowable limits set by FAO for irrigation as well as with WHO for drinking, there is a significant difference in BOD among sites. The maximum value of BOD and the drastic decreased of dissolved oxygen at site 3 is mainly by receiving high concentration of organic waste from residential (*kebele* 14 and 16) and commercial centers, open toilet of *Negedewch* community along the canal two.

Table 3. Mean ± SE of water quality parameters for Canal #2 sites.

Parameters	site1	site2	site3	site4	site5	site8	site 14	P value
BOD mg/L	36.5 ± 0.52	28.5 ± .35	44.99 ± 1.5	40.1 ± 0.8	34 ± 0.67	26.6 ± 0.6	20 ± 0.35	p < 0.05
DO mg/L	3.32 ± 0.16	4.83 ± 0.1	1.78 ± 0.04	2.17 ± 0.04	3.2 ± 0.1	4.10.1	5.9 ± 0.21	P < 0.05
TDS mg/L	288.6 ± 3	445 ± .1	634 ± 2	529 ± 2.5	556 ± 2	977.5 ± 5	166 ± 1.5	P < 0.05
Conductivity' µs/cm	398.5 ± 2.2	587 ± 1.2	870 ± 1.5	723 ± 1.5	733 ± 3	929 ± 2.7	245 ± 4.4	P < 0.05
PH	8.45 ± 0.03	8.95 ± 0.1	8.33 ± 0.1	8.23 ± 0.5	8.2 ± .04	8.2 ± 0.04	7.48 ± .07	P < 0.05
NO_3 mg/L	16.2 ± 0.3	14.84 ± 0.2	15.7 ± 0.1	17.8 ± 0.3	10.4 ± .2	2.76 ± 0.1	5.59 ± .1	P < 0.05
PO_4 mg/L	0.5 ± 0.1	7.7 ± 0.02	3.53 ± 0.05	3.9 ± 0.03	2.5 ± .03	0.43 ± 0.2	0.46 ± .01	P < 0.05
NH_3 mg/L	3.44 ± .1	4.4 ± 0.03	5.8 ± 0.04	4.1 ± 0.03	3.1 ± .06	3.8 ± .02	0.59 ± 0.2	P < 0.05

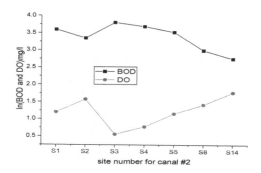

Fig. 4. Absolute value of BOD and DO versus site number for Canal #2

3.4   TDS, Conductivity, Nutrients and PH Variations for Canal #2

In Table 3 and Fig. 5A, the minimum and maximum average values of TDS (range from 166–977 mg/L) and electrical conductivity (range from 245–929 µs/cm) were recorded at site 14 and 8 respectively. The p-value for both parameters show significant variation among the sampling sites ($p < 0.05$) for all cases. The maximum values for both parameters were recorded in site 8. Where this site is a wetland open space that receive municipal wastewater from dividing line of site five along Silassie church, lower reach of *kebele* 14 areas, and partly from peda campus. It is highly encroached by grazing, pollution and informal settlement and open-field slaughter activities, automotive garage, and industrial chemicals.

Ammonia, nitrate and phosphate concentrations range from 0.59–5.8 mg/L, 2.76–17.8 mg/L, and 0.43–7.7 mg/L, respectively (Fig. 5B). The p-value for three parameters show significant variation ($p < 0.05$). Recorded nutrients were higher for three sampling sites (sites 3, 2 and 4). This is because of direct effluent mix from various sources such as commercial and residential domestic wastewater including organic foods. As it moves from the upstream to downstream along the canal two shows a trend of reduction due to many factors such as sediment adsorption, reduction by chemical reaction, microbial activities, vegetation absorption, macro-invertebrate consumption and dilution. Similarly the mean values of pH were the same as to that of canal #1 (Fig. 5C). The minimum and maximum pHs 7.48–8.95 were record at site 14 and 2 respectively. The mean value of pH was significantly different among the sampling sites ($p < 0.05$). High pH was recorded at site two. The rising of pH at this site may be attributed the discharge of detergent waste water from *kebele* 16 condominium and from residence near by the drainage line.

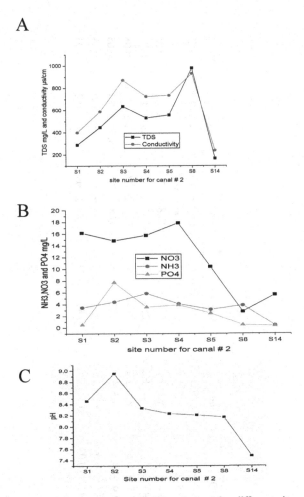

Fig. 5. TDS, conductivity, nutrients and pH variations for different sites of Canal #2.

3.5 Biological Oxygen Demand and Dissolved Oxygen for Blue Nile River Course

Table 4 presents values of water quality parameters for Bahir Dar municipal waste water drainage for. FAO and WHO maximum limits may be referred from Table 2.

In Table 4 and Fig. 6; the minimum and maximum average values of BOD (range from 15.7–33 mg/L) and DO (range from 5,9 – 5.01 mg/L) were recorded at sites 14 and 12 respectively. The p-value for both parameters show significant difference among the sampling sites ($p < 0.05$). The increment of BOD and reduction of dissolved oxygen were recorded at site 12. This reduction is as a result sediment addition and addition of organic matter in to Blue Nile river. Such as a direct effluent mix of organic waste from various sources mainly from residential and commercial centers along the main canal (including kebeles 08, 09 and 10), chimbile stream, car washing, by product

Table 4.

parameters	Site9	SitelO	Sitel 1	Site 12	Sitel 3	Sitel 4	value
BOD mg/L	15 ± 0.28	23 ± .21	27.89 ± .94	33 ± 0.8	15.7 ± 0.3	20 ± 0.35	0.05
DO mg/L	7.1 ± 0.01	7.25 ± 0.1	6.1 ± 0.06	5.0 ± 0.03	5.06 ± 0.1	5.9 ± 0.21	0.05
TDS mg/L	167.8 ± 3	165.3 ± 2	173.6 ± 2.7	175 ± 1.5	170.8 ± .7	166 ± 1.5	0.05
Conductivity' µs/cm	240 ± .28	243 ± 3	244 ± 2.9	269 ± 3.4	237 ± 2.5	245 ± 4.4	0.05
pH	7.74 ± 0.07	7.77 ± 0.6	8.1 ± 0.7	8.4 ± 0.04	7.74 ± .07	7.48 ± .07	0.05
NO_3 mg/L	2.5 ± 0.5	3.9 ± 0.4	4.65 ± 0.1	8.2 ± 0.7	6.68 ± .1	5.59 ± .04	0.05
PO_4 mg/L	0.1 ± 0.1	0.4 ± 0.01	0.13 ± 0.07	.3 ± 0.0	.35 ± .01	0.46 ± 01	0.05
NH_3 mg/L	0.2 ± .0	0.44 ± 0.03	0.14 ± 0.04	0.59 ± 0.02	0.45 ± .05	0.44 ± 0.2	0.05

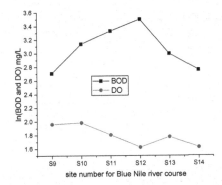

Fig. 6. Absolute value of BOD and DO versus site number for Blue Nile water course

from pig farm, and discharge of textile factory wastes. The drastic BOD reduction and enhancement of DO at site 14 is explained by ecosystem purification and dilution effect of the Blue Nile River.

3.6   TDS, Conductivity, Nutrients and PH Variations for Blue Nile River Course

The minimum and maximum average values of TDS (range from 166–175 mg/L) and electrical conductivity (range from 237–269 µs/cm) were recorded at site 14 and 12 respectively (Fig. 7A). The p-value for both parameters show significant difference among the sampling sites ($p < 0.05$). The maximum values for both parameters were recorded in site 12 where higher concentration due to the collected effluents of wastewater from hotels, residents (*kebele* 9, 10 and 11) garages, Textile waste water discharge, storm water on both side of the river, storm water from Chimbil stream and by product from farm land near to Blue Nile river.

Ammonia, nitrate and phosphate concentration ranges from 0.14–0.49 mg/L, 5.9–8.2 mg/L, and 0.3–0.47 mg/L, respectively (Fig. 7B). Recorded nutrients were higher in site 13, 12, and 11 respectively. This is because of direct effluent mix from various sources such as residential domestic wastewater including organic foods, byproduct from pig farm and textile factory discharging of waste water. As it moves from the upstream to downstream along the canal shows a trend of reduction due to many factors such as sediment adsorption, redox chemical reaction, microbial activities, vegetation absorption, macro-invertebrate consumption and dilution. The pH mean value ranges 7.48–8.4 were recorded at site 14 and 12 (Fig. 7C). The mean value was significantly different among the sampling sites ($p < 0.05$). High pH was recorded at site twelve. The rising of pH at this site may be attributed the discharge of waste water from textile industry and cloth washing by local people near to the Blue Nile river.

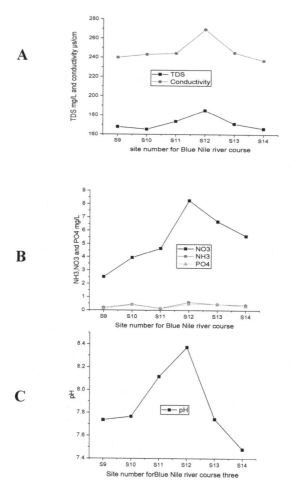

Fig. 7. TDS, conductivity, nutrients and pH variations for different sites of Blue Nile water course

Summary Results

Ecosystems reduced BOD, TDS, Conductivity, pH, NO_3, PO_4, and NH_3 reduced by 66.6%, 75%, 75.5%, 16.4%, 62.5%, 95.4%, 92.4% and increased DO by 70% in waste water drainage canal #1

Ecosystems reduced BOD, TDS, Conductivity, pH, NO_3, PO_4 and NH_3 by 55.5%, 83%, 73.6%, 16.4%, 62.5%, 95.4%, 92.4% and DO increased by 70% In waste water drainage canal #2.

In Lake Tana and Blue Nile river line, BOD, TDS, Conductivity, pH, NO_3, PO_4, and NH_3 was reduced by 52.2%, 5%, 11.89%, 7.85%, 31.83%, 34.8%, 16.95% respectively. while DO was reduced by 18%.

4 Conclusions

Ecosystem purification did not improve conditions of BOD and DO to proximity to FAO and WHO standards.

Even though ecosystem purification and dilution helped improve other water quality indication for both drainage lines, results were found to be under FAO and WHO standards.

With current ecosystem purification, most water quality parameters of effluents at site 14 except BOD & DO were within acceptable levels set by international standards for effluents to be discharged to surface water and FAO maximum permissible level set for waste water to be used for irrigation purposes.

But some water quality parameters of the head of Blue Nile River were above WHO maximum permissible level set for drinking purposes.

Recommendations

To reverse the adverse outcomes of effluents, treating wastes and minimizing their adverse effect on environment the Administration Office of Bahir Dar, community, and institution need to preserve the ecosystem.

Bahir Dar University should develop institutional wastewater treatment plants and management systems to provide clean water to downstream populations and mitigate impacts of development that.

References

1. Mehari, A.K., Gebremedhin, S., Ayele, B.: Effect of Bahir Dar municipal effluents on water quality of the head of Blue Nile River, Ethiopian. J. Environ. Stud. Manage. **9**, 197–208 (2016)
2. Smit, J., Nasr, J., Ratta, A.: Urban agriculture: food, jobs and sustainable cities. New York, USA **2**, 35–37 (1996)
3. Campbell, H.E., Corley, E.A.: Water, pp. 185–216. Urban Environmental Policy Analysis, Routledge (2015)
4. Melaku, S., Wondimu, T., Dams, R., Moens, L: Pollution status of Tinishu Akaki River and its tributaries (Ethiopia) evaluated using physico-chemical parameters, major ions, and nutrients. Bull. Chem. Soc. Ethiopia **21** (2007)
5. Davis, S., Golladay, S.W., Vellidis, G., Pringle, C.M.: Macroinvertebrate biomonitoring in intermittent coastal plain streams impacted by animal agriculture. J. Environ. Qual. **32**, 1036–1043 (2003)
6. EPA U: Guidance on cumulative risk assessment of pesticide chemicals that have a common mechanism of toxicity. Office of Pesticide Programs (2002)
7. Mandaville S: Benthic macroinvertebrates in freshwaters: Taxa tolerance values, metrics, and protocols: Citeseer (2002)
8. Berhe, T.: The degradation of the Abo-Kebena River in Addis Ababa, Ethiopia. M. Sc Thesis, school of Graduates Studies, Addis Ababa University (1988)
9. Mehari, A.K., Wondie, A., Mingist, M., Vijverberg, J.: Spatial and seasonal variation in the macro-invertebrates and physico-chemical parameters of the Enfranz River, Lake Tana sub-basin (Ethiopia). Ecohydrol. Hydrobiol. **14**, 304–312 (2014)

10. Misganaw, T.: Assessment of the ecological impacts of floriculture Industries using physico-chemical parameters and benthic macroinvertebrates metric index along Wedecha River, p. 185. Addis Ababa University, Addis Ababa, Debrezeit (2007)
11. Wosnie, A., Wondie, A.: Assessment of downstream impact of Bahir Dar tannery effluent on the head of Blue Nile River using macroinvertebrates as bioindicators. Int. J. Biodivers. Conserv. **6**, 342–350 (2014)
12. Teferra, A.S., Alemu, F.M., Woldeyohannes, S.M.: Institutional delivery service utilization and associated factors among mothers who gave birth in the last 12 months in Sekela District, North West of Ethiopia: a community-based cross sectional study. BMC Pregnancy Childbirth **12**, 74 (2012)
13. Jain, C., Bhatia, K.: Physico-chemical analysis of water and wastewater. User's manual UM-26, Roorkee: Nat. Inst. Hydrol. (1987)
14. Dagne, M.: Performance Evaluation of Kality Wastewater Stabilization Ponds for the Treatment of Municipal Sewage, from the City of Addis Ababa, Ethiopia, Addis Ababa University (2010)

Analysis of Flexural Strength of Jute/Sisal Hybrid Polyester Composite

Yesheneh Jejaw Mamo[✉] and Ramesh Babu Subramanian

Bahirdar University Institute of Technology, Bahir Dar, Ethiopia
yeshi.jeje@gmail.com, jairameshbabu@gmail.com

Abstract. A flexural strength is one among the predominant factors for the polymer composites under perpendicular loading conditions against the axis of the member. In this study the flexural strength of Ethiopian Jute – Sisal hybrid polyester composite is investigated both analytically and experimentally. Composite test specimens have been prepared at various categories. They are based on different sequence of fibre layers: Jute-Sisal-Jute-Sisal (J/S/J/S), Sisal-Jute-Sisal-Jute (S/J/S/J) and Sisal-Jute-Jute-Sisal (S/J/J/S); fibres arrangement, based on orientation angle of fibres: [0°/45°/45°/0°], [0°/90°/90°/0°] and [45°/0°/0°/45°]; and based on concentration of fibers (weight ratio): [80% Polyester Matrix/20% Sisal/0% Jute], [81% Polyester Matrix/14% Sisal/5% Jute] and [76% Polyester Matrix/14% Sisal/10% Jute]. When comparing the results with different angle arrangement, [0°/45°/45°/0°] of fiber angled laminates is found to be most effective in flexural strength. And with different concentration of fibers in wt%, 10/14/76 [10% Jute, 14% Sisal and 76% Polyester Matrix] is found to be more satisfactory than the others in the flexural strength. From experimental result in sequence of fiber layers (S/J/S/J) has higher flexural strength than (J/S/J/S) and (S/J/J/S). From experimental result of jute/sisal polyester samples [0°/45°/45°/0°] has highest flexural strength which is 111.8 MPa and can resist maximum force of 469.5 N.

Keywords: Ethiopian Jute · Ethiopian sisal · Bending strength · Fiber · ANSYS

1 Introduction

Now sisal is strong and eco-friendly material which can be used to replace asbestos and fiberglass in composite materials in various uses including the automobile industry. Sisal is used commonly for mooring small craft, lashing, and handling cargo. Sisal fibre has several advantages in terms of product design flexibility, insulation, and noise absorption and impact resistance. Due to these properties sisal reinforced composite used in building material (like roofing sheets etc.), locomotive (like gear case, main doors etc.), automobile (like German automotive industry, door panel of E-class Mercedes etc.), aerospace and military (like transportation vehicle, safety equipment etc.) applications [1].

Jute take nearly 3 months, to grow to a height of 12–15 ft, then cut and bundled and kept immersed in water for "retting" process, where the inner stem and outer, gets

F. A. Zimale et al. (Eds.): ICAST 2018, LNICST 274, pp. 599–609, 2019.
https://doi.org/10.1007/978-3-030-15357-1_48

separated and the outer plant gets 'individualized', to form a Fiber. The fiber after drying is taken to Jute mills, for getting converted to Jute yarn and Hessian. There is around 5.6 thousand tons of jute production per year in Ethiopia. Jute is a hydrophobic material and moisture absorption alters the dimensional and mechanical characteristics of jute fibers laminate [2]. Several studies have shown that the strength and stiffness of natural fiber reinforced composites are comparable with those of glass fiber composites on a per-weight basis [3, 5]. Hence, natural fibers have emerged as a green alternative to glass fiber for the production of certain semi-structural parts in various industries such as automotive, packaging and construction [6–10].

Studies have generally addressed hybridizing of fibers for the purpose of improving the performance of natural fiber composites and expand their industrial usage. One of the most effective methods used for improving the properties of natural fiber composites is hybridization which combines at least two different fiber types in a matrix to achieve optimum properties. Several studies have shown that combining natural fibers improves the resulting composite properties and compensates for the weak properties of natural fibers [1]. Li et al. [11] studied that sisal fiber is the promising reinforcement because of low density, high specific strength, no health hazards and finding applications in making of ropes, mats, carpets, baskets and fancy articles like bags etc.

2 Methods and Materials

2.1 Materials

Jute Fiber

Jute take nearly 3 months, to grow to a height of 12–15 ft. in this work jute leaves are cut and Mechanical extraction method is used to extract fibers the following procedures are used.
First sisal leaves are cut.
The fibre is extracted by rasping the leaves with a blunted knife.
Put the raw sisals on the table and rasp it until the resinous material are remove and fiber strands are obtained.

Sisal Fiber

Sisal leaves have a thorn at the tip and grow up to a height of 2 m and yield valuable fibre.
In this research sisal plant is taken from highland of Amhara region specifically debrework wereda and extracted manually.

Matrix and Hardener

The resin used for this study is polyester Resin with product name of OCPOL 711 (GP RESIN), which is manufactured by Ras Al Khaimah, which have low viscosity, consistent performance and doesn't contain any hazardous dilutes or extenders. Polyester resins are quite easily accessible, cheap and find use in a wide range of fields. Liquid polyesters are stored at room temperature for months, sometimes for years and the mere addition of a catalyst can cure the matrix material within a short time. They are used in automobile and structural applications.

The cured polyester is usually rigid or flexible as the case may be and transparent. Polyesters withstand the variations of environment and stable against chemicals.

The catalyst use for polyester resin is methyl ethyl ketone per oxide (MEKP) it helps the resin to solidify. The ratio of polyester to MEKP is 35 g of MEKP to 6 kg of polyester.

2.2   Methods

Alkaline Treatment of Fiber

To study the effect NaOH treatment on the flexural strength of composite jute and sisal fibres are treated at 6% and 10% concentration of fibre.

First 6% (6grams of NaOH with 100 ml water) are mixed and jute and sisal fibre are inserted in the mixture and wait for 24 h then it will be washed with water again and again then dried. For 10% concentration of NaOH the jute and sisal fibres are rinsed in mixture (10 g of NaOH in 100 ml water) for 24 h and washed using water again and again and then dried (Fig. 1).

A-NaOH
B-NaOH mixed with water
C-jute and sisal fibre rinsed in
The NaOH and water mixture
D-dried fibre

Fig. 1. Alkaline treatment process

Preparation of Polyester and Hardener

The matrix used to fabricate the fiber specimen was polyester of density 1.39 g/cm3 at 25 °C mixed with hardener of MEKP. The weight ratio of mixing polyester and hardener will be as per the supplier norms for 1 kg of polyester 6 g of MEKP.

Preparation of Composite Specimen

Sample of jute–sisal hybrid polyester composite will be prepared at different sequence of fiber layers, orientation angle and with different concentration of fibers (weight ratio) and with different percent of NaOH treatment.

The fabrication of the composite material is carried out through the hand lay-up technique. The mold used for preparing composites is made from rectangular wood having dimensions of 112 mm × 170 mm for each sample.

Sample Preparation Steps

The materials used for the experiment is prepared by hand layup process. Extracted sisal and jute fibers are used specimen preparation.

First, the fibers are dried under sunlight for 3 to 5 h.

Step 1- First applying the releasing agent (wax) on the mold;
Step 2 - Implementation of the first layer of resin with a brush over the releasing agent;
Step 3 - Positioning the first jute fiber blanket on the resin;
Step 4 - Apply resin on jute fiber blanket, using a brush;
Step 5 - Elimination of air bubbles using the roller across the surface;
Step 6 - positioning the second layer jute fiber on the resin;
Step 7 - Apply resin on jute fiber blanket, using a brush;
Step 8 - positioning the first sisal fiber blanket on the resin;
Step 9 - Apply resin on sisal fiber blanket, using a brush;
Step 10 - Elimination of air bubbles using the roller across the surface;
Step 11 - Positioning the second layer sisal fiber on the resin;
Step 12 - Apply resin on sisal fiber blanket, using a brush;
Step 13 - Elimination of air bubbles using the roller across the surface;

Finally, these laminas are kept in press for over 24 h to get the perfect shape and thickness (Fig. 2).

Fig. 2. Prepared samples

2.3   Simulation Method

In this work, software package ANSYS version 15 is used to calculate the flexural strength of sisal jute hybrid polyester composite of different angle arrangement of fibres. Specific properties of reinforced composite are given as inputs for ANSYS program and then the results are obtained for the given data.

E11, E22, G12 and vxy of jute and sisal fibers are found from published source [12, 13].

Unidirectional Continuous Fiber Angle –Ply Lamina

The following equations are used to calculate the elastic properties of an angle-ply lamina in which continuous fibers are aligned at angle θ with positive x axis as a reference.

$$\frac{1}{Exx} = \frac{cos^4\theta}{E_{11}} + \frac{sin^4\theta}{E_{22}} + \frac{1}{4}\left(\frac{1}{G_{12}} - \frac{2V12}{E_{11}}\right)sin^2 2\theta$$

$$\frac{1}{Eyy} = \frac{sin^4\theta}{E_{11}} + \frac{cos^4\theta}{E_{22}} + \frac{1}{4}\left(\frac{1}{G_{12}} - \frac{2V12}{E_{11}}\right)sin^2 2\theta$$

$$\frac{1}{Gxy} = \frac{1}{E_{11}} + \frac{2V12}{E_{11}} + \frac{1}{E_{22}} - \left(\frac{1}{E_{11}} + \frac{2V12}{E_{11}} + \frac{1}{E_{22}} - \frac{1}{G_{12}}\right)cos^2 2\theta$$

$$vxy = Exx\left[\frac{V12}{E_{11}} - \frac{1}{4}\left(\frac{1}{E_{11}} + \frac{2V12}{E_{11}} + \frac{1}{E_{22}} - \frac{1}{G_{12}}\right)sin^2 2\theta\right]$$

$$vyx = \frac{Eyy}{Exx} vxy$$

Input Data
See Table 1.

Table 1. ANSYS input values

Angle	Ex (GPa)	Ey (GPa)	Ez (GPa)	vxy	vxz	vyz	Gxy (GPa)	Gxz (GPa)	Gyz (GPa)
00	10.62	6.75	6.75	0.36	0.36	0.44	2.448	2.448	2.32
900	6.75	10.62	10.62	0.23	0.23	0.19	2.448	2.448	2.82
450	6.8	6.88	6.88	0.40	0.40	0.40	3.20	3.20	2.44

ANSYS Simulation Method for Discontinuous Fibers

A thin lamina containing randomly oriented discontinuous fibers exhibits planar isotropic behavior. The properties are ideally the same in all directions in the plan e of the lamina. For such a lamina, the tensile modulus and shear modulus are calculated from

$$Erandom = \frac{3}{8}E11 + \frac{5}{8}E22, Grandom = \frac{1}{8}E11 + \frac{1}{4}E22, vrandom = \frac{Erandom}{2Grandom} - 1$$

2.4 Flexural Test

Samples are prepares according to ASTM D790-10, with dimensions its value became Span length = 128 mm, width = 20 mm, thick = 4 mm & its overall length is greater than 20% of support span length i.e. 170 mm (Table 2).

Universal testing machine with the specification listed below was used during testing, from each type 5 samples were tested and the average of the three sample is taken for the experimental result (Table 3).

Table 2. Source for ANSYS for random oriented fibre

Concentration by weight% of (JSP)	Erandom (GPa)	Grandom (GPa)	vrandom
0/20/80	6.655	2.456	0.355
5/14/81	7.222	2.661	0.356
10/14/76	8.204	3.016	0.36

Table 3. UTM adjusted parameter for the test

UTM capacity	100 kN
Load speed	0.1 kN/s (1 MPa/s)
Displacement	0.2 mm/min
Extension	0.01 mm/s (0.02%/s)

3   Results and Discussion

3.1   ANSYS Result

ANSYS Result
   See Fig. 3

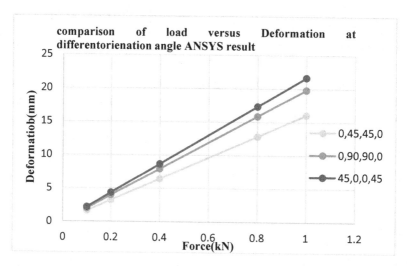

Fig. 3. Comparison of load versus deformation at different orientation angle ANSYS result

ANSYS result for different concentration of fibres
See Fig. 4

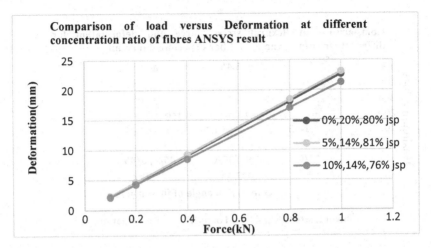

Fig. 4. Comparison of load versus Deformation at different concentration of fibre Weight ratio ANSYS result

3.2   Experimental Result

See Figs. 5, 6, 7 and 8.

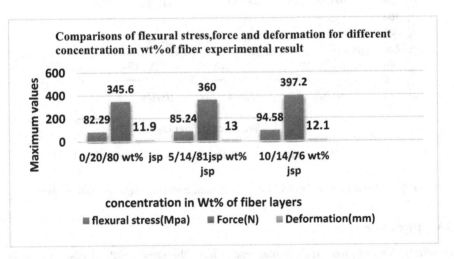

Fig. 5. Experimental results of different concentration of fiber

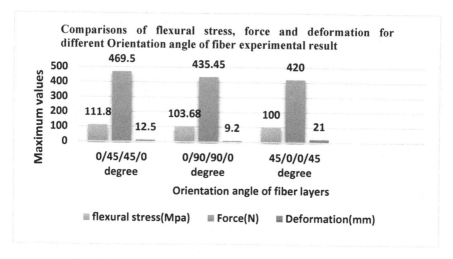

Fig. 6. Experimental results of different sequence of fiber layers

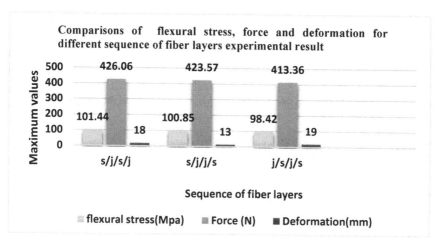

Fig. 7. Experimental results of different arrangement of angle orientation fibers

3.3   Discussion

Generally ANSYS and experimental results have the same result in case of different angle arrangement of fibers and with different concentration of fibers in wt% in both cases [0/45/45/0] and 10/14/76 wt% of fibers have best flexural strength respectively.

From comparison of ANSYS result by angle orientation of fibres [$0^0/45^0/45^0/0^0$] has least deformation. And also it has least induced stress than other arrangements. So it will have better flexural strength.

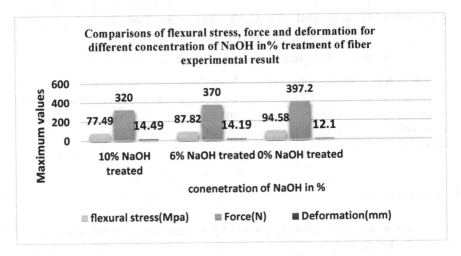

Fig. 8. Experimental results of NaOH treated samples at different concentration

Whereas, $[45°/0°/0°/45°]$ has largest deformation than $[0°/45°/45°/0°]$ and $[0°/90°/90°/0°]$. From experimental result in sequence of fiber layers s/j/s/j has higher flexural strength than j/s/j/s and s/j/j/s. whereas j/s/j/s has least strength. But s/j/j/s has least deformation than others arrangement which shows sequence of layers has effect on flexural strength of composite. From fiber concentration 10/14/76 wt% of fibers (JSP) has highest flexural strength than 0/20/80 and 5/14/81 concentration in wt% of (JSP). But 5/14/81 has better strength than 0/20/80 which shows a positive effect of hybridization.

Failure Modes

The intact and damaged specimens of flexural tests are depicted in figure below. In the case of flexural test, bending failure on the tension surface of specimens was due to matrix and fiber breakage and most of the samples fail at mid-span (Fig. 9).

Fig. 9. Failure modes of samples after test

Comparison of Experimental with ANSYS Result See Table 4.

Table 4. Comparison of experimental result with ANSYS result

Arrangement of layers	Applied Load (N)	Stress (Mpa)		
		ANSYS result	Experimental result	% Error
$0^\circ/45^\circ/45^\circ/0^\circ$	469.5	101.24	111.8	9.4
$0^\circ/90^\circ/90^\circ/0^\circ$	434.5	94.53	103.08	8.29
$45^\circ/0^\circ/0^\circ/45^\circ$	420	81.5	100	18.5

4   Conclusion

From experimental investigation of jute/sisal polyester composite the following conclusions can be made.

- The flexural properties of jute/sisal polyester composite have better strength at $[0^\circ/45^\circ/45^\circ/0^\circ]$ orientation angle than $[0^\circ/90^\circ/90^\circ/0^\circ]$ and $[45^\circ/0^\circ/0^\circ/45^\circ]$ orientation arrangement.
- The flexural properties of jute/sisal polyester composite decreases when it is treated with 10% NAOH in concentration.
- The flexural properties of jute/sisal polyester composite improved when two natural fibers are hybridized.
- The flexural properties of jute/sisal polyester composite depends on sequence of fiber layers and better flexural strength is found on s/j/s/j arrangement than s/j/j/s and j/s/j/s arrangement.
- But s/j/j/s arrangement has less deformation than s/j/s/j and j/s/j/s arrangement.
- The flexural properties of jute/sisal polyester composite improved when continuous fibers are used than chopped fibers.
- From experimental result of jute/sisal polyester samples with concentration 10/14/76 wt% of fibers (JSP) has highest flexural strength which is 43.35 Mpa and fails at force 326.5 N.
- From experimental result of jute/sisal polyester samples $[0^\circ/45^\circ/45^\circ/0^\circ]$ has highest flexural strength which is 111.8 MPa and maximum force 469.5 N.

References

1. Idicula, M., Malhotra, S.K., Joseph, K., Thomas, S.: Dynamic mechanical analysis of randomly oriented intimately mixed short banana/sisal hybrid fiber reinforced polyester composites. Compos. Sci. Technol. **65**, 1077–1087 (2005)
2. Sabeel, K., Ahmed, S., Vijayarangan, A.C., Naidu, B.: Elastic properties, notched strength and fracture criterion in untreated woven jute-glass fabric reinforced polyester hybrid composites. Mater. Des. **28**, 2287–2294 (2007)
3. Mir, A., Zitoune, V., Collombet, F., Bezzazi, B.: Study of mechanical and thermomechanical properties of jute/epoxy composite laminate. Reinf. Plast. Compos. **29**, 1669–1680 (2010)

4. Hachemane, B., Zitoune, R., Bezzazi, B., Bouvet, C.: Sandwich composites impact and indentation behaviour study. Compos. Part B **51**, 1–10 (2013)
5. Wambua, P., Ivens, J., Verpoest, I.: Natural fibres: can they replace glass in fibre reinforced plastics? Compos. Sci. Technol. **63**(9), 1259–1264 (2013)
6. Joshi, S.V., Drzal, L.T., Mohanty, A.K., Arora, S.: Are natural fiber composites environmentally superior to glass fiber-reinforced composites. Compos. Part A **35**, 371–376 (2004)
7. Bledzki, A.K., Faruk, O., Sperber, V.E.: Cars from bio-fibres. Macromol. Mater. Eng. **291** (5), 449–457 (2006)
8. Holbery, J., Houston, D.: Natural-fiber-reinforced polymer composites in automotive applications. JOM **58**(11), 80–86 (2006)
9. Huda, M.S., Drzal, L.T., Ray, D., Mohanty, A.K., Mishra, M.: Natural-fiber composites in the automotive sector. In: Pickering, K.L. (ed.) Properties and Performance of Natural-fibre Composites, pp. 221–268. Woodhead Publishing Limited, Cambridge (2008)
10. Koronis, G., Silva, A., Fontul, M.: Green composites: a review of adequate materials for automotive applications. Compos. Part B-Eng. **44**(1), 120–127 (2013)
11. Li, Y., Mai, Y.-W., Ye, L.: Sisal fiber and its composites: a review of recent developments. Compos. Sci. Technol. **60**, 2037–2055 (2000)
12. Oksman, K., Mathew, A.P., Langstrom, R., Nystrom, B., Joseph, K.: The influence of fibre microstructure on fibre breakage and mechanical properties of natural fibre reinforced polypropylene. Compos. Sci. Technol. **69**, 1847–1853 (2009)
13. Faruk, O., Bledzki, A.K., Fink, H.P., Sain, M.: Bio composites reinforced with natural fibres: 2000–2010. Progess Polym. Sci. **37**, 1552–1596 (2012)

Author Index